SOCIAL ISSUES IN BUSINESS

SOCIAL ISSUES IN BUSINESS
Strategic and Public Policy Perspectives
FIFTH EDITION

Fred Luthans • University of Nebraska

Richard M. Hodgetts • Florida International University

Kenneth R. Thompson • DePaul University

Macmillan Publishing Company
New York
Collier Macmillan Publishers
London

Macmillan Publishing Company
866 Third Avenue, New York, New York 10022

Collier Macmillan Canada, Inc.

3 9082 01538411 1

Library of Congress Cataloging-in-Publication Data

Luthans, Fred.
  Social issues in business.

  Includes indexes.
  1. Industry—Social aspects—United States.
I. Hodgetts, Richard M. II. Thompson, Kenneth R.
III. Title.
HD60.5.U5L872 1987   658.4'08'0973   86–8579
ISBN 0-02-372900-7

Printing: 1 2 3 4 5 6 7 8   Year: 7 8 9 0 1 2 3 4 5 6

ISBN   0-02-372900-7

Preface

The social role of business continues to evolve, but at a faster, more dynamic pace. This more rapid rate of change is reflected by the fact that we have moved from a four-year to a three-year cycle for the editions of this book. Waiting four years before coming out with a new edition was just too long. Things are moving too quickly. The social issues that emerged from the turbulent 1960s (first and second editions of this text), that then began to mature and come of age in the middle 1970s (third edition) and into the 1980s (fourth edition), have now reached a new stage in the middle/late 1980s (this new, fifth edition). About all that remains in this new edition from the book that first came out fifteen years ago is some of the historical foundation. In fifteen short years, the social role of business has changed that much. Not many other fields of study can make that claim.

The major social issues of equal opportunity in employment, employee rights and justice, quality of work life, consumerism, and environmental protection have changed in both emphasis and content. Both business and society recognize that we live in a world of scarce resources in which human values take precedence over material values, a situation reflected in the heightened awareness of both managers and the public of the social responsibility of business. The general public, whose will is eventually expressed through government legislation and enforcement, is making demands on business. This pressure, of course, is nothing new. Through the years the nation's businesses have been buffeted on all sides by competition, government regulation, and powerful labor unions. Companies have found that they are as susceptible to the ominous Darwinian law as are the smallest organisms; only the fittest survive. Those who have survived, however, are not guaranteed a future. The question now facing business firms is whether they can adapt to the new demands of their social role.

Besides the now familiar social issues, the middle 1980s and beyond reveal a much expanded social role for business. In particular, business firms have assumed a broader responsibility; have become, and in many cases have been forced to become, more interested in ethical conduct; have begun to realize that they are living in a shrinking world, and must compete in the international arena; and have begun to plan, implement, and control their social performance more effectively. This fifth edition reflects this new stage in the social role of business.

The book contains five parts. Part I provides a foundation for the modern social role of business, and its four chapters contain a strategic management view of the business-society interface, a historical foundation, a political-economic framework, and a discussion of the ethical conduct of business. Part II is devoted to the role of government in business, with a new chapter on government and public policy and revised chapters on the impact of government on the social role of business and the role of public policy in moderating the power of business. Part III is the heart of the book, with chapters on the major social issues facing business: equal opportunity in employment, employee rights and justice, quality of work life, consumerism, and environmental protection. Part IV recognizes the expanded role and accompanying challenges facing modern business, with a new chapter on business in the international arena, and revised chapters on the broader responsibilities of business and individual social activism. The concluding Part V has three chapters on managing and controlling corporate social performance. There are separate chapters on planning, implementing, and measuring this social performance.

In addition to a significantly revised conceptual framework, this new edition contains three new chapters: Chapter 5, Government and Public Policy; Chapter 9, Employee Rights and Justice Systems, and Chapter 14, Business in the International Arena. There are also new and/or greatly expanded sections in other chapters. Because the book continues to feature topical issues, almost all the statistics, legal actions, and examples have been replaced, expanded, modified, or updated. In addition, there are many new cases/incidents at the end of the chapters and a new feature of this edition—longer case studies for the major parts of the text. These longer cases permit in-depth analysis and the chance to get more realistically involved in the social challenges facing business.

The total package of text, cases, and incidents is intended to be used in business and society (environment) courses and social issues (responsibility) in business courses at the undergraduate or graduate level. It can be used alone or with other materials. In addition, it can be used in such courses as introduction to business, principles of management, business policy, legal environment in business, or an introductory survey course in business administration. Practicing managers should also appreciate this book's attention to the identification and analysis of their social responsibilities. Part V, "Managing and Controlling the Social Performance of Business," should be especially valuable to practicing managers.

We hope this book contributes to an understanding of the important social role of business. How today's managers respond to these tremendous social challenges may well determine the very survival of the business institution in its present form.

We accept responsibility for any defects in the book but acknowledge that any book, including ours, is the product of many others. We are especially grateful to the following individuals who reviewed and gave us helpful feedback on this revision: Jeffrey Lenn, George Washington University; Wilmar F. Bernthal, University of Colorado, Boulder; Richard Pesta, Frostburg State University; Robert Raspberry, Southern Methodist University; Caryn Beck-Dudley, Utah State University; Douglas Fox, Western Connecticut State University; Bernard Goitein, Our Lady of the Lake University; Raymond Vegso, Canisius College; Pamela Stepanovich, Kutztown College.

Finally, we would like to thank our families for their understanding and support.

Fred Luthans
Richard M. Hodgetts
Kenneth R. Thompson

Contents

CHAPTER **3**
The Political and Economic Foundation   63

CHAPTER **4**
The Ethical Foundation   94

PART II
The Role of Government in Business

PART III
The Social Issues Facing Modern Business

PART IV
The Challenges Facing Business

PART **V**
Managing and Controlling the Social Performance of Business

Foundation for the Social Role of Business

1

Business and Society— A Strategic Management Perspective

Chapter Objectives

- To set the perspective for the important role that business plays in society both economically and in terms of quality-of-life dimensions.
- To review the strategy formulation process used by business to determine its social role.
- To identify the various power groups that attempt to influence business decisions and strategy formulation.
- To trace the importance of the chief executive officer in creating the guiding vision that directs the organization toward social responsibility.
- To identify problems associated with defining the social role of business.

A few years ago, Johns-Manville, a large, prestigious corporation, culminated an 80-year history by filing for bankruptcy. The problems came to a head when more than $2 billion in suits had been filed against the company from those whom had suffered serious illness or death from its major product—asbestos. More recently, leaking toxic gas from a Union Carbide pesticide plant killed about 2,500 unsuspecting citizens of Bhopal, India, and provoked more than $100 billion in law suits. If that was not bad enough, there was another toxic leak in a Union Carbide plant in Institute, West Virginia, that sent 135 people to the hospital and prompted another $88 million in suits.

How did these tragedies occur? What role did the compamies play in these tragedies? Could the tragedies have been prevented? The answers to these questions are not easy. Sure it is easy to point the finger in these particular examples, but realistically, Manville or Union Carbide may only be isolated examples of what *Time* magazine called "a modern parable of the risks and rewards originally engendered by the Industrial Revolution: Frankenstein's wonder becoming Frankenstein's monster."[1] The entire business community in modern times has found itself on that thin line between "wonder" and "monster." As the chapters of this book unfold, the relationship between business and society will become clearer and hopefully, some of the answers of the appropriate social role of business will emerge.

The starting point in understanding and analyzing business and society is with management strategies and policies. Strategic management can be defined in many ways. Some example definitions include:

> That set of decisions and actions which leads to the development of an effective strategy or strategies to help achieve corporate objectives.[2]
>
> The process of managing the pursuit of organizational mission while managing the relationship of the organization to its environment.[3]
>
> The formulation and implementation of plans and the carrying out of activities relating to matters which are of vital, pervasive, or continuing importance to the total organization.[4]

Thus strategic management assesses current environmental opportunities and threats and how the organization can best meet those environmental conditions. The purpose of strategic management is to build an organization that will accentuate its strengths and reduce its vulnerabilities in order to survive and prosper in an often turbulent and hostile environment.

In this introductory chapter we use the strategic management and planning function as an overall perspective for the social role of business and to analyze the various constraints and opportunities that society imposes on business. After first defining the role of business in society from two perspectives— economics and the quality of life—the nature and steps of strategy formulation are presented. The final part of the chapter deals more specifically with business strategies toward social responsibility.

[1]*Time*, December 17, 1984, p. 20.

[2]William F. Glueck, *Business Policy and Strategic Management* (New York: McGraw-Hill, 1980), p. 6.

[3]James M. Higgins, *Organizational Policy and Strategic Management* (Chicago: Dryden, 1983), p. 3.

[4]Arthur Sharplin, *Strategic Management* (New York: McGraw-Hill, 1985), p. 6.

THE IMPORTANCE OF BUSINESS IN SOCIETY

Business has a profound effect on the effective and efficient functioning of the economic and general quality of life of an entire country and its individual citizens.

The Economic Role of Business

One way to determine the impact that business has on a country and its people is in terms of the economic contribution. This is generally measured by the value added or wages provided in the national accounting for a specific country. A commonly accepted measure of national accounting is the calculation of a country's gross national product or GNP. GNP is a measure of the total economic activity of a country. GNP can be derived through three separate means: (1) measuring the production or output, (2) measuring the total consumption in terms of economic values of products or services, or (3) determining the incomes that are accrued to various individuals and organizations.

GNP is generally calculated all three ways. Each calculation should be equal to the other two. In other words, consumption should equal production plus or minus imports and exports, and the income received by individuals and organizations should be equal to the expenditures made by individuals and organizations plus or minus income or expenditures made to organizations and individuals external to the home country.

A detailed review of national income accounting is outside the scope of this book; however, a brief overview of the U.S. national income system can demonstrate the important role of business in the economic health of the United States. Figure 1.1 presents a summary model used for national income accounting. This model reflects each of the three approaches to national accounting. Included are the data used to calculate the GNP for 1984 and 1964 so that comparisons can be made between the accounts and the volume of activity time.

In the output method of calculating GNP, each major segment of the country's output is measured as a contribution to national income. Note that under this method, over 84 percent of the production output used in the calculation of national income for the United States was derived from business enterprises.

Besides the output methods, national income accounting by type of income reveals the importance of business. By providing jobs and hence compensation to employees, the wealth of the general population is, to a large degree, the direct result of the ability of business firms to be successful. In addition, corporate profits contribute to the wealth of shareholders in terms of increasing the value of their investment (appreciation of stock values based on the relative success of the organization) and through direct payments of

National Product by Expenditures on Final Product

	1984	1964
Personal Consumption Expenditures	$2342.3	$398.9
Gross Private Domestic Investment	637.3	92.9
Net Exports	- 66.3	8.6
Government Purchases Of Goods & Services	748.0	128.4

	1984	1964
(1) Gross National Product Or Expenditures	$3661.3	$628.7

National Product by Expenditures on Final Product

Income Accruing as:

	1984	1964
Compensation of Employees	$2172.7	$365.3
Proprietor's Income	154.7	51.1
Rental Income of Persons	62.5	18.2
Corporate Profits & Inventory Valuation Adjustment	284.5	64.5
Net Interest	285.	15.2

National Income or Production/Output

Values Added In:

	1984	1964
Agriculture, Forestry & Fisheries	$ 76.3	$ 17.6
Mining	45.4	6.2
Contract Construction	126.6	26.2
Manufacturing	654.9	154.7
Transportation	99.4	21.0
Communications & Public Utilities	135.3	21.4
Wholesale & Retail Trade	431.0	78.1
Finance, Insurance & Real Estate	433.9	57.0
Services	472.0	58.0
Government & Government Enterprises	420.3	70.0
Rest of the World	44.9	4.1

	1984	1964
(3) National Income =	$2954.4	$514.4

	1984	1964
Plus: Indirect Business Tax and Nontax Liability	304.3	58.0
Business Transfer Payments	17.3	2.3
Minus: Subsidies Minus Current Surpluses of Government Enterprises	14.4	1.2
Plus: Statistical Discrepancy	-8.2	- 0.5
Equals: (2) Net National Product	2959.4	573.0
Plus: Capital-Consumption Allowances	701.9	55.7

	1984	1964
Gross National Income of Charges Against Gross National Product	$3661.3	$ 628.7

Supplementary Series

	1984	1964
Minus: Corporate Profits & Inventory-Valuation Adjustment	$ 284.5	$ 64.5
Social Security Contribution	305.9	27.8
Excess of Wage Accruals Over Disbursements		0
Corporate Dividends	100.0	17.2
Plus: Government Transfer Payments to Persons		34.2
Net Interest Paid By Government		9.1
Interest Paid by Consumers	107.4	10.0
Business Transfer Payments	17.3	2.3
Equals: (4) Personal Income	3013.2	495.0
Minus: Personal Tax & Nontax Payments	673.1	59.2
Equals: (5) Disposable Personal Income	2340.1	435.8
Minus: Personal Outlays	2222.0	409.5
Equals: Net Personal Saving	118.1	26.3

FIGURE 1.1 Calculation of Gross National Product in the United States, Comparative Figures for 1984 and 1964. *From Production Output.*

the profits to shareholders through cash dividends. Proprietor's income, that is, the profits that go to people who own their own businesses, also accounts for a significant source of income. Small businesses account for the salaries and wages of literally hundreds of thousands of workers in the United States.

The consumption method of GNP calculates the expenditures of various segments of society. Personal consumption expenditures account for the largest segment of GNP. Personal consumption is greatly facilitated by the ability of individuals to have the money to make purchases of goods and services. The majority of the population acquires money through jobs. The majority of these jobs, of course, come from businesses. Gross private domestic investment, on the other hand, is a measure of the expenditures by private-sector organizations in the development of their facilities and equipment. These expenditures by businesses themselves can be translated into additional jobs in order to provide the products and services bought by businesses. Finally, the needs of government for goods and services are met almost entirely by private-sector organizations. Even municipal services such as transportation, street lighting and repair, and health and legal services are increasingly being turned over to private businesses.[5] Business plays an essential role in meeting the needs of government.

Personal disposable income (PDI), shown in Figure 1.1, can be thought of as the amount of income that is left over for individuals to use for savings or for discretionary or nondiscretionary expenditures. The latter two types of expenditures are combined into a personal outlays account, as shown in Figure 1.1. If business activity determines much of the value as reflected in national income, then much of PDI and personal consumption is also determined by the level of business activity. The importance of business is demonstrated in the ability of governments to function (through tax payments and purchases of goods and services) and through the ability of individuals to acquire resources beyond those needed to cover tax payments (i.e., PDI).

Trickle-Down Effect

The importance of business on PDI and the ability of government to fund social programs can be looked at from two major perspectives. The first views business as a major means to fund social welfare programs. This position would maintain that the privilege granted to business to operate in the country should be compensated by the business through the paying of taxes to fund social programs. This reflects a sharing of profits between business and government. Pragmatically, this approach is favored by many politicians because taxing businesses is more popular than taxing voters.

A second perspective acknowledges the importance of business to the entire economic health of the nation. As such, businesses should be encouraged

[5]"Cities Paying Industry to Provide Public Services," *New York Times*, May 28, 1985, p. 9.

and given incentives so that they can be successful. In this manner, they will be able to provide products and services that will be desired by individuals in both the U.S. and world markets. The success of the business enterprise will lead to more jobs and economic value to the nation. With increased jobs there will be increases in wages and compensations which, through personal and corporate income taxes, will lead to greater tax revenues. According to this perspective, the success of business will lead to a "trickle-down effect" which translates to "if business is successful, there will be more jobs and individuals will have greater economic wealth." More jobs will lead to less demand for government services associated with unemployment and poverty. This, of course, has been the position taken by the Reagan administration in recent years.

Quality-of-Life Dimensions

Economics and GNP calculations have predominated the view of life from the early 1900s until the late 1960s. However, in the last couple of decades there has been an increased sensitivity to quality-of-life issues. There were many reasons for this changed emphasis, but the social awareness of equal opportunity for minorities and women, consumerism, and environmental protection—the major social issues covered in this book—led the American society to interpret quality of life in terms of more than simply the economic criterion. In the 1960s, there was an elevated social awareness that the world in general and America in particular were facing some real social problems. For example, people finally realized that there was irreversible destruction to natural and man-made works of art through industrial pollution. In addition, the exploitation of natural resources in order to obtain the raw materials needed to increase industrial output led to the devastation of massive tracts of land. The disposition of chemicals and spent nuclear fuels led to dangerous pollution of groundwater supplies. This received considerable media exposure when whole areas were declared as uninhabitable. Places such as Love Canal near Niagara Falls, and Times Beach, Missouri, along Interstate 44 near St. Louis, became household words.

The outgrowth of this period was strong public sentiment that an economic criterion is not the only standard that individuals and governments should use to measure success. The idea developed that more qualitative, social dimensions also need to be considered. Analogous to GNP measures, indices of the quality of life were created. These included such things as the quality of health, pollution indices, the level of education, infant mortality rates, life-expectancy ages, the plight of poverty-level families, the quality of housing, and standards of living. Although these measures are more difficult to quantify than the economic indicators, there is an acknowledgment that they and other measures of life quality need to be considered together with the traditional economic ones. The result was the passage of a series of laws in the United States that radically redefined the actions that business may and may not take in striving to reach its goals and strategies. In this book we investigate these new parameters for business.

One thing is certain: Business has a profound influence on the personal lives and success of an entire nation. This can be measured in both economic and noneconomic terms. Society in general is beginning to appreciate and better understand the importance of business. The remainder of the chapter will add to this understanding by discussing the decision- and strategy-making process of modern business. This will serve as a point of departure for the remaining chapters, which are aimed more specially at the social responsibilities of business.

BUSINESS STRATEGY FORMATION

The strategy formation process may be the single most important element in establishing the direction for a business organization. With respect to social responsibility, the strategies that are established can be responsive or nonresponsive depending on the decisions that are made. Because of this important relationship between strategy formation and the level of social responsiveness of a business, an overview of the strategy formation process is needed.

Goals, Objectives, and Strategies

Determining the direction of a business firm starts with setting goals, objectives, and strategies. *Goals* are general statements of direction. For example, Lee Iacocca's goal for Chrysler to "be the best" in the auto industry signals the direction that the top management of this company wants to pursue. The problem with such goals is that although they provide direction, they are not specific enough to provide clear direction to those who must follow them. For example, the engineering design staff may translate Iacocca's goal to mean that "at all cost, the best cars should be made." This interpretation may lead to the financial ruin of the company. Another division, quality control, may translate the goal to mean that each auto should be gone over several times before it is delivered to the dealer. Again, financial ruin may result as quality control costs increase by several hundred percent.

In light of these problems with generalized goals, most strategy experts advocate that specific objectives be established that translate goals and provide clearer direction to the firm and its staff. An *objective* is a specific standard of performance that has a measurable criterion by which to judge progress and normally has some time standard for completion. For example, changing Iacocca's goal to an objective might lead to the following statement: "Chrysler wants to provide the best possible automobiles as defined within the master plan subject to the budgetary and work force standards established." In this situation, the best possible autos have already been specified within the master plan. Criteria such as the number of quality defects and the number of procedures to be carried out on each auto per minute may be specified. The budgetary and materials constraints may limit the expenditures that could be assigned to a department or plant. Notice how an objective gives greater direction than a goal. It is much clearer to all those who are guided by the standard, what specific actions top management had in mind in the development of guidelines for decision making to ensure that specific actions follow the desired directions for the firm.

Strategies are defined as setting a direction as to the means of accomplishing the goals and objectives of an organization. For example, the goal of "being the best" could be translated into a strategy to reach the goal of creating quality circles to get worker input on quality, or installing robotics to speed up the productive process. Table 1.1 gives some guidelines for general or generic strategies that firms may follow depending on the life cycle of the product or industry.

The Role of Goals, Objectives, and Strategies in the Organization

Goals, objectives, and strategies are the backbone of an organization's planning process. Not only do they guide the overall direction of the entire organization, but they serve to link various levels of the organization. The goals, objectives, and strategies at the higher levels of the organization provide direction to the planning processes and implementation at the lower levels. Table 1.2 demonstrates the various organizational levels.

Enterprise-level goals, objectives, and strategies are directed at managing the interface between the organization and the larger society. The degree of social responsibility is addressed mainly at this level.

Corporate-level goals, objectives, and strategies pertain to those areas of activity or business that the organization should pursue,[6] its mission or missions, and the best ways to meet the opportunities, risks, and threats posed by the environment. For example, General Motors may enlarge its mission from being an automobile company to being a transportation company. GM may also decide that transportation includes not only personal transportation by means of internal combustion engines but also the use of electric-, battery-, or solar-powered transportation equipment. This broader mission can be seen in GM's acquisition of railroad-manufacturing companies such as the Electro-Motive Division and its advances in using electric and battery power in railroad and personal transportation vehicles. GM has produced experimental cars that are totally battery powered, and it continues to try to make them commercially feasible. An example of actions taken to reduce

[6]D. E. Schendel and C. W. Hofer, *Strategic Management: A New View of Business Policy and Planning* (Boston: Little, Brown, 1979), pp. 12–13.

TABLE 1.1.   Generic Strategies Based on a Product's Location on the Life Cycle or an Industry's Location on the Life Cycle.

A. Strategies for organizations in industries in the introduction phase
   1. Aim for future growth.
   2. Try to obtain first-mover advantage.
   3. Search out new customer groups, new geographical areas, new user applications, etc.
   4. Build product awareness and create a brand loyalty.
   5. Move if and when technological uncertainty clears.
   6. Prepare for tough competitors to enter the industry.
   7. Prepare for price wars.
B. Strategies for organizations in industries in the growth phase
   1. Improve product quality and add new-product features and models.
   2. Search for new market segments to enter.
   3. Enter new distribution channels to increase product exposure.
   4. Shift advertising from product awareness to product conviction, purchase, and brand loyalty.
   5. Increase price competitiveness to maintain market share and product sales growth.
C. Strategies for organization in the shakeout phase
   1. Increase price competitiveness to maintain market share and product sales growth.
   2. Explore growth segments for entry.
   3. Search for new market segments to enter.
   4. Emphasize product innovation and quality improvements.
   5. Improve product exposure.
   6. Target advertising to growth segments and price/value received competitiveness.
D. Strategies for organizations in industries in the mature stage
   1. Exploit growth segments within the industry.
   2. Emphasize product innovation and quality improvements.
   3. Improve efficiency, thereby cutting the cost of production.
E. Strategies for firms in weak or declining industries
   1. Disinvest.
   2. Cut costs.
   3. Establish product innovation to move product/service back in the product life cycle.
   4. Develop market niche concentration.
   5. Find the growth-stage market segment.

Source: Adapted from Arthur A. Thompson Jr., and A. J. Stickland III, *Strategic Management* (Plano, Tex.: Business Publications, 1984), pp. 78–118.

risk is the vertical integration of the Ford Motor Company in the early 1900s into steel production, mining, and ship and barge transportation in order to avoid supply and price fluctuations, by controlling the supply of raw materials. The acquisition of Marathon Oil by U.S. Steel is an example of a company's attempting to reduce the effects of fluctuations in demand on

TABLE 1.2. Levels of Goal Objective and Strategy Formulation.

Level	Addresses
Enterprise	The organizational and environmental interfaces, including social responsibility
Corporate	The organization's types of business, balancing risks and environmental opportunities
Business	The organization's strategies and policies for a particular business or industry
Functional	The organization's strategies and policies for subunits, such as marketing, research and development, production, and finance
Individual	Individual employee performance expectations through performance standards or unique work plans

Source: Adapted from D. E. Schendel and C. W. Hofer, *Strategic Management: A New View of Business Policy and Planning* (Boston: Little, Brown, 1979), p. 11.

profits. Risk is reduced, too, through the broadening of the business base. A reduction in demand for one type of product will be counteracted by an increase in demand for another.

The *business level* of goal objectives, and strategy formation addresses the issue of "how a firm should compete in a given business?"[7] Whereas previous strategy and goal levels determined the type of business the organization should enter, the business level pertains to how the organization should tactically behave in order to survive and prosper in the market that it has chosen to enter. U.S. Steel, for example, had to decide on the breadth and depth of its product line, its national- versus regional-market penetration, and its quality image versus low-cost volume, all aspects that it considered when formulating goals and strategies at the business level.

Functional area goals, objectives and strategies include establishing the organization's directions for its subunits. For example, the goals, objectives, and strategies for a marketing department or a research and development division all fall under the rubric of the functional level.

Individual-level goals, objectives, and strategies translate the functional-level plan into specific performance direction for operating employees. In essence, all employees ought to have a definite sense of the contribution that they are making to the organization. In like manner, the organization ought to be aware of how employees "fit" into the grand design of the organi-

[7]Schendel and Hofer, p. 13.

zation. Individual-level goals, objectives, and strategies can be met through the development of performance standards as is done with the establishment of procedures in a service firm or production standards, such as making 50 widgets per hour in a manufacturing organization. For more unique tasks, individualized, tailor-made work plans might be employed. The connection of individualized performance plans and organizational plans is often absent in real-world organizations, yet it is a vital link between plans and actions.

Dimensions of the Strategy Formation Process

How does the strategy formation process actually occur? A simplified model is shown in Figure 1.2. The model shows that there are three major dimensions: management's goals and values, the external environment, and the

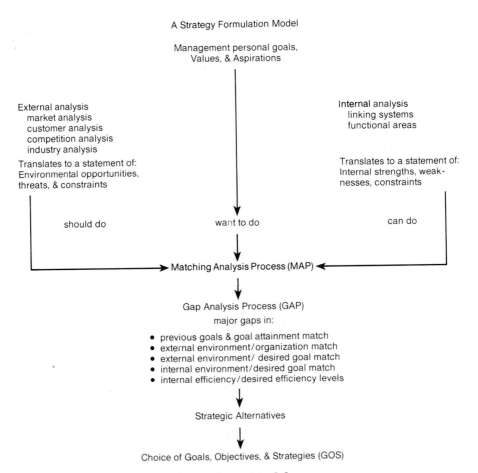

FIGURE 1.2.   Strategy Formulation Model.

internal environment. A closer look at these dimensions will aid in understanding the strategy formation process.

As stated earlier, management's goals and values influence the overall direction of the organization. In essence, this part of the analysis in strategy formation answers questions of what the organization "wants" to do. The most important manager to influence with regard to organization is the chief executive officer or CEO. The CEO's leadership will strongly influence the strategies formulated.

The CEO is the chief decision maker of the organization and sets the tone for the entire firm. The external role of the CEO involves representing the company to external groups such as financial market leaders, bond-rating services, union officials, suppliers of raw materials, and the community at large. All these groups need to have confidence that the organization will be moving in directions that these external groups think is appropriate. For example, if lenders have confidence that a company is following strategies that will enhance their competitive position, lenders would be more likely to provide debt financing. This confidence would be translated into a reduced risk and thus affect the establishment of interest rates. In a similar vein, if suppliers have confidence in the direction of the organization, there is a greater likelihood that they will extend more generous credit terms than they otherwise would. The market price of stock would also increase if there is confidence that the organization is pursuing a course of action that will lead to greater financial returns to investors. Higher stock prices would improve the potential for the organization to sell additional stock if equity financing is desired. In addition, high stock prices reduce the probability that the organization would be vulnerable to an unfriendly takeover attempt.

The CEO's actions and words can do much to build an image for an organization. While the external financial statements (income statement, balance sheet, and changes in retained earnings) provide some historical sense of the degree of success of an organization, the CEO can provide a sense of the plans and expected future of the organization. These future expectations as interpreted by relevant outsiders as well as by the internal staff are vitally important to an organization.

Internally, the CEOs need to do more than just establish strategic plans. They must provide the necessary leadership and be tenacious enough to ensure that the objectives are reached. This involves constant monitoring and measuring (i.e., controlling what is going on in the organization). This internal control function of the CEO is very important. Having a strategic plan is necessary to set the direction, but if there is little follow-up control on the activity of each subunit's contribution to carrying out this plan, there is a strong probability that the strategic process will not be taken seriously. Nowhere has the importance of the CEO been demonstrated more strongly than in the case Chrysler Corporation's Lee Iacocca (see the box "Super CEO").

SUPER CEO

The late 1970s was a disastrous period for Chrysler. Mounting losses from operations led financial analysts to conclude that the third largest U.S. automobile producer was headed for bankruptcy. Between 1978 and 1981 the automaker lost $3.5 billion. Suppliers expecting bankruptcy were less inclined to grant credit to Chrysler, further aggravating a cash flow crisis. The outlook for car sales was bleak for the entire industry, and the general economy was entering its worst recession since the depression of the 1930s.

In August 1982, financial reports for Chrysler contained a different kind of story. The automobile company had profits of $107 million for the second quarter, with expectations that the company would remain profitable for the foreseeable future. The break-even point for Chrysler was reduced dramatically, so that the company needed only one-half the sales that it had needed to make a profit before 1978. By 1982, Chrysler had $1 billion in cash and securities available as a financial cushion. Analysts had a much higher degree of optimism for the future of the company.

What was the cause of the turnaround? Most sources attribute the vast change in the company to the tenacity and drive of one person, CEO Lido Anthony Iacocca, former chairman of the Ford Motor Company. In late 1978, Lee Iacocca was hired by Chrysler as president and later as chairman. Possessed by the drive to "stick a finger in the eye of Henry Ford" for firing him, Iacocca has assured his place in the "Detroit hall of fame" for his leadership and management of Chrysler. Within a very short period, Iacocca had to convince the U.S. Congress to approve $1.2 billion in loan guarantees to Chrysler, coax the United Auto workers union to accept over $1 billion of cuts in pay and benefits, obtain concessions from state governments for loans, grants, and property tax relief, and convince lenders and suppliers that there would be a tomorrow for Chrysler. Auto analyst David Healy has likened Iacocca to Winston Churchill. Iacocca "is a real morale builder. He is for Chrysler what Winston Churchill was for England; he provides the roar."

Note the importance of the CEO to the very survival of Chrysler. The direction that Iacocca provided was imperative for the survival of the organization. The personal style, dynamic nature, personality, and sense of direction were all critical in pulling off the most dramatic turnaround in corporate history. The drive and motivation of CEO Iacocca cannot be underestimated as central factors in Chrysler's survival and now healthy position.

Source: Adapted from Harry Anderson, James C. Jones, and Kim Foltz, "Chrysler Makes a Comeback," *Newsweek*, August 2, 1982, pp. 49–50.

The type of action that CEOs choose to take is influenced by four major factors:

1. The perception of the CEO regarding the external environment.
2. The perceptions of the CEO regarding the capabilities of the organization.
3. The power of external and internal groups to influence the CEO.
4. The CEO's personal goals.

The first and second factors are predicated on an analysis of what the organization can and should do in the current and expected future environment. In a true sense, the "rational man" or "economic man" concept discussed in economics courses would prevail in this consideration. A CEO would opt for the ideal match in the environment. With regard to the third factor, the power of internal and external groups, a CEO's job becomes a matter of balancing personal needs, organizational goals, and groups that have power over different aspects that could influence the organization. These groups, as indicated in the model in Figure 1.3, can be internal, external, or a special-interest group that includes members of both.

Mintzberg's Model of Power and Strategy Formation

The model in Figure 1.3 is designed to demonstrate the various groups that tend to try to influence the top decision makers in a modern organization.[8] These groups try to influence strategy formation so as to reflect their own needs and desires. The model is divided into three specific parts: the external and internal publics and the strategy and policy formation group.

The external publics involve the 10 groups identified in Figure 1.3. Note that owners and employee associations are considered external publics. Owners are viewed as distant to the organization and not really part of the decision-making process. This reflects the notion of the large corporation which has thousands of shareholders, each technically an owner but having little say in the strategy of the organization. Employee associations are also external to the organization. For example, labor has a much different orientation than those of either the organization or the individual employees. It is concerned with its own survival and success, which may be quite different from the goals of the company or those of the individual employee, even though there are obviously some shared goals between the union and employees, such as job security and increased pay.

[8]H. Mintzberg, "Organizational Power and Goals," in D. E. Schendel and C. W. Hofer, *Strategic Management: A New View of Business Policy and Planning* (Boston: Little, Brown, 1979), pp. 64–80.

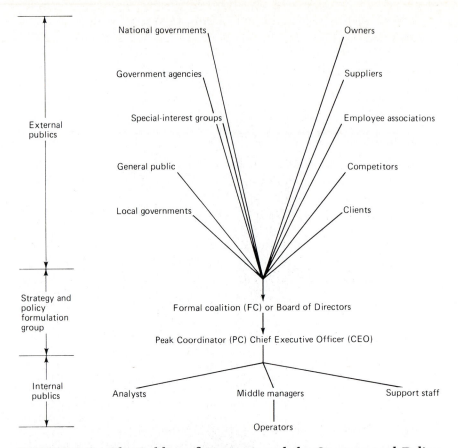

FIGURE 1.3. The Publics of Business and the Strategy and Policy Formulation Group. Adapted from H. Mintzberg, "Organizational Power and Goals," in D. E. Schendel and C. W. Hofer, *Strategic Management: A New View of Business Policy and Planning* (Boston: Little, Brown, 1979).

The internal publics that Mintzberg identifies in Figure 1.3 include the various employee groups, such as operating employees, support staff, middle management, and staff analysts. These reflect the various internal publics that affect strategy formulation.

The third, central group in the Mintzberg model includes the strategy and policy formulators themselves. Mintzberg identifies both a peak coordinator (PC) and a formal coalition (FC). The peak coordinator is analogous to the chief executive officer of an organization. The formal coalition might be considered as the board of directors; both work toward setting the strategies for the organization. The peak coordinator is normally part of the formal coalition. The formal coalition is composed of outsiders (e.g., external members of the board of directors) and insiders (e.g., full-time officers and executives in the corporation). External board members are involved with the decision making of the organization only when they are at board meetings.

Implications of the Mintzberg Model

Mintzberg states that the strategy and policy group will have full say in determining the direction of the organization unless checked by other power sources. In addition, the internal members of the board will have stronger control over the actions of the firm because they will have greater control over information that is given to the external board members.

External and internal publics will attempt to influence the strategy and policy formation group. If one of the publics has power through control over resources or other means to force the organization to comply, there is a strong probability that the organization's goals will be modified to accommodate such groups. If possible, the strategy and policy group may attempt the reduce the power of other groups in both direct and indirect ways. Mintzberg outlines several strategies for doing this. To counter the power of the strategy and policy group, the other groups may band together to form a coalition. This is especially true when the groups do not have the power to do it by themselves. For example, state, local, and federal governments, conservation groups, and tourist groups may form a coalition to stop the stripmining activities of a mining company.

The Mintzberg model points out that management strategy formation is not made in isolation. Rather, strategy is formed after considering the various parameters that are set by groups that have degrees of influence over the organization. The accompanying boxed material on IBM demonstrates some examples of power groups and management strategy making.

IBM: TOO MUCH MUSCLE?

International Business Machines (IBM) is noted for innovation, a well-deserved reputation for quality and service, and a penchant for "playing tough" with its competitors. Although aggressively competing may seem like the "American way" to do business, when the company already has the largest market share in most of the fields in which it competes, such "aggressive" competition might be viewed by some as "unfair" competition. As *Fortune*'s Bro Uttal puts it, "IBM's unprecedented flood of new products, its frequent deep price cuts, and its muscular marketing ploys have been maiming rivals by the

(continued)

score." As a consequence, most of IBM's competitors, such as Burroughs, Univac, NCR, Control Data, and Honeywell, have moved out of the general mainframe computer market into their own specialized niches in an attempt to avoid direct competition with IBM. Soon after IBM entered the personal computer (PC) market, at least 12 other manufacturers, including Osborne, who went bankrupt, dropped out.

The muscle of IBM and the way it flexes it has, of course, raised the hackles of a growing number of critics. Urich Weil, a computer industry analyst from the investment firm of Morgan Stanley, stated that "IBM's behavior is almost reckless, and it invites retribution." In the past, retribution has been attempted with over a dozen private antitrust suits and two federal attempts to split up IBM. One U.S. congressman, Patten Mitchell, from Maryland, thinks that a congressional hearing on IBM's action is inevitable. Although the Reagan administration has a history of being "soft" on antitrust matters, the next administration may not be.

The current actions of IBM may be "legal and ethical," but according to John Opel, its chief executive, following the letter of the law may still invite antitrust suits. This is true particularly if the result of its actions leads to an inability to preserve competition in the industry.

Note that in this case IBM is using its power, but in the exercise of its power there is the chance that outside publics (competitors, government agencies, and special-interest groups) may band together to form a coalition to combat IBM. The actions by the public may be as radical and have as significant an impact on the company as antitrust litigation.

Source: Adapted from Bro Uttal, "Is IBM Playing Too Rough?" *Fortune*, December 10, 1984, pp. 34–37.

The Role of Personal Goals of CEOs

A CEO influence factor in the strategy formulation process identified earlier relates to personal goals. For example, a strategy may be formed to grow in a mature nongrowth industry because of the CEO's own personal goals. This happened when Miller Brewing decided to "upset" a placid, mature market for beer by becoming an aggressive marketing company striving for growth in sales through their product Miller High Life. In addition, Miller grew through segmentation of the market by offering a premium beer, Michelob, and through appealing to the weight-conscious consumer with Miller Lite. The result is an industry engaged in a massive marketing battle for market share in a very competitive market. Why? Because the CEO at Miller Brewing Company wanted to grow.

The importance of personal goals of the CEO should not be minimized. Almost all organizations have rational alternatives available to them in developing an ideal match of the external environment, internal environment, and strategic plans. The alternative that is actually chosen may be based more on the personal preferences of the CEO then on any other single factor.

What about the stockholders—what control do they have over top management of a firm? The board of directors certainly influences the decisions of the CEO, but as Mintzberg pointed out, the stockholders are considered an external group, outside the day-to-day operations and control of the organization. The board of directors can curtail the direction of the CEO, but traditionally, boards have been relatively passive unless the CEO fails to earn a sufficient amount of profit or does something illegal that attracts media attention. Normally, CEOs pursue actions that will, hopefully, lead to profits because CEOs, like most people, want to demonstrate their skills to their colleagues and families. Personal image, reputation, and profits are usually very important to a top manager. These needs strongly influence CEOs in their strategy formulations. Most often, this will benefit both the person and the organization. For example, success of a firm means success for the CEO. Unfortunately, however, there are incidents where the personal goals do not aid the organization, as the accompanying boxed material on "golden parachutes" points out.

External Environmental Analysis

A top manager does not consider simply his or her own wants and those of the various power coalitions. Considerable time and effort are taken to determine the nature of the competitive environment for the industry and the effective market area of the organization. From this analysis, external environmental opportunities, threats, and constraints become evident.

GOLDEN PARACHUTES

Congress is working to change the laws regarding the use of "golden parachutes." A golden parachute is a rich severance contract granted to a company's officers and directors if there is a hostile takeover of the company. Under this arrangement, a director or officer receives very generous compensation if he or she is fired by the new management (thus the term "golden parachute"). There have been some massive payoffs in the past, and legislators are questioning whether a company and its stockholders are best served by these agreements. The most noteworthy of the golden parachute deals was the one William

(continued)

M. Agee received when he was released from Bendix after it was acquired by Allied Corporation. Mr. Agee received a whopping $4 million in severance pay.

The number of companies that have golden parachute provisos increased 42 percent from 1981 to 1984. The trend, however, is for a leveling off of companies granting golden parachutes, due to the adverse publicity surrounding them and the fear that stockholder suits may result.

Source: Adapted from "An Assault on Golden Parachutes and Greenmail," *Business Week,* August 13, 1984, p. 56; "Cushioning the Crash of the Golden Parachutes," *Business Week,* August 6, 1984, pp. 72–73; "Golden Parachutes May Go the Way of the Dodo," *Business Week,* January 9, 1984, p. 34.

The two main problems in determining external environmental opportunities and threats are (1) delineating the various types of external information important to determining environmental opportunities and threats, and (2) determining the essential environmental information needed. The first problem is how to define the data needed by the decision makers to formulate some kind of meaningful information strategy. For example, in projecting the consumer consumption of beer, the factors that influence consumption must be identified. Price is important, but so might be the consumption of wine, hard liquor, and soft drinks. Personal disposable income might be a factor, as well as the drinkers' median income, as socioeconomic class seems to be related to consumption patterns. Are these the key determinants influencing consumption, or are other factors also important, and are these factors vital to predicting demand in the future, or may there be other variables? The complexity of this environmental "scanning" complicates the determination of environmental opportunities and threats. The problem this poses to the business decision maker is exemplified in Figure 1.4.

Once the relevant information has been found, this determination becomes less difficult but often just as problematic. For example, in the decision to locate a McDonald's franchise in a particular city, some relatively complex information bases are generated. The income-potential data for the outlet are found by analyzing the population's median income, the calculated personal disposable income for the market area, and the receptiveness of the local community to this type of food service operation. Some of these data are readily available from the census bureau, the Bureau of Business Research, or the local chamber of commerce. Additional data may have to be generated through surveys and trained observations of customer buying hab-

"INFORMANIA"
It's having to decide with absolute, total uncertainty.

You face a clear-cut decision.

You either increase production or you don't.

Which is to say you either succeed or you fail. Such decisions are your life's work.

So when you've got to sign on the line, but there's not a scrap of hard evidence to help you, momentary loss of vision is entirely normal.

That's "Informania."

The solution is information. The right information. In the right form. For the right people in the right place and time.

Burroughs can help. Because we know how to manage information. We've put 95 years of thought and experience into it. We offer a comprehensive solution to the problem of "Informania."

Our computers and office automation systems can help you collect, compose, analyze, store, recall, reformulate and distribute information.

So that you will know. And act with certainty.

When "Informania" strikes, the answer is Burroughs. Write for our brochure: Burroughs Corporation, Dept. BW-19, Burroughs Place, Detroit, Michigan 48232.

Burroughs
Building on strength

FIGURE 1.4. The Need for Information. Used with permission of the Burroughs Corporation.

its at similar food outlets. Through an analysis of the community, McDonald's can calculate the feasibility of locating an outlet in that community and, further, the optimal location.

The analysis of the environmental data is crucial for an organization's survival. Calculated risk taking is a natural condition for strategic choice, but it becomes less risky if there is solid evidence to indicate that the environment will provide a climate accommodating the decision being made. Just as a major league baseball manager relies on percentages in the match of hitter and pitcher and in the placement of outfielders, a corporate executive also relies on the percentages found in the data analysis, such as current and future trends, to determine the optimal course of action.

From the analysis of the external data, conclusions are made as to what the environment has to offer in terms of quantifiable opportunities, threats, and constraints. For the steel industry, for example, the cost of labor and raw material is increasing. At the same time the cost of compliance with environmental regulations is reducing the industry's competitive position with respect to foreign producers. Added to this combination of events is the problem of technological obsolescence facing the industry at a time when market prices and demand for the product are down and the cost of capital (i.e., interest rates on external money needed to modernize equipment) is high. This hostile environment for steel production is leading some companites to withhold money from steel production and invest in other, more lucrative markets. In essence, the external environment is too hostile or threatening to warrant continued investment, since the probability of profits is not great.

Although the external environmental analysis is critical in determining the environment's opportunities and threats, of equal importance is an analysis of the organization's ability to meet future challenges. This analysis is accomplished through an organizational audit or internal analysis.

Internal Considerations in Strategy and Policy Formulation

An organization's survival and success is predicated on a compatible match between the organization and the environment. The external analysis is only part of the knowledge needed to build an effective strategy. The decision maker must be aware of the organization's strengths, weaknesses, and constraints. A company cannot do more than is possible and will be stronger if it competes on its own strengths rather than on its weaknesses.

Analyzing an organization is viewing an organization through both resource and management audits. The ability of a business to attract sufficient quality resources depends on its technical and managerial capacity to compete effectively in the environment. The organizational audit or internal organizational analysis examines data on several aspects of the organization. Table 1.3 shows some of the variables in such an organizational audit. The quality and quantity of resources and the potential of the organization to obtain additional resources are assessed.

The management audit decides how well the resources are being utilized toward the organization's objectives. Both efficiency and effectiveness are measured in this step. Once the organizational audit is complete, the organization's strengths, vulnerabilities, and limits are known. These organizational capabilities can then be matched with the environment in order to determine

TABLE 1.3. Elements in an Organizational Audit.

Resources

Financial
Human—quality and quantity
Raw materials
Physical plant
Consumer perception
Societal perception

Management Systems

Top leadership style
Scope of operations/menu of services
Differentiation process
Job design
Division of labor
Departmentalization
Distribution of power/decision-making authority
Integration—coordinating a activities to maximize
commitment and organizational effectiveness
Reward systems
Individual role and performance expectations
Management information systems

the organization's ability to meet current and future opportunities and threats.

The goal of the organizational audit process is to develop an organization that will be able to meet the challenges of the environment in such a way as to maximize its long-term survival and success. This process of matching the organization with the environment is called *gap analysis*. The end result of gap analysis is a statement of actions that the organization must take to enhance its own capabilities. This statement then becomes the foundation on which its strategies and policies are based.

Strategy and Policy Formulation from Gap Analysis

There are several sets of strategies and policies that can emerge from gap analysis. Notice that the term *set of strategies* is used. Gap analysis leads to an awareness of actions that ought to be taken. These actions entail not just one simple strategy but action on several fronts. These strategic actions form a set of strategies that guide the organization. For example, with the keen competition in the beer industry, regional brewers have had to develop strategies relating to price, advertising emphasis, acquisition, production, and whether to remain regionalized or become national producers. Each of these strategies is part of a master plan; hence a set of strategies is devised.

The process of strategy and policy formulation is mapping out detailed strategies to meet the organization's needs as defined in the gap analysis process. Strategy formulation is articulating in sufficient detail a set of strategies so that the feasibility of a particular set of strategies, the cost of the proposal, and a realistic time framework can be decided. These three aspects help determine the merits of each proposed strategy set so that a realistic comparison between strategies can be made.

In order to compare strategies, each is often translated into pro forma or predicted financial statements (income statements, balance sheets, and cash flow or funds flow) and operating statements (measures of levels of activity or resource deployment). The main determinant of the strategy's success is the estimated demand or revenue generated from the strategy. Because of the importance and variability of the estimated demand resulting from a proposed strategy, several demand levels often will be calculated. Differing financial and operating statements will be constructed for each, much as in accounting in which several budgets are created. These projections are based on different expectations of levels of demand. For example, Table 1.4 presents optimistic, expected, and pessimistic levels of demand for a retail organization with an associated income statement projecting the effects on profits resulting from each of the environmental conditions (demand levels).

Changes in demand cannot always be readily translated into optimistic, pessimistic, or normal fluctuations in demand. More sophisticated approaches are necessary. One such approach is called *scenario forecasting*, trying out different environmental conditions in a scenario of the organization's future conditions. Table 1.5 shows the expected changes in profits for a railroad in differing scenarios. The scenarios are based on increasing fuel and labor costs and general economic activity. The scenario forecast helps show how different environmental conditions will modify the organization's expectations in meeting its goals vis-à-vis its chosen strategies.

Once a strategy is formulated into detailed effects on the organization

TABLE 1.4.   Example of a Variable Budget.

	Optimistic Demand	Normal Demand	Pessimistic Demand
Demand in units	1600	1200	1000
Revenues	$8000	$6000	$5000
Variable costs	4800	3600	3000
Fixed costs	1000	1000	1000
Planned profit	$2200	$1400	$1000

TABLE 1.5.   Example of Scenario Forecasts.

Scenario		A	B	C	D
Environmental conditions	Fuel costs	$3/gal	$3/gal	$1.50/gal	$1.50/gal
	Labor costs Economic conditions compared with last year's	$10/hr	$15/hr	$10/hr	$8/hr
		95	95	105	105
Expected revenue		$15M	$15M	$20M	$20M
Expected profit (loss)		$ 1M	($2M)	$ 2M	$ 3M

and likely environmental responses are translated into probably consequences, the strategies can be compared. This is done so that an optimal
set of strategies can be chosen to guide the future of the business. In this
manner, it is more likely that a strategy will be chosen that will enhance
the organization's survival and success.

The strategy formulation and evaluation process is one way for an organization to plan for the future through a systematic analysis of the environment
and the organization. The final strategy decision, however, is not simply
based on the most economically rational action. An organization succeeds
because it has the commitment of its employees and the support of the
various publics important to its existence. Strategies are planned in consideration of these publics' needs.

SOCIAL RESPONSIVENESS AND THE
STRATEGY FORMATION PROCESS

Part of the built-in responsiveness of business to societal needs is that organizations rely on society. The goal of a business firm is to survive and grow.
What is society's role in this? Society is the source of the organization's
inputs and outputs, and for its survival, the business organization must
make sure that it will continue to receive the needed inputs so that it can
function. Similarly, the survival of the organization is predicated on a society
that will purchase the product or service the organization provides.

For these needs to be met, three conditions must be present. First, there
must be a supply of needed raw materials at a cost that the company can
afford. Second, society must be willing to purchase the available service or
goods. If there are no markets for the product or service, there is little need
for raw materials. Third, there must be a forum for conducting the exchange
among the organization, the users of the product or service, and the provider

of the raw materials. A legal and social framework is required to conduct business among these parties in an efficient and orderly manner. On a rudimentary level, the firm must ensure that society can, and is willing to provide, the climate and the conditions necessary for its survival. Hence, the responsibility of a business firm is also the preservation of society.

The degree of commitment to the preservation of society is not necessarily a short-term goal. In the short run, a business firm may be faced with conditions that dictate survival as the primary goal, with good relations with society as a secondary goal. For example, in a cash flow crisis, a company may reduce inventories, but the lower levels of inventories can mean that the customer may not receive the merchandise as quickly, which may lead to ill will between the organization and the consumer. Some furniture retailers are examples. Because of the cost of financing inventories, some retailers have only a display model. When customers wish to buy the item, they may have to wait several weeks or even months to receive it. The delay is the result of the furniture store's need to reduce the amount of money tied up in inventories, money not earning a return for the store owner.

The same is true for the cost of borrowing money and the amount of credit that the company is willing to grant customers. Most credit policies give the purchaser free credit for 30 to 60 days after the product is sold. But to finance that credit, the company must commit some financial resources. The cost of such financial resources has increased dramatically in the past few years, leading to a revision of some companies' credit policies. For example, some gas stations are now offering a cash discount in order to reduce the number of sales on deferred payment (credit). In effect, credit card users are charged for deferring their payment for the product.

Although the long-run effects of these policies may hurt the good will between the company and society, the company's short-term needs to survive may dictate that the needs and wants of society be held in abeyance. The limits of the firm's social responsibility are tied, in this case, to its ability to survive. Thus, the degree of social responsiveness may be decided by the organization's financial condition. Although business firms depend on society for many of their needs, society is unable to exist without businesses.

THE EVOLUTION OF BUSINESS RESPONSIVENESS: ACTS OF NECESSITY, ACCOMMODATION, AND VISION

As the reader can readily see, the strategy and policy formulation process is not the result of arbitrary acts by one individual. No business organization can survive long unless its decisions consider the needs of the organization, the needs of its employees, and the desires of the various publics that the organization serves and with which it interacts in the larger environment. In this section we discuss how management decision makers attempt to reconcile these considerations during the formulation of future organizational plans.

Mandatory Constraints for Modern Business Firms

A synthesis of the societal demands on an organization can lead to a dichotomy of mandatory and discretionary constraints. Mandatory constraints are those that an organization must acknowledge and react to in order to remain a viable functioning unit in society. These constraints are represented in Figure 1.5.

Each point in Figure 1.5 may be viewed as a particular goal or option in the execution of a strategy. These mandatory constraints may be considered barriers that keep the organization from executing a particular action or considering a particular option or that force the organization to use a different strategy in order to achieve the desired objective. As an example, if public policy requires that automobiles produced in the United States average 25 miles per gallon of gas, domestic automakers may immediately reduce the number of large cars produced and manufacture only smaller cars that satisfy the public policy edict. Or they may decide to increase research and development to meet the legal constraints while at the same time lobby to change the law so that it is less of a problem (e.g., change the average from 25 miles to 20 miles per gallon). Finally, the auto companies may work to produce cars outside the country in order to circumvent the law.

Notice that in the example, management actions attempt to compensate for the constraint while working simultaneously to change the constraint so that it will be more compatible with the goals of their own company. In any event, the mandatory constraint leads to some actions by management to address the problem. In this fashion, the organization does meet the constraints established by an external public, in this case, the government. Here the external public has the power to ensure compliance through fines and the possible shutdown of operations. Mandatory constraints may also force the company to act in a particular fashion. For example, the Internal Revenue Service forces the company to comply with the federal tax laws or else be fined and its officers jailed. This mandatory action is demonstrated in Figure 1.5 by point A. Area B is an example of mandatory restraint from a particular action.

Although certain constraints may be placed on an organization by external publics, by no means are these mandatory constraints permanent. In the auto company example, note that several actions are the result of the legal constraint. Some are directed at compliance, others at reducing the law's influence over the auto company by modifying the constraint.

Discretionary Constraints for Modern Business Firms

Discretionary constraints are those over which the organization has some control. Even though the organization may not be required to act or be restrained from acting regarding a specific concern, management has decided that the organization will constrain its actions. Although mandatory constraints are imposed on the organization by means of a penalty such as

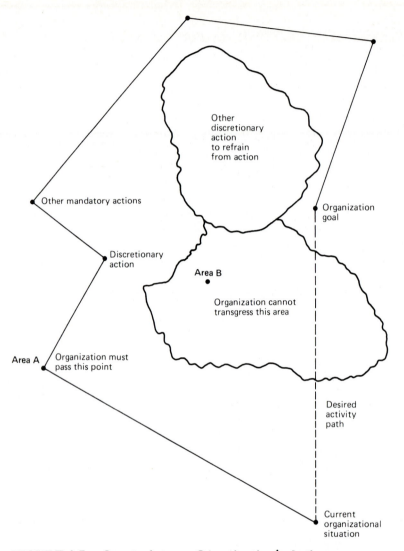

FIGURE 1.5.   Constraints on Organization's Actions.

legal sanctions, which could substantially damage the organization, discretionary constraints are not. Sanctions may still be associated with discretionary constraints, but they would not be as severe as those with mandatory constraints.

Discretionary constraints are determined by management. It is management that decides a particular course of action or discretionary constraint (either to avoid or to carry out a particular action). Management's discretion can be based on cost versus benefit considerations. This cost-benefit analysis calculates the cost of the proposed constraint balanced against the particular gains associated with compliance. Costs and benefits are calculated under conditions of certainty or risk and uncertainty. Under conditions of certainty, all the costs and benefits are known. Under risk and uncertainty, the costs and benefits can be calculated, although the amounts in some cases may have to be based on probability estimates. In either case, it is still possible to make some cost comparisons of the benefits of deciding on particular proposals. If there are intangible benefits or costs, it will be more difficult to calculate those costs and benefits.

Intangible costs or benefits are those that cannot be easily translated into dollar considerations. Items such as goodwill, the value of a patent, the improvement in an organization's image to the general public, and the value of a management development program are all examples whose dollar value of the benefits or costs is difficult to estimate. Intangible costs, though difficult to translate into dollar terms, are still important to the manager in determining an optimal set of strategies to guide the organization's future.

Given the difficulty of determining specific costs and benefits associated with intangibles and the problems associated with cost or benefit estimation in many other projects, it is apparent that the strategy and policy formulation (S&PF) group may have trouble choosing among particular courses of actions. These difficulties are complicated further by the political nature of the organizational setting. Other external and internal publics could be attempting to convince management to constrain its actions further. It is the responsibility of management to reconcile the differences among these groups and their strategic proposals and to devise a strategic plan that meets the needs of these groups and also provides a consistent and coherent focus for the organization's members. Often, this means meeting some of the demands of the various publics and developing strategies that will diffuse particular issues in order to reduce the damaging effect that those demands might have on the organization.

A Diffusion Strategy

Diffusing the power or demands of a coalition group is important in coordinating the demands of the external and internal publics with the goals of the organization. Just as a public must convince the organization of the merits of its proposal, so must an organization be able to articulate its point of view and be able to negotiate effectively that its goals will not be compromised. In some cases, however, nominal compliance by the organization will be sufficent to reduce the coalition's power, by satisfying enough of its members. Nominal compliance requires sufficient minor behavior changes by the organization to satisfy the public while still maintaining its planned course of action. For example, a soft-drink company may agree to a plan for hiring minority employees. Even though the hiring has not begun, the interest group may be satisfied enough to reduce its initial demands.

Other Strategies in Dealing with Constraints

There are several strategies that management can use to comply with the coalition's wishes. In the most conciliatory respect, management can directly comply with the coalition's wishes and develop a strategy to meet the concerns of the coalition. In the least conciliatory strategy, management can refuse to listen to any of the coalition's concerns. The middle ground includes a study of the merits of the action and a review of the reasons that the organization can or cannot acquiesce to the coalition's wishes.

The granting of discretionary constraints must be carefully decided by management. An organization has only limited resources, and its actions must fit its objectives and goals. Each proposed strategy must be measured not only on its own merits but also with respect to the organization's overall strategic plan. One play may be better than another. Limited resources must be allocated in a manner that will ensure the organization's survival and success in meeting its needs. The same is true with one's own personal finances.

For example, if you have savings of $1,000, you can choose how to spend it. You must decide how it can be of the most benefit to you. It might be used for a down payment on a new car or new clothes, be saved to pay for future education, or be donated to a charity. As the decision maker, you must determine which option will maximize your own tangible or intangible welfare. If you then compare the difficulty in making your decision with the millions of dollars affecting hundreds of workers with a multitude of external and internal coalitions attempting to influence your decision making, you will have some idea of the complexity of organizational strategy and policy formulation.

Not only the environmental opportunities, threats, and constraints but also the determination of the organization's strengths and vulnerabilities must be understood. Because of the possible gaps in information and the imprecision of forcasting, determining the merits of proposed strategies will be difficult. In the choice of strategies, not only what is economically best for the organization but also the demands by various publics and the consequences of the proposed strategies must be considered. The end result is a framework of imperfect information, influence pressures, and resource limitations.

In light of all these problems, what are the implications for determining the degree of social responsibility of business? The extent of its social role is important to determining its overall strategies.

DILEMMAS IN DELINEATING THE SOCIAL ROLE OF BUSINESS

There are four dilemmas facing the strategy and policy formulation (S&PF) group in delineating the social role of business: (1) the definition of social needs, (2) the difficulty of prioritizing social needs, (3) the problems associated with selecting and devising strategies that will help fulfill social needs, and (4) the responsibility that the S&PF group has to the organization's owners and employees.

Defining Social Needs

There is almost an unlimited number of actions that an organization can take to meet its social responsibility. Determining the social areas in which a business might become involved includes considering the organization's objectives, the decision makers' value system, and the various publics' desires with which the organization is involved. Difficulties ensue when the S&PF group relies only on popular opinion to select areas for social involvement.

Popular opinion regarding social issues seems to change almost daily. Often the changes occur even though the previous popular issue has not yet been resolved. In the early 1970s antipoverty issues garnered the attention of most of the world. By the later 1970s human rights and social justice seemed to be the major social concern. Now in the early 1980s it appears that nuclear disarmament is the focal concern, closely followed by poverty, violations of human rights, and social injustice. An organization that relies on an issue's popularity may not be serving its best interests, using its resources wisely, or making the most effective contribution to social change. Social actions should be selected after much thought about and research into the areas in which the organization can most effectively meet social needs.

Prioritizing Social Needs

In defining society's social needs, prioritization of those needs can help determine the appropriate actions to take. With the multitude of actions that can be taken, the most important issues must be identified. Top priority should be assigned to those issues that must be dealt with immediately. Other issues are placed into a secondary category for consideration if the organization still has sufficient resources. A final category might be those issues that the organization will consider only after the primary and secondary categories have been satisfied.

Ordering socially responsible actions into categories of importance may become a relatively callous procedure. It is imperative, however, that some clear choices be made by management so that the strategies of social responsibility will lead to the greatest benefit to the organization and have a positive effect on society. Each organization has special competencies and abilities. Maximization of social welfare strategies should require management to pursue actions that blend the organization's resources with its talents.

One approach used by some business firms to choose among social concerns is to establish whether the social action being contemplated directly affects the organization or addresses a broader issue more remote from the organization's routine activities. For example, an organization may decide to choose between committing resources for development programs for women and minority workers and committing funds to air the issues associated with nuclear disarmament. Both issues are topical and important to the organization, but the organization probably would opt for the former proposal because the organization and the immediate community would directly benefit from the development programs, whereas the benefits of the latter program would be less quantifiable or have less perceived direct value. Often an organization will select projects that offer a high degree of visibility; that is, a project may be selected only if it offers a high potential for demonstrating to the public that this particular company is involved with a socially responsible program.

Fulfilling Social Needs

The third dilemma facing business management in determining its degree of social responsibility is selecting effective actions that will induce positive change in social problems. In this respect, the problem is what action is appropriate and whether the organization has sufficient resources and time to induce the necessary change. For example, an owner of a small business may want to take action in order to preserve the downtown business area as a cultural center. The action might be a series of comprehensive meetings of local government officials and business leaders to mount a cooperative effort. Additionally, it might mean voluntary contributions of $1,000 per year for seven years. The sole proprietor may be hesitant to extend his or her commitment because of the money involved and the time needed to get the cultural program under way. In this example, the sole proprietor simply does not have the resources to induce change: therefore, another project may be chosen, one more likely to lead to substantial change and requiring resources more in line with the capabilities of his or her organization.

Determining what an effective action would be is important. There are different directions that can be taken in tackling a pressing social problem, and various actions might lead to the same result. The difficulty with advancing solutions is measuring the tangible results. One organization committing relatively insignificant time and resources to a global social problem may be seen as having little effect on the situation, and therefore, the organization may be hesitant to allocate resources with little chance of seeing positive results.

Organizations' Own Needs

The fourth difficulty facing business managers is their responsibility to their own organization. In carrying out socially responsible actions, managers have to be careful not to violate their responsibilities to their own organization. Resources committed elsewhere are, in essence, taken away from the organization. These other uses are not necessarily in the organization's best interests and, in fact, can deprive the organization of the resources that it may need to survive and prosper. If, for example, the directors of a big auto company decide to make a substantial contribution to study the problems of water pollution, it may take away valuable resources to compete with automobiles imported from Japan and Europe. Questions could be raised as to the correctness of the board's conduct. Was its decision in the best interests of the company's owners and employees and the rest of society? Answering this question becomes paramount to deciding the social role of business, both in a theoretical and practical sense.

In conclusion, the dilemmas faced by modern business managers regarding their companies' social roles are very hard to resolve. Managers are faced with complex social problems with little focus and little means by which to prioritize concerns. Strategies to solve some of the social problems are not very clear in terms of either costs or outcomes. The resources used for social actions directly compete with the resources needed to sustain the organization. Additionally, there are growing concerns that managers' legal and moral responsibilities are such that their first priority is to the organization, its owners, and its employees. These are the constraints under which the managers of today's business organization must operate.

Fortunately, most organizations are managed by reasonable, prudent, and moral people. The typical business firm is not a monolithic entity that is attempting to dominate and exercise its power over all aspects of life in order to meet its goals. Rather, it consists of a group of reasonable individuals who manage so as to meet organizational objectives and also society's needs. As the remainder of the book will show, however, striking this balance is neither easy nor, in the eyes of the various publics, always attained.

SUMMARY

The goal of this chapter was to show the importance of the business sector and provide a strategic management perspective. A business firm is an artificial creation of society, and its role is to serve society. Just as society needs business to meet its needs, so business depends on society to supply its needed inputs and to consume its output.

Strategic management seems like an effective way to begin to analyze the social role of business. The strategy formulation process provides a framework in which the social role for business as a whole or a particular firm can be determined. Strategies evolve through an analysis of the internal organization environment and the relevant external environment. From this comprehensive analysis, environmental opportunities, threats, and constraints are balanced against the organization's strengths, vulnerabilities, and capabilities in a process called gap analysis. It becomes clearer through gap analysis what direction the organization ought to pursue in order to ensure its long-term viability.

The gap analysis facilitates the formulation of alternative strategies. To help select an optimal strategy, each is translated into a detailed plan of implementation. The implementation plan includes detailed financial and operating forecast statements. In certain cases in which environmental outcomes are less certain, additional scenario forecasts may be made. Detailed implementation plans lead to a more objective base from which to select an optimal set of strategies to guide the organization's future behavior.

Economically rational choices are not the only decision criterion used in strategy choice. Various internal and external publics modify the actions of the organization through mandatory or discretionary constraints. It is management's role to negotiate an accommodation of the various demands placed on the organization by its various publics and still maintain the centrality of purpose in meeting the organization's goals.

The social role of business can be determined through strategy and policy formulation. The complexity of this process is matched only by the complexity of the choice of the degree of an organization's social responsibility. The decision as to an organization's social role is hindered by the four dilemmas outlined in the final section of this chapter.

DISCUSSION AND STUDY QUESTIONS

1. What are Schendel's and Hofer's four levels of strategy in an organization? At which level would the degree of social responsibility be considered? Why is it appropriate that social responsibility be considered at this level?
2. What is the interrelationship between the policy and strategy formulation process and the determination of business's social role?
3. What are the social benefits that can be derived from business, regardless of the social role that business assumes?
4. Why would the organization's success in competing in the environment aid society?
5. Why can management not establish policies without regard to the various external and internal publics that influence the organization?
6. Why would an organization not adopt the optimal strategy in order to reach its goals?
7. Distinguish between discretionary and mandatory constraints.
8. What are the four dilemmas facing management in delineating its social role?
9. Why is it difficult to define social needs? Why is it difficult to prioritize social needs?
10. Why might a company's needs influence its choice of social strategies? Give examples of social policies and strategies that reflect underlying business strategies.

CASES AND INCIDENTS

Hire One More

When Helen Thomas became mayor of a medium-sized city last year, she knew she had her work cut out for her. The budget deficit was forecast at $60 million this year. With her administrative staff, Helen got out her red pen and began going through the proposed budgets line by line. Slowly but surely, they began to cut out those items that they felt were not absolutely necessary to the city's overall operation. One of the easiest decisions was to freeze all hirings and to refuse to replace those who quit or retired. This decision alone saved $1.5 million in the budget. By the time Helen and her aides were finished, there was a surplus of around $1.2 million. But this surplus depended heavily on sales taxes. If the amount of money being collected were to dip, the budget might again run into the red.

Two months after implementing this new budget, a major problem emerged. The 3 percent city sales tax was not generating the necessary tax funds. It seemed that with unemployment in the area running at 11 percent and projected to move up to 15 percent by the end of the year, tax revenues were going to dip dramatically. Unless Helen could turn this situation around, she could not save the budget.

Helen and her people hit on what they thought was a great budget-saving idea. In order to generate sufficient budget revenue, they had to get unemployment down to about 9 percent. This, they reasoned, could be done if all the firms in the city hired just one person. Since there were hundreds of small and large businesses, this campaign could bring unemployment down to approximately 7.5 percent. Of course, if not all the companies complied, this percentage would be much higher. But the mayor's office hoped that some of the larger firms would hire two or more people and thus carry some of the smaller ones.

Unfortunately, this was not what happened. After only two weeks of the current campaign, entitled "Hire One More," Helen realized that this strategy would not solve all her problems. She began the campaign by announcing that three national firms with offices in the city would each be hiring 25 additional workers. After this, however, the numbers dropped off quickly. Most large and intermediate-sized firms agreed to hire one more person or said that they would "take the matter under consideration" and get back to her. Of the 700 small firms that Helen's people called on last week, only 25 promised to hire one more person. One of the small business owners explained his situation this way, "Look, I just don't have any slack. I'm just getting by as is. I can't afford to hire anyone else. If things pick up, sure I'll consider putting on another person. For the moment, however, forget it. If anything, I'm considering letting some people go."

ANALYSIS

1. If you were to use a strategy formulation process, what publics would you consider if you were the mayor? Why?
2. How does your answer to the first question tie in with Mintzberg's model presented in the chapter?
3. Why was the mayor's campaign failing? Can you make any recommendations? Give the mayor one detailed suggestion for dealing with her current dilemma.

The Co-Opting Chairperson

In a large midwestern state, there is a metropolis that has an antiquated electric power plant. Three years ago, because of the rising cost of oil and the increasing expenses associated with maintaining the antiquated facilities, the utility management discovered a new approach to reduce long-run costs to the consumer and update the equipment. It proposed a nuclear plant to be built right next to its current facilities. The chairperson of the board thought the idea was good, and all the members of the board concurred. However, they also realized that there were many people who were against nuclear power and that there would be quite a fight over the proposal. So instead of simply making the proposal to the local power regulatory agency, the board began formulating a strategy that would increase its chances of acceptance by both the agency and the general public.

The first thing it did was conduct a cost-benefit analysis to show how the long-run price of electricity would be lower with a nuclear plant than with its current one. Second, it consulted with businesses in the local area to get their opinions and advice regarding how to proceed. Third, it put together a team of in-house personnel to investigate and research the most common antinuke arguments and find out the most successful strategies employed by those utilities that had been able to succeed in their nuclear power plant plans. Having done all of this, the company then asked for a hearing with the public power agency.

The meeting room was filled with people who wanted to hear the company's proposal. In addition to the press, there were many who had brought placards that read, "Down with Nukes" and "Don't Endanger Our Kids' Lives." There were also some who had signs that read "Better Living Through Nuclear Power." Realizing that things could get out of hand, the chairperson of the public power agency restricted the number of people allowed into the hearing room to only those who could be seated. The only people who were standing were 15 police officers, all of whom were determined to maintain law and order. There was no need for them. After presenting the proposal for a nuclear facility, the chairperson asked that the agency appoint a group to serve as a feasibility committee. This committee would review both the benefits and the drawbacks of the proposal. The committee would include members of the power agency, the utility, and the general public. No one in the room was opposed. The agency agreed, and the meeting adjourned within an hour. On the way out, one of the news reporters heard an antinuke person say, "I don't believe it. They just co-opted us."

ANALYSIS

1. What groups in the general public would be interested in attending a meeting of this sort? Describe four.
2. In what way did the company "co-opt" the antinukes?
3. Overall, was the utility's strategy well thought out? Why or why not?

A Case of Quality

The Gallen Corporation produces components for use in personal computers. One of its biggest competitors is the Whaller Corporation. Between them, the two firms account for approximately 23 percent of all the components used in the personal computers of one of the nation's largest manufacturers of these machines. Last year Gallen's profit was 22 percent of sales; Whaller's was 13 percent.

When the salespeople from both companies met with the manufacturer to talk about new annual contracts, both were delighted to learn that each would be given increases of 15 percent over last year's orders. The manufacturer did, however, indicate that the terms of their contracts would be the same as before: all orders had to be delivered on time, and there would be an inspection of all components. If more than 2 percent of any lot were found to be defective, the entire lot would be returned, and all costs associated with shipping and inspection by the manufacturer would be charged to the account of the respective firm. Both component producers agreed to the terms.

Later that day two senior salespeople from the respective firms were having a drink and discussing their good fortune. The conversation eventually turned to profit, and both admitted that they had read the annual statement of the other firm. The Whaller salesman asked his counterpart, "How did you manage to earn 22 percent on sales? We were lucky to clear 13 percent." His friend smiled, "Actually, the answer is simple. We invested heavily in new production machinery and redesigned the jobs in our factory. So we now turn out higher-quality products the first time around, and when there is a mistake, our people pick it up almost immediately. That's why we were able to double our total sales this last year. Many people whom I go to see already know about our manufacturing quality, so I have a signed contract before I leave the premises. As I understand your firm's operations, you work hardest at trying to keep the customer happy, regardless of the cost. With that strategy, you'll always have lots of customers, but do you have to do it at so great a cost? The key to keeping the customer happy these days is better quality. Why, we had some consultants in last month who were showing us that across American industry, the firms with the highest quality also have the greatest market share. If that's true, your firm is going to have to change its managerial and operating philosophies." The other salesman thanked him for the advice. "I'll pass it on to higher-level management. Who knows? Maybe for once they'll listen to me."

ANALYSIS

1. In this case, is increased quality a mandatory constraint or a discretionary constraint? Explain your logic.
2. In what way does this case illustrate how a firm can tie its needs to those of society at large?
3. Why does the Whaller management not use a quality production strategy similar to that of Gallen? What recommendations would you make to the firm?

Historical Foundation

Chapter Objectives

- To provide a historical background for the changing societal perspective as to the role of business in society.
- To develop an understanding of the philosophies that aided business growth during the Industrial Revolution.
- To promote a greater awareness of the shortcomings of pure capitalism in an imperfect market.
- To trace the emergence of the government as a proactive force in a country's economic well-being through monetary and fiscal actions.
- To point out the growing importance of interest groups in shaping the role of business in society.

As one becomes older (and perhaps, but not necessarily, wiser), the importance of history becomes better recognized and appreciated. This is especially true in examining the history of the social role of business. History teaches important lessons, and modern issues and concerns take on added meaning when placed into historical context. For example, in Chapter 1 we mentioned that Johns-Manville filed for bankruptcy because of its problems with asbestos. Historically, it is interesting and very revealing to note that its founder, Henry Ward Johns, who made a fortune mining asbestos and inventing uses for it, died in 1898 of "dust pthisis pneumonitis," called *abestosis*.[1] In other words, history often reveals that we come full circle and that we spend a lot of time reinventing wheels. In this chapter we give a comprehensive treatment of the early historical impact of business on society, through modern times.

THE PREBUSINESS ERA

The period before A.D. 1100 is often referred to as the prebusiness era. There was no commerce as it is known today, though business pursuits, such as manufacturing and trade, did exist. Archaeologists have uncovered silver, spices, and wool that were carried to the major trading centers of the day. Knives, needles, and swords made by Mesopotamian craftsmen were found in Brittany and provide proof that trade routes were established from the Middle East to Western Europe. However, business did not flourish during the period because there was little emphasis on business matters. Even the Greeks, often considered the most advanced culture of ancient history, frowned on commerce; business dealings were left to slaves or low-class citizens. The Romans followed a similar pattern. The elite of these ancient civilizations regarded themselves more as thinkers and organizers than as doers. Business was too much of a bother. One result of this attitude was that early civilizations did not produce significant practical inventions, and they failed to apply their knowledge in functional ways. For example, in China, gunpowder was used for fireworks to keep evil spirits away, and the compass was employed to assure that the head of the deceased was placed in the proper direction.

In the small amount of business that did exist, there were two major influences on the conduct of the manager. First, there was his personal ethics, the standards of conduct or moral judgments based on the conscience and personal dictates. These ethical standards told the manager what was right and wrong and were greatly influenced by his religious beliefs and social affiliations. Second, there were laws or rules of conduct, of which the Code of Hammurabi is an excellent example. Although it was not as sophisticated as modern law, it shows that the commercial activity of the ancient manager was regulated to some degree. One of the laws in the code states: "If a man hire a field laborer, he shall pay him 8 GUR of grain per day."[2] This sounds similar to the current minimum wage law. Other laws were based on the existence of liabilities and responsibilities. "The mason who builds

---

[1]Arthur Sharplin, *Strategic Management* (New York: McGraw-Hill, 1985), p. 21.
[2]Robert F. Harper, *The Code of Hammurabi, King of Babylon* (Chicago: University of Chicago Press, 1904), p. 89.

a house which falls down and kills the inmate shall be put to death.[3] And, "If a wine merchant allows riotous men to assemble in his house and does not expel them, he shall be killed."[4] Still others dealt with agency:

> If the merchant has given to the agent corn, wool, oil, or any sort of goods to traffic with, the agent shall write down the price and hand over to the merchant; the agent shall take a sealed memorandum of the price which he shall give to the merchant.
>
> If an agent has forgotten and has not taken a sealed memorandum of the money he has given to the merchant, money that is not sealed for he shall not put into his accounts.[5]

Although these laws were regulatory, they encouraged business activity. Besides business law, some basic accounting procedures, inventory controls, and wage incentives were developed. Nevertheless, the period is still considered to be a prebusiness era. Production was primarily for consumption. Except for personal dictates and such laws as the Code of Hammurabi, which were restricted to the merchant's immediate customers and not to society as a whole, social responsibility was nonexistent.

PREINDUSTRIAL TIMES AND THE EARLY INDUSTRIAL REVOLUTION

Beginning around A.D. 1100, business moved into the era of petty capitalism (1000–1300). Petty capitalists are often given credit for introducing business to society and are usually associated with the "putting-out" system of capitalism, whereby an owner would advance capital goods or money to an individual in return for a promise to pay interest or dividends. From a social responsibility standpoint, this system is important because it introduced such concepts as charging interest on loans and selling merchandise on credit.

Petty capitalists usually were shopkeepers and merchants and typically bought their wares as cheaply as possible and sold them as high as the market would bear. Their skill in the marketplace was the measure of their success. For this reason they tended to stay close to home and operate in the markets they knew and understood best. They also restricted their product line to items they felt they could handle most easily and most profitably, although in contrast with their predecessors, the petty capitalists were not isolated from social responsibility. In this era the Catholic Church was very powerful, and its teachings affected business philosophy. The basis of these teachings was canon law, which had its origins in theology and Christian

---

[3]E. A. Wallis Budge, *Babylonian Life and History*, 2nd ed. (London: Religious Tract Society, 1925), p. 130.

[4]Budge, p. 126.

[5]Edward C. Bursk, Donald T. Clark, and Ralph W. Hidy, *The World of Business* (New York: Simon and Schuster, 1962), p. 9.

ethics. The Church attempted to determine what kinds of behavior were right or wrong in economic and other areas of society. The two principal doctrines that came to the fore during this period were *just price* and *usury*.

Just price was based on the commandment of Christ, "Whatsoever ye would that men should do unto you, do ye also unto them." St. Thomas Aquinas, in interpreting this doctrine of canon law, stated that everything had only one just price. This price was objective and inherent in the item for purchase but was outside the will of the individual buyer. Thus, just price did not depend on what the individual was willing to pay for the product, but on a fixed value that could not be altered. Accordingly, supply and demand were viewed as not having an effect on the price of the product. Such a concept, of course, undermined the very caprice and skill on which the petty capitalists relied. Nevertheless, the Church fathers frowned on any merchant who attempted to charge more than this just price. The petty capitalist had a social responsibility to uphold this Christian law.

The Church also was concerned with usury. It contended that money in and of itself was barren, an idea espoused earlier by the Greek philosophers. If money was considered barren, it followed that payment for its use could not be justified. This was further supported by the belief that time belonged to God, and hence, no one had a right to charge interest for it.

The petty capitalists attempted all kinds of below-board and devious ways to circumvent these barriers, and they often succeeded. Nevertheless, these examples of canon law represent attempts to define the social responsibility of businesspeople. With the weakening of Church power and the redefinition of liberalization of the concept of usury, some of this kind of social pressure was taken from the shoulders of business. Yet the attempts to define social responsibility, however crude, had begun in earnest.

The petty capitalists eventually gave way to the mercantile capitalists (1300–1800), who did not confine themselves to local markets but instead hired agents to carry their wares to foreign lands. They remained behind and assumed the roles of administrators. The mercantilists were more daring and adventurous than the petty capitalists and were answerable to no one. During this period the Church was losing its power, the Protestant Reformation was in full swing, and military and civil strife on the European continent left little time for interest in the affairs of business or its social responsibilities. Personal ethics were about the only regulator in this period.

By the late part of the eighteenth century the Industrial Revolution was having an effect on all businesspeople. Wondrous new machines were being invented and put into use. Hargreaves's spinning jenny, Arkwright's spinning frame, Watt's steam engine, and Cartwright's power loom appeared on the scene. New factories sprang up to accommodate this machinery, and the beginnings of modern management techniques accompanied these new factories. For example, in Birmingham, England, the Soho Engineering Foundry of Boulton and Watt applied advanced management techniques to manufacturing. This factory was concrete evidence of marketing research and forecasting, machine layout for work flow, production standards, and cost accounting and control. The mercantile capitalists, however, lacked the technical know-how to develop these factory production techniques, and so the golden era of mercantile capitalists and owner-managers drew to a close.

The Industrial Revolution and After

The managers of the period from about 1800 to 1890 are referred to by history as the industrial capitalists. These people were primarily specialists who, by using power-driven machinery and working their employees very hard, mass-produced goods at low prices. In addition, they were strong advocates of John Locke's natural right of property as expressed in his *Two Treatises of Government*[6] and of Adam Smith's economic doctrines of laissez-faire and invisible hand as formulated in his *Wealth of Nations*.[7]

Locke's Natural Right of Property

The central theme of Locke's theory was that the origin of private property was in existence even before the formulation of primitive societies. Ownership of private property was a right that every individual had and one that could not be taken away or annulled by either government or society: it was a natural right of human beings. The other natural rights Locke enumerated were life and liberty. Thus, the concepts of life, liberty, and property provided for in the Declaration of Independence are really Lockean in nature. According to Locke, these inalienable rights should be regulated only to protect them. For example, one person's right to property could be regulated or limited if a second person had a more valid claim to that property. This type of outside control was designed for the sole purpose of protecting the natural rights of individuals.

Private property was of great importance to the industrial capitalists, for it provided a theoretical and moral foundation on which their giant corporations could be built. It followed that as long as these corporations did not interfere with the rights of others, they should not be subjected to government control. But it was not recognized that these giant, powerful enterprises also had a direct influence on the natural rights of people. Thus, according to their own Lockean philosophy, social responsibility was inevitable, but this was almost completely overlooked by the early capitalists.

Adam Smith's Laissez-Faire / Invisible Hand Doctrine

Adam Smith's concept of laissez-faire developed Locke's idea of government nonintervention. Smith's thesis was that the government should have no involvement in business. The role of government ought to be restricted to

---

[6]See George H. Sabine, *A History of Political Theory* (New York: Holt, 1937), pp. 526–528.
[7]Adam Smith, *An Inquiry into the Nature and Cause of the Wealth of Nations* (New York: Modern Library, 1937). (First published in 1776.)

defending against the enemies of the nation, constructing and maintaining public works, and providing services that could not be supplied by anyone else. Business should not be asked to become involved with public service because there was no profit incentive involved. Rather, businesspeople were to be encouraged to compete freely with one another. The invisible hand of supply and demand would dictate the price of goods and services. There was to be no intervention by government. Competition was the most important part of Smith's thesis. He felt that it would ensure such vital societal goals as full employment, economic growth, and the lowest possible prices and operating costs and sincerely believed that government interference would upset the natural phenomenon of competition.

Supporting the laissez-faire doctrine was Herbert Spencer's concept of social Darwinism.[8] As is widely known, Charles Darwin emphasized the survival of the fittest. Spencer's thinking was parallel. He believed that if the environment were not tampered with, the most capable people, by means of natural selection, would rise to positions of leadership. Needless to say, the captains of industry were great advocates of such thinking. Spencer's ideas justified their existence. Although Spencer's concept did not long survive him, during his lifetime it received much public attention and became an excellent rationale for avoiding interference by the public in what the owner-manager felt were the private affairs of the business enterprise.

The Protestant Ethic

The social and religious environment was also compatible with the personal philosophies of the capitalists. Each personified the values and mores contained in the Protestant ethic. Max Weber, in his book *The Protestant Ethic and the Spirit of Capitalism*,[9] pointed out that the Protestants, especially the Calvinists, were greatly responsible for the spirit of capitalism. Although Weber has been criticized for taking too narrow a view of the development of the capitalistic spirit, his overall theory contains a great deal of insight.

Weber noted that the Catholics of the time showed a strong propensity to remain in their crafts, whereas the Protestants were mobile and moved into the upper ranks of skilled labor and took over the administrative positions. Why did this happen? Weber believed that it could be explained in terms of religious beliefs. When Catholics sin, they can obtain absolution by confessing their sins to a priest and performing the penance or good works assigned to them. Such absolution releases tensions and anxieties and compensates for one's imperfections. Weber saw a direct relationship between this absolution and the lack of drive exhibited by many Catholics.

[8]Richard Hofstadter, *Social Darwinism in American Thought*, rev. ed. (Boston: Beacon Press, 1955).

[9]Max Weber, trans. by Talcott Parsons, *The Protestant Ethic and the Spirit of Capitalism* (New York: Scribner's, 1958). (First published in Germany in 1904–1905.)

They were at peace with God, thanks to the sacrament of Confession. There was no evidence of a restless spirit searching for consolation. On the other hand, Weber noticed that for Protestants, especially Calvinists, this was not the case. The Calvinist did not believe that confession or good works performed at one point in time could offset human weakness or thoughtlessness committed at another point in time. Rather, the God of Calvin demanded a life of good works here on earth. No cycle of sin, repentance, atonement, and release was available to the Calvinist. For salvation the Calvinist had to work very hard and be as productive as possible. It only followed that if the person was successful, she or he would begin to acquire many worldly goods. Calvinism saw nothing wrong with these material acquisitions as long as the individual did not squander them on luxuries. High living was forbidden under Calvinism because if people wished to attain salvation, they would have to account for their worldly possessions. Therefore, a good Calvinist should practice asceticism, or self-denial, which would accomplish two important objectives. First, individuals would obtain salvation because they would be able to show God a life of hard work and in addition provide an accounting of all the wealth given to them by Providence. Second, because they did not squander or spend their wealth, they naturally reinvested it. This latter consequence of Calvinism not only helped create but also maintained the spirit of capitalism. In Weber's own words:

> Man is only a trustee of the goods which have come to him through God's grace. He must, like the servant in the parable, give an account of every penny entrusted to him, and it is at least hazardous to spend any of it for a purpose which does not serve the glory of God but only one's own enjoyment. What person, who keeps his eyes open, has not met representatives of this viewpoint even in the present? The idea of man's duty to his possessions, to which he subordinates himself as an obedient steward, or even as an acquisitive machine, bears with chilling weight on his life. The greater the possessions the heavier, if the ascetic attitude toward life stands the test, the feeling of responsibility for them, for holding them undiminished for the glory of God and increasing them by restless effort. The origin of this type of life also extends in certain roots, like so many aspects of the spirit of capitalism, back into the Middle Ages. But it was in the ethic of ascetic Protestantism that it first found a consistent ethical foundation. Its significance for the development of capitalism is obvious.[10]

Many early capitalists were guided by the Protestant ethic. One of the most widely known advocates was Benjamin Franklin, who summed up his philosophy and strategy as follows:

> The way to wealth, if you desire it, is as plain as the way to market. It depends chiefly on two words, industry and frugality; that is, waste neither time nor money, but make the best use of both. Without industry and frugality nothing will do,

[10]Weber, p. 170.

and with them everything. He that gets all he can honestly and saves all he gets will certainly become rich, if that Being who governs the world, to whom all should look for a blessing on their honest endeavors, doth not, in His wise providence, otherwise determine. . . .

In order to secure my character and credit as a tradesman, I took care not only to be in reality industrious and frugal, but to avoid the appearance to the contrary. I dressed plain, and was seen at no places of idle diversion; I never went out a-fishing or shooting.[11]

The Impact of Laissez-Faire and Protestant Ethnic Doctrines on Business Practices

The leaders of commerce and industry at this time readily adopted the philosophies of social Darwinism and laissez-faire government policies. From these philosophies it followed that they had little concern for social responsibility. They were more interested in building giant corporations, as evidenced by the great steel plants and railroad lines that flourished during this era. Although all of this began early in the nineteenth century, the most important changes in America took place during or after the Civil War. In this period businesspersons, to whom history now refers as the robber barons, made their grand entrance. These individuals deserve special attention because of the lasting impact they have had on the history of business in general and social responsibility in particular.

The people often referred to as robber barons or captains of industry are virtually synonomous with the history of American business in this era. They include John D. Rockefeller, J. P. Morgan, Cornelius Vanderbilt, Andrew Carnegie, and Edward Harriman. People with their personal characteristics could not have arrived on the American business scene at a more opportune time. The country was expanding, a transcontinental railroad was about to be built, and industry was growing at a tremendous rate. Between 1820 and 1840 the population of the nation had doubled. The iron, steel, textile, shoe, and construction industries were becoming entrenched in the Middle Atlantic states and the Northeast. The political and economic environment was "ripe for the picking" by the robber barons.

The close association between the captains of industry and the Protestant ethnic might seem to imply that because they were God fearing, they were also kind and generous. This was generally not the case. The hard bargains they drove ruined many competitors, and sometimes, innocent bystanders as well. For example, Rockefeller not only sold oil at a cheaper price per barrel than his competitors did, but he actually forced the railroads, because of the hugh volume of business he gave them, to reciprocate by giving him a rebate on every barrel of oil that *his competitors* shipped. He had the best of both worlds. Eventually, the competitors went bankrupt and sold their wells at his price.

[11]Matthew Josephson, *The Robber Barons* (New York: Harcourt Brace, 1934), p. 10.

Vanderbilt drove the same kind of tough bargain. In one incident he paid key New York politicians for the right to operate a streetcar line from Forty-second Street in Manhattan to the Battery. When the news got out, Vanderbilt's transportation stock rose from $50 to $100 a share. The politicians then sold their stock short and canceled his right to operate the streetcar line. But instead of being able to buy their borrowed stock back at a lower price, they found that Vanderbilt had cornered the market and bought all the outstanding stock. He forced each of his adversaries to repurchase their borrowed securities at $285 a share. These kinds of deals were often made by the robber barons.

When dealing with workers the robber barons were at times ruthless. Henry Frick, who was president of Carnegie Company, broke the Homestead strike of 1892 by bringing in Pinkerton men and scab labor. This occurred even though Carnegie professed to oppose the use of scabs. Within six months Frick had ended the strike. The robber barons generally approved of Frick's methods. Rockefeller wrote to Frick, complimenting him on the action he had taken. In his own factories Rockefeller refused to permit collective bargaining, and he allowed only company unions. To him there was a time-honored relationship between obedient servants and good masters, and non-company unions did not fit into this relationship.

In general, the barons undoubtedly believed they were doing the right things and sincerely felt they had been selected by God to do their work. Rockefeller stated: "I believe the power to make money is a gift of God . . . to be developed and used to the best of our ability for the good of mankind. Having been endowed with the gift I possess, I believe it is my duty to make money . . . and still more money, according to the dictates of my conscience.[12] Rockefeller's use of money for the good of humankind is difficult to understand. While he was supporting missionary work in China, the employees of his Colorado Fuel and Iron Company were being shot or burned alive in industrial strikes.

One of the major failings of these early industrialists was their simplistic view of their fellow human beings. For example, they felt that all workers were basically lazy, would shun responsibility whenever and wherever possible, and could be motivated only through economic incentives. Making these assumptions, later termed *Theory X* by Douglas McGregor, the early capitalists managed accordingly.[13] Rather than trying to understand workers as complex, heterogeneous individuals, they often exploited them, and they usually treated customers the same way. Because all emphasis was directed toward production, they tended to neglect customers, seeking too often to deal with them on a mass-production rather than an individual basis.

This era drew to a close around the turn of the century. Although Rockefeller had built an empire in oil, Vanderbilt in railroads, and Carnegie in steel,

---

[12]Josephson, p. 325.
[13]Douglas McGregor, *The Human Side of Enterprise* (New York: McGraw-Hill, 1960).

not all their contemporaries were as fortunate. Especially in the railroad industry, but in other industries as well, many of the businesspeople eventually went bankrupt. The primary reason was cutthroat competition. For example, enterprising individuals would build a railroad line exactly parallel to an existing one, and this was done with the knowledge that there was not enough business to sustain it.

> Speculators were quick to perceive that they could build new lines on the same routes for much less cost than the old ones (especially after '73) and that, with a lower capitalization, they could easily compel the pool to admit them to membership, with all the privileges of a ready-made traffic, and . . . guarantees of . . . exemption from competition. . . .
>
> New roads were built, or sets of old detached ones were connected, so as to afford additional parallels to the existing trunk lines, with no other object than to compel the latter to support them by dividing with them a portion of their traffic, or to accept the alternative of a reckless cutting down of rates.[14]

Situations such as the preceding emphasized the need for some form of cooperative competition. Heretofore, especially in the railroads, pooling arrangements and informal agreements were made, but no mutual trust existed. The robber barons speculated whether or not breaking the agreement would be beneficial to them. This eventually led to destructive competition, and thus, the era of industrial capitalism was replaced by that of financial capitalism (1890–1933). During their heyday, the industrial capitalists had not established any realistic guidelines for social responsibility. In fact, many historians conclude that they completely ignored their obligations to society.

During the late nineteenth and early twentieth centuries, some degree of order was restored to the chaos that had existed during the waning years of industrial capitalism. Those responsible for this order are known as the financial capitalists (1890–1933). Their primary approach was to form business trusts, an arrangement that made it easier for all companies to exist. Many of these famous trusts are well known to students of history. The largest were the huge Standard Oil Company, put together by Rockefeller, and the giant U.S. Steel Corporation, which was formed by J. P. Morgan when he merged several smaller steel firms.

The hugh combines did reduce some of the cutthroat competition, but there were few benefits for the consumer and the rest of society. The supercompanies were no more socially responsible after eliminating competition. The benefactors were the owners; and economic conditions were still as unstable as ever. Panics and recessions still appeared in seemingly regular cycles,[15] creating economic hardship for the whole country through widely fluctuating prices and high unemployment. Competition that could produce lower prices and greater market efficiencies was stifled by the economic sabotage waged by the monopolies in power. The large oil companies would price well below

[14]Josephson, p. 189.
[15]Josephson, p. 189.

cost in order to drive competition out of an area. Once competition was gone, prices would be greatly increased, creating severe hardship for the people. If another competitor entered the territory, prices again would go below cost to force the newcomer into bankruptcy.[16] If the oil company could not economically force a competitor out of business, a price-fixing agreement could be established benefiting both companies at the expense of the consumer. Railroads would establish low freight rates on routes that had competing sources of transportation such as other rail lines or barge lines. On routes that had little or no competition, rates would be much higher. Situations arose in which the total cost to ship goods 300 miles was cheaper than shipping goods 100 miles.[17] Countless other examples exist indicating that the concepts of laissez-faire and the invisible hand were not working. When commerce and industry consisted of small independently owned companies, the invisible hand doctrine might have been effective. But with the advent of the Industrial Revolution, this doctrine failed. With concentrated pools of capital backing the large organizations and highly capital oriented industries and services, entrance into the market was difficult. The condition was aggravated by the lack of social consciousness by the captains of industry. The highly fluctuating economic conditions, monopolistic price structure, and a "public be damned" attitude by the large corporations led to a precarious situation between the public and business. The death knell for the laissez-faire and invisible hand doctrines occurred during the worst economic slump experienced by the industrial world. The depression of the 1930s led to the birth of a new philosophy of business and government relations. The next section will examine this new philosophy and its impact on modern society and the social role of business.

TWENTIETH-CENTURY COMMERCE AND INDUSTRY

On Thursday, October 14, 1929, there began a series of stock market losses that signaled the end of both the boom period of the 1920s and the government's policy of minimal interference in the activities of business. A week of disastrous drops in the price of stocks ensued. There was a massive selling of securities in all forms. As Galbraith described it,

> In mid-November 1929, the market stopped falling. The low was on Wednesday, November 13th. On that day the Times industrial listings closed at 224, down from 452, or almost exactly half since September 3rd. They were also, by then, down 82 points, about one quarter from the close on that day two weeks before.[18]
> After the great (stock market) crash came the great depression which lasted, with varying severity, for ten years. In 1933, GNP (total production of the economy)

[16]Josephson, p. 269.
[17]Josephson, p. 196.
[18]John Kenneth Galbraith, *The Great Crash* (Boston: Houghton Mifflin, 1972), p. 140.

was nearly a third less than in 1929. Not until 1937 did the physical volume of production recover to the levels of 1929, and then it promptly slipped back again. Until 1941 the dollar volume of production remained below 1929. Between 1930 and 1940, only once, in 1937, did the average number of unemployed during the year drop below 8 million. In 1933, nearly 13 million people were out of work, or about one in every four in the labor force. In 1938 one person in five was still out of work.[19]

Although the stock market crash was not the cause of the Depression, it was symptomatic of the difficulties that the United States and the rest of the industrialized world were in. Through overproduction and a lack of demand for products, the entire economic system in the United States was rapidly stagnating. Because of government inaction, the situation worsened. In the first six months of 1929, 346 banks failed, losing $115 million in assets.[20] The weakening of the economy in some areas, such as in the banking industry, started a domino effect, creating difficulty in other parts of the economy and a general panic. Both political parties still maintained that the cure for these economic problems was balancing the federal budget. "The rejection of both fiscal (tax and expenditure) and monetary policy amounted precisely to a rejection of all affirmative government economic policy. The consequences were profound."[21] Finally, society demanded more from the federal government, and Franklin D. Roosevelt's New Deal provided the change in direction. This new affirmative program by the federal government, following Roosevelt's election as president in 1932, initiated a theory that government expenditures and monetary policy can do much to modify the economy. This active role was reflected in a new economic theory expounded by a British lord, John Maynard Keynes, in his 1936 treatise.[22] A new era had arrived. Society had found that the theory of minimal government intervention was insufficient to meet society's needs. The amount of suffering created during the Depression indicated that the importance of the economy to society as a whole was too great to be left to the haphazard fluctuations prevalent during the past years. The invisible hand of the marketplace was not functioning as Smith had intended. A new approach was necessary.

THE EMERGENCE OF COUNTERVAILING POWERS

Several factors led to the inability of the free marketplace to maintain a stable economic climate. Although Adam Smith's doctrines may have been applicable to a particular type of economy, they were not effective in the

---

[19]Galbraith, p. 173.
[20]Galbraith, p. 184.
[21]Galbraith, p. 191.
[22]J. M. Keynes, *The General Theory of Employment, Interest and Money* (New York: Harcourt Brace, 1936).

new industrial economy of the twentieth century. First, the invisible hand doctrine assumed that when it was economically prudent, competition could easily be created by the formation of new organizations. Such formations could easily take place when businesses were small and consisted of an owner-operator, and little or no startup capital was necessary. With the onset of the Industrial Revolution, and especially with the supercompanies of the 1900s and onward, entrance into an industry on equal footing with the existing corporations was very difficult. As indicated in Chapter 1, established companies had the backing of major banks and pools of resources, and so they could withstand losses for several years in an attempt to underprice any new competition. Against this economic power, most new companies found it difficult to compete with the established companies. Also, with the intertwining of companies and quasi-legal agreements among companies, market forces did not actually have the free competitive spirit necessary under the invisible hand doctrine. Economic power could be more centralized, and the concerted influences could offset the balance of perfect competition. Without government controls, business had unlimited power to ensure that those in command of the situation maintained control.

The public, realizing the inequities in the economic structure, soon demanded some curb on the abuses of business. Public action on many fronts evolved. Later, in 1952, John Kenneth Galbraith coined the term *countervailing powers* to refer to this process.[23] Business at this time had, as society viewed it, too much economic power over society. This pervasiveness included not just the market condition for goods and services but also the realm of the workers' rights. Through this inequity a counterforce was established, and a greater role by the government was demanded. Through government regulations and policies, greater control was placed on the activities of business. In like manner, the government took more action to maintain competition. Laws and the interpretation of the laws became more favorable to the formation of groups to ensure the rights of the consumer, the worker, and society as a whole.

The Changing Role of Government

The first major law affecting the conduct of business was the Sherman Anti-Trust Act, passed in 1890. This act prohibited contracts or business combinations formed to restrain trade or commerce among the states. Any person found to be monopolizing interstate trade or commerce would be guilty of a misdemeanor. The next major piece of legislation was the Clayton Act (1914), passed when it became evident that the Sherman Act failed to enumerate specific acts as being illegal. The Clayton Act prohibited such things as

---

[23]John Kenneth Galbraith, *American Capitalism* (Boston: Houghton Mifflin, 1952), pp. 120–123.

local price discrimination, exclusive selling agreements, tying agreements, holding companies, and interlocking directorates.

The Sherman and Clayton acts were beneficial in helping restrain the monopoly powers of the trusts. Other federal legislation complemented these acts. For example, in 1914 the Federal Trade Commission Act was passed, creating a board of five members charged with preventing the formation and continuation of illegal trade combinations. In 1936, the Robinson-Patman Act was signed into law, forbidding price discrimination and thereby eliminating many of the practices used by chain stores to secure price concessions from their vendors. In 1938 the Wheeler Act prohibited false advertising of certain goods. The purpose of this initial legislation was to protect and promote competition. These early laws are still very much in evidence today. In the post–World War II era the government has brought antitrust suits against many firms, such as the Aluminum Corporation of American, Ling-Temco-Vought when it attempted to add Jones & Laughlin Steel to its conglomerate holdings, and more recently the Justice Department's challenges of International Business Machine's dominant position in the data-processing industry, and the breakup of American Telephone and Telegraph.

Besides a policy of promotion of competition for all industries, the federal government felt it necessary to regulate directly such industries as transportation, public utilities, and communication. The first major act dealing with direct regulation was the Interstate Commerce Act of 1887, aimed specifically at the railroads. The major portions of the law (1) provide that all rates are to be just and reasonable; (2) prohibit personal discrimination in the form of special rates and rebates; (3) forbid undue preference or prejudice to any particular person or company; (4) outlaw pooling; and (5) create an Interstate Commerce Commission to hear complaints of alleged violations. In 1906 pipelines came under government regulation (Hepburn Act). Eventually, laws followed to regulate water transportation (1920), motor carriers (1935), and finally, air transport (1938). The Public Utility Holding Company Act (1935) and the Natural Gas Act (1938) did much to regulate the utilities industry, and the Federal Communications Commission (1934) was formed to regulate the communications industry. These acts represent some, though certainly not all, of the laws regulating industry and commerce between 1890 and 1945.

A logical conclusion would be that social responsibility should have become an integral part of corporate philosophy because of the pressure of public concern expressed through legislative acts. But this does not seem to be the case. Increased attention was given to public interest, but this was legally, not humanistically, based. The pre–World War II corporation seemed interested in what it could and could not do only from a legal standpoint, so the laws served only to police and restrain the corporation. Public policy did not demand that corporations take an active interest in community affairs or concern themselves with social issues.

*"I'm sorry, Mr. Jones. . .You're not
rich enough to pay no taxes."*

Source: Informational advertising
from Taxation with Representation;
Suite 204, 1523 L St.; Washington, D.C.
Used with permission.

Monetary and Fiscal Policies

Since 1936, the increased activity of the federal government in modifying
the economy has followed the theories postulated by John Maynard Keynes,[24]
who proposed that economic conditions such as unemployment and inflation
be modified by governmental monetary and fiscal action. During periods
of high inflation and low unemployment, inflation could be reduced by curbing government expenditures or increasing tax rates. During these boom
years, the government would maintain a surplus budget. During periods of
recession when there was high unemployment and low inflation, government
policy would again attempt to modify the economic conditions. High government expenditures and/or lowering tax rates would increase business activity
and encourage employment. During these periods the federal budget would
be operated at a deficit. Over the long run, it was hypothesized, the budget
would be balanced. Additional government expenditures would have a multi-
plier effect throughout the economy, increasing economic activity.

In summary, both regulatory and economic activism were deemed proper
roles for the government to take to ensure the qualify of life for society.
Additionally, society moved toward a legal structure that enhanced other

[24]Keynes, pp. 120–123.

countervailing groups' ability to check business activities. Both labor unions and special-interest groups became common parts of American life.

The More Active Role of Labor Unions

American labor unions had been trying to organize almost since the signing of the Constitution. A few small craft unions were actually in existence before 1800. The first unions were confined to the northeast and north central sections of the country and involved only a few industries, ship workers, printers, and shoemakers. Although unions in the 1830s showed a substantial growth rate, the panic of 1837 hurt their cause. Employers typically resisted union demands and, in many instances, successfully sought court protection. Under common law, early court cases held unions to be illegal conspiracies.

After the panic in the early 1850s, a resurgence in national prosperity brought workers back to the unions. As evidence of their growth in this period, it was estimated that more than 400 strikes were staged between 1853 and 1854. In 1869 the Knights of Labor came into existence. Formed by a small band of Philadelphia tailors, it was originally a secret organization, although it abandoned this secrecy in 1879. By 1886 its membership had risen from 9,000 to 700,000. Poor leadership eventually led to its demise, but another craft group, the American Federation of Labor (A.F. of L.) that was formed in 1886 under the leadership of Samuel Gompers, managed to survive and prosper. By 1900 the A.F. of L membership was 870,000.

Because the A.F. of L. was craft oriented, there was no union for industrial workers. In 1935 this void was filled by the Congress of Industrial Organizations (C.I.O.), organizing the powerful steel and auto workers. The A.F. of L. and C.I.O. are well known to labor history, but there also were other important union movements during this period. The railroad brotherhoods, started just after the Civil War, and the United Mine Workers, headed by John L. Lewis, made especially significant impacts on their respective industries.

Starting in the late 1800s, unions and management seemed to be in a continuous battle. The industrial capitalists were ignoring and, in some cases, exploiting their workers. Their assumptions about workers closely followed McGregor's Theory X. They believed the workers were lazy, avoided responsibility whenever and wherever possible, and had to be managed by the old carrot-and-stick technique. When the first laws to regulate commerce were passed between 1886 and 1914, most businesspeople failed to recognize the trend that was beginning to sweep the country. The public felt that the corporations had become too powerful, and the pendulum was beginning to swing away from corporate management and toward the worker. The strength of the union movement, accompanied by supporting legislation, was proof of the changes that were taking place.

In 1926 the Railway Labor Act was passed. Although it applied only to a limited number of employees and was confined to the railroads, it provided a precedent for the establishment of collective bargaining. The market crash of 1929 and the following Depression actually provided a great boost to union power in America, as did the Norris–La Guardia Act of 1932, which stated that a union could enjoin a threatened violation of a contract by an employer. Norris–La Guardia protected the union's most powerful tool, the right to strike.

In 1935 the height of union power was reached with the passage of the National Labor Relations Act, commonly called the Wagner Act. The act was the first broad declaration of labor policy and procedure stated and enforced by the federal government. The key part of the act was Section VII, which stated that employees had the right to engage in concerted activities for the purpose of collective bargaining or other mutual aid for protection. The act also listed the following five unfair practices by the employer:

1. Interfering, restraining, or coercing employees in the exercise of their rights in Section VII.
2. Dominating and interfering with the formation or administration of labor organizations or contributing financially to its support.
3. Discriminating in conditions of employment against the employees for the purpose of encouraging or discouraging members in any labor organization.
4. Discharging or discriminating against employees because they filed or gave testimony under the act.
5. Refusing to bargin collectively with the duly accredited representatives of the employees.

The Wagner Act also provided for the establishment of a National Labor Relations Board, to consist of three nonlabor or nonemployer members. The functions of this board were to prevent unfair labor practices and to conduct employee elections to select a bargaining agency. The elected agency, usually a union, would then possess the collective bargaining power of all the workers. Between 1930 and 1945 union membership rose from 3.5 million to approximately 15 million, this growth largely attributable to the Wagner Act. Although our discussion provides only a cursory view of the act, it does show the power it extended to the unions.

The labor laws presented management with a second front. They were not only restricted in the area of trusts, but now they were also forced to recognize and bargain collectively with the union. Yet even with these legislative pressures, there still was no movement toward a truly comprehensive concept of social responsibility. Certainly nothing existed in the pre–World War II years that would even approach the social responsibility concept of modern times. But this does not imply that no new thinking was taking place. Management realized that the workers were determined to have a say about their pay and working conditions. Personnel departments sprang up either to deal with the union or keep the union out. Most managers were convinced that it would be a danger to take the unions too lightly and realized that now corporate philosophy and responsibility must include labor.

The Introduction of Special-Interest Groups

One of the most recent countervailing powers in the world today is the special-interest group. Many individuals feel that governments are slow to respond to their needs, labor unions are unresponsive, and business is indifferent. A solution to this lack of response to concerns and needs is for people to establish special groups in order to protect their interests. These special-interest groups represent such diverse viewpoints as consumerism, environmental protection, for and against the equal rights amendment, social reform, antibusiness, probusiness, and even antitax increase. The Committee for the Advancement of Public Interest Organizations categorized the various special-interest groups in the United States today, and its directory consists of nearly 1,000 pages.[25]

The growing power of interest groups is the result of the people's insistence on their rights; the media exposure available and necessary to popularize a cause; and the favorable rulings by the courts toward court action, especially class action suits.[26] The impact of these special-interest groups will continue to challenge the other countervailing power groups and will offer another means by which the needs of society can be expressed through law reform and publicized private corporate activities.

SUMMARY

The historical foundation for understanding the social responsibility of business goes back to before the Industrial Revolution. Beginning around A.D. 1100, business moved into the era of petty capitalism, during which time shopkeepers and merchants emerged. This was followed by the era of the mercantile capitalists, who expanded business operations into foreign markets. By the early 1800s the age of industrialism had arrived, and business grew even larger under the direction of the industrial capitalists. The philosophy and thinking of their day, as presented by Locke's natural right of property, Smith's doctrine of laissez-faire, Spencer's concept of social Darwinism, and the Protestant ethic subscribed to by so many financially successful businesspersons, all served to spur business activity to new heights, though there was little concern for social responsibility. It was basically an era categorized by cutthroat competition and unethical business practices. This

[25]Gerald R. Rosen, "The Growing Clout of 'Do Good' Lobbies," *Dun's Review*, April 1977, in *A Managerial Odyssey: Problems in Business and Its Environment*, ed. Arthur Elkins and Dennis W. Callaghan (Reading, Mass.: Addison-Wesley, 1979), pp. 475–487.

[26]Claire Wilcox and William G. Shepherd, *Public Policies Toward Business*, 5th ed. (Homewood, Ill.: Richard D. Irwin, 1975), pp. 289–290.

continued well into the twentieth century, until the depression of the 1930s led to the birth of a new philosophy of business. The Great Depression proved a number of important things. One was that Smith's doctrine of the invisible hand did not work. Actually, if one wanted to use a term to describe the actions and reactions in the economy, *countervailing power* would be more accurate.

Before the Depression, the government had been increasing its regulation of business. With the Depression came even more regulation, a trend that continued until the early 1970s. This was not the only countervailing force to emerge during the 1930s; unions also began to grow in power. In particular, the Wagner Act strengthened labor unions and provided them with a new-found impetus for growth. Today, another such countervailing power is the special-interest groups that represent such diverse viewpoints as consumerism, environmental protection, and social reform.

Each of the major power sources attempts to influence the others, leading to a system of checks and balances. The existence of countervailing power thus presents both a solution and a dilemma to a concerned society. On the one hand, it promises equality and fair treatment for all; on the other, it poses the very real danger that one power will become so strong that it will be able to dictate to the others. In the next chapter we put this historical context into a political-economic framework and examine the social role of business in modern society.

DISCUSSION AND STUDY QUESTIONS

1. Who were the petty capitalists? In what kinds of business activities did they engage?
2. What is meant by each of the following: Locke's natural right of property, Smith's doctrine of laissez-faire, the doctrine of the invisible hand, Spencer's doctrine of social Darwinism, and the Protestant ethic?
3. In what way are the Protestant ethic and the spirit of capitalism related?
4. "The robber barons were as socially responsible as any other business people of their day." Do you agree or disagree with this statement? Explain.
5. During the late nineteenth and early twentieth centuries, some degree of order was restored to the chaos that had existed during the waning years of industrial capitalism." What is meant by this statement?
6. In what way was Adam Smith's economic doctrine of the invisible hand an erroneous theory? Explain.
7. What is the theory of countervailing power?
8. How did the following acts regulate business: Sherman Anti-Trust Act; Clayton Act; Robinson-Patman Act; Interstate Commerce Act?
9. What are the unfair employer practices that are forbidden by the Wagner Act? Explain.
10. Do you think that special-interest groups have a positive or negative impact on our society? Cite examples to support your answer.

CASES AND INCIDENTS

The Invisible Hand

Adam Smith is perhaps best known for his concept of the *invisible hand.* Smith believed that if all individuals pursued their own selfish ends without outside interference, they would be guided by an invisible hand. Guidance by the invisible hand would result in the greatest good for the greatest number of people. Smith tied together the individual, society, and the idea of the invisible hand into an overall philosophy. In his classic book *The Wealth of Nations* (1776), he explained it as follows:

> As every individual, therefore, endeavours as much as he can both to employ his capital in the support of domestic industry, and so to direct that industry that its produce may be of the greatest value; every individual necessarily labours to render the annual revenue of the society as great as he can. He generally, indeed, neither intends to promote the public interest, nor knows how much he is promoting it. By preferring the support of domestic to that of foreign industry, he intends only his own security; and by directing that industry in such a manner as its produce may be of the greatest value, he intends only his own gain, and he is in this, as in many other cases, led by an invisible hand to promote an end which was no part of his intention. Nor is it always the worse for the society that it was no part of his intention. By pursuing his own interest he frequently promotes that of the society more effectually than when he really intends to promote it.[1]

For Smith the invisible hand was almost a natural phenomenon that could exist only in a totally free-enterprise economy. If there was any government interference or regulation, the naturalness would be lost. The invisible hand depended on government's leaving everything alone, as any attempt to control or regulate business would be unnatural.

In the developing years of America, this laissez-faire thinking was the dominating influence on the economic and social affairs of business. Many of the industrial and financial capitalists were avid proponents of the invisible hand, and most of the small businesspersons of the times also subscribed to this philosophy. Today total nongovernment intervention is advocated by few in the business community and by virtually none outside it. There are two reasons for this change in philosophy. First, everyone is resigned to the fact that government reegulation is here to stay. Second, Smith's theory of the invisible hand did not stand up to the test of empirical validation. Paul Samuelson, a well-known economist and winner of the 1970 Nobel

---

[1]Adam Smith, *An Inquiry into the Nature and Cause of the Wealth of Nations* (New York: Modern Library, 1937), p. 423.

prize in economics, summarized the current attitude toward Smith's invisible hand:

> In short, Adam Smith . . . had no right to assert that an invisible hand channels individuals selfishly seeking their own interest into promoting the "public interest"—as these last two words might be defined by a variety of prominent ethical and religious notions of what constitutes the welfare of a nation. Smith has proved nothing of this kind, nor has any economist since 1776.[2]

ANALYSIS

1. Take a stand on the invisible hand theory and defend it.
2. Aside from the economic concept, why else might businesspeople between 1850 and 1920 have believed in the invisible hand theory? Be specific.
3. How does the invisible hand theory relate to social responsibility?

Silence Is Golden*

John D. Rockefeller made a fortune in the oil industry, and a long list of the reasons for his success could be compiled. One obvious factor would be his driving ambition. Another factor was his managerial ability. But any analysis of his success would be incomplete without some mention of the importance he assigned to silence. For Rockefeller, silence was golden. He felt that businesspeople who publicized their transactions only encouraged competition, and he reasoned that it was much wiser to be tight-lipped about all business agreements. This philosophy of silence was well demonstrated by his South Improvement Company.

The South Improvement Company was formed in 1872 by Rockefeller and his partner Henry M. Flagler. The formation of this company was promoted by the chaotic situation that existed at that time in the Pennsylvania oil fields. Businesspeople in the industry were facing both severe competition and mercurial changes in the supply and the market value of oil. These conditions were repellent to the orderly and methodical spirit of the two partners. Prompted by Rockefeller, they forged a plan to overcome this crisis. The basic idea was quite simple. The principal oil-refining companies in the industry were asked to join Rockefeller's Standard Oil Company. The result was the South Improvement Company. Each of these oil firms was offered between one-third and one-half its actual value. This was to be paid in either cash or, as Rockefeller advised, in the Standard Oil common stock. Once a sufficient number of the oil refiners had joined the South

---

[2]Paul A. Samuelson, *Economics: An Introductory Analysis*, 7th ed. (New York: McGraw-Hill, 1967), p. 610.

*Much of the data in this case can be found in Matthew Josephson, *The Robber Barons* (New York: Harcourt Brace, 1934).

Improvement Company, they descended on the Erie, Pennsylvania, and New York Central railroads and demanded special freight rates. In return, the Rockefeller group promised to give all of their freight business to these lines. The railroads consented. The final agreement that was worked out between Rockefeller and the railroads was beneficial to the refiners. On all crude oil shipped to the refinery, there was to be a rebate of 40 to 50 percent by the railroads. On all oil the refiners shipped out, the rebate was to be 25 to 50 percent. In addition, the agreement stated that those refiners who were not members of the Rockefeller group were to be charged twice as much as the Standard Oil Company at Cleveland was. In fact, part of the extra rate paid by nonmembers was to be kicked back to the Rockefeller group. To ensure that the railroads lived up to the agreement, the oil executives had it put down in writing. For example, one of the provisions required that the railroads draw up manifests or waybills documenting all petroleum transported over their lines. Included in these manifests was the name of the consignee and the origin and final destination of the shipment that was turned over to the officers of the South Improvement Company. Thus, the Rockefeller combine not only received rebates from the railroads for oil shipments by its competitors, but it also knew, from the railroad waybills, the exact strategy being followed by its competitors. With this railroad agreement backing him, Rockefeller was in an ideal position to pressure those refiners who remained outside his group.

A possible flaw in this arrangement was that someone might inform the competition or the newspapers about what was happening. Should this leak out, the unorganized refiners might band together to stop Rockefeller. More important, the discovery of such "goings on" might result in government intervention and public indignation. Thus, the entire success of the plan depended on everyone's keeping a tight lip and maintaining silence. To ensure secrecy, Rockefeller required each member of his group to sign a pledge:

> I, _____, do solemnly promise upon my honor and faith as a gentleman that I will keep secret all transactions which I may have with the corporation known as the South Improvement company; that should I fail to complete any bargains with the said company, all the preliminary conversations shall be kept strictly private; and finally that I will not disclose the price for which I dispose of any products or any other facts which may in any way bring to light the internal workings or organization of the company. All this I do freely promise.[1]

Despite these measures, opposition to the scheme eventually materialized. The state of Pennsylvania instituted proceedings against the group, charging that they were guilty of conspiring to restrain trade. Finally, on April 29, 1879, a grand jury indicted Rockefeller, Flagler, and others who

---

[1]Josephson, p. 117.

were deeply involved in the scheme. During the hearings, silence continued to be their guiding philosophy. They successfully evaded questions or merely "refused to answer on the advise of the counsel." None was so skillful as Rockefeller himself. When asked point blank by the prosecutor if there was a Southern Improvement Company, Rockefeller answered that he had never heard of such a company. When asked if he was a member of it, he replied "no." He justified his answers by noting that the prosecutor had erroneously named the company. The prosecutor should have said "South" not "Southern," and Rockefeller felt no cause to volunteer this information. After all, silence is golden.

ANALYSIS

1. "The establishment of the South Improvement Company was necessary to remedy the chaos that existed in the Pennsylvania oil fields." Give reasons both for and against this statement.
2. Was Rockefeller justified in not elaborating on his answer to the prosecutor's question? Explain your answer.
3. Based on this story, do you think Rockefeller's actions were unethical? Explain.

FCC Decision*

Governmental regulation of business has gone through its ups and downs. For example, around the turn of the century there was a clamor for more government control. Many of the early regulatory laws were passed in the period 1880–1910. There was more government regulation during the Great Depression as government tried to protect "the little guy" from the clutches of giant corporations.

Beginning in the mid- to late 1970s, however, regulation did an about-face. More and more industries now found themselves facing less government intervention. Today, the airline industry is heavily deregulated; banks can merge or acquire other banks across town or across the country; and large firms, in general, are finding that the government is not opposed to them buying up or merging with other large firms (just as long as there is no attempt to monopolize the industry or restrain trade). All of this is beginning to make some people wonder if the government has not moved too far, too fast. The telecommunications industry is a good example. Consider some of the major decisions made by the Federal Communications Commission (FCC) that have led to deregulation in this industry:

1966–1980 The telephone company (AT&T) monopoly is broken when the FCC permits other companies to sell devices that connect with

*The data in this case can be found in "Has the FCC Gone Too Far?" *Business Week*, August 5, 1985, pp. 48–54.

	AT&T's network and allows consumers to buy their own telephones.
1980	Long-distance phone service competition is promoted when the FCC allows independent companies to resell AT&T service.
1982	The FCC allows smaller, nonmonopoly communication companies to change prices or add services without agency approval.
1983–1984	The agency abandons lengthy comparative hearings in favor of lotteries in awarding licenses for some new services, such as cellular mobile telephones.
1985	The FCC moves toward market pricing of telephone service by shifting costs from long-distance users to local users.

ANALYSIS

1. Would Adam Smith approve of the FCC's decisions? Defend your answer, being sure to include in it a discussion of the invisible hand.
2. In what way will these decisions stimulate the work ethic and help promote capitalism? Explain.
3. Why might many of the critics feel that the FCC is moving too quickly? Be complete in your answer.

CHAPTER

3

The Political and Economic Foundation

Chapter Objectives

- To delineate the role of business in society under the differing political and economic systems of socialism, capitalism, and communism.
- To establish a framework for discussing the degree and scope of activities that business organizations should assume to be considered socially responsible.
- To air arguments against business becoming involved in social problems.
- To begin the discussion of government-business cooperation in dealing with social problems.

This chapter builds on the strategic and historical foundation of the first two chapters. It is becoming increasingly evident that business has an inseparable, interactive relationship with the political and economic environments. These interactions have undergone some drastic changes in recent years. There have been some indications that with the advent of Reaganomics and the accompanying shifts in business-government relations that the trends of the 1960s and 1970s have reversed or at least diminished. As one business ethics professor recently noted: "To postulate a continuation of the business-government trends of the past twenty or even fifty years is to fly in the face of current political directions."[1] Yet as she and we would conclude:

> Yet we hesitate to project out a continuation of current thought and practice in trends toward deregulation, fewer government controls, and decreased spending. This current trend is too unproven. Unusual economic circumstances may produce a revision, even a reversal of today's policies.[2]

In other words, there is a dynamic, continually changing interaction between the political, business, and economic environments.

After first examining the overall nature of this pluristic environment, a comparative analysis of economic and political structures is made. Then the pros and cons of a socially responsible position by business are discussed and the major social issues facing modern business are identified.

A PLURALISTIC ENVIRONMENT FOR BUSINESS

The theory of countervailing powers discussed in Chapter 2 states that each power source tries to influence the others in order to balance the fulfillment of societal interests. Through various means, each of the powers (government, business, and labor unions) checks and balances one another. A business cannot act alone without considering the actions of the other power sources. Each of the three has a value system that helps it identify objectives, strategies, and its relationships with the other power sources. The value system for each evolves in three ways.

First, values are determined internally. An example is a business firm's policy that prime consideration be given to survival. Second, values are brought about by the actions of one of the other power sources. An example is the government's requiring business to bargain collectively with its employees. A third source of values comes from power sources other than business, government, and unions. Two examples are religious and educational groups, but perhaps the best example is the public itself. All show that there are many other power groups in the United States today besides business, government, and unions. With the exception of the public, the other groups do not usually openly exhibit their power; rather, they are indirect power groups and come forward openly only when the other groups reach an impasse. The three traditional power blocks—government, business, and unions—used to be relatively impassive to equal rights, ecology, and consumerism, but now the general public has forced the government to take action in these

---

[1]Karen Paul, "Business Environment/Public Policy Problems for the 1980s," *Business and Society*, Winter–Spring 1985, p. 12.
[2]Paul, p. 12.

social areas. Business has reacted to public and governmental pressures by taking a socially responsible stance on these issues.

The public power source has served as a podium from which members of business, government, and union groups speak as individuals and not as representatives of their respective organizations. In general, the religious, educational, and public-interest groups operate outside the limelight. It is seldom necessary for them to exert direct power. Instead, they work indirectly through religious and educational training and the instillation of moral values that dictate that the welfare of the public be given overriding attention. These indirect methods regulate business, government, and union leaders internally. When this internal regulation is not possible, it becomes necessary for the other two major power groups to limit the actions of the third. If one becomes too powerful for the other two, or all three face an impasse, then the indirect power groups may move to the center of the stage. In order to maintain equilibrium, the value systems of the major power sources must agree with those of the interest groups. When they do not, the interest groups will bring about a new equilibrium by forcing change in one or more of the major power groups. On the other hand, as long as the values of the major and indirect power groups are compatible, no intervention will take place. Hence, although prime attention is devoted to the division of power among business, government, and the unions, the real power of the interest groups should not be overlooked or underestimated.

The diffusion of power by the big three results in what is called *pluralism*.[3] When pluralism exists, the big three may compete individually with one another, but each is sufficiently strong to withstand attacks from the other. No one has overriding power. Just as in the executive, legislative, and judicial systems, there are checks and balances. As long as each is able to hold onto its position of relative power, an equilibrium can be maintained. If, however, one becomes too strong for the others, monism will result. The monolithic structure of the more powerful entity may crush or control the less powerful ones. This seems highly undesirable, and John Taylor explained why: "A pluralist society is obliged to proceed always on a principle of counterpoise: it discovers its equilibrium not by eliminating opposition, but by using them, by making them party to a larger design which exhibits the public dimension of every private act. . . ."[4]

The legitimate question is whether the business segment of economic power has in fact become monolithic. There is not a ready answer; arguments exist on both sides. There is little doubt that large corporations have extended their power outside their walls. For instance, they control their suppliers, buyers, and many other groups. This raises the question of how much power they have in addition to that which is evident from their financial statements.

[3]Joseph W. McGuire, *Business and Society* (New York: McGraw-Hill, 1963), p. 130.
[4]John F. A. Taylor, "Is the Corporation Above the Law?" *Harvard Business Review*, March–April 1965, p. 130.

A few decades ago James Burnham foresaw a "managerial revolution" in America that was dominated by a managerial elite that he felt was unresponsive to the public.[5] He compared this elite with the types of people who controlled Nazi Germany. C. Wright Mills, in his classic work *The Power Elite*, also claimed that big business managers, in conjunction with military and political leaders, ran America.[6] He felt that the most important decisions about running the country were made by these few leaders and not by the common people. For Mills, pluralism was not a reality. He contended that although many different groups may exist in America, they are related in such a way that no real check-and-balance system exists. Thus, he concluded, only the façade of pluralism exists.

Were Mills and Burnham correct in their observations, or were they creating monsters where none existed? If their objective was to warn that the corporation is growing in power, they served a useful purpose. Businesspersons are quick to defend their position by stating that management merely carries out the wishes of the stockholders as expressed by the board of directors. This is not always an accurate picture. The stockholders seldom express their wishes and desires, except to approve the board of directors for another year in office. This may be indirect approval, but it is certainly different from what takes place in the political arena. How often is a board of directors rejected by its stockholders?

There is seldom an internal struggle for formal power in a large corporation. Of course, there are always a few stockholders who will appear at the annual meeting to ask questions or raise issues. For example, social activists own a small block of stock so that they can make their voices heard at stockholders' meetings. It has become increasingly popular in recent years for social activist groups to attend annual stockholder meetings. The board of directors goes through the motions of listening carefully, giving the stockholders their day in court. But if any attempt is made to unseat the proposed slate of directors, the current management group almost always has sufficient proxies to defeat the challenge. Unless there is gross incompetence or dishonesty, the stockholders continue year after year to return the board to office. In effect, it becomes a self-perpetuating body with ownership divorced from control. Although the stockholders legally own the corporation, the management controls it. Thus, the goals to which individual managers subscribe are of major importance in analyzing the modern corporation, for these managers hold the key to how business approaches social responsibility.

The Great Balancing Act

The theory of countervailing power presents both a solution and a dilemma to a concerned society. In search of more responsive environs for society there are special dangers with a system that relies on checks and balances

---

[5]James Burnham, *The Managerial Revolution* (New York: John Day, 1941).
[6]C. Wright Mills, *The Power Elite* (New York: Oxford University Press, 1956).

by opposing groups. First is a danger that power in any one area will lead to a distortion of the process of decision making. Just as the "communism scare" in the 1950s led the movie industry to blacklist actors and writers without due process, much of the same mentality is possible should one of the power groups impose its own will on the other groups. Although many situations raise the question of whether business has too much power, certainly other cases can be made for excess government power or power exerted by interest groups. For example, many feel that environmental protection groups are forcing whole areas of the country into economic stagnation by deterring industrial and energy development with stringent pollution standards.

This problem of one group having inordinate power over another group leads to a second difficulty. Whereas the economic criterion was the standard in the invisible hand doctrine, there is no simple standard in the new economic and social order. It is not easy to determine what is best for society when one considers the quality of life issues. Is pollution control so important that there should be economic hardships invoked on workers facing unemployment? Should the government pass laws to protect society from itself, such as seat belt laws and motorcycle helmet rules? Should a railroad keep unprofitable branch lines for the use of local communities, even though the communities provide no funds to help offset the loss and, in most cases, still assess property taxes on the land that the railroad cannot abandon? These are examples of just a few of the complex problems that occur in determining what courses of action are necessary and proper to enhance the quality of life for our society. A pluralistic society can foster a greater awareness of the divergent needs of society, but to meet those needs the social costs and benefits must be weighed. This task of managing corporate social performance is covered in the last part of the book.

COMPARATIVE ECONOMIC AND POLITICAL STRUCTURES

Differing political philosophies and economic conditions have led to several different forms of governance in the past century. Each of these forms placed radically different constraints on business and society.

Capitalism

The concept of capitalism began with the Greek philosophers and has been expounded through centuries ever since. Plato's *Republic* presented the first concept of democracy.[7] Through Plato, Locke, and Adam Smith, the political framework of democracy and capitalism as an economic doctrine was formulated. The major premise of capitalism is that the state allows and supports

[7]Leo Strauss and Joseph Cropsey, *History of Political Philosophy* (Chicago: Rand McNally, 1963), pp. 7–64.

business. Through the allowance of private and individual rights, open and free commerce and industry can survive. It is the role of the government to furnish a suitable climate in which to conduct business, but little else. Decisions regarding the laws and rights of people and business organizations are made through the democratic process, with all of the electorate participating. Decisions as to what to produce and the price and the quantity to be produced are determined by the laws of supply and demand. The invisible hand would regulate the economic functions of the workplace environment, including the types and quantities of labor demanded and supplied. Through individual freedom of choice, perfectly competitive markets, and open market transactions for resources, efficient and equitable allocations of resources would be made to all of society. America and most of Western Europe used to abide by this doctrine.

The concept of the business corporation is a hallmark in the evolution of capitalism, as it provided the means for capital formation and limited liability that has led to the giant firms of today.

The Concept of the Corporation

The concept of the modern corporation can be traced back more than 900 years. Canon lawyers recognized the corporate form of organization as early as the twelfth century,[8] and by the fifteenth century it was well established in English law. In these early years its use was confined almost exclusively to groups such as boroughs, guilds, and ecclesiastical bodies. The corporation had little to do with business. But in time it began to acquire characteristics favorable to business. By the sixteenth century the corporation had the right to hold property, sue or be sued, and exist indefinitely. This was of obvious value to business; yet it was not until the nineteenth century that the business corporation actually came into existence. This was accomplished by enterprising businesspersons who introduced the concept of the corporation into the joint stock trading company. The corporation's charter provided for indefinite existence, whereas the joint stock trading company allowed for limited liability and a division between owner and manager. Thus, as business organizations grew larger, the owners began to realize that the corporate form of organization had advantages not available to proprietorships or partnerships.

In America during the middle and late nineteenth century, charters were available to any business that could meet the requirements of the state in which application was made. To understand fully the rights and privileges accorded by the corporate charter, the corporation as a legal entity must be defined. Perhaps the most famous is that written by Chief Justice Marshall of the U.S. Supreme Court in the 1819 case of *Dartmouth College v. Woodward:*

---

[8]Richard Eels and Clarence Walton, *Conceptual Foundations of Business* (Homewood, Ill.: Richard D. Irwin, 1961), p. 134.

A corporation is an artificial being, invisible, intangible, and existing only in contemplation of law. Being the mere creature of law, it possesses only those properties which the charter of its creation confers upon it, either expressly or as incidental to its very existence. These are such as are supposed best calculated to effect the object for which it was created. Among the most important are immortality, and if the expression may be allowed, individuality; properties, by which a perpetual succession of many persons are considered as the same, and may act as a single individual. They enable a corporation to manage its own affairs, and to hold property without the perplexing intricacies, the hazardous and endless necessity, of perpetual conveyances for the purpose of transmitting it from hand to hand. It is chiefly for the purpose of clothing bodies of men in succession with these qualities and capacities that corporations were invented and are in use.

In the operation of the corporation, the board of directors is selected by the stockholders, who are the legal owners. This board is then held responsible for the welfare of the enterprise. Even though the liability of the stockholders is limited, they have numerous rights. Some of the more important rights of corporate ownership are

1. To receive any dividend as declared by the board.
2. To subscribe to additional stock offerings before the issue is made available to the public.
3. To sell their stockholdings at any time.
4. To share in the assets of the firm upon dissolution, if anything remains after all outstanding liabilities have been met.
5. To inspect the company books when sufficient cause can be shown for requesting such action.[9]

In addition to these stockholder rights there are five advantages to the corporate form of organization. First, as stated earlier, there is the entity's unlimited life. Second, there is limited liability for the owners. Third, in contrast with the proprietorships and partnerships, the organization is better able to raise funds through the sale of stocks and bonds. Fourth, there is often a division between owner and manager and, hence, the possibility of professional management. Because the owner is not always the most competent manager, this concept has great value; it permits specialization. As the corporation increases in size and decentralization follows, this specialization becomes of even greater importance.

A good example of the advantages of professional management is what Peter Drucker called the *federal principle*. The corporation's top management is concerned with such functions as setting overall company objectives, organizing human resources, and establishing the criteria that will be used in evaluating the company's various divisions. In turn, each of these divisions,

[9]Raymond E. Glos and Harold A. Baker, *Introduction to Business,* 7th ed. (Cincinnati, Ohio: Southwestern Publishing, 1972), p. 105.

which is, in effect, an autonomous unit, is responsible for determining its own product line and method of operation.[10] Thus under the federal principle both the top management and the autonomous units participate in the decision-making process. Such efficiency would not be possible without the corporate form of organization.

A final advantage of a corporation is the present tax structure. This contrasts with partnerships and proprietorships, which are taxed as individuals. The progressive individual income tax goes much higher than does the maximum corporate tax.

Because the corporation has an indefinite life, it is usually very stable. This is in contrast with the partnership, whose existence can be terminated at any time by the withdrawal or death of a partner. This stability provides the necessary basis for the modern corporation to survive and grow.

Communism

Besides the capitalist form of political and economic structure that has dominated the Western world, the communist form has taken on increased importance in modern times. The major doctrine for the political form of communism was conceived by Karl Marx, whose view of history was an economic one. He felt political power in a country is dominated by those in economic power (i.e., the wealthy). Because of this arrangement, there was little momentum to change the existing order. Marx believed that the only true way to change the social order in this situation was through radical revolution. Those in power (the bourgeoise) must be overthrown by the working class (the proletariat) to aid social progress. This constant state of conflict is characteristic of the pure, ideological form of communism.

Economically, communism has little regard for private land and free enterprise. The land, resources, and citizens belong to the state, which in turn is ruled by the common people. The state provides all needs of the individual and controls all prices and supplies. Economic plans predominate over the mechanism of pricing in the marketplace. The incentive for production and performance is pride in serving the country. For example, agriculture was changed after the Russian Revolution of 1917. Most of the land was transformed from small, independent tracts to large expanses of collective (state-owned) lands. The farmers then worked on the state-owned land. There was no privately owned land except for small cottage tracts (less than an acre). In a manner similar to the collectives, industrial concerns operating before the revolution were taken over by the central government.

Today, no country, not even the Soviet Union or the People's Republic of China, follows a strict form of communism as conceived by Marx. The communist countries have a managerial class and do provide incentives

---

[10]Peter F. Drucker, *The New Society* (New York: Harper & Row, 1949), pp. 268–271.

for exceeding production quotas. But even today there is still not a great difference between workers and managers. Recently, however, especially with China opening up to the outside world for the first time in many years and workers striking in Poland, there are definite trends toward at least Westernizing, if not becoming more capitalistic, in politically communist countries.

Socialism

A third prevalent form of political and economic structure is that of socialism. The Scandinavian countries and, to a growing degree, Great Britain, are contemporary examples of democratic socialism. A major premise of socialism is that the government ought to control commerce and industry when it is more feasible and efficient for it to do so. Whereas the communistic form of structure advocates that this will be accomplished by revolution, socialists work more with a democratic system, with control more in the hands of the people through representative elections.

Private property and some individual entrepreneurialism are permitted under democratic socialism. Only dominant industries that are vital to the country's economy and well-being are considered for nationalization. For example, Great Britain has nationalized the steel, coal, power, and transportation industries but left less critical industries in private ownership. The economic environment is to some degree determined by market forces of supply and demand. But under socialism, the government assumes a much more direct role in regulating economic growth and eliminating problems of inflation and unemployment.

Comprehensive economic planning and strict government controls are typical of socialism. Profit-making ventures and individual initiative are still encouraged. The state does assume more responsibility for the welfare of the populace than does a democratic form of government. For example, Great Britain has a comprehensive health care program that provides for the health needs of all the populace with little or no cost to the individual, and in Norway, most schools have a full-time dentist. These social programs sound very attractive to people in capitalistic countries until it is realized that the citizens in socialistic countries are taxed up to 90 percent of their income.

Comparing Political and Economic Systems

Although we shall not make a detailed comparison of each of the systems, several general points will be made to serve as a framework for studying the social issues in business. All three systems have difficulty in determining the public good. In the capitalistic system, determining the public good is left to the marketplace. Protecting the environment is the responsibility of the government but, under a purely capitalistic system, the government does not directly interfere in the system, such as to check inflation and unemployment. In addition, social service programs apply only to those who, through age or disability, cannot provide for themselves. Market employment determines the conditions for the working members of a purely capitalistic society. In the other forms of social structure, the political framework plays a more direct role in deciding the social good. In democratic socialism, this is determined by representative decision, with much decision making left to the government. Communism accomplishes its economic planning through centralized, political decision making, using long-range comprehensive national plans. In both socialism and communism, the difficulty of determining the public good is resolved through the political process. Whereas the invisible hand of the market system under capitalism is probably overly simplistic, the political decision-making process of the other two systems may be too idealistic. The point is that it is difficult to justify the social costs and benefits that are derived from what one considers social good.

Economic political systems are complicated and multivariate. Making changes in these systems can have long-range consequences that are difficult to predict. The large taxes placed on Great Britain's industries may have paid for the social programs of the present decade, but the trend of disinvestment by investors and the lack of capital improvements in British industry currently present some ominous forecasts for the future. In a similar manner, the rigid, central planning of the Soviet and Chinese economies has had at least some disastrous results. As a partial solution, these communist governments have become more capitalistic in recent years.

To assess which is the most humane and socially responsive form of political and economic structure, one should probably measure the total spectrum of the quality of life, but because there are few objective measures of the quality of life, the evaluation becomes a matter of personal belief and preference. Possible inputs include not only economic security but also dimensions of personal liberty and freedom. Such criteria lead to decisions that are quite diverse for each person; to reflect individual differences. When determining which criteria are best for society as a whole, the answer becomes even more difficult. In America, at least, there is still wide support for a capitalistic free-enterprise system, but certainly not the pure capitalism that was once envisioned in earlier times.

SOCIAL RESPONSIBILITY IN A FREE-ENTERPRISE SYSTEM

It is difficult to establish criteria for the degree of social responsibility that a business in a free-enterprise system should assume. To some extent its involvement is dictated by the federal laws, as in the case of pollution control. Without laws or federal guidelines, the degree of social responsibility is much less clear. Organizations have allocated differing amounts of resources to social programs. Establishing a single criterion is not possible because of these differences. For example, to maintain that all firms must be involved in community improvement programs may impose severe hardships on some companies, such as some railroads, that are fighting just for economic survival. To mandate that a company must commit a particular amount or percentage of time and monetary resources would not reflect economic reality. Because of these complexities, a precise prescription of the degree of social responsibility for business is not possible.

The social role of business is not a new concept but one that has concerned theoreticians and practitioners since the advent of the capitalistic system. One of those who pioneered in this concern was a British management philosopher, Oliver Sheldon.

Early Advocates of Social Responsibility

After completing his Oxford education and military service, Sheldon embarked on a career in industry. He spent his entire life at the Coca Works of Rowntree & Company, Limited. His managerial abilities propelled him to the position of assistant to the president, and he ultimately became a member of the general board of directors.

After World War I, Sheldon foresaw the need for a change in management philosophy. Heretofore, the philosophy of scientific management predominated, and production received all the emphasis. Only the "things" of production were considered, often at the expense of the human element. In the postwar period, however, Sheldon observed a new kind of business environment. Industry had reached giant proportions, and the problems facing management had never been so complex. He also noticed another, more subtle change. The public was becoming increasingly cognizant of the need for more business involvement in the whole society. This observation caused Sheldon both to formulate his thesis that management's primary responsibility was service to the community and to become a practicing industrialist espousing heresy. His views were outlined in his book, *The Philosophy of Management*, published in 1923: "It is important, therefore, early in our consideration of Management in industry to insist that however scientific Management may become, and however much the full development of its powers may depend upon the use of the scientific method, its primary responsibility is social and communal.[11]

Sheldon's concept of social responsibility was derived from four observations of the social environment. First, he saw an awakening of public interest in the inner workings of business. This was undoubtedly a result of the close cooperation between industry and the community during the war. Second, he observed a demand by workers for more leisure time and opportu-

[11]Oliver Sheldon, *The Philosophy of Management* (New York: Pitman, 1966), p. xv. (The book was originally published in London in 1923 by Sir Isaac Pitman & Sons.)

nities for self-development. Third, he noted that the association of workers into large groups, such as trade unions and political clubs, introduced an atmosphere conducive to social change. Finally, he discovered a new spirit of inquiry stemming from the application of the scientific approach to problem solving. Sheldon felt that the overall social awakening in Great Britain would have a tremendous impact on human relations in industry. He believed that the future problem of management would be to balance the production and human areas. In formulating such a humanistic-production philosophy of management, he dictated ten fundamentals to serve as the basis for his own managerial philosophy, including

1. The reason for industry's existence is to provide those commodities and services which are necessary for the good life of the community.
2. The governing principles of an industrial management must be based on the concept of service to the community.
3. Management is separate from capital and labor and consists of three main parts: administration, management, and organization. For Sheldon, administration meant such things as the determination of corporate policy, the coordination of marketing, finance, and production, and the ultimate control of the executive. To him, management referred to the execution of policy and the attainment of corporate objectives. Organization meant the combining of the workers, the work, and the available facilities in such a manner that there would be systematic and coordinated effort.
4. While management must be concerned with profit, it must also achieve efficiency in the human and material elements of the factory.
5. Through the use of science in management and the development of human resources, this efficiency could be achieved by the management.[12]

Sheldon was a forerunner of the human relationists of the late 1930s and the 1940s, and his major contribution to management philosophy was his shifting business's emphasis away from the materialistic toward the conceptual. He tried to imbue in managers the idea that they ought to be more concerned with the human and social, not just the mechanical, aspects of managing. Many years passed before Sheldon was given the proper attention he deserved.

America also had early social responsibility advocates, though compared with Sheldon, they did not place as much emphasis on the human side of enterprise.[13] The prevailing thought was that profit came first and social responsibility second. John D. Rockefeller, Jr., was representative of this philosophy. In 1923 he questioned whether industry's only role was as an

---

[12]Claude George, *The History of Management Thought*, 2nd ed. (Englewood Cliffs, N.J.: Prentice-Hall, 1972), p. 134.

[13]Those in the scientific management movement, such as Gantt, Gilbreth, and Taylor, stressed viewpoints somewhat similar to those of Sheldon but were overshadowed by the emphasis given to increased productivity.

institution for creating wealth. He wondered if the health and happiness of workers might not also be a major concern. For him it was time for a new approach to an old problem. He believed that the social well-being of the worker was as important to the manager as was the production of goods and services. He felt that the prevailing management philosophy of production and profit merely served to arouse antagonism and court trouble. Besides a purely altruistic interest in the workers, however, there was a sound business reason for his kindness. Rockefeller intended to keep the courts and the public off his back, as he remembered vividly what had happened to his father's Standard Oil Company when the antitrust laws were enacted. He was determined not to make the same mistake.

Henry Ford also expressed a concern for social responsibility. In fact, he is on record as stressing service before profit, though his interpretation of service meant increases in production and profit. Like Rockefeller, Ford was really saying that what was best for business was best for the society as a whole. In retrospect, the few early statements about social responsibility in the years before the Depression were largely for public consumption and appeasement; they were not literally translated into a personal management philosophy or corporate policy. It took the labor unions to awaken management attitudes toward a new responsibility that incorporated the human element.

Modern Advocates of Social Responsibility

Henry Ford II is a staunch advocate of the new concept of social responsibility, having been instrumental in forming the National Alliance of Businessmen. In a speech, Ford eloquently stated the business community's responsibility.[14] Pointing out that although the early attitude of business toward social responsibility was characterized by such phrases as "the public be damned," there has been a gradual evolution away from this kind of thinking. He noted that by the late 1940s many businesspersons had begun to look for better and more efficient ways of supporting worthy social causes. By the beginning of the 1960s, he went on, the business community was feeling rather smug about the business relationship with society. On the one hand, business had learned that it could live with the public's demand that practices be consistent with public interest. On the other, it had developed effective ways of mobilizing financial support for local projects. But as the 1960s drew to a close, it was evident that the business community did not entirely deserve to pat itself on the back. The seriousness of the problems facing the nation called for renewed business involvement in the social area. Pointing to the problems of a deteriorating environment, which were often caused by manu-

---

[14]Text of remarks by Henry Ford II, chairman of the board, Ford Motor Company. Twenty-first Los Angeles Regional Brotherhood Testimonial Dinner of the National Conference of Christians and Jews, Beverly Hilton Hotel, Los Angeles, Thursday, June 5, 1969.

facturing processes, and of the incorporation of disadvantaged minorities into the mainstream of American life, Ford stated:

> In response to such demands, corporations are rapidly increasing their efforts to help solve major social problems.
> It is clearly in the self-interest of business to enlarge its markets and improve its work force by helping disadvantaged people to develop and employ their economic potential. Similarly, it is in the self-interest of business to help reduce dependency, frustration, crime and conflict in the community. The costs of occasional civil disorder are impossible to overlook, but they are far smaller than the continuing costs of welfare, crime, preventable disease and ignorance. These costs are borne by business as well as by the rest of the community.[15]

Statements such as those by Henry Ford II above represent a point of departure for the social responsibility stance taken by most of today's professional managers. They realize that social responsibility and success go hand in hand. This position is summarized by a leading business textbook as follows: "Business must be responsible in their dealings with employees, consumers, suppliers, competitors, government, and the general public if they are to be successful in the long run."[16]

The Loyal Opposition to Business Involvement

Not everyone, of course, agrees with an enlarged role of business in the social arena. The most noteworthy spokesperson for the opposition is the Nobel prize-winning economist Milton Friedman, who contends that the most socially responsible role for business is to make a profit, use resources efficiently, and obey the law. He believes that to do more than this is irresponsible:

> In a free-enterprise, private property system, a corporate executive is an employee of the business. He has direct responsibility to his employers. That responsibility is to conduct the business in accordance with their desires, which generally will be to make as much money as possible while conforming to the basic rules of the society.
> What does it mean to say that the corporate executive has a "social responsibility" in his capacity as businessman? If this statement is not pure rhetoric, it must mean that he is to act in some way that is not in the interest of his employers. For example, that he is to refrain from increasing the price of the product in order to contribute to the social objective of preventing inflation, even though the price increase would be in the best interests of the corporation. Or that he is to make expenditures on reducing pollution beyond the amount required by law in order to contribute to the social objective of improving the environment. . . .

[15]Ford, pp. 6, 7.
[16]Louis E. Boone and David Kurtz, *Contemporary Business*, 4th ed. (Chicago: Dryden Press, 1985), p. 7.

In each of these cases, the corporate executive would be spending someone else's money for general social interest. Insofar as his actions in accord with his "social responsibility" reduce returns to stockholders, he is spending their money. Insofar as his actions raise the price to customers, he is spending the customer's money. Insofar as his actions lower the wages of some employees, he is spending their money.[17]

In effect, the argument presented by Friedman is that the socially responsible manager is operating outside the realm of the fiduciary relationship and, therefore, is committing an illegal act. Subverting funds to "social acts" may hurt the various constituents of the organization in the long run, according to Friedman. Even in the broader context, if the social contributions are of such a magnitude that they hurt the organization in either acquiring funds from investors for further growth or paying salaries that are no longer competitive, the "socially responsible" actions will hurt society at large. Friedman argues that the best way to be socially responsible is to be as *efficient* as possible and that any further course of action may tamper with the economic standard of efficiency that currently keeps the American economy strong.

Another offshoot of Friedman's argument is that the socially responsible manager decides on the use of funds for society without the funds' owners' participating in those decisions. When socially responsible managers are supposed to serve in a free-enterprise system, they may be serving only their narrow interests and not those of the larger group of owners and customers. Theodore Levitt, a marketing and economic consultant and scholar, made this point many years ago, warning against the possibility of the corporation becoming equivalent to the medieval Church. He saw the conglomeration of employee-welfare programs and community, governmental, charitable, and educational interests producing a social order that would be just as repugnant to the corporation as it would be to corporate critics. "The corporation would eventually invest itself with all-embracing duties, obligations, and finally powers—ministering to the whole man and molding him and society in the image of the corporation's narrow ambitions and its essentially unsocial needs.[18]

Weighing the Arguments For and Against

On balance there seems to be greater support for greater social responsiveness by business. This social responsiveness must be tempered, however, by the various constraints and limitations pointed out by Friedman and others. A private business organization cannot entirely lose sight of its objectives in

[17]Milton Friedman, "The Social Responsibility of Business Is to Increase Its Profits," *New York Times Magazine*, September 13, 1970, pp. 33, 122–126.

[18]Theodore Levitt, "The Dangers of Social Responsibility," *Harvard Business Review*, September–October 1958, p. 44.

pursuit of a particular social program unless the public is willing to assume some of the cost and risk. For example, the federal government, when inaugurating a mass immunization program a few years ago, experienced great difficulty in finding a company to produce the needed vaccine. The pharmaceutical firms rightfully demanded underwriting of the risk associated with the potential liability with a program of that magnitude.[19]

The numerous problems that face society cannot be readily solved by business alone. Although some people blame societal ills on convenient, visible targets such as government or business, there are others (sometimes the same people) who feel that these institutions can readily solve the ills of society. It seems that both of these positions fail to grasp the magnitude of the problems and the complexity of the solutions. The government with its tremendous but limited resources has been unable to solve many of the pressing problems of society. Business, also, with its expertise, resources, and economically centered approaches will not be able to solve these social problems overnight. The greatest difficulty lies in defining the problems and their causes and effects. Solutions are not obvious as they may at first appear. Poverty and hunger cannot be erased by providing only welfare assistance, and equal opportunity cannot be dictated by legal fiat alone. It requires more—educational assistance, job training, improvement in local public transportation, crime prevention, and housing. A comprehensive planning system, not a disjointed patchwork approach, is needed to solve such problems.

The social responsibility goal of business is to improve the quality of life for society. Most modern corporations have established a number of important goals and objectives, and social responsibility is only one.

MODERN CORPORATE OBJECTIVES

Over the years business corporations have had five generally recognized objectives: survival, growth, profit, economic contributions, and social obligations.[20]

Survival is the most basic objective because the other goals depend on the corporation's continued existence. A company cannot possibly grow, earn a profit, or make economic and social contributions if it is shut down. Survival is a matter of secondary objectives, such as meeting the competition, reducing costs, and maintaining a qualified work force.

Growth is also an important corporate objective. Included in growth are such goals as increasing output, capturing a large share of the market, and

[19]"A Risky Exodus from Vaccines," *Business Week*, April 10, 1978, pp. 118–120.

[20]Dalton E. McFarland, *Management: Principles and Practices*, 4th ed. (New York: Macmillan, 1974), pp. 350–357.

improving the rate of return on investment. Firms that find their growth limited in one industry will often turn to another. The growth objective accomplishes more than merely creating profits for stockholders; it also ensures expanded opportunities for company executives. An expanding company with accompanying openings and challenges at the top will draw people who have ingenuity, creativity, and drive. A self-perpetuating situation occurs where success breeds success. Therefore, once the corporation is assured of survival, it will attempt to grow, following the maxim that no business stands still but moves either forward or backward.

Profit provides the basis for continued operations and growth and serves as an effective guideline for evaluating managerial performance. A good illustration is the profit-center concept utilized by General Motors, Ford, Chrysler, General Electric, and other organizations that depend on product departmentation. Each product line is regarded as a profit center. In the prewar era, short-run profit maximization was the guideline of most firms, but in the postwar era, more emphasis has been given to long-run profits. Simple economic analysis reveals that because of the tremendous demand for automobiles in the late 1940s, there is little doubt that the auto companies could have charged higher prices. Corporations reasoned, however, that "charging what the traffic will bear" was not as desirable as the long-run profits that would result in repurchases by satisfied customers. Although long-run profit strategy will be examined in more detail later, it appears that the profit concept has changed from a short- to long-run viewpoint in corporate strategy. Such a long-range strategy is used by the Japanese and is often cited as a reason for their recent tremendous success.

Economic contribution goals focus on the firm's approach to satisfying the consumer's demand for material goods and services. From a corporate strategy standpoint this often calls for continued redefinition and reexamination of the product line or market niche. Firms that used to make electric fans have found they must convert their product line and begin making air conditioners. Those in the food industry have found that the consumer wants convenience goods and items specially prepared and ready to be cooked, rather than foods that must be prepared from several ingredients. The movie industry is another illustration. People want entertainment, and if they cannot find it at the movie theaters, they will stay at home and watch television or buy video cassettes. The concept of Hollywood movies is therefore being drastically changed. Today, the financiers literally run the show. Big-name actors generally are compensated by a relatively small salary and a percentage of the profits earned by the picture. The movie industry is fighting for its life. In other words, the economic contribution of Hollywood movies is not as great as it once was. Another example is the railway industry, which once pictured itself in the railroad business. It was sadly mistaken. Today the railroad industry has finally realized that it is in the transportation business, and freight has replaced the unprofitable passenger operation as its major emphasis. Another example is firms that used to make wooden boxes. They have been displaced by firms with enough vision to realize that they are in the container industry. Wood has been replaced by paper, aluminium, plastics, and other materials. A final example is slide rule manufacturers. Today, of course, the hand calculator had made the slide rule obsolete. In short, all these industries have had to adjust their view of the economic contribution. Even though many critics claim that business corporations leave the public little choice as to what it will receive, there is much evidence to indicate that the firm's economic contribution must be considered if it wishes to survive. If such analytical marketing expertise could be concentrated on social problems, the corporation could make a significant social contribution.

Social obligation, the fifth objective, has received increased attention by corporate management. The emerging issues of equal rights, ecology, and consumerism have been greatly responsible for this interest and have forced management to reconsider its social obligations and reshape its strategy in fulfilling this responsibility. Community relations have always been important to management. Today, however, the area has taken on new dimensions. Affirmative action programs and antipollution equipment are becoming an integral part of its social obligations. So, too, is attention to the consumer. For example, the company is responsible not only for making a safe product but also for telling buyers what is in the package and precisely how much it will cost them if they are purchasing it on credit.

The five objectives discussed here are interrelated, but the priorities assigned to them require that attention be given first to survival and growth. Once the corporation is certain of these two objectives, it can then turn to social problems. The issue is not whether business should assume social responsibility. Rather, the issue is to determine at what point business should realize that its survival and growth are assured and social objectives should take top priority.

While the business community established these objectives, society's new awareness and social activism generated a whole new list of social objectives. These social issues indicate the people's concern for society's major ills and provide the framework for business's current and future social responsibilities.

SOCIAL ISSUES RELEVANT TO BUSINESS

Social problems, which have existed for some time, have become matters of vital concern. During the recent years, there have been many social changes, and a number of social issues have emerged. In particular, business ethics, equal opportunity in employment for minorities and women, employee rights, quality of work life, consumerism, and environmental protection are the most important.

Business Ethics

An issue that has resurfaced in recent years is business ethics, more specifically, how the business environment affects its managers' moral and ethical values. There are many sources at work in society and in the business community that may improve or impair business ethics in the near future. Ethical questions range from on-the-job performance to off-the-job activities.

Equal Opportunity and Employee Rights and Justice Systems

A second issue is the equity of treatment and opportunity in employment and employee rights and a fair justice system in the organization. The 1964 Civil Rights Act, Title VII, prohibited discrimination on the basis of race, color, religion, sex, or national origin in hiring, firing, compensation, or any other condition of employment. This was the landmark legislation for equal rights and opportunities. Amended in 1968 and 1972, this part of the civil rights law (Title VII) provides for the fair treatment of individuals in the workplace. Since its passage, the whole approach to employment practices has changed. The law has been refined through interpretations by the agency charged with administering the law (Equal Employment Opportunity Commission) and through various court decisions.

In the past 20 years, there have been many interpretations and cases involving equal opportunity in employment. The political and general public climate has also played a role. After reviewing all the laws and interpretations, an expert on personnel law concludes: "Antidiscrimination laws do not interfere with employment of a qualified person; they do eliminate subjective employment decisions and force employers to justify their decisions on criteria that reflect job requirements."[21]

Ensuring equal treatment and opportunity has been a relatively slow process. Reverse discrimination does not seem to be the answer. It takes a concerted effort and commitment by business firms to search out and develop qualified candidates among minorities and women for job openings and promotions. In the years to come, affirmative action will become more a seeking out and preparing of *all* interested candidates for more rewarding work experiences.

More recently, employee rights and the employee-employer relationship concerning areas such as employee safety and health, organizational justice systems, and security have received increasing attention. Much legislative and managerial activity has been directed toward this emerging social responsibility of business.

[21]Kenneth L. Sovereign, *Personnel Law* (Reston, Va.: Reston, 1984), p. 175.

Quality of Work Life

The quality-of-work-life issue pertains to several on-the-job areas. Besides demands for a safe, healthy, and humane work environment, people are seeking greater meaning in their lives. Pay alone will not meet these needs. Greater responsibility, growth, autonomy, and rewards contingent on performance all are factors that people are demanding from the work environment, and management is becoming increasingly sensitive to these needs.

An example of an emerging quality-of-work-life issue is employees' rights to privacy. Spurred by the growth of computer information programs and computerized personnel files, the privacy issue is of increasing concern to many employees. All employee information may be contained in a single computer system file, which may be accessible to several departments in

CHANGING CONSUMER TASTES

Just about everyone realizes that smoking and alcohol consumption can be harmful to one's health. This undoubtedly helps explain why more and more Americans are smoking and drinking less. Recent statistics also show that Americans are consuming less pork, fewer eggs, less caffeinated coffee, less sugar, more chicken, more fish, more diet soda, and more bottled water. In short, people are taking better care of themselves.

Does this not bode badly for the cigarette and alcohol manufacturers? Not really. They are already changing their strategies to adjust to these new social mores. For example, the cigarette firms just about concede that the number of smokers will continue to decline. They are beginning to diversify into non-cigarette-related fields. Meanwhile, liquor firms are starting to come out with new products that contain less alcohol. Wine production is a popular choice. So are nonalcoholic offerings that taste like they have alcohol. A third are alcohol fad items such as ice cream drinks that have a low alcohol content. Even soft-drink manufacturers are getting into the act, offering diet and noncaffeinated sodas. In fact, the diet-soft-drink market is increasing at a faster rate than any other segment of the market. Decaffeinated coffee is another big winner. Although the price of coffee has declined in recent years, consumers are not as attracted to regular coffee as they were once. The decaffeinated market niche has increased by 30 percent over the last five years, while caffeinated sales have dropped.

These developments are leading businesses to restructure their product lines, offering goods that are more health related. In the process, the companies are fulfilling their social responsibility not only to the customer but to their owners and employees, who stand to profit from the increased sales.

the organization. For instance, private medical records may be accessible to a department supervisor, a possibility that has raised concern in many quarters regarding the employee's right to privacy. Other privacy concerns are the requirements of some organizations to administer a lie detector test as a precondition of employment. Not only are some of the questions considered a violation of privacy, but the whole process of requiring such a test is disquieting.

Another quality-of-work-life issue is the impact that the new retirement law will have on employment and individual employees. Although the elimination of an arbitrary constraint on continuing employment seems desirable to most, there is an accompanying lack of objective criteria by which to determine when an employee should be considered for retirement.

A final example of the quality-of-work-life issue is the emerging demand for employee assistance programs. Drug and alcohol abuse programs, family and marriage counseling, personal finance advising, psychological counseling services, and other such assistance programs are being advocated and, in some cases, demanded as part of the responsibility of business to improve both the performance and the quality of work life for the individual employee.

Consumerism

Another social issue confronting modern business is consumerism. Management was alerted initially to this responsibility as early as 1906, with passage of the Food and Drug Act, which forbids the adulteration of misbranding of foods and drugs sold in interstate commerce. The initial law was strengthened by the passage of the Food, Drug, and Cosmetic Act of 1938, which defined the terms *adulteration* and *misbranding* and authorized the government to inspect food, drug, and cosmetic factories. But these original concerns only scratched the surface of the consumerism issues now facing business.

One of the prime causes for the rapid rise of consumerism is the new marketing concept that began in the post–World War II era. This concept, still in vogue, holds that the main attention of business must be given to marketing, with production taking a secondary role. This approach is a reverse of management thinking in earlier times, when production was always emphasized; selling the product was secondary. Today the new marketing emphasis has led to a massive increase in the number and kinds of goods being offered to the consumer (see the box "Changing Consumer Tastes"). This expansion of marketing has gone hand in hand with such problems as quality, safety, and product information. Although the purchaser had always wanted these characteristics incorporated in a product, with the new marketing concept in existence, many corners seemed to be cut, and consumers had to try to differentiate between the tremendous number of goods and services being offered to them.

An example of a current consumer issue is that of labeling. Exactly what ingredients are contained in a package? How much of each is there? What danger exists in using the product? Consumers want complete information that will tell them what they feel they must know about the item being purchased. They do not want to spend their money for value not received. Nor do they want to endanger their health or that of their family by buying a potentially dangerous product unless they are warned about its dangers. Examples include the plastic bags used to cover clothing being returned from the dry cleaner. A warning that they should be kept away from young children is now placed on these bags, as there is a real danger that children may put the bag over their heads and suffocate.

The major issues in consumerism are relative ones. How far should business go in providing protection and information to the consumer? These are the major consumer issues faced by modern business firms.

Environmental Protection

Whereas issues such as ethics and even equal opportunity in employment were no surprise to business, the environmental protection issue was an unexpected societal demand. The values of Americans after World War II tended toward the conspicuous consumption of resources and the improvement of one's social status by acquiring material things. But during the 1960s and 1970s society's values changed toward the less material and the more qualitative aspects of life. Oddly, everyone was aware that the air and water were being polluted: no one had attempted to swim in the lower Hudson River for years. Millions of late-night television viewers listened to Johnny Carson's lighthearted attack on Consolidated Edison for polluting the air; yet nobody became excited about the situation. Ecologists had been warning people for years that they were destroying the environment and upsetting the balance of nature. No one seemed to listen. Just before she died, Rachel Carson wrote a significant book entitled *Silent Spring*.[22] She warned of pesticides that not only kill unwanted insects but remain potent for many years and eventually poison the environment. Although the book was well received, there was no public outcry, and little action was taken.

During the early 1960s the social responsibility issue getting the most attention from both the public and business was equal opportunities for minorities. As the decade continued, most businesspeople undoubtedly thought the late 1960s would hold more of the same and that defining social responsibility with regard to equal opportunity would continue to be the only major social issue of the 1960s and beyond. In addition, the business community probably guessed that the public became involved with only one crusade at a time. There was some evidence to support this reasoning. Although pollution was increasing, only a very small group of people was bothered by it. There were very few who thought the ecological concern would spread nationwide. It appeared to be a local gripe against easy targets. Furthermore, if it did draw nationwide attention, there was the general

[22]Rachel Carson, *Silent Spring* (Boston: Houghton Mifflin, 1962).

feeling that because so many firms were polluting the air, the cost of cleaning it up would have to be borne by consumers. Business reasoned that consumers would not want to raise their costs any higher and therefore would hesitate to make pollution an issue. A recessionary economy reinforced their beliefs.

The business community misinterpreted the public's attitude: a change practically unnoticed by business had occurred in the public's attitude toward the environment. What accounted for this unexpected change? One answer was that people were beginning to see environmental deterioration firsthand. The damage, which had started slowly, began to snowball. People were able to notice a marked change in environmental conditions. The change in the environment both worried and angered them, and they realized that deterioration was occurring at a very rapid rate. Everyone agreed that something had to be done. The result was a massive demand for immediate environmental protection. In addition, the American public welcomed an issue on which they could all agree.

Today ecological concern has become a major social issue. For example, a recently released extensive American-Canadian study concluded that toxic chemicals are still getting into the food chain in the Great Lakes area, posing a threat to 40 million people. No fewer than 1,065 "hazardous or potentially hazardous" substances were identified in the 1985 study.[23]

BUSINESS-GOVERNMENT INTERFACE

How far should a company go in the interests of public concern? There is no longer any doubt of the importance of businesses' social responsibilities. Our discussion of monism, pluralism, and countervailing power implied a cause and effect relationship between the growth of the corporation and its need to become more socially responsible. One question still to be answered is whether business redefined its social role because of a genuine desire to fulfill its social obligations, because it yielded to pressure by the public, or a combination of the two. A remaining question concerns how business interacts with the government in trying to solve and combat the current social issues.

As pointed out earlier, there is a growing belief that the problems of society are much too large to be solved by the government alone. The government does not have the expertise or the administrative capabilities to handle such awesome tasks. Thus, there is a growing acceptance of government and business joining hands. Congress has shown a greater awareness of the need for joint planning by government and business to help solve social and economic problems.

The need for the cooperation of government and business can best be demonstrated in the case of multinational corporations (MNCs). For two

---

[23]"40 Million Exposed to Dangerous Toxins," *Lincoln Journal*, December 11, 1985.

reasons, special attention should be given to MNCs in reference to social responsibility. First, the MNC is routinely exposed to global social and economic problems. World hunger, oppression, disease, and economic conditions are important societal issues that are directly relevant to MNCs. Because large MNCs have such a broad interface with the entire world, it follows that they should be concerned with taking a more active stance on social responsibility. Second, MNCs based in the United States have a special position with respect to American foreign policy. What role should the American-based MNC assume in the context of foreign policy? Given the importance of the MNC to the economy of the United States and given the world's political climate, might the best interests of the United States be served by regulating MNCs so that they will assume a greater role in foreign policy? Japan, Great Britain, and Germany all have greater economic and political control over their MNCs than does the United States. This lack of government control may be contributing to the current relatively poor competitive position of the United States in world trade. A better definition of the business-government interface for MNCs seems to be of increasing importance to modern society. In Chapter 14 we look in depth at this international arena for business.

OTHER SOCIAL ISSUES

Besides the business-government interface there are several other emerging social issues facing business which are beginning to affect the country's economic and societal structure. These topics will be discussed in more detail in subsequent chapters, but for now they can be summarized as follows:

1. Accumulating evidence indicates that the largest corporations have *interlocking directorships;* that is, several key individuals have seats on the boards of directors of several large companies. An important consideration is what effect this superconcentration of power has on society.
2. Another important issue is the effect on society of extensive horizontal integration (few firms controlling most of the production or sales of a particular product or service) and/or a high degree of vertical integration (few firms controlling the total operation from top to bottom in terms of raw materials, production process, marketing, and distribution such as is found in the oil industry today).
3. In tough economic times, companies are now being asked to ease the impact of plant shutdowns or cutbacks on workers and communities. As one official in the U.S. Chamber of Commerce noted: "There's a real movement within the business community toward responsible corporate behavior on plant closing."[24]

[24]Plant Closings Spark Fresh Resistance," *U.S. News & World Report,* April 15, 1985, p. 75

4. Another societal issue is the efficiency of public institutions. For example, how can it be determined whether a public utility is operating efficiently? How can it be determined whether a governmental agency is operating efficiently?
5. Still another important societal question is whether government ownership is preferable to private ownership.
6. Finally, a social question that is becoming increasingly important is who should bear the costs of products or services that are not producing a profit but are considered vital to a community. How do we determine whether a service is vital? How should the costs of that service be allocated to the public? How do we safeguard the private industry that is directly or indirectly affected by a decision to provide subsidies to the vital service or product?

SUMMARY

In the first part of this chapter we examined the pluralistic nature of modern society and briefly analyzed each of the major political and economic doctrines—capitalism, communism, and socialism. Under capitalism, the determination of the public good is left to the marketplace; under communism, it is dictated by the government; and under socialism, it falls somewhere between the two. Today, it appears that capitalism is acquiring some of the characteristics of the other two, and vice versa.

Within the political-economic framework, in the last half of the chapter we examined the degree and scope of activities that a business firm should assume in order to be considered socially responsible. One question that must be answered is how involved business should become. As early as 1923, Oliver Sheldon recommended shifting away from the mechanical aspects of managing and toward the human and social aspects; since that time numerous managers have followed his advice. One of the best known is Henry Ford II, who provided a good point of departure for the modern view of the social responsibility of business. There are other people, however, most notable of whom is Milton Friedman, a Nobel prizewinner in economics, who believed that the most socially responsible role for business is to make a profit and that to do more is irresponsible. Overall, most of today's managers support active social responsibility.

Today, there are some social responsibility issues with which business must deal. The first is a renewed interest in business ethics. The second is equal opportunity in employment for minorities and women; the third is the quality of work life; the fourth is consumerism; and the fifth is ecology or environmental protection. All five of these were merely introduced in this chapter; they are covered in more detail in later chapters.

DISCUSSION AND STUDY QUESTIONS

1. "American society today is best described as pluralistic." What is meant by this statement?
2. In your own words, what is capitalism? How does it work?
3. If a person buys stock in a corporation, what rights does he or she receive?
4. What is communism? How does it work?
5. How does socialism differ from communism?
6. "All three systems—capitalism, communism, and socialism—have difficulty determing the public good." What is meant by this statement? What implications does it have for the social responsibility of business?
7. What was Oliver Sheldon's philosophy of social responsibility?
8. Was John D. Rockefeller, Jr., socially responsible?
9. In what way does Henry Ford II symbolize the new business spirit in much of America?
10. What is Milton Friedman's philosophy of business's social responsibility?
11. How widely accepted is Friedman's argument?
12. Should business have social responsibility? Cite reasons for and against such involvement.
13. What are the five generally recognized objectives of corporations?
14. What is the quality-of-work-life issue? Give some examples.
15. Do you believe that equal opportunity in employment is still a vital social issue? Cite examples of why or why not.
16. Does the text indicate that business ethics has resurfaced as a social issue? Cite recent news events that support this contention.
17. The environmental protection issue was an unexpected societal demand. What is meant by this statement?
18. In what way is consumerism a major social responsibility issue?
19. "A special case of the interface of government and business corporations is that of the multinational corporation." What is meant by this statement?
20. In addition to the social issues mentioned here, there are several others. What are they, and what kinds of problems do they present to modern corporations?

CASES AND INCIDENTS

Which is Best?

The three principal economic systems in the world today are modified capitalism, socialism, and communism. Each offers certain benefits to its people, and each has certain drawbacks. Of the three, capitalism appears to offer the best opportunity for a high standard of living and, unlike the other two, provides the greatest chance for consumer control over production. If something does not sell well, for example, it will not be produced in the future.

Conversely, communism appears to offer the poorest opportunity for a high standard of living, if only because everyone is supposed to have the same living standards. This results in only a small percentage of the people living very well, although it can certainly be argued, in support of the

Comparison of Economic Systems.

	Modified Capitalism	Socialism	Communism
Basic goal	To increase economic production	To further social welfare	To develop the economy of the state
Ownership of production facilities	Mostly in private hands except for some government ownership of basic services	Varies, with the government owning some production facilities (as in Sweden) or all (as in Yugoslavia)	All state owned
Allocation of resources	Through competition	Through government planning, often with worker participation	Through centralized government planning
Advantages	Promotion of incentive and freedom of choice regarding work, investment, and consumption	Extensive social welfare programs; less unemployment; smaller gap between rich and poor	Sustained economic growth possible; virtually no unemployment; extensive social benefits
Disadvantages	Wide gaps in income; business ups and downs, producing unemployment and depressions	Less incentive; also danger of economic stagnation	Great inefficiency in serving consumers; lack of free choice regarding occupations and careers; lack of worker incentive regarding productivity

system, that medical care is often quite good and that poverty has been greatly eliminated.

Socialism is somewhere in the middle, more restrictive of individual freedom than capitalism is, but less restrictive than communism is. There is a very definite commitment to social welfare, less of a gap between the very rich and the very poor, and generally less unemployment than there is under capitalism. However, there is also less incentive among the workers, because there are no great rewards (as there are in capitalism) available to those who do the best job. Socialism tends to promote a form of mediocrity. The accompanying table compares the three economic systems in more detail.

ANALYSIS

1. Which of the three systems responds best to social needs?
2. If business begins to become more socially responsible, is this not a step toward socialism or communism?
3. In capitalism, can business firms *really* meet the challenge of social responsibility and still maintain a capitalistic philosophy?

It's What's Up Front That Counts

When Jim Johnson received a bachelor's degree in finance from a major eastern university, he thought there would be no difficulty in obtaining a good job. He had this attitude even though his interviews at the university placement office during his last semester had not been fruitful. He was confident that there were numerous banks in the larger cities that would have openings for a person with his educational background. However, after three weeks of luckless job hunting, he began to have second thoughts. His father mentioned the possibility of the state employment office. "You might go down there in the morning," he said, "and see if they know of any suitable openings." Jim decided this was good advice and the next morning went to the state employment office to fill out an application. After filling out the form he waited for 20 minutes before he was called. "Mr. Johnson," said the receptionist, "go to Mrs. Velding's office, the third door on your right." Jim walked down the hall, knocked, and entered. Mrs. Velding was looking over his application.

"Come in and sit down, Mr. Johnson. I'm Irene Velding. I would like to ask you a few questions; we don't have many college graduates seeking our assistance. What difficulties do you seem to be having?" "Well, Mrs. Velding, I'm looking for a job in a large bank, preferably in the trust department. Things have been going so poorly that I will work for just about anyone, but I am still holding out for a job in the trust area. I've talked to more than a dozen banks, but the only openings they seem to have are for bank tellers. I'm not at all interested in that kind of job."

Mrs. Velding looked through her file to see what job openings might apply. She removed one of the cards and studied it carefully. "Jim, this might be exactly what you want, but before sending you over to this bank, let me call a friend who works there and see if the job is still open." She then dialed the number and asked for Mr. Jack Peterson. "Hello, Jack, this is Irene Velding. How are you? Listen, is your bank still looking for a trainee for the trust department? It is? Good. I think I have just the person for the job. His name is Jim Johnson, and he has just received a bachelor's degree in finance and is very interested in trust work. I'll send him over right away. To whom should I direct him? Mr. Bud Forrest. Fine. Could you do me a favor? While he's on his way over, be a true friend and put in a good word for Jim with Mr. Forrest. I'd really appreciate it."

Mrs. Velding then gave Jim the address of the bank and suggested that he go over there right away. "If this doesn't work out," she said, "come back and see me." Jim thanked her and left for the bank. For the rest of the morning Mrs. Velding caught up on her paperwork, and about noon she left for lunch. Upon her return at 1 P.M. she saw, to her surprise, Jim Johnson sitting in the waiting room. She went over and sat down next to him. "Hi, did you go over to the bank?" "I certainly did," answered Jim. "I visited with Mr. Forrest for about half an hour. He told me the bank would be delighted to hire me as a teller but there were, at present, no openings for trainees in the trust department. Perhaps Mr. Peterson was mistaken." "Listen," said Mrs. Velding, "you wait here and let me go to my office and call Mr. Peterson. Perhaps there has been a mix-up somewhere." A few minutes later Mr. Peterson was on the line. "Jack, I've just spoken to Jim Johnson, and he tells me there are no openings for trainees in your trust department. What happened?" There was a moment of silence, and then Mr. Peterson began to speak. "Irene, if you mention a word of this, I'll deny it, but right after Jim left, Mr. Forrest called me. He said he would have hired Jim immediately except that the young man is black. It seems the bank has taken the position that if it is going to hire minorities, they should be placed in teller jobs or other positions out front where the public can see them. No one will see Jim if he is in the trust department. Thus, they feel there is no sense of hiring him. I'm sorry about this, but there is nothing I can do about it."

ANALYSIS

1. What should Mrs. Velding do now? Explain in detail.
2. Would you recommend that Jim take a job as a teller or continue seeking employment in a trust department? Why?
3. Is the bank guilty of discrimination? Is there any justification for this hiring policy?

Medicare: Political Versus Economic Versus Medical Considerations*

While A. Walter Bergland grappled with pneumonia in a small rural Minnesota hospital early this year, two charts at the foot of his bed tracked daily changes in his situation. One indicated his medical progress; the other alerted doctors and nurses to the fact that he was nearing a point beyond which his Medicare payment would no longer cover his hospital bill.

This might seem routine except for one thing: Bergland's wife, Julie, believes that her husband's discharge after nine days had more to do with the chart revealing his possible costs to the hospital than with the one denoting his medical condition. The doctor even admitted that Medicare had run out and they could not keep him in the hospital any longer. Four days after his release, he was deteriorating so rapidly that he had to be rushed by ambulance to another hospital. Diagnosis: probably pneumonia. He died two months later of a stroke.

Concerns about too-early releases are being raised throughout the country. The early releases are being blamed on the three-year-old Medicare DRG (diagnosis-related groups) program. DRGs are a way that government hopes it will be able to better control health care costs. Before this 1983 change in reimbursement for Medicare, a hospital would simply pass the costs of the patient directly to Medicare. Under the DRG system, the Health Care Financing Administration (HCFA), the agency that administers Medicare, payments are made to hospitals based on the treatment category to which the illness is assigned. Currently, there are 468 treatment categories. A hospital receives a fixed amount for a treated illness in a category. If the hospital's expenses are less than the fixed payment, it gets to keep the difference; if the actual expenses are higher, the hospital will lose money. The hospital *cannot* charge the patient for the additional cost incurred.

The new system was designed to contain the rapidly increasing health costs, which have increased several hundredfold in the past decade compared with the cost of living. The result has been a dramatic reduction in the increase in medical costs. McClain Haddow, acting director of HCFA, says that reduced admissions and the shifting of care to outpatient settings has produced sizable cost savings. Moreover, since the new payment system was instituted in 1983, the average number of days in the hospital for Medicare patients has dropped 20 percent, from 9.5 days in 1983 to 7.5 days in 1985.

As expected, the change led to a totally different orientation for hospitals. Instead of emphasizing high-quality care and follow-up procedures to make sure of the illness and the effectiveness of the treatment, hospitals are pushing for meeting the fixed cost established by the government. The new emphasis leads to skimping on good-quality care. Such skimping is already

---

*Adapted from Elliot Carlson and William Oriol, "DRGs: Surviving Medicare's New Obstacle Course," *Modern Maturity*, December 1985–January 1986, pp. 25–27, 87–88, 94–103.

occurring, asserts Senator John Heinz (R, Pennsylvania), chairman of the Senate Special Committee on Aging. Heinz stirred controversy last summer when he declared that, as of March 1985, the peer-review organizations (PROs) had reported as many as 3,700 inappropriate patient discharges or transfers, including several cases where the patient died.

The 1983 law did consider these potential abuses and placed into effect a peer-review organization to monitor procedures under DRGs. In the Bergland case, as well as all other cases, there are patient rights that can be exercised to avoid hospital actions that might harm the patient. Under the new system, a hospital must issue a written notice when the hospital and either the PRO or physician agree than in-hospital care is not needed. If patients or their family disagrees, they have a right to request an immediate review by the PRO. If the PRO agrees that there is merit in a longer stay in the hospital, Medicare will pay for the extended stay. If the extended stay is not approved, patients or their families will be liable to pay all the hospital costs beginning on the third calendar day after the receipt of the notice of noncoverage.

However, Cyril Brickfield, executive director of the American Association of Retired Persons, maintains that patients are not being informed of their rights under the new law because the hospital personnel, physicians, and Medicare administrators are not telling people of the procedures.

ANALYSIS

1. In what ways might procedures be developed that would be able to ensure high-quality care at a reasonable cost? How can the current system be improved to avoid the tragedy of the death of Mr. Bergland?
2. How would Congress determine if the DRG system is meeting societal needs and wants? First consider the political versus economic considerations that are affected by the law. Now consider how Congress might determine the influence this change in the law will have on meeting the desires of patients and the public at large.
3. For a law of this type, which group might exert the most political clout toward changing the law? Which group might be most effective, and why?

4

The Ethical Foundation

Chapter Objectives

- To define ethical conduct in a theoretical and pragmatic sense so that one is aware of the complexities of the concept.
- To present various alternative philosophical approaches to ethical conduct.
- To describe the process of value formation in society from the initial socialization process that occurs in the family unit to the organizational socialization that occurs when a person enters the working environment.
- To increase awareness of the various approaches used to increase the ethical conduct of organizations and the employees of those organizations.
- To review the legislative efforts in the United States to improve ethical conduct in business.

Texaco is ordered to pay Getty Oil over $11 billion—the largest damage award in U.S. civil court history. A jury determined, and on December 10, 1985, a state district judge upheld, that Texaco illegally enticed Getty out of a merger with Pennzoil Company. Texaco bought Getty for $10.1 billion (the second largest merger in history), but after 17 weeks of testimony, a jury felt that Texaco had illegally lured Getty into backing out of a previous merger agreement with Pennzoil in January 1984. Texaco, of course, argues that there was no existing merger agreement between Pennzoil and Getty when Texaco entered the picture. Texaco argues that Pennzoil merely lost out in a bidding war for Getty and should not be penalized at all.[1] Only time will tell what the results of further appeals will be, but in the meantime, the stockholders of Texaco have suffered a severe blow (the priced dropped from about $40 to $30 a share after the jury verdict and the huge company may not even survive).

The question to be answered in this and an increasing number of similar disastrous and/or tragic situations in big corporate America or the local dairy is: What ethical climate exists? Managing in a socially responsible manner in Texaco, or any other company, includes actions that exemplify a strong ethical posture. Fairness and properness in intraorganizational and interorganizational transactions are hallmarks of such an ethical stance.

Determining a specific ethical code of conduct is complicated by the definition of what ethical conduct actually is. Are standards of conduct fixed in the company's value system, or should its conduct depend on the circumstances? Given intense competitive pressures, how is ethical conduct defined? Is ethical conduct determined by the competition's actions? What is business's responsibility to its owners and employees when standard business practice is considered unethical? Does an organization commit unethical behavior in order to remain competitive or to maintain its ethical standards at the cost of competitive disadvantage? Because of an organization's need for results, how does it reconcile performance objectives and ethical objectives? In highly competitive firms whose stakes in winning or losing are high, the temptation becomes greater to act in ways that will ensure success. Although a firm's top management may adhere to a high level of ethical conduct, the firm's standards for its middle- and lower-level management may reinforce unethical behavior. Therefore, the organization must be able to reconcile its demands of employees to the ethical behavior it wishes to reinforce. Those firms striving to be socially responsible must insist on a specific code of ethical behavior as part of their total performance system.

DEFINING ETHICAL CONDUCT

Ethical conduct is not easy to understand. Although absolute guides exist in some areas, the determination of much ethical conduct is subjective and vague, varying among cultures and environmental conditions.

Ethics may be defined as "a theory or morality which attempts to systematize moral judgments, and establish and defend basic moral principles."[2]

[1]"Judge Upholds Texaco Verdict," *Lincoln Journal*, December 11, 1985, p. 34.
[2]R. T. DeGeorge, *Business Ethics* (New York: Macmillan, 1982), p. 37.

The study of ethics includes the analysis of principles and assumptions that guide individual behavior. Ethical behavior can be distinguished from non-ethical behavior by means of a moral judgment of a behavior's ethical quality. The judgment is predicated on the individual's value systems, but this may lead to several questions. For example, how do individuals acquire the information that enables them to distinguish between ethical and unethical conduct? Is the determination of ethical behavior governed by an immutable standard, or is there a "situational code" of ethics according to which the consequence of actions is based on the action's ethical merits?[3] Is the evaluation of ethical and unethical conduct consistent among cultures and countries? Because of the guide of moral reason, does not ethical conduct vary from individual to individual? Given the variety and complexity of the problems associated with determining ethical conduct, how are ethical standards derived for an organization?

Philosophical Approaches to Ethical Conduct

Ethical conduct is determined by individual evaluations, which can be called *moral reasoning*. Approaches to determining an act's ethical nature fall into two categories, based on the merits of the act and its consequences, known as *deontological* and *teleological* approaches, respectively:

> One approach argues on the basis of consequences. This approach to ethical reasoning is called a teleological approach. It states that whether an action is right or wrong depends on the consequences of that action. . . .
>
> The second basic approach is called the deontological approach. This states that the duty is the basic moral category, and that duty is independent of consequences. An action is right if it has certain characteristics or is of a certain kind, and wrong if it has other characteristics or is of another kind.[4]

Each investigates whether a behavior is ethical or unethical. But each has a different criterion for judging the merits of a particular action. For example, a deontological perspective might view lying as unethical behavior, although lying in order to prevent an organization's financial collapse may be acceptable in a teleological approach.

Deontological Approach to Ethics.   The deontological approaches to understanding ethics have a religious or moral framework, as exemplified in the work of William Paley, Immanuel Kant, and George Edward Moore. William Paley, an eighteenth-century moralist, asserted that ethical and moral behavior follows the will of God and that unethical behavior contradicts the will of God.[5] The will of God is expressed through the Scriptures and "by what

[3]R. Baumhart, *Ethics in Business* (New York: Holt, Rinehart and Winston, 1968).
[4]DeGeorge, p. 37.
[5]A. Castell, *An Introduction to Modern Philosophy in Seven Philosophical Problems*, 2nd ed. (New York: Macmillan, 1964), p. 260.

we can discover of his designs and disposition from His works, or, as we usually call it, the light of nature."[6] In cases in which the will of God is not specified, one must decide whether the actions will promote or diminish the general happiness. An underlying assumption is "that God Almighty wills and wishes the happiness of His creatures."[7] Hence, the Judeo-Christian approach to ethics and morality is deontological.[8]

Immanuel Kant, also in the eighteenth century, argued that ethical behavior was not a function of Judeo-Christian precepts but was based on human rationality.[9] Kant saw morality as universally binding on all rational minds and believed that morality was both categorical (not dependent on conditions) and a priori (valid for all persons and all times and all cases).[10] Although Kant did not fit ethics into a theological framework, he did believe that ethics were fixed precepts, a deontological perspective.

George Edward Moore, a more recent writer on ethics, maintained that ethical conduct was self-evident, meaning that it was evident or true on its own merits.[11] Ethical judgments are primary or secondary. Primary ethical judgments are based on a determination of intrinsic good or evil (i.e., self-evident good or evil). Secondary or derived ethical judgments are based on an action's outcome; an action is ethical if its outcome is intrinsically good.[12] Hence, although Moore did consider the consequences of actions as moderating ethical or unethical behavior, the core of his approach is that ethical behavior, as distinguished from unethical behavior, is obvious because it has self-evident, intrinsically good or evil properties; thus Moore's view of ethical behavior is considered deontological.

The Teleological Approach to Ethics.   Several other philosophers explain ethics using a teleological approach, considering consequences as essential to determining whether a behavior is ethical or unethical. John Stuart Mill, Jeremy Bentham, and Friedrich Nietzsche took this view of ethical behavior.

John Stuart Mill and Jeremy Bentham were nineteenth-century philosophers who advocated a utilitarian approach to ethical and moral behavior. Their approach is called *utilitarian* because they reviewed laws, customs, and institutions to determine their utility or use to society. If they had no value to society, the laws, customs, or institutions should be abolished.[13] Utilitarians evaluated ethical and moral conduct by weighing an action's social benefits against its accompanying costs. An act was moral if it produced more happiness than unhappiness. Note that the test of a moral act was not the happiness it brought to the parties to the action, but to society as

[6]Castell, p. 264.
[7]Castell, p. 265.
[8]DeGeorge, p. 37.
[9]Castell, p. 269.
[10]Castell, p. 271.
[11]Castell, p. 329.
[12]Castell, p. 322.
[13]Castell, p. 286.

a whole. So, for example, although breaking a contract might be beneficial to one of the parties of a contract, society's legal framework for conducting business in an orderly fashion would be damaged. If people could not have confidence in the contracts, all of society would suffer.

There are three forms of utilitarianism: hedonistic, eudaimonistic, and ideal.[14] *Hedonistic* utilitarianism judges the basic morality of an action by estimating the degree of pleasure or pain that it offers to society as a whole. *Eudaimonistic* utilitarianism measures an act's degree of happiness for society. *Ideal* utilitariansim encompasses a larger view of valuable consequences and considers "all intrinsically valuable human goods, which also include friendship, knowledge, and a host of other goods valuable in themselves."[15] In any case, an action's consequences for society measure its moral worth. Less emphasis is given to the action itself and the standards associated with the action, regardless of the consequence.

Based on his viewpoint as a noted cultural historian, Friedrich Neitzsche stated that there is not one morality or standard of ethics, but many based on cultural variations. He felt that the guiding force in establishing values must be the cultural force. In relating the formation of morality to the social group in power, Nietzsche recognized two types of morality, master and slave. Master morality is based on the ruling class's definition of good and bad. Slave morality is based on an action's utility to the individual. This highly situational determination of moral and immoral acts led Nietzsche to equate morals with a "herd mentality" in which individuals follow the ruler's notion of morality. Nietzsche felt that morals were determined by the fiat of the elite and hence were subject to variations across cultures and rulers.

Mill, Bentham, and Nietzsche all supported the idea that the standards used to determine moral and immoral acts or ethical and unethical acts were based on the consequences of those acts, that is, a teleological approach to ethics.

The Emotive Approach to Ethics.   Other philosophers, most notably A. J. Ayer, repudiated the existence of ethics and moral judgments, believing that "moral judgments are meaningless expressions of emotion."[16] When an individual judges an action as being ethical or unethical, that judgment is based on his or her own value system. In this sense, ethics are only a personal viewpoint based on the evalutor's emotions. Ayer codified this view of ethics into his Emotive Theory, maintaining that ethics was not an area of study in itself, but part of the study of human emotion (i.e., psychology).[17]

---

[14]DeGeorge, p. 41.
[15]DeGeorge, p. 41.
[16]Castell, p. 259.
[17]Castell, p. 259.

Defining Moral Behavior

These three viewpoints of the determination of ethical and unethical actions pose some interesting problems in understanding what constitutes moral behavior, which are particularly bothersome for organizations developing a code of conduct. These problems center on defining ethical behavior and codifying ethical behavior as behavior guidelines for employees.

The most problematic of the ethical philosophies is Ayer's emotive theory. This theory contains little to guide those drawing up a code of ethics. If ethics is a completely individualized approach and based on an evaluative judgment, society will have difficulty in judging moral or immoral actions consistently. The theory's underlying supposition is that a firm will want to establish a code of conduct that exemplifies the conduct that society deems desirable. Top management will want to ensure that the actions taken by its employees are legal and acceptable to society (i.e., moral). If society has an inconsistent view of moral conduct, then organizational members will have difficulty in adpating to society's changing values.

If morals are viewed as determined by consequences (i.e., a teleological view), the determination of a code of conduct is again frustrated by the inability to judge particular behaviors as moral or immoral. Moral and immoral consequences must be spelled out.

Problems Faced by Multinational Corporations

The difficulties associated with variances in countries' customs, morals, and values make it difficult to draw up a code of ethics for all. If the purpose of the ethical code is to enhance an organization's image within a given society, but the standards vary from country to country, should the code be adapted to the host country's culture? If a multinational corporation's (MNC) ethical code changes from country to country, is the MNC hypocritical? Can a MNC have several codes of conduct? It seems that a MNC must be consistent, though flexible enough to reflect real conditions. For example, if bribery is considered wrong by the values of the management team yet is accepted in country X, should management accept bribery as a cost of doing business? What if a bribe is the only way to clear customs and to facilitate the shipment of needed materials?

The public often expresses its values on activities such as bribery by the passage of laws. An example is the Foreign Corrupt Practices Act, which is discussed later in the chapter. Such heightened public awareness and interest in business ethics stemmed from the Watergate scandal during the Nixon administration and has been sustained by journalistic and media exposés of very questionable business practices.[18]

[18]Karen Paul, "Business Environment/Public Policy Problems for the 1980's," *Business and Society*, Winter–Spring 1985, p. 12.

The difficulty in defining ethics across cultures by local public reaction is not lessened if one assumes a deontological perspective. There are realistic variations in behavior across countries and even within areas in the same country. Some of the difficulties that MNCs have in transacting business abroad pertain to the relatively elitist attitude of imposing their home country's customs and values on the host country. Succeeding in a country requires the understanding and accommodation of differing values and customs and resulting ethics. The quandary is in not compromising so much that the ethics of the MNC lead to a double standard and, hence, hypocritical ethical norms.

VALUE FORMATION IN SOCIETY

Individual value formation is perhaps best understood in the framework of social psychology theories. Secord and Backman described both intraindividual and interindividual approaches.[19] The intraindividual approaches focuses on the function of variables within the individual: "Psychologists have traditionally limited themselves to the individual, engaging in a quest for 'genetypic' traits which provide the basis for predicting the subject's behavior with many kinds of people in many situations."[20] In this approach, behavioral social patterns reflect "intraindividual structures or mechanisms such as habits, needs, cognitive structures, or, most frequently, personality traits."[21]

The interindividual approach, on the other hand, focuses on the function of external variables: "a person's behavior is mostly a reflection of the situation he happens to be in. Inherent in the situation are the social forces that shape and determine his behavior at any moment, although it is recognized that his previous experiences with such situations has predisposed him to react in certain ways in the particular circumstances."[22] For example, in explaining why an individual robs a gas station, an intraindividual approach would blame the individual's genetic and personality characteristics (internal factors). An interindividual approach would stress that the individual had no job, no cash resources, and lived in a crime-infested area. The individual's disposition set up the action in the first case, and society set up the conditions for the crime in the second case.

Because of the inherent limitations of both approaches, a combination explanation for behavior seems likely and has been called the interpersonal approach to understanding behavior.[23] Both societal values and genetic and

---

[19]P. F. Secord and C. W. Backman, *Social Psychology* (New York: McGraw-Hill, 1964), pp. 576–579.

[20]D. R. Miller, "The Study of Social Relationships: Situation, Identity, and Social Interaction," in S. Koch, *Psychology: A Study of Science*, Vol. 5, *The Process Areas, The Person, and Some Applied Fields* (New York: McGraw-Hill, 1963), p. 641.

[21]Secord and Backman, p. 577.

[22]Secord and Backman, p. 578.

[23]Secord and Backman, p. 578.

internal factors contribute to an individual's action. In the robbery of the gas station, both internal dispositions and situational determinants influenced the resultant antisocial conduct.

Applied to the development of an individual's value system, this combination of external and internal factors seems to be the best explanation. An individual learns societal norms, values, and customs through direct or vicarious experiences, and these values are enforced by society through group pressure. There is usually a range of acceptable behaviors, and the individual chooses a behavior within this range. Behaviors must fall within a "zone of tolerance" in order for the individual to be accepted by society.

Ethical behavioral norms are established in the same manner. Society formulates norms of acceptable behavior, and a particular category of behavior forms the zone of tolerable actions. Behavior outside the zone is deemed inappropriate or unethical. The standards of ethical conduct may change over time as society's values and customs change. For example, in the early 1900s, it was considered highly unethical for a person to purchase something on credit, but in the 1980s, credit purchases are widely accepted by almost all segments of society.

Enforcement or reinforcement of social norms can be accomplished by subtle or overt means of compliance. There are two methods of extracting compliance with social norms. One is using negative sanctions against the violators of social norms, and the second is using positive sanctions or reinforcement for conforming to the desired behavioral patterns. Reinforcement includes praise, acknowledgment, inclusion in activities, and social approval, which make an individual feel good about maintaining the norms of proper behavioral patterns. The application of negative sanctions for violations of the norm is necessary to maintain the order created by the code. Social disapproval, withholding of acknowledgment, and, as a last resort, ostracism are common forms of enforcing behavioral norms. Normally, the enforcement and reinforcement actions to extract compliance are a natural occurrence of events, as opposed to a planned deliberate action by groups in society. Society's values are so well entrenched that compliance (or noncompliance) is typically automatically reinforced (or punished) by society.

There is no monolithic group of society norm makers. Society is too complex and individuals are members of too many groups for a closed set of values to prevail. In more primitive, closed settings, the elders of the tribe maintain the cultural consistency. In more cosmopolitan settings, an individual receives approval or disapproval from several sources. Peer groups, extended and immediate family, religious organizations, interest groups, and friendship groups all contribute to the formation of culture and values. There is a balancing and counter-balancing effect in establishing norms and values. Each group's different values are counterbalanced by other groups so that a society's subcultures still have a degree of social value congruity.

If the subculture varies too far from the norms of the mainstream culture, then the culture will enforce corrections in the subculture's value system. This stabilization comes from reinforcement and punishment by individuals outside and inside the subculture. The value system of the subculture is influenced by the values of each member that also belongs to the larger culture. These values move the values of a specific subculture into the zone of tolerance of cultural norms. For example, a radical political organization will not usually be so radical as to offend its own members' and society's value systems. A group can deviate only to the edge of tolerable behavior. Once it oversteps these limits, the behavior will be considered antisocial. Society then will attempt to influence the subculture to comply with societal norms. Failing this, society will work toward the subculture's demise.

In summary, in developing a value system, an individual is influenced by both the external environment and the internal cognitive structure. This value system is affected by the culture and subcultures to which an individual belongs. Ethical behavior is based on the society's social norms. These social norms then aid in forming the individual's own code of ethical conduct.

The organization is a subculture, and both formal and informal work groups influence its behavior. Work demands placed on individuals and the organization's competitive structure incur reinforcements of and punishments for behaviors different from those of the larger societal culture.

THE SOCIALIZATION PROCESS

Society instills a value system in the individual through general cultural values and modifications of the values of the individual's various groups. One group is the work organization. It is important to the organization that its objectives are met, which requires accommodation by both the employees and the organization. This is called *socialization* and is defined as "the whole process by which an individual, born with behavioral potentialities of an enormously wide range, is led to develop actual behavior which is confined within a much narrower range—the range of what is customary and acceptable for him according to the standards of his group."[24] Two relevant groups influence the organizational socialization process, the formal organization and the informal work group.

The Formal Organization and the Socialization Process

The formal organization includes policies, procedures, work design, and expectations for performance, as shown in a formal organization chart. These activities are guided by the organization's objectives, and the formal organization is guided by managers who ensure that it reaches its goals in the

---

[24]I. L. Child, "Socialization," in G. Lindzey, *Handbook of Social Psychology*, Vol. 2 (Cambridge, Mass.: Addison-Wesley, 1954), p. 655.

most effective manner possible. The employees must be willing to adapt their behavior in order to reach these objectives.

Management can take several actions to foster the socialization of its employees, including informing (directly or indirectly) the employee of the organization's "culture." Management can also pass on to its employees the organization's cultural values and see that they are reinforced.

The organization's culture is usually specified in its policies, rules, and procedures. Employee manuals, labor contracts, and supervisors' explanations outline acceptable conduct. Performance expectations, in particular, are part of the organization's culture and are important to its ethical climate. In specifiying required job duties and expected levels of performance, the organization indicates the amount of discretion an employee has in meeting his or her performance objectives. For example, setting a high number of units that the employee is expected to sell indicates how one should sell the product. With very high quotas, a sales agent may be forced to use a "hard sell," approach to push the product. Although the organization's rules, procedures, and expectations help define its culture, management must also reinforce it through overt actions by the supervisors.

Behavior Modification Strategies for Socialization.   Four behavioral intervention strategies can be used to socialize employees: positive reinforcement, extinction, negative reinforcement, and punishment.[25] Figure 4.1 illustrates these methods.

Positive reinforcement is the contingent application of a desired reward when a particular behavior is exhibited. Examples of positive reinforcement in the workplace include nods of approval for correct behavior such as finishing a report on time. *Extinction* is contingently withholding a desired reward for a particular behavior, so as to discourage and, finally, eliminate that behavior. For example, if an employee engages in a lot of story telling on the job, the supervisor may ignore the stories and not respond to them. In this case responding to the story and giving attention would be the desired reward for the storyteller, and so terminating that desired reward would decrease the subsequent frequency of that behavior. *Punishment* is the contingent application of an undesirable consequence. Words of disapproval, docked pay, and formal reprimand of an employee for exhibiting an undesired behavior are examples of punishment. Punishment reduces the frequency of an undesired behavior, though its efficiency at producing behavioral change is questionable.[26] *Negative reinforcement* entails the contingent withholding of an undesired consequence when a particular behavior is exhibited. For example, a parent stops nagging a child once the child cleans his or her room. The undesired consequence is the parent's nagging, and the desired behavior

[25]F. Luthans, *Organizational Behavior*, 4th ed. (New York: McGraw-Hill, 1985), chaps. 9 and 10.
[26]Luthans.

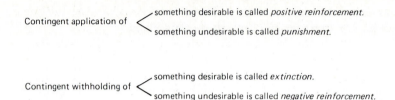

Contingent application of < something desirable is called *positive reinforcement.*
something undesirable is called *punishment.*

Contingent withholding of < something desirable is called *extinction.*
something undesirable is called *negative reinforcement.*

FIGURE 4.1   Behavioral Intervention Strategies.

is cleaning the room. Negative reinforcement is reinforcement of a desired behavior through the withholding of undesired consequences.

It is through a systematic application and withholding of desirable and undesirable consequences that the socialization of the employee into the culture of the organization is achieved. A full discussion of the behavior modification approach appears elsewhere.[27]

Employees' Responses to Socialization Attempts.   The employee has the right to accept or reject the attempts at socialization. If the socialization process is interpreted as being too costly to the employee, the employee may choose not to conform. The cost to the employee includes the restriction of some behavioral patterns and the adoption of some organizational values that may or may not conform to personal values.

In the selection process, the organization and the individual agree on the employee's expectations of the organization and the job and the organization's expectations of the employee's behavior on the job. Any great differences in expectations should be reconciled so as to minimize the chances of socialization problems occurring. Organizations have found that realistically depicting the job and the organization (i.e., reality orientation) is important to long-term satisfaction and tenure. One study found that 71 percent of those exposed to a realistic recruitment booklet remained on the job, but that 51 percent that received a more idealistic image of the job and the organization did not stay.[28]

The individual's responses to socialization attempts can be placed on a continuum. The two endpoints are rebellion and conformity, and the midpoint could be called creative individualism.[29] Rebellion is the rejection of all of the organization's values and norms. At its extreme, conforming is accepting all of the organization's values and norms. Creative individualism, on the other hand, is described as follows:

[27]Luthans.

[28]J. Weitz, "Job Expectancy and Survival," *Journal of Applied Psychology*, August 1956, pp. 245–247.

[29]L. W. Porter, E. E. Lawler III, and J. R. Hackman, *Behavior in Organizations* (New York: McGraw-Hill, 1975), p. 171.

It involves a person's acceptance of the pivotal or absolutely essential (from the organization's standpoint) norms and values, but rejection of many of their relevant or peripheral ones. This, presumably, would be the most successful form of individualization for both parties—the employee gains by exerting some influence on the total collective body (or some subunit of it), and the organization gains by an infusion of fresh ideas and possibly more effective modes of performance.[30]

Remaining creatively independent is difficult because the employee is constantly reinforced for socialization to the organization's values and norms but is not reinforced for preserving his or her own value system. There is a zone of tolerable behavior in which an individual can operate, and creative individualism seems to fall on its fringes.

In summary, the formal organization attempts to influence an employee's behavior so that the employee's behavior will conform to the organization's value system. Conformity is important to the organization because of its social need to "get along" and have a smoother running system and its need to know that there is a congruence between the individual's personal work goals and the organization's performance expectations for the individual. The individual can accept or reject the organization's norms and values. As with society's values and norms, there is a zone of tolerance of behavior that the organization will accept from the employee. Organizational norms are communicated to the individual through specification of job objectives, organizational rules and procedures, and direct and indirect behavioral influence attempts by the organization's management. The organization's culture, however, is not only that created by the formal organization but also that created by the informal organization.

The Informal Organization and the Socialization Process

The informal organization consists of the informal work groups and friendship groups that are a natural outgrowth of the formal organization. Friendships, coalitions of special-interest groups, and groups formed to work on a common task both influence the organization's power structure and provide for the individual's needs. To some degree, the formal organization aids the formation of the informal subculture. The definition and grouping of jobs, authority relationships, hierarchical levels, physical facilities, work flows, and work rules and procedures all help form informal subgroups, which have, to some degree, their own separate culture.

Informal work group culture may or may not reinforce the culture of the formal organization, though there must be some accommodation so that both the formal and informal cultures can coexist. Too much variation may lead to the frustration of each group's goals. The formal organization will

---

[30]Luthans.

tolerate variations in culture as long as its goals are attained. Too much variation may lead to the expulsion of the entire group and the employment of a new group without the "cultural bias." For example, one midwestern computer company terminated an entire department because traditional work norms resisted changes in policy to raise performance standards while reducing compensation. The company felt it was better to begin anew rather than to fight the informal work-group norms.

The communication and enforcement of informal work-group norms follow patterns similar to those of the formal organization, although there are some differences. First, the means of communicating informal group values and norms is less formalized. There is no written employee manual specifying rules and procedures; rather it is only through direct and vicarious interactions with the members (especially leaders) of the work group that the employee is made aware of the group's norms. For example, if the formally designated standard is to produce 200 units per hour, but the work group's norm is 180, the work group must inform the employee of this. Through discussions or comments such as "Ease off a bit" or "What are you doing, trying to make us look bad?" the message will be communicated that the behavior of the employee does not fit the norm of the informal work group.

The informal group influences individual behavior through various social reinforcers. The need to belong is extremely important to most people, and the informal group helps meet this need. First, the members of the immediate informal group are the primary satisfaction of this need. Second, even if the individual is not attracted to the informal group but wants to succeed in the organization, then the informal group will still be important. It is through the cooperation of the informal work group that an individual's performance is facilitated. Without the informal group's help, succeeding becomes difficult, if not impossible, as an informal work group can readily sabotage an employee's efforts. Disruptive activities may lead the formal organization to dismiss or transfer the employee in order to receive the cooperation of the rest of the group. Management's underlying operatings norm is that it is easier to replace one individual than a whole group (often without regard to the merits of the problem). Because of this power, the informal group can influence individual employee behavior. In many cases, the informal group has more influence than does the formal organization.

The Impact of Formal and Informal Groups and Ethics

Codes of ethical conduct are derived from the actions of the formal and informal organizations. The employee is reinforced for behaviors in day-to-day conduct that are acceptable to both the formal and informal groups. Ethical conduct evolves from the norms and values of the organization's formal and the informal cultures. As mentioned previously, the formal organization's demands may require unethical actions by the employee. For example, the formal pressure to meet a sales quota and the informal norm of making sales any way one can may influence an employee's actions to "pressure a client," "to make an unrealistic delivery promise," or "give a personal gift to the purchasing agent" in order to secure the order. Note that the unethical conduct is a function of the formal and informal organizations' value systems and the employee's own values outside the organization.

A cultural environment outside the organization (either formal or informal) that forbids the organization's unethical conduct creates conflict within the individual. The stronger the individual's feeling is that this conduct is wrong, the higher the probability is that the individual will not take these actions. The organization's role, too, in providing the climate for ethical or unethical conduct is central to the employee's actions. Before presenting strategies that management can apply in order to improve the ethical conduct of its employees, we shall review society's attempts to improve the ethical conduct of organizations in general.

IMPROVING THE ETHICAL CONDUCT OF MODERN ORGANIZATIONS

It is probably most accurate to say that ethical conduct is based on a society's mores and values. As Nietzsche indicated, there are variations across cultures of proper ethical conduct. If an organization exists in only one culture, it needs to adapt only to the values of that culture. But if an organization exists in many cultures, as does a multinational corporation, then determining an ethical code becomes more problematic. In the United States, societal values have been translated into several laws that regulate the actions of business. These laws specify the ethical norms that business must follow.

Legislative Efforts to Improve the Ethical Conduct of Business

The right of society to place ethical constraints on business stems from three considerations. First, a society has the right to dictate business's ethical actions because it has given the organization the legal right to conduct business. It logically follows that because society has granted business the right to operate in its environment, it can also determine the conditions that will prevail in that environment. Requiring that business be conducted in an ethical manner in simply another condition of the social contract that a business makes with society when filing for its legal charter of incorporation or beginning business as a partnership or sole proprietorship. By going into business, it follows that the firm's management and employees agree to abide by the laws of the legal political state. The laws reflect the society's values and norms as well as its ethical and moral values.

The second justification rests with the all-encompassing nature of the state.[31] The state is in a better position to regulate ethical behavior than is a single organization. If a single organization assumes an ethical role, it may be to its detriment, especially if other organizations will not also follow that particular code of ethics. For example, trucking company A may decide that it will not give gifts to distribution managers that use their service or that it will not make "under the table" payments to dock workers to expedite the unloading of shipments. But if other companies still follow these unethical practices, the ethical position of company A could impede its success. Because of its ethical position, company A puts itself at a competitive disadvantage. But if all organizations must assume the same basic ethical position through regulation at the state level, no organization will have a competitive advantage because of unethical actions. These unethical actions will now be illegal. The illegality of the actions, coupled with the potential penalties for violating the law, will encourage compliance by all parties.

A third justification for society to define the ethical boundaries of business relates to the failure of companies to regulate themselves. An argument against regulation by the state is that business is in a better position to regulate its own affairs. Although idealistically it seems reasonable that business should be able to establish its own code of conduct, history has not demonstrated that self-policing is effective. An industry-wide ethics formation and enforcement group usually does not have the enforcement powers or the will to compel errant organizations to follow its guidelines. Thus, it seems appropriate for the state to develop and enforce a code of conduct.

The General Legalistic Framework for Ethical Conduct

There are four areas in which the state has established the ethical conduct for business: (1) criminal actions against individuals, (2) civil action against organizations, (3) regulatory guidelines with enforcement powers, and (4) specific legislation directed toward the employees' ethical conduct that forces the establishment of control systems that monitor organizational accountability for ethical conduct. Except for the fourth area, the regulation of ethical conduct has been directed toward specific concerns and issues rather than comprehensive ethical postures. For example, the regulation of ethics has generally been treated on a case-by-case basis, such as the limits to granting discounts as defined in the Robinson-Patman Act. These case-by-case ethical demonstrations have been outlined in legislative fiats, judicial interpretations, and executive actions.

These laws provide mandatory constraints on the actions of a business organization. These constraints spell out those actions an organization can or cannot pursue. For example, the Securities and Exchange Commission

---

[31]"State" refers to the political-legal boundaries of the country in which the organization is operating.

(SEC), created by law in 1934, regulates all publicly traded securities and the markets in which they are traded. The SEC's activities include the procedures for transacting business on the stock exchanges, which can be considered a basic code of ethics for that activity. In much the same manner, other legislative actions have described the ethical climate for operating a business.

The laws themselves are not final edicts that govern ethical conduct. Just as important is the judicial interpretation of specific laws. Through precedential rulings a law is clarified from which an operating code can be surmised. The word *surmised* is used here because the judicial interpretations that occur became a historical basis governing future interpretations of the law. A historical interpretation may be altered under rulings for differing conditions. An example of the importance of these rulings is the various services provided to keep law firms, business organizations, and consultants up to date. For tax court rulings, *Prentice-Hall Tax Court of Reported and Memorandum Decisions* is a weekly tax service that provides the latest information on judicial interpretations of tax laws. There are similar services for other laws and regulatory bodies.

Ethical actions run the gamut of legal decisions regarding both criminal and civil actions. A crime is an act violating a statute and implies a penalty, including fine or imprisonment. A recent application of criminal action against a business was when the Justice Department fined E. F. Hutton $2 million in May, 1985 for being involved in a complex check-kiting scheme.[32] Hutton pleaded guilty to 2,000 separate charges of mail and wire fraud. Hutton played several bank accounts against one another to gain, in effect, interest-free loans. The operation gave the company the use of as much as $250 million a day at no cost; short-term interest rates at the time were about 20 percent. As yet, no individuals have been charged in this action, but in other cases, managers have been sent to jail and/or fined.

A civil action, also called a *tort*, pertains to an invasion of another's right of person, property, or reputation. The commission of a tort gives the injured party the right of redress against the acting party, either by way of damages for an act done or by an injunction against a threatened act. For example, a chemical company that uses its own property as a nontoxic-chemical dumping site may be well within the law. But if there is a threat of polluting the ground water, the affected residents can take legal action to restrain the company from using the site for purposes that may intrude on the rights of adjacent homeowners. Legal decisions covering both criminal actions and torts provide a framework of judicial interpretation that guides ethical activities.

Executive actions are another prescription of ethical conduct by the government. In the United States, the legislative branch of government creates law, and through judicial interpretation the laws are defined and imple-

---

[32]"A Verdict," *Time*, September 9, 1985, p. 56.

mented. The executive branch administers and executes the laws. A law's specifications may offer a wide range of interpretations. An agency head or administrator has much discretion in defining areas of responsibility and deciding the degree of emphasis that particular aspects of the law will receive. For example, in 1914 Congress established the Federal Trade Commission (FTC), which has broad powers to curb unfair trade practices, protect consumers from unsafe products, and maintain competition.

The discretion of executive branch agencies and their heads decides how resources are allocated and what areas will be emphasized in executing the congressional intent of the law. This discretionary power, however, is constrained by the president who appoints the agency officers, who in turn serve at the president's discretion. Congress budgets the agency's funds and can amend its powers. The judicial branch defines the intent of the agency through litigation through civil suits against the agency or criminal suits filed against the agency's officers. Although the judicial branch cannot initiate a suit, it can render a decision when a third party files suit. For example, in 1982 the courts overruled a Department of Transportation (DOT) decision to relax rules governing passive seat restraints, by claiming that the DOT's action was illegal. Congress agreed with the judicial action, in that the Senate restricted funding for an appeal to the Supreme Court of the lower court's decision. In this case both the Senate and the courts rejected the agency's actions. Therefore, even though there is discretion in the actions in executing and administering the legal aspects of business, there still are checks and balances.

In summary, through legislative, judicial, and executive actions covering years of judicial decisions, guidelines for ethical conduct of business have been developed. Although these guidelines are not stated as a cohesive and concise framework, the various laws do help direct the business firm's activities in many areas. One recent piece of legislation, the Foreign Corrupt Practices Act, was directed at the ethical conduct of employees and the responsibilities of management to ensure adequate controls to curb unethical action.

The Foreign Corrupt Practices Act

Society benefits from business's ethical conduct. Owners want to ensure that their investments are safe, as reflected in accurate financial disclosures. Society as a whole wants to ensure that its business firms reflect the values and ethics of a competitive, equal-opportunity environment. In recent years American society has scrutinized many facets of political and corporate life, and its awareness of unethical behavior was heightened when it learned of the degree of air and water pollution resulting from business actions. Additional unethical behaviors were revealed when the Securities and Exchange Commission (SEC) sponsored a voluntary compliance program regarding questionable payments by business firms, especially MNCs, to parties both within and outside the United States.

The involvement of the SEC in business practices was the direct result of the initial statement of the SEC as formulated by Congress 50 years ago. The SEC was charged with regulating all publicly traded securities and security markets. In regulating securities (mainly stocks and bonds), the SEC must see that an organization fairly represents itself to its investors.[33] This fair representation includes public disclosure of material activities, or actions that would significantly affect the investors' evaluation of the organization. The standard of materiality was, until recently, applied primarily to financial considerations. But in 1964, the commission ruled that the integrity of management is also a material factor,[34] though it did not consistently follow this ruling in subsequent decisions. Renewed interest in the SEC's role occurred with the Watergate Special Prosecution Force's discovery that many publicly owned companies had violated disclosure laws and had engaged in a wide variety of questionable practices.[35] In 1976 the findings of the Watergate special prosecutor led to a voluntary disclosure program conducted by the SEC. The results indicated that of those companies complying, over 250 U.S. corporations had made questionable or illegal payments.[36]

The results of these disclosures led Senator William Proxmire (D-Wisconsin) to propose that the SEC be given additional power "to promulgate rules and regulations regarding a corporation's expressed obligation to maintain accurate books, records, or accounts for business transactions."[37] The SEC, however, asserted that more specific legislation would be more effective than would additional SEC powers. On May 2, 1977, the Senate Banking, Housing, and Urban Affairs Committee proposed legislation in its Senate Report No. 95–114.[38] The final legislation, called the Foreign Corrupt Practices Act (FCPA), was signed into law on December 19, 1977.

The act covers foreign corrupt practices and accounting procedures:

> The foreign corrupt practices section of the Act makes it unlawful for SEC registrants (entities subject to registration and reporting requirements of the SEC Act of 1934), both domestic and foreign, and domestic nonregistrant entities to influence foreign governments or officials through payments or gifts. The accounting standard section requires that SEC registrants comply with certain record-keeping and internal accounting control standards.[39]

The first section of the act applies only to SEC registrants engaged in foreign commerce, and the second section of the act applies to all SEC registrants.

---

[33]"The Scale of Government Intervention," *Business Week*, April 4, 1977, pp. 42, 53, 56.

[34]D. N. Ricchiute, *Auditing: Concepts and Standards* (Cincinnati: Southwestern Publishing, 1982), p. 134.

[35]"The Scale of Government Intervention."

[36]H. Baruch, "The Foreign Corrupt Practices Act," *Harvard Business Review*, January–February 1979, p. 33.

[37]Ricchiute, p. 138.

[38]Ricchiute, p. 138.

[39]Ricchiute, p. 138.

Penalties for violating the act's foreign corrupt practice section are up to $1 million in fines for company officials. Violations of the internal control-record-keeping provisions include up to $10,000 for companies and $10,000 and five years of imprisonment for company officials.[40]

Compliance with the record-keeping-internal control section requires the following:

1. *Record-keeping requirements.* Entities must make and keep books, records, and accounts which, in reasonable detail, accurately reflect the transactions and dispositions of the assets of the company.
2. *Internal accounting control requirements.* Entities must devise and maintain a system of internal accounting controls sufficient to provide reasonable assurances that
   - Transactions are executed in accordance with management's general and specific authorization.
   - Transactions are recorded as necessary to permit preparation of financial statements in conformity with generally accepted accounting principles or any other criteria applicable to such statements, and to maintain accountability for assets.
   - Access to assets is permitted only in accordance with management's general and specific authorization.
   - The recorded accountability for assets is compared with the existing assets at reasonable intervals, and appropriate action is taken with respect to differences.[41]

The provisions of the FCPA are administered and enforced by the SEC. In 1979, the SEC proposed that all annual reports include a statement by management as to whether corporate control systems had achieved the FCPA's internal accounting control objectives. In 1980, independent accountants were also to be required to report on the controls' efficiency,[42] though the adoption of these proposals was delayed until 1982, when further considerations of their merits were made.[43]

The FCPA regulates the activities of companies engaged in foreign commerce, and it imposes on business certain record-keeping and internal controls standards. The responsibilities of directors and officers in forming control systems to detect unethical financial activities has profound implications. Management can not only be held accountable for deliberate violation of the first section of the law (corrupt practices) but can also be held negligent by not having a reporting system and a system of internal controls that meets the standards outlined in the act. Although other laws have provided

---

[40]J. E. Connor, *The Foreign Corrupt Practices Act: Implications for Directors* (New York: Price, Waterhouse, 1979).

[41]Ricchiute, p. 140.

[42]Connor.

[43]Ricchiute, p. 143.

constraints defining ethical conduct, no previous law has been as extensive as this in outlining management's responsibilities to provide a system for detecting illegal, unethical actions.

Contemporary public policy has had a significant impact on shaping the conduct of officers and employees. Although laws cannot legislate morality and ethics, they can provide guidelines for the accountability of officers and employees. As a result of these legal constraints and the concern of directors and officers of organizations, actions have been taken to improve business's ethical conduct. The final section of this chapter will present some of the approaches used by companies in establishing ethical codes and will detail one approach.

BUSINESS'S EFFORTS TO IMPROVE ETHICAL CONDUCT

The prescription of a code of ethics for employee conduct has a strong legal and social foundation, and the actions of its employees are important to the organization's success and ethical image. There are legal limits, however, to the activities that an organization can specify as behaviors required on and off the job. For example, requiring ethical behavior on the job, such as forbidding payoffs to clients, is within the organization's jurisdiction. Reprimands and/or dismissal for conduct off the job, is more problematic. For example, if a member of the police department poses nude for a magazine or owns and operates a bar, does the top management of the department have a legal right to fire the individual? These issues are currently being tested in the courts.

There is also the question of whether anyone can ever really determine what is right or wrong. This seems particularly true in recent years. As one professor of business ethics recently commented:

> Culturally we are suffering from the ravages of a metaphysical cancer—a psychological rejection mechanism that questions the possibility of anyone's being able to know right and wrong in absolute terms. This in turn destroys a culture's ability to develop a consensus on matters of right and wrong, which results in ethical schizophrenia—many ethical faces.[44]

Although there are many gray areas to an overall culture's or a specific organization's right to prescribe behavior patterns for its employees, in certain instances there are some legal precedents that do allow an organization to specify behavioral patterns for its employees. These can be stated either as part of the personnel policies or in a code of ethical conduct.

---

[44]Richard C. Cheavning, "Can Free Enterprise Survive Ethical Schizophrenia?" *Business Horizons*, March–April 1984, pp. 5–6.

Developing Ethical Codes of Conduct

An organization's ethical norms do not necessarily have to be written. As discussed earlier, values are developed in organizations through the formal or the informal work groups' activities. Organizational actions include the rules, policies, and actions of the directors and managers, as well as what the organization reinforces or punishes in regard to specific employee behavior. In some cases management may formally articulate its value system through a prescribed code of ethics.

Using Ethical Codes.   A study surveying the extent of use of ethical codes of conduct in recent years found that over 75 percent of the 611 firms responding had a code of ethics,[45] compared with 40 percent of the firms surveyed in 1964[46] and 32 percent of the companies polled in 1968.[47]

Differing conditions make it difficult to standardize a code of ethics for all organizations. Table 4.1 lists items that 30 U.S. companies included in their code of ethics. Caution is in order in interpreting the items shown in Table 4.1. The low ranking of foreign corrupt practices may be the result of many of the respondents' not engaging in multinational transactions. The low ranking of the Foreign Corrupt Practices Act may simply reflect that the FCPA was included in particular actions, though not referred to per se. Table 4.1 does point out a number of items that need to be considered in drawing up a code of ethics. The more specific the code is, the more it will aid in defining and guiding actual ethical practices. Nevertheless, developing a code of ethics does have its problems.

Problems in Developing a Code of Ethics.   Two problems occur when ethical conduct is defined for a specific company. There are many jobs covering many different relationships among organization members and the various publics of a business. When a code of ethics is written, it must be inclusive in order to meet the needs of each of these relationships. If guidelines are not specific, an employee may interpret them to mean that a behavior is allowable, thereby defeating the purpose of the ethical code.

A second problem is establishing too broad a prescriptive statement. If the code is too general, it loses its value in guiding behavior. Employees might view the code as a public relations tool with little practical value. It is apparent that a code of ethics must be an inclusive and meaningful statement of principles.

Transcending the written document is the example set by top management.

---

[45]B. J. White and B. R. Montgomery, "Corporate Codes of Conduct," *California Management Review*, Winter 1980, pp. 80–87.

[46]S. Mathes and G. Thompson, "Ensuring Ethical Conduct in Business," *The Conference Board Record*, December 1964, pp. 17–27.

[47]Baumhart.

TABLE 4.1. Examples of Items to Be Included in a Code of Ethical Conduct.

Item		Percentage of Statements Including Items
Implementation and administration procedures for code enforcement		83
General statement of ethics and philosophy		80
Date code went into effect		77
Conflict of interest with respect to:		73
Acceptance of gifts	77	
Suppliers	57	
Competition	50	
Customers	50	
Relatives or associates	50	
Memberships on boards of directors	30	
Compliance with applicable laws		67
Inside information		63
False entries in books and records		50
Misuse of corporate assets with respect to:		50
Payment to government officials or political parties	63	
Gifts, favors, entertainment	57	
Undisclosed or unrecorded funds or assets	53	
False, misleading support documents	37	
Political contributions	37	
Secret payments	23	
Facilitating payments	20	
Antitrust compliance with respect to:		40
Competitors	30	
Customers	30	
Suppliers	30	
International transactions	13	
Confidential information		40
Equal employment opportunity		30
Arrangements with dealers and agents with respect to:		23
Responsibility for dealer's actions	43	
Commission levels	33	
Foreign third-party payments	13	
Observance of society's moral and ethical standards		20
Specific reference to FCPA		17
Partisan versus issue political activity		13
International trade boycotts		10
Relations with shareholders and security analysts		7

Source: Adapted from B. J. White and B. R. Montgomery, "Corporate Codes of Conduct, *California Management Review*, Winter 1980, p. 84.

The degree of ethical or unethical behavior engaged in or allowed by top management is probably more critical to the acceptance of ethical conduct by its subordinates than any written document is. In particular, top management's own level of ethical conduct, its tolerance of employees' and outsiders' conduct, and its emphasis on performance and ethical values seem most important.

As indicated earlier, people learn directly or vicariously what the acceptable norms of conduct are. If employees directly observe or perceive that ethical conduct is not valued by top management, then the norms and values associated with ethical conduct will probably be disregarded. How can top management's actions influence employees, especially when the employees are removed from management's daily activities? Management's actions are conveyed through rumors, new accounts, and policy pronouncements in the organization. For example, if a newspaper describes the proxy fight between management and another company as a vicious attempt by management to take over the target company, then the employees will learn something of their management's practiced ethics. In the same vein, if management demonstrates that its employees will be unjustly treated in layoff procedures or allows inequitable working conditions and overtime allocation procedures, then employees may not believe that the management values honesty and personal integrity.

A second managerial action important to the development of an ethical climate is the reaction of management to employees' and outsiders' ethical and unethical conduct. Again, the key is how management behaves, not what is written regarding management policies. Its reactions to both internal and external groups is important. Its acceptance of unethical behavior of groups outside the organization, even though it does not tolerate unethical behavior inside the organization, leads to a perception of inconsistency and reduces management's credibility. Management must consistently display ethical behavior in regard to both its own employees and outside groups. For example, an employee found to be padding an expense account must be disciplined according to the severity of the action. The discipline is necessary not only to encourage more ethical behavior in that particular employee but also to communicate to other employees the importance of ethical conduct to management. Reactions to unethical behavior in groups outside the organization include filing suits relating to grievances against the company, promoting ethical conduct in industry and trade associations, and working through groups such as the Better Business Bureau to improve ethical business conduct toward consumer groups.

Third, the value to management of performance reflects the credibility of its ethical posture. If meeting performance objectives at any cost is seen as the most important facet of employee behavior, then the secondary role of ethical conduct will be obvious. For example, if an employee uses hard-sell approaches and is known to give gifts to purchasing agents but is still rewarded for exceeding quotas, then management's value priorities will be evident. If management promotes an unethical employee unknowingly, the climate of the organization will still be affected. It is not only the intentional consequences with which management must be concerned but also the unintentional consequences. Management's responsibility to assess performance *and* ethical behavior in making salary and promotion decisions is obviously essential in order to reinforce the proper value system and subsequent employee behavior.

Developing ethical codes of conduct and providing a climate encouraging ethical conduct are not enough to ensure ethical behavior. The code of conduct must be translated into specific behavioral actions and internal control systems in order to instill high ethical values. This phase of improving ethical conduct may be referred to as implementing ethical values.

Implementing an Ethical Code of Conduct

Implementing ethical values is a four-step procedure. The first step is defining the ethical values or drawing up specific behavioral guidelines. The second step is determining the accountability and responsibility for ethical conduct. The third step is forming a system of internal controls in order to monitor specific practices. And the last step is to formulate a management policy toward responding to deviations of ethical guidelines and procedures for reinforcing proper ethical conduct and punishing unethical conduct.

Figure 4.2 presents the code of ethics for a national pharmaceutical firm, which can be used as an example of some of the problems encountered in implementing business ethics. It is used here only for illustrative purposes and is not necessarily either a good or a bad code of ethics.

The first step in implementing a code of ethics such as the one in Figure 4.2 is to translate the code into specific behavioral guidelines. The code in Figure 4.2 has six areas: customers, suppliers and distributors, employees, immediate community, world responsibility, and stockholders. With respect to the organization's responsibility to its customers, the code lists high quality, reasonable prices, and fast servicing of customer's orders. Note that these goals are interrelated and, to some degree, mutually exclusive. Striving for the lowest price precludes having the fastest filling of customer orders or the highest standards of quality. It is logical to assume that the company intended that a balance be struck between these competing goals. Implementing this portion of the code would necessitate an agreement on the levels of each of the three goals that should be attained. Although it may be impossible to specify these levels in the initial code of conduct, it is important that they be spelled out in organizational strategies.

The difficulty in specifying levels of behavior in the initial code points to the need for flexibility to meet varying conditions in the organization's strategic plan. For example, in one set of economic conditions, customers may value quality and customer service and place less emphasis on price. But during a downturn in the economy, customers may be more interested

Our Credo

We believe our first responsibility is to the doctors, nurses and patients,
to mothers and all others who use our products and services.
In meeting their needs everything we do must be of high quality.
We must constantly strive to reduce our costs
in order to maintain reasonable prices.
Customers' orders must be serviced promptly and accurately.
Our suppliers and distributors must have an opportunity
to make a fair profit.

We are responsible to our employees,
the men and women who work with us throughout the world.
Everyone must be considered as an individual.
We must respect their dignity and recognize their merit.
They must have a sense of security in their jobs.
Compensation must be fair and adequate,
and working conditions clean, orderly and safe.
Employees must feel free to make suggestions and complaints.
There must be equal opportunity for employment, development
and advancement for those qualified.
We must provide competent management,
and their actions must be just and ethical.

We are responsible to the communities in which we live and work
and to the world community as well.
We must be good citizens — support good works and charities
and bear our fair share of taxes.
We must encourage civic improvements and better health and education.
We must maintain in good order
the property we are privileged to use,
protecting the environment and natural resources.

Our final responsibility is to our stockholders.
Business must make a sound profit.
We must experiment with new ideas.
Research must be carried on, innovative programs developed
and mistakes paid for.
New equipment must be purchased, new facilities provided
and new products launched.
Reserves must be created to provide for adverse times.
When we operate according to these principles,
the stockholders should realize a fair return.

Johnson & Johnson

FIGURE 4.2   Example of a Code of Ethics.

in price than service or quality. To meet these shifts in consumer preferences,
management strategy must be flexible enough to be able to respond to these
changes. This seems to be the underlying major goal of the first section of
the code in Figure 4.2.

Our discussion so far may lead you to assume that the code has little
actual value in shaping the organization's conduct. This may be true in
some organizations. But the code in itself offers a standard of accountability
by which the actions of the organization and its employees can be judged.

HELPING CUSTOMERS PROTECT THEMSELVES

While business firms are interested in developing behavioral standards of conduct for their employees, in recent years many of them have also begun trying to protect their customers from unethical practices. This is particularly true among credit card companies.

Every year banks and other finance-related organizations lose millions of dollars because of credit card fraud. There are many ways in which this can happen. One of the most common is for someone (often a waiter or service station attendant) to get a copy of a customer's credit card number, call in a purchase, and then drop by, sign the credit card bill, and depart with the merchandise. Not until the unwary customer gets the bill does the person realize that he or she has been ripped off. Another common approach is for someone to duplicate the card of a customer and use it for two or three weeks. By the time the real card owner learns of the fraud, the person has stopped using the card. Card duplication is fairly difficult, but professional crooks seem to have no trouble doing so.

Can people totally protect themselves from credit card fraud? No. Everyone is a potential victim. However, there are ways of reducing the chances of your getting ripped off by these thieves. Experts recommend four specific steps:

1. When tearing off your copy of the multilayered invoice, also take the carbons. If you crush them up and leave them in an ashtray, a thief can copy your credit card numbers and use them later.
2. Do not give out your account number unless you are making an actual purchase. Do not believe that a phone or mail solicitor who asks for your account number to qualify you for a mailing, a contest, or a prize. Quite often this is nothing more than a ruse to get your card number.
3. Review your monthly bill carefully. A large number of heavy card users unwittingly pay charges they have never authorized. If you report unauthorized charges promptly, it is unlikely that you will even be charged the $50 per card maximum liability.
4. Keep a well-hidden list of account numbers at home so that you can easily report lost or stolen credit cards.

Source: John Merwin, "How the Smart Crooks Use Plastic," *Forbes*, September 9, 1985, pp. 88–95.

For example, in Figure 4.2, the standards for actions toward the consumer determines the quality of performance. In social accountability, an external-public or an internal-interest group could readily ask for an audit of corporate performance to find out if the organization has abided by the stated code. In subscribing to the code, management should demonstrate some specific level of results and be able to show that it is complying with the guidelines established in the code. Hence, the code is a means for directing managerial behavior, and in turn, managerial behavior will be evaluated in light of the code (see the box "Helping Customers Protect Themselves").

Developing Behavioral Standards

In developing behavioral standards, one of three philosophical approaches is commonly followed. One type, the planning mode approach, emphasizes accountability at the strategy and goal formulation level. Because this level is the major source of plans and goals, it makes sense to address the issues specified in the code during the planning process. According to this approach, proposed strategies are evaluated not only by their benefits to the organization but also by the degree to which these proposed strategies comply with the code of conduct. For example, consider a strategy to market a medical product overseas. Within the broad plans are several proposed marketing strategies: through a distributor, through a distributor with an informational advertising campaign, and through direct sales to doctors with an extensive educational campaign to inform them of the proper use of the product. Although the product may not need a prescription for its use, the company may feel that the correct use of the product is essential to meet its responsibility to its customers. The first and second options might be eliminated, as they do not assure the producing company that the instructions for using the product will be clear to the consumer. The third option, therefore, might be chosen, as the company can rely on its own sales force to explain the proper use of the product to responsible dispensers of the product. Note that the third option meets the strategies of expanding into a foreign market and also improves the ethical accountability dimensions desired by management.

The individual accountability approach translates the code into individual behaviors covering all employees of the organization. Whereas the planning approach emphasizes plans and strategy formulation as the major vehicles of accountability, the individual approach focuses on the individual employee's ethical behavior. The logic of this approach is simple. Strategies and policies are formulated by individuals in the organization, and so they will be more responsive to social concerns if they are held directly accountable for them. The burden of ethical and social responsibility is transferred from a nameless corporate identity, committee, or department to individual employees. In the example above, the decision to market a product in a foreign country was made by a committee of upper-level management. The group as a whole was responsible for the decision. In the second approach, each member of the committee is responsible for the committee's decision. At other levels of the organization, each person is also held accountable. For example, a sales representative is directly responsible for marketing a product in a manner that meets the company's code of ethics. If the representative feels that the approach used does not meet the code, it is his or her responsibility to question the practice and raise this concern with upper-level management. If a manager instructs the sales representative to sell the product in a manner that the employee feels violates the code, then the employee has the responsibility to tell this to his or her manager and the manager's supervisor. The end result of this approach, in theory at least, is that each employee will act as a control mechanism to ensure that the formation and implementation of organizational goals and strategies are in accordance with the specified code of conduct.

The third approach is a combination of the two previous approaches. The combination approach, as it is called, guides both goal and strategy formation and individual employee behavior.

Once the approach to establishing the ethical code is decided, ethical behaviors and unethical behaviors can be distinguished. The norm used will probably reflect the value systems of both those drawing up the code and those of upper-level management, with some consideration of society's norms. Because vales change over time, codes should be periodically reviewed and modified to reflect prevailing norms.

It would be impossible and impractical to specify behaviors to meet all conditions that might occur. It is, however, important to establish guidelines to reflect some of the more common situations that an employee may encounter. The advantage of translating a code of conduct into specific behaviors is that it offers guidelines for the employees' conduct, *and* as they adopt the code, an ethical value system or culture will emerge. This value system can be defined as what the organization will tolerate in personal ethical conduct, and it will indicate behavior in other ethical situations the employee may encounter. For example, if there is an item in the code forbidding any form of bribery to customers' purchasing agents in order to encourage product sales, it rationally follows that the company's own purchasing agents should not accept bribes.

Examples of the types of behaviors that might be specified appear in Table 4.2. These behaviors pertain to the section on responsibilities to customers outlined in the general code presented in Figure 4.2. Note that the behavioral translation of the code helps specify acts that would or would not be considered ethical and that the behavioral standards set the tone for other activities not specified by the code.

Other Steps in Implementing an Ethical Code

A second step in implementing ethical conduct in an organization is assigning the degree of accountability and responsibility for monitoring ethical conduct. It is not enough to provide a code and then translate the code into behavioral guidelines. Personal accountability and responsibility must also

TABLE 4.2.   Translating the Ethical Code into Specific Behavioral Policies.

High Quality

1. Each employee has the responsibility to ensure that our products are produced according to the specified standards of quality. If you feel that quality is below acceptable standards, immediately report your concerns to quality control-filing report 41000.

2. If you, as an employer, feel that an unsafe product is being produced, you should inform management. Indicate the nature of your concern and document the reason for it. Management will respond to your concern within two week.

Reasonable Prices

1. In order to reduce costs to the consumer, management solicits your ideas for improving productivity and efficiency. A joint committee of labor and management will review all proposals. If a proposal is adopted, a share of the savings will go directly to the individual or group proposing the idea.

Fast Servicing of Customer Orders

1. Report to management any orders that cannot or will not be filled within five working days after the order has been received.

2. Report any responses to customer complaints that were not handled within 24 hours after learning of complaint.

be spelled out. Obviously, responsibility for specific actions ultimately rests with the individual employee. But to convey its regard for ethical behavior, management at all levels ought to be responsible for monitoring its own employees' ethical behavior. Assignment of managerial authority and responsibility enhances the code's credibility.

The third step is setting up an internal system of control and information that aids in detecting unethical behavior. As part of the Foreign Corrupt Practices Act (FCPA), all organizations registered with the Security and Exchange Commission (SEC) are required to have a system of internal controls to ensure that accounting transactions are in accordance with management's general and specific authorization.[48] It is also reasonable to expect that a general management information system will include standards of control that monitor the organization's ethical behavior. This will make sure that all employees' behaviors are within the guidelines expected by management. Examples of the information that might be gathered appears in Table 4.3. A system of reporting to various levels of management is also part of this process. Normally, the standards in Table 4.3 would require an employee to file a report when an outside agent attempts to influence an employee. Internal ethical behavior can be monitored periodically by auditing expendi-

[48]Securities and Exchange Commission Accounting Series Release No. 242.

TABLE 4.3. Means to Monitor Ethical Behavior.

Occurrence of Unethical Influence Attempts

If you are a target of unethical influence attempts, by individuals or groups inside or outside the organization, you should immediately report these occurrences to your supervisor, followed by a written report filed in the Unethical Practices Form.

Periodic Sign-Off

During their annual performance review, all employees will be required to sign a statement indicating that they have not engaged in, nor plan to engage in, unethical activities as specified in the ethical code. Further, the employees shall indicate that they will abide by the code.

tures documented by receipts or a periodic sign-off by the employee indicating that he or she has not engaged in unethical business practices. These measures could be included as part of the annual review process.

A fourth step in an organizational ethical code is establishing a policy of management responses to reinforce ethical behavior and a policy of appropriate action for infractions of the ethical code. It makes little sense to have an ethical code unless management insists on compliance with it. When these actions are directed toward an individual, they serve two purposes. First, the employee directly learns of management's intent, and second, through the example established by management's actions, other employees learn vicariously of its intent.

Following the four steps outlined in the above discussion will do much to enhance the credibility of the code of ethics that management wishes to advocate and will aid in building the organization's culture so that it relates more readily to its position on ethics. Once a code is agreed on, it must be translated into specific behavioral guidelines. Accountability for ensuring that ethical behavior prevails must be defined and assigned to managers at all levels. Internal information systems should include monitoring and control features to aid in detecting unethical practices. Finally, management must be able to insist on compliance with the code of ethics by means of reinforcing consequences for compliance and disciplinary actions for those who violate the standards.

For a society to trust management's actions, management must establish ethical norms and then see that they are met. An organization's ethical image is important to society's evaluation of it. This ethical evaluation is part of a larger process that leads to a determination of how an organization fits in with the rest of society. An organization with a reputation for high ethical conduct improves its good will in the community. The maintenance of that image dictates that a code of conduct must be more than words, that it must be practiced by and believed in by management and employees alike.

SUMMARY

In this chapter we presented the various problems associated with developing a code of ethics for a business organization. We first reviewed the various philosophical approaches to determining ethical conduct. The teleological approach is based on the moral rightness of an act resulting from its consequences. These consequences pertain not only to the immediate parties involved but also to the effect that these actions have on the rest of society. The deontological approach is based on the correctness of the actions rather than their consequences. In the teleological approach, the correctness of actions is analyzed through the benefits derived, and in the deontological approach, the moral correctness is derived from the precepts established as absolutes in guiding moral behavior. These precepts are derived from religious codes or societal norms. The philosophical differences in defining ethical behavior increase the frustration of operationalizing ethical conduct in an organizational setting. In addition, variations within societies and cultures make it difficult to construct a specific code of conduct that would be universally applicable.

In the second part of the chapter we examined various sources of value formation in society. The employee who enters an organization has some sense of moral right and wrong. Although an individual may not have an absolute standard of uniform behavior, he or she is aware of the zone of acceptable behaviors and societal tolerances. Variations in these standards and tolerances is a function of the various subcultures to which the individual belongs. Each subculture has its own value system, which conforms to the zone of acceptable norms of the rest of society. Individuals or subcultures outside this zone of tolerance are considered antisocial and are ostracized from the rest of society. Through reinforcement or punishment of specific actions, society or a subculture of society shapes the individual's behaviors and value system.

The organization can be regarded as a subculture of society. When an individual joins an organization, the organization will attempt to socialize the employee into exhibiting behaviors that are compatible with its values and norms. Both the formal and the informal organizations affect the individual's behavior and values.

Both society and a segment of the business community have worked to improve the ethical conduct of business. Society has attempted to improve business's conduct by establishing legal constraints on its activities. One such comprehensive act that influences many business organizations is the Foreign Corrupt Practices Act of 1977, which prescribes internal control systems and record-keeping procedures that discourage employees from engaging in actions outside the intentions of management. In addition, the act forbids several corrupt practices with respect to foreign transactions.

Defining and implementing a code of ethics are difficult. Employees' values are a product of both the cultural norms that employees bring to the work environment and those acquired on the job. An organization has a responsibility to build the proper ethical environment for its employees, just as it has an obligation to conduct itself responsibly in society.

DISCUSSION AND STUDY QUESTIONS

1. Define ethics. Compare individual ethics and corporate ethics.
2. Compare a deontological approach with a teleological approach in determining the ethics of an action.
3. Compare the three forms of utilitarianism. Give an example of each.
4. What are some of the problems in defining moral and ethical behavior?
5. Why does a multinational corporation have unique problems in developing a code of ethics?
6. How does a person form his or her own sense of values? How does an organization attempt to influence these values?
7. What is creative individualism? What is its role in making individual values compatible with corporate values?
8. How can the informal organization's value system influence individuals' behavior? How does the informal organization influence corporate values? (*Hint:* Return to Chapter 1 and review goal setting and internal publics.)
9. How does public policy affect business and individual ethics?
10. Trace the provisos of the Foreign Corrupt Practices Act. How does this act help improve business accountability for ethical behavior?

CASES AND INCIDENTS

Mary's Dilemma

The newspapers in Mary Turner's town are having a field day. Much of it seems to be at Mary's expense, and perhaps worst of all, her attorney has requested that she say nothing. "You'll get your day in court," he told her. "Let's save our rebuttal for that time."

Mary is the city manager. One of her responsibilities is to serve on the city commission, which votes on the city's expenditures, including building construction. Over the last five years one of the most successful contractors in the city has been Bill Bassford. During this time Bassford Construction has bid and won over $33 million in city contracts. One of Bill's biggest supporters is Mary Turner. "He has one of the lowest bids on every single one of his jobs," she told the city commission last month. "And he has never come in late or over budget. With rising inflation and the problems of getting and keeping good construction workers, that is something. Bassford Construction is one of the most important assets we have in this town."

Words like this are likely to be turned around and used against Mary during a special hearing scheduled for next week. The problem began about six months ago when Mary and her husband decided to build a summer house on a lake about 150 miles from town. Mary's husband, Karl, is an architect, and he designed a spacious, expensive, two-story home. Initial estimates for the construction put the job at $125,000. Part of the large cost was the expense associated with hauling materials and equipment out to the remote lake area. Mary and her husband then took the blueprints to Bill Bassford and asked him to price the job. He came in with a bid of $92,500. Mary and Karl asked him to do the job.

The mortgage for the cottage was obtained from a bank located in a town near the cottage. Once the papers were signed, Bill had his work crew begin breaking ground and laying the foundation.

Mary's problem developed when her high school son told some friends about the cottage his family was building. One of the reporters for the school newspaper learned about it and went up to the lake to take pictures to back up what was to be a personal interest story. When the pictures were printed along with the story, there in the foreground was one of Bill Bassford's trucks. The edition was released on Tuesday morning, and that evening it was the lead story on the local 6 o'clock news. As the anchorperson put it, "What is Bill Bassford Construction doing building a cottage for the city manager? Did you know about it? Did anyone around here know about it? Why, even the mortgage was taken with an out-of-town bank. This is going to be extremely difficult to explain." The mayor has asked Mary to take a leave of absence pending the outcome of the hearing. Mary has agreed to do so. The hearing is scheduled for next Monday morning at City Hall.

ANALYSIS

1. Is Mary guilty of unethical behavior? Is Bassford Construction guilty of unethical behavior? Explain.
2. How would you answer the anchorperson's comments if you were Mary?
3. How could Mary have avoided this problem? Why did she fail to do so?

He'd Have Done it Years Ago

Every year Tim Raynal's firm tries to put together an annual report that is different from the previous one. Sometimes this is done by means of format. Other times, the firm reports a substantive issue such as the purchase of a new firm or a new discovery by one of its research and development departments. For this year's report, one of Tim's top managers has suggested that the company develop a code of ethics and include it in the annual report. Tim has bounced this idea off a number of different people, including some on the board of directors. For the most part, the reception has been positive. One of the board members noted, "It seems like the thing to do these days. Tell people how ethical your firm is and the fact that you are not going to stand for any unethical nonsense." On the other hand, Tim is a little concerned that much of this code of conduct business is really window dressing. "Does the fact that we have a code of conduct mean that we will be doing things any better than we did before?" he asked. "Will our customers believe that in some way we have changed our ways and are going to be even better than we have been in the past? The question alone indicates that we have been doing something that we shouldn't have, and so we are now in the process of changing."

Nevertheless, the overall idea sounded quite good to most people in management, and Tim went along with it. The code contained 10 statements, all beginning with "We believe. . . ." Each statement related to the way management would conduct its business. Other parts of the code pertained to the manufacture and sale of the company's goods and its advertising and public relations policies.

When the annual report first came out, there were letters from some stockholders indicating that they were pleased with the code. Over the next five months, the number of positive responses increased greatly. Newspapers all around the country began to cite portions of it. A national TV network interviewed Tim in regard to the code and what it meant. Business periodicals referred to it, and one of them reprinted it in its entirety. Some business schools began writing for copies which they wanted to distribute to their students. What started out as a general public relations idea had blossomed into national recognition for the firm. "If I had any idea how well this idea would go over," said Tim, "I'd have done it years ago."

ANALYSIS

1. What is a code of ethics?
2. Assuming that Tim's firm is an insurance company, what types of specific guidelines would you expect to find in the code? Would your answer be different if the firm were in the manufacturing business? The computer business?
3. What practical value does a code of ethics have? How does it help a firm conduct its business more efficiently?

A Way of Life

When Claude Patroni heard that there were a group of dissident stockholders who were going to run their own slate of officers, he was not concerned. Claude was elected to the board of his major multinational corporation in

1958. For the last eight years he has been the chairman, and he believed that he would remain in this position for a long time to come.

Unfortunately, last month there was an unexpected development. One of the sales agents that the corporation used in the Middle East had quit the company over a salary dispute and had written a book. It was entitled, "If You Only Knew" and discussed how the corporation spent a large percentage of its sales and discretionary funds to pay important people in foreign governments to support corporate activities. One of the examples dealt with $100,000 paid to a general in the armed forces of a Western European country. The general, in turn, recommended the purchase of aircraft produced by one of the corporation's American subsidiaries. Another example related how the corporation's board of directors had approved the expenditure of $1 million to support the election of a procorporate official in a Latin American country. The official won the election and almost immediately awarded the corporation a contract worth over $19 million.

When the book was first released, Claude thought the best strategy would be simply to ignore it or to point out that the salesman had an ax to grind with the firm. However, the problem proved to be much more difficult to handle. Within a few days, the dissidents were demanding a special stockholder meeting to discuss the book's charges. They were also threatening to fly the author back to the United States and let him talk directly to the stockholders. Over the next week, the dissidents did manage to get the author to agree to a videotape interview. This interview was conducted by one of the country's most respected television journalists. The results were devastating.

Some of the largest institutional and educational investors that held stock in the firm announced that they were going to support the dissidents. Many small stockholders wrote letters to the company expressing their dismay and indicating that they too were going to vote out the current management. Claude thought about resigning and trying to save the rest of the slate, but they talked him out of it. "We're all in this together," said one of the members of the board. "Let's sink or swim together."

When the votes were counted two days ago, Claude's group sank. They were able to garner only 22 percent of the total votes cast. In his final address to the board, Claude said, "I wish the new management the best of luck. I'd like to see them do business overseas without offering people financial incentives. But it's a way of life with those people, and the sooner the new management wises up to this fact, the better it is going to be for this company."

ANALYSIS

1. Were the actions undertaken by the old board of directors (i.e., financial payoffs) unethical? Explain your answer.
2. Are the stockholders being naive? Do they believe that the new board

of directors can really do business overseas without having to offer bribes?

3. Will the new management be different from the old? Defend your answer.

Codes of Conduct

In recent years a large percentage of business firms, especially large ones, have been showing a great deal of interest in the subject of ethics. In fact, many of them now believe that it is a practical necessity. The public demands it; in many cases the law requires it; and managers themselves think it is good business. Additionally, with the development of modern communication techniques, news of unethical practices can be carried to virtually every corner of the globe via newspapers, magazines, radio, and television. So it is in the best interests of business to develop specific codes of ethical behavior and to enforce sanctions against those who violate these codes. One researcher has put it this way:

> A new age of instant information and public insistence on ethical behavior has transformed business ethics from an ideal condition to a reality, from a luxury to a practical necessity for the survival and success of organizations. The central instrument for making ethics operational and real in a organization is a written code of ethics which is specific . . . is based upon general ethical standards, and is enforceable by appropriate sanctions.[1]

Many companies have codes already in place. In fact, one group of researchers surveyed over 600 businesses and found that 77 percent of them had codes of conduct.[2] These codes cover a series of different areas, including compliance with the law, misuse of corporate assets, observance of moral and ethical standards of society, use of inside or confidential information, antitrust compliance, equal employment opportunity, and guidelines for implementing the particular code. More specifically, companies such as Cummins Engine have set forth the following general guidelines for all their personnel to follow:

1. Obey the law.
2. Be honest—present the fact fairly and accurately.
3. Be fair—give everyone appropriate consideration.
4. Be concerned—care about how Cummins' actions affect others and try to make the effects as beneficial as possible.
5. Be courageous—treat others with respect even when it means losing business.[3]

[1]Harold L. Johnson, "Ethics and the Executive," *Business Horizons*, May–June 1981, pp. 53–59.

[2]Bernard J. White and B. Ruth Montgomery, "Corporate Codes of Conduct," *California Management Review*, Winter 1980, pp. 80–87.

[3]Reported in Oliver F. Williams, "Business Ethics: A Trojan Horse?" *California Management Review*, Summer 1980, p. 20.

ANALYSIS

1. In your own words, what is a code of ethics? Describe some of the most common areas covered in a corporate code.
2. Some researchers have found that those firms that have high ethical standards also tend to have high profitability. Why might this be true?
3. Will we see more companies adopting codes of ethics in the future? Why or why not? Explain.

CASE STUDY FOR PART I

Retail World and PetroTech*

"Perhaps . . . perhaps . . ." he thought as he tossed through another restless night, "perhaps it is time to call it quits." But it wouldn't be easy. One does not easily walk away from 25 years of one's life, from the only company one has ever worked for. Then there were the friends at work, and the still unfulfilled hopes for the company and for himself in the company. And could he in good conscience abandon the people of his division whom he had thus far been able to protect from the wrong-headed policies of the new management? And what of his own security? For, in spite of all, staying still seemed to offer personal security, if not satisfaction. No, it would not be easy to go. But it was getting harder and harder to stay. Of course he had already proven that he had considerable staying power. There had been other periods of indecision, of watching things go wrong and being powerless to do anything about them. But stay he had—one of four survivors from the 38 senior officers who had run the company before the takeover. He had little doubt that the company would continue and that he could continue with it. But should he? What would anyone really gain by it?

Perhaps there had just been too many battles. One gets battle fatigue, gets worn down, even if one is never decisively defeated. One forgets what it is like to have a job one enjoys and to be permitted to do it without constantly fighting to defend one's claim to it and to get a hearing for one's views on larger corporate matters.

Yes, he and the company went back a long way together. But the frustra-

*The research and written case information were presented at a Case Research Symposium and were evaluated by the Case Research Association's Editorial Board. This case was prepared by Paul F. Camenisch of DePaul University. Distributed by the Case Research Association. All rights reserved to the author and the Case Research Association. Used with permission.

tions went way back too. It seemed as though the stage had been set even before his arrival. Retail World, a large retail chain, anticipating a recession after World War II, had dug itself in, had accumulated a large pool of negotiable securities against the coming hard times, and had established no new retail outlets from 1938 to the time he had come to work there almost 20 years later. But shortly after his arrival, the CEO who had authored that conservative policy had retired, and with his own transfer to the home office the following year, George had reason to believe that he and the company were on the move together. But the next four years were disappointing. The new management abandoned the previous defensive policy. But its expansion efforts soon exhausted the accumulated reserves and plunged the company $500 million into debt with no appreciable gains to show for it.

After four directionless years, an executive from a major competitor was brought in to head Retail World. His experience and natural leadership

**Retail World's Earnings Record
(Millions of Dollars).**

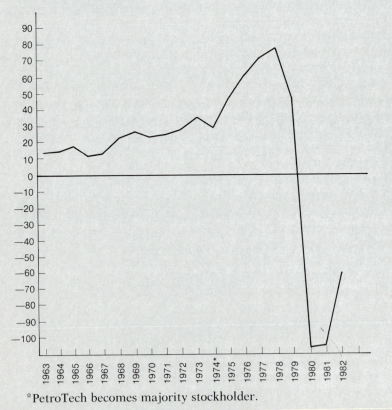

*PetroTech becomes majority stockholder.

abilities enabled him to effect a thorough reorganization of the troubled company. The predictable initial disruption soon gave way to a sense of new opportunties opening up, to considerable excitement and a new team spirit among management. The company was able to offer qualified employees promotions, salaries, and attractive stock options unprecedented in its recent history.

Following a five-year period of rapid growth and increasing earnings, top management began to fear a tender takeover which might exploit the company's potential or at least impede its progress by interfering with management's current policies. The solution settled on was a marriage of convenience with a promising corporation in an unrelated field. Effected in 1968, this created a considerably larger entity more secure from takeover, while the relatedness of the two partners and the structure of the relationship worked out left both companies' leadership free to follow their established successful patterns.

At this point George's career seemed to parallel the company's own success. Although not himself a member of senior management, his immediate boss was a member of the board and he himself had risen to the level of division manager with international responsibilities.

But while the company had been setting its house in order, events on the outside were building momentum which would catch many companies by surprise. The energy crisis hit Retail World with a one-two punch that sent it reeling. It immediately raised the cost of doing business dramatically. Furthermore, increased consumer energy costs and the accompanying recession meant that customers had less disposable income. Sales dropped while the cost of doing business was rising.

But even in the worst of times, some do well. The energy shortage, the scramble for what was available, and the consequent rise in prices generated large profits, including large inventory profits, for many oil companies. One response of the oil companies to the criticism they faced and one way of partially protecting their profits from high tax levies was diversification and acquisitions. And so just six years after its successful defensive merger, George's once again troubled but still potentially profitable company came under the control of PetroTech Corporation, a major oil company.

If George left now, it was clear that this takeover would have to be seen as the beginning of the end. Several dynamics set in motion at that point were converging with an intensity that demanded a decisive response. There was the impact of the takeover on the management team of which he had come to feel a part. In spite of Retail World's troubled state, PetroTech had bought out the stock at prices significantly above market value. In addition, the takeover sent the market price itself up radidly. Virtually the entire team of moderate-income managers who had struggled together to make the company work were suddenly wealthy men. It soon became clear to George that their concern about the future of the company was taking second place to their focus on the joys of sudden wealth—European tours, vacation homes, condominiums in Florida, and personal investment concerns. They seemed more interested in the "war stories" about their past struggles in the company than in the company's future.

George, who had not cashed in as impressively as senior management had, soon began to wonder if one didn't have to be a little hungry to be a good manager. His concern with top management's conduct was not just a question of personal style. It seemed clear that top management, including the CEO, were less and less willing to resist the intervention of the parent company's management who had no experience in the retail business and little knowledge of its distinctive problems. Sadly, he watched managers whom he had respected set aside their own experience and knowledge and let the initiative pass to the PetroTech management.

One particular instance stood out sharply in his mind. When the management of PetroTech and of Retail World realized that discount merchandizing was presenting a significant threat to more traditional firms, they purchased a small profitable discount chain in Texas and began to plan their own discount division. PetroTech, anxious to move decisively in this direction and not realizing the care with which a successful retail operation must be built, pushed for rapid expansion in spite of the caveats of the more knowledgeable Retail World management. Soon the chain was several times its original size, stretched halfway across the continent, and was clearly in deep trouble. It had been stimulated to artificially rapid and unsound growth by the infusion of large amounts of capital until its management and other sectors of the operation could not sustain it at profitable levels. In a relatively short time it had gone from being a profitable chain to generating fully one-half of Retail World's considerable annual losses.

In another matter of general strategy, PetroTech had created problems which Retail World's more experienced management might well have prevented. This concerned vertical or forward and backward integration frequently found in the oil industry but which is much less common in retailing. Retailing requires a flexibility to meet changing situations—the demand for new or redesigned products, the emergence of new and better ways to produce existing products. Without vertical integration, the retailer can switch from supplier to supplier free from worries about the capital investment in its own production facilities. This new policy had directly affected George's division, a major user of printed materials. Because Retail World spent considerable money on printing for advertising brochures and catalogs, PetroTech instructed its management to purchase a printing company for $75 million and to build a new printing plant. All Retail World divisions were then required to use only what its own printers could produce, even though their output was considerably less varied than what had been available externally. Furthermore, costs of printed materials went up instead of down because in an additional attempt to insulate themselves from market fluctuations, PetroTech insisted that the printing operation sign long-term fixed-price contracts for paper. When paper prices later declined, Retail World could not reap the benefits.

George's thoughts were dominated by two concerns. Or perhaps they were two dimensions of the same concern. On the most obvious level, the emerging situation posed financial problems. When experienced competent managers abdicate decision-making and policy-setting responsibilities to less experienced and less competent ones, the company's future and earnings can be expected to suffer.

But the question was not simply economic. It seemed to George that there was a kind of moral failure here also. There was no flagrant immorality or illegality which would interest newspapers. But there was failure to take seriously enough the responsibilities to others one had accepted. Top management positions in a corporation directly affecting the lives of well over 100,000 people, and indirectly affecting many more are not only positions of considerable challenge and reward; they are also a kind of trust, a sort of fiduciary position. Inadequate performance, whether caused by incompetence or indifference, betrayed that trust and needlessly endangered the well-being of employees, of stockholders, and of others.

This concern for people and what was happening to them inside the company was George's second major worry. PetroTech was undoubtedly well managed, but the policies that worked there would not necessarily work well in the retail business. One difference between the two businesses which became increasingly prominent in George's mind was the role of people in them and the way they were treated. PetroTech had three times the annual sales of Retail World, but only one fourth the employees. Thus it was a much less person-intensive operation. Furthermore, in the oil business many employees were highly mobile technical and professional persons who could be expected to change companies frequently during their careers. The personnel policies developed in relation to this sort of employee would be less appropriate in a retail company in which employees tend to be more long term, in which the creative skills needed are not easily measured as in technical fields, and in which, to a large degree, the corporation *is* more the people than it is the tremendously complex and expensive apparatus which dominate an oil company.

It had not been long before George began to feel the inappropriateness of the personnel policies imported from PetroTech. For example, PetroTech's personnel rating practices struck George, who was now responsible for evaluating large numbers of people under him, as highly formal, almost plastic in their impersonality. Employees' performances were rated on the basis of raw statistical data with little or no attention to more personal dynamics, or to more subtle contributions which do not show up in such statistics. Clearly, the parent management viewed the company more in terms of the tremendous capital investment it represented and to which its employees were merely auxiliary, rather than in terms of the personnel themselves. Given the high mobility of its people, that outlook may have been justified. But imported into the retail business, that outlook and its contingent policies made little sense. There the personal contacts and relations and team spirit were crucial to the work itself. Personnel evaluations which omitted those elements would reflect neither the true nature of the work nor the real contributions of various employees.

This failure to appreciate the role of people in retailing seemed, for example, to have been one cause of the fiasco of Retail World's and PetroTech's expansion into discount retailing. PetroTech insisted on rapid expansion and believed that sufficient investment of capital would solve any problems met. What Retail World's management knew but could not persuade Petro-Tech of was that without carefully assembled and well-trained teams on all levels of the operation, capital investment alone would not bring success. George wondered if PetroTech's insistence on vertical integration also reflected a desire to minimize interactions with parties not directly under their control. It seemed that a major goal of PetroTech management was both internally and externally to reduce to a minimum the number of human variables they had to deal with. George was convinced that such a goal put them on a collision course with success in the retail business.

With Retail World management more and more following the often inadequate lead of PetroTech management, and with personnel getting restive and resentful under the new policies, it was not surprising that corporate earnings, while improving, remained below PetroTech's expectations for several years. And when change came it was not for the better. Once again it came in large part through external forces beyond the company's control. This time that force was the unprecedented inflationary interest rates of the early 1980s. During the years of low, stable interest rates and of increasing consumer use of credit, Retail World, like so many retailers, had begun financing more and more consumer debt, both as a service to its customers and as a source of additional revenue. But once interest rates began their rapid rise, it was not long before that source of income became a serious liability, adding to the other difficulties the simultaneous inflation and recession were causing the company. Earnings dropped dramatically and the president was retired by PetroTech.

The new president was clearly a paid savior brought in by PetroTech at a large salary and with a several-year contract to turn things around. George's initial feelings were a combination of relief and hope. He knew that there had been years of neglect, that his company's management had not exercised the needed independence from PetroTech. Now perhaps with a leader of impressive drive, whose long-term contract guaranteed his relative independence, the company's future would receive the attention it so badly needed. As a part of the senior management committee, George thought he was in a good position to help shape that future.

Such salvage operations are seldom smooth. This one was no exception. Numerous changes began to occur among the senior officers, with the dominant pattern being that an officer experienced in the company would be terminated, given the opportunity for early retirement, or would resign and be replaced by someone hired from the outside. Within two years only four of the original 38 senior officers remained. Increasingly, George felt like a survivor. Worse yet, he felt he was being treated like a survivor. While that label carried some positive connotations, it clearly could become a liability. PetroTech policies seemed more and more to reflect an assumption concerning Retail World employees at all levels, that "new" meant "good, competent, qualified," while "old" or "experienced" meant "responsible for the mess we're in."

George was also troubled by the kind of people who were coming to dominate senior management. Most of them had had their success elsewhere, but often not in the area now assigned to them. Furthermore, many of them had a record of frequent moves among various companies. They therefore did not exhibit the identification with and the concern for the company and its people that was so important a part of George's view of his position and its responsibilities. George hoped for the emergence of a new team with some *esprit de corps* and some sense of common purpose. But it did not happen. Whether because they were not team players by nature, or because they were operating in a setting new to them, each seemed more concerned about protecting his territory and his prerogatives within it than about becoming part of a team.

Under these conditions, Retail World's earnings declined sharply. Within two years of its highest earnings ever, the company reported a one-year loss equal to its peak earnings. Company performance obviously justified no management bonuses. Company officers, nevertheless, sent a selected group of managers a kind of consolation payment in lieu of the bonuses they might have earned elsewhere. While the money was welcome and the gesture may have been appreciated, on another level George missed the positive feeling of an honestly earned bonus. Instead, he felt bribed to stay on in spite of the frustration and of his discomfort at the emerging patterns within the company. He did not feel good about being a "kept" executive.

One of the matters that bothered him was the number of people who were being dismissed. From his own level all the way down through the ranks people were being terminated in disturbing numbers—at least 20,000 out of approximately 120,000 over a two-year period. Many were let go—or so he assumed—because of poor performance. Others were terminated because of larger dynamics over which they and the company had little control—population shifts, poor facility locations, and obsolete facilities. George himself had had to close one outmoded facility in his division. It had been difficult to terminate 500 people even though out-placement programs, job fairs, and other efforts had been made to help them find employment. At the same time, George knew that the company that ignored economic necessity imperiled the well-being of more persons than it protected.

But George was becoming convinced that economic necessity and employee incompetence did not explain many of the dismissals. Dismissals from economic necessity would not have permitted so many outside replacements. Increasingly, George sensed a kind of inquisitorial mentality in which the simple fact of long-term employment with the company was itself a weighty argument for dismissal. Such a policy was, of course, never stated explicitly. Nevertheless, those who had been at the company for most or all of their careers were apparently thought to be narrow in their background, and perhaps too uncritically loyal to their co-workers and subordinates. And worst of all, it appeared to him that Retail World veterans were, on that basis alone, being blamed for the current annual losses of over $100 million. They had, after all, been on the scene as the present unprofitable position of the company was emerging and they had not prevented nor subsequently corrected it.

On the other hand, to be new on the scene created a strong presumption that one was competent, broadly experienced, and reliable. The removal of the old soon seemed to be the major strategy for addressing the unacceptable rate of earnings. A system for terminations was put in place by which a person was first rated down, then placed on probation, and then terminated. This process could proceed to its conclusion with few if any of the target's colleagues being aware of what was happening. A close friend of George's, also a long-term employee of Retail World but located in another city, called him one day to set up a meeting when he came to town on business the following week. But the next morning George heard that the friend had resigned and by that evening his replacement had been named. While perhaps stopping short of a purge, there clearly was a well-organized process of removal and replacement established.

Amidst all this George was able to keep his own staff and his division intact and to serve as a buffer between them and what he perceived as the questionable personnel policies he was being urged to implement. He had a staff of good people whom he trusted and respected and he saw no reason to penalize them for their long service to the company. Retirements, voluntary departures, and some company-sponsored buy-outs and early retirements gave him some room for the new talent he was being urged to secure. But his turnover rate was too low for his superiors. Increasingly, he felt driven to defend any promotions from within and to explain his low turnover rate. His suspicion that those making insufficient room for new talent were being given poor ratings was strengthened when a veteran vice-president with the largest number of employees under him was demoted and had his division given to an outsider after having been criticized for generating too little turnover.

Possibly linked to all these developments in ways not entirely clear to George was the emergence of a kind of paranoia among management focused externally on the neighborhood in which Retail World headquarters were located, and internally on employee theft. The headquarters were located near a major public housing project in a largely black neighborhood. Relations between the company and its neighbors had historically been quite good. The corporation had even helped mount educational and recreational programs for the people from the neighborhood. But now, with no apparent provocation, steel gates, guards, security cameras, and even guns in executive briefcases all began to reflect a quite different perception of the company's neighbors.

Simultaneously a similar attitude began to be manifested toward employees and the supposedly massive internal theft which some managers saw as the only possible explanation of the company's continuing losses. Security budgets were increased, electronic admission systems were installed for some areas of the building, and investigations were launched with no real evidence of wrongdoing. Again George felt pressed to treat his people in ways that violated his sense both of good management and of what constituted decent relations among fellow human beings. His refusal to implement policies such as employee surveillance which would clearly have been tantamount to an accusation of wrongdoing again had him on the defensive. There were also other indicators of what George saw as unenlightened personnel policies. Following the firing of a reformed alcoholic whom George had knowingly hired but who had fallen off the wagon twice, the corporation announced that dismissal was to follow an employee's first instance of substance abuse.

Along with these concerns, George found himself having to work harder and harder to avoid being cast as company historian and vestige of the past, a role which would make it difficult for him to become a part of the new team he still hoped would emerge. But when two new high-level outsiders began systematically to isolate George from the president to whom he had been reporting directly, it was clear that his role was jeopardized. George had some heated discussions with the president about the apparent strategy of the two newcomers, and felt afterward that he had gotten the president to understand his position. Nevertheless, he saw his previously frequent meetings with the president dwindle until there was virtually no direct contact between them. It was reasonably clear that the two schemers did not want to eliminate George. They exhibited neither the desire nor the ability to run his division which accounted for 20 percent of Retail World's sales. George nevertheless felt it was time for some decisive action.

He did not think the company would fail, nor that he would be forced to leave. Yet his excitement about what he was doing and about future possibilities for himself and the company together was gone. He still cared about the company and more important, about the people who, for him, finally were the company. Especially, he worried about his own division and the people whom he had thus far been largely able to protect from unjustified firings, denial of promotions, and groundless security checks and investigations. Had he any obligation to stay and to continue to serve as a buffer between them and upper management? If he read the signs correctly, there were indications that were he to depart, there would quite likely be raids on his division by other divisions seeking its most valuable talent. But beyond his concerns for his own division and "his" people, should he stay and try to change those policies and practices which were adversely affecting people throughout the company and which he was convinced were, because of their impact on morale, one important cause of the company's poor earnings?

At the same time George knew he had a right, even a duty, to consider his own interests and those of his family. While he believed that one should bring one's personal commitments and moral standards into the world of work and should be willing to pay the price for applying them there, he also felt that one could legitimately aspire to making a living in a reasonably pleasant and personally fulfilling situation, one that did not regularly send one home preoccupied, frustrated, and irritable. He was less and less certain that these latter needs could be met in his present situation.

And was he being realistic to hope for the emergence of a team of managers more devoted to the future of this company and its people than to their own careers, who saw themselves more as trustees for this company, its people, and their interests than as itinerant management specialists ready, even anxious to jump ship for even a small increment in remuneration or status? Was he, he began to wonder, trying to hold on to an earlier era when loyalty to the company, even gratitude for the opportunities it offered were seen as appropriate, were even expected, rather than being dismissed as sheer sentiment, or even as obstacles to one's advancement and possibly to the company's own interests?

What should the company be able to expect from its managers? What should employees be able to expect from the company and from their superiors? And what—and this was the question that was becoming more and more vexing—should George expect of himself as a conscientious and compassionate moral agent who, among other things was also a manager in a corporation which seemed no longer to understand, much less to value his sense of what it means to be a responsible manager?

Perhaps he should take more seriously the suggestion of a friend a few weeks back that they start their own business.

ANALYSIS

1. What responsibilities does George have to his career and family?
2. What responsibilities does George have to his work group?
3. What responsibilities does George have to Retail World? to PetroTech?
4. Is PetroTech's behavior unethical? Is George unethical in not following the "will" of PetroTech?

5. Is there a conflict between George's values and those of PetroTech? Who is right?
6. Was George's approach to counteracting PetroTech effective? How and Why?
7. What other ways might George try in order to reconcile the differences between PetroTech and himself?

PART II

The Role of Government in Business

5

Government and Public Policy

Chapter Objectives

- To review the many external and internal groups that attempt to influence public policy and the process of government in the United States.
- To identify the various legislative committees that are charged with defining the social role of business.
- To review the legislative process.
- To discuss the role of each branch of government in defining the social responsiveness of business.
- To present a model modifying the theory of countervailing powers to include the important role of society in moderating the power of government, business, and organized labor.
- To present the advantages and disadvantages of using public policy to define the role of business in society.

To America's Founding Fathers, a tyrannical government was one in which a single element assumed a dominant role. Thus, in framing the U.S. Constitution, they created a system of "checks and balances" in the form of three major branches of government—executive, legislative, and judicial. Since George Washington became the first president in 1789, the government has grown immensely, but its fundamental division of powers remains the same.[1]

Part I laid the foundation for the social role of business. This first chapter of Part II presents the role that government has in translating the public will into policies, laws, and actions relevant to the social role of business. Government implements and influences the desires of "the people."

First, the theory behind the role of government in business will be reviewed. Second, each of the branches of government—legislative, judicial, and executive—will be presented and analyzed. Throughout the discussion, there is an attempt to identify the ways in which the public and business interact and separately influence the process. Although business is part of "the public," it will be treated as a separate influence agent in order to demonstrate how business itself may tend to shape the actions of the government, as well as government shaping the conduct of business. Third, in this chapter we refocus on the concept of countervailing powers which was introduced in Chapter 2, and relate the concept to the current forces that shape the political environment for business. Finally, the advantages and disadvantages of strong government involvement in defining the legal limits or corporate responsibility are reviewed.

In this chapter, we provide an important introductory foundation for the role of government in business. It has become very clear in recent years that if there is enough public pressure, either directly, through the media, or in elections, the government will tend to respond to the perceived public will. The response of government will normaly take the form of additional laws or reinterpretation or enforcement of existing laws. Viewed in its totality, this response to the public will can be defined as government's influence in defining the social role of business.

THE THEORETICAL FOUNDATION FOR GOVERNMENT INVOLVEMENT IN BUSINESS

A more fundamental question in defining the role of government in business is the role of government in society at large. A very general definition would be that government is designed to serve the needs of its people. Such a definition is intentionally broad so that it can incorporate the different forms of government that are prevalent in today's society. Although there are many profound theories of government in political science, for the purposes of this discussion, an analogy can be profitably made using a model of organizational goal structures developed by the organization theorist Henry

[1]"The Shape of Government—When It Started and Now," *U.S. News & World Report*, January 28, 1985, p. 38.

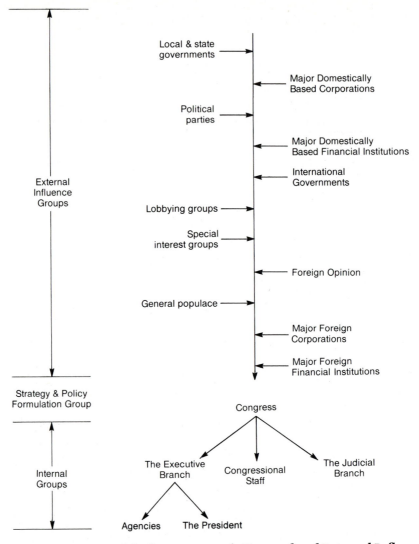

FIGURE 5.1   Model of Government's External and Internal Influence Groups.

Mintzberg.[2] Although oversimplified, the model shown in Figure 5.1 does focus on the role of government in translating the public will into constraints on business.

[2]Henry Mintzberg, "Organizational Power and Goals," in D. E. Schendel and C. W. Hofer, *Strategic Management: A New View of Business Policy and Planning* (Boston: Little, Brown, 1979), pp. 50–80.

Various Publics Influencing Government

Mintzberg's model was originally applied to the goal and strategy process in organizations. If government is substituted for organization, the model shows the people that a government serves. As indicated, the model is divided into three basic parts: external publics, internal publics, and the strategy and policy formation group.

Internal Publics. In the case of government, the internal publics can be viewed as government employees. In the case of the federal government, these would be civil service employes as well as appointed officials. In addition to the congressional staff, the executive and judicial branch can be considered as internal publics of government, as they execute and interpret the laws, respectively.

External Publics. The external publics would consist of various outside groups that influence the government. Just as government serves groups other than business, the original Mintzberg model also recognizes the impact of different groups. These outside groups are reflected in the model.

The external groups affecting government includes those that the government serves, the general public, but also includes various factions of groups, which might be labeled special-interest groups. In addition, government can be influenced by other groups inside or outside the direct control of the federal government. For example, state and local governments are separate entities from the federal government. However, these other government groups tend to moderate federal activities in such a manner that the desires of the state and local levels are incorporated into the policies and strategies that are shaped at the federal level. In the same manner, the general public tends to influence government. However, the general public seldom acts as "a voice of one." In reality, the will of the general public is expressed through a host of special-interest groups that individually tend to shape the actions of the government. This is an important difference to realize and can explain much about the behavior of governments, but first, the other components of the external environment will be explained.

World opinion or perceived world opinion acts as another important influence element. Other national governments, including allies and adversaries, can influence the actions of a government. Both of these groups are not directly controlled or governed by the political entity, but can still be influenced by its actions.

Dominant business corporations and financial institutions are of critical importance to a government in providing needed services. For example, dominant companies can help by providing a product or service that can be used to meet the needs of the public and can provide a product or service that can be exported to other countries. This export is valuable in providing sources of exchange that a country can use to buy products made in foreign countries. Any company in the host government's country that exports a product or service facilitates a favorable balance of trade where more foreign currency is accruing to the host country than money leaving. Large companies are more important to a government than small companies. While, in total, smaller companies may account for a larger proportion of transactions, there are, in most cases, so many of these firms that it becomes more difficult for a government to be influenced or influence these types of organizations. With a large dominant corporation, the government needs to focus on only one group, or in some cases, a single executive head.

Large financial institutions are potential influencers of a government. They can provide capital that a government needs to function, and perhaps just as important, a dominant bank can lend stability for economic transactions in the host country and between the host country and other countries. Both domestic and foreign banks can facilitate these transactions, and both can be sources of operating capital.

The Strategy and Policy Formation Group. External and internal groups or publics tend to influence the direction the government takes. The government attempts to be responsive to the group's desires and goals. For example, government employees may desire job security or pensions. They may then act to influence the government to act to meet these demands. They then attempt to influence the third element shown in the model, the strategy and policy formation group. This policy formation group is considered to be the Congress, because only through Congress can laws be made. These laws provide the direction to guide society and the rest of the federal government in the United States.

What Public Does a Government Serve?

As pointed out, there is a difference between the general public and special-interest groups. The general public seldom acts in unison. It is more likely that many distinct groups with their own special interests may be acting on the government. The government may have different levels of responsiveness to each of these groups.

Different forms of government would also, philosophically, be responsive to different special-interest groups. For example, a democracy would, by design, be more responsive to a wider base of interest groups. Democracies use an open election process with multiple political parties and tend to force a greater responsiveness on the part of the government. Under a dictatorship, the government still needs to be responsive to all interest groups. However, by design, there is greater responsiveness to the special-interest group or groups that are aligned with the current leaders in power.

Under a dictatorship, without free elections, the design of government enables power to flow to fewer special-interest groups. One might then conclude that such a government need not be responsive to other publics. However, this is not totally true. There is always the possible development of a coalition of groups dedicated to a change in government. Even if a government has "control" over the population through fear or coercion, the people that carry out the orders of the government must have enough confidence in the leadership to follow orders (or maybe enough fear in the consequences of not following orders). A government must negotiate between groups in order to balance the personal goals of the leaders of the government with that of the goals and values of each of the external and internal publics.

Importance of the Power of the Public

Which public receives the greater attention by the government depends on the power of the public. The greater potential power that the public can exert to influence the government, the more responsive the government tends to be. If, for example, another national government poses a believable threat that it would invade a country if it did not comply with its threats, the target country, if it did not have a counterthreat, would probably comply. In the same manner, the United States might be more apt to listen to General Motors or Exxon more than it might to Stan's Office Supply. The relative power that each has in influencing the success of the government in reaching its goals is proportionately less with Stan's than with the corporate giants.

In situations where an individual entity may not have very much power, it may form together with others into a collective that will enhance its power. For example, Stan's Office Supply may join an industrial trade association to boost its power with the government. The association may hire a lobbyist to voice and exert pressure for the member's concerns. In addition, several lobbying groups may band together in order to have even greater influence on the government. This combining of efforts is called building a *coalition* (see the box "Business Battles Reagan's Tax Plan"). Developing coalitions is an important part of developing a power base and, as you would expect, power is an important part of influencing governments. Power can range from having a military force to extract compliance to simply writing a letter or making a phone call in order to have a government respond.

A government, on the other hand, also has a desire to have some degree of stability of its own. At one extreme would be the desire of government officials to be left alone to do what they want. At the other extreme would be the desire to meet everyone's needs. These endpoints on a continuum are shown in Figure 5.2. Both extremes represent the ideal in the minds of

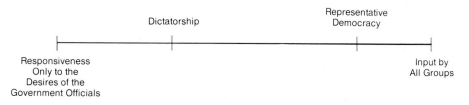

FIGURE 5.2   Continuum of Government Responsiveness.

some governmental officials. However, trying to live the ideal is generally impossible. The reality is that government officials will be striving for various points on the continuum.

Government's Wish to Manage Its Publics

Whatever the orientation, most government officials wish to "manage" the power of internal and external publics. This desire to manage comes from three general reasons:

1. To have control over the environment.
2. To operate in an environment with a manageable amount of turbulence.
3. To have an environment that is compatible with reaching the manager's personal goals as well as reach the goals of the government.

Such a situation can be achieved by

1. Maintaining a reasonable number of power groups to deal with.
2. Ensuring that no single group has too much power.
3. Maintaining a condition where the more critical power groups are supportive, to some degree, of the government's actions.

Maintaining a reasonable number of power groups involves diffusing the power of some groups while enhancing the power of others. The objective is to neutralize the power of some of the external and internal power groups. This can be done through overt and covert actions against the group or through adapting readily to the group in order to diffuse any support that the group might attain.

Ensuring that any one group does not obtain too much power involves the government in a process of diffusing power. Again, this can be done through co-opting the group by incorporating the goals of the group into the goals of government. By eliminating the need for people to join efforts against the government, there is less power to the special-interest group. If there is less collective desire to support the group, and the intensity of the desire is reduced, the group will naturally lose power if that power is based on popular support. Other actions to neutralize power might be to have greater power than other groups or countries, such as that which is done in an arms-buildup program.

Maintaining a condition where the more critical power groups are supportive of the government can involve two processes. First, the government will have to act in a manner that is responsive, at least to a limited degree, to the needs and wants of the interest group. Second, the government must be aware of the external environment of alternatives that special-interest groups might have available to them. For example, in an open-election situation such as those in France, a multitude of political parties are trying to be elected. Each party attempts to accommodate as many interest groups as they can in order to gain strength as an election approaches.

The leaders of the government in power need to be responsive enough to

BUSINESS BATTLES REAGAN'S TAX PLAN

The modified Reagan tax plan that moved out of congressional committee in late November 1985 started industry on a massive lobbying campaign that has crossed traditional industrial lines. These combined efforts arose from fears that Congress and the president would view a specific industry effort to change the law as a special-interest-group approach that might not get as sympathetic a hearing from Congress as that of more concerted and diversified effort cutting across many industries. Charles Walker, a Washington lobbyist, has put together one of four coalitions. These include companies such as Chrysler, Union Pacific, Alcoa, and General Electric. The strategy of Walker's coalition is to have the chief executives of the big manufacturers personally lobby legislators, and to bombard them with mail from home. The goal of the coalition is to slow the momentum for changes in the tax code until the economy becomes less optimistic, the trade-deficit news becomes more prominent, or other economic problems lead to changes in the tax reform proposal that would make it more favorable to business.

In addition to the efforts of the coalitions, various industries are lobbying hard to modify the current tax proposal so that it reflects more closely the desires of particular industries. For example, the entertainment lobby is pushing hard to maintain the business entertainment deduction. The American Council of Life Insurance launched a $2.7 million advertising campaign to solicit public support to keep health insurance nontaxed. Two of the big insurance companies, Metropolitan and Travelers, sent out packets of postcards to their customers protesting the proposed changes in tax laws as they relate to employee benefits. In the literature accompanying the packets, recipients were encouraged to send the postcards protesting the proposed changes to their congressional members and to the president. The result of this effort was that more than 1 million pieces of mail were sent to the federal government.

This is just one example of the role and importance of the lobbying effort in the legislative process. Trade associations and other interest groups normally hire lobbyists to represent them in the legislative process with regard to many important issues, just as was done regarding the tax issue described above.

Source: Adapted from John M. Barry, "Business Battles Reagan's Tax Plan," *Dun's Business Month,* July 1985, pp. 28–35.

maintain the support of these interest groups. The government may have to become more accommodating as an opposing political party becomes more responsive. In the United States, the procedure of having the top vote-getting party win an election tends to make it very difficult to support more than two parties. With only one party as a threat, the government in power has fewer outside sources that are attempting to win-over special-interest groups. However, the strength of the opposing party creates its own difficulties.

The Role of Government in Carrying Out the Will of the People

Given the backdrop of the interaction of the government with its multiple publics, defining and carrying out "the will of the people" becomes difficult. The first problem is that the "will of the people" is not normally voiced in unison. With a host of internal and external groups trying to influence the government, there is often a conflict between what each group desires. Although the will of the group with the most potential power may be heeded, this may not always be the case. For example, the leaders' own goals may run counter to the powerful external group. In any event, the will of the people is seldom so clearly defined.

Second, the will of the people is often more reactive than proactive. Those being governed are often relatively passive. The may also not have a good balance of foresight to judge the technical merits of an action or to judge the significance of the precedent that may be established. For example, a certain segment of the U.S. population is supportive of euthanasia. However, if killing is justified in specific cases, it may become increasingly difficult to convict a person of murder. The courts may be forced to rely on intent, the desires of the person murdered, and the conditions that surrounded the events that led to the killing as a basis to determine guilt. Popular opinion may not be a good standard with which to make a decision in this case. The "larger picture" or broader perspective may need to be examined.

In theory, governments are designed to reflect the will of the people. In actuality, a government is responding to a much more narrow clientele. In more totalitarian forms of government, the clientele becomes even narrower. Hence, as we view the role of government in the next few sections, the imperfections associated with government's intent to serve and the political realities of the government–external/internal publics relationship must be kept in mind.

THE DEMOCRATIC MODEL OF GOVERNMENT

The United States is based on a democratic form of government. In this section we analyze how this form of government attempts to determine and act to meet the public will.

The government of the United States is divided into three branches: the legislative branch, which creates and passes laws; the judicial branch, which interprets the laws and acts to arbitrate when a law is violated; and the executive branch, which executes and administers the law. Each branch attempts to interpret and execute the public will. The legislative branch might be considered as the main planning and policy-creation body. However, as the court becomes less strict in interpreting the letter of the law and moves toward making judgments regarding moral right and wrong, the court is acting as a secondary policy-formation body. It is very clear through recent court rulings that the courts tend to modify significantly, in some cases, the original congressional intent of laws. Finally, the executive branch is charged with executing the will of Congress. However, there is a diffused connection between Congress and specific agencies (i.e., the control of Congress over the actions of a particular executive branch agency is not as well coordinated and monitored as might occur in a business firm). The result is the wide latitude that an executive agency has in the execution of its responsibilities. This results in the executive branch having an important influence on defining and acting in the name of the "will of the people." In the following sections we provide more detail on the three branches of government.

The Legislative Branch

The legislative branch of the U.S. federal government consists of two divisions of Congress, the Senate and the House of Representatives. These two divisions of the legislative branch were formed to reflect more closely the will of the people. The House of Representatives is a body whose membership is based on population. The number of representatives for a given area, such as a state, is based on the population of that area. Districts within the state, in theory, should be of relatively equal population. This form of representation is designed to give an equal voice to each person in the United States through a relatively balanced representation.

The Senate membership is based on two members from each state and territory. This was done, by design, so that each state would have balanced representation and the needs and wants of each state would be fairly represented. Even the length of the elected term of the Senate, six years, was designed so that there would be a stabilizing influence in decision making.

The legislative branch is designed to create laws. A major responsibility in this process is to determine the public will in the design and passage of legislation. In addition, the Congress must determine priorities because the capital needed to execute laws is limited. In addition, time and the capacity to write, research, and pass legislation are limited. Hence, priorities are placed on the laws that proceed through the legislative process.

Determining the public will is not as easy as it may appear on the surface. As discussed earlier, there are many publics with different degrees of interest on legislative topics. There would also be, as mentioned, a segment of the population that would be relatively passive on a topic because (1) they may not have knowledge of the proposed law, (2) they may not have the organization like other groups to articulate their views, or (3) they may not have the financial resources like other groups. Given these possible inequities in learning the "true" public will, the legislator may attempt to research the views of people and have public hearings on proposed legislation. The process of having a hearing on proposed legislation would be too cumbersome for each member of Congress to undertake, so a series of committees has been created. Table 5.1 presents a partial list of committees and subcommittees that directly start the "research" process of determining the "public will" or the "public welfare." This list of committees indicates only those that are particularly relevant to the business-society interface.

The term "public welfare" was introduced here to highlight the responsibility of Congress to go beyond assessing the public will but also to look at the overall social costs and benefits that may accrue through the passage of the legislation.

TABLE 5.1.   Congressional Committees in Business-Related Areas.

Senate Committees

Banking, Housing, and Urban Affairs
   Subcommittees: Consumer Affairs
                         Economic Policy
                         Financial Institutions
                         Housing and Urban Affairs
                         International Finance and Monetary Policy
                         Rural Housing and Development
                         Securities
Commerce Science, and Transportation
   Subcommittees: Aviation
                         Business, Trade and Tourism
                         Communications
                         Consumers
                         Merchant Marine
                         Science, Technology, and Space
                         Surface Transportation
Energy and Natural Resources
   Subcommittees: Energy and Mineral Resources
                         Energy Conservation and Supply
                         Energy Regulation
                         Energy Research and Development
                         Public Lands and Reserved Water
                         Water and Power
Environment and Public Works
   Subcommittees: Environmental Pollution
                         Nuclear Regulation
                         Regional and Community Development
                         Toxic Substances and Environmental Oversight
                         Transportation
                         Water Resources

TABLE 5.1. Continued

Senate Committees
Finance
    Subcommittees: Economic Growth, Employment, and Revenue Sharing
                      Energy and Agricultural Taxation
                      Estate and Gift Taxation
                      Health
                      International Trade
                      Oversight of Internal Revenue Service
                      Savings, Pensions, and Investment Policy
                      Social Security and Income Maintenance Programs
                      Taxation and Debt Management
Foreign Relations
    Subcommittees: African Affairs
                      Arms Control, Oceans, and International Operations and
                          Environment
                      East Asian and Pacific Affairs
                      European Affairs
                      Internal Economic Policy
                      Near Eastern and South Asian Affairs
                      Western Hemisphere Affairs
Labor and Human Resources
    Subcommittees: Aging, Family, and Human Services
                      Alcohol and Drug Abuse
                      Education
                      Employment and Productivity
                      Handicapped
                      Investigations and General Oversight
                      Labor
Small Business
    Subcommittees: Advocacy and the Future of Small Business
                      Capital Formation and Retention
                      Export Promotion and Market Development
                      Government Procurement
                      Government Regulations and Paperwork
                      Innovation and Technology
                      Productivity and Competition
                      Urban and Rural Economic Development
Veterans Affairs

House Committees
Banking, Finance, and Urban Affairs
    Subcommittees: Consumer Affairs and Coinage
                      Domestic Monetary Policy
                      Economic Stabilization
                      Financial Institution Supervision, Regulation, and Insurance
                      General Oversight and Renegotiation
                      Housing and Community Development

TABLE 5.1. Continued

House Committees

International Development Institutions and Finance
International Trade, Investment and Monetary Policy

Education and Labor
    Subcommittees: Elementary, Secondary, and Vocational Education
                Employment Opportunities
                Health and Safety
                Human Resources
                Labor Management Relations
                Labor Standards
                Postsecondary Education
                Select Education

Energy and Commerce

    Subcommittees: Commerce, Transportation, and Tourism
                Energy Conservation and Power
                Fossil and Synthetic Fuels
                Health and the Environment
                Telecommunications, Consumer Protection and Finance
                Oversight and Investigations

Foreign Affairs
    Subcommittees: Africa
                Asian and Pacific Affairs
                Europe and the Middle East
                Human Rights and International Organizations
                Inter-American Affairs
                International Economic Policy and Trade
                International Operations
                International Security and Scientific Affairs

Merchant Marine and Fisheries
    Subcommittees: Coast Guard and Navigation
                Fisheries and Wildlife Conservation and the Environment
                Merchant Marine
                Oceanography
                Panama Canal and Outer Continental Shelf

Science and Technology
    Subcommittees: Energy Development and Applications
                Energy Research and Production
                Investigations and Oversight
                Natural Resources, Agriculture Research and Environment
                Science, Research, and Technology
                Space Science and Applications
                Transportation, Aviation and Materials

Small Business
    Subcommittees: Antitrust and Restraint of Trade Activities Affecting Small Business
                Energy, Environment and Safety Issues Affecting Small Business
                Export Opportunities and Special Small Business Problems
                General Oversight

TABLE 5.1. Continued

House Committees

	SBA and SBIC Authority, Minority Enterprise and General Small Business Problems
	Tax, Access to Equity Capital and Business Opportunities
Veterans' Affairs Subcommittees:	Compensation, Pension and Insurance
	Education, Training and Employment
	Hospitals and Health Care
	Housing and Memorial Affairs
	Oversight and Investigations
Ways and Means Subcommittees:	Health
	Oversight
	Public Assistance and Unemployment Compensation
	Revenue Measures (Select)
	Social Security
	Trade

The Legislative Process

The legislative process therefore involves the process outlined in Figure 5.3. A proposed law is introduced to one of the branches of Congress. On very important issues, several variations of the proposed legislation may be introduced.

After the proposed legislation is introduced, it is referred to the appropriate committee. The responsibility of the committee is to determine the public welfare and desires of the public in the area that the bill or proposed legislation addresses. A *bill* is defined as a proposed law or legislation. (Once the bill is passed and signed by the president, it becomes a *law*.) The committee then researches the bill and holds public information meetings to assess the public viewpoint on the bill. An individual representative may attempt to poll the electorate in her or his district to determine their views. This can be done through surveys or through individual "town meetings" or other formal or informal sessions. Once the bill has been reviewed, researched, and rewritten, and meetings have been conducted to determine the public will and public welfare, the committee votes to accept or reject the bill and to recommend that the bill be presented to the appropriate legislative body for final action.

The means by which the legislative committee determines public welfare range from informal hearings and subjective evaluations to more complicated formulas of environmental impact. Unfortunately, it is normally very difficult to create a formula to indicate how there would be a change in public welfare, as the ramifications of a law may be very difficult to assess in their entirety. The economic and social environment is very complex and it is very difficult

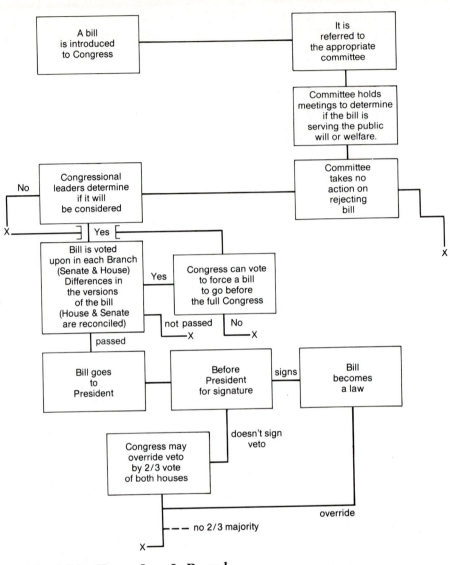

FIGURE 5.3   How a Law Is Passed.

to understand the interactions of all the variables, let alone determine how a change in a law would tend to modify the environment. Limited staff and funding make it difficult for the committee or subcommittee to spend a lot of time developing models, simulations, or scenarios to demonstrate the effects accurately.

Given these limitations, both in staff research time and in having a good sense of the environment and having a desire to determine how a bill might affect the environment, some interesting "cooperative" efforts occur between the government committee and its publics. Often, the legislative committee will rely on the external group for a study of the impact of legislation. For example, a transportation subcommittee may rely on a study completed by the American Association of Railroads as to the effects of a coal slurry pipeline on the economic and ecological environment. Obviously, the railroad group might not be totally objective, as they have traditionally opposed coal slurrying projects. The legislative committee may, to increase the chances for a balanced perspective, try to find a proponent group to the pipeline and also to solicit their input.

Note, however, what occurs during this process. First, the committee must rely on studies done not in the name of determining public will or welfare, but to demonstrate an advocacy for or against the proposal. The different goals of an advocacy study compared to an independent study would tend to distort a true accounting of public good or harm. In these situations, the merits of a proposed law may hinge less on an objective study and more on how well each side of the bill can build a strong case and have the data to support its side of the proposal. Obviously, there would be a better chance for a special-interest group (more practically, called a lobbying group) that had better findings, a professional staff or researchers, copy editors, and writers to obtain an edge in supporting its position.

The Role of Lobbying in the Legislative Process

The result of this legislative process is the formation of lobbying groups that tend to act as a watchdog to support the desires of the special-interest group they represent. Note carefully here that the term *special-interest group* simply means a division of the general public into a group that has a common viewpoint that may or may not reflect the viewpoint of the rest of the population. "Special-interest group," in this sense, does not have the negative connotation that the term is often given during political elections. A special-interest group is any advocacy group. The Sierra Club, a consumer-rights group, and church groups are all special-interest groups. Many groups like these form their own formal lobbying units to express their viewpoints in the legislative process.

Business organizations also form trade associations. These associations commonly create lobbying units on their own. All these special-interest groups try to influence the committee toward the viewpoint of the special-interest group.

Applying public pressure is important to demonstrate to the legislative committee that there is broad-based support for the position being advocated. This can be done through direct organizational actions and by garnering public support for a cause. Public support can be mustered through direct appeals for the public to phone, telegraph, or mail in their concerns to the president, the full Congress, or to the legislative committee that is working on the legislation. For example, Figure 5.4 provides an example that was

MACMILLAN PUBLISHING COMPANY
A Division of Macmillan, Inc.
866 Third Avenue, New York, N. Y. 10022
(212) 702-7903

JEREMIAH KAPLAN
CHAIRMAN

August 1, 1985

To all our authors, agents, and copyright proprietors:

During the past year, there have been many promising signs for the future of American book publishing. Our own experience at Macmillan Publishing Company has given us every reason to be optimistic about the continued growth and success of all our publishing programs in education, in professional markets, and in general trade. This optimism is founded on the cumulative performance of individual books entrusted to us by our authors--a trust, I assure you, we never forget.

But just as authors and publishers share in the benefits of a vital publishing industry, so too we share a common concern when that continued vitality seems most threatened--as it does now. For this reason I bring to your attention an issue of utmost importance to us all--authors, publishers, educators, readers.

At a meeting on June 13th, the Board of Directors of the AAP (Association of American Publishers) expressed the deepest concern over the proposal in the Reagan Administration's tax reform plan to eliminate the deductibility of state and local taxes. Together with the AAP, we believe that this provision will have a profoundly destructive effect on the educational system in every state in the country. In a letter to Congressman Dan Rostenkowski, Chairman of the Ways and Means Committee, the AAP outlined the dire consequences of the proposal as it now stands:

"The negative impact will not be confined to a few 'high tax' states, but will be nationwide in scope.

"As is known, Federal aid to education accounts for only about 6% of the total cost. State aid averages about 40%. This means that more than 50% of the financial support for the public school system, nationwide, depends on local taxes; in large areas

FIGURE 5.4 Example of an Informational Advertisement.

of the country--especially New England, the Middle Atlantic
States and the Great Lakes regions--the figure is even higher."

Obviously, publishers and authors have an economic interest in
this problem. But our real concern is much broader. Across the
country, local and state governments are working to improve our
educational system, which many feel has suffered from
insufficient resources in recent years. Just as these efforts
have begun to bear fruit, the monies devoted to education will be
reduced.

If state and local taxes are no longer deductible from federal
income taxes, there will be enormous pressure to lower those
state and local taxes and thus lower the basic support for our
educational system.

To quote again from the AAP's letter:

"Given the known, severe stresses in the national educational
system and the burgeoning problem of illiteracy, we believe it
would be the height of irresponsibility for Congress to eliminate
a feature of the present tax system that provides the fundamental
prop for education in the United States. If the states and
localities are forced to cut their own budgets by passage of this
aspect of the Reagan tax reform plan, then the commitment to
adequate support levels for education seems certain to be one of
the first casualties."

If you share our concern about the troublesome impact of this
aspect of the Reagan tax proposals, I hope you will join us in
writing promptly to your Representative and Senators, expressing
your views.

Sincerely yours,

Jeremiah Kaplan

Jeremiah Kaplan

used to solicit support to maintain a deduction in the proposed tax law changes discussed earlier in this chapter.

An interesting balance evolves through lobbying efforts. One might think that the lobbying effort would involve intense pressure placed on members of the legislative committee and then the full legislative bodies. However, the long-term development of trust and a working relationship is desired by most professional lobbyists. As such, the working relationship that evolves is based more on developing long-term ties and building relationships, instead of using raw force or special favors. In its totality, the process of lobbying generally provides a positive force to the legislative process.

On the downside, as mentioned earlier, there is a direct relationship between the resources available and the effectiveness of the lobbying effort. Groups with good funding may be able to influence lawmaking more readily than can underfunded groups. The result may be a subversion of public welfare to an enhancement of a limited number of special-interest groups. This fear is a clear and present danger in the current process unless committee members make a special effort to go beyond the normal process to seek out a broader, more representative viewpoint.

One final dimension to the relationship of the lobbyists with legislative committees and the Congress is that, often, a member of Congress may approach a special-interest group to have the group draft the proposed bill for the member of Congress. Consider how this process may lead to a potential subversion of defining public will and welfare.

Regardless of these concerns, the role of the legislative branch of government is to set forth the direction of the government to provide for the public welfare and to reflect the public will. This is accomplished through a process that, at least in theory, enables the change as a result of input from society. With some reservation, this process provides a means to maximize input from affected groups while maintaining an orderly and efficient process of law and policy formation. With adequate congressional funding, the resources would be available to do adequate independent research, and maximizing input would be facilitated. The past decade has, however, been marked by more limited congressional staff support. In sum, the imprecision in determining public will, public welfare, and the potential for subversion of the process through lobbying by interest groups necessitates a high degree of vigilance in the legislative process.

The Judicial Branch

The judicial process is involved with the interpretation of laws in a manner that is consistent with the Constitution. The judicial process tends to influence the defining of public will and public welfare through the modification of laws. After a law is enacted, the law is interpreted through judicial action. When a law is violated, the courts tend to define the law through the decisions that are made regarding what the law means and what the limits of legal and illegal behavior are regarding the law. The normal course of the courts is to view the law in terms of defining the intent of Congress, defining the law in terms of its acceptability in terms of the Constitution; and finally, the law is defined in terms of previous court decisions. Through court interpretations over several years, the current interpretation may or may not match the original intent of the law.

The degree of influence that the public has over the court system is, by design, very limited. A federal judge is normally appointed for life. The logic behind this rather fixed term of office is so that a judge will be less vulnerable to public opinion and can concentrate on points of law and agreement with constitutional intent. The result is a branch of government that is much less responsive than the other two branches.

Under these conditions, a federal judge is less responsive to attempts by interest groups to affect the court's decisions. There are some legal means. A special-interest group may be allowed to file an amicus curiae brief. *Amicus curiae* means "friend of the court." Such a brief can be filed if both lawyers agree to the action, or, barring that, the court decides that it would allow the action. This action is being taken more and more as a means of influencing the outcome of judicial action. For example, in 1985 the American Association of Retired Persons (AARP) filed friend-of-court briefs five times; two of the lawsuits were argued before the Supreme Court. The AARP attempts to become involved in court cases where the organization feels that the outcomes would have ramifications for the membership of the AARP. Four of the five lawsuits in which the AARP was involved were related to age discrimination in employment. The special-interest group would advocate particular viewpoints and back them up with supportive data.

A second means to influence the court is by public opinion, through actions similar to those described in our discussion of the legislative branch. Although judges are generally not subject to reelection, public opinion can still be used to promote greater sensitivity to the issues on the part of judges.

In sum, judicial actions can influence the interpretation of laws and therefore influence the execution of laws. Through the modification of laws, the public welfare or will of the people as defined in the original intent of the law would change, although the public has limited input to this process. In most cases, the easiest way to influence this process is to influence the legislative branch to pass new legislation to clarify the intent of "the public will or welfare."

The Executive Branch

The executive branch of the U.S. government is given the responsibility to carry out the wishes of the Congress through the enforcement and execution of laws. This action can take the form of ensuring that individuals and organizations comply with a broad range of laws. For example, the Justice Department has broad powers to prosecute violations of laws. In other situations, executive agencies have limited power to ensure compliance with the law. For example, the Equal Employment Opportunity Commission

(EEOC) has the power to initiate legal action against violators of all laws pertaining to equal employment.

In some cases, the executive branch agency has broad power even to create social policy, through its powers to create guidelines and establish standards with which organizations must comply. For example, the Occupational Safety and Health Administration (OSHA) has the power to establish standards in the areas of job safety and in providing a work climate that is free from health hazards.

Another group of federal agencies are involved with management functions with limited or no enforcement powers. For example, the National Oceanic and Atmospheric Administration (the weather bureau) is charged with the responsibility of providing a public service. It as little power to force compliance with any laws. The Postal Service and the National Railroad Passenger Corporation (AMTRAK) are both service areas of the government.

A final category of federal executive branch agencies is concerned with internal management of the government. For example, the Office of Management and the Budget (OMB) and Government Accounting Office (GAO) are examples of agencies designed to fulfill internal needs of the government.

The Role of the President

The office of the president of the United States is part of the executive branch. One role of the president is to serve as the presumed leader of the country. His designated role beyond that of chief of state is to carry out the laws of the land. As mentioned earlier in the chapter, there is a weak link between congressional intent and executive actions. As a result, there is wide altitude in the actions that federal agencies, including the president, may take. This latitude has led to several areas that the executive branch may influence in defining the public will and public welfare.

First, most laws are purposely vague. This leaves the executive branch agency a wide degree of discretion in the interpretation of the law and the degree of enforcement that the agency may follow. The choice of direction that the agency may pursue may be a function of the agency, its leader, and the philosophy of the president.

The agency itself will, through its value judgments, create its own climate that will establish norms of behavior. This is part of the culture of the agency. The culture can be influenced, to some degree, by the leader. The extent of the ability of the leader to influence organization cultures is dependent on the personal power of the leader and the status of employees.

In many federal agencies, a majority of staff members are civil service employees. These jobs are more stable than those appointed by the president. A presidential appointee, on the other hand, serves at the "pleasure of the president." When the president changes, there is a good chance that there will be a new appointee. It follows that the appointee has reduced power. The civil service employee may also have more techical expertise about the activities and the administrative procedures of the agency. The appointee must rely on that technical expert to get the agency's goals accomplished. In addition, the appointee may be viewed as a short-timer, one who can be endured, as opposed to a permanent leader to whom one must comply and "live with." However, if the agency head has a lot of tenacity and personal leadership skills, he or she can make substantial changes.

The President's Power to Administer the Government.   The president does have the power to appoint many agency heads. In addition, the agency heads serve at the pleasure of the president. Under these conditions, each agency reflects the president's personal philosophies and how he or she defines public welfare and the will of the people. For example, under President Kennedy, the antitrust division of the Justice Department was very active in prosecuting businesses that were perceived as "restraining trade." Under the Reagan administration, the antitrust division has been less active (see the box "Reagan's Impact on Business").

REAGAN'S IMPACT ON BUSINESS

One of the most interesting changes in the last decade is the change from liberalism to conservatism. This shift was reflected in the second-term election of President Reagan. He is strongly supportive of business as a means to correct many societal ills, more as the result of economic contributions to society by means of jobs than through a specific desire to have business be more socially responsive.

Reagan's view becomes particularly evident through executive branch activity in relation to business. The Department of Labor has been criticized for being too pro-business, at the expense of labor unions. The Equal Employment Opportunity Commission has been attacked as moving in the wrong direction in the area of equal employment rights and opportunities. The Environmental Protection Agency seems to have taken a much less aggressive stance toward inhibiting the actions of business, and the antitrust division of the Department of Justice has also been a target of criticism.

The passage of the Antitrust Improvement Act in 1976 gave the Justice Department additional strength to enforce the various antitrust laws that were on the books. However, the result has not been a more aggressive stance by the Justice Department. The basic reason for the somewhat limp performance of the antitrust division has been blamed on President Reagan's philosophies, which support less government intervention in the marketplace, moving back

(continued)

to a more "social Darwinistic approach" to business (i.e., survival of the fittest). Over 95 percent of antitrust suits (about 2,000 cases each year) in the 1970s and so far in the 1980s have been filed not by the Department of Justice, but by private parties. A landmark example of this turn toward greater leniency by the Justice Department was the dismissal of the IBM case in 1982. The Assistant Attorney General at the time, George Baxter, decided to dismiss the case even though it had been through 13 years of prosecution under five Presidents and was just months away from a district court opinion. The judge on the bench for the trial, the honorable William Edelstein, was quoted in the *Wall Street Journal* as saying that Mr. Baxter suffered from "myopia and misunderstanding of the antitrust laws and this case specifically. . . . Even one with prodigious intellect couldn't be expected to come up with a reasoned evaluation" of the case in the four months that Baxter reviewed it.

The implications were that there was a major shift in the philosophy of the Justice Department toward IBM and business in general. This viewpoint seems to be sustained given the actions (or lack of actions) that have been forthcoming from the Justice Department in the past several years.

The conclusions to be made regarding the enforcement of laws is that enforcement is, to a degree, at the discretion of the executive branch. Vigorous enforcement is possible, as was the case under Attorney General Robert Kennedy during John F. Kennedy presidency, as is the more passive enforcement evidenced under the Reagan administration.

Source: Adapted from *Wall Street Journal*, January 26, 1982, p. 10.

The same is true for the Federal Trade Commission. It was highly active under Presidents Johnson and Nixon. However, under Presidents Carter and Reagan, there as been a substantial reduction in activity. The reduction under the Reagan administration is deliberate and reflects the personal philosophy of the President that government should be less intrusive. This was one the guiding philosophies that President Reagan portrayed during both election campaigns. He won both terms by a wide margin and thus feels that he received a mandate from the people to carry out his philosophy of the role of government. Based on that role, many of the agencies of the executive branch have been much less active in areas such as trade restrictions, price supports for farmers, and affirmative action.

The President's Power over the Judiciary. The president has another way to influence the government's definition of the public will and welfare. The president is in charge of the appointment of federal judges. The appointments normally reflect the philosophy of the president who makes the appointment.

For example, President Reagan's appointment of Sandra Day O'Conner, the first woman justice of the Supreme Court, reflected Reagan's conservative viewpoints. The result of this appointment is a more conservative philosophy on the Court. Appointments, especially to the Supreme Court, may have important long-run ramifications for judicial decisions.

How Responsive Is the Executive Branch?

The term of office for a president is four years. The president can be elected for only two consecutive terms. However, even though the president can be reelected only once, the political party of the president does have an interest in remaining in power. Hence, there is a relatively strong desire to meet the wishes of the public.

What about the agency heads who are appointed? Because these appointees are those of the president, and thus normally support the party in power, there is a strong desire to be responsive. However, occasionally, the connection between the public and an appointee becomes muted because the connection is not as direct as if the appointee were elected.

What about career government service personnel, civil service employees, who are not appointed? This segment of the work force of the executive branch is more similar to employees in the private sector, and because many are covered under civil service laws, they are less prone to change with a change of presidents or political parties. Hence, they are less responsive to the public than are the president and the president's appointees. Of course, a career civil servant may be more responsive because of personal pride in the job and knowing that he or she will be in the position for quite a while. However, the power that the public has over civil service employees has been reduced—again by design. The desire to maintain a basic core of knowledgeable personnel who would be less prone to be changed with every election has led to the protection of many positions under civil service laws.

Because the executive branch acts more in a capacity to execute the will of the Congress, there is less formal seeking out of the will of the public. The president would, however, be quite responsive to public opinion, and therefore, a major way to influence the executive branch is by developing a responsive public. Means to increase the public's response on particular topics were outlined in our discussion of the legislative branch. With the responsive nature of the presidential office, special-interest groups may have a greater probability of influencing executive branch agencies through direct appeals to the president. Media attention may focus on the concern, the government agency's response, and on the fact that the agency head is an extension of the president's office.

The focal point of the president's office for the political party in power also provides special-interest groups with a means of initiating legislation that would be desirable to the interest groups. Although the president cannot introduce legislation into Congress, the office can be used to develop congressional support to have proposed legislation introduced into Congress. The president's office can also be used to apply pressure on Congress to pass legislation.

The power of the president, coupled with the activities of lobbyists, can tend to keep a bill moving through the legislative process. This important lobbyist role of the president is important for special-interest groups. They will often direct their lobbying efforts to the president in addition to the Congress. In that manner, there may be an increased chance for a successful outcome that would be desirable to the interest group.

Executive branch agencies do attempt to gauge the public sentiment for specific proposals. This is normally done to be able to develop a case to Congress for additional funding or to advocate a change in laws governing the agency. For example, AMTRAK, facing reduced funding during the early 1980s, encouraged the public to voice their opinions to their members of Congress. Other agencies have direct public meetings to assess public sentiment.

The three branches of the U.S. government each has the means to interpret and influence the public will and welfare. Each has different levels of responsiveness to the external publics that it serves. However, these branches do not serve in isolation; there is a series of checks and balances that moderate the power of each branch.

How Congress Can Affect the Other Branches

The design of the U.S. government facilitates checks and balances between each branch. This check-and-balance system in and of itself ensures that the public will be served. The legislative branch has influence over the executive and judicial branches in three ways. First, the legislative branch is the only branch that can initiate and pass laws. These laws can force the other branches to reflect the will of the Congress. For example, Congress recently passed legislation that restricted the use of funds by the president to support certain groups in Central America. In a similar manner, Congress established a law that required all states to have and enforce a 55-mile-per-hour speed limit. Although Congress could not directly "force" the states to comply, it did encourage compliance by threatening states that did not comply with a cutoff of federal highway funds.

A second method that Congress can use to check the actions of the other two branches is through the allocation of funds. The Congress decides, through the enactment of a law, allocations that are made to each agency of the federal government, including funding of judicial salaries and support funds. This gives Congress a large degree of power over the other branches. If an agency is not performing to standards that the Congress likes, it can either modify the law that regulates the agency *or* limit the agency's budgetary allocations. For example, some of the outcry of business and labor unions over the involvement of the Occupational Safety and Health Administration

(OSHA) in often trivial standards in the early 1970s led to inadequate funding of the agency by Congress. In the past five years, OSHA has focused on more substantive issues, resulting in more favorable treatment by Congress.

A third method that Congress has to monitor the activities of the other branches is through the need for Congress to approve appointees to both executive and judicial positions. This enables Congress to act to ensure that the appointee is competent and will act in the public's best interest.

How the Executive Branch Can Influence the Others

The executive branch can influence the legislative branch through basically three means. First, the executive branch can mount an intense public relations campaign to try to force the Congress to act. Presidents Carter and Reagan used the media very effectively to try to push the Congress to act. Some analysts believe that the "turnover" in members of the Senate and the House of Representatives is the direct result of a reduction in the public's confidence in Congress. Some of this erosion is the result of the executive branch's somewhat strong attacks on Congress for not acting to balance the budget, not enacting a major tax reform law, and failing to deal with proper funding of welfare programs, such as Social Security and Medicare.

A second means by which the executive branch can influence the legislative branch is through its choice of actions in carrying out the spirit, if not the letter, of the legislation. If there is antagonism between Congress and the executive branch, the president may be less responsive to the desires of the legislative branch. If this is the case, the president will direct agencies to follow the president's philosophy rather than the letter of the law. For example, several presidents have refused to release funds appropriated by Congress. In several cases Congress has filed suit in federal court to force the president to release funds.

Even if the funding is not withheld by presidential action, there is still wide latitude in the means that are available to the president to act in defiance of Congress. Basically, the president can accept or reject the guidelines provided by Congress in meeting the legal requirements in acting in behalf of an agency. Congress cannot run the day-to-day activities of a federal agency. Hence, it is in the best interest of Congress to work with the president to ensure that the executive branch is working toward the interests of the Congress.

Probably the most important action the president can take to influence the legislative branch is through the power of the veto. The president must sign all bills before they can become law. Congress can override a president's veto only if two-thirds of each house votes to override the veto, which is often difficult to accomplish.

The executive branch can influence the judicial branch primarily through public pressure and through the appointment of judges as positions become available. President Franklin Roosevelt, angered at the Supreme Court for declaring many of his programs unconstitutional, tried to increase the number of Supreme Court justices in order to change the philosophical composition of the court. The attempt failed, but it does demonstrate the influence that the power of appointment may have.

How the Judicial Branch Can Influence the Others

The judicial branch can directly influence the other two branches of government through court decisions. Three approaches can be used by the court to check or counter the actions of the other branches. First, the court may grant a restraining order to halt certain actions. A restraining order is issued when a case is made that the action may be illegal and injury to another party may occur if the action is continued.

A second means is through judicial interpretation of laws. These interpretations influence the intent of laws as well as how the laws are carried out through the executive branch. For example, the court took action when a union filed suit claiming that the Occupation Safety and Health Administration (OSHA) was acting contrary to law by not getting safe exposure standards for working with a chemical that is a known cancer-causing substance. The courts maintained that OSHA was negligent and was ordered to develop standards within a reasonable, stated period of time.

A third alternative of the courts is to declare a law unconstitutional. A suit must be filed by parties questioning the legality of the law. The court can declare it unconstitutional only if the law is deemed to be contrary to the provisions of the Constitution, including historical interpretations of the Constitution by the courts.

The checks and balances of each branch of government tend to monitor the actions of the others. Because of these checks and balances, what usually evolves is a greater desire for the branches to cooperate, as each is dependent on the other.

COUNTERVAILING POWERS

Chapter 3 introduced the concept of countervailing powers. By expanding the concept and applying it in a different manner, a better understanding is possible of how the government becomes responsive to the public will. Figure 5.5 demonstrates this relationship expanded to include the public will. Note in the figure that there are four basic groups: government, the public, unions, and businesses. The addition of the public is one element added to the original model proposed by John Kenneth Galbraith.[3] Government acts to express the will of society. As expressed earlier in the chapter, the public has power to act if government does not act in the public's best

[3]John Kenneth Galbraith, *American Capitalism* (Boston: Houghton Mifflin, 1952).

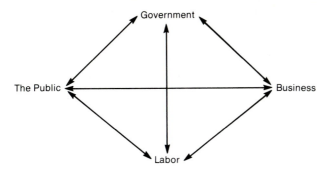

FIGURE 5.5 Adaptation of the Theory of Countervailing Powers.

interest. Business and unions could be considered as special-interest groups; they try to influence government and are influenced by government. In addition, businesses, publics, and labor unions influence each other. These interactions will be considered in later chapters. The interaction of particular relevance here is the interaction between government, the public, and business. Each element is trying to influence the other to be more responsive to its needs. If there is a balance of power, neither element is at an advantage or a disadvantage.

The reason the public has been separated from government in the model presented in Figure 5.5 is that there has been a separation of the will of the people with the actions of government. Galbraith considered government to be the spokesperson of the public. However, the goals of government and the interests of the public are not always the same. For example, this was evident in the turmoil of the 1960s surrounding the role of the United States in Viet Nam.

THE ADVANTAGES OF USING PUBLIC POLICY

So far the discussion has focused on the role of government in defining the will of the public. This becomes a point of departure for defining the role of business in society. Government is involved in defining the will of the public and translating this will into laws that shape the role of business in society. There are several advantages and disadvantages to having government be the interpreter and shaper of the social role of business.

In particular, there are five arguments that support an active role for government in establishing public policy regarding the social role of business. First, business does not have the power to define its own social responsibility. Second, the government's determination of policy toward business is based on representative and democratic choice, not on a single business executive's value system. Third, government can establish policy based on a systematic determination of the public good. Fourth, government has greater resources to effect social change. Fifth, the importance to society of some of the social issues dictates government intervention.

Business Influence on Social Change

One of the arguments supporting the role of public policy in business activity pertains to the comparative power of government and a single business. Government, by having some control over an entire industry, can more readily influence the actions of all businesses. For example, suppose that a paper-cup manufacturer in Wisconsin decides that the current production process is harming the ecology. The company then decides, on its own, to change the production process to make an ecologically safe product. The new process, however, involves an additional cost of 2 cents per cup. The result might be that the ecologically acceptable production process may lead to bankruptcy for the company, if consumers purchase the cheaper but comparable product from the company's competitor. But whether consumers buy the more ecologically safe product depends on whether they have enough monetary slack and elect to spend it on that sort of purchase. "Slack" refers to the amount of available discretionary funds, that is, resources beyond those absolutely necessary for the survival of a business firm or a consumer. In this case, the consumers' discretionary funds are funds beyond those needed for basic comfort and survival. The consumers will decide how to allocate their discretionary funds, if any. They may decide to buy the more expensive paper cups or to use the funds to aid social welfare in their own community and not in a community in Wisconsin. Therefore, the paper-cup manufacturer may lose sales to the less ecologically responsible competition.

The government can alter this scenario by establishing a public policy, that is, a law that mandates that all companies must adopt the new pollution-reducing process. In this way, the goal of less pollution can be maintained in a manner more equitable to the more socially responsive company; that is, it will not suffer for its stand on reducing pollution. Hence, by using public policy, changes to improve social welfare can be made in an entire industry at one time instead of in a single company, with the burden of the potential sales loss borne by the entire industry and not by the more socially responsive, individual company.

Social Welfare Determined by Democratic Process

A second advantage of public policy involvement in determining the social responsibility of business is that the democratic process prevails instead of the more closed process of business policy formation. Through the democratic process of formulating the laws and executing them, the public will is better defined and served than it is without a formal representation. In essence, this argument is that society should determine how it wants to rank social goods by means other than an arbitrary decision by one business. For example, the paper-cup manufacturer's decision to switch to the new, ecologically superior procedure was made by management. Society had little input into the decision process. The company therefore decided on its own that the greatest social welfare would be served by less pollution in the environment, particularly that of the local plant in Wisconsin. This decision was made without regard to the cost to the consumers. Society, in essence, lost its right to determine whether it benefited more from a lower-priced product or from less pollution. Under a representative, democratic government model, society would determine the more judicious allocation of resources.

Greater Cohesiveness of Social Policies

A third advantage of involving public policy in providing a socially responsible framework for business is the consistency that can be created through systematic policy formation. With single businesses determining their social responsibilities, the end result can be many fragmented policies and practices. Under public determination of social policy for business, the representative and public process of debate and compromise would help society determine how the public good would best be served. If each business firm independently denies its own social responsibility and how it will act under that definition, a fragmented and impotent policy can be the outcome. For example, assume that there are five grain wholesalers in the United States. Two of these companies decide that the public good can best be served by selling wheat to the Soviet Union. In this way, prices to farmers will increase as demand for the product increases. Society benefits in that a country that needs wheat for food is supplied at prices that help the U.S. farmer. Three companies, however, feel that the Soviet Union should be punished for disregarding human rights and using armed intervention in the affairs of neighboring countries. These three companies feel that society is better served by boycotting sales to the Soviet Union. The result might be to weaken communism, and the U.S. consumer might be aided in that the reduced demand for wheat would result in lower prices for the commodity. The result of these two conflicting policies is that there would be confusion in the foreign market. As society had no input in the policies, advocates of public policy would maintain that greater cohesiveness is needed in social policy. The government, through its power and agencies, is more likely to provide the degree of order necessary to formulate policy.

Government's Resources to Influence the Social Role of Business

The fourth argument favoring government's determining social policy is based on government resources. Through tax collections and the ability to borrow funds at low cost, the government has greater resources available to influence social change. Business resources, on the other hand, are much more limited and can best be applied to meet the narrower objectives of the firm itself. Social welfare is most often viewed as a secondary product or a by-product of the firm's main objectives. Business is more concerned with making a product or service that fulfills a public need at a reasonable cost. In striving for this objective, the firm is preoccupied with its own survival and therefore must earn a sufficient return for its owners. Government resources, on the other hand, are directed only toward society's public policy dicta, and therefore more funds will be available for various social concerns.

Social Needs and Government Intervention

A fifth argument favoring public policy intervention in business's social activities relates to the importance of business to society. In many respects, business activities are so vital to society that society must have power over business. For example, the importance of the automobile industry to the creation of jobs necessitates that public policy be formulated to guarantee the survival of that industry. Similarly, the importance of transportation systems has resulted in special laws being enacted that ensure that a strike will not impede flow of commerce. The danger of some processes, such as the nuclear power generation of electricity, requires that society have a voice in the location, construction, and safe operation of the facilities.

Although a strong case can be made for socially determined policies that define the role of business in society, there are equally plausible arguments against such intervention.

THE DISADVANTAGES OF USING PUBLIC POLICY

Three arguments can be made for a laissez-faire role of government with respect to defining the social role of business. First, government lawmakers do not know enough about operating a business, and therefore cannot enact equitable constraints. Second, the cost to business of complying with public policy is often not worth the benefits to society. Third, the government does not understand the economic system and therefore should not take an active role in moderating that system to meet society's needs. In reality, most arguments center on the reduction of government's role in business, not on the elimination of public policy as a moderator.

Lack of Government Competence

A major concern with extensive government intrusion into the affairs of business is that government lawmakers do not understand the inner workings of business. Constraints are made on business with little regard for the consequences to business or the consumers of products or services. As discussed in regard to the negative consequences of public policies, the constraints placed on railroads by the Interstate Commerce Commission make it impossible for the railroads to earn sufficient returns for their owners. The result was difficulty in attracting the capital needed to maintain a viable rail system, leading, in effect, to disinvestment in the railroad industry. Other agencies, such as the Occupational Safety and Health Administration (OSHA) and the Environmental Protection Agency (EPA), have had the same debilitating effect on some businesses. A lack of understanding of the inner workings and competitive realities of business by these and other agencies has threatened the survival of many of them.

Compliance Costs Versus Benefits to Society

A second disadvantage of excessive government intervention concerns the costs versus the benefits to society. Costs can be divided into three areas: the costs of compliance, the opportunity costs of compliance, and the administrative costs of compliance. The costs of compliance are obvious. If OSHA, for example, requires new safety guards on equipment, that is a real and calculable cost. The opportunity costs, as mentioned before, are the costs of the opportunities lost by complying with government regulations. Administrative costs include the government's expenditures for making sure that business is obeying the law and the businesses' costs of record keeping and information gathering required to comply with regulations. The general concern is that often these costs are greater than the benefits.

Government and the Complexity of the Economic System

A third argument for less government intrusion is the complexity of the economic system and how government interference in that system could create unforeseen problems. For example, economists have often stated that government borrowing is not a problem, in that it is only borrowing from society, and society is part of government. The unforeseen problem is the restrictive effect on government actions that occurs when debt increases to such a degree that interest payments create a hardship on budgeting. Government expenditures for interest payments restrict government spending for social programs. In addition, the competition to finance the government's debt creates higher interest rates in the investment community and additional burdens on business and increased inflation. The complexity of the effect of government spending was not sufficiently foreseen, so the potential problems were not realistically addressed.

TRENDS IN PUBLIC POLICY TOWARD BUSINESS

The current political environment at the federal level seems to support a reduction of government intervention and the role of public policy in shaping the social role of business. In recent years the rail, truck, and airline industries have been deregulated, and regulations have also eased in the banking indus-try. Under President Ronald Reagan, and with a more conservative political-legal climate in general, equal-opportunity guidelines, health and safety rules, and pollution standards have been relaxed, and tax incentives have been offered to encourage business redevelopment.

The results of the 1984 elections signaled a change in public policy, or at least more deregulation. A swing back to a more liberal perspective may be coming. Traditionally, the liberal viewpoint has been directed toward greater government involvement. In the next few years society will determine whether the substantial changes in its values, as manifested in public policy, will be sustained or be recast into another perspective.

SUMMARY

In this chapter we presented some of the major issues regarding the relation-ship of government and society. A major point made by this chapter is that there are many power groups that attempt to influence government. Government, in turn, is an artificial creation of the state, but is managed by individuals who have their own personal goals, values, and visions as to the role of government in society. Internal and external publics both try to gain input into the process of governing society. Groups with the resources, organization, and a good power base tend to have a larger voice in influencing the policies, goals, and government actions.

A second major facet of the chapter is dedicated to a discussion of the three branches of the U.S. government, how they influence the government process, and how, in turn, they are influenced by external and internal interest groups (business is classified within the category of a special-interest group in this case).

A third major aspect of this chapter relates publics, government, business, and labor into an expanded model of Galbraith's concept of countervailing powers. A difference between government goals and the public it is designed to serve is evident from the turmoil of the 1960s. These differences need to be considered when the government defines public will.

Finally, the advantages and disadvantages of having the government as a major input into defining the role of business in society were discussed.

DISCUSSION AND STUDY QUESTIONS

1. Describe the internal publics, external publics, and strategy and policy forma-tion groups of a government organization.
2. Discuss the relationship between government and dominant companies; fi-nancial institutions.
3. Compare and contrast the different responsiveness levels of government to the general public and special-interest groups.
4. How are coalitions formed, and why are they important?

5. The desire to manage external groups extends from what three desires? How can this goal be facilitated?
6. Why is "carrying out the will of the people" so difficult?
7. Describe the three branches of government in the United States and their functions.
8. What is the logic of each state having two senators who serve six-year terms?
9. Discuss the processes necessary for proposed legislation to become law.
10. What is the role of a lobbying in the democratic process?
11. What is the role of the legislative branch of government, and how is it accomplished?
12. How does the judicial branch influence the definition of the public will?
13. Why are most laws purposely vague when written?
14. Describe how the president may influence the government's definition of the public will and welfare. How do the legislative and judicial branches interpret and influence the public will?
15. Describe the system of checks and balances that exists between the three branches of government.
16. What is the president's most powerful influence over the legislative branch? May it be overturned?
17. Name three ways in which the judicial branch may directly influence the other two branches.
18. Discuss the advantages and disadvantages of government as the major input in defining the social role of business.

CASES AND INCIDENTS

The Advent of AMTRAK

Post–World War II found passenger trains rapidly losing favor in the United States as a means of travel. The unpleasant experiences during the war years of traveling by rail in crowded and makeshift equipment that was used to transport massive numbers of troups and regular passengers led many to search for alternative transportation after the war. The air and auto industries were growing rapidly. Transportation by automobile was being fostered through passage of the 1956 Highway Defense Transportation Act, which established the interstate highway system. In 1929, railroads accounted for 77 percent of all revenue passenger miles; buses, 15.4 percent; and inland waterways, 7.5 percent. By 1960, railroads accounted for only 28.6 percent, buses 14.3 percent, inland waterways 3.6 percent, and air carriers, 42.1 percent. In 1982, railroads accounted for only 4.3 percent of revenue passenger miles, buses 10.9 percent, inland waterway, 1.6 percent, and air carriers, 83.2 percent.

By the mid-1950s, passenger trains were being canceled at an alarming rate even with strict Interstate Commerce Commission (ICC) guidelines and jurisdiction over train abandonments. Even with the great reduction in the number of trains, railroads complained that they were losing millions of dollars each year by having to maintain passenger service. The public complained that the service provided was deplorable.

The railroads' viewpoint was that the drop in passengers that was occurring led to conditions that made it impossible to provide service at a profit. The public, on the other hand, believed that the drop in ridership was the result of slow trains, trains that were never on time, dirty and poorly maintained equipment, and a lack of customer responsiveness. Some people even accused the railroads of wanting to discourage business so that they could justify train discontinuances before the ICC.

In February 1969 the Association of American Railroads advocated that the federal government subsidize passenger trains. The House and Senate held hearings later that year to determine the public will and welfare. The result was the passage of a bill on October 14, 1970, signed by President Nixon on October 30, 1970, that created AMTRAK on May 1, 1981, but not before unsuccessful suits were filed in U.S. district court and appeals were made to the U.S. circuit court challenging the concept. In addition, Senate Democratic leaders Mike Mansfield and Warren Magnuson tried to block the implementation of AMTRAK through amendments to the original law, although the original law passed the full Senate by a vote of 78 to 3.

The mentality of a conservative Congress to allow AMTRAK to survive in some very tight budget years has rested on the belief that society desired a railroad transportation alternative even though there was insufficient demand to make the service profitable on its own. Rail service has survived even though less than 50 percent of the cost of rail service is covered through revenues. The Congress has determined that rail service is a service desired by the public and one that the public is willing to pay tax dollars to maintain. This congressional sense evolved through strong lobbying efforts of the railroads (during its inception), consumer groups such as the National Association of Railroad Passengers (NARP), cities and states that advocate the importance of rail service, and of course, AMTRAK itself. AMTRAK ridership has increased over the past 10 years, but revenues are still not nearly enough to cover costs, and AMTRAK finds that 2,000 passenger cars can meet current ridership needs in most cases, even though in 1944, 8,700 passenger cars were in service.

ANALYSIS

1. Do you think AMTRAK service reflects the public will?
2. Have you ridden AMTRAK? What has been your experience?
3. Do you think the government should subsidize AMTRAK even when it loses so much? Why or why not?

The Scapegoat*

Charles Bellman, 53, is in a federal prison in Rochester, Minnesota, serving an 18-month term for converting mortgaged property: in this case, selling grain being used as collateral and buying cheaper, lower-quality grain to feed his cattle. Bellman maintains that this is common practice among farmers and is done with the banks' full knowledge of the practice. Bellman maintains that he was prosecuted primarily because the banks and lawyers do not like the other activities of Bellman (i.e., being the chief organizer of FAMINE). FAMINE is an acronym for "Farmers of America Merge," a nonprofit organization that is dedicated to informing farmers on procedures by which to avoid having their farms taken over by creditors in a bankruptcy settlement. In addition, Bellman has another organization, the National Farm Management, Ltd., which works with farmers on bankruptcies and estate planning.

Philip Hogen, the federal prosecutor in the case, said he sought to make an example of Bellman because "this defendant has held himself out as an expert to farmers who are encountering financing difficulties." The result is that a farmer is in jail and his farm is not being managed well because he is in prison 400 miles away. If the farm fails, the creditors will lose additional sums—all for the sake of making the farmer an example.

Did the execution of the law serve justice? The prosecutor would say, yes, it will act to deter other farmers from similar actions (even though it is apparent that the action is already widespread and has the tacit approval of creditors). Did execution of the law deter farmers from being active advocates of their rights in farm foreclosures? According to Bellman, definitely yes. In lawyer parlance, this will have a chilling effect on farmers' actions to protect their property. The farmers will become more passive, as they fear the legal consequences, or even if they are in the right, they fear having to commit financial resources to defend themselves.

Bellman philosophizes—about the farm problem, bureaucracy, and "justice gone wild," about creditors that he says are so hung up on policy that they achieve less by prosecuting farmers than by letting them run their farms. He says that the solution lies with lenders working with farmers. "We didn't go broke willingly," he said. "Debtors prisons are not the answer."

ANALYSIS

1. Do you feel that Bellman deserves to be in prison?
2. What arguments would you make to defend Bellman? To prosecute him?
3. What impact will this case have on FAMINE?

*Adapted from John Cunniff, "Debt-Burdened Farmer Says He's in Prison as Scapegoat," *Tulsa World*, October 6, 1985, p. A-15.

A Move Toward Conservativism

Many feel that there has been a major shift in the mood of the public in the 1960s to the 1980s. This mood has been toward a more conservative viewpoint. Many members of Congress had to learn the hard way. The Presidential elections over the past two decades were the first indicators of change. The more conservative candidate won readily over the more liberal candidate. Also, congressional leaders noted for their liberalism had much more difficult elections in their own respective districts. The populace had never been as responsive in voting a change in approach toward improving the quality of life in the United States. The changes toward a new philosophy are represented by the following:

- Government should be less intrusive in the lives of individuals and in influencing the action of business.
- Business should be deregulated so that market forces and economic conditions prevail. The sentiment was that government interference seemed to have only aggravated problems instead of curing them. For example, although Reagan has not been very responsive to the farm problems in the country, there has been continued strength in the rural states for the president.
- There should be fewer controls on foreign competition, even though the lack of import controls may mean a loss of domestic jobs. Overall, the advantages in lower prices and reciprocal trade agreements ought to benefit society.
- Entitlement costs, such as Social Security, Welfare, Medicare, and Medicaid, need to be contained.
- Taxes should be reduced, and the deficit needs to be controlled. The only way to meet these goals is to have fewer government services. It is assumed that the general population is willing to live with less government.

There seems to be a mood of much less trust in big government, much more than has ever been experienced in modern times. It is a healthy mistrust, less destructive than the demonstrations of the 1960s over the Viet Nam action. The new breed of distrust is willing to challenge the system through legal actions, willing to lobby to change the conditions that have led to the perceived inequity.

ANALYSIS

1. Do you agree that there is a shift toward conservatism?
2. Why do you think there has been (or not been) a shift toward conservatism in recent years?
3. What do you think the future holds? Why?

Food on the Table Versus Clean Air

The City of Prinville, Wisconsin, recently faced a terrible problem. The Environmental Protection Agency (EPA) was threatening to force closure of a local paper-producing plant because of the amounts of air and water pollution that it was creating. Boston Paper, the owners of the plant, maintained that the plant was a marginal producer of paper and the company could not afford to spend the $3 million that it would take to comply with the EPA order. The town would lose 300 jobs if the plant closed. In addition, it was estimated that another 100 jobs would be lost in retail stores and material suppliers in the surrounding area as an indirect result of the plant shutdown. One estimate was that the unemployment rate would increase another 10 percent over and above the current 30 percent rate. This translated into almost $1 million in lost income for the area and almost $100,000 in lost tax revenues.

Under the EPA provisions, an exception to compliance could be granted if the economic consequences of compliance would create extensive damage to the community. However, downstream and mainly downwind of the plant was the city of Lake Behere. The city council of Lake Behere issued a strongly worded statement that the pollution of its water and air was harming the attractiveness of their city and hurting the potential industrial growth that they badly needed. At stake, they claimed, was the very survival of Lake Behere.

ANALYSIS

1. How might the EPA quantify the costs and benefits to each community? Develop means to measure both direct and indirect effects.
2. How might the EPA assess the quality-of-life and health dimensions given different levels of pollution so they could include that in their consideration?
3. Given that public policy dictates that the United States should have improved air and water quality, how should the EPA view the request for a variance?

EPA Failure?*

A Heritage Foundation report says that the Reagan administration should receive poor marks for the performance of the Environmental Protection Agency (EPA). The administration seems to be moving in two directions—to give businesses relief from stringent and unfair EPA regulations, and to reduce EPA's budget, thereby reducing its effectiveness to deal with envi-

*Adapted from "EPA Failure Seen by Conservative Unit; Reagan Is Criticized," *Chemical Marketing Reporter*, December 10, 1984, pp. 5, 14.

ronmental problems. Both of these efforts have seemingly failed because conservation groups have attacked any weakening of the EPA.

Regardless of the intense groups' efforts at maintaining the effectiveness of the Environmental Protection Act, there has been a definite movement toward less active enforcement by the EPA. The 500-page Heritage Foundation report maintained that there were a number of poor decisions at the EPA during the first few years of the Reagan administration. Although those decisions were reversed, the credibility of the EPA was severely harmed. In addition, the jail term that Rita Lavelle was given as a result of her actions at the EPA and the turmoil that occurred in the mid-1980s all indicated an agency that has not been able to carry out public policy as specified in the EPA act.

The Heritage Foundation advocated four major steps that the EPA could pursue to improve its effectiveness and credibility. However, if the philosophy of the Reagan administration is that it wants less government interference with business, it is expected that there will be less than an all-out attempt to move the EPA into active advocacy of pollution control as in the 1970s. However, the Congress will take action if the agency does not make at least a half-hearted attempt to comply with the intent of the act.

ANALYSIS

1. How could Congress take action? What sorts of things could it do?
2. What legal range of actions does an executive branch have in the enforcement of the law? What creates this range of actions? It is practical to define an agency's conduct precisely?
3. How might the general public influence a public agency to be more responsive? What can it do directly or indirectly?

The Impact of Government on the Social Role of Business

Chapter Objectives

- To identify specific government agencies that moderate the actions of business and carry out the will of society toward defining the social role of business.
- To demonstrate how business can be used as an instrument of American foreign policy.
- To illustrate how the government can use business to further domestic policies.
- To discuss the positive aspects that public policies and government have for business.
- To show how public policies and government can inhibit business.

In this chapter we build on Chapter 5, in which we outlined the overall nature and dimensions of government and public policy. In this chapter we examine more specifically the role of public policy in shaping the social role of business. First we review the current impact of government on business.

THE ROLE OF GOVERNMENT IN BUSINESS

For the past 25 years the general trend of government has been to assume a more active role in the regulation of business. This regulation has generally been quite comprehensive in scope. One way of viewing the degree of public policy intervention is to divide the government's emphasis into four categories: (1) laws to protect the legal rights and safety of the employee, (2) laws to protect the consumer, (3) laws to protect competition and the marketplace, and (4) laws to protect the ecological environment. Table 6–1 presents a summary of the federal agencies that regulate business, including the agency's major functions, and a synopsis of its activities. At the state level there are often parallel organizations, but the variations among states and the number of state agencies make their inclusion outside the scope of this table.

TABLE 6.1.   Federal Agencies Pertaining to the Social Role of Business.

1. Agencies Protecting Employees' Legal Rights and Safety
a. Protection of Legal Rights

Agency	Major Functions	Synopsis of Activities
Equal Employment Opportunity Commission	Investigates and mediates complaints of employment discrimination based on race, religion, and sex.	Although it has filed—and won—some big court cases involving millions of dollars in back-pay awards, the commission is essentially without powers or real authority. It may be folded into a unified antidiscrimination agency
National Labor Relations Board	Regulates labor practices of unions and companies and conducts representation elections.	Basically a judicial agency, the board conciliates or decides thousands of cases brought each year by individuals, unions, and companies complaining of unfair or illegal labor practices. The board is considered one of the slowest agencies in Washington.
Pension and Benefit Welfare Programs[a]	Oversees pension plans under the Employee Retirement Income Security Act.	The full force of the act has yet to be felt, so the agency is something of an unknown quantity. But of the 1.8 million pension plans in the United States, the agency has exempted 1.2 million from filing.

TABLE 6.1. Continued

1. Agencies Protecting Employees' Legal Rights and Safety
a. Protection of Legal Rights

Agency	Major Functions	Synopsis of Activities
Office of Federal Contract Compliance Programs[a]	Administers prohibitions against discrimination by race or sex by employers holding federal contracts.	The office oversees enforcement activities of about 1,800 people in contract compliance sections in other federal agencies involved in federal contracting. It is generally considered a weak agency with limited powers.

b. Employee Safety and Health

Agency	Major Functions	Synopsis of Activities
Occupational Safety and Health Administration[a]	Responsible for regulating safety and health conditions in all workplaces—except those run by governments.	Few regulators have been the target of as much vituperation and antagonism. Both labor and business have accused it of everything from triviality to harassment. Major administrative reforms are expected.
Mining Enforcement and Safety Administration[b]	Enforces all mine safety regulations, including air-quality and equipment standards.	Caught between management and labor and subservient to the Secretary of the Interior, the agency now has a vigorous pro-enforcement administrator.

2. Agencies Protecting the Consumer

Agency	Major Functions	Synopsis of Activities
Consumer Product Safety Commission	Tries to reduce product-related injuries to consumers by mandating better design, labeling, and instruction sheets.	Notorious for concentrating on trivia, it has been reorganized to stress rational priorities. But its administrators' effort to reach into too many new areas means poor follow-up.

TABLE 6.1.   **Continued**

2. Agencies Protecting the Consumer		
Agency	*Major Functions*	*Synopsis of Activities*
Federal Aviation Administration[c]	Regulates aircraft manufacturing through certification of airplane airworthiness and licenses pilots.	A tough enforcer. But officials tend to be chummy with top aircraft industry executives. Result: some big flaps, such as the DC-10 cargo-door controversy.
Federal Trade Commission	Has broad discretion to curb unfair trade practices, protect consumers, and maintain competition.	Once so absorbed in trivia that there were serious plans to disband it, the commission is now both aggressive and innovative in fulfilling its mandate. But it still stumbles on complex procedures.
Food and Drug Administration[d]	Responsible for the safety and efficacy of drugs and medical devices and the safety and purity of food, and regulates labeling, and oversees about $200 billion of industrial output.	An entrenched bureaucracy notorious for caution and close identification with the industries it regulates. Bold actions can usually be traced to legislative mandates that give the FDA no leeway to stall.
National Highway Traffic Safety Administration[c]	Regulates manufacturers of autos, trucks, buses, motorcycles, trailers, and tires so as to reduce the number and severity of traffic accidents.	An aggressive young regulator, it has promulgated hundreds of regulations on everything from auto bumpers to mandatory seat belt installation.

3. Agencies Protecting Competition and an Orderly Marketplace		
Agency	*Major Functions*	*Synopsis of Activities*
Antitrust Division[e]	Regulates all activity that could affect interstate commerce, from trade restraints and illegal agreements to mergers.	Enormously influential because of the criminal and financial sanctions it can obtain through the courts, the division is a factor in every company's strategic planning. But it has not managed to stem industry concentration.

TABLE 6.1.   Continued

3. *Agencies Protecting Competition and an Orderly Marketplace*		
Agency	*Major Functions*	*Synopsis of Activities*
Civil Aeronautics Board	Regulates airline fares and routes.	Its enforcement of laws that limit competition to the airline industry has built substantial pressure for reform that would ease restrictions on fare and route decisions. A reform bill is in Congress.
Commodity Futures Trading Commission	Regulates futures trading on commodity exchanges.	With very few resources, the commission has had little impact so far on an industry with no regulatory tradition.
Comptroller of the Currency	Charters and regulates national banks.	The most permissive regulator. It opened the door to the go-go banking era of the 1960s. The comptroller has belatedly developed a top-notch system for early warning on bank problems.
Federal Communications Commission	Regulates broadcasting and other communications through licensing and frequency allocation, and interstate telephone and telegraph rates and levels of service.	One of the most heavily "judicialized" of the independent commissions, it takes forever to reach decisions. It is bogged down in things such as a new radio station license applications.
Federal Deposit Insurance Corp.	The New Deal's response to bank failures, shares regulatory powers with the states over state-chartered banks not in the Federal Reserve System and over mutual savings banks.	As a regulator of smaller banks, it is subject to less criticism than are other bank regulators. But its procedures lag behind the industry's problems.
Federal Home Loan Bank Board	Charters and regulates federal savings and loan institutions and insures S&L deposits through a subsidiary.	The bank board quietly drifted for most of 40 years and is very chummy with its industry. But new demands on S&Ls as a

TABLE 6.1.   **Continued**

3. Agencies Protecting Competition and an Orderly Marketplace

Agency	Major Functions	Synopsis of Activities
		primary source of mortgage financing may wake up the board.
Federal Maritime Commission	Regulates foreign and domestic ocean commerce, mainly by overseeing agreements reached by a variety of rate-making conferences of ship carriers.	Concentrates on maintaining stability in ocean shipping and policing discrimination in rate making. Known as a rubber stamp for the shipping conferences, the commission has shown its teeth on rate kickback cases.
Federal Power Commission	Regulates interstate transmission and wholesale price of electric power, rates, and routes of natural gas pipelines, and, under a court ruling in the 1950s, the wellhead price of gas for interstate shipment.	The archetype of the reluctant regulator, it is unremitting in its efforts to escape regulating the prices charged by thousands of natural gas producers.
Federal Reserve Board	Regulates state-chartered banks that belong to the Federal Reserve System, has jurisdiction over bank-holding companies, and sets money and credit policy.	At the Fed, bank regulation has always been secondary to making monetary policy. Now that big banks are having problems, the regulatory staff is considered not quite adequate to meet the challenge.
Interstate Commerce Commission	Regulates rates and routes of railroads, most truckers, and some waterway carriers.	The oldest and most hidebound independent regulator, it spends most of its time adjudicating motor-carrier tariffs and operating rights, is deeply committed to keeping competition among carriers in delicate balance.
Securities and Exchange Commission	Regulates all publicly traded securities and the markets on which they are traded,	Most prestigious of the independent agencies, the commission has a

TABLE 6.1.   Continued

3. Agencies Protecting Competition and an Orderly Marketplace

Agency	Major Functions	Synopsis of Activities
	administers public disclosure laws, and policies securities fraud.	reputation—occasionally unmerited—for aggressive policework and zealous protection of investors. Curent preoccupations: foreign bribes and creation of a national securities market.
Corps of Engineers[f]	Regulates construction along waterways and marshlands and in dredging operations and mine dumping.	A river dredger and dam builder, it was long viewed as the enemy by environmentalists. But sensitive to political winds, it has turned zealous environmental champion, and may get more powers from Congress.
Environmental Protection Agency	Develops and enforces standards for clean air and water, controls pollution from pesticides, toxic substances, and noise, approves state pollution abatement plans, and rules on environmental impact statements.	Preoccupied with developing standards and writing broad rules, it prefers negotiating compliance to twisting arms.
Nuclear Regulatory Commission	Regulates civilian nuclear safety, meaning licensing atomic power plants.	It has a record of fast approval of plant construction. Some critics say it is too fast. The commission's weaknesses, inconsistent national standards and a jurisdiction that overlaps the EPA's.

[a]Labor Dept.
[b]Interior Dept.
[c]Transportation Dept.
[d]Health and Human Services Dept.
[e]Justice Dept.
[f]Defense Dept.

Source: Adapted from *Business Week,* April 4, 1977, pp. 52–53, 56.

Agencies Protecting Employees' Legal Rights and Safety

There are many laws to protect employees; several federal agencies have been created in order to administer these laws or to help establish policies regarding employee rights and safety. The Equal Employment Opportunity Commission, National Labor Relations Board, Pension and Benefit Welfare Division of the Department of Labor, and Office of Federal Contract Compliance all administer and protect employee's legal rights. Both the Occupational Safety and Health Administration (OSHA) and the Mining Enforcement and Safety Administration oversee compliance with federal laws regarding employees' safety.

Agencies Protecting Consumers' Legal Rights

The legal rights of consumers with respect to product quality and safety will be discussed in Chapter 11. Table 6–1 summarizes the five agencies that protect the consumer. The Consumer Product Safety Commission works to eliminate unsafe products. The Federal Aviation Administration certifies the air worthiness of aircraft, maintenance procedures, and scheduling, and licenses pilots. In addition, the agency manages traffic control in the air and aircraft on the ground. The Federal Trade Commission protects consumers against deceptive advertising and selling practices, and establishes policies with respect to warranties and service practices. The Food and Drug Administration is responsible for ensuring that drugs and medical devices are effective and safe and that foods are safe and pure. The National Highway Traffic Safety Administration works toward safer highways and vehicles.

Agencies Protecting Competition and the Marketplace

Government agencies protecting competition and the marketplace are concerned with providing a competitive environment within the industry, that is, that there is an efficient and orderly marketplace for conducting business. These agencies' duties are to maintain the stability of financial and monetary markets and to protect the competitive structure in certain industries in which there is a public need to maintain certain services.

The Antitrust Division of the Justice Department is responsible for maintaining competition in interstate commerce. The Civil Aeronautics Board is charged with monitoring rates within zones, determining rates between cities, and maintaining service to cities that some carriers have decided to abandon. The Commodity Futures Trading Commission ensures a stable commodity exchange market. The Comptroller of the Currency, the Federal Deposit Insurance Corporation, the Federal Home Loan Bank Board, and the Federal Reserve Board all maintain stability in the financial markets. The Federal Reserve Board also influences the economy through its monetary and fiscal policies.

The Federal Communication Commission (FCC) regulates competition of public utilities such as the telephone and telegraph industry. In addition, because of the limited number of frequencies of radio and television signals, the FCC regulates the licensing of these media.

The Federal Energy Administration, currently named the Department of Energy, regulates the price of natural gas and oil and is formulating a national energy policy. After the oil crisis of 1973, the Federal Energy Administration was formed because of the importance of energy to the country's well-being.

The Federal Maritime Commission regulates foreign and domestic ocean commerce, and the Interstate Commerce Commission regulates the trucking and railroad industry, and some waterway carriers. The Federal Power Commission regulates the electrical, pipeline, and natural gas utilities having interstate commerce. The Securities and Exchange Commission oversees securities, security markets, and disclosures of all publicly traded securities to prevent fraudulent practices.

Agencies Protecting the Environment

Three agencies are charged with protecting the environment. The Corps of Engineers is responsible for protecting the waterways and the public interest and for fostering the economic development of various areas of the country if economically feasible. The Environmental Protection Agency (EPA) sets and enforces air, water, and noise pollution standards and standards for handling and using pesticides and toxic wastes. Finally, the Nuclear Regulatory Agency (NRA) regulates the use of radioactive materials in civilian operations. A major portion of its activity is overseeing and approving the construction and granting of operating licenses for nuclear powered reactors for generating electricity.

Legislative Committees

Society has mandated that government action be taken to control business. In total, these government actions might be regarded as public policy toward business. However, public policy is manifested not only in the consequences of legislative actions by the executive branch of government. The *U.S. Government Manual* has a comprehensive list of congressional committees active in business-related areas. These committees act as fact-finding bodies in order to determine whether the social good is served by the current policy. They judge the efficacy of current public policy and the efficiency and effectiveness of the current environment for business. Although public policy is decided by executive or administrative actions by the president or agency chiefs, the actions of the congressional committees are central to the formation or restatement of major shifts in public policy. Government policy can also influence business in another way. Because the government grants licenses for the export and import of goods, business can also be used to advance foreign policy.

BUSINESS AS AN INSTRUMENT OF AMERICAN FOREIGN POLICY

Multinational corporations have often found that their home governments use them to promote their own policies. For example, the Japanese government uses its steel companies as a means of maintaining full employment. Through government subsidies, Japanese steel companies can operate at full output and can underprice many of the world's other steel producers. The U.S. government, in the same way, has blended its policies with the actions of many of the U.S.-based multinational corporations (MNCs). The MNCs of most countries find this practice operates in varied ways. In lieu of direct military threats, the new mode of international diplomacy is to use economic sanctions and moral suasion. Economic sanctions affect the MNCs' activities. In some cases the MNC is directly involved in political intrigue and actions in foreign countries. The well-publicized role of ITT in the coup of Salvador Allende in Chile is an example of the degree of involvement of government and business in foreign policy. The United States often uses MNCs to implement foreign policy by means of trade concessions and subsidies, weapons trade programs and permits, and economic development programs for Third World nations.

Trade Restrictions and Allowances

One of the most effective means by which the government persuades MNCs to abide by its policies is through the use of trade restrictions and subsidies. Most countries establish tariff restrictions on both exports and imports. For example, the United States, in order to protect the steel industry, has placed import quotas and tariffs on imported steel. The tariffs are taxes on the steel entering the United States, and the quotas are the maximum aggregate amount that can be imported into the country. Most other countries have similar policies. For example, the European Economic Community is a trade community to protect Western European businesses from those of the rest of the world and to promote trade among its members.

A second means of restricting the actions of an exporting industry is by means of trade permits. In most cases, firms that do business outside the country must obtain a permit to export from the originating country *and* a permit to import into the country of destination. In each case the country can restrict the MNC to reflect its own government's policies. Most countries' systems of trade permits, restrictions, and tariffs are more comprehensive than that of the United States. In European countries, for example, there is greater government involvement in economic planning for the country than there is in the United States. Japan, too, has a comprehensive economic plan that includes direct subsidies to businesses for complying with the plan. In Japan all foreign trade permits are reviewed to determine if they reflect the government's economic plan. Full employment, as a Japanese national policy, has led to massive subsidies to particular industries. As previously mentioned, Japan's steel industry is considered vital to the government's economic policy. The policy of full employment dictates that the steel mills operate at full capacity, and this requirement cannot be met if there is insufficient demand for the product or the price of selling the product is not economically feasible. If these conditions occur, Japan will infuse the steel industries with money to offset the losses incurred. This policy has, in the past few years, led to charges that the Japanese dump steel on foreign markets in an effort to force foreign steel makers out of the market.

Another example of using trade as a political weapon is the manipulation of oil production and pricing. OPEC (Organization of Petroleum Exporting Countries), reduced oil production and raised prices in an effort to acquire a peace settlement that would have been favorable to OPEC interests. In retaliation, Earl Butz, then Secretary of Agriculture, proposed withholding food exports.

Relations between the Soviet Union and the United States are a third example of the effect of economic policy and restrictions on business firms. Relations between the Soviet Union and the United States are not good. One point of contention is the violations of the Helsinki Accord by the Soviet Union and its aggression in Afghanistan. In response, Presidents Jimmy Carter and Ronald Reagan revoked the licenses of several U.S. firms to sell technical equipment to the Soviet Union.

Economic Development of Third World Nations

Private firms are also involved in governmental policies toward Third World development. Private investment and technological knowledge from U.S. firms have contributed to the economic development of the Third World nations. For example, the Bank of America headed a private consortium that arranged loan programs for several world agencies to aid Third World nations. The financial programs amounted to more than $420 million. The U.S. government has also worked with several MNCs in economic development projects that Third World nations need for growth and modernization. The MNCs provide the technical assistance, and the federal government provides the necessary funding, through either outright grants or low-interest, long-term loans to the developing country.

BUSINESS AS AN INSTRUMENT OF GOVERNMENT'S DOMESTIC POLICY

Direct or indirect domestic policies of America's government sector use business firms as a means to further their interests. As we brought out in Chapter 5, these government interests may or may not be to further the public interest, but all governments act to use business to reach their own goals. This is done in the United States, the Soviet Union, and in South American dictatorships. Business is vital to the internal economic and political welfare and stability of a country. Governments realize this and act accordingly. This

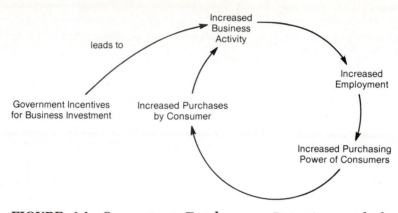

FIGURE 6.1 Government Employment Incentives and the Business Cycle.

means that in some cases, government decision making is influenced by business as well as business being influenced by government. There is a give-and-take relationship between business and government. It would not be in either group's best interest to weaken the other critically.

Employment Policies

Business is a major force in carrying out the employment policies of the government. If government maintains a domestic policy of full employment, or more realistically minimum unemployment, business, of course, is the major vehicle for carrying out this goal. Government actions through tax law changes, actions by the Federal Reserve to stimulate the economy to improve the employment picture, and job training programs sponsored by the federal government are dependent on business for implementation.

For example, the policies of the Reagan administration were tied directly to improving the climate for business so that business would be stimulated. A revitalized business sector would hire additional employees to meet the higher demand for goods and services. The result would be improved purchasing power of consumers, which would further boost the economy. This cyclical relationship is indicated in Figure 6.1. Obviously, the more the government can influence the purchase of domestic products by consumers and facilitate the competitive position of domestic organizations, the higher the probability that the goal of high levels of employment will be reached.

Economic Stability and Growth

Another major domestic goal of government is economic stability and growth. The role of business in the economic sphere is very similar to that of reaching high levels of employment. If there is a sustained upward level of business activity, there will be improved revenues for business, employees, and the government. The government benefits through increased tax revenues and increased economic stability. In addition, the levels of economic activity are further enhanced as employees save some of their income. These savings become sources of capital to finance future business growth and economic activity. Business is the vital link in this economic process.

As with employment policies, the government can make changes in monetary policy, tax policy, other laws, and changes in government purchases for goods and services that would tend to stimulate business activity. Such reasoning was behind the "trickle-down effect" used by the Reagan administration in their attempt to solve the economic ills of the country.

Regional Development Programs

The government also uses business to facilitate regional development programs. For example, many state governments have specific policies, often called *enterprise-zone legislation.* Through such legislation, areas can be designated as special incentive zones. The government provides a host of tax credits and special grants for businesses that locate in the designated areas.

The philosophy behind such regional development programs is that the location of private enterprise in depressed areas will tend to develop its economic base. With the establishment of an economic base in a community or region, it follows that there will be an increase in spending power of employees, which will attract other service and ancillary businesses, such

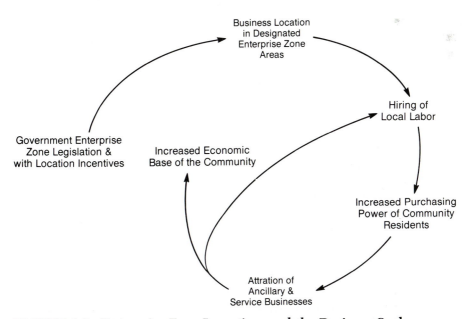

FIGURE 6.2   Enterprise-Zone Incentives and the Business Cycle.

as home-repair companies, restaurants, retail stores, gas stations, and service-based organizations. The addition of these support businesses would further assist the economy of the area and thus the long-run improvement of the local citizenry. This cyclical pattern is demonstrated in Figure 6.2.

Obviously, businesses have a predominate role in improving depressed areas. Government could not do the job itself without severalfold increases in the resources that would be needed to support an enterprise-zone designation. Interestingly enough, the federal enterprise zone was not passed in Congress. Hence, although several states have some form of enterprise-zone legislation, the federal government does not have a comprehensive program to attract industry into specifically designated areas except through several separate programs.

Business Input into Government Service

A major role of business is to provide the development and production of goods and services for government. For example, the federal government relies on private business firms for the development of defense and military hardware. Either direct purchases are made of existing products, such as in the purchase of clothing or computer equipment, or the government will contract with a private firm to do research and development of a product or service. For example, the current state of the art military tank was developed and produced by a division of Chrysler. Much of the nuclear submarine fleet was developed and produced by General Dynamics.

Over the years, the government has relied on business for many of its products and services. This mutual dependency has led to a host of interesting potential conflicts of interests that have been highly publicized: for example, high costs for replacement parts, ashtrays that cost $500 each, or toilet facilities that cost several hundred times more than they would if a private citizen would purchase the product. The mutual dependency tends to lead to less vigilance in costing of products and an apparent willingness to allow excessive costs to be charged.

Energy Exploration

Another area of government using business is energy exploration. Through a tax policy of energy credits for conservation measures and through accelerated depletion allowances for energy exploration, the government has facilitated reaching its energy policies through private enterprise activities. To further its energy goals, the federal government also deregulated the price of oil so that market forces could aid the process of exploration. There was some concern before deregulation that energy prices were too low, thereby reducing the incentive for business to find new supplies. The end results were shortages of natural gas and spot shortages of fuel oil and gasoline. After deregulation, prices increased but supplies became more abundant. For the U.S. government, there were increased energy supplies increased exploration activities, a stabilization of oil prices, and a larger percentage of supplies coming from domestic sources such as Alaska and off the U.S. coast in the Pacific Ocean and the Gulf of Mexico.

A Policy of "Privatization"

The Reagan administration accelerated the process of using business to further governmental and eventually societal goals. President Reagan defined this process as less government intervention and the increase of *privatization* of traditional public-sector enterprises. Translated, this means that there has been a deliberate policy in the Reagan administration to transfer many government programs away from government control to the private sector. For example, the Comprehensive Employment Training Act (CETA) was dismantled in favor of the Manpower Development and Training Act (MDTA). The CETA program involved the government directly in providing many of the funds for the employee training process. The emphasis of the MDTA is to provide additional incentives for businesses themselves to conduct training programs for hard-core unemployed. However, the government subsidizes the program and the wages of disadvantaged workers while they progress through the program. The program, too, is quite liberal in that a training program can be broadly defined as simple on-the-job training.

In sum, there is increasing recognition by the U.S. government that the private sector can be an important instrument in the development and execution of domestic policies. Instead of massive government resources dedicated to domestic programs, the same level of results can be achieved with tax and government incentives. It looks as if the future trend will be toward even greater use of business to accomplish government aims. This has particular implications for large firms and certain industries, such as those in energy, aerospace, heavy equipment, and high tech, which will be major targets of government because of the scope of influence that they have on society as a whole. There are some positive and negative consequences for business from such attempts by government to influence business.

POSITIVE CONSEQUENCES OF GOVERNMENT INTRUSION

There are a number of benefits that accrue to business through government actions. There are some obvious benefits, such as the highway and water systems and the actions taken by government to facilitate air traffic control and the development of airports. In addition, government is a good customer for many business firms and, of course, government can facilitate domestic business through import quotas or duties. But perhaps the most important benefit may be the order and stability that the government brings to the open marketplace. This relates to the economic forum that government provides, a regulatory ordering, and actions that facilitate the movement of goods and services.

Economic Order

The economic order that government brings to the marketplace relates to the support provided to the economic system for both domestic and international transactions. For example, the Federal Reserve system in the United States takes direct actions to influence interest rates, money supply, and inflation rates. This direct action tends to stabilize the value of the dollar, which facilitates an orderly system of transactions.

Confidence in the value of the dollar is an important factor in facilitating the transaction of goods and services. Without confidence in the value of the dollar, there is a probability that individuals and businesses will not want to make long-term price and supply commitments, and will be less prone to want to save for future expansion. Instead, a consumption mentality will take effect, as material possessions are more likely than the currency to have stable value. For example, during the intense inflationary period in the world in recent years, there has been lower confidence in a stable value of money. As a result, people save less money and acquire goods and services. Also under these conditions, people contract greater debt because during inflationary periods the future value of the currency is anticipated to be less. Investments are directed at items that are appreciating more quickly and are of more enduring value, such as precious metals, land, and high-quality paintings. Under such conditions there is a chaotic economic environment. Business has difficulty in planning for the future, cannot obtain the financing it needs to support future growth, and faces difficulty in foreign transactions. A strong government presence in maintaining a stable economic environment is therefore very beneficial to business.

Maintaining a Competitive Marketplace

Government can promote a competitive environment for business through regulatory actions. At first glance, it may appear that business would be adverse to government controls of any kind. However, the reality of most regulation is that it applies uniform control on *all* business firms. This control applies the same ground rules to each organization. The consistency has important ramifications for socially responsible behavior.

As presented in Chapter 3, Milton Friedman maintains that the only responsibility that business has to society is to do the best job it can in making a good product at a low cost. This school of thought maintains that there should be little social responsibility besides meeting the parameters that the government mandates. A manager who goes beyond this narrow definition of social responsibility is acting not in the best interest of the employees, owners, customers, or public at large. Hence, the chief executive officer (CEO) who may want to act more responsibly and commit resources to a safer product, better working environment, or provide a cleaner, safer environment may not feel that it is appropriate to do so given that the competition may not act in the same way. If the competition does not act in the same manner, the result is that the socially responsible company is working at a competitive disadvantage. By having greater government regulation, the CEO can act in a more socially responsive manner, knowing that the same regulations apply to his or her competitors as well.

This benefit of uniformity applies to all sorts of business regulations: pollution control, product safety, labor safety and health, wage and salary policies, pension programs, environmental protection, and marketing practices as well as the obvious competitive practices.

Consumer and Public Confidence

A closely related aspect of facilitating the competitive market conditions is the confidence that consumers have in business. Government standards and regulations tend to increase consumer confidence in the products and services that business can provide. For example, consumer safety laws aid to build consumer confidence that the product they are buying is safe and has had some implied and limited warranty with regard to the product's quality. In addition, the government actions tend to drive out the less scrupulous businesses. Without the government's restrictions, the marketplace motto "let the buyer beware" would prevail, leading to less consumer confidence in business in general.

NEGATIVE CONSEQUENCES OF GOVERNMENT INTRUSION

Besides the positives, there can be negative consequences for both business and society from either direct or indirect government actions. These consequences can also be intended or unintended. Intended consequences are those resulting from public policies carried out as planned and having the desired effect on business. Unintended consequences are those resulting from the execution of public policy, because of overregulation, excessive costs associated with compliance, or the effects of government influences on the marketplace.

The Effects of Overregulation

Almost every organization is influenced by several government regulations, executed by differing federal agencies. At times, the demands placed on business by these agencies have threatened the survival of many of them, and critics argue that the regulatory agencies sometimes do not seem to be serving the public. For example, the Interstate Commerce Commission (ICC) was established in 1881 to regulate the railroads. At that time the railroad monopoly was, in many cases, harming the general public, and the ICC did much to curb the abuses. However, after years of regulations and bureaucratic procedures, some of the laws that at one time protected the consumer

SUPERCORPORATION: IS BEING BIG EVIL?

The question of size and potential power of organizations is not a new issue. During the end of the last century and through the early part of this century through the administration of Theodore Roosevelt, there was much public debate over the actions of corporations. One thing is certain, corporations are big and getting bigger (see the box). Some political groups advocated that size, in itself, was evil and should be controlled by government. The Sherman and Clayton Acts are major pieces of antitrust legislation that evolved from this period. The acts attempt to establish a legal guideline between proper and improper activities of business in influencing the marketplace and fostering a competitive environment.

The backdrop of legislation has been directed toward five major concerns: collusion, monopolization, exclusionary practices, mergers, and unfair and deceptive practices.[1] These are the direct result of government's concern to ensure

1. Maintenance of competition.
2. Fair conduct in the marketplace both between businesses and customers and between businesses competing against one another.
3. Desirable economic performance or market efficiency. This is different from ensuring that an industry or company is profitable, more directed to the premise that there has been an efficient allocation between parties in that there is not undue control of one party distorting the transaction of goods or services.
4. Limitation of big business.[2]

Only one of the four concerns above is related to size per se. Yet size has been a concern even in the current political arena. The most recent legislation proposed was that of Senators Ted Kennedy, Howard Metzenbaum, Lawrence Pressler, John Melcher, and George McGovern. The legislation proposed in 1979 was referred to as the Small and Independent Business Protection Act. Under the proposed legislation, businesses having revenues exceeding $2 billion or assets exceeding $350 million could not merge. Section 3 of the proposed legislation allowed mergers in cases where it could be demonstrated that competition would be enhanced or that substantial efficiencies would result or if the parties involved have divested themselves of the same or greater assets and revenues as had the smaller party to the transaction.[3]

The thrust of this proposed law and of much of the concern over supercorporations is that size, in itself, is undesirable even though misuse of power

---

[1]Douglas F. Greer, *Business, Government, and Society* (New York: Macmillan, 1981), p. 107.
[2]Greer, pp. 105–106.
[3]See S600 Business Protection Act of 1979.

BIG AND GETTING BIGGER

In recent years many firms have begun merging or acquiring other companies. The result is that firms holding a sizable portion of one industry are now becoming even larger, and those that have purchased firms in other industries are proving to be serious competitors in more than one arena. Over the last decade, some of the biggest mergers ($2 billion or more) have been the following:

This Firm:	Bought This Company:	For This Much Money:
Chevron	Gulf Oil	$13,200,000,000
Texaco	Getty Oil	10,100,100,000
DuPont	Conoco	8,000,000,000
U.S. Steel	Marathon Oil	6,600,000,000
Mobil	Superior Oil	5,700,000,000
Royal Dutch/ Shell	Shell Oil	5,500,000,000
Elf Aquitaine	Texasgulf	4,300,000,000
Occidental Petroleum	Cities Service	4,100,000,000
Capital Cities	American Broadcasting Company	3,500,000,000
Nestle	Carnation	2,900,000,000
Flour	St. Joseph Minerals	2,700,000,000
General Motors	Electonic Data Systems	2,500,000,000
Beatrice	Esmark	2,500,000,000
Peter Kiewit et al.	Continental Group	2,500,000,000
Kuwait	Sante Fe International	2,500,000,000
Broken Hill Proprietary	Utah International from General Electric	2,400,000,000
Sun Co.	Texas Pacific Oil from Seagram	2,300,000,000
Standard Oil, Ohio	Kennecott	2,100,000,000

that comes with large organizations has not been demonstrated. Where does this mistrust of size come from? Part of the feeling may be in the rapid growth of large organizations over the past several decades and in the sheer size of many supercorporations. As Table 7.1 indicates, the revenues generated by many supercorporations far exceed the gross national product of many

TABLE 7.1. **Countries with the Highest Gross National Product Compared with U.S. Firms and Non-U.S. Firms with the Highest Sales Volumes (Millions of Dollars).**

Country or Company	1980 GNP or Revenue	Home Country of Company
United States	2,582,160	
Soviet Union	1,212,030	
Japan	1,152,910	
West Germany	827,790	
France	627,700	
Great Britain	442,870	
Italy	368,860	
China	283,250	
Brazil	243,240	
Canada	242,530	
Spain	199,780	
The Netherland	161,440	
India	159,430	
Mexico	144,000	
Australia	142,240	
Poland	139,780	
East Germany	120,940	
Belgium	119,770	
Sweden	111,900	
Exxon	110,469	United States
Switzerland	106,300	
Saudi Arabia	100,930	
Czechoslovakia	89,260	
Nigeria	85,510	
Royal Dutch Shell	79,418.1	Netherlands, Great Britain
Austria	76,530	
South Africa	66,960	
Argentina	66,430	
Denmark	66,350	
Turkey	66,080	
Mobil	63,652	United States
Indonesia	61,770	
South Korea	58,580	
Yugoslavia	58,570	
General Motors	57,728	United States
Venezuela	54,220	
Texaco	52,486	United States
Romania	52,010	
Norway	51,610	
AT&T	50,233	United States
British Petroleum	49,471.1	Great Britain

TABLE 7.1.   Continued

Country of Company	1980 GNP or Revenue	Home Country of Company
Finland	47,280	
Hungary	44,990	
Standard Oil of California	42,900	United States
Greece	42,190	
Iraq	39,500	
Bulgaria	37,390	
Ford	37,088	United States
Algeria	36,410	
Philippines	34,350	
Columbia	31,570	
Thailand	31,140	
Kuwait	30,900	
Standard Oil of Indiana	27,800	United States
Gulf Oil	26,884	United States
United Arab Emirates	26,850	
Englehard Minerals & Chemicals	26,570	United States
IBM	26,213	United States
Libya	25,730	
ENI	24,985	Italy
General Electric	24,960	United States
Pakistan	24,870	
Unilevel	24,311	Great Britain, Netherlands
Atlantic Richfield	24,156	United States
Chile	23,980	
ITT	23,819	United States
New Zealand	23,160	
Egypt	23,140	
Portugal	23,140	
Sears	23,037	United States
Malaysia	22,410	
Cie Français de Pétroles	22,311	France
Hong Kong	21,500	
VEBA	21,288	Germany
Shell Oil	19,959	United States
Petroles de Venezuela	18,822	Venezuela
Conoco	18,800	United States
BAT ind.	18,310	Great Britain
Renault	17,687	France
Siemens	17,629	Germany
Israel	17,440	
Morocco	17,440	
Philips	17,234	Netherlands
Elf Aquitaine	16,936	France

TABLE 7.1.   Continued

Country or Company	1980 GNP or Revenue	Home Country of Company
Volkswagen	16,896	West Germany
Peru	16,470	
Nippon Oil	16,246	Japan
Ireland	16,130	
Fiat	15,800	Italy
Diamler-Benz	15,757	West Germany
Peugeot	15,700	France
Toyota Motor	15,688	Japan
Hoechst	15,179	West Germany
Safeway Stores	15,103	United States
Thyssen	14,964	West Germany

Source: Adapted from Standard & Poor's Compustat Service, Inc., *World Bank Atlas,* 1981.

countries. In addition, the rapid growth of many organizations has alarmed many interest groups that influence the formation of public policy.

There are four types of growth patterns for organizations. One type is *horizontal growth,* where an organization grows through aggressive sales or through the acquisition of other organizations that are in the same business. The organization stays in the same industry but grows through an increase in market share. For example, General Motors has grown through aggressive marketing to obtain about 47 percent of the domestic market for new automobiles and to almost 60 percent of the domestic market for railroad diesel and electric locomotives.

A second type is *vertical growth,* which is accomplished as an organization develops its own or acquires other organizations in different stages of the production or distribution process. For example, U.S. Steel, starting in the 1860s, integrated backward—moving from steel production to ownership of iron ore and coal mines, ships, and railroads. This helped to ensure that they would have a reliable supply of material and service at a controllable cost. In fact, U.S. Steel has the largest fleet of ships in the Great Lakes, with 44 ships registered, nearly double its nearest competitor. Vertical growth can be forward or backward.

Backward vertical integration is growth moving toward the raw material stage of production, as in the U.S. Steel example. *Forward vertical integration* is directed toward the final distribution stages of the product or service. For example, General Motors' acquisition of its own dealer network is an example of forward integration. GM moved from just producing automobiles to direct selling.

A third type of integration is *concentric diversification,* where an organization acquires or develops organizations that produce complementary or related products. For example, the movement of United Parcel into the overnight air express market is an example of concentric diversification.

Finally, *conglomerate diversification* is movement of an organization into unrelated product or service areas. For example, the acquisition by PepsiCo (Pepsi Cola's holding company) of North American Van Lines is an example of a conglomerate growth.

Conglomerate growth has been particularly troublesome to some because the size of conglomerates seems to have no limits. Whereas vertical growth and horizontal growth are limited by the size of the market for a particular set of products or markets, conglomerate growth is not (see Table 7.2). While conglomerate growth does not imply higher levels of control, some public policymakers feel that the potential is there to influence society and competition unjustly, and that size, by itself, ought to be contained.

TABLE 7–2. Examples of Conglomerate Ownership.

Parent Company	Subsidiaries
Amfac	*Food:* C&H sugar, Fisher cheese, Monterey mushrooms, Lawb-Western frozen potatoes, Pacific Pearl seafoods, Puna papayas
	Department stores: Liberty House, Kavai Stores
	Restaurants: Fred Harvey
	Hotels: Airport Marina, Amfac, Island Holidays, Metropolitan Motels
	Country clubs: Silverado Country Club (Napa, California)
	Resorts: Grand Canyon National Park Lodges, Coco Palm Resorts (Hawaii)
	Financial services: Amfac Commercial Credit
	Nurseries: Amfac (Hawaii), Glenn Walters (Oregon), Selest (California)
	Insurance: ARMS
	Tours: Hawaiian Discovery
City Investing	*Air conditioning:* Rheem, Ruud
	Motels: Motel 6
	Mobile homes: Great Lakes, Magnolia, Leisurama, Staler, Wayco
	Insurance: Home Insurance
	Fast foods: Red Barn
	Banking: Southern California Savings & Loan
	Plastics: Alma Plastics (Alma, Michigan)
	Aircraft maintenance: Hayes International
	Property: Sterling Forest (north of New York City)
	Substantial stock in: Stokely-Van Camp foods

TABEL 7.2.   Continued

Parent Company	Subsidiaries
Dart & Kraft Industries	*Kitchenware:* Tupperware
	Cookware: West Bend
	Batteries: Duracell
	Cosmetics: Vanda
	Plastic coverings: Wilsonart
	Dairy products: Kraft, Sealtest, Breakstone, Light n' Lively, Parkay, Velveeta, Philadelphia Brand, Cracker Barrel, Breyer's
	Other grocery products: Miracle Whip salad dressing, Kraft dinners, snacks, peanut butter, salad dressings and condiments, Cheez 'n Crackers
	Houseware: Chilton, Slick-Kote, Globe
	Toys: Fun Trend
Gulf & Western Industries, Inc.	*Movies:* Paramount
	Book publishing: Simon & Schuster, Summit, Sovereign, Pocket Books, Archway, Fireside, Touchstone, Wallaby, Monarch, Julian Messner, Wanderer
	Sports arenas: Madison Square Garden, Roosevelt Raceway, Arlington Park
	Sports teams: New York Knickerbockers, New York Rangers, Washington Diplomats
	Cigars: Don Diego, Don Marcos, Don Miguel, Flamenco, H. Upmann, Montecristo, Montecruz, Por Larranaga, Primo del Rey, Dutch Masters, El Producto, Muriel, Capitan de Tueros, Ben Franklin, Harvester, La Palina, Lovera, 1886, Tipalet, Dutch Treats
	Tobacco: Mixture No. 79, Old Grand Dad, Sutliff Private Stock, Heine's Blend pipe tobacco, Rogers Pouch tobacco
	Pipe lighter: Nimrod
	Candy: Schraffts, Lewis, King Kup, Wallace, Terry
	Auto parts: A.P.S., Big A
	Swim and sportswear: Cole of California, Catalina, Sandcastle, Going Places, Bay Club, Malibu, Bob Mackie, John Newcombe
	Lingerie: Kayser
	Gloves: Kayser, Halston
	Sleepwear: Her Majesty, Nazareth
	Men's wear: Excello, John Weitz, Oscar de la Renta, Mavest, Tassel, Champion
	Belts: Paris
	Hosiery: No Nonsense, Easy To Be Me, Sheer Indulgence, Supp-hose, Mojud, Kayser, Interwoven, Esquire

TABLE 7.2.   Continued

Parent Company	Subsidiaries
	Slippers: Jiffies
	Shoes: Bostonian, Stetson, London Character, Pacer, After Six, Jack Nicklaus, Sandler of Boston
	Paper products: Nibroc, Pert, Purity towels and napkins, Paper Maid, Handi-Pac, Aristocrat food containers
	Matches: Monarch, Superior
	Loan offices: Associates
	Insurance: Capital (life), Providence (property and casualty)
	Sugar mill: World's largest (Dominican Republic)
	Resorts: (Dominican Republic)
	Dock and shipping facilities: (Dominican Republic)
	Railroad: (Dominican Republic)
	Office buildings: (Florida)
	Refinery: (Florida)
	Substantial stock holdings in: Sherwin-Williams' Paint, Uniroyal tires, Amfac (see above), Cummins Engine, Jonathan Logan women's apparel, West Point Pepperel bedding and linens
	Miscellaneous: 250 manufacturing plants, 5 quarries, 16 concrete plants, Zinc mines
I.C. Industries	*Roadside restaurant and gift shops:* Stuckey's
	Party supply stores: Vendome (California), 9–0–5 (Missouri)
	Soft drinks: Dad's Root Beer, Bubble-up
	Auto parts: Midas
	Candy: Whitman's, Stuckey's
	Mexican food: Old El Paso
	Canned milk: Pet
	Cereal: Heartland
	Snack food: Laura Scudder's
	Diet food: Sego
	Nuts: Funsten, Haig Berberian
	Fruit products: Musselman's
	Seafoods: Gulf Belle shrimp, Orleans oysters
	Bakery goods: Aunt Fanny's, Pet, Pet Ritz pie crusts, Downyflake waffles and frozen foods
	Railroad: Illinois Central Gulf, 8,850 miles of track, 45,000 freight cars, 1,000 locomotives
	Miscellaneous: 65 Abex factories, 65 pet food plants, 311 Stuckey's, 10 Midas factories, 10 Pepsi plants in the Midwest, real estate in Chicago and New Orleans
International Telephone & Telegraph Corporation	*Bakery products:* Wonder Bread, Hostess Twinkies, cupcakes, and Sno-Balls
	Frozen food: Morton

TABLE 7.2. Continued

Parent Company	Subsidiaries
	Lawn-care products: Scott's Turf Builder, Turf Builder Plus 2, and Grass Seed
	Meats: Gwaltney Ham, Great Dogs (chicken dogs), Genuine Smithfield
	Books: Bobbs-Merrill, Marquis Who's Who
	Soft drinks: C&C Cola
	Hotels: Sheraton
	Insurance: Hartford
	Miscellaneous: $23 billion of factories, real estate, forests, coal, oil, and securities in United States and abroad
Northwest Industries	*Underwear:* Fruit of the Loom, Underoos, B.V.D.
	Boots: Acme, Dingo, Polo, Ralph Lauren, Dan Post
	Liquor (imports): Cutty Sark, Cutty 12 Scotch whiskys, Finlandia vodka, Mouton Cadet and Marquisat wines
	Bottled water: Arrowhead Puritas
	Miscellaneous: Microdot Corporation, Coca-Cola bottling plant in California
RCA	*Televisions and radios:* RCA
	Rental cars: Hertz
	Frozen foods: Banquet
	Rugs: Coronet
	Records: RCA
	Greetings cards: Gibson, Buzza, Cleo Wrap, Pleasant Thoughts, Success
	Office furniture: All-Steel
	Video cassettes and discs: SelectaVision
	Miscellaneous: 65 plants: 47 in United States and 18 in foreign countries, 9 TV and radio stations
Transamerica	*Rental cars:* Budget
	Consumer loans: Pacific Finance
	Insurance: Occidental, American Life of New York, Transamerica, Wolverine, Riverside, Premier, Automotive
	Moving: Lyon Moving & Storage
	Films: United Artists
	Airline: Transamerican Airlines
	Miscellaneous: Transamerica DeLand, 10 plants producing turbines, compressors, pumps, and condensers, United Artists Building (New York City), Occidental Center (Los Angeles), Transamerica Building (San Francisco)

Source: Adapted from Milton Moskowitz, Michael Katz, and Robert Levering, *Everybody's Business: An Almanac—An Irreverent Guide to Corporate America* (San Francisco: Harper & Row, 1980), p. 862.

While size may be an easy way to categorize companies and as a determinant of "goodness" or "badness," a more real concern probably relates to the potential concentration of economic and market power that a corporation may wield. This power is related to size, to some degree, but there are other important dimensions to also consider.

CONCENTRATION OF POWER: A THREAT TO COMPETITION?

Most of government's concerns relating to antitrust legislation really refer to the fear of misuse of power by big corporations. Interestingly enough, the concern of government relates primarily to the balance of power in the marketplace. Given the potential influence that firms may have as a counterforce against government through lobbying and campaign contributions, it would seem that there should be some real concern with power along this line. In reality, however, this potential abuse of corporations has been addressed through disclosure acts, Securities and Exchange Commission (SEC) rules, and campaign contribution laws. What seems to be lacking, however, is a realization of the economic clout and the ability to develop support that is possible with a large organization through advertising, letters to employees, and funding to professional lobbying organizations or trade associations. For example, Wal-Mart Stores, Inc., the second largest department store chain in the United States, has over 100,000 employees and over 950 retail outlets, and this is a relatively undiversified organization. Consider Dart & Kraft Industries, Gulf & Western, or Exxon. The potential to influence is ever present.

How real is this threat of concentration of power, or what might be called superconcentration? Consider Figure 7.1. It shows the power structure of the Penn Central Company, a holding company formed after the merger of the New York Central and Pennsylvania railroads. Notice the percent ownership of the Penn Central Company in other firms indicated in Figure 7.1. Realize that controlling interest can be guaranteed with over 50 percent control over another company and effective control can be maintained with less than 30 percent control in most cases. In Penn Central's case, almost all the holdings indicated were under the potential direct control of the chief executive officer, who at the time was Stuart Saunders.

The Penn Central, the largest railroad in the United States before it became the largest single bankruptcy of a U.S. railroad in 1970, is not unique. Compared to some of the supercorporations of today, Penn Central was in a junior league. Most large to very large organizations have the same, if not greater potential to control. They direct thousands of employees and millions of dollars of assets while controlling substantial segments of the market directly. For example, consider Exxon, with its 130,000 employees and sales of $110 billion, which is the largest company in oil, natural gas, and retail gasoline sales industry and also has the world's largest shipping fleet. The company itself has higher revenues than all but 19 nations, with revenues

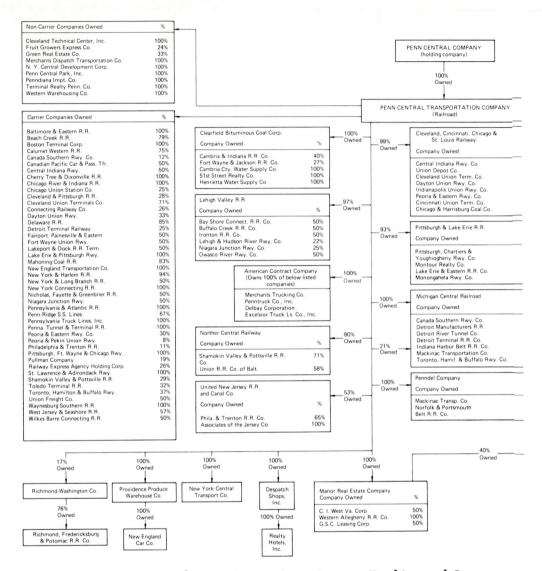

FIGURE 7.1 Penn Central. From House Committee on Banking and Currency, p. 113.

comparable to the gross national product of Sweden and Switzerland. The potential concentration issue becomes of great importance when considering corporations of this magnitude.

What of the argument that most corporations are not family controlled anymore, but are owned by thousands of stockholders—thus control is maintained through many, not few individuals. Edward S. Herman's work[4]

[4]Edward S. Herman, *Corporate Control, Corporate Power* (Cambridge: Cambridge University Press, 1981).

The Penn Central empire. A chart prepared by the House Committee on
Banking and Currency staff. The immense scope of what was once a $6.5
billion corporation is shown. (House Committee on Banking and Currency)

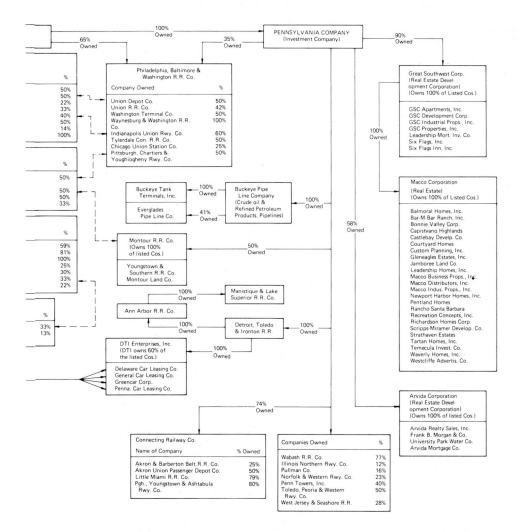

would, on the surface at least, support this claim. Family control of businesses
has been substantially reduced over the past 45 years. In addition, of the
largest 200 nonfinancial corporations, the number of shareholders for each
firm has increased substantially over the past 45 years. This would tend to
support the claim that ownership, and therefore control, is less concentrated
than it was previously. Or is that the case?

Following Mintzberg's model, presented in Chapter 1, the concept of shareholders as an external group was introduced. In essence, Mintzberg believes
that shareholders are an external group, virtually removed from the decision-

making capacity of the organization.[5] The formal coalition and peak coordinator, as described by Mintzberg, make the major decisions in the organization. The peak coordinator is normally the chief executive officer, and the formal coalition is the board of directors. However, in many organizations, the major power base rests with the operating team of professional managers. They have greater power because they have much more day-to-day information about the company.

By maintaining control over this information, operating managers have much greater control than outside directors on the board. Through the use of proxy statements, the management team can maintain effective control over the organization even to the company's detriment. For example, the $4 billion cost of Phillips Petroleum's efforts to avoid hostile takeover bids by T. Boone Pickens and Carl Icon was considered by some to damage Phillips ability to compete. Management won the war but not without great costs to the shareholders in terms of the future viability of the company.

The shareholders' alternatives, because their power is so diffused, is to sell their stock if they are not happy, buy enough stock to be elected to the board, or form a coalition of other shareholders. Through voting procedures and other acts, management can do much to diffuse their power.[6]

The result is that even though there is less of concentration of corporate ownership through shareholders, there is increased power wielded by the professional management team, as there is less power held by individual shareholders. Given the size of the many firms and the degree of control that is possible through a holding company network, the power of the chief executive officer (CEO) can be great indeed.

Concentration can go beyond direct control over a particular firm or family of firms. Many organizations, particularly large financial institutions, have expanded their influence potential through the routine use of interlocking directorships. *Interlocks* are of two types. *Direct interlocks* exist when one person is on the board of directors of two organizations, for example, when William O. Beers served as director of both Kraftco and Manufacturers Hanover Trust. An *indirect interlock* exists when two directors, each from a different company, meet on the board of a third company. An example existed in the late 1970s when William O. Beers, from Manufacturers Hanover Trust, and Norma Pace, a director of Chase Manhattan, were members of the board of directors of Sears. Obviously, a direct interlock is more relevant than an indirect interlock in terms of concentration of power.[7]

Control and concentration of power need not be relegated only to control over the internal company structure or contol of economic resources. There is also a significant relationship between business and government. The influence of big business on government goes beyond lobbying efforts and

[5]Henry Mintzberg, *Power in and Around Organizations* (Englewood Cliffs, N.J.: Prentice-Hall, 1983).

[6]Ford S. Worthy, "What's Next for the Raiders," *Fortune*, November 11, 1985, pp. 20–24.

[7]Herman, p. 198.

can become much more direct. Consider the importance of big business in a government's domestic and foreign policies. This was introduced in Chapters 5 and 6. It was shown that big business and government develop a working relationship that often leads to things such as co-mingling of individuals from industrial positions to government positions. For example, W. Graham Claytor was the former CEO of the Southern Railway, then became an Assistant Secretary of the Navy, and currently has the position of the chief operating officer of AMTRAK. Some firms have had longer histories of such relationships. James Knowles[8] traced the influence of the Rockefeller financial group in the government sector and found a host of connections between government and the Rockefeller financial group's operating management over the years. Table 7.3 traces his findings.

In summary, there is a clear concentration of power in corporate American life. This concentration is the result of size, control over subsidiaries, through direct and indirect interlocks, and through appointments of business leaders to government positions. Concentration of power and the misuse of that power has been at the forefront of public policy in antitrust matters. At the core has been the identification of potential abuses. However, before considering the major problems of concentration, the potential benefits will be reviewed.

BENEFITS OF SUPERCORPORATIONS/SUPERCONCENTRATION

Do superconcentration or supercorporations offer a threat to or an opportunity for society? If the potential disadvantages seem unacceptable, then it may be appropriate for public policy to curb the potential for abuse or to eliminate the large corporation, interlocking directors, or large conglomerates. But if society determines that there are potential public benefits, the public policy should foster the development of these supercorporations. There are degrees of public policy: discouraging or encouraging the formation of superconcentration or supercorporation or passing laws to reduce the possible abuse of supercorporate powers. There are two kinds of possible benefit from supercorporation or superconcentration: the benefit of the superpower to the corporate entity and the benefits to society as a whole.

Benefits to the Company

The company benefits in four ways when it decides to become a conglomerate or when it becomes the dominating company in a particular industry. These benefits are stated as general relationships, which depend, of course, on

---

[8]James C. Knowles, "The Rockefeller Financial Group, in *Superconcentration/Supercorporation,* ed. Ralph L. Andreano, (Andover, Mass.: Warner Modular Publications, 1973), pp. 343–344.

TABLE 7.3. Government Positions Held by Persons with Close Ties to the Rockefeller Group.

Name	Rockefeller Group Connection	Government Position
Winthrop Aldrich	Rockefeller family (son-in-law of John D. Rockefeller)	Ambassador to England, 1953–57
Eugene Black	Dir., Chase Manhattan Bank (and one-time executive officer of the Chase Manhattan Bank)	Pres., World Bank, 1949–62; Special Advisor to President for Economic and Social Developments in Southeast Asia, 1965–69; chairman, Council of Economic Advisors for N.Y. State
Roger Blough	Dir., Equitable; past Chairman of U.S. Steel	Member, General Advisory Committee of U.S. Arms Control and Disarmament Agency
Arleigh Burke	Dir., Freeport Sulphur and Texaco, Inc.	Chief, U.S. Naval Operations, 1955–61
John Connor	Dir., Chase Manhattan	Secretary of Commerce, 1963–65
Arthur Dean	Partner, Sullivan & Cromwell (Standard Oil of New Jersey's law firm)	Special Ambassador to Korea, 1953–54; Chairman, U.S. delegation, 18-nation disarmament conference, 1962; Chairman, U.S. Geneva Conf. Delegation, 1961–62
C. Douglas Dillon	Dir., Chase Manhattan	Ambassador to France, 1953–57; Under Secretary of State for Economic Affairs, 1958–59; Under Secretary of State, 1959–60; Secretary of Treasury, 1960–65
Allen Dulles	Partner, Sullivan & Cromwell; Pres., Council on Foreign Relations	Dir., CIA, 1953–61
John Foster Dulles	Partner, Sullivan & Cromwell; Ch., Rockefeller Foundation Trustees	Secretary of State, 1952–59
Gilbert Fitzhugh	Dir., Chase Manhattan; Ch., Metropolitan	Ch., President's Blue Ribbon Defense Panel
Peter Flanigan	Partner, Dillon, Read & Co.	Assistant to President for Economic Affairs 1969–72
Lincoln Gordon	Dir., Equitable	Ambassador to Brazil, 1961–66; Asst. Secretary of State-Inter-Am. Affairs, 1966–67

ket dominance or
In a conglomerate,
result is that if on
should still remain
will be able to infl
stable demand for
actions of others. I
is, in essence, sprea
with multiple inves
sentation on the b
loaned money to f
interlocks between
the extensive loans
tions.

A second benefit i
ing resources. Toge
better able to attrac
Motors Acceptance
the financial marke
Machines) enables i
lower than smaller
entrepreneurships c

A third benefit of
diversity, the compa
Transamerica Corpo
until antitrust laws
that time the comp
oriented industries
sumer loans (Pacific
cal competence in
Although each divis
of one may be calle
marketing family fil
ing department of I
a large corporate er
tence.

A fourth benefit i
greater technical co
favorable competitiv
capital, the larger c
needed in order to i
to adapt to new techi
ing campaigns. In t
can be staggered so
while making invest

TABLE 7.3. Continued

Name	Rockefeller Group Connection	Government Position
Alfred Gruenther	Dir., New York Life, Fed. Dept. Stores	Retired army officer; Member, Gen. Advisory Committee of Arms Control and Disarmament Agency, 1966–69; Pres. Comm. on all volunteer army, 1969
Ben Heineman	Dir., Metropolitan, First National Bank of Chicago	Ch., White House Conference on Civil Rights, 1966; Ch., President's Task Force on Govt. Organization, 1966–67; President's Commission on Income Maintenance programs, 1967–
William Hewlett	Dir., Chase Manhattan	Pres. Gen. Advisory Comm. on Foreign Assistance, 1965–68; Member, President's Science Advisory Committee, 1966–69
Paul Hoffman	Dir., New York Life	Dir., UN Development Program, 1966–
Amory Houghton	Dir., First National City Bank, Metropolitan Life	Ambassador to France, 1957–61
Henry Kissinger	Dir., Special Studies Project for Rockefeller Bros. Fund, 1956–58; Nuclear Weapons & Foreign Policy Dir., Council on Foreign Relations, 1955–56; Editor of *Foreign Affairs*; Nelson Rockefeller's personal advisor on foreign policy	U.S. Arms Control & Disarmament Agency Consultant, 1961–67; Assistant to Pres., Foreign Policy, 1969 and later Secretary of State
John J. McCloy	Past Ch., Chase Manhattan Council on Foreign Relations	U.S. High Commission for Germany; Pres. World Bank, 1947–49; Asst. Secretary of War, 1941–45; Coordinator, disarmament negotiations, 1961–63; long-time advisor to U.S. Govt. on national security affairs
Neil McElroy	Dir., Equitable	Secretary of Defense, 1957–59
Paul Nitze	Past partner, Dillon, Read & Co.	Secretary of Navy, 1963–67; Deputy Secretary of Defense, 1967–69; Director foreign policy planning staff; Dept. of State, 1950–53

TABLE 7.3. (

Name
David Packard
Charles Percy
James A. Perkii
John D. Rockefeller I\
Nelson Rockefel
Winthrop Rockefeller
Dean Rusk
Lewis Strauss
R. D. Stuart

Source: James C.
ration, ed. Ralph
344.

the vitality an
of the compa
increased size
earlier, shows
One benefit

An example of an MNC's actions is that of a soft-drink manufacturer that expanded into a Third World nation. This company built a plant and trained local people to operate it. Next, it helped develop a bottle plant, a wooden-case manufacturer, cooler and machine manufacturers for dispensing the soft drinks, and a truck repair facility to maintain the vehicles used to distribute the soft drinks. This type of an approach may do much more for a less developed country than can government grants. A private company can more readily control expenses and ensure that available funds are used in the most efficient manner possible.

DISADVANTAGES OF SUPERCONCENTRATION OF POWER

There are four potential disadvantages of superconcentrations of power. These relate to the potential harm of misused economic power for the corporation's own interests. If the organization's principal goal is its survival, then that goal will take precedence over more socially based goals. A supercorporation's potential for abuse is also greater than that of a smaller business. Furthermore, size and power do not necessarily mean greater profits and more ability to attract capital. The Penn Central Railroad is an example of a company that was large (the largest railroad in the United States), yet went bankrupt. The problems of Chrysler in the early 1980s also show that size does not always mean success.

A disadvantage of supercorporations to society is their ability to influence public policy, thereby weakening the process of democratic representation. Knowles and others questioned whether the influence of big business, affected the independence of decision making *on behalf* of government.[9] There seems to be little evidence that this has been the case, but an improper relationship may still ensue. For example, ITT allegedly attempted to influence the Central Intelligence Agency to intervene in the elections of Chile. Other companies have been implicated in bribes and payoffs to foreign and domestic officials in the hope of influencing legislation and obtaining permits to do business. It is these types of abuses that become possible whenever much power is concentrated in one or a few companies.

A second disadvantage is the possibility of stifling competition. With their ability to attract large amounts of capital, supercorporations have the economic power to drive out competition. A company with many resources can price its product below cost. Other companies, without such cash reserves, may not be able to survive in a market in which goods must be sold below cost. When there is no longer any competition, the surviving company can raise prices to higher levels than before, as there is no competition left to check the surviving company's actions. New entrants into the marketplace may be deterred, knowing that the supercompany can again price below

[9]Knowles, pp. 349–359.

cost. The result of this strategy is a few companies effectively controlling the market.

A third disadvantage is the economic dominance of big business over other aspects of the marketplace. Just as a supercorporation can dominate the competitive environment of the sale of the company's goods or services, so can a supercorporation dominate the market for resources. For example, a supercorporation can arrange large contracts for raw materials at a low price because it can guarantee large quantities of purchases.

The supercorporation's dominance of the marketplace can also determine its stability. Just as government purchases can influence the marketplace (see Chapter 6), so can the purchases and sales of a supercorporation. For example, some financial analysts believe that the American stock market system is unduly influenced through the market activities of large investment and insurance institutions that have interlocking directorships. Over the past years, insurance companies have been able to grow because of the willingness of the American public to buy insurance in order to spread the risk of loss over a large segment of the population. The increased payments received for insurance and the growth of the industry have enabled insurance companies to acquire large pools of capital for investment. This is also true of companies that manage pension funds, as the investment portfolios of these companies are enormous. Herein lies what a growing number of people consider a problem. The actions of the investment companies can radically affect the price of a given stock. If, for example, a large investment concern decides to buy large blocks of a particular company's stock, the price of the stock will be favorably affected. The reverse is also true. If the investment institution decides to sell its large holdings, the price would fall. The consequence of such power places the small individual investor in a difficult situation. Not only must small investors be concerned with general economic conditions that influence the price of their stock, but they also are at the mercy of large institutions' purchasing and selling. This situation is confounded by possible concerted actions by institutions that have common board representation. Just as J. P. Morgan greatly influenced the market during the crash of 1929, a power elite with control through interlocking directorships or economic dominance could have the same effect today.

A fourth potential disadvantage of supercorporate growth is the company's goals if they conflict with the public welfare. A supercorporation's economic power and its goals of survival and growth may conflict with the safety and health of society. For example, a supercompany can develop services and products that are unsafe and potentially harmful and sell the product or service in foreign countries that do not have extensive legal protection against unsafe products or services. Some examples are the corporations that sell to overseas markets sleepwear that is flammable, pesticides that are banned in the United States, and chemicals that are highly toxic. Even with products that are considered safe by the United States, sales to Third World countries may cause problems. For example, Nestlé Company, which sells baby formulas and baby bottles, was criticized for selling its products in the Third World countries without concern for their possible misuse. When used with little knowledge or without understanding the proper operating conditions, there may be dangerous consequences to the foreign consumer. Under more primitive conditions in which a baby may not receive other forms of nourishment, a mother's milk may be more beneficial to the child than the prepared formula. Nestlé initially showed little regard for the possible consequences of selling the formula under conditions that could harm the children.

The critical aspect of these practices is the size of the supercorporations engaging in them. A small company also may make an unsafe or harmful product, but a small company does not have the resources to mass-produce, advertise, and distribute the product as extensively as a supercorporation can. Any harmful effects of the smaller business's product would have less effect on society than would a mass-distributed product made by a supercorporation.

A comparison of the potential advantages and disadvantages of superconcentration and supercorporations does not mean that corporate power is inherently good or bad. Only society can decide that.

CURRENT PUBLIC POLICY TOWARD CORPORATE POWER

Antitrust laws have been directed toward the resolution of market problems associated with the concentration of power within one organization. The best contemporary example was the breakdown of AT&T (see the box). The major elements viewed in the analysis of desirable or undesirable conditions for antitrust action relate to considering three major aspects of the market environment: structure, conduct, and performance.[10]

Elements Considered in Antitrust

Structure relates to the design or infrastructure of the marketplace. Structure, as it relates to antitrust considerations, includes five major elements. The degree of market concentration prevalent in the market is one element. Obviously, if there is tight control of a market by only a few organizations, there is much more potential control possible by a single company or colluding companies than in markets that might be considered as more free-competition situations. Second, if there are major barriers to entry of new organizations into an industry or market, the current companies in the industry have greater power. Third, if considerable product differentiation or market segmentation exists, there is increased ability for an organization to dominate a segment of the market. Fourth, diversification of an organization increases

[10]Greer, p. 90.

BREAKING UP MA BELL

A few years ago the federal government decided that American Telephone and Telegraph (AT&T) was a monopoly and should be broken up. Many people in the general public agreed. "The phone company charges us too much," they argued, "the government should do something. There is no reason for Ma Bell to have a monopoly." Unfortunately, many people are now beginning to have doubts regarding their original opinion. It seems that with the break up of the $75-billion-a-year giant, service is not quite what it used to be.

Why? The primary answer is that there now are many small firms where there used to be just one large one. The local telephone companies have been broken away from AT&T, and many newly formed firms have entered the long-distance market. Now if something goes wrong, the customer has to figure out who is providing the service as well as the equipment. A lot of people who have gone out and bought their own telephones are finding that unless the phone company sold them the phone, it is not responsible for repairing it. For many Americans, the moral of the story is: Don't fix things that are going well.

its influence in the total market and, as such, increases its relative power. Finally, other factors, such as technology and price elasticity, can moderate the power of organization over the market relative to the other considerations and must be considered in determining the relative power of an organization or colluding organizations. The major concern in antitrust is to ensure that the structure of the market or the regulation of companies in the market are such that competition is present. With structural elements, the potential for power abuse is considered, as opposed to demonstrated actions to distort market conditions unreasonably.

Antitrust regulation is concerned with the behavior or *conduct* of organizations, specifically if collusion or exclusionary actions are occurring. *Collusion* occurs if competing companies act jointly to achieve monopolistic aims. *Exclusionary practices* are those that tend to help one competitor at the expense of another. For example, predatory pricing, price discrimination, tying arrangements, and exclusive dealerships are examples of exclusionary practices and are grounds for antitrust action.

Whereas conduct issues are concerned with management actions, performance issues are concerned with the effect of market structure and its consequences on the market. Thus, analysts look at profit levels of firms, relative social costs, and benefits that are occurring to all parties (buyer, seller, and society) in the marketplace.

In light of these concerns, a body of laws have evolved that attempt to maintain a balance of power in the marketplace. The laws are the basis for antitrust actions currently available and reflect current public policy on corporate power concentration.

ANTITRUST LAWS

Eight laws have formed the cornerstone of antitrust legislation: the Sherman Act, the Clayton Act, the Federal Trade Commission Act, the Robinson-Patman Act, the Wheeler-Lea Act, the Celler-Kefauver Act, the Consumer Goods Pricing Act, and the Anti-Trust Improvement Act.

The Sherman Act.   Before the passage of the Sherman Act in 1890, the courts had ruled that monopolies were illegal, though the basis of these rulings rested in common law. The concern of lawmakers was that court rulings on monopolies or restraints of trade could be initiated only by private parties and not by the federal government. The government wanted a stronger voice in eliminating monopolistic practices. Hence the Sherman Act, named after Senator John Sherman, was made into law. The act prohibited contracts, combinations, and conspiracies that were in restraint of trade (Section 1) and monopolies or conspiracies to monopolize (Section 2). The act gave the Justice Department enforcement powers and provided for criminal penalties for violation.

The Clayton Act.   Problems with enforcing the Sherman Act led to the passage of the Clayton Act in 1914. Section 2 forbade price discrimination in the sale of goods of like grade and quality. Sellers could not sell the same or similar product to two different buyers at different prices unless they could prove that there were cost differences (such as selling in quantity or the necessity to meet competition). Section 3 severely limited exclusive dealer contracts in which the seller forbade the buyer to sell or use a product of one of the seller's competitors. Section 7 prohibited the acquisition of stock of a competitor or the stock of two or more firms in competition with each other. But Sections 2, 3, and 7 were enforced only when their effect might lead to a substantial lessening of competition or create a monopoly in any line of commerce in any part of the country. Section 4 pertained to the initiation of private suits under both the Sherman and Clayton acts. Injured parties could sue violators of the acts for treble damages. Section 8 prohibited interlocking directorships, primarily in the banking industry.

Both the Department of Justice and the Federal Trade Commission have the authority to enforce the Clayton Act. Private litigants (private parties and state attorney generals) also have the power to sue.

Federal Trade Commission Act. The Federal Trade Commission Act was also enacted in 1914. Section 5 outlawed "unfair methods of competition in commerce, and unfair or deceptive acts and practices in commerce." In addition, the act empowered the Federal Trade Commission (FTC), created under the act, to work toward eliminating deceptive acts and practices that may not otherwise violate antitrust laws. The FTC also helps enforce the Clayton Act.

The Robinson-Patman Act. Ineffective wording of Section 2 of the Clayton Act and court interpretations because of that wording led to the passage of The Robinson-Patman (R-P) Act of 1936. The R-P Act is concerned mainly with the preservation of competition by making it illegal to price products at different levels for different customers without the ability to demonstrate that there is a real cost savings by dealing with the client receiving the lower cost as compared to the one receiving exactly the same product or service at a higher cost. The major provisions of the act include the following:

1. Price discrimination among different purchasers of commodities of like grade and quality is prohibited if the effect of such discrimination may lessen competition substantially or tend to create a monopoly.
2. Price differentials are legal if they can be justified as cost savings or as meeting competition in good faith. Price differentials per se are not illegal.
3. Paying, receiving, or accepting anything of value as a commission, brokerage, or other compensation—except for actual services rendered—is prohibited.
4. It is unlawful to knowingly induce or receive discriminatory prices when prohibited by this law.
5. The furnishing of services or facilities to purchasers on terms not accorded to all purchasers proportionately equally is illegal.[11]

The seller and the purchaser can be held for violations of the act. Triple damages, the cost of the suit, and reasonable attorneys' fees can be awarded to the injured party for violations under the R-P Act. While the Clayton and Sherman acts tended to provide a framework for antitrust activities, the R-P Act and the acts that follow direct their attention to more specific sorts of activities that can distort the competitive environment.

The Wheeler-Lea Act. The Wheeler-Lea Act of 1938 is essentially an amendment to Section 5 of the Federal Trade Commission (FTC) act. "Essentially, the Wheeler-Lea Act makes unfair and deceptive acts or practices unlawful, regardless of whether or not they injure competition. It specifically prohibits false advertising of food, drugs, therapeutic devices, and cosmetics."[12] The

---

[11]William M. Pride and O. C. Ferrell, *Marketing* (Boston: Houghton Mifflin, 1985), p. 479.
[12]Pride and Ferrell, p. 478.

amendment was the result of a court decision, *FTC* v. *Raladam Company*,[13] where the courts ruled that the FTC law does not forbid false advertising unless it tends to lessen competition. Although this act, on the surface, is not directed toward maintaining a competitive environment, it really is, in that it is providing clearer ground rules for competition. The act strengthens the hand of the FTC in maintaining some degree of ethical ground rules for business in the marketing arena.

The Celler-Kefauver Act.   The Celler-Kefauver (C-K) Act of 1950 strengthens Section 7 of the Clayton Act and forbids not only the acquisition of a competitor's stock but also of the acquisition of a competitor's assets when the acquisition would tend to substantially lessen competition or tends to create a monopoly. Hence, the acquisition of Muse Airlines by Southwest Airlines in 1985 might be considered illegal *if* it could be demonstrated that the combination would *substantially* lessen competition. The injured party would not have to demonstrate that the combination would hurt competition in the entire industry, only in the effective market area, the southwestern United States. The courts, as will be indicated later in this chapter, have made some interesting decisions as to what constitutes monopoly and in defining an effective market area.

The Consumer Goods Pricing Act.   The Consumer Goods Pricing (CGP) Act of 1975 is an attempt by Congress to reduce the potential power of manufacturers to establish a fixed retail price for their product if they are operating through wholesalers or retailers that deal directly with consumers. The CGP Act specifically prohibits the use of price maintenance agreements between manufacturer and reseller and voids state laws that permit such activities if the participants are engaged in interstate commerce. State may, at their option, still enact such laws for intrastate commerce. These "fair trade laws" were survivors from the early growth period of large chains. At this time, many states enacted legislation to protect the entrepreneur from discount pricing. The 1975 change reflects the changing sentiment of public policy, moving from protecting the smaller outlets to providing a climate that would lead to lower prices for the consumer.

The Antitrust Improvement Act.   The Antitrust Improvement (AI) Act of 1976 strengthened the government's role in enforcing all antitrust regulations. First, all large organizations are required to notify the Justice Department and the Federal Trade Commission of proposed mergers or acquisitions. Second, the 1976 Act empowered state attorney generals to file suit against companies that fix prices and to recover damages for injured parties from violations of antitrust laws. Third, the AI Act expands the Department of

---

[13]Federal Trade Commission v. Raladam Company, 283 U.S. 643 (1931).

Justice's investigatory powers in antitrust matters. Finally, the Federal Trade Commission (FTC) obtained the authority, through the AI Act, to issue guidelines that restrain the entire industry instead of merely initiating actions against a specific organization. Hence, the FTC can provide some guidance to industry as to which sorts of activities might be acceptable and which might not. This is especially helpful in those situations where the actions of business are in the "gray" areas of the law.

FEDERAL ADMINISTRATION OF ANTITRUST ACTIONS

The Sherman Act designated the Justice Department as the principal enforcing body for antitrust actions. The Federal Trade Commission Act designated the Federal Trade Commission (FTC) as having the responsibility to ensure compliance under the Federal Trade Commission Act. Of the two, only the Department of Justice can initiate criminal proceedings.

Prosecution under antitrust acts can lead to criminal or civil remedies. Criminal prosecution can lead to fines or imprisonment, or both, and is directed at punishment of the officers of the corporation. The objective in civil proceedings is to correct the damages that have been made with, in some cases, the awarding of triple damages to deter the organization and others from committing illegal actions. Under civil proceedings, however, the objective is to correct damages, whereas with criminal proceedings it is to punish offenders.

The FTC and the Justice Department are not the only bodies that can initiate proceedings against organizations under antitrust statutes. Private parties and state attorney generals may also initiate antitrust actions. What the plaintiff must demonstrate is that there were violations under the law. In addition, if the plaintiff is attempting to recover damages resulting from those violations, the degree to which the damages were incurred must be demonstrated. As a practical matter, the federal agencies are more concerned with correcting imbalances (i.e., "righting the wrong") than they are with awarding damages. Hence, the suits initiated by federal agencies are directed toward proving that the law was broken. Once that is determined, additional suits can be filed by "injured" parties, who would then need only demonstrate that they were damaged by the actions of the convicted organization and to what degree they were damaged. The determination of damages is much less cumbersome than proving that illegal activities did occur.

The Antitrust Division of the Department of Justice

The antitrust division of the Department of Justice consists of lawyers and economists organized around several major divisions (see Figure 7.2). The nature of prosecution in this division is such that there is a need for an

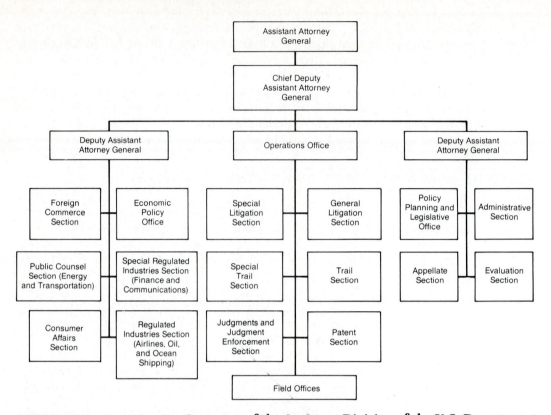

FIGURE 7.2   Organization Structure of the Antitrust Division of the U.S. Department of Justice.

immense amount of legal and economic research in substantiating that the law has been broken. The division must be able to demonstrate that there has been either direct or indirect activity that tends to lessen competition in the industry or the effective market area. The burden of proof is on the plaintiff to demonstrate that the law was broken. In antitrust litigation, not only does this take a great understanding of the judicial interpretation of the law, but it also takes a gathering of economic market data that support the claim. Delineation of the criteria that need to be demonstrated under current law and case precedents will be discussed in the next section.

The economic data that are amassed must be such that there is a clear determination, beyond the shadow of a doubt, that the market structure has changed because of the actions of the defendants, not just because of changing market preferences, demographics, or technological advances. One of the points of defense in the now famous IBM antitrust case was that even though there was a greater concentration of the market, with IBM having greater market share, this concentration was the result of aggressive

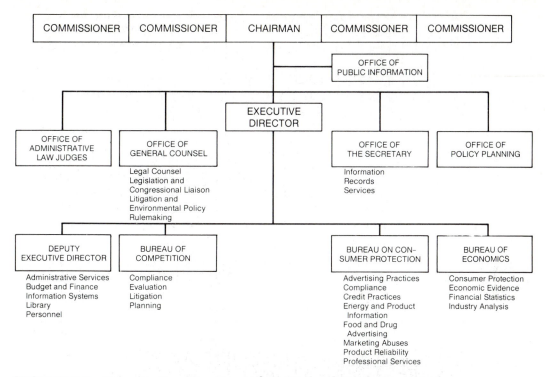

FIGURE 7.3 Organization Structure of the Federal Trade Commission.

marketing and product development, not through illegal activities. Hence, there is a need for highly skilled data gathering, with high-quality, quantified interpretation, in order to develop a case supportive of illegal activity. Therefore, there is much need for a highly skilled law and economics research staff in an antitrust division. In 1985, the antitrust division of the Department of Justice had a budget of $48 million and a staff of over 800.

The Federal Trade Commission

The structure for the FTC appears in Figure 7.3. The FTC is somewhat different from the antitrust division, in that it has the power to make decisions on its own through an FTC administrative law judge. The judge can issue "cease and desist" orders to stop a company's activities. In addition, a daily fine of $10,000 can be levied if the parties do not comply. The FTC can also issue "trade regulation rules," similar to the guidelines that the Equal Employment Opportunity Commission issues, to aid in defining legal and illegal trade and competitive behavior within an industry or industries. If the target of a decision of an administrative law judge disagrees with the decision, it may be appealed to a full FTC board hearing. If the board's decision is not accepted by the target organization, it may move the deliberations to a federal appellate court.

The FTC and the antitrust division of the Department of Justice are guided by the various antitrust laws reviewed above. Equally important is the precedential case law that has shaped interpretation of the legislation over time. To obtain an understanding of the current status of antitrust actions, the major court case decisions need to be considered.

Judicial Interpretations

Since the beginning of prosecution under the Sherman Act, the courts have moved from the premise that restraint of trade must be proved, to the premise that the potential for illegal actions is grounds for antitrust action. With this change in philosophy, the courts' concern shifted from determining a firm's illegal actions to defining a monopoly.

Potential Versus Actual Behavior

Initial prosecution under antitrust laws focused on demonstrated restraint of trade. The first case tried under the Sherman Act was *Knight* v. *United States* in 1895. The Supreme Court ruled that even though the manufacturing company controlled 98 percent of sugar refining, the government had failed to prove that there was any intent to restrain interstate commerce. Proof of intent and actual acts or a conspiracy to violate provisions of the antitrust laws was needed in order to demonstrate violations under the law.[14] The principle followed by the courts in determining antitrust violations was called the *rule of reason*, which asked, "were the company's actions reasonable business practices or was the intent of the business to create or sustain a monopoly?"[15]

From Intent to Potential to Restrain Trade

The Court's reasoning shifted as the result of its different philosophical approach and changes in antitrust regulations. Modifications and additions to the laws clarify Congress's intent and, thus, the intent of public policy. In the 1899 suit of *Addystone Pipe and Steel Co.* v. *United States*, price fixing among independent companies was deemed illegal, regardless of whether or not the fixed price was unreasonable. This decision was reaffirmed in the *U.S.* v. *Trenton Potteries Co.* case in 1927. Price fixing was illegal even if there was no direct conspiracy to control the market (*Interstate Circuit,*

---

[14]U.S. v. American Can Co., 230 F.859, 861 (1916); U.S. v. U.S. Steel Corp., 251 U.S. 417 (1920); and U.S. v. International Hervester Co., 274 U.S. 693, 708 (1927).

[15]Standard Oil Co. of N.J. v. U.S., 221 U.S. 1 (1911) and U.S. v. American Can Co., 230 F. 859, 861 (1916).

Inc. v. *U.S.*, 1939), but this was reversed in a later decision (*Theatre Enterprises* v. *Paramount Film Distributing Corp.*, 1954). Hence, the Court paradoxically disallowed control of market actions through the cooperative actions of competitors, regardless of intent, though it did allow single companies to control markets unless it could be proved that monopolistic or restraint of trade was the intent of the single company's actions. Interestingly enough, the Court's interpretation of the law encouraged mergers, the exact opposite intent of the antitrust laws; however, later Court rulings reversed this policy.

The *U.S.* v. *Aluminum Co. of America* (Alcoa) case of 1945 and the *U.S.* v. *Atlantic & Pacific* (A&P) case of 1949 also demonstrate a change in the courts' philosophy. Alcoa was convicted because it built up its capacity in anticipation of increases in demand, thereby discouraging entry. A&P was convicted "for vigorously seeking discounts from suppliers and cutting prices in highly competitive markets."[16]

Determining Potential Threat

The change in the Court's philosophy from the rule of reason to not permitting combinations because of the possible domination of a market raises some interesting problems. Paramount is the criterion determining whether a firm has dominant control of a market. The problem occurs because of differences across markets, industries, and combinations of companies. For example, should the same criterion be used for a horizontal and a vertical combination? For a conglomerate? Should conglomerates be allowed to grow unchecked unless any one of its subsidiaries attains a dominant share of the market? The law is purposefully vague regarding these points.

Market Share.   One criterion used is market share. Market share is the share of total sales that one company has in a market, compared with that of its competitors. For example, in 1982 General Motors had approximately a 45 percent share of the domestic market for automobiles. In the Alcoa case cited above, Justice Learned Hand ruled that the threshold share of the market was 60 to 64 percent. *Threshold* means the point that market concentration becomes so great that there is a potential for monopolistic or restraint of trade actions. In the A&P case, the threshold point was much lower, at 40 percent, and not in all the markets served by A&P Foods.[17] In *U.S.* v. *Pabst Brewing Co.* (1966), the Court held that this concentration need not be total. Hence, market concentration need not be total domination but only domination in particular geographical regions of specific products. Market dominance thus seems to change with the industry.

Marketing concentration also seems to apply regardless of whether it is

[16]F. M. Scherer, *Industrial Market Structure and Economic Performance* (Chicago: Rand McNally, 1971), pp. 460–461.
[17]Scherer, pp. 460–461.

a horizontal, vertical, or conglomerate merger. The Brown Shoe case (*Brown Shoe Company* v. *United States*, 1962) expanded the antitrust acts to vertical and conglomerate mergers. In 1956 Brown acquired G. R. Kinney Company, a large retail chain of family shoe stores. This merger was an example of vertical integration, and the courts disallowed the merger on several grounds because it felt that the merger would discourage manufacturers from selling to Kinney's because Kinney probably would purchase predominantly from Brown. The combination of Kinney and Brown would deter entrants into the field, and therefore it was in restraint of trade, even though the combined sales of shoes by Brown and Kinney averaged only 5 percent in 47 cities. The Court said that a merger achieving even 5 percent control of the market was excessive concentration. The major argument with respect to vertical integration was related to the possible deterrent to other entrants into the industry. Note that it was not necessary to prove that there was a clear and present danger to current competitors in the field but only that there was a potential for harm. Obviously, market concentration is of less concern in a vertical merger.

Asset Size.   A second major criterion for determining the potential for restraint of trade is asset size, which seems to be the strongest line of attack against conglomerate mergers. In asset size, the power wielded by the size of the company is enough, by itself, to deter competition. For example, in the Reynolds Metal Company case, Reynolds acquired Arrow Brands, a maker of colored and embossed aluminum foil used by florists. The courts held that the merger was illegal because the size of Reynolds created a competitive imbalance in the florist-foil market. The ability of Reynolds, as the rich parent, to support and finance the activities of its subsidiary could either allow actions to restrict trade or deter other companies from entering the field.

The size of the parent was also a factor in the *FTC* v. *Procter & Gamble Co.* case of 1957. Procter & Gamble acquired the Clorox Company, the country's largest producer of bleach. The Court held that the merger was in restraint of trade for three reasons. First, the size of the combined companies would discourage other competitors for entering the market. This was the same logic used in the Brown Shoe case. Second, the Court noted that before the combination, Clorox was already the industry's dominant force in pricing and that the combination would only increase that power. Finally, the Court said that if Procter & Gamble were not allowed to acquire Clorox it probably would develop its own bleach product. Hence, if the merger was allowed, there would not be new competition for Clorox, thereby harming competition in the field.

Determining what constitutes a large enough size is problematic. In cases of horizontal integrations, the degree of market concentration seems to be the most logical criterion. Variations among industries make it difficult to specify the degree of concentration that might be legal or illegal. In cases of vertical integration or conglomerate formation, market concentration seems insufficient to measure the potential to restrain trade. The Court seems to feel that economic power should help determine the potential for influence. Economic power can be measured by both market concentration and asset size. A conglomerate's asset size and, to a lesser degree, the target subsidiary's market concentration seem to be the favored criteria.

The courts seem to be interpreting the laws inconsistently. Currently there does not appear to be one guideline or criterion that a company can use to direct its own policies and strategies. Prosecution by the Federal Trade Commission and the Justice Department does not follow a consistent path. It seems that only certain violators are prosecuted, not all those who have the potential to influence. According to Ford and Ratchford, "Perhaps the major villain in this case is the vagueness of the Sherman Act itself, and the poorly-defined anti-trust policy which has evolved from this law over the past 85 years. Precedents are often in conflict, and cases appear to be decided largely on an ad hoc basis (perhaps influenced by prevailing political climate)."[18]

CURRENT TRENDS AND FUTURE PERSPECTIVES

The growth of conglomerates has made problems for lawmakers, law administrators, and the courts. Conglomerate mergers are on the blind side of antitrust laws. When market concentration is not affected in a merger, the criterion to allow or disallow a merger becomes many times more problematic. Asset size, or arguing that bigness leads to potential restraint, is an insufficient demonstration of monopolistic action. It becomes more difficult when bigness in this country might mean medium size in terms of foreign competition. As Table 7.1 indicates, many international firms are of comparable size and can be formidable competition. If the United States restricts the size of industries, as proposed in the Kennedy legislation, it may create some serious problems in maintaining a competitive advantage in the world markets. However, there is merit in the claim by some analysts that the resources available to a conglomerate might give the subsidiary of that conglomerate an advantage over other competitors or deter new entrants into the field.

The main theoretical question seems to be when corporate power potential starts influencing the competition. Would a brewer of beer be concerned if a company with 1.8 percent of the market, such as C. Schmidt & Sons,[19] is acquired by a huge conglomerate such as W. R. Grace? Would other companies be deterred from entering the market if they knew that C. Schmidt &

---

[18]Gary T. Ford and Brian T. Ratchford, "Public Policy, the Sherman Act and the IBM Antitrust Case." *The Challenges and the Opportunities, 1975 Combined Proceedings Series 37* (New York: American Marketing Association, 1975).

[19]"Anheuser-Busch: The King of Beer Still Rules," *Business Week,* July 12, 1982, pp. 50–54.

Sons had the resources behind it of a company such as W. R. Grace, with sales of $6 billion and profits of $283.8 million?[20] At what point would there be concern? Would it be when a company has greater market concentration, for example, 10 to 20 percent of the market? Would it be when the company exhibited rapid growth? In any event, this issue will have to be determined when a more rational criterion is developed to decide whether a conglomerate or vertical merger is illegal.

The antitrust laws are currently administered by the Justice Department and the Federal Trade Commission. The current philosophy of the Reagan administration, which appointed the current agency heads, favors less antitrust action, particularly with respect to conglomerate mergers. As the Assistant Attorney General for Antitrust, William Baxter, philosophized:

> There is nothing written in the sky that says the world would not be a perfectly satisfactory place if there were only 100 companies, provided each had one percent of every product and service market. In that case, there would be extremely high aggregate concentration and, at the same time, perfect competition. So you see, the two have nothing necessarily to do with one another. Consequently, I do not see a war against aggregate concentration as part of this department's mission.[21]

The same philosophy is evident at the Federal Trade Commission whose Reagan appointee, James C. Miller III, indicated that much of the previous antitrust activity had too much emphasis on "attacking bigness for its own sake."[22] There may be a major shift in the FTC's role when its operating charter comes up for renewal.

The practical result of this shift in policy was reflected in several recent actions: a cabinet-level task force recommended to the Justice Department that it drop the AT&T case; the FTC dropped a suit against the major oil companies; and the Justice Department narrowed its case against IBM.[23] The current trend seems to favor less antitrust action, but as the recent Texaco case indicates[24] (see Chapter 4 for details), there may be more indirect ways, such as questioning the ethical and criminal motives of mergers and acquisitions to limit companies from getting bigger.

SUMMARY

Concentration of economic and market power is a natural by-product in the formation of the supercorporations. Industry has grown in the past 20 years, including all possible types of power concentrations, through horizon-

[20]Standard & Poor's Compustat Service, Inc., 1980.

[21]"Big Shift in Antitrust Policy," *Dun's Review*, August 1981, pp. 38–40.

[22]Richard L. Gordon, "Anti-trust Policy: Back to Basics," *Industrial Marketing*, June 1981, pp. 10, 32.

[23]"American Antitrust Law: On the Side of Big Battalions?" *The Economist*, June 27, 1981, pp. 75, 78.

[24]"Judge Upholds Texaco Verdict," *Lincoln Journal*, December 11, 1985, p. 34.

tal, vertical, and conglomerate mergers. There are several arguments that support superconcentration because it can contribute to social goals. It is also true that superconcentration can lead to power being used to advance the narrow interests of those managing that power. The abuse of this power can subvert social welfare and goals by affecting the marketplace and the political process.

Public policy toward supercorporations and superconcentrations of business power has been articulated in three laws: the Sherman Act, the Clayton Act, and the Federal Trade Commission Act. Amendments to these acts include the Robinson-Patman Act of 1936, the Celler-Kefauver Act of 1950, and the Anti-trust Improvement Act of 1976. The administrative agencies for these acts include the Anti-trust Division of the Justice Department and the Federal Trade Commission.

Court rulings have defined the intent of public policy toward antitrust actions. Original interpretations of the Sherman Act seemed to view mergers as illegal, collusive behavior between competitors, whether or not intent to restrain trade was proved. In the case of a single company or merged partners, it was necessary to prove intent to restrain trade. Over the years, the courts modified their position. Currently, the potential to restrain trade is sufficient to prosecute under the antitrust laws. In the case of a horizontal merger, the amount of relative market share is an important criterion in proving potential market abuse. The criterion used for vertical and conglomerate combinations seems to be market concentration and asset size. Current public policy, as reflected by the administration of antitrust agencies, reflects a rededication to viewing market concentration, as opposed to asset size, as a major criterion to judge potential market abuse.

There seems little doubt that the role of supercorporations will be questioned in the future. Although current antitrust laws provide some protection, they tend to be inadequate in dealing with the new form of holding-company conglomerates or multinational corporations. Public policy must more clearly determine in the years to come whether or not the benefits of supercorporations are worth their associated shortcomings. Currently, several experts question large size as a desirable attribute for modern corporations. Others question whether there is an optimal size for business organizations, and if, in many cases, this optimal size has already been reached.[25] Movies such as *Network* and books such as *The Wreck of the Penn Central* and *The Seven Sisters: The Great Oil Companies and the World They Made* indicate the potential abuses of the supercorporation. Society must define its essential needs and the role of the MNC in fulfilling those needs. Likewise, the superconcentrated business relationship must be assessed to determine its benefits to society. Today's supercorporation and superconcentration have already made an important influence on society, and tampering with them would certainly bring about some profound changes in much of society. The influence of

[25] E. F. Schumacher, *Small Is Beautiful: The Economics As If People Mattered* (New York: Harper & Row, 1975).

these changes on public policy regarding corporate formation, conglomeration, and mergers must be weighed carefully before these changes are made. Society must ascertain not only immediate but also long-run changes in the free market system. The future may show that supercorporations are efficient tools in improving the quality of life for millions of people all over the world. On the other side of the coin, safeguards are needed to ensure that superconcentrations of power will not lead to collusions with governments and other institutions to the detriment of society.

DISCUSSION AND STUDY QUESTIONS

1. What is meant by "superconcentration"? How does superconcentration differ from supercorporation?
2. Distinguish vertical, horizontal, and conglomerate integrations. Cite an example of each.
3. What are some of the reasons for a company to become a supercorporate power?
4. What are some of the benefits to society for allowing superconcentrations of power in business?
5. How can having supercorporations help promote a country's self-interest and foreign policy?
6. How have foreign grain sales been used as an instrument of U.S. foreign policy?
7. What are some of the disadvantages to society superconcentrations of corporate power?
8. What are some of the ways public policy might reduce the influence on supercorporations? For example, how could investors' concern about institutional trading in the stock market be reduced?
9. Outline the major points in the Sherman Act, the Clayton Act, and the Federal Trade Commission Act. How did each contribute to defining public policy toward superconcentrations and supercorporations?
10. How did the Robinson-Patman Act, the Celler-Kefauver Act, and the Antitrust Improvement Act clarify public policy toward antitrust actions?
11. Trace the history of judicial interpretation of antitrust laws from *Knight* v. *United States* to the current philosophy.
12. What is the current criterion to determine potential monopolistic influences in an horizontal combination, a vertical and a conglomerate combination?
13. What are some of the shortcomings of using asset size as a criterion to judge corporate influence? Why is asset size used as a criterion?
14. What is the current trend with respect to the actions of the Justice Department and the Federal Trade Commission toward antitrust violations?

CASES AND INCIDENTS

Historical Precedent*

Many members of the public are surprised to learn that there are 50 or so major corporations that wield most of the economic clout in this country. However, students of history know that there is historical precedent for this development. As early as 90 years ago there were a small number of firms that held economic sway in most industries. The Rockefeller family, for example, had interests everywhere from the oil fields of Pennsylvania to the Mesabi iron range of Minnesota. Drawing on the expertise of people in their clique such as James Stillman, president of the National City Bank, it was able to gain control of many different types of businesses.

According to Matthew Josephson's *The Robber Barons*, the 15 directors of the Standard Oil Company of New Jersey held directorships in innumerable banks, insurance companies, traction companies, electric light, gas, and industrial concerns of every sort. Through Stillman they dominated a constellation of banks: the National City, Hanover, Farmer Loan and Trust, Second National, and United States Trust; they were involved in the new American Smelting and Refining combination, in the copper mines of Montana, and the iron deposits of Minnesota; and in United Gas Improvement Interborough Rapid Transit, Brooklyn Rapid Transit, and Metropolitan Securities. Rockefeller even approached Carnegie and "tried to buy him out." It was Rockefeller's desire to solidify his interest in ore land, his ore railway in Minnesota, as well as his fleet of freight vessels on the Great Lakes.

Nor were the Rockefellers alone. There were others who had trusts of their own. H. O. Havemeyer, for example, had the sugar trust. Consolidating seven refineries into the American Sugar Refining Company in 1897, following the example of Standard Oil, Havemeyer achieved a firm grip on the market. Holding the margin of profit at 1.1 cents per pound, regardless of the price of sugar, the company was able to pay dividends of 10 percent and more per year. Additionally, with competition now out of the picture, Havemeyer began quietly to raise the price by one quarter of one cent per pound. He also made a deal with customs officials whereby, for a bribe, they would reduce the recorded weight of the sugar that was being imported, reducing the import tax duty in the process.

Of course, this type of combination did not go unnoticed by Havemeyer's competitors. But when challenged in the state of New York as a monopoly, the company appealed to the Supreme Court and won its case. The high court ruled that there was nothing in the state's case to indicate any intention by the company to restrain trade or commerce, and the fact that trade or

---

*The data in this case can be found in Matthew Josephson, *The Robber Barons* (New York: Harcourt Brace, 1934).

commerce might be indirectly affected was not enough to entitle the complainants to a decree.

ANALYSIS

1. Is the concentration of wealth and power among business people and corporations today as great as it was at the turn of the century?
2. Some people believe that it is impossible to legislate the concentration of economic power out of existence. We can hope only that those who have it will use it wisely. Do you agree with this philosophy?
3. Are those who hold economic power today more responsible than those in power at the turn of the century? Explain.

An International Audit for an International Firm*

As noted earlier in the chapter, there is currently a proposal at the United Nations that would set a committee to establish accounting and reporting standards for multinational corporations (MNCs). This proposal would require multinationals to provide balance sheets, income statements, and funds statements for the parent company and each subordinate company. Similar financial statements would also be required for every major subsidiary of the MNC that is doing business in any particular part of the world. Geographical and product-line information, similar to that recently set forth by the Financial Accounting Standards Board, would be required from both groups. Additionally, details on accounting policies and company ownership would be required.

N. T. Wang, director of the information analysis division of the United Nation's Center on Transnational Corporations, says that most large American firms would have little difficulty providing such familiar financial items, although they might balk at having to reveal product-line data, country by country. "It's easy to know IBM as a whole," he says, "but harder to know a shipping magnate" who may operate through interlocking family companies.

The group's more controversial recommendations are in the area of nonfinancial disclosure: employment and production data, transfer-pricing policies, significant new products and processes, new capital investment programs, the cost and effect of announced mergers, and environmental-impact information. Considerably more detailed data would be required for subsidiary companies within individual countries than at the parent level.

A few companies in Germany, Sweden, and the United States are experimenting with that kind of special "social accounting" report. And the UN group insists that nonfinancial reporting is as important as financial in appraising transnational corporations.

*The data in this case can be found in "The U.N. May 'Audit' Business," *Business Week*, June 26, 1978, pp. 98, 100.

Of course, multinationals compete with companies that are strictly national in operation and some that are state owned. This raises the question of whether these latter firms should be subject to the same accounting requirement that the UN is attempting to place on multinationals. The UN accounting group says they should be, but this recommendation has yet to be endorsed by [former] Secretary General Kurt Waldheim or the transnational commission. The Financial Executives Institute (FEI), an American business organization, says that it has serious reservations abut the ability of a UN commission to ensure equal treatment, particularly when state-owned enterprises or other arms of government are involved. What also worries the institute is that the UN might confuse or duplicate significant voluntary efforts already being made by multinationals. For example, the Organization for Economic Cooperation and Development, through its guidelines for MNCs, has taken steps to improve disclosure; and the relatively new International Accounting Standards Committee (IASC), an association of national accounting bodies from ten of the more developed countries and some two dozen smaller or developing countries, has made important progress toward drawing up some common worldwide standards.

In an effort to achieve a working agreement, one of the partners in a large American public accounting firm that recently suggested the IASC offer to help the UN work toward developing common international accounting standards, thus freeing any new UN group to make recommendations in the nonfinancial area. "They ought to turn over the independent auditing procedures to the professional bodies," he said, "and then appoint a group that can work with the professional bodies on the other, more socially oriented matters."

ANALYSIS

1. Is there really a need for some international agency to control multinational corporations, or at least look into their operations? Explain.
2. Is the UN proposal feasible? Defend your answer.
3. Does this new development at the UN indicate the beginning of a trend toward demanding more socially responsible multinational corporations? Explain.

Supercorporations: Fact or Fiction?*

Mention the term *supercorporation* to the average person on the street and ask the individual to name one, and you are likely to get an oil company such as Gulf, Texaco, Exxon, or Mobil. In the minds of many people these multinational corporations transcend national boundaries and have a great influence on both foreign government policy and American living standards.

*The data in this case can be found in Richard M. Hodgetts, *The Business Enterprise: Social Challenge, Social Response* (Philadelphia: Saunders, 1977), pp. 229–254.

For example, recent research shows that many Americans believe there is no real gas shortage, just one that was created by the large oil firms.

On the other side of the coin is the argument put forth by the supercorporations in the oil industry. For example, Mobil Oil argues that there is *no* oil monopoly because there are far too many firms in the industry for any two, three, or four to dominate the others. Counting the total number that produces and refines oil and markets its own products (including independent wholesalers and fuel oil and liquefied petroleum gas distributors but omitting service stations), Mobil found more than 43,000 American firms in the oil business. Additionally, the firm pointed out:

> The cost of a large, modern refinery, which can easily exceed $250 million, does not encourage thousands to enter that end of the business, but neither does anyone dominate it. There are 239 refineries in this country, operated by 127 companies. The largest accounts for less than nine percent of total U.S. refining capacity. No other major manufacturing industry is so little dominated by any one company. Or any seven.
>
> The oil business does include some of the world's largest industrial companies. Mobil among them. This industry breeds big companies because it takes an enormous complex of men and machines to meet the worldwide demand for energy. U.S. oil demand has more than doubled over the past 20 years, and it will almost double again by 1985. The world will require more oil just in the Seventies than in the past 100 years.
>
> Competition clearly is good for the consumer. It has kept oil products—especially gasoline—among the best bargains in the marketplace. We think competition is good for the companies in the oil industry, too.
>
> We face some of the toughest competitors in the world. We are determined not to let them monopolize the business.

Despite such claims, critics argue that the oil companies are urging the public to examine the wrong end of the marketing channel. It is not the retail part of the operation that is being monopolized by the super oil companies—it is the acquisition part. Only the very large firms can afford to drill for their own oil or set up large facilities overseas for purchasing and shipping the oil to the United States. By restricting the supply, the oil firms maintain a stranglehold on the nation.

At the present time there is not enough information to judge the merits of either side's arguments, but one thing is clear. The major oil companies believe that it is fiction to refer to them as supercorporations, but most members of the general public believe that it is fact.

ANALYSIS

1. Are there any benefits from supercorporations? Explain.
2. Are the major oil companies supercorporations? Defend your answer.
3. What social responsibilities do these companies have to the public? Are they meeting these responsibilities, or are they attempting to manipulate prices and supplies for their own ends? Explain your answer.

CASE STUDY FOR PART II

The Westinghouse Uranium Contracts: Commercial Impracticability and Related Matters*

Westinghouse Electric Corporation surprised and shocked the business and legal communities when, on September 8, 1975, it announced that it would not deliver about 70 million pounds of uranium under fixed-price contracts to 27 utility companies.

Westinghouse supported its position by relying on a relatively obscure and little used provision of the Uniform Commercial Code, Section 2–615, which provides that a party may be excused from performing contractual obligations on the basis of "commercial impracticability." It claimed that the potential loss of $2 billion made it "commercially impractical" to meet its obligations.

The utilities responded predictably enough, by filing civil suits in 13 different federal jurisdictions. All 13 cases were combined and sent to the U.S. District Court for the Eastern District of Virginia[1] on the basis that the commonality was greater than the differences, particularly Westinghouse's defense of commercial impracticability and the problem of how to distribute the uranium that Westinghouse had on hand. Three utilities brought suit in a Pennsylvania state court, and three Swedish utilities took action in Stockholm.

This is only part of the picture, as ripples from this bombshell spread out. In an effort to protect its interests, in 1976 Westinghouse brought suit against its suppliers of uranium, claiming that an international cartel had caused an unforeseen and precipitous increase in the price of uranium. Preliminary maneuvers resulted in a decision from the Supreme Court of Ontario[2] and one from the British House of Lords[3] that prevented Westinghouse from getting documents and testimony relating to their case from foreign corporations. Similar action was taken in South Africa and Australia.[4]

*Abridged from "The Westinghouse Uranium Contracts: Commercial Impracticability and Related Matters" written William Eagan, University of Notre Dame, used with permission.
[1] *In re* Westinghouse Electric Corporation Uranium Contracts Litigation 405 F. Supp. 316.
[2] *In re* the Evidence Act No. GD 75–23978 (June 29, 1977).
[3] *New York Times*, December 2, 1977, IV 9:3.
[4] *Wall Street Journal*, May 4, 1979, 1:6.

The Westinghouse Positon

When Westinghouse announced in September 1975 that it would not honor its contractual obligations to deliver 70 million pounds of uranium under price-fixed agreements, it claimed that dramatic, unprecedented, and unforeseeable events occurred that raised the price of uranium from about $6.50 to $9.00 per pound to $26 per pound in September 1975.[5] This could lead to a potential loss to Westinghouse of about $2 billion. By July 1978 the price had risen to about $44 per pound and the potential loss escalated to approximately $3 billion.[6]

Westinghouse contended that the unexpected Arab Oil Embargo of 1973–1974 was one of the factors that resulted in a major increase in the price of all energy resources, including uranium. Later it argued that an international cartel was establishing prices for uranium and thus artificially increasing the price. For these reasons, Westinghouse sought refuge under Section 2–615 of the Uniform Commercial Code, arguing that it would be "commercially impracticable" to complete a contract that could result in bankruptcy. One problem that existed was the fact that the code does not define the terms and there is little precedent available for the parties of the courts to refer to.

On October 27, 1978, after having arrived at several out-of-court settlements, Westinghouse contended that Section 2–712 of the Code requires that if the injured party is to cover, they must do it "without unreasonable delay." Although the plaintiffs could have covered for $26 to $30 per pound. Thus, Westinghouse argued that if they were to be assessed damages, or if out-of-court settlements should be arrived at, it should be on the basis of the cost of uranium at the date of recession and not the current $43 per pound.[7]

The Uranium Cartel

There seems to be little question at this time that a uranium cartel did, in fact, exist.[8] D. J. LeCraw, for example, even lists all the players as well

[5]Joskow, Commercial Impossibility, the Uranium Market and the Westinghouse Case, 6 Jr. Legal Studies 119–74 at 137 (1977).

[6]New York Times, July 9, 1978, III 1:1.

[7]Transcript, *Virginia Electric Power Company et al. v. Westinghouse Electric Corporation,* U.S. District Court for the Eastern District of Virginia, October 27, 1978, 22295–98.

[8]See Probyn and Anthony, The Cartel that Ottawa Built (Development of a Canadian Uranium Cartel), 50 Canadian Business 36–38 November 1977; D. S. Le Craw, The Uranium Cartel: An Interim Report 42 Business Quarterly (Canada) 76–84, Winter 1977; U.S. House Committee on Interstate and Foreign Commerce, Sub Committee on Oversight and Investigations Hearings International Uranium Supply and Demand, 94th Congress 2nd Session; U.S. House Committee on Interstate and Foreign Commerce, Sub Committee on Oversight and Investigations Hearings. International Uranium Cartels 95th Congress 1st Session.

as the companies and governments they represented.[9] Gulf Oil admits that its Canadian subsidiary was a member of the cartel but only on the insistence of the Canadian government and with assurances that this activity would not violate U.S. antitrust laws.[10] Why Gulf relied on Canadian authorities for an interpretation of U.S. law is not clear. Gulf also contended that the cartel broke up because the international price for uranium rose so rapidly as the result of natural economic forces that the cartel could not keep up.

How Widespread was the Knowledge of the Existence of the Cartel?

The Nuclear Exchange Corporation (Nuexco) was aware of the cartel from its first meeting in August 1972 and reported this and subsequent meetings to the industry through its publications.[11] Therefore, when the Canadian government confirmed the existence of the cartel on September 22, 1976.[12] according to George White, president of Nuexco, it should have come to no one's surprise.

The literature aimed specifically at the uranium industry in 1973–1974 devoted much space to the increased activity of public utilities as they struggled to meet their requirements and the problems involving capacity shortages and even obtaining contracts.

The TVA became aware of the cartel at least by January 1974.[13] In the summer of 1976 the Australian Chapter of Friends of the Earth released to the California Energy Commission materials indicating the existence of an international uranium cartel.

It is not clear why it took Westinghouse until this time to become aware of the situation. Again, Westinghouse was not alone. Reserve Oil and Minerals did not get around to suing General Atomic Company and Gulf Oil and Scallop Nuclear, Inc. until after the release of the congressional hearings in 1977.[14]

Effect of Cartel

What effect did the existence and operation of the cartel have on the price rise from $6 per pound to $44 in five years?

D. J. LeCraw concludes that:

[9]Le Craw, p. 81.
[10]*New York Times*, May 10, 1978 IV 1:6.
[11]Supra Note 8 Hearings 2nd Session at 4.
[12]Id. at 12–15.
[13]Supra Note 8 Hearings 1st Session at 351.
[14]*New York Times*, September 23, 1977 IV 1:3.

The supply-demand imbalance existed independent of the cartel. The cartel—especially through its actions toward Westinghouse—was only one of the factors which triggered the rise in price which was necessary to equalize supply and demand.[15]

Nuexco listed the following events as being primarily responsible for the increase:

First, a long-overdue correction in uranium prices from subnormal levels to recognize rapid and large increases in production costs of the mining industry.

Second, major short sales of uranium in the fuel fabrication sector of the industry.

Third, ERDA's, that is, the Energy Research and Development Administration's, adoption of the long-term, fixed-commitment enrichment contract with the coincidental requirement that uranium deliveries be rigidly fixed both in time and quantity.

Fourth, the adoption of nationalistic policies relating to all energy sources by foreign governments, including Canada, Australia, France, and of course, the Arabs, with their much-publicized action of implementing an oil embargo.

Finally, fifth, severe and continuing problems resulting from the actions or inactions of the government relating to the reprocessing and recycling of fuel, the timing and extent of changes in the diffusion plant tails assay, the importation of foreign uranium, the construction requirements of government agencies such as the Nuclear Regulatory Commission and the Environmental Protection Agency, and the effect of such government actions and inactions on both supply and demand.[16]

It is interesting to note that Westinghouse's short sales are listed and the cartel is not. At the congressional hearings a Gulf official admitted that "to the extent they bought overseas, they probably paid a higher price."[17] Westinghouse, of course, claims that the cartel had a significant impact on prices.

LeCraw supplies the following information:

The cartel members engaged in a wide range of activities aimed at reducing international competition from middlemen; especially Westinghouse, who bought uranium from producers and resold it to utilities. The producers acted to dissuade the Australian government from allowing Westinghouse to participate in uranium producing properties there; refused bids by Westinghouse below cartel prices; only made bids to Westinghouse at above the price at which they quoted the utilities, and finally refused to make any bids to Westinghouse at all.[18]

If Westinghouse had difficulty arranging for future contracts for the delivery of uranium and there is considerable evidence that the cartel made

---

[15]Le Craw, p. 83.
[16]Supra Note 8 Hearings 2nd Session at 3–4.
[17]Supra Note 8 Hearings 1st Session at 338.
[18]Le Craw, p. 82.

sure that it happened, this would seem to assure an upward bias for prices. TVA and Duke Power, among others, found themselves in the same type of bind but not in such serious proportions.

Utilities in general were willing to bid up the price of uranium to ensure that their facilities would go on-stream as scheduled. Because the price of fuel was only 5 percent of total operating costs, they felt that it was worth the extra cost to prevent any delays.

Impact of Short Sales

The impact of Westinghouse's short sales on the price of uranium is difficult to determine with a high degree of accuracy. However, George White, president of Nuexco, estimated that this activity upset the orderly function of the market enough to raise the price to $41 per pound rather than about $30 per pound under a more orderly market.[19] Without the short sales, the prices would have started to increase gradually in 1968–1971 rather than so sharply in 1973–1974. Paul L. Joskow comes to a similar conclusion.[20]

As of January 1, 1975, Westinghouse had commitments to supply 60,000 tons of uranium but had only 20,000 tons available, either on hand or contracted for. Westinghouse did not publically admit this until July 14, 1975. The admission was a shock to the U.S. market, which in 1975 was producing about 13,000 tons per year and would have a capacity of only 18,000 to 20,000 tons per year when facilities then under construction came on-line.[21]

The Organization for Economic Co-Operation and Development predicted in 1973 that "no shortages of uranium supply are to be expected in the 1970's.[22] The report went on to say that:

The rapid growth in demand in the coming decade cannot be satisfied on the basis of existing uranium exploration levels. Given the necessary lead time of about eight years between discovery and actual production, it is therefore essential that steps be taken to increase the rate of exploration of uranium so that an adequate forward reserve may be maintained.[23]

A latter report indicated that worldwide demand for uranium in 1975 would be about 18,000 tons, with a production capacity of 26,000 tons, in what was called a "tight uranium market."[24]

[19]Supra Note 8 Hearings 2nd Session at 8.
[20]Joskow, pp. 142–143.
[21]Joskow, p. 144.
[22]OEDC Nuclear Energy Agency and the International Atomic Energy Agency, Uranium: Resources, Production and Demand, Aug. 1973 9.
[23]Id.
[24]OEDC Nuclear Energy Agency and the International Atomic Energy Agency, Uranium: Resources, Production and Demand, Dec. 1975 9.

It would seem reasonable to conclude that Westinghouse's activity in the market had to have some effect on demand and therefore on price.

Evaluation

And now after all the discussion, where does this leave Westinghouse in its attempt to chart new applications to the concept of impossibility and specifically, to commercial impracticability as contained in U.C.C. Section 2–615?

Several studies have been done concerning the relationship and application of economic theory to the interpretation of impossibility and commercial impracticability. Posner and Rosenfield[25] apply macroeconomic theory to the general area of impossibility, while Joskow[26] does the same in relationship specifically to Section 2–615 of the U.C.C. with special application to the Westinghouse case. Ashley[27] and Birmingham[28] apply microeconomic theory to the same area. None of these studies lend much support to the Westinghouse position.

Although Westinghouse is arguing commercial impracticality rather than impossibility, because of the unsettled state of this concept, the question of supervening and antecedent impossibility would still have to be faced. The cartel existed before most of Westinghouse's short contracts were made in 1973–1974, and it would seem that Westinghouse knew or should have known of its existence. The oil embargo of OPEC occurred in 1973 as a supervening impossibility, but Westinghouse continued to make contracts after the impact of the embargo and subsequent price rise became apparent.

There seems to be serious questions that can be raised concerning Westinghouse's management's handling of the whole problem. In March 1973, John Simpson, then president of Westinghouse Power Systems, told financial analysts that "we have firm commitments that match our requirements throughout the terms of our contracts." The board of directors was not notified of the problem until September 1974 and the board did not give it serious consideration until March 1975.[29] In fact, as of January 1, 1975, Westinghouse had commitments to supply 60,000 tons of uranium but had only 20,000 tons available either on hand or contracted for.[30]

Paul Joskow raised the point that Westinghouse may not have had a

[25]Posner and Rosenfield, Impossibility and Related Doctrines in Contract Law: An Economic Analysis, 6 Jr. Legal Studies 83–118 (1977).
[26]Joskow.
[27]Ashley, The Economic Implications of the Doctrine of Impossibility, 26 Hastings L. J. 1251 (1975).
[28]Birmingham, A Second Look at the Suez Cases: Excuse for Non-performance of Contractual Obligations in Light of Economic Theory, 20 Hastings L. J. 1393 (1969).
[29]New York Times, February 17, 1977 57:2.
[30]Joskow, p. 144.

well-thought-out corporate policy and that as a consequence the uranium situation may have evolved, at least in part, by accident. During the years that the large short position was developing, particularly 1973–1974, the nuclear power division was run essentially autonomously from the rest of the corporation, and at the same time Westinghouse was facing a serious depletion of its cash flow and a substantial reorganization. At this time it was apparently emphasizing plant construction and operation, on which it had lost between $200 and $250 million.[31]

In relation to allocation of risk, the major reason for a purchaser to agree to a fixed-price contract for future delivery is to have assurance of the availability of the goods or services at a predetermined price, in other words, to shift the risk to the seller. Westinghouse, on the other hand, was making the offer to supply the uranium fuel as an added inducement to prospective customers to buy its power-generating equipment. It would appear that Westinghouse was assuming the risk of a price change as part of its marketing strategy. If there was to be a ceiling on the risks involved or a different allocation of risks, that should have been included in the contract.

Following his analysis of the impact of Section 2–615, Duesenberg concludes:

> The foregoing review demonstrates that, short of a physical or scientific incapability, identifying what is impracticable is proving no less difficult than it has always been. Notwithstanding the Code's announced purpose to loosen up on the tight restraints imposed by the common law there is little sign of any judicial appetite to use section 2–615 to jeopardize the certainty of contractual duties on which parties have a right to rely. Additionally, the consequences of foreseeability, risk assumption and causation of one's own misfortune are as severe and relevant as they were prior to when excuse of performance took its place in the Code as a codified contract principle.[32]

> Few cases have aided burdened sellers. More precisely, it can be said that not one has although operation of this section has been implicitly accepted in one or two decisions.[33]

> The point is that whether the cause be an increase in costs, shortages, or other extraordinary event, section 2–615 is not a ready exit from contract liability. As had often been observed, the law is a jealous mistress, and she isn't yielding gracefully to the new code term.[34]

Joskow arrives at a similar conclusion specifically as it applies to Westinghouse:

---

[31]Joskow, pp. 147–148.

[32]Duesenberg, Contract Impracticability: Courts to Shape Section 2–615, 32 Bus. Law 1089 at 1100 (1977).

[33]Duesenberg, p. 1101.

[34]Duesenberg, p. 1101.

At least as the law is currently interpreted, Westinghouse appears to fail on all counts to justify a discharge of its contractual obligations under U.C.C. Section 2–615. To hold otherwise would mean a major change in the interpretation of the impracticability doctrine, serving to shift business risks ordinarily borne by the seller of the commodity to the buyers.[35]

A decision in favor of Westinghouse would increase the uncertainty associated with U.C.C. Section 2–615 itself, leading at least in the short run to a substantial increase in litigation and delays in performance on contracts.[36]

ANALYSIS

1. What is Westinghouse's position regarding their interpretation of the law?
2. What is the position of those companies that negotiated to have Westinghouse provide uranium under the fixed price?
3. What would be the effect on Westinghouse if the contracts were enforced by the courts?
4. What would be the effect on the utilities if the court would decide against them?
5. What do you suppose the underlying purpose of the Uniform Commercial Code is? How does it serve the public welfare?
6. Discuss the social welfare and good that would be served by a decision that would favor Westinghouse. Would favor the utilities.
7. Taking each of the six questions above into perspective, what decision would you make to resolve the dispute between Westinghouse and the utilities?

[35]Joskow, p. 175.
[36]Joskow, p. 176.

PART III

The Social Issues Facing Modern Business

8

Equal Opportunity in Employment

Chapter Objectives

- To illustrate the past and present levels of structural discrimination in modern society.
- To review the federal laws enacted to reduce the amount of employment discrimination.
- To present the ways that today's firm can implement affirmative action and the effectiveness of the federal mandates.
- To trace the role of organized labor and the federal government in training and job/employee matching programs.

This chapter is concerned with the demands of society for equal opportunity for all employees.

BACKGROUND OF GROUPS TRADITIONALLY DISCRIMINATED AGAINST

There are four significantly large racial minorities in America today: Native Americans, Mexican Americans, Puerto Ricans, and blacks. Collectively, they account for about a fifth of the U.S. population. Census figures, however, reveal that the racial minorities in the United States are gaining in relative numbers to whites. One study of the Population Reference Bureau estimated that by 2000 more than 30 percent of several states will be members of minority groups and that by 2080 whites will be a minority group in this country. In other words, the number of minority group members will increase, and the problems of discriminating against them will become worse unless something is done and done soon.

Most would agree that Native Americans have suffered more than any other ethnic group in American history has. They are the wards of the federal government and fall under the protection of the Bureau of Indian Affairs (BIA). About 750,000 live on reservations, and about the same number live elsewhere. Although the amount of economic support has increased since the 1930s, the statistics reveal a disheartening story: about 75 percent of those living on reservations earn less than $7,500 per year and unemployment rates are extremely high. Native Americans still suffer greatly from malnutrition and disease. Ninety percent of their housing is below minimum standards, and their literacy rate is a mere 50 percent. The average life span is only 65.1 years, the lowest of any population group. Pneumonia and influenza are the fourth leading causes of death, and infant mortality is fifth, three times the national average. Cirrhosis of the liver (caused by alcoholism) is the sixth leading cause of death, and suicide is the tenth. Between the ages of 19 and 35, Native Americans kill themselves at a rate that is three times the national average. Their average income is the lowest of any group in the nation: there is no question that Native Americans are far behind the mainstream of American prosperity.

Mexican Americans are the second-largest minority. A fair overall assessment is that they are better off than the Native Americans are and are about on an equal footing with black Americans. Practically all Mexican Americans were born in the United States and live in the Southwest, particularly California and Texas. In California their average income is 80 percent that of whites, and in Texas it is 60 percent. Most are employed as common laborers or farmhands. Their work pattern is irregular, unemployment is high, and working conditions are generally very poor. Except for the efforts of César Chavez to unionize the farm laborers, they have traditionally lacked organization and leadership.

The Puerto Ricans are primarily located in the urban centers of the Northeast. Three-quarters of all Puerto Ricans living in the 50 states are in New York City. The Puerto Ricans' problem may be worse than that of the blacks. Although both the Puerto Rican and black poor live in ghettos, the Puerto Ricans' housing may even be poorer. Their income is very low, and language is a major barrier when seeking employment. Furthermore, the Puerto Ricans are only beginning to become politically strong.

Black Americans, who account for 75 percent of all minorities, are not confined to any particular region of the country. Since 1940 millions of blacks have left the South, and the exodus continues. Most blacks live in the large urban centers of the North. Today, almost two-thirds of blacks reside in cities. In contrast with the other minorities, they have gained much political power. They are organized and recently have made some progress in income and educational levels.

Although most people would agree that blacks are better off than they were a couple of decades ago, the fact remains that the median income for black families is still below that of whites. Only for black families in the South in which both husband and wife worked have there been substantial gains in narrowing the income gap. It should be noted that young black families in which both spouses worked actually had a higher average income than did white families. Yet the annual earnings of black men working full time averaged much below those of whites.

The unemployment levels remain about twice as high for blacks as for whites, and unemployment for blacks is three times higher than for whites among younger workers (16 to 24 years old).

There have always been unequal employment opportunities for females, as well as inequities in male and female salaries and job promotions. Overall, there are far fewer female than male managers and administrators, though the percentage has recently improved. But for black women, the statistics are even worse. Black female managers account for a negligible percentage of all managerial positions.

The median earnings for these positions are considerably higher for white male managers than for black male managers, and both are higher than for women managers. Despite the obvious gains that women have made in recent years in the workplace, there is still no evidence that the wage gap has narrowed. The average working woman still earns far less than her male counterpart.[1] The problem may be more pronounced in executive ranks, as shown in the box "Women Are Still Absent from the Executive Suite."

In summary, the statistics indicate that equal employment opportunity remains an important social issue. Although the recent political climate has tried to cool the equal-opportunity issue, civil rights groups are beginning to react.[2] The statistics clearly indicate that minorities and women do not fare well in employment. Although the civil rights laws enacted over 20 years ago prohibited sexual and racial discrimination, the statistics cannot enumerate the amount of human suffering that discrimination creates. Those who have no will to succeed because they feel it would be of no use or those who become alcoholics as a way to forget their plight represent only a few of the victims of discrimination. Society and business must work

---

[1]Barbara Mackey Carlson and Mary Pat McEnrue, "Eliminating the Gender-Based Earning Gap: Two Alternatives," *Business Horizons*, July–August 1985, p. 76.

[2]"Battle Heats Up over Sex, Race Bias in Jobs," *U.S. News & World Report*, May 27, 1985, p. 49.

WOMEN ARE STILL ABSENT FROM THE EXECUTIVE SUITE

The popular press likes to write about how discrimination barriers are falling and more and more women are getting promotions and higher salaries. However, recent research shows that although this may be occurring at the middle ranks of the hierarchy, it is not taking place in the executive suite. *Fortune* magazine reports that "no women are on the fast track to the chief executive's job at any Fortune 500 corporation. That's incongruous, given the number of years women have been working in management. The reasons are elusive and tough for management to deal with."

Some researchers argue that the reason women are not paid more money or do not occupy top management positions is that they choose occupations that traditionally are low paying. For example, they gravitate toward jobs with the government instead of those in investment banking and real estate, where the money and opportunities are much better. Other researchers contest these findings. One researcher recently matched 45 men and women who graduated from the Columbia Business School from 1969 through 1972. Each was paired on the basis of background, and the starting salaries of the women were 98 percent of the men's. Ten years later the salary gaps were much greater. The women were earning $41,818 annually compared to $59,733 for the men; in finance the average salaries for the women were $42,867 versus $46,786 for the men; in service industries it was $36,666 for the women versus $38,600 for the men. What accounts for this? Some of the reasons that were examined included: women have low motivation; they tend to take jobs in low-paying industries; and they are interested in motherhood rather than a career. None of these hypotheses were found to be supported by the research data. The conclusion of was that low salaries are a result of discrimination. Whether or not this conclusion is totally accurate, it does point out that the challenge of providing equal opportunity for women in the workplace continues to be a major one for business.

Source: Susan Fraker, "Why Women Aren't Getting to the Top," *Fortune,* April 16, 1985, pp. 40–45.

together to stamp out discrimination and the resultant hopelessness. Later in this chapter we review some of the affirmative action programs initiated by business firms for recruiting and training disadvantaged, discriminated workers to enable them to compete in today's work force. First, we examine the federal legislation against discrimination so as to analyze equal opportunity employment.

FEDERAL LAW AND EMPLOYMENT DISCRIMINATION

There are five major federal laws that directly affect the discretion that a business firm has in personnel matters. These five laws are the Equal Pay Act, Title VII of the Civil Rights Act, executive orders, the Age Discrimination in Employment Act, and the Rehabilitation Act.

Equal Pay Act of 1963

The Equal Pay Act was passed as an amendment to the Fair Labor Standards Act of 1938. The Equal Pay Act was not designed to protect all groups from discrimination in levels of compensation, only discrimination based on sex. The provisions of the law prohibit an employer, in the matter of compensation, from discriminating on the basis of sex. Compensation may be based on a seniority system, merit system, piece-rate system, or another differential based on any other factor besides sex. Violations under the law can lead to the payment of damages equal to the inequity for a period of three years from the violation (i.e., there is a statute of limitations of three years on violations). In addition, damages can be awarded that would equal, at most, the amount of damages in back pay. Until July 1979 the agency in charge of interpretation and enforcement of the Equal Pay Act was the Department of Labor. President Carter's organization plan of 1978 shifted responsibility to the Equal Employment Opportunity Commission (EEOC).

The initial focus of the act was to forbid payment of a different wage for employees of different sexes doing the same work. The focus of litigation in the past decade has been directed toward uncovering immaterial differences in job classifications that would tend to hide pay discrimination. For example, the titles "administrative assistant" and "executive secretary," used for the same job but the first held by a male and the second by a female, would be a guise for pay discrimination. The courts attempt to uncover discrimination through a determination if there are a significantly higher number of females in one job compared to the other. If so, the question becomes: Is there a material difference in the nature of each task? The key indices would relate to comparing the skill, effort (mental and physical), and level of responsibility, and whether the task was performed under similar working conditions. If there is a material difference between any of the four dimensions, the two jobs are considered different and the pay differential not discriminatory.

A company's primary defense in granting a difference in the level of pay would be based on demonstrating that there are differences in the task. Barring that defense, a company may demonstrate that there is a bona fide training program for training to the higher-paying position and that the program is open to both sexes equally and there has been a recruiting effort to encourage people of both sexes to apply. A third defense is for a company to demonstrate that the higher-paying task is a "red-circle" job. This is a job that is designated at a lower wage rate than is currently being paid because employees in this job were already in it before the rate was lowered.

Comparable Worth: Going Beyond the Equal Pay Act

Related to the concept of equal pay for equal worth is the concept of comparable worth. *Comparable worth* can be defined as a systematic evaluation of all jobs with a determination of each's comparable contribution to an organization. The comparable worth position is that the contribution made, and not market forces, should determine the level of compensation one receives. There are some real philosophical differences between comparable worth and equal worth. The comparable worth controversy is a debate about the causes of the pay gap between traditionally "male" and traditionally "female" occupations and what, if anything, should be done to reduce them.[3]

Comparable worth is more inclusive and considers comparing dissimilar jobs and the contribution each makes to an organization. For example, do clerical workers (predominantly female) and construction workers (predominantly male) make comparable contributions to the same organization? If they do, then under the comparable worth doctrine the clerical workers should be paid the same as the construction workers. However, under the equal pay act, only similar jobs are compared to determine if they are, indeed, paid at the same rate.

With the continued disparity between pay levels between sexes in organizations, there is increasing pressure for a change in the equal pay law toward the direction of comparable worth. However, there is also strong resistance against comparable worth because it would involve a complex and subjective job rating system and fails to account for market forces in the determination of compensation.[4] At first, some court decisions, such as for government employees in Washington state, upheld comparable worth, but more recently, for political and economic as well as legal reasons, the decisions have been going against such cases.

Title VII of the 1964 Civil Rights Act

The Civil Rights Act was signed into law on July 2, 1964. It contains 11 major sections. Title VII is the most relevant to business, for it prohibits discrimination in employment on the basis of race, color, religion, sex, or national origin. Employees fitting these targeted criteria are considered protected groups. The act specifically forbids employers from discriminating

[3]Sara Rynes, Benson Rosen, and Thomas A. Mahoney, "Evaluating Comparable Worth: Three Perspectives," *Business Horizons*, July–August 1985, p. 82.
[4]Danial Seligman, "Pay Equity Is a Bad Idea," *Fortune*, May 14, 1984, p. 133.

in hiring, training, compensating, promoting, or discharging workers and prohibits segregating or classifying in any way that would deprive, or tend to deprive, a person of equal employment opportunities. The law covers virtually every employer, including religious and educational institutions. In addition, the act forbids employment agencies to segregate, expel, exclude, or classify workers. An employment agency is defined to include all private and public employment agencies, newspapers that have employment want ads, labor organizations, and college placement activities. The act established the Equal Employment Opportunity Commission (EEOC), composed of five members appointed by the president and approved by the Senate. The commission's responsibility is to investigate complaints, seek to attain settlements through conciliation if it finds violations, and ask the Attorney General to bring suit if conciliation is unsuccessful. A 1972 amendment gave power to the EEOC to file its own suits and expanded coverage of the act to public service employees.

There are three general standards that are applied to determine if there is discrimination against one of the protected groups. First, it is determined if there is any evidence of overt, disparate treatment against a protected group. A second criterion is whether there are any rules that tend to perpetuate past intentional discrimination or segregation. A third criterion is whether there are any rules that have an adverse impact on a protected class but which are not justified by "business necessity."

If any of these three conditions exist, discrimination has occurred. The penalties for violation under the act include back pay and remedial seniority to correct the discrimination, and attorney fees, but punitive damages are excluded. However, the remedies allowed under the Equal Pay Act are often included in litigation.

In recent years, most litigation has been directed toward de facto discrimination or in cases where rules or policies have led to adverse impact on a protected group. A major consideration under this criterion is whether the rules, restrictions, or employee selection techniques utilize *bona fide occupational qualifications* (BFOQs). Determining whether a requirement for a job is a BFOQ has been relatively troublesome for the courts. Some cases are obviously relatively clear. For example, requiring that a police officer be of a particular height has been struck down by the courts as being discriminatory. Under Title VII, the organization, in this case the police department, has the burden of proof to demonstrate that a particular height is critical in the execution of the normal duties of the task. If it cannot, this criterion may be declared as discriminatory, as women are, on the average, shorter than males.

In other cases, a BFOQ might be more troublesome to determine. For example, a dress code is legal unless it can be demonstrated that compliance creates a hardship for a protected group. However, the courts attempt to weigh the needs of business with the impact that the code may have on a protected group. For example, a "Big Eight" accounting firm, because of its need for a professional image, may be allowed to prescribe a particular dress code. However, this code may inhibit the rights of an employee who is a member of a particular religious order that wears religious garb while on the job.

Requiring an employee to work on his or her Sabbath may be an acceptable BFOQ if other people would be forced to cover for the employee granted time off with work that is essential, but educational institutions operated by religious organizations may discriminate in their hiring based on religion. In the latter case, the needs to reflect the values of the religion outweigh the need to protect specific groups of employees. In addition, restricting a particular job to a specific sex may be allowable if it is part of a company image, for example, a Playboy Bunny.

As the examples demonstrate above, the determination of what conditions are BFOQs and what are not becomes an important part of the interpretation of the law and a matter of judicial interpretation. It is clear, however, that the court is ready to balance the legitimate needs of firms for BFOQs with equal opportunity in employment. However, the burden of proof is on the organization to demonstrate that each qualification or criterion is necessary.

Executive Orders and the Current Legal/Political Climate

Executive orders are not laws but administrative guidelines that are issued by the executive branch. For example, Executive Order 11246 was issued to guide the purchase of goods and services by the federal government. Title VII of the Civil Rights Act would have an influence on most private-sector organizations from which the government would purchase services, and an executive order provides some additional restrictions on the activities of those sellers. The philosophy for these restrictions is based on the notion that suppliers for the government sign contracts at their own free will. The government can therefore specify the terms and conditions that contractors must follow if they wish to do busiess with the federal government. Executive Order 11246 lays down some very specific groundwork regarding affirmative action and employment discrimination guidelines.

Executive Order 11246 requires that all contractors that do business with the federal government with agreements worth $10,000 or more must

1. Not discriminate on the basis of race, color, religion, or national origin.
2. Have an acceptable affirmative action program.
3. Provide information required under the executive order.
4. Indicate in all advertising that it is an affirmative action employer.
5. Ensure that all subcontracting work is also under a bona fide affirmative action program.

An *affirmative action program*, which is also required under Title VII of the Civil Rights Act, is a program that attempts to attract, retain, and promote protected classes of individuals in that organization. It is given detailed attention toward the end of the chapter.

Although quotas are illegal under Title VII, they are legal under government contract work. Hence programs in construction work using federal funds have been required to submit *Philadelphia Plans*. These are specific plans to demonstrate how the contractor will have representatives of protected groups on the work force in sufficient numbers to meet the goals outlined by the administrator of the Executive Order 11246, the Federal Office of Contract Compliance, which is part of the Department of Labor. The term "Philadelphia Plan" evolved from the first application of Executive Order 11246 for federal contracts.

Penalties for violations of Executive Order 11246 are the same as for violation of any contract. Violations may lead to the company's exclusion of eligibility for future federal government contracts. However, when the Philadelphia Plan concept of quotas has been extended to areas other than those doing contract work for the federal government, there has been much resistance, legally and politically. For example, in a case involving layoffs of Memphis, Tennessee, firefighters, the Supreme Court ruled in 1984 that employers cannot interfere with a seniority system to protect minorities from being laid off. The court then went on to say that this principle applied to hiring and promotion as well.

The Reagan administration has generally not supported the idea of quotas and feels that the whole idea is attacking the wrong problem and is devisive. For example, in a recent interview, Morris Abram, vice-chairman of the U.S. Commission on Civil Rights, stated:

> I oppose quotas because they create an ethnic spoils system for certain groups to grab more power for their members—at the expense of individuals outside the group. That's contrary to our civil-rights laws that guarantee equal protection of civil rights for *all* Americans, not just for blacks, women, and other minorities. . . . Just as discrimination done in the name of white supremacy was wrong, discrimination done in the name of racial or sexual preference is wrong.[5]

The Age Discrimination in Employment Act

The Age Discrimination in Employment Act is similar to Title VII of the Civil Rights Act except that it focuses on age. Under this act, the protected group is defined as anyone between the ages of 40 and 65. The act was amended in 1974 to expand coverage to include public-sector employees. In 1978, the act was further amended when the maximum age of the protected group was modified from 65 to 70 years of age. Until 1979, the Department of Labor was responsible for the enforcement and interpretation of the act;

[5]Morris Abram, "End Sex and Race Goals in Hiring," *U.S. News & World Report*, May 27, 1985, p. 50.

then the responsibility was transferred to the Equal Employment Opportunity Commission.

The act was designed to curb many of the seemingly arbitrary rules regarding retirement age and abuses that occurred regarding employment decisions for older workers. For example, not hiring salespersons because they were in their 40s and considered too old for the job would be considered illegal under the act. Since the protected group is between 40 and 70, mandatory retirement ages of 65 became illegal. However, manadatory retirement ages of over 70 years of age are not. Apparently, Congress felt that only those between 40 and 70 needed to be protected.

The Age Discrimination Act makes age a factor in hiring, firing, promotion, training, and compensating. It also makes tests and other requirements illegal if they are given because of age; this is the "age-plus" notion. For example, it is illegal to require an employee to take an annual physical exam after age 50. The taking of the physical exam is not at issue if it is a bona fide occupational requirement. However, making an older employee take a physical is illegal even if age is not the deciding factor in determining whether or not the employee may retain employment. The same standard is held for other personnel policies, such as performance standards, misconduct, and attendance policies.

The courts have also taken a dim view of terminating an individual's employment because of benefit plan restrictions or in situations where an employee might only be covered by health insurance if the employee is under 65 or not working. Some companies have tried to force "elective" retirement at age 65 through the use of lack of benefit program coverage.

The Rehabilitation Act

Similar to Executive Order 11246, the Rehabilitation Act is directed at contractors who do work with the federal government. The act aids the disabled and handicapped in securing rehabilitation training, access to public buildings, and equal opportunity in employment. More specifically, the act does the following:

1. Section 501 requires federal agencies to have affirmative action programs directed toward hiring of the handicapped. Rights specified under Title VII of the Civil Rights Act apply to the disabled. This section of the law is administered by the Equal Employment Opportunity Commission.
2. Section 503 includes disabled persons in affirmative action programs that are imposed on federal contractors similar to those imposed in Executive Order 11246. This section of the law is administered by the Federal Office of Contract Compliance and covers contracts of $10,000 or more.
3. Section 504 prohibits discrimination for federally funded programs

on the basis of being disabled. This section is administered by the Department of Health and Human Services.

4. The Veterans Readjustment Assistance Act addresses disabled veterans and is similar to Section 503 of the Rehabilitation Act except that the disabled veteran is the targeted protected group. This act is administered by the Federal Office of Contract Compliance and covers contracts of $10,000 or more.

The act is not as broad-based as the Civil Rights Act. It does not cover employers who are not federal contractors.

EMPLOYMENT DISCRIMINATION LAWS AND THE CONSEQUENCE TO BUSINESS

Table 8.1 summarizes the federal laws that attempt to ensure equal opportunity employment for all citizens. In addition to the major pieces of federal legislation discussed so far, the table indicates that most states have enacted their own laws to stamp out discrimination in employment. The consequence to business of these federal and state laws have been dramatic.

In general, the guiding rule for business is to be more careful to ensure that decision criteria used for personnel actions are bona fide occupational qualifications that can be justified both through logical arguments and well-documented backup and analysis. In addition, the courts are viewing uniform quantified decision criteria as much more acceptable than subjectively based evaluations.

Appropriate antidiscrimination requirements for an organization can be found in the guidelines set forth by the Equal Employment Opportunity Commission (EEOC). These guidelines primarily affect the personnel process, such as recruitment, selection (especially the use of employment tests and application forms), promotion, and the resultant record-keeping requirements.

Recruitment Procedures

By assuming an affirmative action responsibility, a firm should do everything possible to recruit minority applicants, including advertising in newspapers with a high minority readership or advertising on television and radio programs that are relevant to minority interests. In determining whether an organization uses discriminatory practices, the EEOC requires some indication that the organization is actively attempting to recruit minorities in good faith and has some working plan to reach a more equitable balance. A second area of the civil rights law's impact on recruitment is the use of want ads. It is illegal to state a sex pereference for a particular task unless sex is a bona fide requirement for the task. Most ads should also state that the firm is an equal employment opportunity employer.

TABLE 8.1. **Summary of Antidiscrimination Laws.**

Federal Law	Type of Employment Discrimination Prohibited	Employers Covered
U.S. Constitution, 1st and 5th Amendments	Deprivation of employment rights without due process of law	Federal government
U.S. Constitution, 14th Amendment	Deprivation of employment rights without due process of law	State and local governments
Civil Rights Act of 1866 and 1870 (based on 13th Amendment)	Race discrimination in hiring, placement, and continuation of employment	Private employers, unions, employment agencies
Civil Rights Act of 1871 (based on 14th Amendment)	Deprivation of equal employment rights under cover of state law	State and local governments (private employers if conspiracy is involved)
National Labor Relations Act	Unfair representation by unions, or interference with employee rights, that discriminates on the basis of race, color, religion, sex, or national origin	Private employers and unions
Equal Pay Act of 1963	Sex differences in pay for substantially equal work	Private employers (state and local governments uncertain)
Executive Order 11141 (1964)	Age discrimination	Federal contractors and subcontractors
Title VI, 1964 Civil Rights Act	Discrimination based on race, color, or national origin	Employers receiving federal financial assistance
Title VII, 1964 Civil Rights Act (as amended in 1972) by the Equal Employment Act of 1972	Discrimination or segregation based on race, color, religion, sex, or national origin	Private employers with 15 or more employees; federal, state, and local governments; unions and apprenticeship committees; employment agencies
Executive Orders 11246 and 11375 (1965)	Discrimination based on race, color, religion, sex, or national origin (affirmative action required)	Federal contractors and subcontractors
Age Discrimination in Employment Act of 1967	Age discrimination against those between the ages of 40 and 65	Private employers with 20 or more employees, unions with 25 or more members, employment agencies, apprenticeship and training programs (state and local governments uncertain)
Title I, 1968 Civil Rights Act	Interference with a person's exercise of rights with respect to race, religion, color, or national origin	Persons generally

TABLE 8.1.   Continued

Federal Law	Type of Employment Discrimination Prohibited	Employers Covered
Executive Order 11478 (1969)	Discrimination based on race, color, religion, sex, national origin, political affiliation, marital status, or physical handicap	Federal government
Revenue Sharing Act of 1972	Discrimination based on race, color, national origin, or sex	State and local governments receiving revenue-sharing funds
Education Amendments of 1972	Sex discrimination	Educational institutions receiving federal financial assistance
Rehabilitation act of 1973; Executive Order no. 11914 (1974)	Discrimination based on physical or mental handicap (affirmative action required)	Federal contractors, federal government
Vietnam Era Veterans Readjustments Act of 1974	Discrimination against disabled veterans and Vietnam era veterans (affirmative action required)	Federal contractors, federal government
Age Discrimination Act of 1975	Age discrimination	Employers receiving federal financial assistance
State laws. State fair employment practices laws	Similar to Title VII and Equal Employment Act of 1972	Varies by state; passed in about 85 percent of states

Source: William F. Glueck, *Personnel: A Diagnostic Approach,* rev. ed. (Plano, Tex.: Business Publications). p. 602. © 1978 by Business Publications, Inc. Used with permission.

The Use of Employment Tests

Although most firms are committed to eliminating employment discrimination, a fine line still exists between what is and what is not discriminatory. Testing is a good illustration. Traditionally every major business organization in America depended on tests in the selection procedure. Intelligence, aptitude, physical skill, and personality are only a few of the things that were tested. But it is extremely difficult to determine whether discrimination enters into the evaluation of the results. If a particular test measures what it is designed to measure and does so consistently, then it is both valid and reliable.

However, being valid and reliable does not necessarily mean that the test is not discriminatory. Intelligence testing is a good example. If a middle-class white person scores high, and an impoverished black person scores low, are the results a fair test of intelligence? Many scholars contend that the typical intelligence test is designed so that people with middle-class values and education will do better, as the questions deal with topics and examples they know and understand. For the black who grew up in the ghetto, the entire exam may be befuddling. The vocabulary is likely to be strange, and the math questions use unfamiliar examples. The test may accurately measure a specific achievement but not intellectual capacity or potential. The Motorola Company encountered this problem when it gave a general aptitude test to a black applicant for a job. He failed the test and was not hired. The black then filed a complaint claiming that he was discriminated against because of the nature of the test. The case received national publicity but was never clearly settled. But the U.S. Supreme Court took a stand on testing in the case of *Griggs* v. *Duke Power Company*. In this case, 13 black laborers had asked to be promoted to coal handlers in the North Carolina utility. The company insisted that the men take a general intelligence test containing verbal and mathematical puzzles. The men scored low and were not promoted. In the suit that followed the Court unanimously ruled that the Civil Rights Act prohibits an employer from requiring a high school education or a standard general intelligence test as a condition of employment in or transfer to jobs when neither is related to successful job performance. In other words, companies must now be able to prove the validity of a test used for selection, transfer, or promotion. Instead of trying to validate their employment tests, which they should have been doing all along, most companies today have simply eliminated them.

The Use of Application Blanks and Interviews

The EEOC generally defined what is legal and illegal to include on an application blank or what questions may or may not be asked during the preemployment interview. The general guideline with respect to employment tests and recruitment programs is that an employer should ask only those questions that are necessary for the particular task for which the individual is applying. If the questions are not essential to that end, then they should not be asked. Table 8.2 presents a comprehensive list of legal and illegal question topics.

The courts have generally ruled that just asking certain questions before the selection decision is made can unduly influence the decision makers and therefore can be considered discriminatory. For example, a previous arrest record or a particular marital record is not an equitable criterion to use to select an employee and cannot be allowed to influence the decision. A survey of seventy-four directors of placement services found that the most common questions in screening interviews involved the applicants' sex.[6] especially females' marital and family plans.

---

[6]"Use of Discriminatory Questions in Screening Interviews," *Personnel Administrator*, March 1982, pp. 41–44.

TABLE 8.2.   Guidelines for Preemployment Inquiries.[a]

	Lawful Inquiries	*Unlawful Inquiries*
Name	"Have you worked for this organization under a different name? Is any additional information relative to change of name, use of an assumed name, or nickname necessary to enable a check on your work and educational record? If yes, explain."	Inquiries about the name that would indicate applicant's lineage, ancestry, national origin, or descent. Inquiries into previous name of applicant when it has been changed by court order, marriage, or otherwise.
Marital and family status	Whether applicant can meet specified work schedules or has activities, commitments, or responsibilities that may hinder the meeting of work attendance requirements. Inquiries as to a duration of stay on the job or anticipated absences that are made to males and females alike.	Any inquiries indicating whether an applicant is married, single, divorced, engaged, etc. Number and age of children. Any questions concerning pregnancy. Any such questions that directly or indirectly results in limiting job opportunities in any way.
Age	If a minor, require proof of age in form of a work permit or a certificate of age. Require proof of age by birth certificate after being hired. Inquiry as to whether or not the applicant meets the minimum age requirements as set by law and requirements that upon hire, proof of age must be submitted. If age is a legal requirement: "If hired, can you furnish proof of age?"/ or statement that hire is subject to verification of age.	Requirement that applicant produce proof of age in the form of a birth certificate or baptismal record.
Handicaps	Whether applicant has any handicaps or health problems, sensory, mental, or physical, that may affect work performance or that the employer should consider in determining job placement.	General inquiries (i.e., "Do you have any handicaps?") that would divulge handicaps or health conditions that do not relate reasonably to fitness to perform the job.

TABLE 8.2.   Continued

	Lawful Inquiries	*Unlawful Inquiries*
Sex	Inquiry or restriction of employment is permissible only if a bona fide occupational qualification exists. (This BFOQ exception is interpreted very narrowly by the courts and EEOC.) The burden of proof rests on the employer to prove that the BFOQ does exist and that all members of the affected class are incapable of performing the job.	Sex of the applicant. Any other inquiry that would indicate sex. Sex is not a BFOQ because a job involves physical labor (such as heavy lifting) beyond the capacity of some women, nor can sex be used as a factor for determining whether or not an applicant will be satisfied in a particular job.
Race or color	General distinguishing physical characteristics, such as scars or moles.	Applicant's race. Color of applicant's skin, eyes, hair, etc. or other questions directly or indirectly indicating race or color. Applicant's height or weight when not relevant
Address or duration of residence	Applicant's address. Inquiry into place and length of current and previous addresses. "How long a resident of this state or city?"	Specific inquiry into foreign addresses that would indicate national origin. Names or relationships of persons with whom applicant resides. Whether applicant owns or rents home
Birthplace	"Can you after employment submit a birth certificate or other proof of U.S. citizenship?"	Birthplace of applicant. Birthplace of applicant's parents, spouse, or other relatives. Requirement that applicant submit birth certificate or naturalization or baptismal record before employment. Any other inquiry to indicate or identify denomination or customs.
Photograph	May be required after hiring for identification.	Request photograph before hiring. Requirement that applicant affix a photograph to his application. Request that applicant, at his or her option, submit photograph. Requirement of photograph after interview but before hiring.

TABLE 8.2. Continued

	Lawful Inquiries	Unlawful Inquiries
Military record	Type of education and experience in service as it relates to a particular job.	Type of discharge.
Citizenship	"Are you a citizen of the U.S.?" If you are not a U.S. citizen, do you have the legal right to remain permanently in the U.S.? Do you intend to remain permanently in the U.S.? Statement that if hired, applicant may be required to submit proof of citizenship." If not a citizen, are you prevented from lawfully becoming employed because of visa or immigration status?"	"Of what country are you a citizen?" Whether applicant or his parents or spouse are naturalized or native-born U.S. citizens. Date when applicant or parents or spouse acquired U.S. citizenship. Requirement that applicant produce his or her naturalization papers or first papers. Whether applicant's parents are citizens of the United States.
Ancestry or national origin	Languages applicant reads, speaks, or writes fluently.	Inquiries into applicant's lineage, ancestry, national origin, descent, birthplace, or mother tongue. National origin of applicant's parents or spouse.
Education	Applicant's academic, vocational, or professional education; school attended. Inquiry into language skills such as reading, speaking, and writing foreign languages.	Inquiry asking specifically the nationality, racial or religious affiliation of a school. Inquiry as to what is mother tongue or how foreign language ability was acquired.
Experience	Applicant's work experience. Other countries visited.	
Conviction, arrest and court record	Inquiry into actual convictions that relate reasonably to fitness to perform a particular job. (A conviction is a court ruling in which the party is found guilty as charged. An arrest is merely the apprehending or detaining of the person to answer the alleged crime.)	Any inquiry relating to arrests. To ask or check into a person's arrest, court, or conviction record if not substantially related to functions and responsibilities of the prospective employment.
Relatives	Names of applicant's relatives already employed by this company. Names and	Name or address of any relative of adult applicant.

TABLE 8.2.   Continued

	Lawful Inquiries	Unlawful Inquiries
Notice in case of emergency	addresses of parents or guardian of minor applicant. Names of persons to be notified.	Names and address of relative to be notified in case of accident or emergency.
Organizations	Inquiry into the organization of which an applicant is a member, providing the name or character of the organization does not reveal the race, religion, color, or ancestry of the membership. What offices are held, if any?	"List all organizations, clubs, societies and lodges to which you belong." The names of organizations to which the applicant belongs if such information would indicate, through character or name, the race, religion, color, or ancestry of the membership.
Credit rating	None.	Any questions concerning credit rating, charge accounts, etc.
References	By whom were you referred for a position here? Names of persons willing to provide professional and/or character references for applicant. Who suggested that applicant apply for a position here?	Require the submission of a religious reference. Request reference from applicant's pastor.
Miscellaneous	Notice to applicants that any misstatement or omissions of material facts in the application may be cause for dismissal.	

[a]These are only *guidelines*. The courts, EEOC, and state and local fair employment practices agencies may make different interpretations.

Source: Compiled by Clifford Coen, December 1976 *Newsletter* of the American Association of Affirmative Action.

Promotion Criteria

Not only has the EEOC enforced rigorous selection guidelines, but it also has taken several organizations to task for discrimination after employment. Discrimination can exist in disparity between salaries and a lack of minorities and women in supervisory/managerial positions. For example, a few years ago, the EEOC obtained a consent decree that cost American Telephone and Telegraph $45 million and drastically changed its promotion and hiring procedures. The EEOC favors an objective promotion plan. Promotion decisions must be based on rational, quantifiable criteria such as the individual's work record and ability, and not on any subjective whim.

Although to date the courts have not provided specific guidelines for evaluation systems, many traditional promotion procedures could be considered discriminatory. Most of the existing systems depend heavily on trait assessment. For example, one of the categories on a typical appraisal form asks the supervisor to rate work habits. Such categories include subjective judgments, rating habits from excellent to poor. This sort of subjective approach may provide data for making wage increases or job promotions but does not provide a quantitative base. Many experts believe that this aspect of discrimination may be the basis of the EEOC's future activities and of resulting court actions.

Personnel Record-Keeping Requirements

As part of the process to prevent discrimination in organizations, the EEOC requires large amounts of employee data. The EEOC also recommends that a specific affirmative action program be developed and implemented. The specifics of this program should be well documented. (Examples of such affirmative action programs appear later in this chapter.) Such record-keeping requirements can be costly and time-consuming for business firms. An example of the types of data requested by EEOC during a legal proceeding follows:

List all job classifications.

List all grade classifications within each job classification.

List all job descriptions.

Indicate all starting salaries for each job.

Indicate the number of jobs in each classification at the present time.

List the number of blacks employed in each job by job during 7/2/65; 7/2/68; presently.

List the number of whites employed in each job by job during the same periods.

Indicate each job promotion ladder; the salaries of each job promotion, and the number of blacks and whites in each progression, and how rapidly they progressed.

Indicate for each current employee the date hired, starting salary, and job, present salary and job and intermediate promotions and salary levels, with dates of promotions.

Describe criteria of promotion and hiring that are used.

Indicate how the company recruited for personnel.

Indicate for each job the requirements for the tasks and the specific screening devices used. Indicate validation procedures for these devices.[7]

[7]William F. Glueck, *Personnel: A Diagnostic Approach* (Plano, Tex.: Business Publications, 1974), pp. 543–549.

These are just some of the data required, but they indicate the scope and pervasiveness of the EEOC in current business personnel practices.

AFFIRMATIVE ACTION TRAINING AND RECRUITMENT PROGRAMS

In light of the Court decisions, many firms have been moving away from hiring quotas and toward special training programs and increased recruitment efforts to reduce discrimination and institute affirmative action. The argument in favor of affirmative action programs was recently stated by the mayor of Indianapolis, William Hudnut: "A lot of progress has been made with affirmative-action goals. Without them, we would regress into a situation where overt or covert discrimination against blacks, Hispanics, and women would prevent them from taking their rightful place in the mainstream of community activity."[8] Almost all modern organizations have reexamined job entry requirements and testing techniques to determine if they are really related to the task. There are several approaches that can be used in hiring and training minorities and women.

Hiring the Hard-Core Unemployed

Although hard-core unemployment programs are cut back in a recessionary economy, as the economy picks up, they can proceed in three directions: (1) random hiring from walk-in applicants or through regular channels; (2) working through minority group and/or government organizations; (3) using private firms that specialize in matching hard-core applicants with appropriate jobs in cooperating companies.

Companies that have been successful in hiring the hard-core unemployed have most often sought the help of relevant minority group organizations and the government. The case of Western Electric is a good illustration. Its experience with hiring hard-core unemployed for a plant in the Newark ghetto determined that it was absolutely necessary to obtain support from grass-roots minority organizations and the government. Western Electric obtained this support in two ways. First, it became acquainted with relevant national and local government agencies which provided valuable information about recruiting, hiring, training, and placing disadvantaged persons. After this information was exhausted, the next step was to turn to the target area it was trying to help and to identify the informal leaders at the ghetto level, whom it used to establish meaningful dialogue with the grass-roots populace.

The Social Research Corporation of New York City is a program in which a private job awaits the trainee at the end of the training period. This is extremely valuable in training the new employee, for frequent reference

[8]William Hudnut, "End Sex and Race Goals in Hiring?" *U.S. News & World Report,* 1985, p. 50.

• In 1965, 54 percent of the men and 50 percent of the women responding said that women rarely expect or want authority. Today, only 9 percent of the male respondents and 4 percent of the female respondents felt that way.

The findings, in general, reveal that both men and women in the workplace feel that a woman has a better chance to succeed than she had two decades ago. As one female respondent put it, "Women must keep knocking on the door. The women who are there must keep the faith for those who will follow. It will be easier in the future."

ANALYSIS

1. Based on the data in the case, do men believe that women are getting equal opportunities for employment? Do women agree? Explain.
2. Although not reported in the case, the thing that women feel most disheartened about is that their salaries are not equal to those of men. Why might this be so? Is it a sign that women are not being given equal opportunity? Defend your answer.
3. What would you expect the survey results to look like if this study were replicated in 20 years? Explain.

Employee Rights and Justice Systems

Chapter Objectives

- To trace the evolution of the employee-employer relationship over the past 100 years.

- To review current worker safety and health laws and the employees rights under these laws.

- To trace the various philosophies governing employee job security actions taken by governments, unions, and socially responsibe business organizations.

- To indicate the rights of employees such as ex-offenders and AIDS victims and the use of lie detector tests and drug and alcohol abuse tests.

- To improve awareness as to what constitutes harassment in the workplace and the rights of employees in harassment situations.

- To review the various structural and procedural methods that can be implemented to safeguard employee rights.

In Chapter 8 we stressed the role of government and business in combating discrimination and providing equal opportunity for all. In this chapter we continue with a consideration of the rights of employees and employers in the work setting. Whereas in Chapter 8 we enumerated the various antidiscrimination laws that influence business activity, in this chapter we view several different conditions of employment and how the organization can act legally and responsibly to ensure that there is a balancing of the rights of the individual employee, other employees as a group, and the employer. This balancing is essential to ensure that the rights of each of these three are preserved. It is a balancing of the three that the courts consider along with the letter of the law in determining whether the organization is acting responsibly.

In this chapter we first consider the evolution of the employee-employer relationship over the past 100 years. This will set the stage for understanding the current state of legal and social philosophies that are guiding public and private organization policies regarding the nature of the employee, his or her rights, and the organizational responsibility to the employee. The chapter will then view four specific dimensions of the employee/employer relationship: employee safety and health, organizational justice systems, employee personal rights, and worker security.

There is an interesting evolution that is occurring in the area of the employee-employer relationship, one that will have profound effects on the employment relationship. Through the actions of the courts and legislative activity with regard to both private- and public-sector employment, there is a clear movement to provide the employee with increasing rights and responsibilities in the employment relationship. In this chapter we review this evolution and describe the current state of employee's rights and employer responsibilities.

EVOLUTION OF EMPLOYEE-EMPLOYER RELATIONSHIPS

The Bill of Rights and the Fourteenth Amendment to the U.S. Constitution protect an individual only from government action. In no manner was the intent of this historic document to protect the individual from other individuals or from the acts of an employer. As such, a private organization could, in the absence of laws, contract and suppress an employee's rights for cause or even for no cause. The framers of the United States had little concept of the power that would be wielded by large corporations in the twentieth century. The United States, at the time of the signing of the Constitution, was primarily an agricultural-based economic system. There seemed little cause to worry over the action of corporate giants. If an employee were dissatisfied with his or her employer during the eighteenth century, there was easy recourse—to quit and be hired by another employer. In addition, at the time, the U.S. legal environment was governed by English common law, which recognized a status-based concept of employee relations.

Status-Based Doctrine of Employment

The status-based concept views employment in terms of a master-slave relationship. The master has decided control over the relationship with the employee. However, the master-slave relationship carried with it a prescribed set of responsibilities of the employer to the employee. The employer had the responsibility for the employee's health and well-being, protection, and job security. The status-based concept placed much more of the responsibility for employee welfare on the employer and restricted the rights of the employer to act in a capricious and arbitrary manner toward the employee. The status-based doctrine is still the guiding principle in some Western European employee-employer relationships.[1]

Countries in the Far East apparently have a similar status-based doctrine. For example, in Japan there is common practice that a company will employ a loyal employee for life (i.e., the policy of lifetime employment) and has a responsibility to the employee's entire family.[2]

In the United States, on the other hand, laws governing the employment relationship took a radical turn away from the status-based model in the late nineteenth century. This departure paralleled the development of the notions of manifest destiny, social Darwinism, and laissez-faire. The reason for the change in the United States and not in the rest of the world may be attributed to the spirit of self-determination at the time, the lack of deep-rooted tradition in the employment relationship, or the repugnancy of the master-slave concept after the Civil War. In any event, the judicial decisions at the time moved aside the status-based concept and introduced the notion of an "implied employment contract" doctrine that governs the employee-employer relationship in the United States to this day.

The Implied Employment Contract Doctrine

The implied employment contract doctrine supports the notion that an employee enters a contract with an employer at the time of hiring. This contract is entered in with an "equal footing" and with "open eyes" by each party.[3] It is assumed that each party has equal say in the construction of the contract and , as such, each party would include any specific restrictions in the contract if they desire. In the absence of any specific contract provisions, the more restrictive aspect of contract law would prevail, as has been the custom through judicial precedence in applications of contract law in other business transactions. As courts moved toward the application of contract law in the employment relationship, the traditional status-based concept was replaced.

Initially, the resulting court interpretations under the implied employment contract doctrine led to some harmful consequences to the employee. For example, in the cases of *Tiller* v. *the Atlantic Coast Line Railroad*[4] and *Farwell*

---

[1]C. Summers, "Individual Protection Against Unjust Dismissal: Time for a Statute," *Virginia Law Review*, 1976, p. 485.

[2]W. Ouchi, *Theory Z: How American Business Can Meet the Japanese Challenge* (Reading, Mass.: Addison-Wesley, 1981), p. 58.

[3]"Protecting At Will Employee Against Wrongful Discharge: The Duty to Terminate Only in Good Faith," *Harvard Law Review*, 1980, pp. 1816–1818.

[4]318 U.S. 54, 58–59 (1943).

v. *the Boston and Western Railroad,*[5] the courts held that companies were not responsible for compensation for the loss to the employees from injuries that occurred to the employees while they were employed with the railroads. The basis for the courts' decisions rested with the notion that there was nothing in the implied employment contract that specified the company's responsibility for losses that the employee would have. In both cases, the courts felt that employees had the responsibility and the power to negotiate with the railroad to ensure protection and compensation for injuries. In both cases, the courts maintained that the employee chose, at their own free will, not to include injury compensation and income-loss protection. This was done at the employee's own risk. A second reinforcing principle that was applied in these cases was the notion that the wages for the tasks involved were higher than those of less risky tasks. The premium paid for employment with the railroad in the task was "just" and "adequate" compensation for the risk associated with the task. The railroad had transferred its responsibility for the risk to the employee through providing a premium level of compensation.

The doctrine of the implied employment contract has been sustained into the 1980s and currently is still the major force guiding litigation.[6] However, through recent legislation, judicial interpretations, and changes in the court's philosophy, there have been some major shifts in the responsibilities of employers and employees in the employment contract.

Expanding the Employer's Responsibility to the Employee

While contract law still prevails as the guiding doctrine in U.S. employee-employer relations, there have been some major inroads to management rights that have tended to moderate the responsibilities of the employer. These changes have been the result of laws and court decisions. Court decisions have moved more to a philosophy of the "deep pocket" theory. The *deep pocket doctrine* maintains that the entity with the higher capacity to sustain a loss ought to be made to sustain the loss rather than the entity with less capacity. For example, recently a person was involved in a fatal automobile accident. The killed driver was drunk and parked his car on the center lane of an interstate highway, then turned off the lights and went to sleep. A trailer truck proceeding at interstate speeds rammed the car from behind. The family sued the car manufacturer for having an unsafe product, as the gas tank exploded when hit from behind by a truck and "contributed" to the death of the driver of the car. The courts maintained that the manufacturer did contribute to the death and awarded $2 million to the family.

---

[5]45 Mass 49, 57 (1842).

[6]T. Moore, "Individual Rights of Employees Within the Corporation," *The Corporate Law Review*, 1983, pp. 39–48.

Similarly, the courts would view the overall organization as having a higher capacity to withstand a loss than an individual employee. As such, companies are successfully being challenged more and more by employees who have sustained a loss because of personal rights violations, invasion of privacy, or other types of personal loss.

Laws have been passed that have tended to modify the employment contract through further restricting management rights. These laws can be grouped into four categories: employee health and safety, protecting the employee from employer abuses, employee security, and antidiscrimination laws.

Employee safety and health laws relate to the various laws that have been established to protect the employee. Most publicly visible of these laws is the 1971 Occupational Safety and Health Act (OSHA). A principal purpose of the law is "to assure so far as possible, every working man and woman in the Nation safe and healthful working conditions as to preserve our human resources. . . ."[7] The practical aspects of OSHA was to change many of the previous safety and health codes of voluntary compliance into specific mandatory directives. In the absence of providing a safe environment, the employer should inform the employee of the working hazards. In addition, employer responsibility is reflected in state worker injury and disability compensation (worker injury compensation) programs that are funded through employer contributions.[8]

Protecting the employee from employer abuses accounts for a second category of laws. Specific areas of legislation under this category include pension reform, hours of work, minimum pay, child labor, and similar legislation. The focus of this body of laws is to protect the employee from "exploitation" by the employer. For example, the Welfare and Pension Plan Disclosure Act is designed to eliminate pension program abuses by the employer through making the administrators of pension plans more accountable through mandatory reporting requirements. The Employee Retirement Income Security Act further restricts management's or organized labor's use of funds in a pension plan, mandates more generous vesting requirements, and restricts exclusionary provisions. These acts protect the investment that the employee has in his or her pension that the company or the employee has contributed to in the employee's behalf.

A third category relates to employee security. Unemployment compensation programs and the passage of the Social Security Act are obvious responses to public policy sentiment that the employee should be safeguarded in times of need or in old age. In addition, the employer has some obligation to the employee to meet these needs, as evidenced by the mandatory employer contributions associated with each of these programs.

---

[7]U.S. Department of Labor, *All About OSHA* (Washington, D.C.: U.S. Government Printing Office, 1972), p. 3.

[8]J. Ledvinka, *Federal Regulation and Personnel and Human Resource Management* (Boston: Kent Publishing, 1982), pp. 137–154.

Equal Employment Opportunity legislation, such as that discussed in Chapter 8, provide a distinct framework of laws that safeguard protected classes of employees (and unprotected under Section 703j of the Civil Rights Act). In an employer-employee contract framework, the antidiscrimination legislation specifies the responsibilities of employers to ensure that personnel actions are appropriate and consider the personal rights that employees do have and bring to the workplace.

The laws discussed above and the evolution of the courts reflect the changing sentiment of society for the responsibilities of the employer to the employee. There is a clear evidence that society desires that employing organizations have a more extensive obligation to employees than the narrow view held many years ago. In addition, there seems to be an accurate assessment that the implied contract of employment that an employee enters when agreeing to work for an organization is not made, in most cases, on an "equal footing" basis. Under current realities of employment, the employee needs additional protection that probably could not be "negotiated" at the time of employment.

In the rest of the chapter we review specific aspects of the current law and the status of management and employee rights in the area of worker safety and health, workplace justice, employee personal rights, and worker security.

WORKER SAFETY AND HEALTH: THE RIGHT TO SAFE AND HEALTHY WORKING CONDITIONS

Two concerns are focused on in consideration of worker safety and health: first, the protection of workers, and second, what the role of business should be to provide for the worker or the worker's family when he or she is injured, becomes ill, or dies. The Occupational Safety and Health Act (OSHA) covers the former condition and worker compensation covers the later.

Defining Business Responsibilities for Worker Occupational Safety and Health

The extent of society's concern about the safety and health of employees surfaced with the passage of the Occupational Safety and Health Act (OSHA), which established a federal government organization to research occupational diseases and unsafe practices, to establish standards of workplace safety and health, and to enforce these standards.[9] The act covers almost every business organization in the United States. OSHA, sometimes known as the Williams-Steiger Act, covers 4.1 million businesses and 57 million employees, and its mission is

[9]U.S. Department of Labor, p. 3.

To encourage employers and employees to reduce hazards in the workplace, and start or improve existing safety and health programs.

To establish employer and employee responsibilities.

To authorize OSHA to set mandatory job safety and health programs.

To provide an effective enforcement program.

To encourage the states to assume the fullest responsibility for administering and enforcing their own occupational safety and health programs that are to be at least as effective as the federal program.

To provide for reporting procedures on job injuries, illnesses, and fatalities.[10]

OSHA has been a controversial law. The notion of worker health and safety and the government's role in regulating them is in direct contrast with the philosophical view of the rights of private property. Some managers believe that the law violates their right to manage and their right (as owners) to conduct their business and use their resources as they see fit. An even stronger complaint comes from the problems of meeting OSHA's stringent safety standards. Many organizations, especially the smaller ones, believe that the rules are complex, covering areas that are superfluous, and that the standards do not really improve safety and health as the law intends.[11] For example, the OSHA standards for noise exposure indicate only the levels of intensity that an employee may withstand, not the tone frequency. Yet tone frequency is considered by some hearing experts as an important aspect of human noise tolerance. Criticisms have also been leveled at OSHA for acting too rapidly and for issuing standards before sufficient research has established realistic standards.

The overall evaluation of OSHA's impact has not been very positive. For example, General Motors, after spending $29 million and 11 million work-years in reaching compliance, reported little reduction in its accident rate.[12] But business is still working with OSHA to improve conditions in the working environment for millions of Americans. There is also growing evidence that OSHA requirements are beginning to be toned down.

Defining Business Responsibility for Employee Injury Compensation: Worker Compensation Laws

While the federal government has designed a law that addresses worker safety and health, there is no federal law that addresses the responsibilities of business to the employee in the event of work-related injury. The major driving force for this sort of legislation, called worker compensation laws, has been the individual states. Wisconsin passed the first worker compensa-

[10]U.S. Department of Labor, p. 3.

[11]Tom Alexander, "OSHA's Ill-Conceived Crusade Against Cancer," *Fortune*, July 3, 1978, pp. 86–90.

[12]"Why Nobody Wants to Listen to OSHA," *Business Week*, June 14, 1976, pp. 64–68.

Another area of importance to an employee is job security. Although job security is not a legal right of employment, there have been substantial curtailment of management's rights to hire and fire at will.

EMPLOYEE JOB SECURITY

Job security pertains to the stability of employment for the individual employee over time, an issue unheard of at the turn of the century. At the whim of the owner/manager, individual employees could lose their jobs, but the current thinking is that the employee invests his or her own life in the organization. Just as health and insurance policies help protect the individual from harm, some security measure ought to be provided to meet the possible economic loss of employment.

Guaranteed Employment

The first widely recognized program of guaranteed employment was established by Japan after World War II. Through national planning and an active fiscal policy, the goal of the Japanese government was to ensure that each person who wanted employment would be employed. Under the Japanese system, when an organization hires a person, the organization is expected to retain the employee until the employee either quits or retires or the company closes down. During periods of recession, a company will place employees in different jobs or send employees, at company expense, to further their education and training. The Japanese government subsidizes business firms when they incur a deficit under this system.[15] This lifetime employment policy is recognized to be one reason for the phenomenal productivity rate of the Japanese.

The United States has no national guaranteed employment program, but the federal government does provide unemployment compensation and other programs offering job training/retraining, supported work, subsidized wages, and apprenticeship aid.[16] Through the Social Security Act, unemployment programs were established. These programs were to be self-sufficient and were to be paid totally from business contributions. The states administer the fund and establish some of the policies for eligibility and length of time that one can receive payments. In more recent times, the federal government has taken more and more responsibility for administering the program, as federal funds are needed to meet the high expenditures for the unemployed. Although this program does not ensure job security per se, it does offer employees some security.

Privately sponsored programs of guaranteed employment have evolved

[15]"Japan: The End of Lifetime Jobs," *Business Week*, July 17, 1978, pp. 82–83.
[16]Robert Kuttner, "Getting Off the Dole," *The Atlantic Monthly*, September 1985, p. 75.

in several industries. The unions in the large industries, such as the steel and auto manufacturing, have pushed for a guaranteed annual wage (GAW) for a number of years. The auto industry also has a highly publicized supplemental unemployment benefits (SUB) program. The SUB plan supplements the government unemployment compensation so as to, in effect, give the employee a GAW. This SUB plan, however, has recently run into monetary problems because of the slowdown in the economy, which has forced many auto employees out of work. Demands for the supplemental benefits have consumed the program's resources.

There are a few examples of guaranteed employment policies in American companies that are similar to that of Japan. One such company is Lincoln Electric, which guarantees that its employees will have at least 49 working weeks of at least 30 hours per week. The agreement covers all full-time employees with continuous service of two years and more. The Ohio company has had relative success with the program.[17]

Limiting Management's Rights to Hire, Promote, and Fire

Management's right to hire, promote, and fire has been substantially limited through laws, judicial interpretations of those laws, executive orders, union agreements, and common practice by management. Most of the legal infringement on hiring and promotion was presented in Chapter 8. These laws, taken in the entirety, force more objectivity in managerial decisions.

Management's right to fire an employee has come under similar attack, and legal and judicial actions have greatly reduced the latitude that a manager has in capricious and arbitrary terminations.[18] At the turn of the century, managerial prerogatives clearly included the right to dismiss an employee. This right was perhaps best stated in the *Payne* v. *Western and Atlantic Railroad* case of 1884, in which the judge stated: "All may dismiss their employees at will, be they many or few, for good cause, for no cause, or even for cause morally wrong, without thereby being guilty of legal wrong."[19] This traditional viewpoint was not challenged until recently. Now with the greater demand for job security, both unions and the courts demand that an employee must be chosen, promoted, transferred, and fired with just cause. In effect, management's dismissal actions must be based on objective criteria and not simply on traditional managerial prerogatives. Union-secured seniority systems have helped secure rational and objective personal decisions. Union contract agreements have reduced the general sphere of managerial preroga-

[17]Robert Zager, "Managing Guaranteed Employment," *Harvard Business Review*, May–June 1978, p. 103.

[18]Tony McAdams, "Dismissal: A Decline in Employer Autonomy?" *Business Horizons*, February 1978, pp. 67–72.

[19]McAdams, p. 67.

tives, especially with regard to protection from unjust dismissals. But only about one-fourth of America's work force is covered by union contracts, and hence most of the work force does not have formal protection against arbitrary management dismissals. Because of this lack of protection and the overall society's changing philosophy of the right to employment, court cases have begun to limit managerial dismissal abuses. For example, the *Holonak* v. *Avco* case upheld the right of an employee to free speech.[20]

Another landmark case for employee protection against unfair dismissal was the *Beebe Rubber Company* case. In this case, the court held that "a termination by the employer of a contract of employment at will which is motivated by bad faith or malice, or based on retaliation is not in the best interest of the economic system or the public good and constitutes a breach of the employment contract."[21] This ruling was again affirmed in the *Barnes* v. *Costle* case,[22] in which a female employee was transferred because she would not succumb to the advances of her male supervisor. Although the suit was aimed at discrimination, the results again signaled that capricious actions by management in regard to personnel actions would not be tolerated by the courts.

Including affirmative action legislation discussed in Chapter 8, the status of management's right to "fire at will" leads to the following three conclusions. First, firing without cause may lead to a suit filed based on discriminatory action against protected groups or nonprotected groups as discussed. The court's definition of what constitutes bad faith, malice, or being in the best interests of society seem to be broadening and will cover additional issues not covered heretofore. Third, it would be reasonable to expect that the courts will look at management's previous actions as "setting precedent" in determining whether a firing was reasonable and proper,[23] much as is done in union-management proceedings reviewed later in this chapter.

Pension Protection: Legislation and Retirement Security

An obvious concern of employees is security in the retirement years. Over 70 percent of organizations with more than 100 employees have some form of pension program to contribute to the security of employees after they retire. In addition, two major pieces of federal legislation are directed toward improving the security of private-sector employees.

Social Security.   The first act was an outgrowth of the Depression era and "New Deal" legislation. The Social Security Act of 1935 provided a level of

---

[20]Holodnak v. Avco Corp., Avco-Lycoming Division, Stratford, Conn. and Local 1010, United Auto Workers of America, Stratford, Conn., 381 F. Supp. 191, 193, 194 (1974).

[21]Monge v. Beebe Rubber Co., 114 N.H. 130, 316 A 2d 549, 551 (1974).

[22]Barnes v. Costle, 561 F. 2d 983 (D.C. Cir. 1977).

[23]Summers, pp. 39–48.

compensation for retirement-age individuals and families based on the amount of years employed. In addition, later legislation led to the inclusion of Medicare and Medicaid health care benefits. The latter benefits were intended to ensure a higher level of medical care for retirement-age people. Medicare is part of a federal program and Medicaid is a state-sponsored program.

Funding for Social Security benefits is based on equal employer and employee contributions. This reflects the philosophy that business, as well as the individual employee, has a responsibility to its employees to provide for their needs after retirement. The initial intent of Social Security was to provide a minimal level of retirement income. The result is that for several millions of people, Social Security is the only income that they now receive. As a result, the monthly income paid under Social Security has substantially increased over the past 40 years and the program itself, along with Medicaid and Medicare, has been attributed with keeping millions of retirement-age individuals above the poverty line and in some instances, the program has literally saved their lives.

Social Security has been in financial trouble several times over the past decade. The basic problems stems from the fact that people are living longer and there are more people at or above retirement age, creating a large financial burden on the system. Although these financial problems occur periodically, there is strong public sentiment in favor of continuation of the Social Security system in its current form.

Private Pension Plans.   Besides Social Security, another major source of income for retirees is in the form of pension payments. Pensions are normally private-sector programs where there is employee or employer contributions toward an individual's retirement income. Pension investments are managed by a trustee and payouts are normally made at the employee's retirement. In the 1950s, concerns were raised over several aspects of pension management practices. Behind the concern was the feeling that employees were being denied the right to benefits that were normally theirs through promises made by the company or the union. The view held by many members of Congress was that employees granted wage concessions in order to receive a pension or allowed deductions in wages in order to have the union manage a pension. Employees deserved some return for their contribution or contributions made in their name. Several abuses in the management of pensions led to a public outcry for reform. These abuses centered around forfeitures and termination of plans.[24]

Five elements of forfeiture were of particular concern: eligibility requirements, vesting requirements, complicated restrictions in the plan, nonportability, and intentional dismissal before an employee becomes vested. *Eligibility* refers to the time when an employee can join a pension program. *Vesting*

---

[24]Ledvinka, pp. 213–217.

refers to the time when an employee can qualify for receiving benefits in the plan. *Portability* relates to the ability of an employee to transfer rights to benefits from one employer to another. The abuses before the 1958 and 1974 Acts, which dealt with forfeiture, was that there were many unwarranted and highly restrictive exclusionary provisions. These tended to serve only those pension managers who wanted to exclude potential pensioners. Under these exclusionary provisions there were more funds that could be used for the goals of pensions managers, who were often closely associated with the union or the company. This led to a conflict of interest.

A second major area of abuse related to the termination of programs. These terminations occurred because of inadequate funding of programs, misuse of funds, changes in management, and bankruptcy of the company. However, in some instances, these terminations benefited the company rather than the pensioners.

The abuses led to a call for pension reform. The first legislation was the passage of the Welfare and Pension Plan Disclosure Act in 1958. This act forced pension administrators to greater accountability through public financial disclosures. However, in actuality, the law did little to curb major abuses.

The call for reform in pension practices continued after the 1958 Act; however, there was no further action in Congress until a major event solidified public opinion. This event was the 1964 closing of the Studebaker Plant in South Bend, Indiana.[25] This plant closing left net pension assets of only $3.3 million to those that had not retired. Full benefits were given to employees 60 years and older, but only 15 percent of benefits were given to employees 40 to 60 years of age. This translated to a lump-sum payment of only $350 to an employee of 40 years of age with 20 years of experience with Studebaker. No benefits were given to workers under 40 years of age. This amounted to no benefits for over 2,000 former employees. The outcry of these and a few other such tragedies led to the passage of the 1974 Employee Retirement Income Security Act (ERISA).

ERISA.   This act required that an employee is eligible for a pension at a maximum of 1,000 hours of employment in a calendar year. In addition, vesting must occur after 10 years of service, or with a specified schedule of vesting, or under conditions where age plus seniority equals 45. The company may choose which of the three approaches it will use. Language in pension provisions must be stated in clear terms so as not to confuse the participants. ERISA mandates portability and makes it clear that the Age Discrimination Act (presented in Chapter 8) makes firing an employee to avoid vesting illegal.

ERISA provides restrictions on pension funding to avoid terminations of programs. A employer must remain current in its own or its employees' contribution to the program. A company or union must make up below-average returns from investments made with pension funds. Only 10 percent

---

[25]Ledvinka, p. 218.

of pension funds can be invested in the company that is supporting the pension. ERISA restricts changes in pension programs even if there is a change in management. To protect bankruptcies, a pension program must be protected through Pension Benefit Guaranty Corporation, an insurance company, and the employer pays the premium.

The end result is a standard model of pension management conduct that has reduced previous abuses and insured, to a greater degree, that there would be improved retirement security for today's employees.

COMPANY RIGHTS AND EMPLOYEE RIGHTS

The area of employee rights is a dynamic topic in current legal and moral discussions. The organization has a unique capacity to influence individual employees and, in turn, demand certain concessions from them. The legal and moral questions focus on the definition of limits. The limits definition spells out the extent to which the organization may require the employees to surrender their own personal rights in order to remain employed with the organization. A second important question relates to the degree that the organization should intervene in order to balance an individual employee's rights with the rights of the rest of the work group. As the other dimensions of the employee-employer relationship, there are certain minimal guidelines of behavior that have been specified through legislative and judicial actions. In this section we review the current state of the legal environment on the topic of employee rights and will indicate the questions that the organization must consider when it defines its own posture with respect to defining the rights of the employer, the individual employee, and other employees.

Organizations are generally motivated by their own self-interest, and given the equal bargaining relationship between employee and employer, the chances for abuses to personal rights of the employee are clear and present. A second major concern is how the organization arbitrates between employees. The major concern in these sorts of situations is the balancing of the rights of the individual employee with that of the remainder of the employees. For example, with the current concern over acquired immune deficiency syndrome (AIDS), an organization may be called to make a choice between the other employees and the individual. This area of balancing rights does not have easy answers for the organization.

Legal Rights of Employees Under the National Labor Relations Act

Employee rights are treated through a host of legislative acts and court decisions. For example, antidiscrimination legislation has specified the conduct of organizations with respect to equal treatment. However, the focus of antidiscrimination laws has been more toward equal treatment as opposed to specifying whether this treatment protects individual personal rights.

The National Labor Relations Act (NLRA), also called the Wagner Act, was passed in 1935 with major additions to the act made with the passage of the Taft-Hartley Act of 1947 and the Landrum-Griffin Act of 1959.[26] Section 7 of the act guarantees all employees the right "to engage in concerted activities for the purpose of collective bargaining or for other mutual aid or protection." Section 7 refers "to all employees," not just those represented by a union. Section 8(a)(1) of the act prevents the employer from interfering with these protected rights by making it an unfair labor practice to "interfere with, restrain or coerce employees in the exercise of the rights guaranteed in Section 7."[27]

The NLRA has been liberally interpreted by the courts and provides a haven for unionized and nonunionized employees in the protection of their personal rights. The key element in the application of the act is whether the individual employee or employee group is working for the mutual aid or protection and the actions must be directed toward improving their working conditions. For example, in the *NLRB* v. *Washington Aluminum Company*[28] case, nonunion employees walked off the job after repeated complaints over the cold working conditions of the plant went unheeded by management. The company subsequently fired the employees for leaving. The courts upheld the employees right to work toward improved working conditions.

Under NLRA an individual employee can act alone as long as it is for the mutual benefit and protection of all. For example, in the Alleluia Cushion Company[29] a person was fired for complaining about numerous safety hazards at the plant. The complaints went unheeded and the employee filed a complaint with the California Occupational Safety and Health Administration. The National Labor Relations Board (NLRB) upheld the employee's right. This right is also guaranteed in the National Occupational and Safety Act (OSHA). In fact, the right of individual employees goes so far as to allow them to refuse to work in an abnormally unsafe environment without fear of being discharged. However, the employees must (1) have reasonable belief that they will be placed in jeopardy of injury or death if they executed the task, and (2) believe that there was no other alternative but to disobey the employer's order.[30]

The rights of the unionized employer are protected under the NLR act, in addition to the general protection cited above. The act generally supports the right of employees to unionize and the role of the employer and union in the process of certifying a union, contract negotiations, and in the process of dispute settlement in situations where there is an impasse in the process.

[26]Kenneth L. Sovereign, *Personnel Law* (Reston, Va.: Reston, 1984), p. 178.
[27]Sovereign, p. 178.
[28]NLRB v. Washington Aluminum Co., 370 U.S. 9 (1962).
[29]Alleluia Cushion Company, 221 NLRB 999 (1975).
[30]Sovereign, p. 184.

The Employee's Right to Privacy

There are three areas of potential employer-employee dispute regarding the right to privacy. The first is in the collection and use of data to be maintained in the personnel file. The second is in the use of lie detector tests, and the third involves the use of tests to determine the employee's use of controlled substances.

Personnel Files. Data maintained in the personnel file raise two concerns for the employee. First is the question of access to the file by the employee so that the employee may ensure its accuracy. Second is the right of the employee to control the release of the information.

The courts have generally upheld the notion that employee records are the property of the employer and it is the choice of the employer to release or not to release the information.[31] In essence, the employee has little right to control the dissemination of any part of the records. The interesting paradox is that not only does the employee not have the right to control his or her own employee records from being used as the company sees fit (i.e., dissemination to individuals inside or outside the organization), the employee also has no rights to inspect the file to ensure that it is accurate. Hence, incorrect information may be disseminated that could adversely affect the career of the employee without the employee's knowledge or with limited recourse by the employee.[32]

There are statutory conditions that do require that information be granted by organizations to outside bodies. For example, the Equal Employment Opportunity Commission (EEOC) may require documentation of an employee's personnel file in a determination as to whether an organization's actions are discriminatory or not. The Occupational Safety and Health Administration (OSHA) requires that organizations furnish employee data regarding accident severity and frequency. However, none of these laws limit the use of employee records for other uses. That is at the discretion of the employer. This has many individual and civil rights groups concerned.

The Privacy Act. The government is also concerned about personal privacy as reflected in their control of personnel record keeping in the public sector. In 1974, the Privacy Act was passed, which allows a government employee access to his or her own personnel file. In addition, the act allows federal employees to contest inaccurate information in the file and include these exceptions in the file. The Privacy Act also restricts the disclosure of information to individuals or groups outside the employing organization without the consent of the employee except in some relatively restrictive situations.

Tests

[31]Cort v. Bristol-Myers, 431 N.E. 2nd 908 (Mass., 1982).
[32]David W. Ewing, "What Business Thinks About Employee Rights" in Allan F. Westin and Stephen Salisbury, *Individual Rights in the Corporation—A Reader on Employee Rights* (New York: Pantheon Books, 1980), pp. 120–131.

guidelines that can be used to give some relative sense of the degree of impairment.

A third concern relates to management reaction. If a test leads to a positive conclusion that drugs or alcohol are present, what should management do? If they fire the employee, is there any recourse? If the results of the drug test are entered in the personnel file, is that information then available for disclosure? These are areas of the law that are currently being treated in the courts, as this whole area is a relatively new aspect of employee rights and justice.

Fourth, the whole process of drug and alcohol testing is relatively dehumanizing and demoralizing. Employers feel that legally, they are in a better position regarding antidiscrimination laws in requiring all personnel to take the tests, but there is a clear cost in the testing procedures in the resultant distrust and lower morale that occurs. It may be more appropriate to establish expected modes of conduct and performance and create greater accountability for managers to be more sensitive to detecting drug and alcohol problems and reacting to those problems than submitting all employees to these tests.

Ex-offender Rights

So far, the discussion has focused on regular employees and their rights. Now attention is shifted to the rights of special types of employees and balancing their rights with that of others and of the organization. The first is the rights of ex-offenders.

An *ex-offender* is a person who was convicted of a crime and has completed the punishment that was specified by the sentence. This sentence may or may not have consisted of a jail term.

Technically, there is no law that particularly specifies the rights of the ex-offender. However, the Civil Rights Act, through a court decision, became an important source of ex-offender rights. In the famous *Griggs* v. *Duke Power Company* decision,[36] the courts held that neutral laws that may not, on the surface, affect a protected group, may be discriminatory if the neutral law does, in fact, operate to exclude a disproportionate percentage of a protected group.[37] This decision helped pave the way for a 1975 decision in *Green* v. *Missouri Pacific Railroad*.[38] The court maintained that a company policy that excluded all persons with a prior conviction was contrary to public policy and violated Title VII of the Civil Rights Act. The court view, since this 1975 decision, is that a blanket exclusion is inappropriate. However, a person may be excluded if it can be demonstrated that the exclusion has

---

[36]Griggs v. Duke Power Company, 401 U.S. 424 (1971).

[37] Eric Matusewitch, "Employee Rights of Ex-offenders," *Personnel Journal*, December 1983, p. 951.

[38]Green v. Missouri Pacific Railroad, 523 F. 2d 1290 (8th Cir. 1975).

been done for job-related consideration. The burden of proof, however, is on the company to demonstrate job-relatedness. For example, if a person had prior convictions of theft and the job entailed the handling of money or company property, an exclusion might be sustained. However, even with a prior conviction, the courts will look at additional factors in determining whether the exclusion was appropriate.

Specifically, the court will consider four factors in dealings with ex-offenders:

1. The number of offenses and circumstances of each offense.
2. The length of time intervening between the conviction and the employment decision.
3. The person's employment history.
4. The person's efforts at rehabilitation.[39]

The overriding concern of the court is to balance the company's necessity for security and customer relations with the rights of the ex-offender, who has "paid" for a crime that was committed.

"Business necessity" is a purposely vague term. However, through court decisions, it can be defined as directed toward the efficient and safe operation of an organization. This does not mean that a company can fire ex-offenders because other employees may not want to work with them.[40] However, if an ex-offender lies on his or her application blank and does not indicate a conviction if requested, the employer may legally fire the ex-offender.[41] Having valid and accurate application blanks is an important need of an organization in order to judge accurately the merits of applicants.

The courts have generally ruled that an organization must try to accommodate the ex-offender. The law requires that the ex-offender be treated the same as others. Only when business necessity is proven will an exception be allowed. The enlightened employer will recruit and hire on an objective basis and work with other employees to ensure that ex-offenders have their personal rights.

AIDS Victims

A difficult question is currently being faced in the courts and the general public across the country. What are the rights of individuals who may have a contagious disease? In a company, what are the rights of other employees? This becomes more difficult when there is not a full understanding of the causes of a strange disease and how those affected may transmit the disease. One can obviously empathize with both sides in this ordeal.

[39]Matusewitch, p. 952.
[40]EEOC Decision No. 80–18 (August 18, 1980).
[41]King v. Girard Bank, 17 EDP 8455 (E.D. Pa. 1978).

For example, in the case of the individual employee with AIDS, there seems to be enough knowledge about the disease to be able to take reasonable precautions in the work setting to ensure that other employees will not contract it. The denial of employment to the AIDS victim may be considered as discriminatory if it can be ascertained that protected groups of people are more apt to contract the disease than other groups. It should be noted that at this time homosexuals are not considered a protected group under Title VII of the Civil Rights Act.[42]

Relating to other employees, the rights of employees to be free from workplace hazards has already been discussed. However, there are still many unknowns regarding a disease such as AIDS, and this may cause concern with other employees. For example, asbestos was once thought to be safe. Yet, through additional research, it was found to be a carcinogen. Accordingly, it may be wise to take extra care until there is greater knowledge of a communicable disease. A business firm also has an interest in balancing the rights of others. What sort of disruption might having an AIDS employee create? Is this enough grounds to dismiss the employee on grounds of business necessity? Probably not; however, might the company be liable if other employees contracted the disease? What is the moral responsibility of the employer to ensure that the disease does not spread, and what is the responsibility of the employer to the AIDS victim? These questions are in the courts and in the media currently and are as yet unresolved, and may never be to all concerned.

Harassment

Harassment directed at a protected group is considered illegal under Title VII of the Civil Rights Act. This is true if it is initiated by the employer or if the employer does not act to stop other employees from harassing another employee.[43] The employer therefore does have a responsibility to ensure that the employee's rights to be free from harassment are assured. Although successful legal remedies are available only in cases of harassment directed at a protected group, the whole notion of other employees or members of management harassing employees ought to be repugnant to top management, as it demonstrates to employees that top management is not in control of the situation and has little regard for its employees.

One manner in which to provide for the safeguarding of the rights of the individual employee, whether it be harassment or other problems, is to provide a mechanism of dispute or grievance resolution. Having a system to handle complaints that employees might have is an excellent way for employers to avoid costly litigation and to maintain good morale.

[42]DeSantis v. Pacific Telephone & Telegraph Company, 608 F. 2d 327 (9th Cir., 1979).
[43]Higgins v. Gates Rubber Co., 578 F. 2d 281 (10th Cir. 1978).

EMPLOYEE JUSTICE SYSTEMS

There are three major means for employees to obtain just treatment: (1) the establishment of a formal grievance procedure, (2) a collectively bargained agreement, or (3) the establishment of an employee contract.

A Formal Grievance Procedure

One means to safeguard the rights of employees is through the establishment of a formal process that employees might use if they feel their concerns or rights are not being addressed by their immediate supervisors. This formal mechanism is normally called a *grievance procedure*. An example of one form of grievance procedure is outlined in Figure 9.1.

The grievance procedure can take various forms. Most include several levels of appeal from the initial supervisor-employee representative meeting, to a higher-level manager or human resources staff member-plant employee representative, and finally, to binding arbitration. The process becomes more formal each step of the way, and documentation becomes more important as the filed grievance moves higher in the dispute settlement process.

The value of a grievance procedure can be reflected in the importance that is placed on the process in labor agreements. Almost all union contracts specify a formal means of employee and labor dispute settlements. In addition, in the public sector, a formal grievance procedure is specified in civil

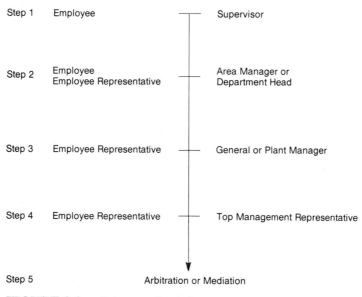

Step 1	Employee	Supervisor
Step 2	Employee Employee Representative	Area Manager or Department Head
Step 3	Employee Representative	General or Plant Manager
Step 4	Employee Representative	Top Management Representative
Step 5		Arbitration or Mediation

FIGURE 9.1   *Grievance Procedure.*

service laws at both the federal level and in most states. Thus, it is obvious that employees value a grievance procedure. Even if they choose not to use it, there is satisfaction that there is a process that one can use when he or she feels that concerns are not being addressed or rights are being violated by the organization.

Beyond the individual employee satisfaction that results from the adoption of a formal grievance procedure, the organization also receives a means to protect itself from litigation. The organization is protected from litigation because court decisions have specified that an employee must first exercise the grievance procedure before seeking redress in the courts. Thus, the process would help to resolve problems before they become costly legal battles. Additionally, the grievance procedure can act as a means to relieve pressure and inform management when problems are occurring, before they grow into major issues.

Another major advantage of a formalized grievance procedure is that the decisions made in the resolution of disputes become a basis of precedent to guide the future actions of employees and management. What evolves from several years of grievance decisions is a body of precedent that tends to further ensure that there is a balancing of the rights off employees and the organization.

Examples of the types of issues that reach arbitration in a grievance process appear in Table 9.1. Although the great majority of the grievances that are filed are settled before reaching arbitration, the table still gives a sense of the broad-based issues that are involved in the grievance procedure. These are cases that have been from both nonunion and union organizations. The

TABLE 9.1.   Profile of Grievance Arbitration Cases.

Major Issue	Number of Cases
Discharge	
for physical violence and threats (19 cases)	124
Discipline	
for refusal of work assignment or order (20 cases)	91
Fringe benefits	33
Assignments and schedules	39
Promotion and transfer	43
Wages	52
Arbitrability	
procedural arbitrability (36 cases)	53
Affirmative actions disputes	0
Discrimination	2
Union security	3

Source: Perry A. Zirkel "A Profile of Grievance Arbitration Cases," *The Arbitration Journal,* March 1983, pp. 35–38. Based on a survey of 400 Arbitrator's Case Reports filed with the American Arbitration Association National Headquarters Files.

trends for the future indicate that grievance procedures will maintain their great importance as a means of ensuring employee justice.

The Collectively Bargained Agreement

A second means to assure justice of individual employees is through the collectively bargained formal agreement. The contract specifies the rights and responsibilities of the employee, the employee association, and the organization. There has been a long history of improved organizational responsiveness to employee concerns through the process of having an employee association or union represent the employee in the establishment of a contract, the administration of employee rights under the contract, and through representation of the employee in dispute resolution under the contract. The rights of the employee to form an employee association is specified in the National Labor Relations Act of 1935 and its amendments, the Taft-Hartley Act of 1947 and the Landrum-Griffin act of 1959.

The number of the employees who are unionized has stayed relatively constant over the past decade and the percentage of workers covered by a union contract has decreased, as there is an increase in the percentage of white-collar workers over blue-collar workers. Current worker sentiment toward unionization is relatively negative, especially among white-collar employees. The average white-collar employee feels that unions are not being responsive to worker concerns, and white-collar workers identify more closely with management than with labor. Regardless of the present sentiment, there is a role for a responsive union in ensuring worker rights and employee justice. This role is particularly important in the absence of an executive branch of federal government that is vigorous in its role of safeguarding employee rights and safety.

Employee Contracts

A third method of securing the rights of the employee is through the development of an employee contract. Whereas the collectively bargained union contract protects the rights of all union employees covered by the agreement, the employee contract specifies the rights and responsibilities of the employer and employee covered under the contract. These individual contracts are normally developed between employees that are very valuable to the organization and, as such, have more leverage than the average employee.

There is a clear and substantial legal precedent for individual employee agreements. These are legal, enforceable, and can substantially protect the employee and the employer from damaging actions by either side. Employee agreements affect only about 5 percent of the work force. About half of the agreements are initiated by the employer.

The interest of the employer in these employee contracts is to protect the employer from action by the employee. In certain jobs, the employee learns highly privileged information about the company. For example, an employee may learn of a production process, a list of clients, or a specialized marketing approach. The employer establishes an employee agreement to protect the company from misuse of this information by the employee: for example, having the employee start his own company and underbid for contracts, or making intense contacts with the customers of the employer once the employee leaves the organization. The contract would, in these cases, include clauses that would restrict the employee from using his or her services in the market area of the organization for a stated period. The courts have upheld the legality of such contracts.

THE IMPLICATIONS OF EMPLOYEE RIGHTS AND JUSTICE SYSTEMS

The state of employee rights and justice in the workplace may be the single most important aspect of employer-employee relations in the next decade. This is because there seems to be a pronounced shift in favor of the rights of the employee through judicial interpretation, proposed legislation, and through the degree of litigation and media coverage. There is momentum in public sentiment that may tip the balance of employee and employer rights more in favor of employee rights. Confounded with these rights are the rights of other employees to be protected from the capricious acts of individual employees and, of course, the employer. There already is evidence of this shift of philosophy, as shown in the passage of legislation to further protect the rights of public-sector employees.

In addition, there is evidence that there is dissatisfaction with current antidiscrimination legislation in that it is very limited with regard to the employee's rights that are included. One remedy to this problem is the development of an employee "Bill of Rights" that would be more inclusive of individual rights. This movement is assisted by the questionable tactics of some organizations in the overuse of lie detector tests and/or mandatory drug and alcohol detection tests. Movement toward passage of this type of legislation is currently hampered by the current wave of conservatism in the Congress and President Reagan's real or projected views.

Finally, there is a clear trend for less passive employees. They are more concerned about their own personal rights and are willing to take action when they feel that their rights are being violated. Management needs to take these tendencies into account and ought to be sure that the actions that management takes, down to that of the first-line supervisor, should be legal and necessary for the orderly conduct of business in a secure and safe fashion. Determining what is necessary conduct is not that easy. The best preventive action that upper management can take is to establish clear policies governing the behavior of all management personnel and offering a means for aggrieved employees to air their concerns in-house without having to seek litigation.

SUMMARY

In this chapter we first explored employee rights and the means for individual employees to exercise their rights through organizational justice systems. Within this chapter the evolution of employer-employee relations was traced from the common law concept of status based or master-slave relationship to the implied contract doctrine that is currently prevalent in the United States. The implied contract doctrine has been the guiding force in exercising employer-employee rights for the past 80 years. However, this doctrine has been modified over the past two decades to reflect a change in public policy in favor of greater employee rights in the workplace.

Employee rights were viewed through three major perspectives: the right to a safe and healthy working environment, the right to job security, and the rights of the individual employee for privacy and to work toward a better working environment.

The federal law applicable to a safe and healthy working environment is the Occupational Safety and Health Act. Additionally, in cases where an employee is injured, worker compensation laws tend to moderate the personal loss suffered by the employee. These two laws reflect the enlarged responsibilities that the employer has toward the employee.

Employee job security was first presented in terms of organizational agreements to ensure a guaranteed annual wage. In addition, the legal restrictions placed on an employer to make arbitrary promotion and termination decisions was discussed. Various pension protection laws were reviewed as a public policy response to ensure that employees are protected in their retirement years.

Employee personal rights to work for the common good of the other employees and the rights of the employee to privacy were reviewed through several different situations: the use of personnel files, lie detector tests, tests of drug and alcohol abuse, the rights of ex-offenders, the rights of AIDS victims, and employee rights in harassment situations.

Finally, we considered employee justice systems and pointed out that management ought to adopt some means for an employee to address concerns in a fashion that will reduce the need for formal litigation.

The rights of employees and employers are being redefined in the courts and through public policy. This reformulation is the result of the failure of "the implied contract doctrine" to protect the rights of the employee in the employment contract. As employees become more aware of their personal freedoms and have an increasing sense of what are reasonable and unreasonable demands on management, there will be increasing sentiment for management to become more responsive to employees' personal rights. This emphasis will be felt in the business environment and in the public policy arena in the years to come.

3. If you were a consultant to a retail store that had a rash of stealing, would you recommend using a lie detector? Would you recommend that any guidelines be used when employing the machine? Explain your answer.

Managers Fired at Will*

Thomas R. Wagener climbed the executive ladder of Alex Corporation, a subsidiary of IC Industries, for 17 years. The company manufactures castings and hydraulic equipment. "Not too long ago we all talked about the fast track in management," he says. Wagener, a corporate purchasing manager, had his career derailed at Alex last June while the company was "downsizing" its headquarters staff as part of a move from New York City to Connecticut.

Companies, from Alex to Xerox, are all following the mentality that they need to be "lean and mean" to compete in the world economy. This translates to less overhead burden—translated to less middle management. This mentality is fueled by the advent of computer systems and management information systems that can place top management "closer to the action." The end result is a layoff of white-collar workers at a level that exceeds all years since the depression.

Unemployment can come in a variety of guises, some even benevolent. Companies may tempt managers into early retirement with extra-sweet pensions and bonuses. Organizations can encourage employees to leave through limited-time offers of generous packages. For example, Polaroid, one of the most generous companies, offered managers over 50 years of age one month's pay for each year of service. Other companies are less openhanded. In one instance, International Harvester offered a manager with 22 years' experience 19 weeks' pay or severance, but the company shorted the weekly checks by the amount the employee would receive in unemployment benefits. To obtain the additional $133, the manager had to stand in line in the unemployment office.

The fringes, cutbacks, and forced retirements are sending an ominous message to managers. Although most of them have no formal employment contract, they did perceive an implicit contract that practically guaranteed lifetime jobs in exchange for competence, honesty, loyalty, and hard work. Some companies have unilaterally changed the rules. According to Wilton Murphy, a human resource consultant at William M. Mercer-Meidinger of New York, "More large organizations in effect are telling people, 'You have some skills we currently need; we have a job available. As long as that is there, we have a relationship—but don't count on anything beyond that.'"

*Adapted from John Nielsen, "Management Layoffs Won't Quit," *Fortune*, October 28, 1985, pp. 46–49; Felix Kessler, "Managers Without a Company," *Fortune*, October 28, 1985, pp. 51–56.

Those managers who survive initial cuts by an organization are much more prone to be either more security conscious and tend to "play it safe" or become much more career—as opposed to company—oriented. The latter types are oriented toward self-advancement and being highly mobile. They care less about the long-run direction of the organization and more about those activities that will mean more advancement potential to them—either inside or outside the organization.

Managers asked to leave a company usually feel shock, humiliation, grief, and a sense of financial uncertainty. Their whole notion of self-worth and personal competence is questioned. Organizations do not help much, as "they try to do what is right in the legal and actuarial sense. Period. Do they also show consideration and sensitivity? Not a lot," says Richard Holan, director of the Center for Management Development at Duqueswe University. Says Murphy of Mercer-Meidinger, "People invest a lot of emotion in their companies and companies encourage it: They give them T-shirts and pens with the company logo, they issue newsletters. They talk about the company as 'family.' Then one day they reject you." It can come when least expected. Jerome Metz, a former JI Case manager, had just received a solid raise and one of the highest performance evaluations in his 11-year career when he was terminated last November.

ANALYSIS

1. Given the degree of involvement that is expected in organizations, should organizations have greater responsibility to their managers than they currently have legally? Why or why not?
2. Is this change in management orientation healthy for organizations? What about individuals? Managers?
3. How can an employee protect themselves from unjust firings? What does the law currently say regarding just and injust firings?

Drug Abuse at Nuclear Power Plants*

It was computer specialist K. G. Hensley's first day on the job at Carolina Power and Light Company's Shearon Harris nuclear power plant. Before two hours had passed on that day last November, Hensley had purhased $100 worth of cocaine from a fellow worker. Hensley would buy narcotics more than 20 times over the next eight weeks. This is just one example of the scope of the drug abuse problem in the work environment. With an estimated 4 to 8 million regular cocaine users in the United States, drugs in the workplace have become a common problem.

Although drug abuse is a problem in most industries, it is a particularly

*Adapted from Barbara Staff, "Drug Abuse at Nuclear Plants: The Alarms Are Ringing," *Business Week,* October 26, 1986, p. 35.

alarming potential problem in the nuclear industry, both in the construction and operation of plants. Construction defects could result in operational failures that could lead to massive death and destruction. The same potential destruction is possible if an operational staff employee makes an error in the execution of his or her job. Up to now, no one has documented the use of drugs in any utilities' power-plant control rooms. However, increasing concern for safety has led to pressure being placed on the Nuclear Regulatory Commission (NRC) to establish basic fitness standards for anyone in a sensitive nuclear job. However, according to Barbara Staff, a *Business Week* Washington, D.C., staff member, the NRC is reluctant to become a drug detection agency. As it currently exists, there is no uniform policy on screening and drug detection. The reluctance of the NRC is echoed by the Edison Electric Institute, a trade association, which has issued a 68-page guidebook for a drug program.

The result of this lack of policy is that there is a wide degree of difference between drug screening programs at nuclear power plants—both with respect to program and to those who are screened. Some utilities, such as Georgia Power, order urine testing of any employee who shows signs of drug use. Others, such as Arizona Public Service, require employees to submit to urine tests at random. Both Georgia Power and Carolina Power and Light also have used drug-sniffling dogs to search employee property and vehicles.

Even if the NRC can come up with an enforceable drug policy, the nuclear industry is unlikely to remain drug-free. "We are not oblivious to the fact that our workers represent a cross section of society, and there is drug abuse in society," says A. Lee Orsen, Boston Edison's Company's vice-president for nuclear operations. But the nuclear industry hopes that it can avoid the unthinkable.

A major concern is balancing the rights of the individual employee with the needs of the organization and of society. The NRC has been delegated by Congress the responsibility to ensure the safety of the nuclear power industry. As such, they must look not only at the procedures and facilities, but also at the fitness and competency of the human resources employed at the facility. Society also has a vested interest in ensuring that nuclear plants are safe.

Considering the rights of employees, however, makes most organizations reluctant to specify standards and detection methods. No detection method is fail-safe. In addition, there are some concerns that mandatory screening of all employees may violate the employees' civil rights. The testing itself can be considered as dehumanizing. Some people think that the tests treat all employees as criminals. There is some concern that the approaches used are not 100 percent acurate, with little chance for recourse if there is a positive indication on the test. In addition, the detection measures traces of drug use that could have been taken off the job. Even though the drug's effects have "worn off," the employee may still be reprimanded or fired.

Some think that this is an unfair intrusion into an employee's personal life.

ANALYSIS

1. Suggest a policy that the NRC could use to determine what it should require of nuclear plant employee conduct and how to determine which employees should apply to the requirements specified. This policy should be stated as an industry standard.
2. Should there be mandatory screening of all employees? Why? How can the NRC balance employee rights, company rights, and the NRC's responsibility to society?
3. How might an employee's rights be protected under mandatory drug screening?
4. What legal liability do organizations have to ensure that their employees are competent?

The Quality of Work Life

Chapter Objectives

- To discuss the causes of worker alienation.
- To review job context and content dimensions of workers' quality of work life.
- To review the job design efforts by business firms to improve worker satisfaction and productivity.
- To trace union involvement in improving workers' quality of work life.
- To trace some of the problems of implementing job design changes in organizations.

In this chapter we focus on the changes in societal demands for a more enriching job experience. Today's employees are awakening to their entire work experience. Contemporary employees are expecting much more out of life in general and their work experience in particular. Organizations must work toward meeting these new needs, or they will suffer the consequences of alienated, less motivated, and perhaps less effective employees.

Two dimensions of the work experience are considered in this chapter, job context and job content. *Job context* dimensions are those elements in the job environment that pertain to an employee's job and work experience. *Job content* factors are those that relate directly to the work itself. Hence, job context considers the job environment in which the work is accomplished, and job content considers the elements of the task that is being accomplished. The demands of employees are focused around both dimensions. Management must be concerned with each of these areas, and the success that an organization has in providing a desirable context and content will do much to attract and sustain a well-qualified, highly motivated work force.

This chapter is organized into three major parts. First, the problem of worker alienation is reviewed. Next, elements of job context are reviewed. Alternative strategies are proposed to improve context factors. Third, elements of job content are presented with a review of what can be and is being done to improve the content of tasks.

WORKER ALIENATION

Alienation (job boredom and the feeling of powerlessness) seems to be widespread. Estimates indicate that millions of employees are dissatisfied with their jobs. There is growing evidence that the present work force considers the job as less important to their lives than ever before.

Going hand in hand with employee alienation are problems with employee performance. For example, in recent years in the United States, the growth rate of worker productivity has slipped way below that of foreign countries such as Canada, Japan, and West Germany. Although there are several explanations for this turn of events, at least to some degree the declining productivity can be traced to the way human resources are managed in the United States.

Given the somewhat alarming trends regarding worker alienation and dissatisfaction, it must be remembered that a sizable portion of the work force is satisfied. Management cannot ignore these satisfied, dedicated employees. But there is growing resentment at all levels of modern organizations, as indicated by the growth of professional unions and the activism of lower supervisory personnel.[1]

The dissatisfaction of employees is complex and has several causes. Most experts would agree, however, that two of the most important causes are the values of employees and the structure of their jobs. The jobs at most organizations were designed in the 1950s or earlier. The philosophy of many of these design efforts is rooted in the principles of scientific management set forth by Frederick W. Taylor in the late 1800s and early 1900s. The major premise of scientific management is to make jobs as efficient as possible and then match them to the employees' needs. At the time Taylor devised this approach, the work force was largely immigrants, who had difficulty

[1]"The Unhappy Foreman at Wheeling-Pittsburgh," *Business Week*, May 22, 1978, p. 32.

with the language, had rather low educational levels, and were economically motivated. The job was to be designed so that anyone could be trained to do it in a short period of time and would be well paid for efficiency; that is, the employee was regarded as a machine. This scientific management approach to job design met the needs of the work force at that time, but there is now a recognized incongruence between the needs of the modern, mature employee and this scientifically designed job.

The values of work have changed in recent years, and the old value systems of even a few decades ago just do not reflect the values of modern employees. The values of the 1950s and 1960s can be summarized as follows:

1. If a woman did not have to work, she would not.
2. If a job paid a decent living, it would be acceptable.
3. Money and status were prime motivators for employees.
4. Loyalty to the organization and a strong commitment to meeting the family's economic needs tied individuals to the organization.
5. Most people identified with their work role. Their own desires and needs were subordinated to that of the demands and needs of their work role.[2]

In contrast, the new values of the current work force can be summarized as follows:

1. The increasing importance of leisure to the employee.
2. The symbolic significance of the paid job.
3. Insistence that the job becomes less depersonalized. The individual is the center of life, not the work environment.[3]

In a sense, the new values are that employees are entitled to decent working conditions, a living wage, and a job with a content that fits their expanding needs. The job exists for the employee, not the employee for the job. The job can symbolically offer much to the young man and especially the new working woman. In the 1950s there were not as many working women as there are today. Holding a job is considered by many women as a sign of their independence; the role of housewife is no longer desired by many women. A job with its accompanying pay and social acceptability offers many new options and a greater sense of security for today's woman. But the job itself is not so central to an individual's (male or female) life as it once was. For example, one used to hear expressions such as "I am John Doe; I am a car salesman." Now the emphasis has seemed to shift to John or Jane Doe, the person.[4]

The new work force seems to be much more impatient, which may be the result of exposure to the instant solutions that television provides. Today's

[2]Daniel Yankelovich, "The New Psychological Contract at Work," *Psychology Today*, May 1978, p. 47.

[3]Yankelovich, p. 47.

[4]Yankelovich, p. 50.

younger, better-educated work force asks more questions and is not willing to accept things as they are or have been. They want to take part in the organization that employs them; they want to stimulate and participate in its change; and they want jobs that offer them an opportunity to grow. A job cannot excite them just by providing money and possible occupational status as it could for employees of previous generations. A job must have much more for today's employees, and they expect much from the work environment. For example, employees want praise for a task well done, feedback on performance, the opportunity to participate in decisions that affect their job, opportunity to control their work, greater autonomy, more challenges to their skills, opportunities for professional growth, and greater discretionary time. These demands on business to improve the quality of work life are challenging, and the changes needed to meet these needs are profound and cannot be made overnight. Yet, the new work force is impatient with management and unions for not moving faster in these directions. Much of the labor unrest exhibited in recent strikes can be attributed not only to workers' dissatisfaction with management but also to their dissatisfaction with the union leaders for not meeting their expectations. Is this an exception or a sign of things to come in the workplace environment?

In response to these changing expectations and demands, many business firms have begun to improve the content of jobs. Several popular human resource programs to improve job content have been developed in the past few years. In the remainder of the chapter we examine several of these techniques and some examples of firms that have used these programs.

In response to these changing expectations and demands of employees, many organizations have begun to take a more active interest in assessing and improving the quality of work life for their employees. For example, General Motors recently conducted a survey of their employees to assess their quality of work life. An example of one page of the instrument used appears in Figure 10.1. Both content and context dimensions are assessed. The following two sections consider those elements that are part of each dimension of the quality of work life and what strategies organizations use to improve the job content and context for their employees.

JOB CONTEXT DIMENSIONS

Once again, job context factors deal with the job environment. These contextual factors consist of such things as security, salary, fringe benefits, working conditions, personal status, company policies, quality of technical supervision, and quality of interpersonal relations among peers, supervisors, and subordinates.[5] It is interesting to note that although research has consistently found these contextual factors to be important to employee satisfaction,

[5]Dennis W. Organ and W. Clay Hamner, *Organizational Behavior: An Applied Psychological Approach* (Plano, Tex. Business Publications, 1982), pp. 173–176.

THE QUALITY OF YOUR WORK LIFE
IN
GENERAL MOTORS

This survey is aimed at getting your ideas about what it is like to work here. We are trying to learn more about the quality of work life where you work. The purpose of this survey is to measure the attitudes, opinions, and work climate of GM organizations from the employee's point of view.

Please indicate how much you Agree or Disagree with each statement. Each question should be completed by circling one of the numbers.

1 = strongly disagree   2 = neither agree nor disagree   3 = strongly disagree

1.	What happens to GM is really important to me.	1 2 3
2.	I could care less what happens to GM as long as I get my pay check.	1 2 3
3.	I used to care about my work more than I do now.	1 2 3
4.	My job requires that I keep on learning new things.	1 2 3
5.	My job gives me the chance to learn new skills and techniques.	1 2 3
6.	On my job I have a chance to do some things that really test my ability.	1 2 3
7.	My job makes good use of my skills and abilities.	1 2 3
8.	I have a great deal of say over what changes are made in my work place.	1 2 3
9.	Around here, I am asked for my ideas.	1 2 3
10.	In this part of GM, getting ahead is based on ability.	1 2 3
11.	Job experience is financially rewarded in GM.	1 2 3
12.	GM management is really interested in my getting ahead.	1 2 3
13.	I think more job opportunities should be given to women and minorities around here.	1 2 3
14.	I really expected to make more job progress than I have up to now.	1 2 3
15.	I feel that I deserve to have been promoted higher by now.	1 2 3
16.	My immediate supervisor is interested in listening to what I have to say.	1 2 3

FIGURE 10.1 Quality of Work Life Survey. *Adapted from:* Quality of Your Work Life, *General Motors Corporation, 1978.*

they are not sufficient in themselves to produce satisfaction or to instill a high level of motivation. Job *content* dimensions, on the other hand, seem to be more strongly related to employee satisfaction and motivation.[6] However, most would agree that another desirable objective is the development of a dependable, high-quality work force. This does seem to be accomplished through not only having jobs that have positive content factors, but also a work environment (i.e., job context) that is conducive to attracting and retain-

[6]Organ and Hamner, pp. 173–176.

ing high-quality employees. Thus, job context factors can contribute to overall human resource management goals as well as supporting and supplementing job content factors.

Job security was discussed in Chapter 9, but a closer look at the other major job context dimensions of compensation, working conditions, personal status of the employee, company policies, supervision, and interpersonal relations will now be taken.

Compensation

Compensation is a relatively complex issue in contemporary business organizations. In fact, the whole meaning of pay is complex. Determining equitable levels of pay and pay increases is difficult. What an employee considers as just reward is high subjective, and many do not view pay as adequate compensation for the skills and effort they give to the organization. Compensation involves much more. Many tasks are highly paid, not for the skills and effort needed, but as compensation to an individual accomplishing a particular task. Examples of this type of compensation for an undesirable task are pay for a garbage collector or a domestic servant. Because of many possible variables, it is difficult to establish and maintain a system of rewards that all employees will consider equitable. However, in light of the quality-of-work-life issue, pay becomes important.

Another aspect of compensation is the various nonfinancial rewards provided in the workplace. Rewards such as office location, office furniture, a special parking space, and use of company facilities all are important considerations in equitably managing a compensation system. If the system is not equitable, worker discontent will result in a deterioration of the quality of work life. Thus, an equitable compensation system is not confined to comparisons of pay within the company. A compensation system must be relatively equal with regard to the nonfinancial rewards, and if there is any real or perceived injustice, the workers will be dissatisfied. The primary concern, however, is that the compensation that employees receive is just and equitable for their efforts and skills. Most compensation plans are not based on the amount of effort and skills that an individual contributes, but on length of service, and minimal attention is given to the quality and quantity of work effort. The result is that employees do not exert much effort; they are not rewarded for output, and so many see no reason to work hard. Several plans have been suggested to increase the performance of individuals and their feeling of equity. The objectives of these plans are to motivate employees by rewarding performance and efficiency. In designing a compensation system that recognizes an employee's effort, the company should benefit from higher employee satisfaction and better performance.

Scanlan Plan. The Scanlan Plan was formulated by Joseph Scanlan several decades ago and advocates that workers participate in determining the work and that any gains attributable to the employees' input be shared with all employees. This program has not been widely adopted. Although the plan does include changes in job content, its main feature is the participation and compensation approach, and so it is treated here as a job context factor.

The plan generally calls for a joint team of management and rank-and-file employees. This team considers ways to improve the organization's productivity. The entire work force may submit suggestions for changes in the production process, which are discussed and either accepted or rejected by the joint committee. When accepted by the committee, the actual amount of annual savings that resulted from the proposed change is estimated. These savings are divided among all employees and the company. It should be emphasized that the productivity improvement saving accrues to *all* employees, not just to the individual making the suggestion. This is to foster a cooperative team effort rather than pitting the individual against the group. The resulting spirit of cooperation between management and employees and among the employees can create a positive climate that adds much to the quality of work life.

Cafeteria-Style Compensation Plans. More recent than the Scanlan Plan are efforts to tie compensation plans more closely to the needs of the individual employee. One such approach is called *cafeteria-style compensation*. The basis of this approach is to find the method of compensation that best fits the individual employee's needs. The compensation includes both direct monetary compensation and fringe benefits. For example, since World War II, fringe benefits have increased from nearly nothing to almost 40 percent of the payroll costs. Fringe benefits include such diverse items as vacation time, sick leave, insurance programs, pension plan contributions, medical payments, use of company facilities, and even prepaid legal fees. They are offered to help meet the needs of employees and thereby enhance their quality of work life. However, as Edward Lawler found, many of the fringes are not really wanted by the employee,[7] in essence, all those costly fringe benefits may not really be having the intended effect.

The cafeteria approach to compensation attempts to meet employees' needs and give them a choice of fringe benefits. This approach suggests that employees receive some compensation. They may choose to receive all of their compensation in cash or in various fringe benefits available. Each fringe benefit has a cash basis so that they can weigh the value of each choice. For example, an employee may receive a base amount of $14 per hour and may choose to take the full $14 per hour in cash or in benefits such as medical insurance at $0.25 per hour, vacation pay at $0.10 per hour, sick pay at $0.05 per hour, and prepaid legal expenses at $0.02 per hour. In this way, employees will be able to select the compensation program that

[7]Edward Lawler, "Reward Systems," in J. Richard Hackman and J. Lloyd Suttle, *Improving Life at Work* (Santa Monica, Calif.: Goodyear, 1977), pp. 180–182.

best fits their needs. The ideas behind the cafeteria approach are that freedom of choice will make employees more satisfied with the organization and make it more responsive to its employees' individual needs and give them more control over their work lives.

Although few cafeteria compensation plans have been adopted, it is becoming technologically easier to accomplish. With the computerization of work and pay records, little effort is needed to adapt existing systems to this more flexible system. Potential problems include insurance companies that provide only low-cost group coverage rates if the whole organization participates. A side benefit to management is its ability to determine through the choices made just how important a particular fringe item is to its employees. Management may find that many costly fringe benefits are not worth their cost and effort because employees do not find them particularly desirable. In any event, a cafeteria compensation system seems to offer an alternative to meeting employees' needs for an acceptable quality of work life.

Working Conditions

"Working conditions" might be considered as an umbrella term that can be used for the quality of the physical surroundings of the work environment and the degree of inconvenience that the worker must endure, such as poor lighting, hot or cold conditions, noise, being in an isolated area, or the number of hazards that may be present in the work environment, such as explosion hazard, fire hazard, radiation hazard, or other health and safety hazards. Some of these health and safety concerns were discussed in Chapter 9.

The physical facilities and surroundings of the work environment seem to be important to employee satisfaction. Obviously, having a new facility with a well-landscaped surrounding can do much to improve the mental state of employees and the positive feelings that these have about the work experience.

The levels of inconvenience that an employee may have to endure can be moderated in most organizations either through the protective clothing that an organization may provide or through the construction of specialized work areas to reduce the inconvenience. For example, the printers on word processors can be irritating and noisy to an operator or those surrounding the operator. One solution offered by most word-processing-equipment manufacturers is a housing that reduces the noise by half. For working conditions outside, construction companies or shipping lines will reduce the time that employees must be in the hostile environment. Shipping lines have employees on "watch" for 4-hour periods instead of 8-hour periods. In severe weather, construction crews will have a 2-hour work period with a half-hour warmup break to reduce exposure time; the same is true in isolated conditions. A work crew of an offshore drilling rig may be on a 30-day on/30-day off schedule to make the job more appealing to the crew, which must endure long periods of being away from their family and friends.

Personal Status

Personal status refers to the self-image that the employee has regarding the job and how the employee perceives that others (such as family or friends) view the employee's job and employer. It is very important to most employees to have the recognition and respect of relevant others. Job status includes both the perception of status that is placed on the job title and the nature of the task, as well as appreciation for the level of excellence achieved in that job. For example, an employee may have a job that some consider as low status, such as a porter on a train. Yet the porter may receive high status for being the best porter on the train.

Organizations have some degree of difficulty in meeting status issues. Often, an organization is not sensitive to the status needs of employees. One problem is that status perceptions may be different for each person, and the degree of demonstration that may be necessary for sufficient recognition of desired status is also highly individualized. The organization, is therefore faced with a very nebulous perceptual need to fulfill that it may not be aware of, and because status also comes from other sources, may not even be in control of the ways to fulfill employees' status needs.

Perhaps the best way that organizations can fulfill the status needs of employees is by providing recognition for performance (performance-related status), be responsive to the individual as a person (individual-based status), and try to design tasks in a manner that makes them more significant in the eyes of the employee. Then the organization must be responsive to the contribution that each job makes to the organization. Task design and job content issues are discussed later in the chapter.

Company Policies

Company policies can do much to improve or harm the job environment for employees. Rules that are perceived as arbitrary or capricious tend to display management in an uncaring light and in a role of using power because they have control. This situation tends to impose arbitrary barriers between management and employees, leading to less trust and satisfaction. On the other hand, company policies that are perceived as reasonable and facilitate the accomplishment of the task will be accepted by employees.

Company policies include any rule or set of rules that guide the behavior of employees, customers, or clients in the organization. To illustrate how company policies can influence the work environment, two areas in which company policies are made—hours of work and employer special services—will be considered.

Hours of Work.   The workweek has not always been 40 hours. In 1901, the average workweek was 58.4 hours, and at the end of World War II, the average workweek was 42 hours. Since the war years, the emphasis in collective-bargaining negotiatons has beeen for more pay and better working conditions with little regard for reducing the numbers of working hours, but there is some indication that this attitue is now changing.

Time-Off Provisions. In their initial offers in contract negotiations, many unions are demanding a reduction of the workweek. If contracts do not demand this outright, the unions try to get more time off with pay. For example, some contracts demand a program called paid personal holiday (PPH). Along with the regular vacation time, PPH grants an additional five personal days off per year after an employee has been with the company for one year. After two years, seven PPHs are granted. The intent of many of these programs is to increase this amount until a person has, in effect, a four-day workweek.

Four-Day Workweek. Under a four-day workweek plan, each individual works a 10-hour day for four days per week. This plan has had some mixed results, as the employee's efficiency has been found to fall after eight hours, leading to lower productivity, increased accident rates, and greater discontent.[8] On the other hand there is evidence indicating that these fears may be unfounded.[9]

Another new approach is called flexiweek. Under this program, the employee works eight-hour days but works four days one week and six days the next. This program offers a change of pace without creating the hardships of a 10-hour day. More common is the flexitime approach.

Flexitime. Under flexitime programs there is one time when all employees must be present. For example, an employee may be able to report for work between 7 and 9 A.M., Employees can schedule departure time between 3 and 6 P.M. Lunch breaks can also be taken anytime between 11 A.M. and 2 P.M. The only restriction is that the person must work at least 40 hours per week. The main benefit of flexitime systems is that the time may be scheduled more to the tastes and needs of the individual employee, thereby increasing an employee's control over the job. The employee can schedule work time around the rush-hour periods to avoid traffic congestion, to meet such family commitments as getting children off to school, or to sleep longer in the morning. To date, the results of flexitime programs have been fairly positive.[10]

[8]Frederick D. Sturdivant, *Business and Society* (Homewood, Ill.: Richard D. Irwin, 1977), p. 156.

[9]For example, see John Ivancevich and Herbert Lyon, "The Shortened Work-Week: A Field Experiment," *Journal of Applied Psychology* 62 (1977): 34–37; Cheedle W. Millard, Diane Lockwood, and Fred Luthans, "The Impact of a Four-Day Workweek on Employees," *MSU Business Topics*, Spring 1980, pp. 31–37.

[10]J. D. Owens, "Flexitime: Some Problems and Solutions," *Industrial and Labor Relations Review*, January 1977, pp. 152–160; Barron Harvey and Fred Luthans, "Flexitime: An Empirical Analysis of Its Real Meaning and Impact," *MSU Business Topics*, Summer 1979, pp. 31–36.

Such scheduling allows more opportunities for women to pursue full-time careers. An example is Elizabeth Carlson. She is 42, has three young children, a Phi Beta Kappa key, and a MBA. She had to quit a responsible position in a Chicago bank because it would not be flexible about hours, and she asserted, "I cannot work without flexible hours."[11] She then took a job with another company that had flexitime. The bank then realized that it was losing too many good people like Mrs. Carlson, and so it instituted a flexitime program and rehired her. The personnel manager of the bank commented: "When enough good people like Mrs. Carlson begin to leave because your hours are not compatible with theirs, you get the message."[12] In other words, there are advantages of programs like flexitime to parties other than the individual employee. Programs such as flexitime has given employees greater discretion and self-control in planning their schedules. With the overcrowding of many of the recreation spots during the weekends, the congestion of transportation during peak rush hours, and more women employees with family commitments, employees are finding that these new alternatives to work scheduling improve the quality of their work life.

More and more employees are becoming disenchanted with the encroachment of the organization on their personal time and quality of life. People want to live their own lives and do not want the company to rule their lives for them. Fewer and fewer purely organization men and women exist today. The company is still in their lives, but it is certainly not everything in their lives.[13]

Employee Special Services

Chapter 3 raised the question of the extent of social responsibility that an organization should assume in society as a whole. In the organization, the same question might be raised as to the extent of responsibility an organization should assume for its own employees. Some believe the latter question should be addressed first. Their reasoning is that business firms should "get their own house in order before they try to change the world." Traditionally, business firms took the position that when an employee agreed to work for them, the obligation was for a payment of money for the services rendered. Little or nothing else was provided. If an employee did not demand enough for her or his services, then that was the employee's fault. If the employee did not have enough foresight to save for retirement, illness, or other contingencies, this was his or her problem and of no concern to the company. At present, few organizations are this callous about their responsibility to their own employees. As Chapter 3 pointed out, business is currently taking a different perspective as to its role in modern society. There are more and

---

[11]"Working Around Motherhood," *Business Week*, May 24, 1982, p. 188.
[12]"Working Around Motherhood," p. 188.
[13]"The Growing Disaffection with 'Workaholism'" *Business Week*, February 27, 1978, pp. 97–98.

more indications of the business organization's changing from a provider of pay to a provider of a multitude of services.

Employee special services are becoming an increasingly popular way for business firms to meet employee needs. Companies are offering a variety of services unheard of a few years ago. These services usually evolve from problems found in the workplace, which may be the result of on-the-job activities but often are problems that employees bring to the job. Special services are offered to help solve these problems, including such as alcohol- and drug abuse-counseling programs, psychological counseling, financial and family economic-planning programs, career counseling, retirement planning, and investment programs. Many of these programs are initiated by a true concern for the employees, though most are started when the organization perceives that the performance of many of its employees is deteriorating because of such problems.

It is generally agreed that about 10 percent of the total work force are alcoholics and that another 10 percent are borderline alcoholics. The annual loss to industry in sick time and lost production is in the billions. Because of this great loss and the human suffering that accompanies alcoholism, both business and unions have begun to provide services for counseling and rehabilitating the alcoholic worker and include counseling for both the alcoholic and his or her family. The counseling is aimed at improving the situation that caused the worker to become an alcoholic in the first place.

Drug addiction is a problem that many business firms realize needs some positive action. As with alcohol rehabilitation programs, drug programs usually offer counseling to the employee and to the family so as to correct the underlying causes of the addiction as well as to eliminate the drug problem itself.

Career counseling is another employee service. More and more companies are assuming greater openness with their employees regarding the opportunities available to them. Formal counseling services are available at many companies to aid in charting a career path that will benefit the individual. Development of education and experiential programs that will best fit the needs of the employee are often proposed, even if they lead to careers outside that organization.

Another employee service is retirement planning. More companies now offer options for early retirements and counseling to help the retiree adapt to retirement. Investment opportunities, travel activities, hobbies, and community programs designed for senior citizens all are discussed with the retiring employee.

Employee services of all kinds are expanding. Problems in the employee's personal life may affect job performance, and often they are too sever to ignore. In some cases, the very life of an employee or, more pragmatically, the loss of a good employee, may be at stake. These service programs recognize that the firm is obligated to offer more to the employee than pay alone.

As the discussion above implies, the policies that management makes have a big impact on the work environment. A responsive management carefully considers policies and the extent of services that are to be offered to ensure that they will lead to the desired employee behavior, will be accepted, and will be worth the potential undesired consequences that may sometimes occur.

The Quality of Supervision

The quality of supervision relates to the technical competency of the management team, and more specifically, the immediate supervisor. Management can ensure that it has quality supervision through the recruitment and selection process. In addition, management can have continuing programs of supervisor development. These development programs can include the technical aspects of the supervisor's performance, interpersonal skills in dealing with employees, and conceptual skills such as planning, organizing, and controlling.

Many organizations have continuing development programs for their supervisory/managerial staff. For example, Wal-Mart Stores, Inc. has a multi-million-dollar program in cooperation with the University of Arkansas, Fayetteville, that is designed for development programs for all managerial staff. Every manager in the Wal-Mart organization attends at least a one-week development program each year. Topics include technical skills such as merchandising, interpersonal communication skills, team building, and planning. Most large organizations have similar formal training and development programs. For example, McDonald's University, "Hamburger U," in Elk Grove Village, Illinois, is a separate facility that trains employees to become managers of McDonald's fast-food outlets. Holiday Inns, Inc. has a training facility outside Memphis dedicated to the development of new and existing managers of their hotel and motel facilities. The General Motors Institute (GMI) at Flint, Michigan, is designed to prepare managers for General Motors' facilities worldwide. The management training program at GMI involves classroom work combined with on-the-job experience.

In general, organizations need to be more responsive to the development of high-quality supervision. In the complex environments that organizations face in contemporary society, it is essential that there be managers and supervisors who can face the challenges and meet the needs of a more demanding work force. It is not sufficient just to promote an employee to supervisor without training. It places the organization and the employee at a distinct disadvantage.

Interpersonal Relations

The final area of job context factors is interpersonal relations. The employees' concern with this factor is that there must be a climate that is conducive to meeting the needs of the employees for social interaction. This social interaction includes peers, subordinates, and supervisors.

Having a climate conducive to social interaction involves the organization in the design of tasks, work layout, and physical facility design, in addition to direct management actions to facilitate employee interaction. Outside the direct control of the organization, however, are the personalities of the individual employees and the employees own needs for social interaction. In addition, the organization must be concerned with the performance goals of the organization.

The design of the job is considered in the next section. Physical work layout and facility design is one of the more important "emerging" issues in the field of industrial design. "Emerging" is placed in quotes because research has been conducted in this field of industrial management for years at places such as schools of architecture. Only recently have organizations become aware of the importance of work area design.

Management can facilitate social interaction through the development of company-sponsored picnics, baseball teams, and family outings, where the employee's family comes to the job site to learn more about the organization and to meet the other employees' families. For example, the Union Pacific Railroad has sponsored family outings throughout its railroad with a high degree of success. Wal-Mart has a family picnic for its corporate staff and a picnic for over 7,000 employees and guests at its Bentonville, Arkansas, corporate offices. In addition, the organization could have a newsletter or magazine such as the Union Pacific's *Info* magazine, which has won national honors for the quality of its articles and use of graphics.

It is of great importance to employees to have an environment that is conducive to meeting their needs. Employees of today are not the passive, accepting employees of yesteryear. Organizations need to address these needs in order to attract and retain a highly qualified and motivated work force.

JOB CONTENT DIMENSIONS

Research has generally supported the importance of the content of the job over the contextual environment of the job in improving performance and satisfaction. In particular, research has concentrated on identifying those job characteristics that are important to performance and satisfaction. Hackman and his colleagues have developed the most widely accepted job characteristics model (see Figure 10.2).[14]

There are five key job characteristics in this model: skill variety, task identity, task significance, autonomy, and feedback. *Skill variety* refers to the variety of things or tasks that are accomplished in the execution of the employee's job. *Task identity* relates to the manner in which the employee can relate the entire accomplishment of the job to his or her contribution.

[14]J. R. Hackman, G. Oldham, R. Janson, and K. Purdy, "A New Strategy for Job Enrichment," *California Management Review*, Summer 1975, p. 62.

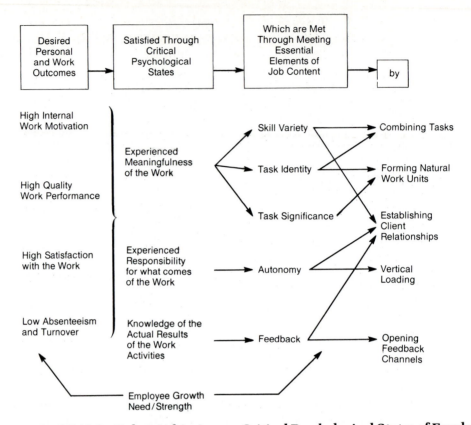

FIGURE 10.2   Relationship Among Critical Psychological States of Employees, Elements of Job Content, Examples of Ways to Meet Job Content Dimension, and Personal and Organization Outcomes of Meeting Core Dimensions.
Adapted from J. R. Hackam, G. Oldham, R. Janson, and K. Purdy, "A New Strategy for Job Enrichment," California Management Review, *Summer 1975, p. 62.*

Autonomy is the degree of personal control or independence that the employee has over planning and execution of the task. *Feedback* refers to the information that the employee receives about the quality and quantity of performance. This information can be generated internally through the job itself or given by supervisors.

The five core dimensions of the job are based on the critical psychological states identified in Figure 10.2. In addition, Figure 10.2 provides some suggested ways to facilitate implementation of the core dimensions in an actual job setting. The result of improving the content of the job around these core dimensions will lead to high work motivation, quality work, job satisfaction, and reduced absenteeism and turnover. As indicated at the bottom of the figure, the success of improving the core dimensions of the task are dependent on the growth needs of the employee. If there are low growth needs, there is less need to improve the job content.

The application of models such as this is that many organizations are directing their efforts toward improving the content of jobs so that they meet the needs of their employee. Two areas have received the most attention: improving the design of jobs so that they include higher levels of the desired dimensions, and the development of techniques to improve employees' involvement in the task.

Job Design Efforts

Job design changes require jobs to be restructured so that they become more meaningful for the individual. The changes usually mean restructuring the job content so that it gives greater autonomy to the employee. Instead of a highly defined, low-skill task, the employee is given greater latitude in the type and nature of operations that he or she can undertake in the job. Two methods of job redesign are widely recognized in both a literature and actual practice, called *job enlargement* and *job enrichment*.

Job Enlargement.   Job enlargement is a process whereby the job is enlarged to include a greater variety of tasks. For example, instead of having the employee work at one machine for the full work period, he or she is assigned to many different tasks throughout the day. An assembly line employee in an auto plant would not just install the seats of the automobiles but might also bolt on the tires, attach the windshield wipers, and tighten the engine mounts. The purpose of varying the task is to reduce the worker's boredom. It is sometimes called horizontally loading the job.

Job Enrichment.   A newer technique of task redesign is called job enrichment which vertically loads the job. Whereas job enlargement adds to the variety of duties of the job (horizontal loading), job enrichment adds vertical dimensions such as greater amounts of personal discretion, participation in decision making, and more independence in creating and performing the task. Job enrichment can be traced to motivational theorist Frederick Herzberg. In his two-factor theory of motivation, he advocated that organizations should pay more attention to job content factors such as achievement, recognition, responsibility, advancement, and the work itself as key motivators for employees.[15] If a job contains these enriching elements, Herzberg believed it would improve performance and the quality of work life for the individual employee.

Since the early 1960s, job enrichment has been used at a number of organizations. The essential characteristic of the program is to increase the employ-

[15]Frederick Herzberg, "Motivation-Hygiene Profiles," *Organizational Dynamics*, Fall 1974, pp. 18–29.

ee's control over work pace and provide greater recognition and opportunity for growth. A sampling of the programs of job enrichment that have been implemented follow. The applications of job enrichment are too numerous to mention, but a few have been widely publicized.

Eaton Corporation's Program of Job Enrichment.   The Eaton Corporation was concerned about the stagnation in its employees' productivity and the deterioration of employee-management relations. As the corporation opened new plants, it attempted to change the work environment so as to reduce worker alienation. The resultant organizational structure was initially the same as in the older established plants, except that basic policies were changed to let the blue-collar employees participate more in the entire work process.[16]

The policy manual was rewritten so that it stressed the positive aspects of employment. This was in marked contrast with the former policy manual that was written for blue-collar workers and stressed the rules and penalties for violations. The approach was to establish a climate of managerial respect and trust for the employees instead of the paternalistic and exploitive environment that formerly existed. The hiring process was also changed. More emphasis was placed on the employees' questions and concerns about the job. Formerly, the selection process was much like that of other organizations. An employee filled out an application blank; there was a structured interview with the company interviewer asking a series of questions; and then a decision was made based more on the company's needs, with little regard for the employee's understanding the format. Now there is no formal probationary period for the new employee. It is assumed that the employee wants to do a good job. Time clocks and structured coffee breaks have been eliminated. Employees fill out their own time cards and take breaks when the time is right for them, not when a bell rings at a specified time. Staff position personnel are encouraged to do more of their work with line employees at the latter's job site. In other words, the personnel department is encouraged to keep an open shop policy instead of an open door. Grass-roots participation is allowed at the weekly staff meetings, and employees are encouraged to perform activities outside the scope of their job design. For example, some employees volunteer to help when there is a problem in the work flow somewhere else in the plant. Other employees volunteer to lead plant tours for visitors, and still others may edit the company newsletter. The whole process attempts to change the feeling of all rank-and-file employees that they are less important than the rest of the organization's employees. For example, blue-collar employees are now treated in the same fashion as white-collar employees. They both have more opportunities to participate in the operations and actual decision-making process. The employees' decision making

[16]Donald N. Scobel, "Doing Away with the Factory Blues," *Harvard Business Review*, December 1975, pp. 132–142.

includes areas of the production process and personnel actions, such as how to lay off workers during a production downswing. The emphasis is on increasing the human dignity of the blue-collar worker and at the same time maintaining a high level of performance.

The results of this approach to job enrichment at Eaton have been very encouraging. At the new plants, the absentee rate ranged from 0.5 to 3 percent, compared with 6 to 12 percent at the traditionally structured locations, and the turnover rate was 4 percent compared with more than 60 percent at the other locations.[17] Performance and quality are also much higher than at the traditional Eaton plants. Production figures at the plants under the new program are up to 35 percent higher for the same processes than those at the traditional ones, and scrap rates are 15 percent lower. Employee satisfaction is also much higher. Employees under the new system are noted to be more relaxed in the work environment and to take an active interest in the company. They make more suggestions as to how to improve performance and feel more involved with the company.

AT&T's Job Enrichment Program.   American Telephone and Telegraph's job enrichment program has received a great deal of publicity.[18] The program first was used in the phone books' compiling room in Indiana. Before the program, the phone books were compiled by a large work force, with each individual assigned to a small part of the process. One would compile listings, and another individual would check the first person's performance. More than 33 employees were involved in this single process. Turnover and worker dissatisfaction were high. In the year before the job enrichment program was started, 28 of the 33 employees were replaced. Job satisfaction was low, and the employee error rate had not really improved, even when a large number of clerks were assigned to check each person's work.

The job enrichment program used in this situation consisted of a series of work modification stages. The first stage was to ask the high-quality performers if they could check their own work and thereby eliminate the separate checkers who verified their work. After this process was successfully completed, the next phase consisted of asking good employees if they wanted to work exclusively on the thinner phone books and become totally responsible for compiling these smaller books assigned to them. The final process was dividing the work on the larger phone books so that an individual employee would be responsible for all aspects of the listings for a particular letter of the larger phone books. This afforded the employees an opportunity to become more involved with their jobs and to develop greater pride in the total process. An employee developed the feeling that "this is my particular section of the phone book." The results were an increase in the quality

[17]Scobel, pp. 138, 193.

[18]Robert N. Ford, "Job Enrichment Lessons for AT&T," *Harvard Business Review,* January–February 1973, pp. 96–107.

and quantity of performance, less turnover, and greater job satisfaction. Currently, this type of job enrichment program is being expanded to a number of other areas in the huge AT&T system.

Volvo's and Saab's Experiments.   There are many innovative programs used by business firms in Europe that attempt to enhance the employees' quality of work life. The best known are those of the Swedish automobile manufacturers Volvo and Saab. The traditional assembly line operations, which are similar to those in American automobile plants, are no longer used. In the Volvo plants, the employees are organized into work teams of twelve to fifteen people, each of which is in charge of the particular production process to which it is assigned. Decisions as to job assignments within the work group are made by that group. Although the work group concept is in itself an important aspect of job enrichment, the process goes much further at Volvo. A work group committee is also directly involved with upper-level planning. Worker involvement is standard procedure in most of Volvo's decision-making process.[19]

In the Saab plant, the work groups are assigned to the engine assembly. Three member groups have complete autonomy in the work operation. An American team of blue-collar workers spent one year working at the Saab plant and had mixed reactions to the experience, though the job enrichment program at Saab and Volvo has reportedly improved the satisfaction of the Swedish workers.[20]

Nationally, the Swedish government has made worker participation in their employing organizations almost mandatory. A law passed in Sweden in 1973 requires that all firms with more than five hundred employees appoint two union representatives to the board of directors.[21] Similar to Sweden, many other European countries are involving the rank-and-file worker more in the total organizational process through job enrichment and industrial democracy. In some cases, of course, such participation goes hand in hand with the political system in force. Chapter 3 discussed these political-social systems.

Increasing Job Involvement

Job enrichment programs stress the job's redesign to appeal to the employees' growth needs and induce greater satisfaction. A second approach is directed more at managerial practices and how they may be changed to increase the employees' quality of work life. These programs are especially directed

---

[19]Nancy Foy and Herman Gadon, "Worker Participation: Contrasts in Three Countries," *Harvard Business Review*, June 1976, pp. 71–84.

[20]Arthur S. Weinberg, "Six American Workers Assess Job Redesign at Saab-Scandia," *Monthly Labor Review*, September 1975, p. 52.

[21]"What Foreign Firms Are Doing to Fight 'Blue-Collar Blues,'" *U.S. News & World Report*, July 23, 1973, p. 76.

toward improving supervisory and managerial skills for interacting with employees. Through these programs, an analysis is made of the communication process, the reward structure, and the clarity of the work role for the employee. The theory behind this approach is that if an employee understands what should be accomplished in the work setting and he or she is rewarded for its accomplishment, greater satisfaction and performance will result (see the boxes "Dow and the Work Environment" and "Guidelines from Volvo").

DOW AND THE WORK ENVIRONMENT—A POLICY STATEMENT

The Dow Chemical Company, like many other business firms in this country, is concerned with the quality of work life. As a result, it has developed a health policy statement to clarify its responsibilities to employees and to establish practical goals for maintaining a healthy work environment. Some of the things it intends to continue doing include the following:

1. Establish and maintain the lowest practical exposure levels for all materials and forms of energy used by the company.
2. Notify employees who are exposed to materials at levels that present a potential risk to health.
3. Provide industrial hygiene and medical surveillance services to determine present levels of exposure and to evaluate their effects, if any, on employees.
4. Predict reasonable exposure control guidelines through properly developed data for hazardous materials and forms of energy.
5. Review and modify, if necessary, company exposure guidelines when new findings become available.
6. Assure that the work environment is considered when plants are designed, operating practices developed, processes changed, and employees trained.
7. Provide employees with necessary protective equipment and conduct training programs in its effective use.
8. Work toward the goal of annually informing employees about (1) the chemical, biological, and physical stresses in their work environment; (2) the methods of protection and control; (3) the consequences of overexposure; and (4) the individual's responsibility under this program.
9. Furnish contractors on Dow sites with pertinent information on the safe handling, use, and disposal of Dow products.
10. Cooperate with government agencies by providing information useful in determining hazards and setting reasonable standards.

Source: Dow and the Work Environment: Policy Statement, July 1978. Reprinted with permission of the Dow Chemical Company.

Several broad categories of programs are directed toward these ends, of which we shall discuss two of the more popular and promising: management by objectives (MBO) and organizational behavior modification (O.B. Mod.).

Management by Objectives.   MBO was first advocated more than 20 years ago by management consultant Peter Drucker and involves setting objectives and appraisal by results. Each supervisor–subordinate pair formally establishes objectives for a stated period of time (usually a fiscal year). The overall MBO process can best be described as a series of five stages. Stage 1 is establishing the overall organizational objectives. Although these objectives are actually decided by the higher managerial levels, an input from lower-level participants is encouraged. The theory behind this initial stage of MBO is that the individual determining his or her own specific objectives needs some information and guidelines as to the direction of the overall organization. Stage 2 of MBO is helping the organization personnel understand, accept, and implement the system. Through a series of training sessions, the employees become acquainted with the MBO process and acquire the skills needed to write their own objectives. This second stage may last for a couple of weeks to a couple of years and may be a total reorganization process. Stage 3 is the negotiation between each supervisor and subordinate pair concerning the subordinate's individual objectives for the given time period. This is the "guts" of the MBO process. Stage 4 begins the appraisal of results. The progress in reaching the objectives set in Stage 3 is reviewed at least quarterly. The fifth and final stage is an overall appraisal and the establishment of objectives for the next period.

One purpose of the MBO process is to improve the quality of work life for the individual by allowing greater participation in the establishment of work goals and appraisal of results. Of secondary benefit is the clarity of actions that the subordinate should receive through a consensus of activities by the subordinate and superior during the third phase.

The results of MBO programs have generally been favorable. For example, Raia conducted an extensive MBO program at Purex. Purex's entire managerial staff helped establish and enact the objectives for organizational units and for themselves. The program was determined to be successful. Performance and the quality of work life improved. The staff reported that the MBO program did much to eliminate the arbitrary method by which a manager might evalute an employee's contribution to the organization. Instead of relying on subjective evaluations, the subordinate now knew what criteria the superior was using to evaluate performance. The subordinate was allowed input into the criteria and better understood the expectations of performance.[22] For example, one manager indicated that this was the first

---

[22]See A. P. Raia, "Goal Setting and Self Control," *Journal of Management Studies,* February 1965, pp. 34–53; "A Second Look at Goals and Control," *California Management Review,* Summer 1966, pp. 49–58.

The work w
able to turn c
month she fou

There was
nents did not
it into the un
appear to be
her that the s
however, this

The units t
brought to the
something wc
work. At the e
the number of
to 3 P.M. of th
in the work ar

Mary notice
everyone the
had done. Usu
cases the num
to be more cc
part fit proper
a faulty teleph

Three mont
team of job re
investigate wc
could be made
group. "We he
them and tell
in grammar s
Lots of times t
times, it's our
was something
jobs. If we get

Apparently,
jobs in the de
tests all incom
tests it to mal
units that eack
company has c
ment, and ove
during the las
standard, and
the manageme

GUIDELINES FROM VOLVO

Perhaps the most successful job enrichment principles in the workplace have been used by Volvo, the Swedish auto maker. Over the last 10 years Volvo has introduced the concept of work teams into its assembly line operations and has had very good results. The following relates some of the guidelines the company followed in implementing job enrichment on the assembly line.

1. Each unit should be free to develop individually, without detailed control or interference from headquarters.
2. An active and positive top management attitude toward change is a prerequisite for positive results.
3. Headquarters is most effective when its role is sanctioning investments for new approaches and challenging local managers to take more radical initiatives and risks.
4. Our positive achievements seem related to how well our managers understand that the change process will sooner or later affect several organizational levels, regardless of where it started.
5. We encounter problems if we formalize change and request targets, minutes, and figures too early. Change requires time and freedom of action. When people view it as a continuing search-and-learning process of their own, the chances of lasting effects are increased.
6. Progress seems to be fastest when a factory or company starts by forming a joint management and a union steering committee to look at its own problems.
7. The fastest way to get ideas flowing seems to be to set up decision groups in each working area. A working area in this sense (and in a group-working sense) should probably contain fewer than 25 people.
8. A new investment in one new facility or one group area often results in spontaneous changes in related facilities or groups. These can be encouraged by alert managers.
9. Most factories have a number of tasks that need not be done on assembly lines. Once a few have been found and changed, others will be revealed.
10. Some of the most effective changes in work organization at Volvo have taken place naturally, without projects, without scientific sophistication, and without being reported to anyone. Those changes occur simply because people are keen and interested. Finding ways to encourage such changes is management's challenge.

Source: Adapted from Pehr G. Gyllenhammar, "How Volvo Adapts Work to People," *Harvard Business Review,* July–August 1977, p. 111.

mc
ass
an

DISCUSSI

1. Is
   a l
2. Hc
   yes
3. Wl
   in
4. "T
   the
5. Hc
   of
6. Jo
   mc
7. Hc
8. Hc
9. Hc
10. Hc
    of
11. W
12. Hc
    of
13. W
14. Dc

When
introdu
Mary's
table o
phone.
them or
telephc

be given an extra 15 percent bonus this year, and the firm was looking into redesigning the work of similar departments in other geographic locations.

ANALYSIS

1. In redesigning the work, did the specialists use job enlargement or job enrichment? Explain your answer.
2. In what way was vertical loading or vertical dimensions used to change the work? Give some examples in your answer.
3. What do Mary and her work associates like about their job? In what way has the new work made the employees more enthusiastic?

Organizational Behavior Modification in Action

Can organizational behavior modification really help a manager reorganize the work environment and increase employee output? A growing number of researchers and consultants report that it can. Consider, for example, the following illustration:

A particularly disruptive female machine operator was selected as a target for [behavior modification] by one supervisor/trainee in the program. She often complained bitterly about the production standards to the supervisor. In addition, she seemed to adversely affect the productivity of her co-workers by talking to them about their rates and production sheets. According to her, everyone else in the plant had an easier job. Close review of her case revealed that her complaints were unfounded.

After identifying the complaining behavior, the supervisor gathered baseline data on this behavior during a 10-day period. No new contingencies were introduced during this "before" baseline measure. In conducting a functional analysis of the target response during the baseline period, the supervisor determined that *he* was probably serving as a reinforcing consequence by paying attention to the complaints.

Armed with this baseline data and information gathered in the functional analysis, the supervisor decided to use a combination extinction/positive reinforcement intervention strategy. Extinction took the form of his withholding attention when she complained. Satisfactory production and constructive suggestions were socially reinforced by praise in an effort to strengthen the compatible behavior. In addition, her constructive suggestions were implemented whenever possible.[1]

The supervisor found that this combination intervention did in fact have the desired effect. The complaining decreased in frequency, and the number of complaints declined from four per day, before behavior modification was introduced, to zero at the end of 45 days.

[1]Fred Luthans and Robert Kreitner, *Organizational Behavior Modification* (Glenview, Ill.: Scott, Foresman, 1975), p. 153.

ANALYSIS

1. What types of rewards did the supervisor use to modify the worker's behavior?
2. How does O.B. Mod. link performance and rewards?
3. How successful was the supervisor?

Back to Square One

Bob Fanchar had been a counselor at Todren Community College for three years. The work was interesting and Bob liked his job, though the pay was not very high. If the school system in town had not had more applicants for teaching positions than it needed, Bob would have landed a much higher paying job doing what he really wanted to do. Nevertheless, in time Bob settled into his job and began to realize that unless he took employment in industry, he would never really be able to improve his salary; and the nearest large industrial center was 125 miles away.

Six months ago, however, one of the large national manufacturers announced that it was going to convert an old local warehouse into an assembly line plant. Starting salaries were almost 45 percent higher than what Bob was making at the community college. After giving the matter a great deal of thought, Bob applied for a job at the plant and was hired. The president at the community college was sorry to see Bob go but wished him the best and told him that there would always be a job waiting for him at the college should he decide to return.

For the first three weeks, the job at the assembly plant was very interesting; in fact, it was challenging. Bob had all he could do just to keep up with the work, but after mastering the job, Bob found that he had more time to himself. It was then that he realized that it was virtually impossible to interact with anyone else on the line. The nearest worker was located almost thirty feet away, and with the noise on the line, Bob had to shout to make himself heard. As a result, he realized that it was best to just do the work and try to daydream his way through the day. This upset him, and so he went to his foreman to see if there were any other job openings in the plant that afforded more social interaction, such as he used to have at the community college. Unfortunately, there was none.

Bob then began to consider his alternatives. If he stayed at the plant, he could continue to earn a large salary but would suffer from alienation. If he quit, he could go back to the community college, but the pay would be quite low. After thinking it over for three weeks, Bob decided to quit. On the last day of his employment, he went to the personnel department to sign some forms and pick up his paycheck. He noticed that there were seven other people who had begun work the same day as he had who were also quitting. One of these people said that to date almost 40 percent of the original people had quit and that this Sunday the company was going to place a large employment ad in the newspaper in hopes of attracting more people to the firm. Bob also learned that the company was going to raise salaries across the board by 7 percent as an incentive both to attract more people and to keep the ones that were currently on board.

ANALYSIS

1. Describe Bob's job at the community college in contrast with his job at the manufacturing assembly line plant.
2. Why did Bob leave his job at the community college and go to work at the assembly line plant?
3. Why is Bob now returning to his old job? Explain, incorporating into your answer a discussion of worker alienation.

CHAPTER 11

Consumerism Issues: Challenge and Response

Chapter Objectives

- To present the major consumerism challenges facing business in the areas of advertising, packaging, pricing, product safety, service, and legal actions.
- To describe and analyze the business response to consumerism, including giving more information to consumers, handling complaints, the role of trade associations, self-regulation, and product safety, especially auto safety.
- To probe the future directions of the consumerism issue.

Societal demands on business have continued to focus on consumer needs and reactions.[1] Although the consumerism issue is not new (in fact, it can be traced back to the muckraker days of the early 1900s), the consumer movement in modern times can probably best be traced in Ralph Nader's actions. His various action groups of a decade or so ago, known as Nader's Raiders, received worldwide attention. College students from across the coun-

[1]Lee E. Preston and Paul N. Bloom, "The Concerns of the Rich/Poor Consumers," *California Management Review*, Fall 1983, pp. 100–119.

ing, the FTC looks at the entire ad. Sometimes there are ambiguous statements. For example, if a government-supported study shows that cigarette X is the lowest in tar and nicotine, can the advertiser use the statement "government supported," or will the reader construe this to mean that the cigarette has been approved by the government as "safe"?

In addition, the FTC is concerned with the substance of statements. For example, Colgate Palmolive ran an advertisement showing how simulated sandpaper, covered with Palmolive Rapid Shave Cream, could be shaved, thanks to the cream's moisturizing qualities. The FTC objected to the ad because it failed to tell the listener that the sandpaper could be shaved only after an extended period of soaking.

Recently, the commission has been making companies prove their claims. If the claims cannot be substantiated, the FTC can take the company to court. For example, the agency took court action against the manufacturers of painkillers. The FTC's concerns were that it could find no proof for various claims, such as the following:

1. Bayer products are superior to other aspirins.
2. Cope is more effective in eliminating headaches than is any other non-prescription internal analgesic.
3. In contrast with other painkillers, Vanquish upsets the stomach less frequently.
4. Bufferin or Excedrin have twice the painkilling power of aspirin.
5. Excedrin PM is a mild sedative or is a better pain reliever than aspirin.
6. Anacin is superior to any other nonprescription painkiller on the market.

The drug industry, in particular, is a visible target for consumer protection groups. The FDA was given a mid-1982 deadline to take action against 211 drugs that were "deemed to lack evidence of effectiveness."[3] Some of the consumer protection groups feel that the FDA is dragging its feet in this area of over-the-counter (OTC) drugs. For example, the Ralph Nader Public Citizen group sued the FDA to end a nine-year delay and take action against all OTC drugs that have been given sufficient time to complete safety and efficacy tests, and have not. This would affect about 69 percent of all OTC drugs. This review process was intended to take four years when it began in 1972, but as of the beginning of 1982 the FDA had responded to only four of the 81 reports it had received.[4]

At the present time, the Federal Trade Commission is continuing its surveillance of advertising. One of the most difficult is drawing the line between mere puffery, such as calling one's product "the greatest," and deliberate deception. In deciding whether an ad is appropriate, the FTC uses criteria such as

[3]"FDA Shakedown Challenges Efficacy of Top Rx Drugs," *Drug Topics*, June 21, 1982, p. 85.

[4]"Consumerist Want to Wipe Out 69% of All OTC's," *Drug Topics*, January 4, 1982, p. 24.

1. Would the public be adequately informed of the alleged deception and thus able to protect themselves from future recurrences?
2. Are there sufficient assurances that the alleged violations will not be repeated in the future?
3. What are the extent and type of the deceptions that take place?
4. Is there a danger to health or safety of consumers?[5]

The way that the FTC enforces its regulations has changed dramatically. Now the commission goes after individual companies on a case-by-case basis rather than issue industrywide rules. The commission now feels that too much regulation may stop advertisers from including truly useful information. Although there are some abuses of loosening up the regulations, Amanda Pedersen, the current deputy director of the FTC's consumer protection operation, estimated that prosecuting an advertiser, even in drawn-out litigation, took almost half the time and effort needed to develop a trade regulation rule.[6]

Truth in Packaging Act Besides the assistance provided to the consumer by the FTC, there are several consumer laws. The Truth in Packaging Act, formally called the Fair Packaging and Labeling Act, passed on November 3, 1966, is one of the most important. The packaging legislation calls for both uniformity and simplification of labeling through both mandatory and discretionary provisions. The mandatory provisions are

1. The identity of the commodity shall be specified on the label.
2. The net quantity of contents shall be stated in a uniform and prominent location on the package.
3. The net quantity of contents shall be clearly expressed in ounces (only) and, if applicable, pounds (only) or in the case of liquid measures, in the largest whole unit of quarts or pints.
4. The net quantity of a "serving" must be stated if the package bears a representation concerning servings.

In addition to the mandatory provisions, if the representative agency charged with enforcing this act believes that consumer deception can be avoided or value comparisons facilitated, it is authorized to

1. Determine what size of packages may be represented by such descriptions as small, medium, and large.
2. Regulate the use of such promotions as "cents off" or "economy size" on any package.
3. Require the listing of ingredients in the order of decreasing predominance.
4. Prevent nonfunctional slack fill.[7]

---

[5]Robert E. Freer, Jr., "The Federal Trade Commission—A Study in Survival," *The Business Lawyer*, July 1971, p. 1516.

[6]"Back to Cases at the FTC," *Business Week*, July 5, 1982, p. 90.

[7]Stewart H. Rewoldt, James D. Scott, and Martin R. Warshaw, *Introduction to Marketing Management* (Homewood, Ill.: Richard D. Irwin, 1969), pp. 186–187.

The Packaging Act authorizes the secretary of commerce to insist that all manufacturers and packers develop voluntary standards. The Food and Drug Administration has jurisdiction over the food and cosmetics contained in these packages, and the Federal Trade Commission regulates the labeling of all consumer commodities. Table 11.1 provides additional information on this subject.

Consumer Protection and Pricing Policies

Pricing-policy problems have been a constant source of concern for consumers. Several sorts of problems come under this broad area of consumer complaints. Examples are information about discount practices; secret and discriminatory rebate practices; policies that keep prices at an artificially higher rate than free competition would dictate; hidden costs; and complex charges.

Discount practices include the pricing of a product or service below the suggested retail price. This is done through a series of discounts or markdowns. Although there seldom is a consumer complaint about discounting per se, the problem arises when this practice discriminates against particular groups, either through the direct application of the policy or by de facto discrimination because certain customers were not informed of the discount. Since deregulation, the airlines have offered a wide variety of fares, but the complexity of some of the fare discounts is upsetting many people. With the wide variety of packages and restrictions on some of the fares, there is a growing feeling that the airlines are being unfair to certain travelers and in general may be deliberately trying to confuse the public. Passengers sitting side by side on a plane may have as much as a 50 percent difference in the fares they paid. Other examples are complaints by smaller retailers against companies that cater to the very large retailers. In the pre-Robinson-Patman Act era, warehouses could offer substantial discounts to purchasers of large quantities. At times these discounts were very large, sometimes bringing the prices below actual production costs. This practice offered a great competitive advantage to the larger retailers because the small purchasers could not handle the large quantities needed to get the discount. This abuse has largely been curtailed by the Robinson-Patman Act passed a few decades ago.

The currently popular rebates used in the auto and major commodity industries are another form of price discount that has potential problems. The rebate is given as a cash benefit for purchasing the product or service; as indicated in the introductory historical chapters, the robber barons used this type of discount. For example, part of the deal that Rockefeller had with the railroads was to guarantee to use a particular railroad to ship goods if the railroad granted a rebate for the service guarantee and charged an additional surcharge for shipments of competitive oil companies using the same railroad. This practice was subsequently discouraged by the Robinson-Patman Act.

TABLE 11.1. Summary of U.S. Standardization and Disclosure Policies.

Policy	Enforcement Agencies[a]	Products Covered
A. Standardization		
1. Fair Packaging and Labeling Act (1966)	FTC, FDA	Grocery store items (e.g., foods and detergents)
2. Size uniformity and simplification	Various state authorities	Bread, margarine, flour, dairy products
3. Unit pricing	Various state authorities	Grocery store items
4. Truth in Lending Act (1969)	FTC, FRB	Consumer credit
5. Warranty standards	FTC	Durables over $15 with written warranty
B. Quality Disclosures		
1. Ingredient labeling:		
Wool Products Labeling Act (1939)	FTC	Wool products
Fur Product Labeling Act (1951)	FTC	Furs
Textile Fiber Identification Act (1958)	FTC	Textiles, apparel, etc.
Food, Drug and Cosmetic Act	FDA	Food products
2. Open dating of perishables	Various state authorities	Grocery perishables
3. Antitampering Odometer Law (1972)	NHTSA	Cars and trucks
4. Performance disclosures:		
Fuel efficiency	FEA, FTC	Autos, appliances
Octane rating	FTC, FEA	Gasoline
Tar and nicotine	FTC	Cigarettes
On-time performance	ICC	Moving van services
5. Grade rating	USDA	Meat, eggs, butter, etc.
	NHTSA	Tires

[a] FTC, Federal Trade Commission; FDA, Food and Drug Administration; FRB, Federal Reserve Board of Governors; NHTSA, National Highway Traffic Safety Administration; FEA, Federal Energy Administration; ICC, Interstate Commerce Commission; USDA, U.S. Department of Agriculture.

Artificially stabilized pricing is a third form of price discrimination. In this approach, the selling price for a product or service is artificially maintained at an agreed-upon level, regardless of supply and demand. Manufacturers' suggested retail-price contracts that compel retailers to sell at the particular manufacturers' price are a form of price maintenance. Manufacturers have been guilty of this practice, and the federal government, in effect, also actively supports price maintenance. Crop price supports, import and export quotas, and minimum wage laws all are examples of government price maintenance. Governmental price controls are also accomplished through the regulation of pricing. Much recent debate has centered on the beneficial and/or harmful effects of these actions on the price levels of the products and services that they regulate.

Still another source of price support comes from the unions' establishing wage rates for their members. In effect, labor is a service, and the wage rate is a price for this service. Under labor contract agreements, the unions are, in effect, establishing the cost of a particular service. In each of these examples of price supports, a case for or against it is not necessarily being made. The stabilizing mechanisms for prices are identified, not evaluated. But, consumers are becoming increasingly aware that these regulated prices may affect the competitive free market price for the goods or services they buy. In this context, society wants to be assured that the public good is in fact being served by these artificial pricing mechanisms.

The final price-related issue is that of confusing and hidden cost agreements. In the past, many contractual agreements were so confusingly worded that the customer did not understand the service that was provided or the real cost of goods being purchased. Customers making a large purchase with easy credit terms often paid more than twice the original cost of the goods or services because of exorbitant interest rates. Fortunately, much of this abuse has been curtailed, but there are still vaguely worded contracts for goods or services that confuse the customer, usually at his or her expense.

Business is attempting to police itself and is taking steps to reduce the problems with pricing policies, which will be discussed later in the chapter. Government, of course, is also taking steps to curb pricing abuses.

Federal Laws to Reduce General Pricing Abuses.   Three laws at the federal level have been directed at reducing pricing abuses. The Sherman Act passed before the turn of the century, made illegal some types of price fixing. This act is directed at industries that act in collusion to maintain prices. The second piece of legislation was the Clayton Act, which stated that price discrimination was illegal unless there was evidence that the discount was justified by the price savings realized by the seller. The third piece of legislation was the Robinson-Patman Act, mentioned earlier, which defined price discrimination more thoroughly than did the Clayton Act. The Robinson-Patman Act made quantity discounts legal only if the amount of discount equaled the savings realized by handling the larger quantity. Furthermore, it charged the Federal Trade Commission with regulating the amount and limits of quantity discounts. In effect, this act narrowed the amount of discounts or rebates that could be offered to consumers and retailers.[8] Although the federal laws have in some cases aided in price maintenance (i.e., permitting manufacturers to protect their outlets through suggested price level agreements), the courts have made the enforcement of these contracts very difficult.[9]

Truth in Lending Act. The Truth in Lending Act, passed on July 1, 1969, is another important piece of legislation designed to protect the consumer. Any person or business that extends or arranges credit to individuals for personal, family, household, or agricultural purposes falls under the act. This law requires that customers be told all the charges they are paying, direct and indirect, to the nearest 0.25 percent. This requirement gives the borrower valuable information. Monthly statements sent with open-end accounts, such as revolving charges, must include the following information:

1. Unpaid balance at the beginning of the period.
2. Amount and date of new purchases unless provided previously.
3. Payments made by the customer.
4. Finance charge in dollars and cents.
5. Periodic rates that were used to compute finance charges on the amount and the range of balances that were applicable.
6. Annual percentage rate.
7. Unpaid balance on which the finance charge is computed.
8. Closing date of the billing cycle and the unpaid balance as of that date.

For loan transactions, the borrower must be told

1. The amount of credit.
2. All charges, itemized individually, are included in the credit but are not part of the finance charge.
3. Prepaid finance charges and required deposit balance.[10]

The lending law also protects the consumer against the unauthorized use of credit cards. If a card is stolen and used before the theft is reported to the card issuer, the maximum liability to the customer will be $50. If it is reported before the card is used, there is no liability on the part of the consumer. Furthermore, a card issuer cannot hold a person liable for any unauthorized use unless

[8]Ronald R. Gist, *Marketing and Society* (New York: Holt, Rinehart and Winston, 1971), pp. 138–139.

[9]Gist, pp. 120–122.

[10]"What Must You Tell Your Customer?" *Nation's Business*, June 1969, pp. 42–44.

1. The person either requested or used the card.
2. The issuer provided some means, such as a signature panel or photo on the card, for identifying the user.
3. The user was told of the potential $50 liability.
4. The issuer provided a form for use in notifying him of the loss or theft of the card.[11]

The law also forbids the issuer from sending new, unsolicited credit cards, but it does allow renewal cards to be sent without being requested.

Other features of the lending law pertain to advertising credit terms and the need to provide complete information. For example, if the advertiser tells the amount of the down payment, other important terms such as the number, amount, and periods of payment must also be included so that the purchaser has the necessary information for making an intelligent decision.

Another important provision of the law is designed to protect homeowners when they use their home as security in a credit transaction. This law gives the owner three days to think about the transaction and requires the creditor to give written notice to the potential borrower regarding the right to cancellation. Then, if the homeowner decides not to go ahead, the deal can be terminated by merely notifying the creditor in writing.

Government legislation such as the acts forbidding price fixing and the Truth in Lending Act has done much to curb past abuses in pricing, but there still is much to be done. Business is also attempting to police itself by providing full information as to price and pricing policies.

Product Safety

Product safety is a key dimension of consumerism. The other concerns we examined reflect deceptive practices, but product safety reflects practices that not only can harm the customer financially but also can bring physical harm and even death to the user of the product or service. Although declining, the most recent data indicate about 33 million consumer-product-related injuries and 20,000 consumer-product-related deaths annually.[12]

General Product Safety. The courts have greatly modified the concept of product safety. At one time the manufacturer had limited liability for a product after it was produced. But as McGuire reported, "Under the now-prevailing doctrine (held by the courts), an individual seeking damages for product-related injuries need not prove that the product's manufacturer

---

[11]"What Truth in Lending Means to You," pamphlet distributed by the board of governors of the Federal Reserve System.

[12]Terrence Scanlon, "We Want to Work with Companies, Not Against Them," *U.S. News & World Report*, April 15, 1985, p. 74.

had been negligent or had violated an expressed or implied warranty. The producer can be held liable simply by reason of having produced an inherently dangerous or defective product."[13] In fact, recent interpretations of liability laws protect the consumer from the company's product, even if the product is misused. For example, a man successfully sued a lawn mower manufacturer when he was injured while holding the lawn mower up so that he could cut his bushes with it.[14] One case was cited in which a football helmet manufacturer was successfully sued by a family when their son was injured in a football game. Whether the player was or was not wearing the helmet at the time of injury was not even proved in the case.[15] The end result is that product safety is becoming a great concern not only to consumer groups but also to business firms and their insurance companies who sell liability insurance. It should be pointed out that liability insurance rates have increased several hundredfold over the past few years, and some small firms have gone out of business because they could not afford the high cost of liability insurance.

Automobile Safety. The critic of auto safety and the person most credited for initiating the consumerism movement is Ralph Nader. His now classic book *Unsafe at Any Speed*[16] was directed primarily toward the GM Compact Corvair, but its effect was and is still being felt throughout the auto industry.

Consumer Product Safety Act. Although most of the safety complaints have been aimed at autos, there is also concern for general product safety, as reflected in the Consumer Product Safety Act. In essence, the act is designed to

1. Protect the public against unreasonable risk of injury from consumer products.
2. Assist consumers in evaluating the comparative safety of these products.
3. Develop uniform safety standards for consumer products while minimizing any conflicts with state or local regulations.
4. Promote research and investigation into the causes and prevention of product-related injuries, illnesses, or deaths.

To carry out these directives, the act established a Consumer Product Safety Commission consisting of five members appointed by the president with the advice and consent of the Senate.

One goal of the commission is to establish and maintain product safety standards. For example, it is empowered to order a manufacturer, wholesaler,

---

[13]E. Patrick McGuire, "Manufacturer's Malpractice," in *A Managerial Odyssey: Problems in Business and Its Environment*, 2nd ed., ed. Arthur Elkins and Dennis W. Callaghan (Reading, Mass.: Addison-Wesley, 1978), pp. 307–308.

[14]McGuire, p. 308.

[15]McGuire, p. 312.

[16]Ralph Nader, *Unsafe at Any Speed* (New York: Grossman Publishers, 1965).

distributor, or retailer to recall, repair, or replace any product that it feels constitutes an unreasonable risk to the consumer. Failure to comply can bring fines ranging from $50,000 to $500,000 and jail sentences of up to one year. However, these penalties serve only as warnings. The commission prefers that business firms comply voluntarily and institutes such drastic action only when all else fails.

Another objective of the commission is to reduce the many product-related accidents that occur every year. One way is to demand safer products. A second is to familiarize both industry and the public with some of the most hazardous products. In 1985, the commission was examining 50 products, including kerosene heaters, upholstered furniture, gas heating systems, portable electric heaters, chain saws, riding mowers, and garage door openers. The commission hopes that by identifying hazardous products and investigating product safety, the problems can be reduced (see the box "Product Liability").

PRODUCT LIABILITY

The A. H. Robins Company recently put off its annual meeting until it could determine how many millions of dollars it should set aside to pay women injured by its Dalkon contraceptive device. The FMC Corporation decided not to make precision bearings for helicopter rotors because the profit it stood to make did not justify the losses it would suffer if the helicopters crashed. These developments all underscore the importance today of product liability. So many companies are being hit with lawsuits and huge awards that they are asking Congress to step in and help.

Hardest hit is the pharmaceutical industry. Take the case of Merrell Dow Pharmaceuticals. Its prescription morning sickness drug, Bendectin, was used by an estimated 33 million women over a 27-year period. In 1983 the firm had so many lawsuits against it that its annual insurance premium was $10 million, while its sales were only $12 to $13 million. The firm withdrew the product from the market and in July 1984 agreed to pay $120 million to settle 700 outstanding lawsuits. Cases such as this help to indicate why product quality continues to be of overriding importance to businesses in their efforts to develop and manufacture consumer goods.

Warranties.   A warranty can be defined as an obligation that the seller assumes to the buyer. Quite often it is in writing and promises to substitute a good product or return the purchase price if the product is of poor quality or proves to be defective. In other words, warranties protect buyers against poor quality. Many types of products have warranties—refrigerators, vacuum cleaners, television sets, and hair dryers.

If the buyer relies on this information when purchasing the product, there are legal grounds for recourse. For example, if Ford Motor Company advertises its windshields as shatterproof, a consumer whose window is broken by a flying pebble has grounds for legal action. Furthermore, the courts have broadened their interpretation of expressed warranty to include some types of general statements in advertising copy.

The history of product warranties and the liability that business must assume for its products' performance is a history of court litigations that effectively broaden the responsibility of the business organization for the quality of its product or service. Initially, business was covered under the doctrine of privity of contract. In effect, if the individual purchased the goods from another source, the liability for the safe, quality performance of that product was the responsibility of the seller. If a consumer was dissatisfied with the product and wanted some form of restitution, the consumer had recourse to sue only the party from which the consumer had purchased the product. If that suit was successful, the retailer could then sue the party from whom the retailer obtained the product, usually a wholesaler. The wholesaler would then have the right to sue the manufacturer. But this notion of privity of contract as protecting the manufacturer was not upheld in the case of *MacPherson* v. *Buick Motor Company* more than a half century ago.

> Mr. MacPherson purchased a new Buick automobile from a local dealer. Shortly thereafter defective wooden spokes in a wheel collapsed, and Mr. MacPherson was injured as a result. He sued Buick. The company claimed that MacPherson had purchased the car from a dealer and not from Buick and therefore Buick had no obligation to him. The judge ruled that Buick had been negligent because the wheel had not been inspected before it was put on the car. He further ruled that Buick was responsible for defects resulting from negligence, regardless of how many middlemen were in between.[17]

As a result of this landmark decision and further interpretations by the courts, the notion of privity of contract has been ruled as an ineffective means for business to avoid responsibility for the safety, quality, and performance of its products.

The current legal environment makes all parties involved in transactions between the manufacturer of the product and the user liable for that product's performance. In fact, a recent decision still under appeal holds the personalities who advertise the product (a movie star or popular athlete) responsible and liable if the product does not live up to expectations. A singing and acting personality was successfully sued recently when the product that he was advertising (a blemish remover and facial cream) did not live up to the advertising claims that he made for the product. The dissatisfied customer

---

[17]MacPherson v. Buick Motor Company, 217 N.Y. 382, 111 N.E. 1050 (Court of Appeals of New York, 1916). Cited in Keith Davis and Robert Blomstrom, *Business, Society and Environment*, 3rd ed. (New York: McGraw-Hill, 1975), pp. 282–283.

sued not only the product manufacturer but also the personality whose word the consumer was following. Under present law, an aggrieved consumer may attempt to find recourse by suing the retailer, manufacturer, wholesaler, and/or advertiser. Each of the parties is responsible for providing a safe, quality product or service and making honest advertising claims.

Within the present legal framework there are implied warranties and expressed warranties. An *expressed warranty* is one that is in writing. An *implied warranty* is one that is an unwritten responsibility of the manufacturer or provider of the service to offer a product or service that is reasonably safe and functional for the purposes for which it was intended. Under the Magnuson-Moss bill, a major law governing warranties, written liabilities fall into two categories, either full warranties or limited warranties. A full warranty must stipulate that the product will meet specific standards of performance and the reasonable needs of the consumer. If the product is defective, under the full warranty proviso, it must be repaired in a reasonable time and without charge. If the product is not performing after several attempts to repair it, the price must be refunded or replaced with no additional charge. Any warranty less than a full warranty is considered a limited warranty and must be so indicated. In addition, this law provides that warranties must be written in plain and simple language that the consumer can understand. Attempts to reduce the manufacturer's liability through the warranty or through disclaimers were voided in a landmark decision:

> In this case, Mr. Claus Henningsen purchased a new automobile which he and his wife drove around town for several days. Then, while his wife was driving out of town, the steering mechanism failed and the car crashed into a highway sign and then into a brick wall. Mrs. Henningsen sustained injuries, and the car was a total loss. Mr. Henningsen went to court. The automobile company claimed that Mr. Henningsen had signed a disclaimer when he bought the car and this limited the liability of the company to replacement of defective parts. The court held that the company could not avoid its legal responsibility to make automobiles good enough to serve the purposes for which they were intended.[18]

Today, business organizations cannot, through warranty language or disclaimers, avoid responsibility for reasonable demands for the reliability of their products or services.

Service Issues

Although much of the previous legislation and court actions has been directed toward manufacturing organizations, there is increasing concern about service organizations and the service that they should provide.[19] This concern

---

[18]Henningsen v. Bloomfield Motors, Inc. and Chrysler Corporation, 32 N.J. 358, 161 A 2d 69 (Supreme Court of New Jersey, 1960). Cited in Davis and Blomstrom, pp. 282–283.

[19]Leonard L. Berry, Valarie A. Ziethaml, and A. Parasuraman, "Quality Counts in Services, Too," *Business Horizons*, May–June 1985, pp. 44–52.

is not surprising, as the number of service-based organizations has gone up rapidly since the postwar years. At present, service-based organizations account for more than half of all business organizations and offer a range of special services for the consumer. Most firms, of course, are reliable and try to meet consumer needs with the best possible service. However, enormous growth has brought an increasing number of fraudulent businesses that provide inadequate, slipshod services. There have been widespread media coverage and several congressional hearings on service-based organizations. For example, one hearing tried to assess the quality of automobile repair services. The congressional committee's findings cited thousands of instances of faulty repairs, unfair repair charges, and unnecessary repairs not needed to correct the problems. In similar studies of household repairs, it was found that some television repair firms are fraudulent and that some construction companies do not do the required repairs and bilk the public out of millions of dollars each year. Retail stores have been found to use poor billing procedures and collection tactics that often intimidate customers. Credit agencies were found, in congressional hearings, to write erroneous reports about clients. As a result of these abuses in the service industry, several laws have been passed to correct the problems.

Many of the laws previously discussed apply to service industries, but there are also special laws to curb abuses in the service-based industries. These include the Right of Privacy Act of 1976, the Fair Credit Reporting Act of 1971, and the Truth in Lending Act of 1969. The Truth in Lending Act was discussed earlier. The Right to Privacy Act not only protects an individual's privacy from questions that may be asked by private and public organizations but also gives the consumer the right to see information about him or her that an organization has in its file. This act helps consumers correct mistakes in the organization's information that may be used to determine eligibility for particular services.

The Fair Credit Reporting Act is aimed at consumer credit issues, and its purpose is to protect the consumer against inaccurate or obsolete credit information and to ensure that credit agencies treat the consumer in a fair and equitable manner. In essence, the act is designed to prevent business firms from unfairly denying credit to consumers.

This consumer law permits individuals to obtain information that was heretofore denied to them. For example, if a person is denied credit, he or she is entitled to be told the name and address of the credit agency that prepared the report on which the denial was based. The person is also entitled to take anyone of his or her choice to the consumer reporting agency and be told the nature, substance, and sources (except investigative sources) of the information (except medical) collected about him or her. In addition, the act permits the consumer to

1. Be told who has received a consumer report on him or her in the last six months.

2. Have incomplete or incorrect information reinvestigated and revised.
3. Have the agency notify, free of cost, those individuals named by the consumer who have received erroneous information.
4. Sue a reporting agency for damages if it willingly or negligently violates the law and, if successful, collect attorney's fees and court costs.[20]

Additionally, a consumer is protected by state laws against consumer fraud and federal laws relating to breach of warranties and consumer fraud. Although these laws are effective to some degree, there is concern that not enough is being done to protect the consumer. Proposals to further regulate service-based organizations are presently under consideration at both federal and state levels. Service organizations are proposing and enacting several self-regulation programs to aid in curbing abuses in their industry.

Legal Action by Consumers

In addition to assistance from the safety commission, consumers who suffer product-related injuries can take legal action, and the courts are becoming more liberal in awarding damages. An example is the case of an Illinois housewife who was blinded when a can of drain cleaner exploded in her face. The court awarded her almost $1 million. This type of verdict greatly worries many businesspersons who see the cost of liability suits increasing faster than the rate of sales. There are "tens of thousands of suits filed each year alleging defects in everything from step-ladders and chain saws to birth control devices, tampons, toys, and drugs."[21] There are two types of liability that are relevant to the safety issue: negligence and strict liability.

Negligence. Liability laws concerning product safety have recently undergone drastic changes. Under old English law, business concerns were liable for negligence only to the person who bought the goods. Eventually the courts began to recognize exceptions, and in 1916 an important precedent was established. A court in New York ruled that if a manufacturer produces a defective product, it has a duty to exercise reasonable care not only to the person who bought the product but to others as well. Today the generally accepted rule is that if negligence can be shown, manufacturers as well as intermediaries, such as wholesalers and retailers, will be liable for the defective products. This is true regardless of whether a contractual relationship existed between the parties. One example of this situation is provided by *Noel* v. *United Aircraft Corporation*. In this case Mr. Noel sued the aircraft company that built the plane that crashed while he was a passenger in it. One of the engines had begun to overspeed almost an hour before the crash, at which time the pilot had tried unsuccessfully to feather the propeller.

[20]*FTC Buyer's Guide No. 7: Fair Credit Reporting Act*, pamphlet distributed by the Federal Trade Commission.
[21]"The Product-Liability Debate," *Newsweek*, September 10, 1984, p. 54.

The court ruled against United Aircraft, stating that for six years the manufacturer had been aware of sticking valves in the engine governor and had been slow to make the necessary changes. The court said the firm should have exercised reasonable care, a duty that did not end with the delivery of the plane to the airline. In other words, United Aircraft, as well as the airline that bought the plane, was guilty of product negligence to the passenger.

Strict Liability

A second area is strict liability, which holds that a manufacturer has unlimited liability for unfit or unsafe products that injure the consumer or user. Negligence does not have to be either alleged or proved. As long as it can be established that the manufacturer made a defective or unsafe product, suit can be brought. Most states enforce strict liability.

Strict liability laws have been challenged as tipping the balance of justice in favor of the consumer. *Suvada* v. *White Motor Company* provides an illustration. The plaintiffs in the case purchased from White Motor Company a reconditioned tractor truck to use in their milk-distributing business. The tractor's brake system had been made by Bendix-Westinghouse and installed by White Motor. Three years after the purchase, the brake system failed, causing a collision. The plaintiffs sued both Bendix-Westinghouse and White Motor Company. From the state's intermediate appellate court, the plaintiffs received a ruling in their favor, the court basing its decision on the implied warranty of fitness for use. The decision was appealed. The state's supreme court also upheld the verdict, but on the basis of the strict liability in tort and not implied warranty. In brief, the state supreme court ruled that because the plaintiffs were able to prove that the product left the manufacturer's control in an unsafe condition, they were entitled to damages.

Another well-known case of strict liability is *Greenman* v. *Yuba Power Products, Inc.* Mr. Greenman purchased a shopsmith combination power tool he saw demonstrated in a California dealer's store. Two years later he bought some attachments so that the tool could be used as a lathe. After he worked the block several times with no problems, it suddenly flew out of the machine and struck him on the forehead, causing serious injury. Mr. Greenman sued both the dealer and the manufacturer. Yuba Power Products claimed there was no contractual arrangement with Greenman, but the court pushed aside this defense. Meanwhile, Mr. Greenman's lawyer was able to show that the machine was unsafe when used in the manner recommended by the company. Damages were awarded to Mr. Greenman. Yuba appealed to the California Supreme Court, but again lost, although this time the court added a new feature. It said that even if the company had not been negligent, it would still have been liable for damages. A manufacturer is strictly liable in tort when an article he places on the market, knowing that it will be used without inspection, proves to have a defect that causes injury to a human being.[22] Thus an injured plaintiff can recover, regardless of whether the manufacturer is negligent.

Effectiveness of Current Federal Laws.   The diverse demands of consumers that they be treated fairly and honestly and given a safe and reliable product or service have stimulated a host of federal legislation. This legislation, although solving some consumer problems, has also created considerable controversy. Several problems plague governmental agencies in attempting to carry out the laws and, at the same time, meet the needs of the public at large. These problems include overlapping jurisdictions, a lack of research into the problems, and confusing and watered-down directives issued by the agencies.

Overlapping jurisdictions have always been a problem in federal programs that try to meet consumer needs. With the maturing of the consumer movement and a more comprehensive approach, many of the problems have been eradicated. According to several consumer groups, however, the problem will not be truly solved until comprehensive consumer practices legislation is enacted at the federal level. Such legislation would bring together all the various regulatory bodies under one command and make more efficient use of resources and work power.

Funding has been a constant source of irritation for the federal agencies charged with enforcing consumer-oriented legislation. Although the law may be specific for certain abuses, many of the federal agencies do not have the personnel to police all businesses so as to ensure that the law is being carried out. Several agencies must rely on business's self-reports. For example, the Department of Agriculture came under attack for allowing the companies, themselves, to place quality standards on meat and fish products.

Consumer groups have attacked legislation for not having sufficient clarity or power to combat the abuses that need to be eliminated. They argue that the powerful business lobbies reduce and water down legislation through amendments and revisions before the bills are actually passed into law. The final bill, the groups argue, has lost much of the essential provisos that would make it an effective deterrent to unethical business practices.

It is hoped that future government action will curb the problems outlined here. Consumer groups are presently mustering support for legislative reform and for the formation of a federal agency for consumer protection. This will be successful, however, only if public officials feel that the support is nationwide and that people are genuinely concerned about improving the environment of the marketplace and the protection of the consumer.

THE BUSINESS RESPONSE TO CONSUMERISM

Business is doing many things to respond to the consumerism challenge. In the following section we examine some of the most important.

[22]Greenman v. Yuba Power Products, Inc., 377P. 2d 897 (1963).

Giving More Information to Consumers

One possible solution to consumers' problems is giving more information to consumers, and this is done in three ways. Informational advertising that provides basic consumer information on a variety of topics is one popular approach. A second approach offers information about the exact service or product price before a consumer buys it. A final type of information program spells out warranty and service guarantees.

Informational Advertising. Informational advertising is not necessarily directed at selling a product or service. Instead, its purpose is to offer enough information to increase a consumer's knowledge and awareness of particular topics. An example is an informational guide to aid consumers in their purchase decisions. Sears has used this type of advertising in some of its campaigns. Another approach is improving a consumer's knowledge of current topics. Examples of this are General Foods' and Hunt-Wesson's nutritional information advertising and the St. Paul Insurance Company's advertisements regarding insurance and arson. It must be remembered that these are only representative; more and more businesses are taking greater responsibility in their advertising, enabling a more informed consumer and society.

1. The Sears Approach. Sears sponsored a number of ads designed to improve the consumer's knowledge of a group of products. In one case the company's refrigerator department placed advertisements in more than 30 magazines to educate consumers on defrost systems. The purpose of the ads was to clarify the often-confusing claims about automatic defrost and frostless refrigerators. In another instance Sears launched a campaign to help consumers choose the right color television set. In the advertising copy, which began with "what to look for in any brand," an item checklist was provided. Although Sears acknowledged that not all consumers, once educated about the things to look for in a television set, would choose a Sears TV, a company spokesperson indicated that the firm hoped its frankness and honesty in dealing with the issue would create a positive attitude toward the company.

Sears uses a similar informational policy on all labeling and package copy in which there might be any doubt or confusion about the product's use. For example, the pressure-sensitive labels on its ladders do more than identify the product. They also describe the exact type of ladder, the preferred uses based on standards established by the American National Standards Institute, the directions for inspecting the ladder before using it, and specific safety recommendations and suggestions for care in order to prolong the ladder's life. Sears identified its goals in the product information area as follows:

> Advertising and product labeling must . . . meet rigid standards of accuracy, all aimed at honesty, integrity and straightforwardness, in information. All such information must meet a rigid test. Literally every statement about the goods and

services shall be worded in a manner which will be clearly understood. Nothing will be obscured or concealed, no promises made that cannot be kept, and there shall be nothing ambiguous or incomplete in representation or suggestion.[23]

Another Sears policy is to offer consumer credit counseling. Its Consumer Information Services Division provides pamphlets and texts showing consumers how to use credit intelligently, and it also creates educational materials for use in schools. In fact, these materials are being currently used by about 10 million teenagers in schools, as well as thousands of teachers, family counselors, and social workers throughout the country. By offering information on credit, selling, and consumer economics, Sears hopes to help purchasers receive top value for their dollar.

2. General Foods' Approach.   General Foods (GF) has also undertaken an informative advertising campaign to acquaint consumers with a variety of topics. In its ads it has covered subjects such as packaging and labeling, food additives, freshness, and nutrition. In addition, each advertisement recommends that the consumer buy a booklet entitled "The Family Guide to Better Food and Better Health." Although GF has played no role in writing the book, it has agreed to distribute it at no profit. The ads also suggest that consumers write to the firm's vice-president for consumer affairs regarding any questions they might have.

The purpose of the GF ads is to provide useful information to consumers. For example, in its ad on food additives GF tells consumers that unless they grow their own food and are satisfied with eating what is in season, it is impossible to avoid using additives. It is pointed out that these additives should not be viewed as harmful; they have many benefits, including reducing mold, preserving crispness, holding moisture, providing flavor, reducing spoilage, and increasing nutrition. The company points out that

> Di-hydrogen oxide is probably the world's most common food additive. It's used to add moisture and change texture. Its safety is accepted without question. In fact, it's absolutely essential to life. But the name di-hydrogen oxide on a label might make you uneasy. You won't even see it, though, because di-hydrogen oxide is always called water.[24]

It is not clear what impact the GF campaign has had on consumers. In addition, other firms such as Kraft Foods are considering incorporating nutritional messages into their regular advertising. Thus, there seems to be a trend, at least in the food industry, to use informational advertising.

3. Hunt-Wesson Foods' Approach.   For the past several years, Hunt-Wesson Foods has had a nutritional assistance program for poverty families. The approach is to offer special packets of information and to conduct food preparation seminars and demonstrations in high-poverty areas. The pro-

---

[23]"Corporate Social Responsibility: Whose Business Is It?" paper sent to authors by Sears.
[24]"GF Nutrition Ad Series May Go National After Test," *Advertising Age*, May 27, 1974, p. 2.

gram is geared not only to individuals' nutritional needs but also to what Hunt-Wesson officials call "low-cost cookery." The purpose of the program is to teach less-educated groups how to prepare nutritional and appetizing meals at a low cost. The program includes meal planning, food purchasing, food storage, and food preparation, and the U.S. Department of Agriculture rated it as a substantial success in the first two years that it was offered.[25]

Once again we should emphasize that the objective of these companies is to inform the consuming public. Nutritional advertising on package labels has improved the consumer's diet, and labeling a package as to its toxicity has added to consumer safety. The "Mr. Yuk" symbol being used on poisonous products and the requirement that instructions for an antidote be added are examples of educating the consumer about the product and its safe usage.[26]

4. St. Paul Property and Liability Insurance's Approach. Figure 11.1 presents an example of the informational advertising conducted by the St. Paul Insurance Company. The company has run several advertisements relating to various topics in the insurance field. Topics included no-fault auto insurance, concern over the high cost of liability court settlements, and the problem of arson and its cost to society. Although these advertisements are not directly related to the sale of insurance per se, they are directed to the very survival of the entire insurance industry. In this case, St. Paul is giving the consumer additional insight into the problems and costs facing the industry and recommending what can be done by the individual consumer to reduce these costs. In Figure 11.1, the company asserts that tougher laws would reduce the loss from arson-related fires. Note that the advertisement also indicates where more information about the topic can be obtained.

This type of informational advertising has been used by other industries as well. Several oil companies, a paper manufacturer, a copy company, and a computer corporation, to name but a few, all have spent great sums of money on topical information advertisements. For example, Mobil Oil directed its advertisements to a better understanding of basic economics and the free-enterprise system. Although these advertisements probably do little to increase a company's sales, they may aid in the long-term survival of the business institution and the free enterprise economic system.

Unit Pricing. One result of the consumerism movement has been a new system of providing price information. Unit pricing was designed by retail organizations to help the consumer determine the exact price for a particular item. Previously, the consumer found comparative pricing difficult because there was little standard packaging for most items. The consumer wishing to purchase a product such as soap found packages from various manufactur-

---

[25]David A. Aaker and George S. Day, *Consumerism: Search for the Consumer Interest*, 2nd ed. (New York: Free Press, 1974), pp. 214–217.

[26]K. C. Schneider, "Prevention of Accidental Poisoning Through Package and Label Design," *Journal of Consumer Research*, September 1977, pp. 67–74.

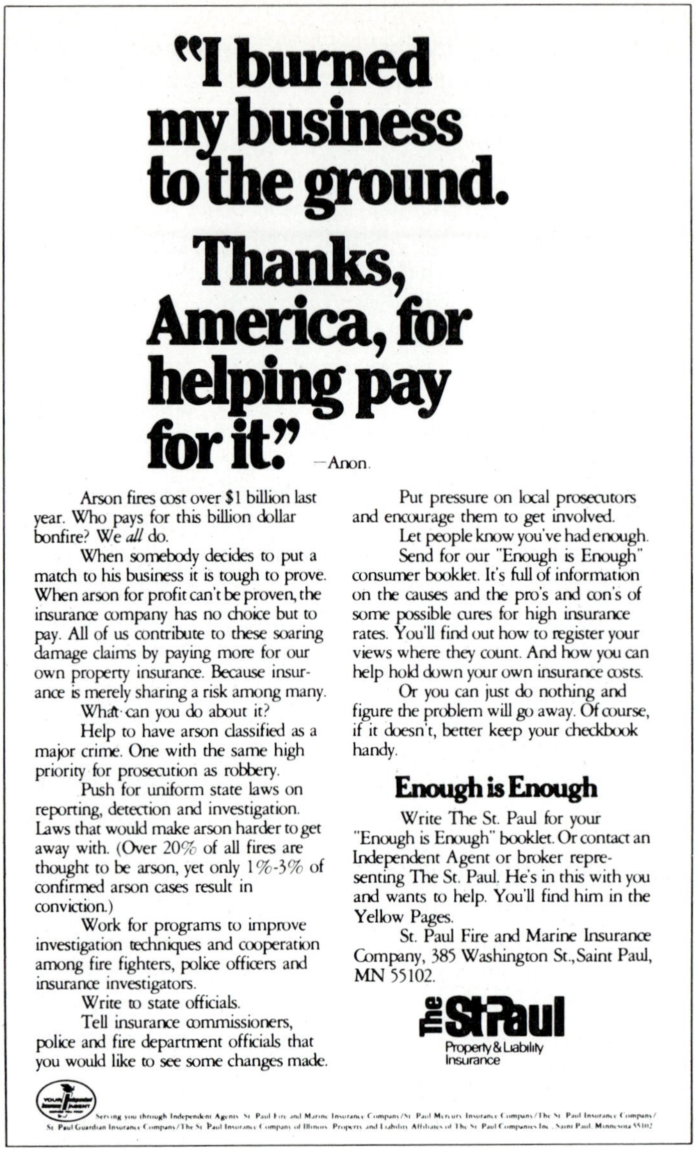

"I burned my business to the ground.

Thanks, America, for helping pay for it." —Anon.

Arson fires cost over $1 billion last year. Who pays for this billion dollar bonfire? We *all* do.

When somebody decides to put a match to his business it is tough to prove. When arson for profit can't be proven, the insurance company has no choice but to pay. All of us contribute to these soaring damage claims by paying more for our own property insurance. Because insurance is merely sharing a risk among many.

What can you do about it?

Help to have arson classified as a major crime. One with the same high priority for prosecution as robbery.

Push for uniform state laws on reporting, detection and investigation. Laws that would make arson harder to get away with. (Over 20% of all fires are thought to be arson, yet only 1%-3% of confirmed arson cases result in conviction.)

Work for programs to improve investigation techniques and cooperation among fire fighters, police officers and insurance investigators.

Write to state officials.

Tell insurance commissioners, police and fire department officials that you would like to see some changes made.

Put pressure on local prosecutors and encourage them to get involved.

Let people know you've had enough.

Send for our "Enough is Enough" consumer booklet. It's full of information on the causes and the pro's and con's of some possible cures for high insurance rates. You'll find out how to register your views where they count. And how you can help hold down your own insurance costs.

Or you can just do nothing and figure the problem will go away. Of course, if it doesn't, better keep your checkbook handy.

Enough is Enough

Write The St. Paul for your "Enough is Enough" booklet. Or contact an Independent Agent or broker representing The St. Paul. He's in this with you and wants to help. You'll find him in the Yellow Pages.

St. Paul Fire and Marine Insurance Company, 385 Washington St., Saint Paul, MN 55102.

The St.Paul
Property & Liability
Insurance

Serving you through Independent Agents St. Paul Fire and Marine Insurance Company/St. Paul Mercury Insurance Company/The St. Paul Insurance Company/
St. Paul Guardian Insurance Company/The St. Paul Insurance Company of Illinois Property and Liability Affiliates of The St. Paul Companies Inc., Saint Paul, Minnesota 55102

Used with permission of The St. Paul Companies, Inc.

FIGURE 11.1 **Institutional Advertising to Benefit the Insurance Industry.**
Used with permission of The St. Paul Companies, Inc.

ers in 10-, 12-, 14-, 16-, and 20-ounce sizes. Even price comparison among the regular, large, and giant "economy" sizes of the same brand was complicated. Except for a conscientious few using calculators, consumers could not readily calculate the true price savings, if any, of buying one brand and/or size of product over another. To alleviate this problem, several enlightened business organizations developed unit-pricing methods to indicate price. Along with the overall price for the product was the unit price for the product (e.g., cost per pound for meat products, cost per ounce for soup, etc.). Through unit pricing the shopper could more easily compare products and sizes of products. Most merchandising firms now use unit pricing in their stores.

1. Giant Foods' Approach. An organization with a particularly successful approach to providing consumer information is Giant Foods, Inc. One of the innovative consumer aids instituted by the company is called *open dating* in which dates are printed on packaged foods so the customer can determine the product's freshness. Most supermarkets and wholesalers put this information on selected products to meet legal requirements of the law, but in Giant's case open dating and unit pricing are applied to almost all its products.

Giant Foods also lists the ingredients and nutritional values of foods sold under its private-brand labels. This nutritional value labeling program was devised by one of its early consumer advisory committees, headed by the well-known nutritionist, Jean Mayer. The labels on the products tell the consumer the amount of essential nutrients such as protein, iron, and vitamin C.

Another aspect of Giant's approach is to recommend bargains to their customers. For example, when beef prices rise sharply, the company's stores may urge the customers to buy substitutes such as fish or poultry. Then, when meat prices decline, the firm encourages consumers to switch back to beef.

2. Jewel Food Stores' Approach. Jewel Food Stores, like Giant Foods and many other firms, has made a concerted effort to offer more information to its customers. Jewel started a pilot unit-pricing program several years ago,[27] but found that after the six-month initial test, only 7.4 percent of the customers had used unit pricing in their purchase decisions. The program had cost Jewel approximately $1,000 per store to change over to unit pricing. More recently the company introduced another form of price reduction. Under the generic-brand food program, Jewel presented products without specific brand names. The foods were packaged for Jewel in plain white and black labels with few of the frills and art typical of most national brand packaging. The generic foods can be sold at a much lower cost and therefore have become quite popular. Many supermarket chains across the country now use this approach.

Unit pricing and other variations are major steps in giving additional

[27]Aaker and Day, pp. 194–195.

information to the consumer. However, it is interesting to note that Jewel found that the consuming public does not seem to use unit pricing when making purchasing decisions. Jewel indicated that it had explained the benefits of unit pricing through institutional advertising; yet only a small percent of the customers used this price information. This finding, of course, may not necessarily mean that the unit price system is a failure and not wanted by customers. Rather, it may indicate that once consumers learn of the price difference, they have decided to continue purchasing the national brand item because it is of known quality and the price difference is not that significant. But there is some evidence to suggest that consumers may be suffering from information overload. The results of one study found that

- Only 9 percent of consumers used nutritional labels at least once.
- 30 to 50 percent of consumers used unit pricing in the buying decision.
- 10 percent of all credit buyers used information supplied by the Truth in Lending Bill in the last purchase of a durable.
- 39 percent used open dating information on one or more products during the last shopping trip.[28]

Warranty Information and Service Guarantees.   Providing clear warranty and service information is another way that business can inform its customers. With this form of informational advertising the product or service is not stressed as much as is the explanation of the warranty and what can be done if the product does not live up to expectations. The Whirlpool appliance company has done much in this consumer information area. So has the maker of Zippo lighters, which tells where to send defective products and also gives lifetime warranties for its products.

The FTC has made it mandatory that warranties be expressed in language that the consumer can understand. The FTC has also made it much easier for the consumer to return a defective product. But many companies go beyond what is required by the law in order to provide a quality product, a good warranty, and a reliable service system to back up their responsibility to consumers. Whirlpool Corporation is an example of this enlightened approach.

Figure 11.2 shows a Whirlpool advertisement that stresses the quality of and the service behind its product. Note than this advertisement says little about the actual products that Whirlpool makes, only the customer service provided by the company. Although this does not represent all of Whirlpool's advertising, it is a considerable part of its overall media exposure program.

Other organizations have also used this sort of advertising. Zenith Television and Radio has often promoted its products' reliability and warranty. American Motors' buyer protection plan is another example. In trade journals, Pullman Standard, a railway car and transportation equipment manufac-

---

[28]George S. Day, "Assessing the Effects of Information Disclosure Requirements," *Journal of Marketing*, April 1976, p. 46.

Lesson from a dying breed.

Extinction is a dreadful word. Like Donne's bell, it doesn't ring. It tolls. And it's tolling for the eagle now, which puts us in danger, too.

We're in danger of losing the living symbol of our highest standards: Pride. Honor. Honesty. To lose the eagle would be sad. To forget him would be tragic.

At Whirlpool we believe it's our duty to remember. Remember what these standards mean to us. In our lives. And in our business.

We start with pride. To make something of quality is a challenge these days. An appliance is either quality built or it isn't. And if it isn't good enough for us, we know it's not good enough for you.

The test of honor and honesty comes after the sale. We believe a customer should always be treated like a customer. Now, or years from now. With this in mind, we've developed several ways of extending our services for as long as anyone needs them.

For example, we have Cool-Line® service. A toll free telephone number you can call with any problem or question. Try it. We're always glad when people do. (800) 253-1301. In Michigan, (800) 632-2243.

And if you ever do need service, just call Tech-Care® service. It's our nationwide franchised service . . . from a group of service technicians who know what they're doing. And who will be happy to come out and help you whenever you need them. They're in the Yellow Pages.

Or our warranty. It's written clearly, simply. It can be read, understood and used with confidence. We feel that's the way a warranty should work.

These services are really extensions of our way of thinking. Our way of life. They represent our standards: Pride. Honor. Honesty.

They may be in danger. They may be impractical. But at Whirlpool, we believe it's our duty to keep them very much alive.

Whirlpool
CORPORATION

FIGURE 11.2 Example of Informational Advertising. *Used with permission of the Whirlpool Corporation.*

turer, boasts of the quality of its products and included some educational advertising to inform the consumer about the free-enterprise system.

Handling Complaints

In addition to desiring more information about the products and services they are buying, consumers also want their complaints handled quickly and judiciously. In meeting this consumer demand, most companies have created a consumer affairs office headed by a top-level executive.[29] Although these departments have functions other than handling complaints (e.g., they represent consumer interests to the company, keep on top of regulatory/ legislative activities, and develop and run some of the consumer programs), this is their main function. For example, Western Union's consumer affairs department feeds all consumer complaints into one central file, analyzes them, and then disseminates them to appropriate areas in the company.

Visible targets of consumer complaints, such as grocery stores, have found that a unified approach works best. To begin to meet the problem of handling complaints, Armour, Swift, Coca-Cola, Pepsi, General Mills, and United Fruit contributed a total of $300,000 to start the Consumer Research Institute (CRI). The major purpose of this institute is to explore consumer complaints about the food industry. The first thing that the CRI did was hire a management consulting firm to determine precisely what the complaints were. The consultants identified six: advertising, health and safety, deception, information and confusion, cost, and nonprice competition. These six factors were placed down the side of a grid. Across the top of the grid were listed various marketing practices, such as advertising, packaging, labeling, promoting, pricing, branding, personal selling, new product development, marketing research, and product composition. In this way a matrix model was constructed in which the consumer problems and the marketing areas in which they existed could be pinpointed. This approach allows for quick and accurate problem identification, and as a follow-up, the food industry is now concentrating its attention on handling complaints and reestablishing rapport with the customer.

Firms in other industries have devised tailor-made approaches to handle customer complaints. Corning Glass has a manager of consumer interests whose job is to represent the consumer and make sure a complaint does not get lost. As shown in Figure 11.2, Whirlpool offers the consumer a 24-hour "cool-line" free of charge. This escape-valve concept enables the customer to call collect from anywhere in the country to ask about service or to lodge a complaint. Many firms are finding if the customer has the opportunity to discuss his or her problem with a company representative, he or she will be more willing to do repeat business with the company. In some cases top executives in the company personally answer complaints. Others placate

[29]Henry Assael, *Consumer Behavior and Marketing Action* (Boston: Kent, 1981), p. 596.

the caller by turning him or her over to the individual they have assigned to handle complaints. In contrast, an unhappy consumer is one who demands satisfaction but is shuffled around and justifiably becomes infuriated. Those who have been treated this way have been known to call a company chief executive at his or her home.

Fortunately, business does seem to be making progress in dealing with consumer complaints. Pillsbury, for example, maintains a staff of 10 to answer the 2,500 complaints they receive each month, and most customers seem to be satisfied with the results. American Airlines has also had success, not only in answering complaints, but also in reducing their overall number.

Trade Associations—Self-Regulation

Many businesses have formed or joined trade associations. There are hundreds of professional trade organizations in the United States. The motives for joining trade associations are quite diverse. Some of the more socially conscious organizations join in order to help set standards of conduct for their trade or industry. These businesses are working to reduce the number of unscrupulous firms in their ranks. Other firms join professional organizations in the hope of discouraging federal control by indicating that the industry already has a workable code. A third reason for joining the associations is to work as a lobby group in curtailing federal legislation. Whatever the reason, there has been a proliferation of trade associations in this country in the past several years, and these trade organizations are becoming stronger and more active in consumer affairs.

A second area of self-regulation comes from business firms, regardless of their membership in trade associations. This self-regulation aids in building the credibility of the modern firm and enhancing its good will. One sector of business conducting self-regulation is the various media. For example, television, newspapers, and radio, for the most part, subscribe to a code of ethics and behavior. As subscribers to this code, they analyze much of the advertising they present to the public.

Screening Advertising. By providing more information, firms are offering more opportunities for the consumer to get more for the dollar. However, there may still be a problem with erroneous or misleading advertising, so there is a movement to make the media more responsible for the ads they run. For example, newspapers would be required to screen all ads before printing them; in this way, only legitimate ads would be presented. Although one can argue that consumers should exercise reasonable judgment in dealing with a company, the fact is that many consumers assume that an advertisement automatically has a degree of legitimacy attached to it. Otherwise, they reason, why would the media carry the message? Unfortunately, this is sometimes not the case. For example, a retired machinist in Maryland read an ad in the *Sunday Baltimore Sun* guaranteeing three rooms of wall-to-wall carpeting for only $109 and a free vacuum cleaner. But when the salesman arrived he talked the man into buying more expensive carpeting—$309 worth, to be exact—and that was for only one room. In addition, the consumer was given neither a guarantee on the product's workmanship nor a free vacuum cleaner. As might be expected, this man later became very angry at not only the carpet company but the newspaper as well. One reporter covering the case noted "Whatever his own responsibility for his plight, he isn't alone these days in calling for newspapers, magazines and other print media to exercise greater responsibility for the truthfulness of the advertising they accept."[30]

To meet this new responsibility, more and more newspapers are screening the ads submitted to them. For example, the *St. Petersburg Times* in Florida refuses to print any questionable advertisement until it has run a check on the ad's claims. In addition, the newspaper has a weekly column in which it exposes ad deceptions. Another newspaper with a similar policy of checking its ads is the *Louisville Courier-Journal.* In one case this paper refused to carry a butchershop ad and wound up in a law suit. However, a state circuit court judge issued a final ruling in the paper's favor, stating that a newspaper "has a categorical right to accept or reject advertising."[31] Such decisions are lauded by most newspapers because screening can provide a dual benefit. On the one hand, screening ads can help the paper protect its readers, and on the other, the newspaper's own reputation will be enhanced. As one newspaper executive stated, "We have to protect our public image because unethical ads undermine the credibility of our news and editorial comment."

Better Business Bureau.   The Better Business Bureau (BBB) is one of the major self-regulation attempts by business. The BBB is an association of local business people, formed as a place at which consumers could inquire about a particular firm's reputation or complain if they had been wronged by a business. The BBB assumes the role of consumer's advocate to seek out restitution when the consumer has been wronged. The BBB will even go as far as to take a business to court for restitution.

Although the BBB has been under attack for not being aggressive enough as a champion of consumer rights, it has tried to become more active in meeting consumer demands for protection. One of the newest directions that the BBB has taken is to administer an arbitration board for consumers. If the consumer has a complaint against a local business, the BBB will mediate the complaint through an informal hearing and decide, from the facts given, how to make restitution, if warranted. The benefits of this approach are that the process is much speedier and less costly than is a formal trial or small claims court proceeding. If either party is not satisfied with

[30]Karen J. Elliott, "Consumer Advocates Push Print Media to Screen Advertising," *Wall Street Journal,* June 27, 1974, p. 1.
[31]Elliott, p. 1

the arbitration board's decision, the dissenting party can appeal it to a local court. However, most courts will usually support the arbitrator's decision. This approach by the BBB has done much to bring the consumer's voice to the ears of business, and in the process, the BBB has regained much respect from both business and consumer as being a fair consumer advocate.

Problems of Self-regulation.   Self-regulation by business in consumer affairs can create problems. One is the possible restraint of trade. If consumers trust the seal of membership in a trade group, can businesses use that to limit the number of companies that can receive certification? The FTC has reviewed trade associations to ensure that this will not happen; yet the potential certainly exists. The Supreme Court has ruled that a trade association can be held liable for the misdeeds of its standards-setting committee. In one case, the vice-president of a company used his influence in the American Society of Mechanical Engineers to declare a competitor's product unsafe, eventually leading to the competitors being forced out of business. The estate of the competition's now deceased owner was awarded $3.3 million by the court.[32]

A second problem with self-regulation is plaguing some of the federal regulatory bodies. If the group is composed of business people governing themselves, may the agency be more receptive to the business point of view than to that of the consumer? This argument has also been voiced in federal agencies, that over time the regulatory bodies become extensions of those industries they regulate and thus may often work *against* the consumer and competition and *for* the industry.

A final complaint is that the self-regulating associations have little sanction-power. If a member or nonmember violates the code that the association has adopted, what can the association do? Little recourse is available. On balance, however, the advantages of such self-regulatory attempts seem to outweigh the potential problems. Over the long run, as most professions have discovered, self-regulation may be the most effective approach to ethics and social responsibility.

The Safety Issue

Another consumerism challenge identified earlier is safety. Product information alone cannot solve this problem, and business is finding that it must incorporate more safety features into the products themselves if it is to meet the social responsibility of providing a safe product. The response to the safety issue can best be discussed in terms of auto safety, which has received the most publicity, and general product safety.

---

[32]"Who Is to Guard the Guards?" *Sales and Marketing Management*, July 5, 1982, p. 20.

Auto Safety. In the past several years autos have had more safety features added than at any time in the history of the industry. Yet, before any safety feature is installed on a car, it has generally been subjected to years of sophisticated research and testing. The auto manufacturers have come a long way from the days when they merely crashed cars into walls to test safety equipment. An example of today's approach is the use of a simulated human model in safety testing. The model's lifelike bones fracture under the same pressure as those of a human being. In addition, equipment has been developed that can tape, film, and play back simulated crashes, relating everything in thousandths of seconds or inches. Using these sophisticated data, automotive engineers can determine, for example, the ideal shoulderbelt anchor location or the effectiveness of a new energy-absorbing dashboard.

As a result of extensive safety research, new lifesaving items continue to appear each year. Some of these safety features are designed to help avoid accidents, others to reduce injuries. Ford, for example, uses a sophisticated computer system called CYBER 176 that permits engineers to try different designs without the cost and time of having to build prototypes. The computer simulates driving conditions and tests various design components in an attempt to make the vehicle safer and to improve gas mileage. Other automobile manufacturers have similar systems. Each auto manufacturer tries to make a safer, more efficient automobile, thereby helping avoid accidents, or at least reducing the severity of injuries in unavoidable accidents.

1. Auto Weight and Size. To many safety experts, auto safety is not just a matter of collapsible steering wheels and passive restraining systems; it is also the auto's weight and size. Because of gasoline prices and foreign competition, consumers have been turning to smaller, lighter autos. Statistics show that the occupants of these cars run a much higher risk of severe injury than do their counterparts in large, heavy autos. One study, conducted by the New York State Motor Vehicle Department, analyzed the results of 420,000 auto accident cases. The statistics revealed that over 9 percent of all foreign subcompact cars involved in crashes were associated with severe injury, in contrast with 3 percent for domestic full-size luxury cars. Figure 11.3 shows that there is a definite, positive relationship between serious injuries and the auto's weight.

In addition, when a large and a small vehicle collide, the fatality figures are always much higher for the small car. The New York State study put the ratio at 3 to 1. A Maine study found the ratio to be 5 to 1, and a federal government study concluded that 8 to 1 may be the most accurate figure.

2. Safety Restraints. For over 15 years there has been much controversy and confusion surrounding passive safety restraints in autos. President Reagan would prefer to do nothing, but his Secretary of Transportation, Elizabeth Dole, struck a compromise with consumer safety groups and the auto companies. Starting in September 1986, 10 percent of all new cars must have either air bags (at a cost of about $800 per car) or automatic seat belts in the front seat. The percentage will rise to 25 in 1987, 40 in

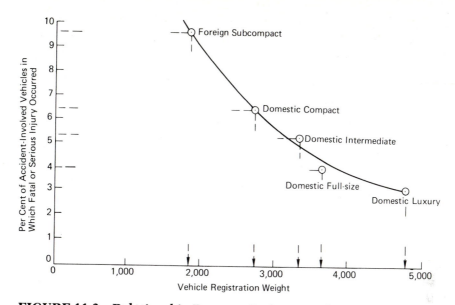

FIGURE 11.3   Relationship Between Serious Accidents and Vehicle Weight.
Reprinted by permission of the Chrysler Corporation and the Insurance Institute for Highway Safety.

1988, and 100 in 1989. If the states passed mandatory seat belt laws, this federal program would be canceled.[33]

General Product Safety.   In addition to the automakers, other manufacturers are also responding to the safety issue. Most firms are now giving more attention to quality control, and product safety committees are becoming popular. Firms are attempting to overcome the common problems in the following ways.

1. Product Use.   One safety lesson that firms have learned is that they can take little for granted in terms of how their product will be used. Companies have found it necessary to point out carefully how their product can be used safely. An example is the Hoover Company, which now informs the operator not to use its vacuum to suck up puddles of water. In the past the company merely assumed that no one would do such a thing. A similar safety problem is the dangerous shortcuts that many product users take. After the consumer has correctly used the product for a while, he or she may develop a faster but more dangerous method of doing the job. The Toro Manufacturing Company is one firm that tries to discourage dangerous habits through instructions in its owner's manual.

2. Product Safety Engineers.   A popular approach that business has taken

[33]"Air Bags: A Modest Proposal," *Newsweek*, July 24, 1984.

is to put an engineer in charge of safety who reports directly to the president. With a direct line to the president, the engineer does not have to sell the safety ideas first to manufacturing and marketing. Those who use this approach are convinced that it leads to better safety and that it pays for itself through lower liability insurance costs.

3. Managing Product Recalls.   Another area of product safety is product recall. One reason for the interest is the civil fine that can be leveled against manufacturers who knowingly market a product that fails to comply with the quality standards put forth by the Consumer Product Safety Act. These fines range from $500,000 up to a year in prison for a related series of violations and a $50,000 fine for marketing a "noncomplying" consumer product. It is much more cost effective to establish and maintain a good quality-control system ensuring safe products than it is to pay such penalties.

One approach being taken by manufacturers to handle more effectively product recalls is to place a coded identification number on each product (or batch of products) and then keep track of the units as they move through the distribution channel. Another method is to ask the owner of the product to fill out a prepaid warranty card so that the firm has the name and address of the user. In these latter cases, it is a lot easier to recall defective products. It should be remembered that not all units recalled are defective. In fact, a company may recall thousands of items just to find a few defects or potential defects. For example, the Zenith Corporation had to find the owners of 23,000 television sets and check every one in order to find a defect present in 2 percent of them. In other cases, perfectly safe but mislabeled products have had to be recalled. For example, Goodyear Tire and Rubber accidentally inverted a numeral on one of its models so that instead of saying the tire could bear a load of 1,680 pounds, it read 1,980 pounds. These tires had to be recalled.

To deal with general product recall problems, many companies are looking to the automobile industry for answers because they have had a great deal of experience in this area. One thing they are learning is that when a defect is discovered, company dealers should be notified before consumers get the word. Otherwise purchasers will be returning defective merchandise to a confused and probably angry retailer. Another guideline is to spell out, in all news releases or letters, the exact nature of the defect and the severity of the problem. Unclear explanations encourage rumors that can damage the company's reputation. A third important lesson for effective recalls is that there should be replacement parts or substitute units immediately available.

The recall procedure can be extremely costly and time consuming. Some of the largest recalls undertaken were GM's notification of 6.5 million owners to bring in their cars for inspection of the motor mounts and Firestone's recall of one of its most popular tires. In the GM recall, each notice had to be sent by certified mail, resulting in an expense of about $3.5 million for postage alone. Nevertheless, these costs cannot be avoided, and a company must take corrective action. The Consumer Product Safety Act requires all manufacturers to notify the Consumer Product Safety Commission within 24 hours of discovering that something they manufactured and sold constitutes a substantial product safety hazard.

4. Avoiding Product Recalls.   The best way to avoid recalls, of course, is to turn out a product with no defects. In the past, too much emphasis was placed on quantity of production and not enough on quality. Today, the companies that are concerned with product safety are separating production and quality control.

The evidence indicates that business is both aware of and generally responding to consumers' demands for better and safer products, though a great deal remains to be done. For example, auto safety continues to be a problem, and there is considerable controversy over the best way to meet this challenge. Yet despite the problems and controversies, there seems to have been some progress.

HOW ABOUT YOUR OWN LIABILITIES?

Negligence and strict liability are two issues of concern to modern businesses, and recent court rulings have also made these issues of concern to the average person. For example, if a houseguest slipped and was injured while attending a party, it was common for the host or hostess to plead "contributory negligence" on the part of the guest so as to protect himself or herself from costly lawsuit. Now, however, this old standby has been greatly watered down in many states, and now contributory negligence holds that the host is at least partially responsible for any accidents. Today, in many states, for example, if someone has too much to drink at a party and trips into the swimming pool, injuring himself or herself in the process, he or she can claim that the hosts had a duty to stop serving him or her liquor and that the failure to do so contributed to the accident.

Many homeowners argue that they cannot be sued if they use reasonable care to protect their guests from danger. However, this is easier said than done. For example, at a backyard party for more than 200 guests, the host's son was tossing around a football. The ball accidentally flew into an open charcoal grill, flipping a hot chip onto a man who was sipping beer. He jumped up, tripped into the grill, and was badly injured. The host was sued for $50,000. When the host agreed that he was negligent in letting his son play football too close to the grill, his lawyers settled out of court for $10,000.

Of course, if the host is unable to anticipate problems beforehand, such as a bee flying into the backyard and stinging someone or a snake crawling into the yard and biting a guest, there is little likelihood of a successful suit. And if the law has no special swimming-pool requirements, such as a high

(continued)

fence, a host will not be responsible if a tipsy guest wanders into the pool and drowns. But in the case of children, this is not so. Children at pools get special attention. Generally, pool owners cannot defend themselves by proving that a youngster who was injured in the pool was a trespasser. The pool, in some states, is regarded as an "attractive nuisance" that lures children into peril, and it is the owner's duty to prevent it or to pay the price. In many states, if the child is under age 6, there is virtually no defense for the pool owner. If the child is 6 to 12 years of age, the owner's position is a little better, although still weak. If it is a teenager, the homeowner can argue contributory negligence with some hope of success.

Commenting on this area of person liability, *Business Week* reported:

"Jury awards have been climbing rapidly, partly because juries sympathize with an injured person," notes San Francisco lawyer Richard J. Stratton. In a negligence case, the suit is for "actual damages," with punitive damages normally applying only in cases of willful wrong. But as a partygiver who is open to lawsuit, you can take little comfort, since actual damages include medical expenses, loss of income, property damage, and "pain and suffering"—which is a wide-open item for a jury.

"If medical income and property damage are $1,000 each, 'pain and suffering' can easily amount to $3,000—or $30,000." . . . In a typical negligence case . . . "the recovery range is $5,000 to $50,000—but it can go a lot higher."

Houston's Joseph Jamail tells of a recent client, an oil pipeline executive, who slipped on a small tapestry rug at a private party hosted by a business associate. "He has a screw holding a hip together and has had surgery twice," says Jamail, noting that the money settlement was "in six figures." It was split between the partygiver's own insurance company and his employer's insurer, because the injured executive was being entertained for business purposes.

Many homeowners are asking how they can deal with the problem of personal liability. Some experts advise maximum care, from limiting the amount of liquor you serve to a guest at a party to hiring a lifeguard for your pool if you are going to have a large gathering. Other experts believe that accidents are sometimes not preventable. As a result, they recommend purchasing personal liability insurance of $1 million and higher.

Source: Adapted from "Backyard Liabilities," *Business Week*, July 10, 1978, pp. 102–104.

FUTURE DIRECTIONS FOR THE CONSUMERISM ISSUE

One of the questions that must be asked in determining the future direction of business's responsibility to consumers is whether it is currently doing all that is reasonably possible. Although it is obviously impossible to generalize about all businesses, the answer is that more can and probably must be done. But another question that needs to be asked is whether the present law is balanced or unbalanced with respect to consumer liability. Many argue that court cases award far too much to the aggrieved consumer. There is growing public support for changes in the law to protect business from unreasonably high liability claims. Several proposals have been offered, such as a statute of limitations on product claims (e.g., five years after the manufacture of the product). For instance, an individual harmed by a product five years after its manufacture date could not raise any charges against the company. Other proposals limit the amount of liability that can be assessed. One law limits the liability of utilities in the event of a nuclear accident at electric generating stations.

It is difficult to balance the merits of the arguments on both sides of the issue. However, if high awards to injured consumers lead to more extensive product-safety engineering and safer outcomes, will the cost be worth it? At what point will manufacturers and insurance companies realize that the consumer's safety is an important part of product engineering? Would reducing the effectiveness of current laws discourage businesses from making safe products? Who should suffer the loss resulting from unsafe products, the unwary consumer or society? These are questions that must be considered when formulating policy and laws regarding consumer protection. The direction of future court decisions and laws will do much to change the scope of many business firms' future activities.

It now seems evident that Congress will replace state product-liability laws with a more comprehensive federal law.[34] Once wary of such a solution, business now favors it. Such a law would create federal standards stating who is responsible, and under what circumstances, when a consumer or worker is injured by a product. To create such a law raises many questions, ranging from the possible encroachment on states' rights to whether the burden of injuries will be shifted from the manufacturers or distributors of defective products to the victims of those defects. The drafting of any such law, however, leaves the consumer open to abuse by industry unless care is taken to avoid it.

SUMMARY

In this chapter we examined major consumer challenges: Advertising claims cover a broad range of topics, from bait and switch and incomplete advertising to high-pressure sales techniques and packaging practices. All of these fall under the heading of deceptive practices. How can the consumer cope with such problems? One way is by reporting the allegedly guilty company to

---

[34]"A Liability Patchwork Congress May Replace," *Business Week*, May 31, 1982, p. 34.

the Federal Trade Commission (FTC), an agency created to protect the consumer from, among other things, false advertising. Another consumer aid is the Truth in Packaging Act, which provides for the uniformity and simplification of labeling through both mandatory and discretionary provisions.

Another consumer problem is the pricing policies of business firms. Many of the consumers' complaints are related to discount practices, secret and discriminatory rebate practices, policies that keep prices at an artificially higher rate than would be the case if free competition reigned, and hidden costs and complex charges designed to fool or mislead the consumer. Many companies are taking steps to regulate their actions in these areas, and there are also laws designed to assist the consumer. One is the Sherman Act, which makes price fixing illegal. Another is the Clayton Act, which is designed to make price discrimination illegal unless there is evidence that the discount is justified by price savings realized by the seller. A third is the Robinson-Patman Act, which defines price discrimination more thoroughly than does the Clayton Act. A fourth is the Truth in Lending Act, which provides borrowers with full disclosure of the terms of their consumer loans. This has been particularly helpful to those with revolving charge accounts.

We also considered product safety. One of the major concerns is general product safety. Today if a consumer can prove that the purchased product is either inherently dangerous or defective, it is possible to sue the manufacturer successfully. In addition, there are warranties, both expressed and implied, that the consumer can use in bringing suit against a manufacturer. More and more attention is being directed toward service organizations such as auto and television repair firms and credit agencies that deliberately write erroneous reports on clients. Legislation that has been enacted to protect the consumer includes the Right to Privacy Act and the Fair Credit Reporting Act.

The federal government is continuing to enact legislation to protect the consumer, and there are a growing number of consumer protection groups. Additionally, state and local governmental agencies are now serving as consumer watchdogs in bringing suits against deceptive and fraudulent business organizations.

In the latter part of the chapter we examined business's response to consumerism. One area of consideration was providing information to consumers, through: (1) informational advertising, (2) information regarding service and/or price, and (3) understandable warranty and service guarantees. Examples of business informational advertising practices were those used by Sears, General Foods, Hunt-Wesson Foods, and the St. Paul Property and Liability Insurance Company. Examples of unit pricing were those used by Giant Foods and Jewel Foods. Also cited were examples of effective complaint handling by such firms as Western Union, Coca-Cola, Corning Glass, and Whirlpool. It was pointed out that many businesses have formed or joined trade associations to regulate both themselves and their members.

The last part of the chapter dealt with the safety issue, noting that auto safety has increased dramatically in recent years as car manufacturers have produced safer cars. In the area of general product safety, product engineers are more important than ever before and business firms are developing techniques for managing product recalls and, at the same time, working to avoid their occurrence.

DISCUSSION AND STUDY QUESTIONS

1. One of the problems that concerns consumers is the bait and switch tactic. How does it work?
2. What is the Federal Trade Commission? What are its functions?
3. What is the Truth in Packaging Act?
4. Problems related to consumer protection and pricing policies include discount practices, secret and discriminatory rebate practices, policies that keep prices at an artificially higher rate, hidden costs, and complex charges. What is meant by each of these?
5. What is the Truth in Lending Act?
6. How does an implied warranty differ from an expressed warranty?
7. Is privity of contract still a defense used by manufacturers of goods, or has it been set aside by the courts?
8. How does the Fair Credit Reporting Act help the consumer? Cite some of the act's provisions.
9. Have federal laws been effective in protecting the consumer?
10. How does negligence differ from strict liability?
11. What is informational advertising? How does it help the consumer?
12. What is Sear's approach to informational advertising? How about General Foods? Hunt and Wesson Foods? St. Paul Property and Liability Insurance?
13. One result of the consumerism movement was the start of a new system of providing price information to consumers. How does this system benefit the consumer?
14. How does Giant Foods use unit pricing in its product marketing? What about Jewel Food stores?
15. How does the Whirlpool Corporation convey service information to its consumers?
16. Consumers complain that no one listens to their complaints. What is business doing about this?
17. In what way are trade associations attempting to regulate their members? Explain, and include the role of the Better Business Bureau.
18. In dealing with product safety, what are some general guidelines that can help business firms? Cite at least five.
19. What appears to be the future direction of consumerism?

CASES AND INCIDENTS

A Bone to Choke On

Harvey Wilson worked for a well-known brokerage house in a large eastern city. Harvey's best friend was Dan Smith, who owned a small restaurant located a few blocks away. Every day at noon Harvey walked over to the restaurant, ate lunch, and chatted with Dan. Because business was so hectic at the brokerage, Harvey did not like to eat a very big lunch and usually had only a sandwich and glass of milk. Later, as he talked with Dan, he would sip a cup of coffee. At 12:50 P.M. sharp he would pay his bill and head back to the office. Harvey enjoyed his noon routine, especially because the food was good and the conversation enjoyable.

Harvey especially liked the chicken sandwich special on Wednesdays, and on Wednesday, January 21, he ordered the special. The sandwich consisted of several slices of chicken and a few pieces of lettuce served between two slices of bread. As Harvey and Dan sat talking, Harvey bit into the sandwich and swallowed the first bite. An instant later his face flushed a deep red, and he began coughing and gasping for breath. It was several minutes before Harvey could breath normally. Even then he still felt as if something was caught in his throat. Not wishing to aggravate the situation, he requested that Dan call his office and tell them he would not be in for the rest of the afternoon. Dan was happy to comply. He also called Harvey's physician and, after explaining the symptoms to the nurse, was able to get him an appointment that afternoon.

After a brief examination, the doctor confirmed Harvey's fear. A thin, elongated chicken bone was lodged in the lower portion of his throat. Preliminary signs indicated that there had been a laceration and that an infection was beginning to develop. The doctor recommended immediate surgery, and Harvey agreed. He entered the hospital that evening, and the next morning the operation was performed. Although the bone was not very big, nor had it been lodged in his throat very long, the operation proved to be very difficult. Complications ensued, and finally a tracheotomy had to be performed. Nonetheless, the operation was completed successfully. The doctor afterward explained that Harvey had been quite lucky and that it would be two weeks before he could go home and an additional week before he could return to work.

Harvey bore Dan no grudge. In fact, the first day back he dropped into the restaurant and ordered a chicken sandwich. "It's like almost drowning," chuckled Harvey. "If you don't go back into the water immediately, you never will." However, his initially positive attitude soon disappeared. Harvey received a bill from the hospital for $2,900 and learned to his dismay that his insurance covered only $2,000 of the cost. Harvey then called Dan and learned that although his friend was distressed over the matter, business had not been good and he carried no insurance to cover such an accident.

Harvey became angry, and in desperation he called his attorney. The lawyer recommended that a suit be brought against Dan. Harvey concluded that he had no choice and agreed to sue.

In court, Harvey's lawyer argued that the implied warranty of reasonable fitness of food for human consumption had been breached. The lawyer reasoned that when Harvey was served a chicken sandwich, he assumed that the sandwich was fit to be eaten. When a restaurant serves food, the diner should not have to sift through each morsel, searching for foreign substances. It is logical to assume that the cook or chef has already taken this precaution. Because this was not true in the case under consideration, Dan's restaurant had breached its implied warranty and was responsible for all damages to the customer.

Dan's lawyer replied that there had been no breach of implied warranty because the error rested with Harvey and not the restaurant. The lawyer pointed out that chicken is known to have many bones. The same holds true for fish, steak, and many other foods. Because of this common knowledge, it is the duty of the diner to exercise due care. Harvey was surely aware that chicken often had bones, but instead of eating slowly he gulped the sandwich. To support his argument further, Dan's lawyer cited similar court precedents. In all these cases the court had ruled in favor of the defendant. "The law," Dan's lawyer stated, "is clear on this point. If a harmful substance present in the food is natural to it, no breach of implied warranty of reasonable fitness for food exists. Therefore, we request judgment for the defense."

After some deliberation, judgment was rendered in favor of the plaintiff. The court reasoned that although a chicken sandwich may have bones in it, this does not free the restaurant owner from the implied warranty that the food is fit for human consumption.

ANALYSIS

1. Do you agree with the judgment in this case, or do you think the restaurant was treated unfairly? Explain.
2. What implications does such a judgment have for consumers in general?
3. Do you see a trend toward increased consumer protection? Give your reasons.

Buckle Up or Pay Up

In Australia the wearing of seat belts is mandatory. The same is true in Puerto Rico, and in the United States many have recommended similar legislation. On the positive side, it is believed that by "buckling up," between 10,000 and 20,000 lives a year could be saved. One official of the National Highway Traffic Safety Administration concluded that mandatory buckling up would cut highway deaths and injuries "more dramatically than any other measure yet implemented." Some states have laws requiring the use of seat belts. Others are also thinking of making shoulder straps mandatory.

Yet the going is slow. One reason is undoubtedly the belief that the law would infringe on the rights of individual citizens. One critic argued that if this trend were carried to the extreme, it could result in all sorts of new laws. For example, wearing seat belts might be helpful but so, too, might weight control. Therefore, why not pass a law requiring how much people can weigh? Another useful law might be one designed to make everyone, except those with a doctor's excuse, take physical exercise. Of course, the latter illustrations are made somewhat in jest, but they do illustrate the type of argument being raised against mandatory seat belts.

Nevertheless, proponents of the legislation are unswayed. They point to the great success that Australia and New Zealand are having in saving lives because of their new seat belt laws. In Australia, for example, highway deaths have declined by 24 percent. At the same time, spinal-injury and eye-injury cases have also dropped dramatically. In light of these statistics, some Americans are proposing mandatory buckling up, with fines of up to $25 per offense. If such a law does pass, auto occupants will have the option of either buckling up or paying up.

ANALYSIS

1. How effective do you think a mandatory seat belt law would be in reducing auto fatalities and injuries?
2. Do you think such legislation will ever become mandatory in all 50 states? Explain.
3. How effective would a $25 fine be in encouraging compliance with the law? What other steps or actions could be taken to ensure compliance?

Accident Information

Shell Oil puts out free booklets to help auto owners and drivers cope with common problems. The booklets describe such problems as foul-weather driving, emergency repairs, and unexpected dangers on the road. The following is an excerpt from the booklet entitled "Accidents."

Q. What's the most important thing to remember when a serious accident occurs?

A. There are three things to remember:
1. Don't panic. You need your wits about you.
2. Think. Do what needs to be done *in logical order*. When giving first aid, don't do more than you're qualified to do.
3. Don't try to be a hero. Call or send for help as soon as possible.

Q. What if I see an accident but don't stop or render aid?

A. We all have a moral obligation to stop and help if we can. But if you're involved in the accident, you *must* stop. All states impose severe penalties on those drivers who don't.

Q. "Involved in an accident" means actual physical contact involving my car. Right?

A. Wrong! You can be involved in an accident even if your car never comes into contact with anything. According to Ed Kearney, Executive Director of the National Committee on Uniform Traffic Laws and Ordinances, if you *contribute in any way* to a crash by another driver, you are involved in the accident.

For example, if two cars collide because one was trying to avoid your double-parked car, you are a part of that accident.

You are also involved in the accident if you pass a car and force it off the road into another object.

In both examples, you are required to stop just as if you had actually run into someone.

Q. I'm the first to arrive at a bad accident. What should I do?

A. The paramedics of the Los Angeles County Fire Department suggested five things to do before help arrives.

1. Avoid a second collision. *Don't park behind* the wreck, or on the *opposite side* of the road. Pull up several yards *beyond* the accident. Turn on your flashers.

2. If it's safe, reduce the chance of fire by turning off the ignitions in the wrecked cars.

3. Assist the injured. Ask them where they hurt. Check to see if anyone is not breathing and look for those with severe bleeding.

   But don't move the victims unless absolutely necessary! Many traffic accidents inflict neck or spine injuries, and moving the victims could be fatal. An exception to this rule is if the car is burning or there is some other immediate danger involved.

   Note: If "smoke" is rising from the wreck, look closely. It may be steam from the radiator, and not smoke from a fire.

4. Get help. Radio or phone for the police, an ambulance, or the fire department. If you're busy giving first aid, ask others who stop to warn approaching traffic. Always use flares or reflectors if at all possible.

5. Search the area for victims who might have been thrown from the cars involved.

Q. I've just had an accident myself. What do I do?

A. Mr. Kearney told me: "Remember, you are legally bound to *stop*. You should also *identify yourself*, and *aid the injured*."

Stop as near to the scene as possible. Move the cars out of the flow of traffic if you can. But note their location for the accident report.

Give your name, address, and the license number of your car to the other driver. Never leave the scene without identifying yourself.

Under many circumstances, you'll have to notify your insurance company, the police, and probably file an accident report. (It's a good idea to keep a blank form with you, so you'll have it if you need it. Your insurance agent can get one for you.) Be sure to find out exactly what the requirements are in *your* state.

Q. Can I direct traffic around an accident?

A. Yes, according to Sergeant Chuck Brady of the California State Highway Patrol, but only until the police arrive. Then the job of traffic control is theirs, not yours.

Tip: If you have to direct traffic, be sure to position yourself so you can get of of the way of an uncooperative driver. Keep your mind on what you're doing.

ANALYSIS

1. Can booklets such as these really be of value to motorists?
2. Why is Shell giving away these free booklets?
3. Could other firms profit by following a similar example?

McDentist*

Over the past five years there have been some dramatic changes in the way that goods and services are delivered to consumers. One of the most significant has been the rise in dentists' offices in shopping centers. Just like any other retail outlet, dentists rent space in a shopping mall, but offer the same type of care that they used to provide in their private offices. What has caused this change in the delivery system? One is convenience. It is easier for many people to go to a shopping mall than it is to drive to an office building or residential area, where parking may be a problem. A second reason is quality of care. In some of these dentist offices there are five or six dentists who team up to handle all the case loads. This means that a person who needs root canal work may see Dr. Jones, while Dr. Smith does the fillings and Dr. Anderson does most of the periodontal work. Even when the doctors are not this specialized, it is not uncommon to find one doctor filling the first tooth and a second doctor taking over on the next visit and filling the second tooth. A third reason is price. By advertising their location and getting a large number of people to visit their office, dentists are finding that their fixed costs can be spread over many patients and their charges are lower than they were when operating out of a private office. A fourth reason is that the dentists have more flexibility in terms of scheduling their hours. When they had their own office, they had to be

---

*Some of the material in this case can be found in "Moving the Dentist's Chair to Retail Stores," *Business Week*, January 19, 1981, pp. 56–58.

there from, for example, 9 to 5. However, when there are a group of dentists, it is easier to schedule time off. In fact, some dentists have retired from their first practice in order to go to work in a retail store location because they find the work easier, the money just as good, and the risk associated with running their own business nonexistent.

Is the quality really that good? Many patients feel that it is. "For too long," some of them contend, "there was the belief that good dentistry could be done by only a small number of dentists. With modern training and technology we're finding that most dentists are excellent. So it comes down to a matter of price and convenience."

Because they are located in so many different locations, just like fast-food franchises, these dental outlets are now being referred to as "McDentist," an obvious reference to McDonald's, the fast-food chain.

ANALYSIS

1. In what way does this new development represent an attempt by the dental industry to address the needs of the consumer?
2. Most dentists work for an association that owns the office and pays them a salary. If a patient decides that the dental care was defective and decides to bring a lawsuit, whom would the individual sue: the dentist or the association? Give your reasoning.
3. Some medical offices are also beginning to offer fast, efficient, low-price medical care. Known as "Doc in the Box," like the dentists' offices described in this case, they are beginning to spring up all around the country. What particular consumerism problems might these doctors face? Would they be of the same type as faced currently by doctors? Explain.

chapter 12

Ecological Issues: Challenge and Response

Chapter Objectives

- To present the major ecological challenges facing business in the areas of population and food, energy, natural resource use, and pollution.
- To outline the major federal and local regulations for environmental protection.
- To describe and analyze the business response to ecological issues, including birth control; food production; natural resource use; energy demands; air, water, and solid-waste pollution; disposal of hazardous chemicals and radioactive materials; and noise pollution.
- To discuss the burdens and methods of paying for pollution control.

Although the ecology problem means different things to different people, there is one common fear—the problems with the environment may threaten the continued existence of modern society in its present form. In one way or another, the environment is changing, and some plan of action is required.

THE ECOLOGICAL CHALLENGES FACING BUSINESS

The ecological challenges confronting business fall into four major categories: population and food, energy, natural resource use, and pollution. We examine each category, beginning with a discussion of ecosystems.

Ecosystems

The term *ecology* is freely used but seldom precisely defined. Webster's dictionary defines it as "a branch of science concerned with the interrelationship of organisms and their environments especially as manifested by natural cycles and rhythms, community development and structure, interaction between different kinds of organisms, geographic distributions, and population alterations."[1] The key to understanding ecology lies in the word *interrelationship*. Organisms must be able to adapt to the environment if they are to survive. If they do not adapt, they will go the way of the dinosaur. Because there are natural cycles or rhythms, changes are always taking place, and new interrelationships are formed between organisms and their environments. Some organisms die; others are created.

Ecology takes a general systems viewpoint and can be presented as an *ecosystem*, "an ecological community considered together with the nonliving factors of its environment as a unit."[2] Because the living and nonliving elements interact with one another, a change in one subsystem will very likely lead to changes in the others. Ecosystem analysis is analogous to the physics law that states that for each action there is an equal and opposite reaction. One problem that puts the ecological situation on an intimately personal basis is overpopulation; in fact, many ecologists consider population growth as the primary problem facing the world today.

The Population Issue

Is overpopulation really a serious problem? A brief look at the available statistics leaves little doubt that it is. In 6000 B.C. the population of the earth was around 5 million people. Empirical evidence reveals that a million years earlier it had been 2.5 million; thus, it took a million years for the population to double. Between 6000 B.C. and A.D. 1650 it doubled every 1,000 years. By A.D. 1650 there were approximately a half billion people on earth. By A.D. 1850 the total stood at 1 billion—the population had doubled in 200 years. The next doubling took only 80 years, and at present it is doubling approximately every 35 years.

Those who have studied economic history know that Thomas Malthus

[1]Webster's *Third New Intercollegiate Dictionary*, Vol. 1 (Chicago: Encyclopaedia Britannica, 1966), p. 720.
[2]Webster's, p. 720.

realized the danger of overpopulation many years ago. Malthus's theory has often been considered to be interesting theoretically but factually incorrect. He contended that the population would always increase at a rate faster than that of its ability to feed itself.

The Malthusian thesis was that food increased at an arithmetic rate but that the population increased at a geometric rate. Only famine, war, and ill health could be counted on to hold the population in check. Since Malthus's time, tremendous strides made in medicine have reduced the mortality rate. And unless there is a nuclear holocaust, war will not be a serious deterrent to population growth. In fact, even though the United States lost approximately 600,000 troops in combat in all its wars, it would take the world population growth only a few days to compensate for this loss. Furthermore, a growing population places tremendous strain on the world's existing resources. It has been estimated that by the year 2000, for the United States to accommodate another 100 million people, it would be necessary to construct a city the size of Tulsa, Dayton, or Jersey City every 30 days for 30 years.

Was Malthus right? A study sponsored by the Club of Rome (an international group of scientists, businesspersons, and educators) and conducted by researchers from the Massachusetts Institute of Technology (MIT) stated that if population and industry continued to grow for much more than 100 years, even if there were important advances in birth control, food production, pollution control, and natural resource production, a catastrophe of major proportions would surely strike. The only way to avert this impending disaster would be to stabilize the population and limit capital investment to replacing worn-out plants and equipment.

The MIT forecast was based on a computer analysis of five world trends: population growth, food production, industrial output, resource consumption, and pollution. Each of these factors is growing exponentially, according to the study, and each interacts with the others. By feeding all of these interacting trends into the computer, various combinations were obtained. For example, in one case the researchers assumed that by A.D. 2100 recycling technology would reduce by 25 percent the raw materials needed to obtain a unit of output. They also assumed that birth control would eliminate unwanted children, and current environmental pollution would be cut by 75 percent of its present level. What would the overall results be under these conditions? Resources would be adequate, but industrial growth would be so great that the higher output would offset the 75 percent decline in pollution. Furthermore, even if growth were slowed, the population would be large enough to trigger a food crisis.

Of course, any computer forecast is only as good as its underlying assumptions, and many have challenged those made by the MIT researchers. One argument is that to assume an exponential growth of the world's problems without an accompanying growth in its problem-solving capability is erroneous. Another criticism challenges the link between pollution and health, because little is currently known about this area. A third argument is that the MIT computer model has a built-in "collapse factor" and that no matter what happened by A.D. 2100, the human race would be in desperate trouble.

Such criticisms indicate that the MIT conclusions may be overly pessimistic. But on the other hand, no one would argue that the basic problems of population, pollution, and food production are not real.

Meeting the World's Demand for Food

The future massive increase in the population will necessarily put pressure on the production of food. Although the reliance on science and agricultural technology to increase yields has been sufficient up to now, the time is fast approaching when there just will not be enough land to meet our needs. Following World War II, crop yields began to increase in almost every industrialized country, and fertilizer-responsive varieties of wheat and rice also increased output in the Third World countries. But since 1970 the rate of increase in cereal yield per hectare has fallen from 2.2 percent annually to 1.6 percent. Possible explanations for the decrease are a lower quality of new cropland, reduction in fallow area in dryland-farming regions, soil erosion, and diverting water to uses other than food production. In a recent 10-year period, nearly a million acres of U.S. cropland each year were converted to nonfarm uses.[3] The productivity of farmlands can increase only so much, and even now some are suffering the effects of overuse and overfertilization.

Technology that enables the U.S. farmer to produce the high yields that have historically been a part of American agriculture is not available to the less developed countries (LDCs). The seed may be available, but the cost of fertilizer and equipment needed to produce the crop is financially outside the reach of many of the Third World nations. Climatically, too, the United States has been fortunate. In some parts of the world, the climate has been changing, leading to destructive changes in the region's agriculture. An example is the long drought periods in central Africa. The poor harvests have been partly the result of changing climate and partly the result of poor farming methods. The consequence was a severe famine that left thousands dead of starvation. At the present time, the desert is encroaching upon the farmland at the rate of 25 to 30 percent per year. Even though this area has land as rich as that in the San Joaquin Valley of California, there is little capital to provide the necessary water resources and programs to educate the farmers in proper farming techniques that would reduce the amount of acreage lost to soil erosion and the desert. This situation is repeated in many of the other Third World nations. Giving surplus food to these countries is doing little to improve the long-run situation. Too little

---

[3]Lester R. Brown, "World Population, Soil Erosion, and Food Security," *Science*, November 27, 1981, pp. 995–1002.

is being done to change the farmers' practices. World development programs, such as the United Nations' economic development program, are not extensive enough to make the necessary changes in many of the Third World nations.

Changing diets are also affecting the food supplies. For example, as a country becomes more prosperous, like some of the oil-rich Third World nations, there is a marked shift from cereal to meat consumption. This shift puts an additional strain on both land and grain supplies, as an animal requires much more grain per pound to produce an equal amount of meat. Animal-grazing land also competes with cropland, forcing more cropland out of production. Although animal production yields have increased over the years through breeding and chemical injections, there is some indication that some of the chemicals used may be harmful to humans, and a drive has been started to limit the amount and types of drugs that can be used to increase the weight gain of animals raised for human consumption. Further restrictions have been placed on the use of pesticides and plant-yield fertilizers.

The problems encountered by the use of pesticides merits additional attention. Although pesticides have done much to increase crop yields, by eradicating pests that can ruin crops, the damage done by the by-products of some pesticides sometimes has been more costly than the damage that would have been done by the insects if no pesticide had been applied. The next section will look at pesticides in more depth.

The Use of Pesticides.   The use of pesticides was one of the first ecological problems to be identified. Conservationists had expressed concern about pesticides for years. For example, in 1962 Rachel Carson wrote about the dangers of pesticides in her classic book, *Silent Spring*.[4] This book is often given credit for instigating the entire environmental protection movement.

Since *Silent Spring* was first published, there has been a great deal of progress and a number of high-level government officials have made pesticides a personal cause. There has also been visible progress at the state level. Numerous bills have been introduced in state legislatures, requiring the regulation and control of pesticides. Kansas and Iowa now have laws requiring professional applicators of pesticides to be licensed. California has taken more positive action than any other state.

The current dilemma is to find an acceptable pesticide substitute. There seems little doubt that something is needed to control pests in order to increase food production. Some experts argue that a total ban on pesticides would result in starvation for hundreds of millions of people around the world. Estimates of the impact of a ban on pesticides in the United States predict a 30 percent decline in agriculture products and threatened starvation for 50 million. The solution to this dilemma may come through increased research and development. To date, too much effort has been directed toward

[4]Rachel Carson, *Silent Spring* (Boston: Houghton Mifflin, 1962), pp. 12–13.

developing effective killing chemicals, while research on effective, economical, and safe control methods has been neglected. In the future, there must be more research in order to walk the fine line between increased food production and environmental safety.

The Use of Natural Resources

The food shortage resulting from the population growth and the improved conditions of some segments of the world's population, allowing them to upgrade their diets from grain to meat, has been highly documented. Not so widely publicized but receiving increasing notice in recent years has been the use of other natural resources, especially energy fuels. Raw materials such as coal and various metals are necessary for the production of goods that millions of people consider essential to today's way of life.

The world's principal natural resources are rapidly becoming more scarce. The increased demands for most of these resources is far outstripping the new discoveries. Although in the past many of the raw materials were made synthetically, the future production of synthetic materials to meet declining raw material supplies is not automatically assured. In some manner the use of these rapidly depleting reserves must be curtailed.

The Energy Issue

Although the depletion of natural resources in general is an important issue, the energy situation, and oil in particular, is a dominant concern today. Since the oil embargo in the mid-1970s, national attention has been focused on energy supplies, though the issue of energy did not immediately ensue as the result of the embargo. Natural gas supplies had already been interrupted in the northern and eastern United States in both 1971 and 1972.[5] The shortages of the early 1970s, however, underscored the precarious situation in the United States.

Those concerned about energy consumption and those concerned about environmental protection have come to loggerheads several times in the past few years and will likely remain so.[6] Balancing the concern for the environment with the needs of conserving energy is one of the issues presently in the forefront of the national policy.[7]

[5]Council on Environmental Quality, *The Fifth Annual Report of the Council on Environmental Quality* (Washington, D.C.: U.S. Government Printing Office, 1975), p. 95.

[6]Robert C. Seamans, Jr., James L. Liverman, and Frederick I. Ordway, "National Energy Planning and Environmental Responsibility," *Environmental Affairs*, Vol. 6, No. 3, 1978, pp. 283–300.

[7]"The Oil Glut Isn't Going Away," *Business Week*, November 8, 1982, pp. 38–39.

Pollution Issues

In terms of environmental protection, society's concerns have mainly centered on curbing the amount of pollution that befouls the world. Concerns cover air, water, solid-waste, and noise pollution and hazardous-material disposal. Through years of neglect, the world has become burdened with large amounts of materials that have upset the earth's capacity to cleanse itself. Society is now demanding that government and business do something to restore this balance. Demands range from halting present pollution by business to demanding that business assume an active role in cleaning the environment of pollutants for which business was not necessarily responsible. In the United States, the federal government has even directed, through the EPA, that areas with high levels of pollution cannot assume any further economic growth until pollution reaches safer levels.[8]

Air Pollution.   A critical environment problem facing the modern world is air pollution. This takes two major forms: automobile exhaust and industrial "smokestack" pollution.

1. Automobile Exhaust.   One of the major causes of air pollution is the automobile. Initial attention to automobile-caused pollution came as a result of research on Los Angeles's smog done in 1953 by Haagen Smit. He theorized that when auto emissions of hydrocarbons and nitrogen oxides are exposed to sunlight under certain meteorological conditions, smog will result. From this time on, auto engineers were alerted to the hazards of air pollution. The three main auto emissions are carbon monoxide, hydrocarbons, and nitrogen oxides. Of the three, carbon monoxide is the most polluting, and nitrogen oxide is the least polluting. Fortunately, the actual auto pollution amounts per mile have been reduced in recent years.

2. Industrial "Smokestack Pollution.   Another major source of air pollution comes from the industrial smokestacks. All one needs to do is view the skyline over any city in America to see this smokestack pollution. The utilities are among the worst industrial air polluters. Manufacturing plants are a second source of industrial air pollution. Large copper refineries, for example, can put tons of solid copper, copper oxides, and fly ash into the air each year. Steel makers are also big polluters.

The situation has become so bad in some areas that local and federal governments have had to demand that firms clean up the mess. Although near-zero pollution is virtually impossible for most factories, environmental agencies are demanding that firms install the "best practicable technology." In addition, many firms are being put on a timetable to adapt the latest technology to their organizations with accompanying mandatory, interim stop-gap measures. Once it was felt that taller smokestacks would alleviate the problem as they would disperse the pollution over a wider area so it

[8]"A State Face-Off over Dirty Air," *Business Week,* April 17, 1978, p. 134.

would not be as concentrated in one area. However, taller smokestacks do not reduce pollution and they have been shown to produce acid rain, which kills aquatic life in even distant rivers and lakes. For example, power plants in Ohio can cause sulfate health problems as far away as New York City.

Water Pollution.   Water pollution is still a great concern in the United States today, though the types of water pollution are changing to some degree. Originally, the concern was about the visible pollution in the nation's water supplies and waterways. Much has been done to curb this visible pollution, and so now interest has been directed toward the less obvious but often more dangerous effects of water pollution on nature and human health. Studies indicate that often invisible chemical wastes, bacterial contamination, and other such water pollutants are far more dangerous than are the highly visible solid water pollutants. Cancer-causing substances, long-lived chemical wastes, and life-destroying industrial discharges have become of increasing concern. In particular, water pollutants, such as industrial discharge (heavy effluent, particulate matter), chemical discharge, bacterial contamination, phosphorus, and untreated urban sewage are receiving attention, as is acid rain. Such pollution comes from many sources, including inadequate sewage systems, industrial dumping, untreated industrial wastes, runoffs from farms and previously mined areas, pesticide residue, and soluble fertilizer runoff. Some of the ways that these pollutants have been handled are also controversial. Here are some of the ways.

   1. Underground Dumps.   In addition to dumping liquid wastes directly into bodies of water, firms often use underground dumps. The dump generally consists of a hole 5 or 6 inches in diameter, approximately 2000 to 3000 feet deep, ending in a layer of sandstone and limestone. These porous rock formations act as a petrified sponge to soak up the liquid wastes. The hole is encased in steel so that there is a minimum danger of seepage. Such an underground dump has a surprising capacity: if the sandstone is 100 feet thick and covers 20 square miles, which is a relatively small formation, sewage can be pumped in at the rate of 500 gallons a minute for 200 years before the saturation point will be reached.

   Although underground dumps appear effective at first glance, they, too, can be dangerous. If there is a leak, underground water and surface water will be polluted. Another problem is that the dumps often create underground pressure, causing abandoned oil and gas wells to leak.

   The use of underground dumps has been offered as an alternative to the disposal of hazardous wastes, though in some cases, this has led to tragic consequences. For example, Niagara Falls, New York, discovered that a school and a residential area had been built on top of a chemical dumping ground. After a particularly rainy season, the chemicals were drawn closer to the surface, creating dangerous fumes, a high risk of cancer, and a potential for serious illnesses in the area. Women living in the area experienced a higher than normal rate of miscarriages and incidence of birth defects. Obviously, such newsworthy happenings open the floodgates for questioning the social responsibility of business for environmental protection and even life and death.

2. Industrial-Waste Dumping.   Mining and manufacturing processes generate much waste material. Traditionally, this was dumped into rivers and lakes; there was no thought given to the side effects. It appeared that the waste material just settled to the bottom, but current research indicates that this is not necessarily true. The water can react to the waste material by dissolving some of its chemical elements.

In addition to rivers and lakes, the ocean has also received attention as a waste site. John Knauss, an oceanographer with the National Advisory Committee on the Ocean and the Atmosphere (NACOA), contends that seawater neutralizes acids and alkalis and that the movement of the ocean disperses waste materials.[9] Disposing of sewage sludge, industrial wastes, and mud dredged from harbor channels would be worse on land dump sites than on ocean sites.

There is no question that industrial wastes can be harmful, as more is learned about the harmful effects that industrial water pollution can have on aquatic and human life. Environmentalists believe that more attention must be given to recycling wastes (e.g., converting them into fertilizers after the contaminants have been removed.)[10]

3. Thermal Pollutants.   Another water problem is thermal, or warm-water, pollution. Most thermal pollution is caused by very hot water's being poured back by hydroelectric plants into bodies of water. To generate electricity, such plants bring in water from nearby lakes or rivers and heat it with coal, oil, or nuclear fuel. The resulting steam is used to turn the plant's turbine engines to generate electricity. The steam is then passed through a condenser in which it is cooled and turned back into water. Simultaneously, more fresh water is brought in to cool the generator. The water that is used as a coolant is then released into the lake or river, but at ten to twenty degrees above its original temperature. This warm water is the cause of the thermal pollution. Its principal effect is that it can change the basic ecosystem of the body of water to which it is returned. Many of the plant organisms and fish cannot adjust to the higher temperature and so change or die.

America's demand for electric power is growing larger every year. Toasters, refrigerators, stoves, and air conditioners for millions of people require tremendous amounts of power. To meet these demands, the utilities are expanding their power-producing facilities, but this often produces more air and water pollution. Some experts believe that the demand for electric power will thermally pollute all the nation's water. These forecasts are forcing utilities to devise new methods of creating electricity. Currently, it is not

[9]"Waste Sites in the Ocean," *Science Digest*, April 1982, p. 21.
[10]"Waste Sites in the Ocean," p. 21.

possible to have both less thermal pollution and more electric power, except at a very high cost.

Solid-Waste Disposal.   Solid-waste disposal an is often-ignored form of pollution; yet it exists everywhere. Basically, solid waste is garbage and other discarded solid materials. In recent years this form of pollution has increased. For example, in 1930, households generated about 2.2 pounds of solid waste per day. Forty years later this figure had grown to approximately 5.3 pounds a day. If the same rate of increase were maintained, by 1990 the total will stand at about 24 pounds per day, or an 1100 percent increase in 60 years. Furthermore, if one added in the commercial and other municipal solid waste, the annual total would rise to around 250 million tons. Then there is the approximately 140 million tons of industrial solid waste from productive processes. If all of this were combined, there would be enough garbage to cover over 4,700 square miles at a depth of 1 foot, an area about as large as the state of Connecticut.

Of this annual 450 million tons of solid waste, approximately 50 percent is not collected by any agency, public or private. Most of it is thrown out of car windows, dumped along country roads, flushed down toilets, or burned in fireplaces or private incinerators. The cost of handling the rest is surprisingly high. For example, excluding agricultural and mining wastes, about $8 billion is expended annually to store, collect, process, and dispose of the nation's solid-waste materials. This makes it the third most expensive service, preceded only by education and highway expenses.

Hazardous- and Toxic-Substance Pollution.   Hazardous materials are substances that can cause ill health and death in human beings and/or widespread destruction of animal and plant life in the environment. Of the various types of pollution, toxic substances merit special attention because of their potential threat to the environment. The main dangerous substances are from chemical and nuclear production, handling, storage, usage, and disposal. The danger comes from the hazards of handling these materials during their useful life and continues after their disposal. As pointed out earlier, in some instances, the materials are buried in containers, which when they rust and deteriorate, permit the substance to leak into the soil and contaminate not only the land but also the nearby ground and surface water supplies. Additionally, the many spills, fires, and transportation accidents involving hazardous materials is raising concern about their use and has stimulated federal legislation for the stricter control of these substances.

Noise Pollution.   Another ecological problem is excessive noise. The blaring of horns, the shouts of pedestrians, the staccato blasts of construction workers' pneumatic drills, and the roar of low-flying airplanes are daily occurrences in every big city in America. The cacophony seems to be getting worse. As

TABLE 12.1. Decibel Scale for Noise.

Decibel Rating	Noise Effect	Example
140 130	Physical damage	Jet takeoff
120 110	Painful	Siren
100 90	Deafening	Power mower
80 70	Very loud	Cocktail party
60 50	Loud	Average traffic
40 30	Moderate	Conversation
20 10 0	Faint	Rustling leaves

the sounds of "progress" increase in number and intensity, noise pollution will become a more common by-product.

Noise pollution can be measured in terms of decibels of measurable units of sound. Table 12.1 presents some of the effects of certain levels of noise. As noise becomes louder, a number of other things can happen. People performing tasks make errors in observation, misjudge time, and have difficulty remaining alert. These effects can occur from noise levels as low as 90 decibels. In sleep experiments, noise as low as 55 decibels (city traffic noise) disturbed the subjects' sleep. In addition, noise may contribute to physical problems. The most common ailment, of course, is hearing damage. Noise can impair or destroy the receptor organs in the inner ear. Other problems attributed to noise pollution include sore throats, sleeplessness, heart attacks, dizziness, irritability, and impotence. In addition to physical problems, there are mental problems. Noise definitely contributes to stress and anxiety, which can bring on emotional crises. For example, studies in London established a correlation between noise levels and admissions to psychiatric hospitals.

NOISE IN THE HOME

Ask people to list those things that cause a lot of noise, and you will get responses such as auto horns, low-flying aircraft, and noisy machinery. But there is one type of noise to which people have been subjected for years that often goes unmentioned, namely, noisy appliances.

Today the Environmental Protection Agency (EPA) is trying to crack down on the amount of noise given off by household appliances. One of the things the EPA wants to do is require manufacturers to label appliances as to the amount of noise they emit. Some critics charge that the cost of reducing appliance noise will be high, because the product will be bulkier and will add cost in the form of transportation, handling, shipping, and materials associated with reducing the noise. EPA supporters counter with the claim that the noise and bulk of household appliances could be reduced if the manufacturers properly designed the product.

One scheme currently under consideration would require the labeling of each product to indicate both its own noise-generating characteristics and the range of noise emitted by similar products on the market. However, rather than requiring a label that gives a product's exact decibel count, the EPA is leaning toward a type of color-coding or numbering system to make the comparison easier for the average consumer.

Will this new idea work? That is a difficult question to answer because of what is called "noise psychology." People have come to associate noise with certain appliances and machines. For example, if a typewriter begins to make a loud noise, there is probably something wrong with the machine, and the individual will have it checked out. If one's car begins to "knock" or there is some grinding sound whenever one turns the corner, the driver will take the car into the shop and have it checked out. There are unacceptable sounds and are interpreted as warnings. But the reverse is often true for household appliances. Noise is equated with power. If the machine is too quiet, the consumer may think the appliance lacks the power or strength to get the job done properly. In fact, in the early 1960s, a manufacturer introduced to the market a quiet vacuum cleaner that failed to sell because consumers thought it had no cleaning power. Conversely, another manufacturer brought out a vacuum cleaner that had a clicking noise. This concerned the company engineers but not the consumer. The vacuum's users believed the noise indicated that it was working. The noise in a home can approach the decibel level of a busy airport, but the question is whether people want to reduce this form of pollution or have become so accustomed to it that they will accept it and all of the physical problems, including hearing loss, that often occur after people are subjected to excess noise for extended periods of time.

Source: Adapted from "The EPA's Next Target: Noisy Appliances," *Business Week*, October 10, 1977, pp. 100–102.

The Environmental Protection Agency set forth proposals for regulating noise, and some cities have taken action on their own. For example, in New York City a driver can be fined up to $50 for honking his horn in other than an emergency situation. Other municipalities, including Baltimore,

Boston, Chicago, Honolulu, and Minneapolis, also have noise regulations. With such antinoise pollution action, America can, it is hoped, become a more tranquil place in which to live.

FEDERAL AND LOCAL ENVIRONMENTAL REGULATIONS

In order to correct the ecological problems discussed thus far, a number of national, state, and local laws have been enacted to reinforce the rights and duties spelled out by former President Lyndon Johnson's guidelines for environmental legislation as

1. The right to clean water, and the duty not to pollute it.
2. The right to clean air, and the duty not to befoul it.
3. The right to surroundings reasonably free from man-made ugliness, and the duty not to blight it.
4. The right of easy access to places of beauty and tranquility where every family can find recreation and refreshment, and the duty to preserve such places clean and unspoiled.
5. The right to enjoy plants and animals in their natural habitats, and the duty not to eliminate them from the face of this earth.

Federal Regulation for Environmental Protection

Several federal laws to protect the environment are being vigorously enforced by the government (see Table 12.2 for a summary of these laws). The most important ones include the Air Quality Act, the Water Quality Act, the Water Quality Improvement Act, the Solid Waste Disposal Act, the National Air Quality Standards Act, and the Resource Recovery Act. The Air Quality Act set up control regions around the country and established air-quality standards for each and also deals with auto air pollution. The Water Quality Act gave states the option of either setting water-quality standards themselves or having the federal government (the Interior Department) do it for them. The Water Quality Improvement Act strengthened the earlier act by emphasizing pollution from oil and other hazardous materials and requiring the installation of marine sanitation devices for controlling sewage from vessels. The Solid Waste Disposal Act authorized a program for improving the economic disposal of solid wastes, such as trash, garbage, paper, and scrap metal, by giving technical assistance to state and local governments.

The National Air Quality Standards Act, one of the stiffest antipollution bills passed to date:

1. Requires that all new factories use the latest pollution-control equipment.
2. Orders auto makers to cut exhaust emissions from their automobiles.
3. Authorizes the federal government to set emission standards for 10 major pollutants, ranging from soot to sulfur dioxide.

TABLE 12.2.   Outline of Major Federal Legislation on Air and Water Pollution Control.

Popular Title and Official Citation	*Key Provisions*
Water	
1899 Refuse Act (30 Stat. 1152)	Required permit from Chief of Engineers for discharge of refuse into navigable waters.
Water Pollution Control Act (62 Stat. 1155)	Gave the federal government authority for investigations, research, and surveys; left primary responsibility for pollution control with the states.
Water Pollution Control Act Amendments (70 Stat. 498)	Established federal policy for the period 1956–1970. Provided (1) federal grants for construction of municipal water treatment plants; (2) complex procedure for federal enforcement actions against individual dischargers. (Some strengthening amendments enacted in 1961.)
Water Quality Act (79 Stat. 903)	Sought to strengthen enforcement process; provided for federal approval of ambient standards on interstate waters. (Minor strengthening amendments enacted in 1966 and 1970.)
Water Pollution Act Amendments (86 Stat. 816)	Set policy under which federal government now operates. Provided (1) federal establishment of effluent limits for individual sources of pollution; (2) issuance of discharge permits, (3) large increase in authorized grant funds for municipal waste treatment plants.
Water Pollution Control Act as Amended by the Clean Water Act	Modified earlier clean-up deadlines
Air	
Air Pollution Control Act (69 Stat. 322)	Authorized, for the first time, a federal program of research, training, and demonstrations relating to air pollution control. (Extended for four years by amendments of 1959.)
Clean Air Act (77 Stat. 392)	Gave the federal government enforcement powers regarding air pollution, through enforcement conferences similar to 1956 approach for water pollution control.

Table 12.2.   Continued

Popular Title and Official Citation	Key Provisions
Motor Vehicle Air Pollution Control Act (79 Stat. 992)	Added new authority to 1963 act, giving the Department of Health, Education and Welfare power to prescribe emission standards for automobiles as soon as practicable.
Air Quality Act (81 Stat. 485)	(1) Authorized HEW to oversee establishment of state standards for ambient air quality and of state implementation plans; (2) for the first time, set national standards for automobile emissions.
Clean Air Amendments (84 Stat. 1676)	Sharply expanded the federal role in setting and enforcing standards for ambient air quality and established stringent new emission standards for automobiles.
The Clean Air Act Amendments	Set new deadlines for cleaning up polluted areas, added protection for clean air areas, and required review of existing air quality standards.

Each state is charged with setting factory-emission levels that accord with federal standards. If a state fails to comply, the Environmental Protection Agency (EPA), after giving 30 days' notice, can take over the job and make sure that it is done. The bill also gives the EPA the right to sue polluters directly. If the EPA is lax in its job, the law declares that a private citizen may sue the agency or the alleged polluter. In the case of those firms that, despite all efforts, are unable to meet these stiff regulations within the allotted time period, the law provides for a one-year extension. But after the one-year period, only Congress can grant delays. Violators of the law are subject to a maximum fine of $25,000 per day or one year in jail.

There has been much public support of legislative action regarding environmental protection. In the passage of the Environmental Protection Act, protection of natural resources was a recognized national priority. A National Industrial Pollution Control Council consisting of 50 industrialists was also formed, whose goal is to improve environmental quality by means of a joint industry-government effort. In addition, the Council on Environmental Quality was established, to

1. Assist the president in preparing an annual report on environmental quality.

2. Develop and recommend national policies for promoting environmental quality.
3. Accumulate data for analyzing trends in the national environment.

One of the council's projects was to create unconventional vehicles that would curb air pollution—for example, turbine-, steam-, and electric-powered cars. Finally, the EPA was also formed, to bring together in a single organization all the major federal pollution control programs, which were previously handled by four separate agencies and one interagency council. The goal of the EPA is to organize the fight against all types of environmental pollution.

The Resource Recovery Act was designed to reduce solid-waste disposal by encouraging firms to recycle their products, in essence, to

1. Promote solid-waste management programs and resource-recovery systems.
2. Give financial and technical assistance to local government, state, and interstate agencies involved in solid-waste disposal and resource-recovery programs.
3. Promote national research and development for better solid-waste management and disposal.
4. Offer guidelines for solid-waste disposal.
5. Provide training grants for programs pertaining to solid-waste disposal.

After a trio of railroad accidents involving hazardous cargoes several years ago, the Department of Transportation required greater safety measures for the transportation of dangerous substances. Occupational accidents with hazardous materials led the Occupational Safety and Health Administration (OSHA) to establish new standards restricting employees' exposure to toxic materials and requiring greater safety in the handling of hazardous substances. The Toxic Substances Control Act was passed to provide a mechanism for pretesting new chemicals to determine their toxicity and to make rules for the safe handling, use, and disposal of toxic substances. The Atomic Energy Commission, with the cooperation of the EPA, is responsible for the safe handling and disposal of radioactive material and wastes.

Recent court decisions are evidence of the courts' recognition that not all environmental risks can be eliminated by regulation and that risks must be weighed against the costs of environmental legislation. The Supreme Court ruled in *Industrial Union* v. *American Petroleum Institute* that OSHA was required, before issuing a standard, to demonstrate the existence of a significant risk of material health impairment. The National Environmental Policy Act (NEPA) mandates the "balancing of the environmental costs of a project against its economic and technological benefits."[11]

---

[11]Paolo F. Ricci and Lawrence S. Molton, "Risk and Benefit in Environmental Law," *Science*, December 4, 1981, pp. 1096–1100.

THE RESPONSE OF BUSINESS TO ECOLOGICAL ISSUES

Business is making many different responses to the ecological challenge. In the following sections we examine some of the major ones.

Birth Control

As noted earlier in the chapter, the potential debacle of an overpopulated world is of great concern to much of society. Business has responded by providing research and development on safer and less expensive birth control methods. Birth control pills have been a great boon in reducing the number of unplanned births. It has been determined that with the pills the number of unplanned births for 1000 women between the ages of 18 and 40 will be approximately 30. But with more traditional methods, such as diaphragms, spermicides, condoms, or the rhythm method, the number of unwanted pregnancies have been 80 for the same number of women. Although the pill has proved to be effective as a contraceptive, there is concern that it has dangerous side effects for its users. But because of conflicting evidence, no conclusion has been made as to the degree of risk; however, many pharmaceutical organizations are trying to produce a safer, more effective alternative to the pill. One of the alternatives is an oral contraceptive that can be used after intercourse but that need not be taken regularly. Other research efforts have been directed toward making the present pill safer. Other alternatives include sterilization and vasectomy.

While research is trying to find a safer birth control method, pharmaceutical companies are working with local and federal agencies to publicize the various methods available and the safety and cost of each. Part of the reduction in the worldwide birth rate is attributable to the efforts to make birth control methods better known and used more throughout the world. Although countries in North America and Europe have not increased their percentage of use of contraceptives, the less developed countries have, though they are still way behind the degree of use in developed countries.[12]

Food Production Methods: The Green Revolution

Providing greater amounts of food has been a concern of business and government alike. Some organizations have attempted to increase the yield of crops by means of genetic improvements of plant and animal species; the use of fertilizers to boost crop yields; nutrients and vitamins to improve animal yields; the use of better pesticides to combat diseases that can affect yields; and teaching better farming methods, such as crop rotation, in order to maintain the soil. Planting and tilling methods to reduce the amount of

---

[12]Steven Mumford, "Population Growth and Global Security: Toward an American Strategic Commitment," *The Humanist*, January–February 1981, p. 13.

soil that is lost to wind and water erosion is part of this approach. The means and methods of distribution, storage, and transportation are being improved so that there are less loss of grain and less weight reduction when shipping livestock. Cattle feedlots are an example of the changes in animal feeding and fattening methods. A final method is finding different food sources.

Increasing Food Supplies: Business's Response.   The yields of crops in the United States have increased 200 percent in the past thirty years, largely attributed to the growing use of fertilizers and the improvement in the strain of seeds used for planting. For example, many seed grains now can combat particular diseases, tolerate dryness, and produce shorter stalks that strengthen the grain head. The same is true for fruit products. Most apple orchards now have dwarf trees that bear more fruit and permit easier harvesting.

Different food sources are also being introduced. Meat extenders and meat substitutes have been produced commercially in the United States for several years. The first patent for meat substitutes was granted in 1907 to J. H. Kellogg of the Kellogg Food Company. In most cases, regular meat is mixed with soybeans to produce a product that tastes like meat. More recently, a meatlike product was made out of just soybeans.

Aquaculture is also being promoted as a means of increasing food supplies. Food sources of the sea are harvested, including fish and shellfish as well as less familiar foods such as squid, plankton, and algae. Ice cream has been commercially produced from algae. In addition to aquaculture, more and more uses of plant material not commonly used in foods has been promoted commercially. For example, a bread currently on the market is made not from grain but from plant fibers, including wood fibers. Algae, bacteria, fungi, and some yeasts have been suggested as means to improve food supplies, to be used in processed foods or in the food supplies of animals grown for consumption.

Many innovative programs have increased yields of both plant and animal foods. Average corn yields in the United States have more than doubled since 1950. The 100 pounds of feed formerly required to produce less than 30 pounds of meat, today produces 40 to 50 pounds. Hens that laid 170 eggs per year are now laying more than 220 eggs per year. Twelve million cows today give as much milk as 25 million cows did 30 years ago. Although the long-term food crisis has not been solved, forecasts of mass starvation have been delayed for several more decades. Estimates indicate that better diets will be available for the world's population through the year 2000.

Pesticides: The Search for Alternatives.   The pesticide issue is a major problem for business. On the one hand, pesticides contribute to bigger crop yields, thus keeping food production ahead of population growth. On the other hand, these chemicals cause serious ecological problems and can be dangerous not only to all who come in contact with them but also, in some cases, to the food they help produce. The solution to this problem can only come about through more research, though the costs can be very high. Dow Chemical estimated that for every 10,000 compounds they test, only one new pesticide is found. In addition, the length of time from discovery to market often is eight to 10 years, at a cost of over $10 million. As a result, firms have to identify "losses" early and concentrate their resources on the others if they hope to salvage any favorable cost-benefit from research on pesticides.

Some chastise the chemical industry for being overly profit oriented, but from a company perspective, there must be adequate return on investment. One chemical executive defined a profitable pesticide as one with a market that lasts at least nine years, has annual sales of $10 to $20 million, and provides a 40 percent before-tax return on investment. This seems high to the outsider, but the successes must offset the failures and enable the company to recoup its investment.

Business firms have also developed biological controls of viral and microbial insect pathogens and steril insecticides to halt population growth. An example is Dipel, a microbial insecticide developed by Abbott Laboratories. It causes fatal poisoning in leaf-eating caterpillars and worms and thus has become a standard worm killer for the leafy vegetable industry. The industry is also investigating sex attractants that interfere with insect growth. For example, Gossyplure was developed by Albany International. This chemical sends out a scent similar to that of the female pink bollworm moth. When spread on the cotton field, the male first becomes excited but later is unaffected by the chemical's scent or even by the actual scent of the female. This lack of sexual activity reduces the moth population. A third way of eradicating insects is by finding insect pathogens—natural enemies of the insects. This can be other insects or birds or a microbial agent to make the insects ill. Through these various techniques and a program of selective application of pesticides, the use of pesticides in the United States should decrease by more than 30 percent by the mid-1980s.

Natural Resource Use

To maintain the high levels of production to meet the needs of modern society, business must find alternatives to limit raw materials and must conserve existing material as well as find new supplies of existing natural resources.

Avoiding the Depletion of Raw Materials. Several means are available to business to meet the problem of the diminishing supply of raw materials. One method is to find new sources of raw materials, which is being done primarily through new research and discovery techniques. Businesses are joining together to explore for new raw materials. For example, some of the companies involved in consortia for joint exploration and development are Kennecott Copper, U.S. Steel, Ocean Mining Associates, Atlantic Richfield, Tenneco, Deepsea Ventures, Sun Company, and Lockheed.

Raw materials have been discovered through oceanic research. Some of the world's richest veins of ore and other raw materials can be found under-seas, and many materials can now be removed using the newest techniques of underwater mining.

A second way of improving the supplies of raw materials is through the invention of synthetic products. For example, the invention of nylon helped reduce the dependence on rubber. Research is now being directed to the commercial applications of synthetic oil, so as to reduce the demand for the rapidly depleting and expensive crude oil. Some feel that because of the development of alternative sources of raw materials, there should be little concern for the rapid depletion of resources. Some experts believe that alternatives will always be found. Although this position is not shared by most of the business community, it does indicate the confidence that some groups have in private and public research and development.

Business Response to Energy Demands

Energy has been a topic of concern over the past few decades, especially since the oil embargo of 1974. The possible solutions are similar to those pertaining to the shortage of raw materials: (1) finding new supplies of existing energy fuels, (2) finding new sources of energy, (3) conserving existing supplies by curtailing the uses of energy, and (4) making structural changes in the production process. To date there still is no widely accepted comprehensive federal policy regarding the energy crisis; the attention of both the federal government and business has been on the preceding three means of solving the energy crisis.

Much has been done toward obtaining new supplies of existing energy products. The recovery of oil off Alaska and the North Sea and the exploration in the Atlantic Ocean near the Baltimore Canyon are some of the efforts that energy companies are making to meet the higher demands for fuel. Besides oil exploration, there are renewed searches for other energy products, such as natural gas and coal. The exploration and development of western coal has occurred in recent years because it has a lower sulfur content than does eastern coal and thus more closely meets pollution standards. A second approach to mitigating the energy shortage is to find new sources of energy. Business has joined the government to develop alternatives to fossil fuels.

Although it is still in its early stages in the United States, the use of solar power is much more extensive in Europe and Australia. For example, a cooperative effort of Australian industry and the Australian and Saudi Arabian governments is a project that uses solar central heating and cooling facilities for a large community. Australia has several towns that are mostly heated by solar power.

Solar power, of course, is not the only alternative source of energy. The use of wind-powered electric generators are one alternative. However, few locations have sufficiently stable wind velocities to generate constant amounts of power. This has been remedied to a degree through the use of wind power in conjunction with existing electric power as complementary sources. Coal gasification plants convert lower-grade fossil fuels into gas to help meet the energy demands placed on natural gas firms. Energy companies have also looked at hydroelectric power with renewed interest. Electricity is generated by using water power to propel turbines. Although this process is not new, many organizations are turning to smaller hydroelectric plants to meet the needs of small communities and industries.

Another method of finding alternatives to the scarce supply of energy fuels is through conservation. Business is responding to conservation needs through a number of programs. For example, most utility companies are actively encouraging their customers to use conservation measures. Another device that utilities are using is to fly at night over residential areas in planes that have heat-sensitive filming equipment aboard. The pictures taken indicate the house's heat loss. Homeowners can use this information to decide whether they need more insulation. Private industry also is encouraging energy conservation. For example, the Adolph Coors beer brewery in Golden, Colorado, has switched some of its natural gas-fired boilers to coal in order to conserve gas. Several organizations also have stressed the recycling of oil.

A fourth way that business has responded to energy demands has been through structural changes in production processes. Fuel economies and pollution control have resulted from major structural changes in the production process of steel, from smelting and refining iron ore in huge integrated iron and steel works, to scrap in electric-arc furnaces. American companies, including Jones & Laughlin, have torn down their blast furnaces, feeding them as scrap into the new electric furnaces. Electric-arc steel making rose from about 15 percent in 1970 to about 25 percent in the 1980s. To undertake major changes such as this, it must be cost beneficial. Companies are saving money under these changes in the production process.[13]

Pollution: The Great Challenge

Pollution control is undoubtedly one of the most pressing problems facing modern society. It is actually three problems. First is the problem of cleaning up the mess accumulated over years of pollution. Second is the problem of minimizing present pollution and, finally, is the problem of balancing energy, growth, and pollution in the future. Business has done much to contribute to the pollution problem, though it is now trying to correct its pollution practices, sometimes because of legal fiat, but often because of a greater

[13]"Changing Patterns of Energy Use," *World Press Review*, February 1982, pp. 34–35.

awareness of the gravity of the problem and a commitment to become socially responsible for environmental protection.

Progress in Eliminating Air Pollution. The auto firms have made some progress toward overcoming air pollution by automobile exhaust. Most of these successes are the result of engine modifications. For example, researchers at General Motors discovered that a principal cause of air pollution was the large percentage of unburned hydrocarbons being emitted by automobiles. The company therefore designed a device that recirculates the hydrocarbons back into the carburetor. All GM autos contain this device. Chrysler and Ford use similar devices. To control the amount of hydrocarbons and carbon monoxide, they use such approaches as higher coolant temperatures, retarded-spark timing, altered valve timing, and double-diaphragm distributors. To reduce nitrogen oxides, another pollutant, a number of approaches are presently being explored. The main method is to modify the design and technical aspects of the engine itself. A second technique is to reduce peak combustion temperatures by using water injection or exhaust-gas recirculation. A third method is to use a reducing-type catalyst to treat the exhaust gas.

New Fuel Developments. The petroleum industry, also, must face up to the problem of air pollution. For some time now Detroit automakers have been urging oil firms to develop a fuel that gives better mileage and lower emissions of harmful gases. In particular, General Motors wants a lighter fuel that will burn cleaner when the engine is cold, because this is when the high-carbon gasoline components do not completely vaporize and burn. GM's catalytic converter helps, but it has to be hot in order to operate effectively. As a result, most of the emissions that escape do so in the first couple of minutes.

About half of the crude oil input into a refinery is turned into gasoline. In the case of nonleaded gasoline, this output drops to 47 percent. A move to even lighter leaded gas could reduce the yield to as low as 35 percent. Yet the leaded gases are very hard on the antipollution devices, and so the oil companies are currently producing nonlead gasoline and are looking into ways to reduce air pollution further through new and modified fuels.[14]

In addition to the changes taking place in gasoline fuels, the feasibility of new fuels such as steam, alcohol, or hydrogen as substitutes or additives is being investigated. For example, in a conventional internal combustion engine with a slightly modified carburetor, hydrogen was mixed with gasoline, air, and water to produce a relatively pollution-free exhaust while simultaneously obtaining a 10 percent saving in gasoline. In another case, using gasoline as the main fuel, a car was equipped with a new carburization system for converting gasoline into hydrogen, carbon monoxide, and carbon

---

[14]"Why Refiners Bought the EPA's Lead Rule," *Business Week*, November 1, 1982, p. 33.

dioxide by a reaction with water. In this way, the engine could burn most of the harmful elements before they reached the exhaust system.

Overcoming Smokestack Pollution.   Business firms around the country have taken steps toward eliminating smokestack pollution. The steel industry, one of the prime polluters, has spent more than $1 billion on antipollution equipment since 1975. For example, in Allegheny County, Pennsylvania, U.S. Steel replaced 11 old open-hearth steel-making furnaces with more modern equipment, thus reducing particulate emissions in the area by 15 percent, or 16,500 tons a year. In addition, U.S. Steel built a "smokeless" coke battery and replaced 28 open hearths with more modern furnaces in Gary, Indiana, and installed expensive equipment for removing phenols, cyanides, and other poisons from its coke works in Clairton, Pennsylvania. Other steel makers have taken similar steps. In overcoming smokestack pollution, firms rely heavily on technological advances, including power plant scrubbers, fluid-bed boilers, and cyclonic burners. Let's look at these in detail:

   1. Power Plant Scrubbers.   A number of firms, especially utilities, now use power plant scrubbers. Most of the scrubbers contain pulverized limestone for removing sulfur. A slurry of rock and water is sprayed into the dirty gas as it moves from the boiler to the scrubber, and the limestone combines with the sulfur in the gas to form a liquid that settles out as sludge waste. The remaining "scrubbed" gas continues up the smokestack.

   This scrubber technique can be very useful to fossil-fuel power plants which create sulfur dioxide as they burn sulfur-laden fuels. Sulfur dioxide often ends up as dangerous sulfuric acid and undesirable sulfate salts that can affect visibility and destroy vegetation. One way to eliminate the problem would be for the utility to switch from high-sulfur fuel, particularly coal, to low-sulfur fuel, but the current energy crunch makes coal, which the United States has in relative abundance, an attractive energy source. Thus, the most promising way to clean up stack gases appears to be by means of wet scrubbers.

   Utilities are trying out power plant scrubbers, although many are finding technical problems and frequent breakdowns. The Japanese have used scrubbers successfully, but some American firms believe that fuel and operating conditions in the United States are vastly different; thus what works in Japan may not work here.

   2. Cyclonic Burners.   Another development in reducing smokestack pollution is an offshoot of the cyclonic furnace, an air-fed machine designed a generation ago to extract the last ounce of combustion from coal. This time the principle of the cyclonic furnace is used to help the lumber industry get rid of its waste products while at the same time preserving clean air and improving company profits.

   The cyclonic burner is able to achieve near total combustion of solid mill wastes by "grinding them up and suspending the particles on blasts of air in the fire box. The generated heat provides a handy and economical source of energy." Because the system is virtually closed-loop, exhausts are fed back into the firebox rather than out the smokestack. Two of these systems already in operation show that the heat from the burner can be used to fire kilns in the mill. As a result, it is possible for a mill that cuts 1 million board-feet a year to save $115,000 in carting costs and $85,000 on fuel needed to fire the kilns.

Fighting Water Pollution. To fight water pollution, business has taken steps to cease dumping untreated wastes into nearby bodies of water, to halt the use of underground dumps wherever possible, and to recycle water after cleansing it. Here are a couple of illustrations of recycling programs to help fight water pollution.

1. General Motors' Waste Treatment System. GM has no less than 40 control processes set up for handling water pollution from operations. Their waste treatment system is designed not only to render potential pollutants harmless but also to recover resources whenever possible. For example, as a result of its water pollution–control system, the Chevrolet Division is able to reclaim almost 9 million gallons of oil a year. Oldsmobile has a similar program and also sells the recovered oil (about 1 million gallons) to the nearby municipal utility.

One of the most common techniques that GM uses to achieve these significant statistics is a recycling water system. Water from a foundry is pumped into a large lagoon or settling basin in which the foundry solids gradually settle to the bottom. The clean water is then pumped back into the foundry for use in operations. General Motors is also looking into a new technique to purify water to a degree suitable for reuse in any plant process. In essence, the purifying process involves passing waste water through sand filters to remove suspended solids, through activated carbon towers to remove organics, and, finally, through reverse osmosis units to reduce dissolved solids. Similar purifying techniques are also being studied and tested by other manufacturers.

2. Lake Restoration Projects. Many firms are also studying ways of restoring already heavily polluted bodies of water. Union Carbide undertook restoration projects at Lake Waccabuc, in Westchester County, New York; the Attica, New York, reservoir; and the Ottoville, Ohio, quarry. All three of these lakes had developed oxygen deficiencies and minimum water currents in their bottom zones. Under these conditions, nutrients that should be trapped in bottom sediments are instead released into the water, promoting the growth of algae and unwanted surface plants. In addition, the water has high concentrations of noxious gases. Cold-water fish, such as salmon and trout, found survival in these conditions virtually impossible.

In an attempt to solve the lakes' problems, Union Carbide withdrew water from each, saturated it with oxygen, and then returned it to the bottom of the lake. After six weeks of "aeration" at Lake Waccabuc, the oxygen level at the bottom increased from zero parts per million (ppm) to 5 ppm, which is adequate for the support of cold-water fish life. The company then stocked the lake with 2,100 trout, which survived. At the same time the firm was able to report a 30 percent reduction in dissolved phosphates at the bottom. This means that these nutrients will no longer be available to support the growth of undesirable algae. The cost of the aeration was $50,000 for the initial installation and $6,000 a year for maintenance. In the case of the Ottoville quarry, the same basic technique resulted in dissolved oxygen rising from zero ppm to 8 ppm, with stocked trout surviving. The Attica reservoir had similar results. In both of these cases the cost of initial installation ran to $25,000, with $11,000 a year for maintenance.

With such good results at a relatively low cost, Union Carbide is currently thinking of expanding its operations and taking on projects from private lake associations, large land developers, and municipal governments. One of the greatest advantages of the restoration technique is that there is no limit to the size of the lake that can be treated. For example, a body of water 1,000 feet long and 29 feet deep requires 60 pounds of oxygen per day. A lake one-fifth the size requires 30 pounds of oxygen a day. Because some oxygenators are capable of turning out 400 tons of oxygen a day, smaller lakes are no problem, using the present oxygenator capacity.

Reducing Solid-Waste Pollution.   To reduce solid-waste pollution, many firms are beginning to recycle their waste products. Steel firms, automakers, and plastics manufacturers are examples. Other companies (e.g., tire manufacturers) are searching for alternative uses for their discarded products. Still other firms such as General Electric are working closely with local communities to develop solid-waste management systems. Here are some closer looks at these approaches:

1. Disposing of Solid Wastes.   There are several feasible methods of disposing of solid wastes. One of the most common is to use wastes as landfill. Garbage or contaminants are dumped into a chosen site and then covered over. In addition, the site is usually contoured, and leaking gases or liquids are collected and treated or eliminated. The purpose of filling in the land in this way is to make it suitable for future development, for example, for parks, playgrounds, golf courses, and residential areas. Some of the advantages are that

1. It is often an economical waste-disposal method.
2. Submarginal land can be reclaimed through such a process.
3. These landfills can receive most types of solid waste.

On the other hand, some of the drawbacks are that

1. In highly populated areas, suitable land may not be available within economical hauling distances.
2. Without proper planning, gases produced from the wastes' decomposition can become a hazard or nuisance, interfering with the use of the completed landfill.
3. A completed landfill will settle and require periodic maintenance.

A second method of disposal is the open dump in which solid wastes are left uncovered. In contrast with landfills, this technique creates both a health hazard and an eyesore. Yet because many villages and smaller cities are not required to operate solid-waste disposal sites, dumps are prevalent throughout the country. On the positive side, few operators are needed, and the maintenance costs are low. But on the negative side, the dumps serve as breeding grounds for rats and other disease-carrying vermin, and there is often accompanying air, water, and landscape pollution, and land value in the local area declines.

A third and supplemental disposal approach is to reduce the volume of solid waste by means of such methods as incineration and grinding or shredding. Incineration reduces the need for hauling wastes to external dumps and can generate steam or electric power. On the other hand, of course, it causes air pollution, some of the residue still needs to be disposed of; and the incineration equipment and personnel can be expensive.

A fourth method of waste disposal is grinding or shredding, which can minimize the odor of solids during shipment and landfill. Also, wastes handled in this way can be spread and compacted in landfills up to 50 percent faster than umshredded waste can. But the machinery to handle this shredding function is expensive, and the wear and tear from grinding is great.

A final method of disposal is composting, a method of handling and processing solid wastes so as to produce a humuslike end product that can be used as a soil conditioner. In essence the process is a biological degradation of organic matter through the use of aerobic microorganisms under controlled conditions. Some of the advantages of composting are that

1. It can be used to dispose of many industrial wastes.
2. It can be used as a soil conditioner.
3. Revenue from its sale can be used to offset some of its costs.

On the other hand, some of the disadvantages are that

1. Not all wastes will compost.
2. There are few outlets for compost and salvaged material.
3. Capital and operating costs are relatively high.

Regardless of what method of solid-waste disposal is used, something must be done. Part of the problem's solution is the creation of less waste. Americans must move away from being a "throw-away society." In addition, attempts must be made to recycle the waste material for reuse.

2. Recycling Solid Wastes.   There is new emphasis on recycling. Spurred by rising costs and diminishing supplies, more and more organizations are finding additional ways for recycling waste materials for reuse or for sale to other users. The recycling of tin and aluminum cans in an example of resource conservation. Every year more than 60 billion metal cans are manufactured, which are a great part of the current solid-waste pollution problem. To remedy the situation, several of the nation's major steel and aluminum firms—Alcoa Aluminum, Bethlehem Steel, Jones & Laughlin, Kaiser Steel,

National Steel, U.S. Steel, Wheeling-Pittsburgh Steel, and Youngstown Sheet and Tube—announced a program to recycle these cans, by increasing the number of can collection centers around the country.

The automakers are following a recycling strategy both within their plants and in the external environment. Internally, they reclaim millions of tons of material. For example, almost all metal scrap is reused; the rest is burned, and the residue, fly ash, and core are put into sanitary landfills. Externally, the car companies are cooperating with local law enforcement agencies and dealers to collect abandoned cars and process them into reusable scrap. In order to encourage even more recycling, the Ford Motor Company is urging financial incentives such as tax deductions for manufacturers who buy recycled or recyclable solid-waste material and accelerated tax amortization of the costs of solid-waste recycling facilities and equipment. Metal is not the only material being recycled. Western Electric, for example, is studying ways of recycling parts from the more than 20 million telephones it repairs every year. The Hoffman Plastics Company of Chicago is running tests to determine whether concrete paving with 30 percent of the sand replaced with scrap plastic is more resistant to cracking than standard concrete is. Gulf Oil is gradually replacing its 100 million motor-oil cans with high-density polythene containers that can be shredded and recycled.

Business's Response to Problems with Hazardous Chemicals and Radioactive Materials

Hazardous chemicals and radioactive materials are difficult to control. Business has striven to attain a high degree of safety in the use and disposal of radioactive wastes. Most of this program has been carefully monitored by the Atomic Energy Commission, though the use and handling of hazardous chemicals has not been as carefully controlled, exemplified by the many chemical-related disasters and near disasters. The government is now moving to ensure that these substances are used with care. Business firms are improving their techniques of using and disposing of these hazardous materials. Earthline has done much in this area, and with an enviable safety record. Earthline is a private organization that treats industrial wastes and combines dangerous wastes in such a way that the toxicity of one is canceled out by the other. This process is called a waste-to-waste-treatment method.

Although the use of dangerous materials seems virtually unavoidable because they are necessary for today's society, the minimization of accidents and injuries is absolutely essential. Nuclear energy, although dangerous, provides a needed fuel in the world's diminishing energy supply. Chemicals provide necessary ingredients for the pesticides used in agriculture, in the production processes used to make many vital industrial goods, and in the production of medicines and fertilizers. Without them, there would be setbacks in meeting the world's demand for food, health, and material needs.

Although 100 percent fail-proof protection systems are probably not possible, business has done much to improve safety in handling and disposing of these materials. Safety agencies of the federal government and of private liability insurance companies are also trying to minimize these potential dangers.

CALMING THE PUBLIC'S FEARS

Ever since the Union Carbide plant's gas leak in December 1984 in Bhopal, India, the American public has been wary of chemical plant accidents. And to some degree, their fears are well founded. On August 11, 1985, Union Carbide's plant in Institute, West Virginia, had a major toxic-chemical leak. The safety and health director for the International Association of Machinists reported that gas clouded up the room so badly that the workers could not see. They were able to find only one respirator and they used it among themselves until a rescue unit arrived on the scene. The workers had no warning before the accident occurred. Outside the plant a cloud of aldicarb oxime gas rose over the area. When things were finally under control, 32 people were hospitalized.

The next day on the Capital Beltway around Washington, D.C., a tanker truck carrying chemicals sprung a leak. Nearby residents had to be evacuated until the chemicals could be transferred to another tanker. Meanwhile, on this same day in Arizona, a train wreck caused the release of dangerous chemical fumes and 250 residents had to be evacuated. On the following day a chemical leak occurred at a Union Carbide plant.

These developments are making more and more people uneasy about safety in the chemical industry. Yet this industry has one of the best safety records of any. For example, the number of transportation-related incidents between 1981 and 1984 fell from 10,070 to 5,756. At the same time the Chemical Manufacturers Association has been revamping emergency-response networks and information systems, and companies have done audits of their safety and back-up systems for handling potential releases. Union Carbide, for example, has spent $5 million on new safety equipment at its Institute, West Virginia, plant.

Despite these measures many people are worried and want to see even more done. On the other hand, more regulation is going to mean more taxes. Commenting on the problem, *Business Week* recently noted that "the ultimate responsibility for the safety and health of chemical workers and the public remains where it has always been—with the industry."

Source: "Calming the Public's Fears: It's Up to the Chemical Workers," *Business Week*, August 26, 1985, p. 33.

Abating Noise Pollution

In the last few years business has tried to reduce still another form of pollution—noise. To date, most efforts have been directed toward factory and machine noise and the roar of aircraft.

Reducing Factory and Machine Noise.   In the early 1970s, the Occupational Safety and Health Administration (OSHA) succeeded in getting the sound level to which workers are subjected in an eight-hour day lowered to 90 decibels. Now OSHA is attempting to reduce this level to 85 decibels.

As a result of OSHA's and other efforts, many initiated by business itself, the workplace is becoming quieter. An illustration is the case of the General Motors plant in Saginaw, Michigan. The steering gear factory has $1 million worth of built-in noise suppressors and, with 88 percent success, has been able to reach its self-imposed goal of 80 decibels. All around the plant, ceilings and walls are covered with sound-absorbing materials. Over and around particularly noisy departments are draft curtains, rigid, wall-like panels stuffed with noise-reducing fiber glass. In areas around the factory containing power tools, the company has attached hoses to the machinery to carry the noise out of the building. To quiet its conveyor systems, the plant has slowed the machines, and to reduce the din from its automatic screw machines, it has placed sound-absorbing hoods over the tubes.

Other firms are following the GM example by using shields and padding to stifle plant noise or having workers wear protective ear devices in areas in which the noise is more than 90 decibels. One textile company developed polyurethane replacement parts for looms. Now those parts of the machine involved in throwing and catching the shuttle used in textile manufacturing make far less noise, and "weaver's deafness" is being reduced. In riveting, the hammer-type riveters are being replaced by orbital and spin riveters. Now, instead of the rivet head being slammed into the ground, the tool compresses the rivet head with an orbital or revolving motion. With these and similar developments, factory and machinery noise is being reduced.

Cutting Aircraft Noise.   Another and more noticeable form of noise pollution to the general public comes from airplanes' turbo fans or jet engines. At the present time many different approaches are being used to stifle this form of noise pollution. The most common is to redesign the jet engine. One of the redesigns widens the spacing between the rotating elements of the turbo-fan engine and the stationary elements. Another design puts sound-absorbing materials on the walls of the exhaust duct and the inlet duct of the turbo-fan engine.

Unfortunately, it is impossible to eliminate all noise from a jet engine, though every little bit helps. For example, a cutback of ten decibels translates into a 50 percent decrease in a person's awareness of the noise. Thus if acoustical engineers can reduce 15 to 20 decibels from the roar of a jet engine, the sky will be a lot quieter. At the present time, aerospace firms are stepping up their efforts to accomplish this goal as they experiment with the number, spacing, and position of inlet vanes, blades, and outlet vanes. Another idea under consideration is the addition of a third shaft in the engine that would allow the fan to spin independently, which would permit the pilot to slow the fan speed during an approach while simultaneously maintaining efficient engine thrust. Efforts such as these promise to reduce aircraft noise in the future.

Paying for Pollution Control

Cleaning up the environment costs a great deal of money. This is especially true if the goal is to approach zero pollution; costs tend to rise almost geometrically as pollution decreases arithmetically. Some experts believe that it will cost just as much to clean up the last 1 percent of pollution as it did to eliminate the first 99 percent. In any case, everyone agrees that the expenditures are going to be very, very large.

Financial Burden. It is becoming clear that the costs for fighting pollution may be even greater than anticipated. The EPA is now defining exactly how much pollution will be allowed for all types of businesses, including power plants, steel mills, chemical plants, petroleum refineries, food processors, and paper mills. In the areas of air and water pollution, for example, it appears that billions of dollars will have to be invested by these industries if they are to meet existing pollution control standards.

Table 12.3 shows the amount of money spent for pollution abatement

TABLE 12.3. Constant-Dollar Spending for the Pollution Abatement and Control Program (Millions of Constant 1972 Dollars).

	1980	*1981*[a]	*1982*[a]	*1983*[b]
Pollution abatement and control	26,353	25,536	24,304	25,182
Regulation and monitoring	728	701	661	555
Air	180	165	147	140
Water	295	262	234	216
Solid	72	112	118	85
Other[c]	181	162	162	114
Research and development	927	853	689	680
Air	521	477	374	355
Water	123	117	105	108
Solid	29	31	30	35
Other[c]	254	228	180	183

TABLE 12.3. **Continued**

	1980	1981 [a]	1982 [a]	1983 [b]
Pollution abatement	24,698	23,983	22,955	23,947
Air [d]	10,216	10,822	10,315	11,004
Mobile sources [e]	5,545	6,452	6,393	7,411
Devices	3,432	4,398	4,300	5,211
Operation of devices	2,113	2,054	2,093	2,200
Stationary sources	4,672	4,370	3,922	3,593
Facilities	2,726	2,440	2,189	1,682
Industrial [f]	2,541	2,255	2,000	1,527
Other [g]	185	185	189	156
Operation of facilities	1,946	1,930	1,733	1,911
Industrial	1,867	1,865	1,668	1,831
Other [h]	79	64	65	80
Water [i]	10,596	9,276	8,871	9,026
Point sources	9,940	8,689	8,282	8,449
Facilities	6,485	5,167	4,746	4,511
Industrial [f]	1,698	1,425	1,329	1,239
Public sewer systems	4,178	3,211	2,866	2,595
Other [j]	609	531	551	677
Operation of facilities	3,455	3,522	3,536	3,938
Industrial	1,530	1,564	1,472	1,687
Public sewer systems	1,782	1,853	1,955	2,071
Other [h]	143	105	109	180
Nonpoint sources	656	587	589	577
Solid	4,526	4,505	4,248	4,349
Industrial	1,859	1,883	1,593	1,658
Other [k]	2,667	2,622	2,655	2,691
Other [c]	−640	−621	−478	−433

[a] Revised.

[b] Preliminary.

[c] Consists of "other and unallocated" spending.

[d] The Clean Air Act classifies sources of pollutants as either mobile, such as passenger cars, or stationary, such as factories.

[e] Excludes spending to reduce emissions from mobile sources other than cars and trucks; such spending was insignificant during 1972–1983.

[f] Consists of new plant and equipment expenditures for pollution abatement according to results from the plant and equipment expenditures survey by BEA.

[g] Consists of spending for fixed capital of government enterprises such as the Tennessee Valley Authority.

[h] Consists of spending to operate government enterprises and all spending by government; separate data on spending to acquire and operate government pollution abatement facilities are not available.

[i] The Federal Water Pollution Control Act defines point sources as facilities that discharge to a body of water through a pipe or ditch.

[j] Consists of spending for private connectors to public sewer systems, capital spending by owners of feedlots, and spending for fixed capital of government enterprises such as the Tennessee Valley Authority.

[k] Consists of spending by federal, state, and local governments for the collection and disposal of solid waste and spending by households for collection and disposal of solid waste by business.

Source: Survey of Current Business, March 1985, p. 21.

and control (PAC) during the early to mid-1980s (expressed in 1972 dollars).[15] Over $100 billion was expended. These costs fall more heavily on some industries than on others. For example, air pollution abatement hit the auto and electric industries most strongly. Water pollution creates the heaviest burden for steel, metal finishing, and pulp and paper firms. The chemical industry feels the brunt of the blow for toxic substance controls.

These costs have sometimes resulted in plant closings (see Figure 12.1), especially in the industrialized northeastern and Great Lake states. The U.S. Department of Labor reports that 118 plants were closed during the 1971–1977 period and 12,900 workers were affected.

Methods of Financing Pollution Control.   In dealing with this challenge, many firms are looking into ways of financing PAC equipment. There are several ways of doing so. One of the most obvious is to use profits after taxes and dividends. A second, traditional approach is to use bank financing. A third way is to sell stock or long-term bonds. A fourth is to buy the equipment and recoup the investment through rapid depreciation. A fifth method available to business is to obtain a subsidy loan, guarantee, or grant from the federal government, which has made available billions of dollars in subsidy payments for antipollution equipment. A sixth approach is to get someone to buy the equipment and lease it to the company.

SUMMARY

In this chapter we examined ecological issues, noting the challenge to, and responses by, business firms. We began by noting that the projected increase in population without a sufficient increase in food production is leading to a specter of mass starvation on a world level. Changing world diets are also aggravating the problem, as the shift from cereal to meat consumption puts an additional strain on both land and grain supplies.

A second ecological challenge is the use of pesticides. These chemicals have been found to remain in the soil, rather than breaking down, and as a result they end up in food products. The dangers faced by the consumers of these foods are varied and, in some cases, fatal. Yet supporters of pesticides point to the importance of these chemicals in the current battle to keep food supplies in line with the growing population.

A third ecological issue is the energy crisis. The United States uses an enormous amount of energy each year and, as a result, is depleting such

---

[15]"Pollution Abatement and Control Expenditures, 1980–83," *Survey of Current Business,* March 1985, pp. 18–22.

Region	Number of plant closings	Number of affected employees	Labor force (thousands)	Regional unemployment rate
I			5,871	8.4
II			7,830	9.2
III			13,906	7.4
IV			15,884	6.7
V			20,905	5.9
VI			10,251	5.6
VII			5,550	4.4
VIII			2,974	5.7
IX			12,242	8.5
X			3,443	8.5

FIGURE 12.1   Plant Closings Allegedly Resulting in Part from Pollution Abatement Costs, April 1978. *From* Council on Environmental Quality, *Environmental Quality*, 1978, p. 433.

vital raw materials as oil and gas. Currently, the battle continues between those concerned with environmental protection and those interested in using natural resources for energy consumption.

A fourth major ecological issue is pollution. Auto and industrial smokestack pollution, water pollution, underground dumps, thermal pollution, solid-waste disposal, hazardous- and toxic-substance pollution, and noise pollution are among the main types. At the present time, the federal government, state governments, and local communities are trying to regulate pollution effectively.

In the latter part of the chapter we sought to discover what business is doing to meet its ecological responsibility. There is evidence to indicate, despite what the general public may believe, that business is doing a great deal in the environmental area.

The first issue discussed was birth control. It was noted that business has responded to this challenge by providing research and development for safer and less expensive birth control methods.

The next issue, food production, efforts to increase the yield of crops through genetic improvements of plant and animal species, improvement of fertilizer to boost crop yields, and the use of more effective pesticides, were identified.

In the area of pesticides, business is continuing to search for safer alternatives. Meanwhile, in mitigating the depletion of raw materials, business involvement in oceanic research, the discovery of synthetic products, and the increasing use of raw materials through recycling were examined. In a corollary area, energy demands, business is trying to find new sources of energy and working to develop conservation measures to reduce current use.

In the area of pollution control, auto engineering developments in the form of catalytic emission systems and new fuel developments were discussed, as were efforts to reduce smokestack pollution, including power plant scrubbers, fluid-bed boilers, and cyclonic burners. In reference to water pollution, General Motors' waste treatment system, business efforts to reduce thermal pollution, and lake restoration projects currently under way were considered.

As for reducing solid-waste pollution, efforts in disposing of solid wastes, and recycling these wastes were discussed, as was business's effort to deal with problems caused by hazardous chemical and radioactive materials.

In the last part of the chapter we examined noise pollution. Some of the business efforts discussed were the reduction of factory and machine noise and aircraft noise. Finally, the issue of who will pay for all this pollution control was broached, and the methods of financing pollution control were explored.

Overall, it is evident that business is aware of its social responsibility to the environment and has taken some steps to meet this obligation. However, research indicates that a great deal more needs to be done.

DISCUSSION AND STUDY QUESTIONS

1. What is meant by the term "ecosystem"? How is it relevant to our study of environmental protection?

2. In what way are changing diets affecting food supplies? In turn, what is the overall effect on world starvation?

3. What dangers are there in using chemical pesticides? What arguments can you cite in favor of their use? Overall, who has the better argument: those in favor or those opposed? Give your reasons.

4. Can the United States do much about energy conservation and Americans' ravenous appetite for energy? Additionally, would you support environmental damage, at least in the short run, to ensure that American's energy needs are met and then develop a long-range plan for preventing this continued damage, or would you limit energy consumption immediately and require Americans to live within these constraints, even if it meant rationing supplies? Explain.

5. How much air pollution do automobiles cause? Is the situation becoming worse, or is it starting to improve?

6. Is industrial smokestack pollution greater or less than that caused by automobiles? Can it be eliminated?

7. What kinds of dangers do underground dumps create? How about industrial-waste dumping?

8. What are some of the effects of noise pollution?

9. How is the federal government trying to protect the environment? How about the state governments? Community agencies? Explain.

10. How is business helping increase food supplies? Cite some examples.

11. What is business doing in its search for alternatives to pesticides?

12. Several means are available to business to meet the problem of a diminishing supply of raw materials. What are these means? What is business doing to meet the problem?

13. How is business responding to the energy crisis?

14. One of the biggest air polluters is the automobile. What is business doing to reduce auto air pollution?

15. How are power plant scrubbers helping reduce smokestack pollution? What about fluid-bed boilers? Cyclonic burners?

16. What is meant by the term "thermal pollution"? How can this type of pollution be reduced and/or eliminated?

17. What are some of the ways that business is dealing with solid-waste pollution? Cite some examples.

18. Hazardous chemicals and radioactive materials are difficult to control. What is business doing in response to this ecological challenge?

19. Business is currently working to reduce noise pollution. What are some of the ways?

20. How expensive will it be to clean up pollution?

CASES AND INCIDENTS

The Problem is Garbage

Wehrler Industries is a paper-manufacturing firm situated in the northwestern part of the country, on the outskirts of a major metropolis. A management-consulting team was called in to study the firm's operations, and one of its recommendations was to install a furnace to burn waste products. Before, waste had been hauled away by a privately owned garbage service. The consultants pointed out that by burning the waste itself, the company could save enough to pay for the furnace within five years. After studying the cost figures, management accepted this recommendation.

After the first year of burning the waste, it appeared that the purchase of the furnace had been a wise decision, but then the city council passed Ordinance 341–22, which forbade the burning of garbage or waste products except in a furnace that had been checked and approved by the city's fire department. The primary reason behind the new ordinance was that the city had just built a giant, highly efficient plant for disposing of waste material. Thus, the city fathers saw a dual purpose for the facility: on the one hand, air pollution would be reduced because inefficient furnaces would be closed down, and on the other hand, there would be a demand for the new disposal plant.

To enforce the new regulation, the city's fire department was given an extra $36,000 in its annual budget. In turn, the fire department was charged with checking all city furnaces that burned waste materials. Those that did not meet the new requirements were to be either upgraded or prohibited from doing any further burning. In all, 763 such furnaces had to be inspected. Because of the large number, it was two months after the ordinance went into effect before the fire department sent someone out to the Wehrler plant. The inspector checked the furnace, noted the amount of pollution emitted during the burning of the firm's waste products, wrote down some of the figures regarding the design and capacity of the furnace, and then said he would let them know.

Two weeks later Wehrler's president, John Thurbing, received a letter from the chief of the fire department. The letter stated that the company's furnace did not meet the standards specified by the city ordinance. Part of the message read, "in light of the fact that your firm's furnace does not meet the new specifications as set for it by Ordinance 341–22 passed by the city council, your company must either comply with this new rule by Friday, October 1, or show cause as to why compliance should not be required." Mr. Thurbing immediately called the fire chief and was told that although Wehrler's furnace was quite new, it was not very efficient. Therefore, unless Wehrler could obtain a waiver from the council, the company would be required to comply with the ruling. This order would entail calling the city's sanitation department and arranging a time every week to pick up the waste products at the company's expense.

Mr. Thurbing was very unhappy with this situation. He called the secretary of the city council and was politely but firmly informed that no one was going to be given a waiver. He then called in the head of his engineering department, Thomas Badger. He explained the situation to him and asked how difficult and expensive it would be to make the necessary changes on the furnace. Mr. Badger said it would take about a day to analyze the problem but that he would immediately put two men on the assignment.

The next afternoon Mr. Badger told Mr. Thurbing, "You're not going to like this, but my engineers inform me that for all practical purposes, it is impossible to make the requested changes on the furnace. The only way to meet the required specifications is to purchase an entirely new furnace. The city's sanitation department has capabilities that we cannot hope to match with our equipment. They must have a couple of million dollars invested in the new garbage disposal plant. As far as I'm concerned, we have no alternative; we'll have to go along with the ordinance." An hour later Mr. Thurbing called Mr. Badger back. "I've been thinking over your advice, and I see no reason to doubt it. Call the city and make the necessary arrangement to get rid of our waste every week. But I would like you to do some thinking about what we might do with our furnace. Perhaps one of our competitors in another city might be willing to take it off our hands." Mr. Badger promised to look into the matter and make a report in two weeks.

ANALYSIS

1. Was it fair of the city to pass such an ordinance? Explain.
2. Was there any way that Wehrler Industries could have avoided this problem? How?
3. Did Mr. Thurbing take the right action? Explain your answer.

Sopping Up a Liquid Spill

Dow Chemical invented a way of dealing with oil spills—"imbiber beads," tiny plastic spheres that unlike many plastic products, do not dissolve in a solvent. Rather, when they are placed in liquid, they drink in the substance and entrap it in their molecular network. The entrapped fluid cannot leak or be sqeezed from the beads. In fact, a fully imbibed bead can be cut in half, and no fluid will escape.

These imbiber beads will swell to three times their initial diameter and, in the process, capture and contain 27 volumes of the solvent. The beads are designed to capture and contain a broad spectrum of organic fluids, including gasoline; numbers 1, 2, and 3 fuel oils; jet fuels; benzene; toluene; and many complex organic compounds. As Dow explained:

Imbiber Packets or Imbiber Blankets can be used nearly anywhere a spill occurs. Since these products float, they are ideal for control of spills in aquatic areas. And remember, once the spill is imbibed, it won't leak out of the packets as it will from many absorbents such as polyurethane foam, spun fiber mats, straw, ground corn cobs, pearlite, and the like. Imbiber Packets and Imbiber Blankets can also be weighted to recover spills in lakes or streams of those heavier-than-water materials such as methylchloroform, carbon tetrachloride, and PCB's. That's something we're sure you can't accomplish with straw or ground corncobs. As a matter of fact, we know of no competitive product that will work under these conditions.

Two unique properties of Imbiber Beads are put to good use in another series of Imbiber products—Imbiber Valve devices. Remember, we mentioned that Imbiber Beads are spheres, and these spheres, when contacted by a great many hydrocarbon solvents, imbibe and swell. When you pack a lot of spheres into a container with porous ends, you can still cause liquids to flow through the container. This happens because any bed of packed spheres has a measurable free space between the particles, and it's through this space where liquid flow occurs. This is just what happens in the Imbiber Valve, but with one important additional factor. The Imbiber Beads within the valve member are unaffected by water, but organic solvents cause them to swell and soften. Thus, when solvent enters an Imbiber Valve that is being used for water drainage, the beads swell and soften, squeezing against each other to seal the free space and stop all flow. This means that Imbiber Valve devices can be used in nearly every application where you must normally drain water but are required to guard against hydrocarbon escape. A few examples are water drawoff from bulk hydrocarbon storage tanks, sidestream monitors on large aqueous lines to prevent process upsets due to hydrocarbon introduction (some customers monitor boiler condensate lines with Imbiber Valves attached to pressure-drop alarms), and as drainage devices for diked hydrocarbon or chlorocarbon storage areas. One progressive petroleum company uses layers of Imbiber Beads in its gasoline station fill-pipe pits and under the fuel dispensers to allow water drainage but insure positive seal of these areas in the event of a fuel leak or spill. Thus, they insure against costly undetected produce loss while protecting the environment by preventing contamination of soil and subterranean water.

ANALYSIS

1. Are imbiber beads valuable in helping contain an oil spill? Explain.
2. For what other pollution problems could these beads be used? Give two examples.
3. Would the beads be of any value to the average homeowner? When?

Energy-Saving Windows

One of the ways in which business is helping with the energy problem is by using energy-saving window products. This is certainly welcome news for the average homeowner for whom such products can represent sizable reductions in their utility bills.

One of the most important types of window-related products helps home-owners insulate their premises more effectively. For example, the National Metalizing Division of Standard Packaging Corporation is now offering insulating draperies. Virtually indistinguishable from conventional blinds and draperies, they come in a wide range of colors, weaves, and types of fabrics. On the window side, the draperies are coated with metalized plastic film that remains completely pliable and can be pleated, gathered, folded, rolled, and sewn without damage. The film acts as insulation and creates a dead-air space between the drapery or blind and the window, thereby increasing its insulating value. The product also filters out ultraviolet rays that are responsible for fading fabrics in the room.

The company reports that some of these fabrics are nearly transparent, others are translucent, and others permit light to enter when the draperies are drawn or the shades are down. Others are opaque. The insulating film is bonded to the fabric, and this film is similar to that made for use directly on the glass, which National Metalizing says will reject 80 percent or more of the sun's heat in the summer and retain up to 90 percent of the home's heat during the winter.

What makes this product so attractive is that it helps reduce energy loss through plate glass, one of the biggest energy wasters. But this is not the only product currently available for reducing heat loss through windows. The Andersen Corporation and Capitol Products Corporation have demonstrated triple-glazing—double-pane insulating glass plus removable storm panels. This type of glass offers many of the fuel-saving benefits of single-glazing with storm windows, with only half of the cleaning chores. The addition of removable storm panels increases the insulating value of these window units by more than 35 percent, according to company representatives.

Similar products to reach the market recently include a variety of thermal break windows. These windows combine vinyl with aluminum framing, thus minimizing or eliminating aluminum's tendency to "sweat" in cold weather, causing moisture problems. They also cut heat loss through the frame. These thermal break models may be single- or double-glazed. All are designed to eliminate metal-to-metal contact and to expose only vinyl sections to the elements. Recent independent tests report that the heat saving is substantial.

ANALYSIS

1. Some people believe that consumers are not energy conscious because many of the energy-saving products take a year or two to pay for themselves. Rather than accept the higher cost now, people will buy less efficient, but cheaper products and let the long run take care of itself. Do you think there is any truth in this argument?

2. Besides using energy-saving windows and insulation, how else can people reduce the amount of energy they are using in their homes? Cite some examples.

Everybody Pays

Who should pay to clean up toxic wastes? Some people say the industry doing it should bear the burden. Others say that it should be taken care of through higher taxes. In truth, it appears that everyone is going to be paying for this cleanup. A recent decision in the House Ways and Means Committee approved a toxic-waste cleanup package that includes a controversial broad-based tax on manufactured goods.

Toxic waste used to be handled through a "Superfund" cleanup program which was budgeted at $1.6 billion. Most of this was paid for by the oil and chemical industries. Now, however, Congress wants to pump up the fund over the next five years into the $7.5 to $10 billion range. Oil and gas lobbyists argue that it is unfair for them to have to pay all of this, and Congress seems to agree. The result—a value-added tax. It will work this way. All manufactured goods of companies with more than $10 million in sales (except for processed food firms) will pay a 0.08 percent value-added tax (VAT). This tax, of course, will be passed on to the consumer.

The Grocery Manufacturers Association is opposed to this tax, as are a number of congressmen, who feel that a VAT hits lower-income people a lot harder than anyone else. Why should the poor pay for toxic waste cleanup, they ask. Nevertheless, unless there is a drastic change in congressional thinking, this is exactly what will happen.

ANALYSIS

1. How does a value-added tax work? Explain.
2. Why would a VAT hit poor people harder than anyone else? Explain your reasoning.
3. Is the approach to the funding of toxic waste cleanup a fair one? Defend your answer.

CASE STUDY FOR PART III

The Coca-Cola Company Does "What it Ought to Do"*

Here in hot Atlanta on August 19, 1981, at a press conference at Coca-Cola's headquarters, the working press was reminded of the turbulent 1960s when the civil rights movement came of age. There was Coretta Scott King, soft-spoken, refined, very strong, the widow of the slain leader and Nobel Peace Price laureate Martin Luther King, Jr. Over there was the Reverend Jesse L. Jackson, older certainly than in the days when he marched to Selma with the Reverend King, but at 39, still brash, enigmatic, controversial, charismatic. He had grown to power through the Chicago-based activist organization People United to Save Humanity (PUSH), which he founded in the early 1970s, and had sought to extend black unity beyond the boundaries of the United States. Talking with him was the Reverend Joseph Lowery, another King protegé, who was president of the Southern Christian Leadership Conference (SCLC), which was holding its annual convention in New Orleans this week. Present also was the Honorable Maynard Jackson, no longer simply an attorney but the seasoned mayor of Atlanta, Georgia, which had a metropolitan area population of almost 2 million, who was retiring after two terms in office.

The dusty roads near Selma, the marble steps of the capitol, the streets of Birmingham were a far cry from the paneled conference room of a corporate giant where the group gathered today. Trying to get a word in and announce his company's expanded Minority Participation Program was Donald R. Keough, president and chief operating officer of the Coca-Cola Company.

Coke and PUSH had invited the black leaders to the historic press conference called for August 10, 1981, at the multinational company's headquarters in Atlanta. Purpose of the conference was to announce expansion of the company's entire minority participation program, a "moral covenant" that

---

*This case was prepared by Robert D. Hay, University of Arkansas, with the assistance of Jane Lobell and others. Used with permission.

would channel $34 million from Coca-Cola's general system into black economic development. President Keough addressed the press.

Good morning. First, I want to acknowledge the presence today of so many of America's prominent black leaders, especially the mayor of our city, the Honorable Maynard Jackson. I am happy to be part of this historic occasion for the company, Reverend Jackson, and the black leadership assembled here. As an employee of the Coca-Cola Company I am proud for many reasons, not the least of which is that the company, through its decades under the guidance of Mr. Woodruff and other outstanding leaders, has always merited a place in the forefront of social justice.

Over the years, the Coca-Cola Company has maintained a high level of involvement in the black community through corporate gifts, scholarships, and executive time devoted to such organizations as United Negro College Fund, Atlanta University, Morris Brown, Spelman College, and Morehouse Medical School. In addition, the Company has provided financial aid to the Martin Luther King Center and to many civil rights organizations, created career development films for black youth, and has been involved in other endeavors too numerous to tick off here.

As a result, when we were approached by Reverend Jackson and his associates in Operation PUSH last November, we had no reason to hesitate to enter into discussions with them to hear their views on minority participation in the company's system.

Over the months, we listened very carefully, and we matched their comments, suggestions, and concerns with our own agenda for the black community, which we recognize as a significant segment of our society in the decade of the '80s.

From the beginning, however, we listened on a broader scope than just across the conference table or a telephone line. We had self-imposed tests to apply to the discussions—and the ideas arising out of them—to determine whether what we are now doing, and plan to do, is *what we ought to do*.

Several months ago, the chairman of the Coca-Cola Company, Roberto Goizeuta, set forth his strategy for the Company for the decade of the '80s. This strategy statement has been shared with all our employees and stockholders. In it, Mr. Goizeuta states, and I am quoting for the document: "All employees will have equal opportunities to grow, develop and advance within the company. Their progress will depend only on their abilities, ambition, and achievements." In addition, it is a focal point of Mr. Goizeuta's strategy to nurture the sensitivity to adapt to change and to manage our enterprise in such a way that we will always be considered a welcomed and important part of the communities in which we operate.

Those are not idle words, but the essence of what we fully intend to be. With nearly a century of operation behind us and our strategy for the '80s as a guideline, it was indeed easy for my associates to move forward in discussions with Reverend Jackson. In any human endeavor of this kind, there are inevitable periods of misconception which interrupt discussions. However, throughout the process, our discussions have maintained the integrity of forthrightness, courtesy, and respect.

Let me pause here to say that special words of gratitude are due to Mrs. Coretta Scott King, Rev. Joseph Lowery, and his associates at the SCLC and

I charge you to mobilize your congregation, mobilize your community, the P.T.A.'s, the fraternal organizations, the civic clubs, the block clubs, yes, and even go into the streets and to the neighborhoods and knock on doors and ring door bells. We must let this country know we mean business.

Finally, my brethren, we must trust in God. When Moses trusted God, the Red Sea parted. When He said, "Why I speaked thou unto me? Cry I speak to the children that they might go forward." When they stepped forward the Red Sea backed up. Moses trusted God. When Joshua trusted God, Jericho fell. When Abraham trusted God, Sarah bore a son. When Jacob trusted God, his cattle outnumbered Laban's. When Shadrach, Meshach and Abednego trusted God, Nebuchadnezzar's firery furnace could do them no harm. When Gideon trusted God, he defeated the Midianites with 300 men. When the widow at Zarephath trusted God and the man of God, her meal barrel ran over and her oil never failed. When Naaman trusted God and the man of God, when he dipped in Jordan seven times, he lost his leprosy.

Mr. Reagan can do what he likes. He can cut out food stamps. We made it without them. He can cut out C.E.T.A. We made it without it. He can cut out medicare. We made it without it. He can cut out Social Security. We made it without it. But, let me tell you something. I know somebody that sits high and looks low. HE PROMISED NEVER TO LEAVE ME, NEVER TO LEAVE ME ALONE!

I've heard the lightning flashing. I've heard the thunder roar. I've felt sin breakers dashing, trying to conquer my soul. BUT I'VE HEARD THE VOICE OF JESUS TELLING ME STILL FIGHT ON. HE PROMISED (you don't hear me!) HE PROMISED, HE PROMISED NEVER, NEVER, NEVER TO LEAVE ME, NEVER TO LEAVE ME ALONE! The song writer says, "He walks with me, He talks with Me and tells me I am His own." Let me tell you, preachers, go back to your churches, go back to your congregations. Tell them if they rise up and walk, trust in God and follow your leadership, He'll bring things out alright. Ain't He alright? Ain't He alright? Have you tried Him? Ain't He alright? Won't he fix it if you trust him? Ain't He alright? Ain't He alright? Ain't He alright? Ain't He alright?

ANALYSIS

1. Does Coke have a social conscience? Explain.
2. What strategies does Coke have to improve the quality of life for society?
3. Does the philosophy of Coke's management play a part in the Company's strategy with Operation PUSH? Give evidence.
4. What factors in the external environment affect Coke's strategy with PUSH?
5. Does Coke have the necessary internal resources to carry out its strategy?
6. What external factors influence operation PUSH's strategy with Coke?
7. Discuss and summarize four determinants that influence Coke's strategy with PUSH.

PART IV

The Challenges Facing Business

13

Broader Responsibilities for Business

Chapter Objectives

- To air the issues favoring business assuming a broader social role.
- To indicate the various alternative actions a business can pursue in meeting a broader social role.
- To show the importance of businesses working together to improve industry, community, national, and world welfare.

In this chapter we examine the responsibility that business has to its industry, community, host country, and the world in general. Although there are several logical arguments against the broader social role advocated in this chapter, the practice of many businesses has demonstrated that they can influence the quality of life on both the local and international level.

A BROADER SOCIAL ROLE FOR BUSINESS

In Chapter 3, Milton Friedman was quoted as stating that by obeying the law and applying all resources to making a better product at a lower cost, a business would fulfill its social obligation.[1] Friedman maintained that this

[1]Milton Friedman, "The Social Responsibility of Business Is to Increase Its Profits," *New York Times Magazine*, September 13, 1970, pp. 33, 122–126.

was the extent of business social involvement and that to go beyond this would be a disservice to society. Society should decide, through public policy, government expenditures, and private contributions of time and money, how the public welfare should be served. Allocation by business managers beyond that needed to run a business is, in essence, a misallocation of funds, as further social welfare expenditures subordinate the interests of the owners. The consumers are not being served either, as expenditures for social improvement programs increase the price of the product or service, which is a forced welfare expenditure that the consumer must assume without any voice in forming the policy. Similarly, there are fewer profits because of the business's social welfare programs, which means fewer profits to distribute to owners. Therefore, the owners of the company will be prevented from deciding how they want to contribute to society.

The strongest argument against broadening business's social responsibility is that individuals such as customers and owners should have the right to decide how much will be spent for social programs. This can be done better by the individuals themselves or through representative government's (public policy) allocation of tax dollars instead of by a private decision in the boardroom or company president's office.

The arguments against this limited perspective of business' social responsibility is the basis of this chapter. For business to survive, there must be consumers, sources of raw materials, and a viable marketplace. Business therefore has a vested interest in creating a favorable climate for business. Instead of being passive, business should be active, so as to preserve its own self-interest. This self-interest requires actions beyond making short-term profits and producing a useful, low-cost product or service. It means building a market for the product or service and ensuring that there is a future for the business. Business is best served by influencing its future, directly, through actions such as community development programs or, indirectly, through shaping public policy. In the long run, there must be a functioning society for there to be successful transactions of commerce.

There are several means of assuming this broader social role. An organization can work alone in instituting social welfare programs. For example, the Crown Center in Kansas City was built with the help of Joyce Hall, the founder and owner of the Hallmark Card Company. Hallmark cards is one of the largest privately owned companies in the United States. Or a company may work with a volunteer group. McDonald's support for the Special Olympics Program and Ronald McDonald Houses is an example of such cooperative efforts. A third means of assuming a greater social role is through joint actions with other companies. For example, the Committee of Economic Development is a nonprofit business organization that works to improve society through research and social projects. A fourth means to become more socially active is through joint projects with government. For example, the former CETA (Comprehensive Employment and Training Act), now reformulated as the Job Training Partnership Act, offers federal block grants to states to allocate to private industry to develop and implement training programs.

Only with a healthy economy with a stable marketplace will a company's chances for survival be enhanced. As J. Irwin Miller, a former chairman of Cummins Engine, pointed out, "We save ourselves, our business, only by making this society work equally well for all its members. To me, that means, among other things, voluntary giving—giving knowledge, time, money, whenever we are convinced it will improve quality, correct evils, extend equity in America. The case for corporate giving is an essential part of corporate survival."[2]

Current corporate involvement in these broader social issues is difficult to calculate. Indirect expenditures and the cost of time commitments must be included. Direct expenditures alone can give only some idea of the involvement of business, because often the expenditures reported are only the outright grants, as opposed to indirect program support. Corporate giving represents a small percentage of all private giving in the United States.[3] The rate of corporate giving has been stable over the past 30 years, and the rate of 1 percent of pretax income is well below the legal limit for tax-deductible contributions of 5 percent.[4]

The outright grants of a couple of billion per year seem significant. But when one realizes that this represents only 1 percent of pretax net income and only 4.5 percent of all private giving, it seems that corporate philanthropy is not as great as one might expect. In most cases, business seems only nominally involved in charitable activities and not really dedicated to a broader social role.

INDUSTRY WELFARE

Industry welfare means direct actions by a company to improve the industry as a whole. The company's main goal is to survive, which is more likely if the whole industry is strong. The usual means of improving the industry is by forming industry trade associations, several of which are listed in Table 13.1. Note the variety of industries represented. So complex and numerous are these trade associations that they are outlined in the three-volume *Encyclopedia of Associations* published by Gale Research Company, along with a brief statement about their purpose, membership, and publications.

Industry welfare is directed toward creating a favorable climate for business, and thus for the entire industry. For example, industry efforts to change

---

[2]Quoted in Frank Koch, *The New Corporate Philanthropy: How Society and Business Can Profit* (New York: Plenum, 1979), p. 3.

[3]Koch, p. 71.

[4]Frederick D. Sturdivant, *Business and Society: A Managerial Approach* (Homewood, Ill.: Richard D. Irwin, 1981), p. 422.

TABLE 13.1.   Leading Industry Associations in the United States.

The Advertising Council
Aerospace Industries Association of America
American Accounting Association
American Advertising Federation
American Apparel Manufacturers Association
American Association of Advertising Agencies
American Association of Exporters & Importers
American Booksellers Association
American Car Rental Association
American Collectors Association
American Compensation Association
American Council of Independent Laboratories
American Dairy Association
American Finance Association
American Forest Institute
American Hotel & Motel Association
American Importers Association
American Institute of Certified Public Accountants
American Institute of Food Distribution, Inc.
American Insurance Association
American Iron & Steel Institute
American Mining Congress
American Newspaper Publishing Association
American Petroleum Institute
American Rental Association
American Savings & Loan League, Inc.
American Textile Manufacturers Institute, Inc.
American Trucking Association, Inc.
Apartment Owners & Managers Association of America
Associated Builders & Contractors, Inc.
Associated Equipment Distributors
Association of American Publishers
Association of American Railroads
Association of Home Appliance Manufacturers
Association of National Advertisers, Inc.

Association of Physical Fitness Centers
Building Owners & Managers Association International
Building Service Contractors Association International
Chemical Manufacturers Association Inc.
Chemical Specialties Manufacturers Association, Inc.
Commercial Food Equipment Service Agencies of America, Inc.
Conference Board of Major Printers
Council of Better Business Bureaus
Direct Mail Marketing Association
Food Marketing Institute
Graphic Arts Technical Foundation
Independent Bankers Association of America
Independent Insurance Agents of America
International Advertising Association, Inc.
International Communications Association
International Council of Shopping Centers
International Quorum of Motion Picture Producers
International Radio & Television Society, Inc.
International Television Association
Investment Company Institute
Manufacturers Agents National Association
Medical-Dental-Hospital Bureau of America
Motor Vehicle Manufacturers Association
National Association of Credit Management
National Association of Exposition Managers
National Association of Home Manufacturers
National Association of Realtors
National Association of Service Merchandising

TABLE 13.1. Continued

National Association of Wholesaler-Distributors	National Retail Merchants Association
National Automobile Dealers Association	National Trade Show Exhibitors Association
National Beer Wholesalers Association of America, Inc.	Packaging Institute, U.S.A.
National Business Forms Association	Pharmaceutical Manufacturers Association
National Coal Association	Printing Industries of America, Inc.
National Coffee Association of U.S.A., Inc.	Private Truck Council of America, Inc.
National Cotton Council of America	Radio Advertising Bureau
National Council of Physical Distribution Management	Risk & Insurance Management Society, Inc.
National Electrical Manufacturers Association	Securities Industry Association
National Newspaper Association	Society of the Plastics Industry
National Restaurant Association	Transportation Association of America
	Travel Industry Association of America
	U.S. Independent Telephone Association
	U.S. League of Savings Associations

Source: Adapted from *Encyclopedia of Associations,* 1980, and *The Business Week Almanac,* 1982.

tax laws, pollution requirements, and worker safety and health laws all are designed to improve the industry's profitability. Through favorable legislation, the costs of doing business would be decreased, thereby improving competition between the target industry and foreign competitors and between the target industry and substitute products. Industry associations also may act as a single business representative for all companies in bargaining with the union, as is done in the automobile industry.

A second way to improve industry welfare is to ensure fair competition within the industry. For example, collective action with the Better Business Bureau supports fair and honest business practices and discourages unscrupulous firms. Efforts to improve market competition can also include actions such as working for legislation to ease usury laws. A third method is directed toward improving business in general. For example, a business's joining the local chamber of commerce helps business in the entire community, not just the industry.

Industry's welfare activities fall into four categories. First is the formation of a trade association which can act as a focal point for gathering industry's concerns and as a dissemination point for industry's efforts to further its goals. By acting as a focal point in gathering concerns, a trade association can determine the nature of the industry's problems, which can be technical, environmental, service connected, or competitive. For example, the American Association of Railroads is making technical studies to determine rail car and track dynamics. Its goal is to find out more about track- and equipment-operating characteristics in order to help design new equipment and maintenance procedures for tracks and roadbeds.

The second category of actions to improve the industry in attracting public support. For an industry to survive, it must be supported by society. An industrial association can help by providing information and institutional advertising to explain the industry and its position on various issues. For example, Figure 13.1 presents institutional advertising to benefit the insurance industry. Figure 13.2 is an example of the chemical industry's advertising, and Figure 13.3 is an example of institutional advertising to benefit the railroad industry.

The third category is political action committees.[5] Through lobbying and contributions to political parties and candidates, an industry can influence public policy. This process is the same as that used by individuals or environmental groups (see Chapter 15). As a focal point for disseminating industry information, a trade association can try to convince government officials of the merits of laws beneficial to the industry.

Legal actions are the fourth category. An individual organization or trade association can sue to change conditions in order to facilitate the industry as a whole. For example, Sears sued several government agencies for conflicting laws, including the Equal Employment Opportunity Commission. Sears felt the actions of several government agencies were creating hardships in record keeping and compliance. The outcome of the suit was to improve conditions in the entire industry through the precedents that it established.

COMMUNITY WELFARE

Some of the arguments favoring a more active social role for business hinge on its need to have a viable market for its products or services. This market includes having access to resources (human, monetary, and raw materials), customers, and an organized marketplace in which to transact business. Safeguarding these needs means that business should not transact commerce without regard for the future. To compete better, a business must not only invest in itself to renew its plant and equipment, but it must also invest to maintain a viable marketplace.

Community welfare, one of the four areas of social concern, entails the investment of business in the local community of which it is a part. Employees will not be attracted to a company that is located in an area of urban decay or to a community that does not or cannot provide the basic services demanded by its residents. Similarly, customers will not seek out a company that is located in a dangerous neighborhood or is hard to get to.

Most businesses will remain in a community until it harms their viability.

---

[5]George A. Thoma, "The Behavior of Corporate Action Committees," *Business and Society*, Spring 1985, p. 55.

Auto Safety.

We're doing what has to be done.

Crashes kill. They maim and cripple. And they are costly to Society. That's why Property-Casualty insurance companies support safer automotive engineering.

It's nine o'clock at night. Visibility is poor and rain is turning to sleet. You're driving home after an unusually hard day. Preoccupied, you don't realize the road is icy until, suddenly, you reach a curve. You struggle to maintain control, but you can't. You skid off the road at 40 miles an hour and smash head-on into a large tree. The sound of the crash is thunderous.

Then—silence. And you open the door and walk away. Impossible? In today's car, yes. But not in tomorrow's.

Today, automobile accidents injure more than five million people a year... and kill over 50,000. A national tragedy and a national problem.

Many serious accidents involve drinking drivers, youthful drivers, or tired drivers. Human error can never be eliminated. But a great many deaths and crippling injuries can be avoided by stressing safety in automotive design and engineering.

That's why Property-Casualty insurance companies support the Insurance Institute for Highway Safety. IIHS is an independent scientific organization that studies the causes of highway crashes and injuries and then suggests what can be done to reduce them.

IIHS has found that automobile design is a major contributor to crashes and injuries. In frontal crashes, for example, some designs allowed the hood to slash through the windshield and invade the passenger compartment. Partly because of IIHS investigations, the Federal Government in 1977 adopted a performance standard to prevent this.

Another example: after a crash, many car fuel tanks were prone to rupture or leak, heightening the chance of lethal post-crash fire. Again, IIHS research ultimately led to action: Congressional hearings and adoption of a corrective safety standard.

The Research Safety Vehicle (RSV) is a prototype automobile that demonstrates today's "state of the art." When all cars embody RSV's features, a 40-mph. head-on crash won't have to mean death or even serious injury. That's why IIHS and insurers strongly support the RSV program.

The RSV is stylish, seats 4 comfortably, gets good gas mileage (City 27, Highway 37), would cost approximately $7,000 to mass produce—and can thoroughly protect driver and passenger in ways no contemporary auto can.

The RSV features a unitized, foam-filled body shell for improved crash protection, an interior 'clean' of knobs and gadgets that can injure and maim; improved protection in side-impact crash or rollover; plus, seat belts and an automatic air-bag protection system. (The RSV also includes such amenities as air conditioning and citizens' band radio/AM-FM stereo cassette combination.)

You can't buy the RSV today. But we hope that tomorrow, these improvements in auto safety will be standard in automotive designs.

The IIHS research program and the RSV are positive efforts. They show that tomorrow's cars—the ones being designed right now by the world's auto manufacturers—could be much, much safer than those on the road today.

Obviously, for Property-Casualty insurance companies, auto safety is an area where social responsibility and self-interest are joined.

Our primary concern is to save lives and reduce injuries, wherever possible. But we also realize that the fewer claims we receive and the lower the cost of medical bills, the more policyholders will benefit—both from improvements in auto safety, and from positive effects auto safety features have on auto insurance costs.

The RSV. Designed and built for the Government by private industry contractors.

We're working to keep insurance affordable.

This message presented by the **American Insurance Association**, 85 John Street, NY, NY 10038

FIGURE 13.1 Trade Association Advertising—American Insurance Association. *Reprinted with permission.*

FIGURE 13.2   Trade Association Advertising—Chemical Manufacturers Association. *Reprinted with permission.*

At that time, the business will move to a place where conditions are more conducive to its goals. Unfortunately, the business will leave in its wake additional problems for the community, such as higher unemployment, smaller tax base, and vacant buildings. The social costs of these moves are devastating to some communities, and business that decides to move also

FIGURE 13.3 Advertisement from the Association of American Railroads. *Reprinted with permission.*

incurs high costs for replacing buildings and finding and training new workers. Hence, it seems prudent for businesses to help stabilize their community and encourage it to support their needs.[6]

The following examples describe the consequences of business's assuming, or not assuming, this broader social responsibility to the local community,

---

[6]Plant Closings Spark Fresh Resistance,'' *U.S. News & World Report,* April 15, 1985, p. 75.

showing the public and private costs of business inaction and that positive activities can be beneficial to both business and the community.

The Effects of Plant Closings—The Youngstown-Warren Case

Youngstown and Warren, Ohio, are cities of 115,000 and 56,000 population, respectively and are heavily dependent on the steel industry for jobs. In essence, these cities might be considered one-industry towns. Unfortunately, the steel industry has been depressed for several years. Part of the problem is foreign imports and the reduction in the demand for steel in the United States. The automobile industry, a major user of steel, has reduced its consumption of steel as it has switched from steel to aluminum and plastic. This switch to lighter materials was a direct result of the oil embargo and federal demands for more fuel-efficient automobiles. The general demand for automobiles has also been down. Complicating the issue in the Upper Midwest is the depletion of iron ore reserves in the Mesabi iron range in northern Minnesota. The last mine that had rich enough ore to ship without processing was closed in 1981. Several mines are still open, but the available grade of ore requires expensive processing into taconite pellets. This in turn makes production of midwestern steel more expensive because of the cost of the domestically processed ore. The alternative is transporting foreign ore to the Midwest.

This combination of factors led U.S. Steel to close its marginal facilities. Some analysts feel that the closures represent shifts by the steel companies to pull away from steel manufacturing and invest in more profitable activities. Joel Garreau observed that "there is a certain merciless logic to that, from a market perspective. A corporation naturally wants to make money, not necessarily steel. If there is more money in making chemicals. . . . The problem is the enormous social cost the shift entails."[7]

The Youngstown-Warren area was particularly badly affected by the plant closing. "Starting in 1977, three major steel mills in a row folded in Youngstown, starting with the Campbell Works of Youngstown Sheet and Tube (Company), followed by U.S. Steel's Ohio Works and its McDonald Works."[8] The first mill closing created additional unemployment of 4,000. By the time the third mill closed, over 10,000 workers were unemployed. The closings, as well, affected basic services in the area. The loss of the 4,100 jobs at the Campbell plant was estimated to have created a loss of 1,600 to 3,500 additional jobs because of the retail and allied industrial jobs lost. The combined loss of jobs can be translated into an annual payroll loss of $88.77 to $102.59 million and a loss of $68.89 to $79.61 million in retail

[7]Joel Garreau, *The Nine Nations of North America* (New York: Avon, 1981), p. 79.
[8]Garreau, p. 80.

and service sales.[9] The human cost was also high, with estimates, based on one study,[10] that 97 additional deaths from psychological trauma would occur as the result of prolonged unemployment in the area.[11] Fifty-four of these deaths would be the result of heart attacks, one from cirrhosis of the liver, two suicides, and two homicides. One study estimated that the public sector "would bear costs of $60 to $70 million in adjustment assistance, unemployment compensation, revenue reduction, and increased government expenditures."[12]

This case shows the effects of plant closings on a community. The plant closings were justified, given the economic problems. But what other influences did these plant closings have on the area? Should there have been some cooperation among the steel companies, the employees, and the communities? Given the cost to a business and the communities of relocation, it seems that public policy and social welfare would be helped by a joint effort.[13] What is the role of the steel companies in the city, and what is their obligation to Youngstown and Warren? What are the limits of their ethical and moral involvement?

Business and Urban Redevelopment

There are also examples of more positive business involvement in the community. Many firms are interested in redeveloping their communities. For example, the Marriot Hotel Chain located a unit in downtown South Bend, Indiana, following its policy of aiding depressed areas. The location program was financed with municipal bonds that lowered the cost of the project. Holiday Inn Motels also has a policy of locating some of its units in downtown areas as part of its urban renewal program. A unit built in downtown Chicago was deliberately placed at the fringe of a "skid row" area in an attempt to revitalize that area.

Kansas City's Crown Center is an example of private industry's (Hallmark Cards) working to rebuild a depressed area of a community. Over $400 million was committed to a 21-square-block tract. The center includes office buildings, apartment houses, a bank, 65 retail stores, and a 730-room hotel. This

[9]*Socioeconomic Costs and Benefits of the Community-Worker Ownership Plan to the Youngstown-Warren SMSA* (Boston: Policy & Management Associates, Inc., 1978).

[10]Harvey Brenner, *Estimating the Social Costs of National Economic Policy: Implications for Mental and Physical Health, and Criminal Aggression.* (Prepared for the Joint Economic Committee, Congress of the United States). (Washington, D.C.: U.S. Government Printing Office, 1976), p. 88.

[11]*Socioeconomic Costs*, p. 79.

[12]David Smith and Patrick McGuigan, *Towards a Public Balance Sheet: Calculating the Costs and Benefits of Community Stabilization.* (Washington, D.C.: National Center for Economic Alternatives, 1979), p. iii.

[13]Don Stillman, "The devastating Impact of Plant Relocations," in *The Big Business Reader: Essays on Corporate America*, ed. Mark Green and Robert Massie, Jr. (New York: Pilgrim Press, 1980), pp. 72–88.

single private project has been given credit for reviving Kansas City's downtown center.[14] In much the same way, Cummins Engine in Columbus, Indiana, has aided in developing segments of its community. Columbus has over thirty public buildings designed by well-known architects, all paid for by the Cummins Engine Company, which has its corporate offices there.

One final example of business involvement is Detroit's Renaissance Center, a joint venture by 51 Detroit firms to "bring back life into what used to be one of the most run-down, decaying and crime-ridden city centers in the United States."[15] The $350 million investment, instigated by Henry Ford II and 50 other firms, including General Motors, consists of a complex of offices, shops, and hotel accommodations. It was estimated that 30 percent of the businesses located in the center would not have located in the city without the urban development program. When the center first got under way, it accounted for $4 billion of revenue and 9,000 employees, 688 of whom had previously been unemployed.[16] Although economic problems in the 1980s have caused some problems with this development, it serves as an example of what can be done.

Business and Improved Housing

General Motors (GM) in Detroit has a program to rehabilitate eighteen blocks of homes around its headquarters. GM persuaded several other local companies to join in forming the New Center Development Partnership (NCDP).[17] NCDP developed a $20 million plan to restore a majority of the buildings and to build a shopping center, a retirement home, and low-income housing. Federal authorities contributed $3.5 million, and city officials agreed to repave streets and improve traffic patterns in the area. General Motors is also involved in other home improvement programs such as those with Urban Revitalization, Inc.,[18] which teaches carpentry, plumbing, and electrical skills to local unemployed individuals.

One roadblock to home rehabilitation is the problems caused by "redlining." Redlining is the practice of denying loans to people who want to improve homes situated inside redlined areas, that is, poor-risk areas, as defined by lending institutions. They are poor risks in that its property values have fallen. Lending institutions are reluctant to loan money to residents of these areas because the loans, based on mortgages, will be less secure if property values drop. The paradox is that because of redlining an area will deteriorate

[14]Milton Moskowitz, Michael Katz, and Robert Levering, *Everybody's Business: An Almanac—An Irreverent Guide to Corporate America* (San Francisco: Harper & Row, 1980), p. 862.

[15]David Clutterbuck, "The Renaissance of the Inner City," *International Management*, February 1981, pp. 12–16.

[16]Clutterbuck, p. 13.

[17]Clutterbuck, p. 14.

[18]Clutterbuck, p. 14.

faster, since without funds, homeowners will not be able to make the improvements necessary to maintain their homes.

Many companies have home rehabilitation projects, most notably Honeywell in Minneapolis, Continental Bank in Chicago, and the Battelle Memorial Institute, a research organization in Columbus, Ohio.[19]

NATIONAL WELFARE

The emphasis on business's becoming involved in broader social concerns is not limited to issues such as community or industry welfare. As indicated earlier, the survival of business is predicated on the survival of society. In other words, what is good for the country is good for business.

National welfare, as an area of business attention, is concerned with the establishment of a democratic form of government, economic stability, and an acceptable quality of life for the populace that will ensure a favorable climate for business. As mentioned earlier, a business must have sources of raw materials for manufacturing its products or providing its services. In addition, business must have consumers for its products and a marketplace that encourages the transaction of business. The state's economic-social-political entity can help fulfill many of these needs. It is reasonable, therefore, for business to be concerned with preserving the state in a form that will meet these needs.

The economic stabilization of the marketplaces within the host country includes the economic stabilization of its currency and the preservation of commercial law. If economic stability is a result of a stable currency, would it not then be appropriate to include the factors associated with a stable currency in business's broader responsibility? For example, if high government debts influence the stability of a nation's currency, does business not have a vested interest in working toward government fiscal responsibility? In the same vein, if an imbalance of foreign imports to exports threatens the stability of a foreign currency, should that not be a concern for businesses in that nation?

The quality of life can also be translated into business concerns. For example, if high inflation and high unemployment lead to frustration and social unrest, might not business be the loser? The heavy regulation and taxation of business in the 1960s and 1970s were the results of society's distrust of and disdain for business. Might not continued high unemployment lead to more regulations and taxes against business? In order to counter these frustrations, does not business have a responsibility to help eradicate these problems?

The actions that can be taken by business to improve the national welfare can be divided into three groups. First, business can work directly to eliminate

[19]Clutterbuck, p. 15.

some of the problems facing the country. Job-training programs are one approach for direct business actions. The second and third approaches are influencing and providing information to the public. Business may also try to influence public policy formation. Actions taken by political action committees (PACs) and lobbying organizations are an example (see the advertisements in Figures 13.1, 13.2, and 13.3).

A business can accomplish any or all of these goals by using one of two approaches. First, a business may decide to take action by itself. An example is the McDonald Corporation's sponsorship of the Ronald McDonald houses, for families to use while their child is in the hospital or receiving treatment. The second approach is to cooperate with others. A business may decide to work with other businesses, the government, or a volunteer organization.

Trade Policies and the National Welfare

Three aspects of trade policies and the national welfare are (1) the stability of the U.S. dollar abroad, (2) the equalization of competitive advantages in domestic markets, and (3) the reorganization of American industries so as to compete better in foreign markets.

Stability of the U.S. Dollar in Foreign Markets.   The relationship between the amount of imports and exports and the value of the dollar is well established. When the value of the dollar falls in comparison with that of other countries' currencies, it makes American exported goods more attractive and American imported goods more costly. The result is that the changes in the value of the dollar automatically balances distortions in the value of trade among countries. In the 1970s when the energy prices of the Organization of Petroleum Exporting Countries (OPEC) forced up oil prices, oil-consuming nations incurred deficits in their balance of trade. Payments to the oil-producing countries shot up, leading to a devaluation of the oil-consuming countries' currencies. The United States, a major importer of oil, found that the value of the dollar fell as more dollars left the country to pay for imported oil. The result was the destabilization of the world's money markets. The U.S. government finally intervened by means of conservation measures and deregulation of domestic oil prices.

Equalization of Competitive Advantage in Domestic Markets.   International support for and constraints on business vary across countries. One of business's concerns is creating equal competition, particularly in domestic markets in the United States. Simply having free competition (i.e., few tariff barriers between countries) may not guarantee free competition. If some countries give indirect or direct subsidies to their own industries to support full employment, those companies may have a competitive advantage. Similarly, if U.S. companies are faced with pollution, employee safety, and other regulations not faced by business in other countries, the foreign firms may have a competitive advantage, thus possibly weakening the American firms and leading to unemployment and economic destabilization. Advocates for the equalization of competitive advantages maintain that tariffs and trade restrictions should be imposed when the variations between the United States and foreign countries might harm American industries.

Reorganization of Industries to Compete Better Abroad—U.S. Agriculture. A final example of business action influencing trade policies is the recommendation that the United States support the growth of an industry that is vital to world stability and contributes to American economic well-being. This proposal suggests price supports, production adjustments, pressure on foreign countries to ease import restrictions, reserve stocking of foods for use in emergencies, research and development, and food aid to poor nations be a central part of a cohesive agriculture policy for the United States. Production adjustments would include allowances to farmers who take land out of production to reduce surplus supplies of food.

With respect to agricultural trade policies, U.S. business has helped the stability and economic vitality through its active participation in changing public policy to enable fair competition among countries and to see that American interests are served in international trade. In Chapter 14 we give more detailed attention to these international concerns.

Unemployment

Another great problem is unemployment. With the passage of the Job Training Partnership Act that became effective on October 1, 1983, there are now further incentives for business to train workers. The Job Training Partnership Act replaces the Comprehensive Employment and Training Act.[20] The new act gives federal funds to states in the form of block grants which will then be given to private industry councils to develop and operate training programs.[21] The private industry councils are composed of local government appointees but are dominated by employers. Many American companies have training programs for disadvantaged workers.

Economic Stabilization

A final area of national welfare is economic stabilization, which includes the first two areas already reviewed (trade policies and unemployment) and also inflation, energy policies, and the restoration of real economic growth.

Inflation. The negative consequences of sustained high inflation have been well documented. As the Commitee for Economic Development (CED) pointed out:

[20]"New Training Bill Stresses Partnership," *American Machinist*, November 1982, p. 51.
[21]"New Training Bill Stresses Partnership," p. 51.

Continued high inflation is very damaging to the national well-being. Inflation redistributes incomes and wealth in a highly arbitrary and inequitable fashion. Society, as a whole, loses because of the adverse effects of inflation on productivity, output, and economic growth. Inflation seriously interferes with rational corporate and personal savings and investment decisions, undermines financial markets, exacerbates industrial and social strife, and causes a diversion of the country's productive energies away from long-term productive investment into speculative or defensive efforts.[22]

Many groups, including businesses, are working to change public policy to reduce inflation and maintain economic stablilty. The CED, after some research, developed a plan of action to guide public policy.[23]

Energy Policies.   The energy issue seems to have faded from popular concern, because of the current moderation of prices, though some businesses and government leaders are still aware of the effect that an oil embargo could have on economic stabilization. These threats are real and become more important as less emphasis is placed on conservation and planning for future shortages. But the businesses that entered alternative energy source industries have been affected also by the poor economy; major oil companies have virtually stopped all shale oil projects because of the current lack of profitability of such ventures. There is still a need for energy planning, but for the most part, it seems that the bulk of business energy conservation will be the result of a corporation's actions to reduce its own energy costs through individual conservation efforts. Current tax allowances are aiding this process.

Economic Growth.   Economic growth is a function of many of the factors already indicated. The key to economic growth is the expected profitability from a venture that encourages investment. Savings also must accumulate so that monies are available for investment.

A major concern of business is to foster the government's economic policies that encourage savings and profitable innovation. Profitable innovation can be supported by tax and patent laws. Organizations also cooperate in joint ventures so as to reduce risks. Business groups such as the CED,[24] the Financial

---

[22]Research and Policy Committee of the Committee for Economic Development, *Fighting Inflation and Rebuilding a Sound Economy* (Washington, D.C.: Committee for Economic Development, September 1980), p. 384.

[23]Research and Policy Committee, pp. 2–6.

[24]See Committee for Economic Development, *Stimulating Technological Progress* (Washington, D.C.: Committee for Economic Development, January 1980) and *Fighting Inflation and Rebuilding a Sound Economy* (Washington, D.C.: Committee for Economic Development, September 1980).

Executive Research Institute,[25] and the Business Roundtable[26] have addressed the need for changes in public policy in this area.

WORLD WELFARE

Working to improve conditions in the countries other than the home country expands business's social responsibilities to world welfare. A company need not be a multinational company with outlets in various countries. For example, a company conducting research in only one country on new strains of corn, wheat, and rice that can be grown in the poor soil of Third World nations is helping improve the world's welfare. In Chapter 14 we give attention to all dimensions of the internationalization of business.

SUMMARY

In this chapter we reviewed the various activities included under the broader definition of the social role of business, including the arguments favoring business's pursuing a broader social role. This basis of business social responsibility was enlarged to include industry, community, and national and world welfare.

Industry welfare refers to actions that a business can take to protect the economic and competitive viability of the industry of which it is a part.

Community responsibility requires a business to see that the community in which it is located remains economically healthy. A specific concern was the need for business to maintain its community to preserve the business itself. Several examples were presented that showed both responsible actions taken by a business and the consequences of no community involvement.

National welfare is served by actions taken by business to preserve the legal and social entity of the state so as to provide an effective and efficient marketplace for the orderly transaction of business. Actions to promote national welfare include direct attempts by business to improve economic and social conditions and indirect actions to influence public opinion and public policy formation.

World welfare is advanced because of actions taken by business to improve world economic and social stability. The difficulty in initiating improvements in Third World nations centers on their misgivings about multinational corporations and foreign governments. Examples demonstrated the actions taken

[25]N. B. Ture and B. K. Sarden, *The Effects of Tax Policy on Capital Formation* (New York: Financial Executives Research Foundation, June 1977).

[26]See, for example, Francis Steckmest and the Resource and Review Committee of the Business Roundtable, *Corporate Performance* (New York: McGraw-Hill, 1982).

by governments, governments and business, and business alone to facilitate economic development among Third World nations.

DISCUSSION AND STUDY QUESTIONS

1. Why should business pursue a broader social role?
2. Why should business *not* pursue a broader social role?
3. How can a business improve the environment for the industry?
4. Why does industry welfare often depend on government actions? How does business attempt to influence public policy?
5. Why is influencing public opinion important to improving industry welfare?
6. Why should business be concerned with community welfare? How can business improve community welfare?
7. What could business have done to moderate the effects of unemployment in the Youngstown-Warren area? What could the community have done?
8. Why does business try to influence public policy in order to improve national welfare?
9. Why is the stability of the U.S. dollar important to national welfare? How can business influence the dollar's stability?
10. How can business help reduce unemployment?
11. What changes in public policy might stimulate economic growth? What can business in depressed industries do to stimulate economic growth?

CASES AND INCIDENTS

Nothing He Can't Handle

Everyone likes to bring good news. When Jack Jackson entered the stockholders' meeting last week, he was sure that what he had to tell the group would be well received. For the most part, he was right. Company earnings were up 12 percent over the previous year, and sales for the coming year were predicted to grow at an annual rate of 19 percent. But there was one agenda item that did not go over well. It related to a minority small-business program that Jackson had thought up and wanted to describe to the stockholders.

Since the firm was doing so well, Jackson believed that it could afford to become more actively involved socially. One area that had long intrigued Jackson was minority small-business entrepreneurship. Approximately 15 percent of all goods and services that his company purchased from outside suppliers were from minority enterprises. These contracts generally cost between $1,000 and $25,000. Jackson began thinking about how important these minority businesses were to the firm. Often they took jobs that other contractors were not interested in bidding on because they had a lower overhead and were willing to accept a smaller return on their investment.

Jackson decided that in the future the company should give a fixed percentage of its business to minority entrepreneurs. Approximately 25 percent of the local community consisted of minorities, and Jackson felt that this was a logical percentage. He, therefore, announced to the stockholders that at the first board meeting of the new year he was going to ask the board to approve a resolution that 25 percent of all outside contracts be given to minority entrepreneurs. The announcement was meant to be strictly informational, and Jackson did not think that there would be any discussion about it. He was wrong.

Almost immediately, one of the stockholders stood up and began to protest the president's decision. "We ought to give our business to the lowest bidder, regardless of who that happens to be," he said. From the murmur of approval around the room, Jackson realized that there were others at the meeting who agreed with this position. Quickly recovering from his initial shock, Jackson said, "I certainly understand what you are talking about, and you can be sure that we are not going to make any decision that is going to jeopardize our return on investment or our growth potential. However, this matter merits far more than the one or two minutes that our agenda will allow us to spend on it. But please be assured that the members of the board and I will be looking at this proposal from every angle before we decide exactly how to proceed." This seemed to satisfy the stockholder, and he sat down. After the meeting Jackson saw the man in the hallway with a few other stockholders, and they were talking with three members of the board whom they had cornered. The three board members appeared to be very ill at ease. "I may have a problem on my hands," Jackson thought to himself, "but I don't think it's anything I can't handle."

ANALYSIS

1. Is it all right for the firm to adopt the policy that Jackson is recommending? Under what conditions would his decision be justified?
2. What arguments can you think of that would support the dissenting stockholder's position?
3. Overall, who had the better argument: the president or the stockholder? Why?

No Substitute for Humanistic Management

The Willowby Corporation ended an era last year with the retirement of its founder and president, Peter Willowby. Willowby had run the company for over fifty years, and Ted Crownwall, the executive vice-president, had hoped to fill his shoes, but this was not to be. The board of directors decided to look outside, instead. Willowby probably could have stepped in and insisted on an inside person, in which case Crownwall would have gotten the job. But Willowby decided to allow the board to make the decision that it felt was best. As a result Chuck Manfield was hired nine months ago.

Manfield is well respected in the industry. He had been the chief executive officer of two large firms before coming over to Willowby. In each case, Manfield took a company that was having trouble and turned it into a winner. His motto is "control of return on investment (ROI)." If a division or unit is not making money, Manfield closes it down or sells it. One of the firms he took over was losing $1 million a month. Within eighteen months, Manfield had the firm back in the black. "I cut my losses and let my profits run," he likes to tell luncheon groups when he is the speaker. Business magazines find Manfield to be interesting copy, and he is continually being quoted by industry spokespeople.

Last month, after making a thorough analysis of Willowby's operations, Manfield presented some preliminary recommendations to his top management team. One of the things he wanted to do is to close or sell off all operations that are not generating an annual ROI of at least 12 percent. In the main, Crownwall thinks this is a good idea. However, there are two assembly plants that the firm operates in depressed areas of a large metropolitan area that fall into the "under 12 percent ROI" category. These were set up by Willowby over six years ago, and Willowby himself went on record as saying that the corporation wanted to "do its fair share to help out all of the people in this great nation of ours." Crownwall told Manfield about this during the meeting, but the latter seemed to have ideas of his own. "That was okay five years ago," he told Crownwall, "but today we have to be more bottom-line conscious. I'm going to recommend to the board that these two plants be sold off as quickly as possible." Crownwall found himself getting angry over the decision, but he said nothing. Later that day he called and talked to Willowby. The founder was genuinely surprised to learn of Manfield's decision. He let Ted finish talking and then said, "Okay, I'll take care of things at our board meeting next week."

At this meeting, Manfield presented his idea for selling off the two plants. The members of the board said nothing but it was obvious that all eyes were on Willowby. When he spoke, he chose his words carefully. "Chuck, we built this firm by following one basic rule of strategy that is important to every industry. It's my cliché for success and it goes this way: anything that isn't good for everybody isn't good for anybody. Closing this plant is going to hurt the people we most need to help in this country—the hardworking, lower-middle class. ROI is a great idea, but it is no substitute for humanistic management. I think I speak for the entire board when I say that we can live with a little less profit if it means keeping these two plants open." Manfield immediately agreed with the founder and suggested that the matter be dropped from further consideration. The rest of the board members nodded their assent.

ANALYSIS

1. What employment responsibilities does a business firm have to the residents of the local community?
2. Is it common to find business people thinking the way Manfield did? What is the logic behind their actions?
3. How would you describe Willowby's philosophy of business? What does he think the responsibilities of a business firm ought to be?

Taking a Risk

The recession of the early 1980s had a dramatic effect on many world economies. Some of the hardest hit were those in the Caribbean. In an effort to help out these governments, the United States began encouraging business firms to invest more money in the Caribbean. One of the firms giving serious attention to this request was the B. F. Harcott Corporation. Harcott manufactures industrial equipment and finds that in many cases it is cheaper to set up operations overseas and import the parts back into the United States. Some of its largest facilities are located in Ireland.

Two months ago the firm's top management started looking into the feasibility of building a plant on one of the largest islands in the Caribbean. Management believes that the labor force on the island is sufficient to turn out the needed production parts. However, there is a big question regarding the government. Five years ago the island had a socialist-communist government, which made decisions that almost wrecked the national economy. During the elections two years ago, this government was thrown out, and over 80 percent of the seats in the parliament were won by the opposition party, which is pro-Western. The new prime minister has been to the United States at least four times a year since his election, continually looking for business investment in his country. What worries the business firm is that very few American firms have chosen to invest in this Caribbean country, and the economy has not improved very much. In fact, the previous government left things in such a sorry state that during the first year of the present prime minister's term of office, prices rose faster than salaries did. A recent poll showed that the prime minister is now less popular than is the social-communist leader whom he defeated in the general elections.

The Harcott people are concerned that if they invest and build a plant in this country, the economy may not turn around enough to ensure that the prime minister will remain in office. Should he be defeated, the new government would probably renationalize industry again, and the firm would lose all of its investment. On the other hand, a government representative was in to see the members of the firm and to encourage them to proceed with their discussions regarding a manufacturing plant. "If you do not come to our island," he said, "and no other American firms will either, then we shall most assuredly lose the next election. We need support from our American friends. When we won the election, it was with a mandate to turn things around. If we cannot improve the situation, then the people will go back to the old leader and things will get even worse. You also should look at your responsibility. Sure, you want to help out your local community and your country. But Harcott is an international firm, and your obligations transcend national boundaries. You have an obligation to help people in general as well as your nation. I appeal to you as a citizen of the world. Do not turn your backs on us." His impassioned plea did not fall on deaf ears. Last week the board of directors voted unanimously to open a manufacturing plant on the island. Construction will begin as soon as the government gives it clearance to proceed.

ANALYSIS

1. What kinds of responsibilities do business firms have to other nations and the world? What did the government representative mean?
2. What advantages does the company's decision offer to the host country? What advantages does it offer to the firm itself? Identify and describe two of each.
3. Are there not some risks in regard to expropriation? How should these be allowed to influence the decision-making process in regard to international expansion?

chapter 14

Business in the International Arena

Chapter Objectives

- To define and discuss the pros and cons of multinational corporations.
- To identify and describe the three major environments that affect multinational operations: cultural political, and economic.
- To describe the challenges that multinationals face, including expropriation, culture shock, value conflict, and the problem of controlling operations.

Since the end of World War II, business's presence in the international arena has increased dramatically. In the beginning, American and European firms dominated the multinational markets. Over the last two decades Oriental businesses, especially Japanese, but also Korean, Taiwanese, and Hong Kong–based firms have begun to make their presence felt.

The main objective of this chapter is to examine business in the international arena. Particular attention is devoted to the general nature of multinational firms, why businesses choose to go international; the cultural, political, and economic environments in which these firms compete; and the social responsibility challenges that these companies face. The role of women in the multinational business arena is also addressed, and consideration is given to the need for more nationals in the management ranks of overseas operations.

NATURE OF MULTINATIONAL CORPORATIONS

There are many businesses that operate in the international arena. The largest of these are multinational corporations (MNCs). Many are based in the United States, although every industrialized nation has them.

What Are MNCs?

A *multinational corporation* can take many different forms. However, there are some criteria that all of them seem to meet. One is that they have operations in more than one country. This usually takes the form of subsidiaries, branches, or other structural forms. A good example is provided by the joint ventures currently under way between American firms and the People's Republic of China. Table 14.1 reports some of these.

Under this first criterion of having operations in more than one country, there are often stages through which a company progresses on its way to

TABLE 14.1.   U.S. Joint Ventures with the People's Republic of China.

Company	Product
American International Group	Insurance
American Motors Corporation	Four-wheel-drive vehicles
Baker Marine Corporation	Oil rig construction and leasing
Beatrice Foods	Processed foods
Brown & Root, Inc.	Offshore engineering services
Dresser Industries	Oil exploration services
Florasynth Inc.	Flavors and fragrances
Foxboro Company	Electronic process-control instruments
Gillette Company	Razor blades
Korwin Xian Hotel Company	Hotel
Parker-Hannifin Corporation	O-ring seals
R. J. Reynolds Tobacco International, Inc.	Cigarettes
Seahorse Inc.	Supply vessels for South China Sea exploration
E. R. Squibb & Sons, Inc.	Pharmaceuticals
United Technologies–Otis Elevator	Elevators

Source: John D. Daniels, Jeffrey Krug, and Douglas Nigh, "U.S. Joint Ventures in China: Motivation and Management of Political Risk," *California Management Review*, Summer 1985, p. 47.

becoming an MNC. This transition typically entails such phases as (1) exporting products to foreign countries, (2) licensing the use of patents and know-how to foreign firms, (3) establishing a sales organization overseas, (4) developing foreign manufacturing facilities, (5) establishing multinational management at all levels, and (6) having multinational ownership of corporate stock. Many would argue that the firm does not really become an MNC until the third step, until operating units are actually set up in a foreign land.

A second criterion often used to determine an MNC is foreign sales. Some would argue that until a firm reaches a particular level of foreign sales in either dollars (e.g., $100,000) or percentage of sales (10 percent in other countries) it is not an MNC.

A third generally recognized criterion is the nationality mix of managers and the distribution of ownership. If the firm uses more than just home-based managers and has its stock held by people in all corners of the globe, it would be considered an MNC under this criterion.

Although any one, or more, of these criteria can qualify a firm for MNC status, the important thing to remember is that multinationals have a pres-

TABLE 14.2. Largest U.S. Exporters (Thousands of Dollars).

Company	Products	Exports
General Motors	Motor vehicles and parts, locomotives, diesel engines	7,276,500
Ford Motor	Motor vehicles and parts	6,041,000
General Electric	Aircraft engines, generating equipment, locomotives	3,935,000
Boeing	Commercial aircraft	3,621,000
IBM	Information-handling systems, equipment and parts	3,074,000
Chrysler	Motor vehicles & parts	2,706,900
E. I. DuPont	Chemicals, fibers, polymer and petroleum products	2,650,000
United Technologies	Aircraft engines, helicopters, air-conditioning equipment	2,387,810
McDonnell Douglas	Aircraft, missiles, space systems	2,133,700
Eastman Kodak	Photographic equipment and supplies	1,949,000

Source: Fortune, August 5, 1985, p. 61.

ence in more than one country and impact on the economy of the latter. Some of the largest American MNCs, presented in Table 14.2, certainly fit into this category.

Why Firms Go International

There are a number of reasons associated with going international. Most of these can be explained in terms of four basic causes.

One of the major reasons for going international is that of resource extraction. For example, a company that wants to sell bananas in the U.S. market must go where the product is grown, outside the continental United States. A major oil company, on the other hand, must have operations in the Mideast or some other foreign location where oil is located, if only to complement and supplement its domestic sources.

A second reason is that of tariff jumping. Many nations have tariff barriers that discourage imports. However, if a firm sets up a factory in the country and produces the products there, the tariff can be avoided. Japanese auto makers are beginning to take this strategy in the United States.

A third reason is comparative advantage. Quite often it is cheaper to manufacture or assemble goods outside the country and then import them. Taiwan and Korea have become well known for their low labor costs. Many American firms in labor-intensive industries, such as textiles, use these sources to help reduce the overall labor cost associated with their products.

A fourth major reason is profit. Many firms make higher returns on their investment (ROI) in foreign than in domestic markets. This is because the product has already been tested and perfected, so the costs of producing it are quite low. Additionally, the company is often unable to increase market share at home because of competition or market saturation, so overseas sales, if nothing else, are an excellent way to bolster ROI with little added indirect expense.

Societal Implications of Multinationals: Pros and Cons

Multinationals have definite societal implications because they offer some very distinct benefits to their host countries. At the same time, however, there are drawbacks to domestic societies that must be considered in evaluating MNCs and putting them in perspective.

Benefits of MNCs to Society. One of the major benefits of MNCs is that they hire local people and thus help a country deal with unemployment. A second benefit is that the MNC invests money in the country and helps promote a higher standard of living for all citizens. A third benefit is that the MNC often helps the country become more competitive in terms of local businesses and thus improves products, services, and prices. A fourth benefit is that the MNC typically transfers technology to the host country and thus saves it the funds that would have been spent creating this technology from scratch and also supplies the needed talent that may never have existed. The United States, of course, has shared its advanced technology with the world.

Drawbacks of MNCs to Society.   On the negative side, MNCs often worsen their home country's balance of payments problem by substituting capital outflows for exports. They also substitute overseas jobs for home jobs.

Besides the problems for the home countries of the MNCs, the host countries also have problems with MNCs. One is that the MNC often finances its local operations with local capital and credit. Thus, there is no large inflow of foreign investment into the country. A second problem for the host country is that the overseas operation often buys materials, parts, and so on, from the home country and pays whatever the latter charges. The result can be overcharging or at least noncompetitive prices that is eventually passed on to customers in the foreign country. A third is that imported technology often displaces local workers. A fourth is the creation of new product tastes or demands and expectations brought about by the MNC, which result in different habits of eating, drinking, recreation, sanitation, and so on. A fifth is the real or imagined belief by many Third World countries that the MNCs are out to exploit their resources and take advantage of them.

On balance, from a societal perspective, the advantages and disadvantages must be weighed by a business firm in making a decision regarding whether to remain in a specific country or to expand operations into a particular part of the world. If a firm does enter the international arena, it must deal with the cultural and political environments.

THE CULTURAL, POLITICAL, AND ECONOMIC ENVIRONMENTS FOR MNCs

In the multinational business arena, companies face a number of environments that are often quite different from those they encounter back home. The major ones are cultural, political, and economic.

Cultural Environment

Although there are many definitions, for present purposes culture can be thought of as the norms, attitudes, values, and beliefs members of a given society hold. These are generally a result of the person's upbringing and are generally very localized. Thus, unless overseas managers understand the local culture, they are likely to make serious mistakes in their everyday and crucial business dealings. For example, many American managers like to single out those who do the best job and reward them in some way, such as a bonus or salary increase. However, in Japanese culture, the group is considered more important than the individual, and to single out someone for a special reward would be inappropriate and embarrassing. Thus, in Japan, individual incentive payment plans should not be used. The same caution could also be applied in dealing with managers. One of the authors was recently told the story of the young Japanese manager who completed his work early and was given the rest of the day off by his American boss. When the person returned home, his mother was upset. She thought he had been fired or sent home for making a major mistake. When she learned the truth, she begged her son not to come home early again but rather to stay in town, take in a movie, and get the late bus back. Otherwise, she complained, "the neighbors will ask questions and I will have to explain your behavior."

The above are but a few examples of the effect of culture on doing business in foreign lands. Consider the case of Apple Computers, which ran a big Christmas sale in the Netherlands in mid-December only to discover later, to their dismay, that St. Nicholas Day is celebrated on December 2. Or the American-based conglomerate that encouraged its Caracas customers to shop early for Christmas and then offered a major price reduction in its post-Christmas sale. The company failed to realize that many Latins exchange gifts on January 6 (the arrival of the Wise Men at the stable) and its after-Christmas sale coincided with their normal shopping period. Many people found that they were able to stay well within their holiday budget that year.

Culture and its stereotypes even affect the way managers function. Table 14.3 provides some insights regarding the differences between Mideastern and Western management styles. These "stereotypes" are a result of the fundamentally different cultures, histories, and socioeconomic characteristics of the two regions of the world.

Political Environment

The political environment has a number of important aspects for multinational business operations. One of these is nationalistic emotions and drives. In many countries the citizens want to be free of any substantial domination by foreign nationals. They do not want MNCs holding power over them. There are a number of ways in which domestic governments limit and control MNCs in order to comply with the nationalistic desires of their people.

Such government controls can take many different forms. These include: the need for MNCs to obtain licenses in order to operate; required forms and reports that need to be periodically supplied so the government knows what the company is doing; abiding by foreign exchange limitations which restrict (if not outright forbid) the company's ability to convert local currency back to dollars; and laws regulating the percentage of ownership that a host country's citizens must hold in the MNC. Depending on the government's attitude toward the MNC, these rules and regulations can be complied with quite easily or can prove to be so burdensome that it drives the MNC out of the country.

TABLE 14.3. Differences in Mideastern and Western Management.

Managerial Function	Mideastern Stereotype	Western Stereotype
Organizational design	Highly bureaucratic, overcentralized with power and authority at the top; vague relationships; ambiguous and unpredictable organization environments	Less bureaucratic, more delegation of authority; relatively decentralized structure
Patterns of decision making	Ad hoc planning, decisions made at the highest level of management; unwillingness to take high risk inherent in decision making	Sophisticated planning techniques, modern tools of decision making, elaborate management information systems
Performance evaluation and control	Informal control mechanisms, routine checks on performance; lack of vigorous performance evaluation systems	Fairly advanced control systems focusing on cost reduction and organizational effectiveness
Manpower policies	Heavy reliance on personal contacts and getting individuals from the "right social origin" to fill major positions	Sound personnel management policies; candidates qualifications are usually the basis for selection decisions
Leadership	Highly authoritarian tone, rigid instructions; too many management directives	Less emphasis on leader's personality, considerable weight on leader's style and performance
Communication	The tone depends on the communicants; social position, power, and family influence are ever-present factors; chain of command must be followed rigidly; people relate to each other tightly and specifically; friendships are intense and binding	Stress usually on equality and a minimization of differences; people relate to each other loosely and generally; friendships not intense and binding
Management methods	Generally, old and outdated	Generally, modern and more scientific

Source: M. K. Badawy, "Styles of Mideastern Management." Copyright © 1980 by the Regents of the University of California. Reprinted from *California Management Review*, No. 2, p. 57, by permission of the Regents.

One of the most difficult problems for an MNC occurs when the domestic government insists that local partners be taken on. The logic is that with these partners the country has representation in the decision-making process and the chances of the MNC doing anything detrimental to the nation are greatly reduced. For the MNC, local partners are often more of a headache than anything else. Quite often, they have no knowledge of the business, they invest but a small amount of money, and their only saving grace is that they are well connected with some government official(s). Unfortunately, a change in government often results in an end to their usefulness—but not their presence.

Another problem occurs when the domestic government decides that foreign businesses are becoming too strong. The result is a fanning of protectionist fires. Many industrial nations claim that it is unfair to keep out international businesses with such measures. On the other hand, even in the United States we are beginning to feel the pressure for protectionism. (see the box "Here Comes the Foreign Competition").

HERE COMES THE FOREIGN COMPETITION

All over the world it seems that governments are using protectionism schemes to keep out foreign goods. The United States would never do a thing like that, right? Wrong! At the present time, there is a growing number of people who want America to take action against foreign imports. One of their primary targets is Japan, a country, they contend, which ships billions of dollars of goods to the United States but refuses to buy American products in turn. The result? More and more politicians are talking about protectionist measures. Some of those getting the greatest attention are the following:

- *Country bashing.* Under this arrangement, any country whose exports to the United States exceed its imports from the United States by 65 percent would be subject to a 25 percent customs surcharge on any goods it exports to the United States. A country could earn an exemption from the surcharge in any year in which it reduced its trade surplus by 10 percentage points. The countries most directly affected by this measure would be Japan, Korea, Taiwan, and Brazil. A less harsh measure, which is also under study, calls for the president to retaliate within 90 days by imposing countervailing duties, quotas, or embargoes on specific imports.

- *Industry safety nets.* These nets are designed to protect specific industries. One proposal calls for quotas or tariffs on specific imports. Another calls for the refusal to allow certain exports to the United States unless the other country allowed American firms to compete in the same market in

(continued)

its country. An example is the telecommunications business, where American firms argue that they cannot get into the Japanese market but that Japanese firms are allowed to sell over here.

- *Tougher enforcement.* This approach calls for stronger enforcement of current trade laws. It includes speeding up the process of investigating complaints from domestic industries and having the Customs Service crack down on copyright and trademark violations by U.S. trading partners, specifically Taiwan.
- *Counter-subsidization.* To offset the assistance many foreign exporters get from their own governments, the United States is considering increasing its own export subsidies. For example, the administration has subsidized some agricultural exports in an attempt to match European practices.
- *Market sharing.* As protectionism measures have grown, more and more thought has been given to dropping out of the competitive game and, instead, carving up markets. Under this type of arrangement, governments agree not to compete in certain areas of the world or in certain world markets. Those that remain get these market shares. These types of agreements avoid many of the problems associated with trying to choke off another country's imports.

Returning to the U.S. market, does America really need to take protectionism steps? Aren't American businesses strong enough to beat the foreign competition in head-to-head combat? The answer is: not always. Consider, for example, the inroads that foreign imports have made into U.S. industry from the early 1970s to the mid-1980s.

A third problem is that of nationalization or expropriation of the business, in which case the government seizes the assets of the firms. In some instances, the company is paid for these assets, although the final price is often much lower than that established by the company. Socialistic countries typically reimburse the firm in some way. Communist countries do not. For example, in 1959–1960 Cuba seized American businesses worth $1.5 billion and never compensated the owners. Fortunately, expropriation occurs less frequently than commonly believed.

In recent years many MNCs have begun reducing the likelihood of nationalization or government interference in their business. One pragmatic way is by purchasing political risk insurance with private insurance firms.[1] Another

[1]Frank Vogl, "Revolution Insurance New Trend for Firms," New York Times News Service in *Pittsburgh Post-Gazette*, January 30, 1979, p. 33.

Product Line	Imports as a Percentage of the U.S. Market	
	1972	1984
Blowers and fans	3.6	29.2
Converted paper products	10.4	20.1
Costume jewelry	10.4	28.6
Dolls	21.8	54.7
Electronic computing equipment	0.0	14.2
Lighting fixtures	4.2	17.4
Luggage and personal goods	20.7	52.4
Men's and boys' outwear	8.7	26.8
Men's and boys' shirts and nightwear	17.8	46.1
Musical instruments	14.9	25.2
Nitrogen fertilizers	4.3	19.4
Power-driven hand tools	7.5	23.2
Precious metal jewelry	4.9	24.9
Primary zinc	28.4	51.5
Printing trades machinery	8.5	22.9
Radios and TV sets	34.9	57.5
Semiconductors	12.3	30.5
Shoes	17.1	50.4
Sporting and athletic goods	13.0	23.2
Telephone and telegraph equipment	2.1	12.1
Tires and inner tubes	7.2	15.1
Women's blouses	14.9	33.0
Women's suits and coats	7.3	24.5
Wool yarn mills	6.1	17.4

It is statistics such as these that have many Americans convinced that foreign MNCs are taking advantage of them and that some protectioism steps must be taken.

Source: The data in this story can be found in "The New Trade Strategy," *Business Week,* October 7, 1985, pp. 90–96.

strategy is to make it extremely difficult for the firm to seize the company. Example include the following:

- Design operations so that they are highly complex and above the skill level of most people in the local labor force. (Even if the company is seized, the government is likely to give it back so as to at least derive some benefits from its use.)
- Export as much as possible to other countries. (Forty percent or more is a good target; the government is unlikely to shut off such a source of economic wealth.)
- Hire as many foreign nationals as can be justified. (The government is not likely to close down an operation that is providing employment to its people.)
- Be of little, if any, strategic value to the country. (This lessens the chance of the government wanting to seize the firm.)
- Remain fairly small. (Large firms call attention to themselves; small ones often avoid attention.)
- Maintain aggressive management contact and communication with influential host nationals in the government. (These contacts can help if the issue of nationalization is ever raised.)[2]

Economic Environment

The economic environment contains a number of important dimensions with which MNCs are concerned. One is the potential stability and growth of the economy. Large firms, in particular, are interested in stable, consistent sales growth. Countries that cannot offer this are often identified as high risk and require careful scrutiny before making a decision to enter the market.

In recent years, inflation has been one of the primary areas of concern. Latin American countries, in particular, have been hard hit with inflation rising as much as 2 to 4 percent a month in some cases. This has resulted in economic instability and difficulty repaying foreign loans. At the present time, many American banks that loaned money to these countries are in the process of restructuring the loans, extending the repayment schedules, and revising the interest rates. Critics argue that these are merely stalling tactics because the countries cannot repay the loans and the banks are merely postponing the final day of reckoning. In any event, inflation and poor economic growth have accounted for the present situation.

In making an evaluation of the economic climate, many MNCs use an "upside gain, downside loss" approach. They estimate the largest annual ROI they might attain from their investment and largest loss they might sustain. Based on these two extremes and the likelihood of various points

[2]For more on this, see Thomas A. Poyntor, "Government Intervention in Less Developed Countries: The Experience of Multinational Companies," *Journal of International Business Studies*, Spring–Summer 1982, pp. 9–25.

in between, the company makes a decision. Unfortunately, in recent years many MNCs, especially large banks such as Chase Manhattan, have taken financial baths in the international arena. More accurate economic environmental forecasting (coupled with realistic political forecasts) can reduce the likelihood of such disasters.

CHALLENGES FACING FIRMS DOING INTERNATIONAL BUSINESS

There are many challenges that MNCs face. In addition to the environmental ones discussed so far, there are also culture and value conflict challenges, and the ever-present challenge of managing ongoing international operations. In the following sections we examine each of these.

Culture Shock

Culture shock occurs when employees enter another country and become disoriented or encounter feelings of insecurity brought on by the strangeness of a new culture. There are three ways in which an MNC can prevent this: (1) careful selection of overseas personnel, (2) proper orientation and training before the people arrive on-site, and (3) careful repatriation back to the host country.

Careful Selection.   Choosing the right people can be a difficult assignment. Some organizations attempt to sidestep the problem by using local nationals whenever possible. Figure 14.1 traces a very comprehensive selection-decision process. As shown, if it is not possible or desirable to select a local national, they begin a search for the best person to send over. The guidelines used in this process are often a result of past experience gained over the years:

> For example, many like to employ unmarried people who have learned to make quick and easy personal adjustments to transfers and who will not have families to worry about. On the other hand, one U.S. oil company operating in the Middle East considers the middle-aged man with grown children the best risks. Economic conditions of the country and the specific operations of the firm can have an effect on who is most suitable for the job. So too can the geography. Companies with desert surroundings find that people from Texas or southern California tend to be better risks than those from New England. By employing such guidelines, the firm can often pick those most suitable for the job.[3]

Proper Orientation and Training.   Once the best personnel have been selected, attention is focused on providing them appropriate orientation and training. There are many procedures that are useful in doing this. Some of

[3]Richard M. Hodgetts, *Management: Theory, Process, and Practice,* 4th ed. Orlando, Fl.: Academic Press, 1986.), p. 707.

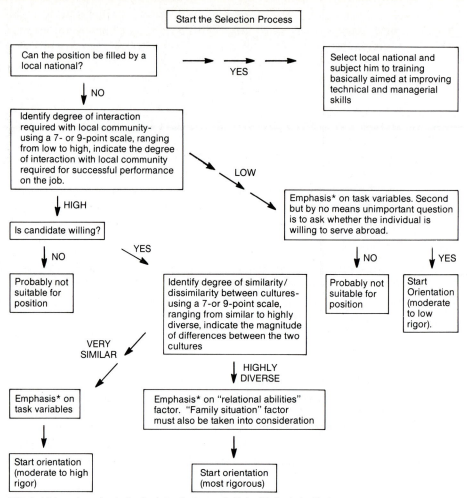

FIGURE 14.1.   Flow chart of the Selection-Decision Process. *From Rosalie L. Tung, "Selection and Training of Personnel for Overseas Assignments,"* Columbia Journal of World Business, *Spring 1981, p. 73.*

the most common include (1) providing the individuals with a previsit to the country and/or audio/visual presentation, during which the people are given a visual frame of reference; (2) training the personnel in the host country's language and communication, including informal and nonverbal communication; (3) providing detailed input regarding the specific culture's attitudes, heritage, politics, social structure, economics, and religion; (4) developing a country-specific handbook that relates everything the personnel ever wanted to know about the country, including how to use a telephone, how to get clothing dry cleaned, and what to do in an emergency; (5) in-company counseling on company or tax-related matters, contract terms, career path decisions, and the acculturation issues that are so important when an executive's family will also be going along; and (6) meetings with personnel who have recently returned from the country, including a spouse's viewpoint regarding what to know about the area.[4]

Careful Repatriation. Another problem facing overseas personnel is their repatriation to the host country. Anyone who has been overseas for an extended period of time is likely to suffer reverse culture shock. The person has to readjust his or her life-style. For example, it is quite common to find companies giving their overseas personnel a housing allowance. This often allows them to live better than they could back home. If the employees have children, educational supplements are often provided, allowing them to send the kids to the best private schools in the area. This often could not be done back home on the individual's base salary.

Another adjustment comes in the form of social and cultural life-style. Americans overseas often live much better than anyone else. The manager has a car, eats at the best restaurants, is a member of the golf or racquet club, and finds that the associated expenses are largely, if not totally, paid for by the employer. The person can also take advantage of fact that vacations to other countries often require but a short plane trip. For example, a manager stationed in Paris can visit other countries on the continent quite easily. Flying over from the states for such a vacation would cost a great deal of money. Added to all of this is often a cost-of-living allowance and a hardship allowance. Cost of living is particularly important in countries undergoing rapid inflation. The company will ensure that the manager's purchasing power is not eroded. A hardship allowance is given to those who are located in far-away places or cities where life can be quite boring.

When the person is transferred back home, he or she will lose all these "extras." The adjustment for many people is quite difficult, and in recent years businesses have begun taking steps to help their people deal with it. One of these is giving them a bonus for overseas assignments, but withholding it until the person returns. In this way, the person can use the money toward the purchase of living quarters or a house that is much better than that commanded by his or her American salary. Since the person is used to a standard of living that is above this salary, the bonus helps the person maintain that standard somewhat.

Another way of easing the transition back to the States is by making up

[4]Michael G. Harper, "The Multinational Corporation's Expatriate Problem: An Application of Murphy's Law," *Business Horizons*, January–February 1983, p. 72. For more on this subject, see Nicholas Sleveking, Kenneth Anchor, and Ronald C. Marston, "Selecting and Preparing Employees," *Personnel Journal*, March 1981, pp. 197–202; and Yosup Lee and Laurie Larwood, "The Socialization of Expatriate Managers in Multinational Firms," *Academy of Management Journal*, December 1983, pp. 657–665.

the difference between the value of the house the person sold before leaving and its current value. For example, a person who bought a $40,000 house in 1975 might have to pay $80,000 for it today. Because the person took an overseas assignment, he or she "lost" $40,000.

Still another approach is to provide counseling to returning executives in the form of guidance and advice. This is often given by trained counselors and/or financial advisors, since the person will be making a personal and a financial adjustment back home.

Finally, most firms make it a point to tell the manager up front what his or her position with the firm will be upon repatriation. Without such a promise, the overseas manager may find that all the best jobs at the home office are already filled by those who did not go overseas or who got back first. MNCs have learned that they have a major responsibility toward repatriated personnel.[5]

Value Conflict

Managers transferred to overseas positions often find themselves confronted with value conflicts. Such conflicts have important ethical and social responsibility implications.

Questionable Payments.   One of the biggest surprises to some newly assigned overseas managers is the various types of financial payments they are expected to make to government officials or others who help put business deals together. Many of these payments would be considered illegal in the United States and land the executive in jail.

One of the most common forms of questionable payments is that of making contributions to political parties. Since there may be three or four parties in an election, firms will cover their bases by giving to all of them. Does this ensure better treatment? Most international management experts answer this question by saying, "Maybe, maybe not. But if you don't give, you can be sure you will get poorer treatment than anyone else. So you pay just to stay even with the competition."

Another common form of payment is the sales commission paid to the person who puts together a business deal. For example, the brother of the defense minister contacts the manager and offers to serve as an intermediary in helping the firm secure a defense-related sale. The person asks for 5 percent of the total sales price as a commission.

Another example is paying someone to expedite a particular matter. In many countries, who you know is more important than what you know. Influential individuals, who can hurry along the approval of a license or

[5]For more on this, see D. W. Kendall, "Repatriation: An Ending and a Beginning," *Business Horizons*, November–December 1980, pp. 21–25; and Cecil G. Howard, "The Expatriate Manager and the Role of the MNC," *Personnel Journal*, October 1980, pp. 838–844.

reduce the amount of time needed to secure approval for importing machinery, can become important to a company. The question is whether these people are performing legitimate tasks that warrant compensation or are simply in a position to extort money from the firm.

How Companies React.   In the examples above, most MNCs would go ahead and pay. If nothing else, they would reason that "everyone else does it," or "it's simply the price of doing business in this country." On the other hand, these practices are often in direct conflict with ethical values, and some companies refuse to comply. Table 14.4 provides an example of an antibribery company policy developed by one company.

In some cases, firms have even stopped doing business altogether in certain countries because they are unable to accept their basic value structure. A recent example is South Africa, where an increasing number of American firms have now announced that they will not do business and/or are pulling out their operations because of apartheid (see the box "Leaving South Africa").

TABLE 14.4.   Example of an Antibribery Company Policy.

Recognizing the international nature of our business and our commitment to be good citizens of the world community, the following is a Corporate Statement of Policy regarding payments to foreign government officials or employees:

1. It is against the policy of the Company to authorize, encourage or tolerate unlawful payments by the Company, directly or indirectly, to foreign government officials.
2. The Company shall not knowingly pay or incur liability for, or enter into any agreement or understanding to pay or incur liability for, any unlawful fee, commission, payment or consideration, to any foreign sales agent, representative, or consultant or other person that, directly or indirectly, in whole or in part, incurs to the personal financial benefit of any foreign government official or employee in connection with or in order to promote or influence the Company's business.
3. The Company has developed a standard clause embodying the policies stated in paragraphs 1 and 2 and will include such clause in all contracts with foreign representatives to the extent not prohibited by the laws of the country or countries in which the contract is performed.
4. The company has developed and implemented procedures requiring certain levels of review and approval of contracts or other arrangements with foreign representatives, in relation to the amount of the fee, commission or other consideration to be paid by the Company to a foreign representative.
5. Company officers and employees are required to report to the General Counsel any information indicating that a violation of the policies stated in paragraphs 1 and 2 has occurred, is occurring, or appears reasonably likely to occur.

Source: Corporate Mission and Philosophy of Management (McLean, Va.: Dynalectron Corporation, 1977), p. 8.

LEAVING SOUTH AFRICA

Since 1984, American firms have begun changing their posture regarding South Africa. Many are either reducing their investment or halting operations. In 1984, six American firms stopped part or all of their operations. In 1985, this number rose to 18, and it is still on the rise. Some specific examples include the following:

This Company:	*Took This Action:*
Apple Computer	Closed down operations
BBDO International	Sold 75 percent ownership in its South African agency to local directors
Blue Bell	Sold its jeans manufacturing plant
City Investing	Sold its financial services group as part of a corporate liquidation program
Coca-Cola	Sold a majority interest in its bottling operation
Ford Motor	Merged its auto operation into Anglo American Corporation's Signa Motor Corporation, reduced its stake to 40 percent and is in the process of surrendering management
Helena Rubinstein	Closed its cosmetic operation
International Harvester	Sold its truck operation
Oak Industries	Sold its electronic components plant
Pan American World Airways	Closed its operations
Pepsico	Sold both of its bottling plants
Perkin-Elmer	Sold its manufacturing instruments and electrical components, as well as its sales office, to former employees
Phibro-Salomon	Closed its Johannesburg office
Singer	Sold its marketing and distribution operations
Smith International	Sold its affiliate
Tidwell Industries	Sold its homebuilding subsidiary to a local construction company

What has caused this movement? One reason is that many American firms are finding apartheid repugnant and believe that their presence in the country helps support this political philosophy. Additionally, apartheid retards economic growth making South Africa a less desirable place to do business. Commenting on this, *Business Week* reports:

The high cost of apartheid are staggering—even those that can be measured in economic terms. For years, South Africa's gold and diamond riches have financed the maze of laws that keep blacks, Indians, people of mixed race—called coloreds—and whites in distinct, parallel societies. Even in good times, the system hurt economic growth by limiting labor mobility and creating an artificial shortage of skilled workers. Some experts estimate that without apartheid, the country's economy could grow at a 12 percent annual rate vs. the 2.6 percent of the past decade.[1]

A second reason is that many businesses are beginning to follow the Sullivan Code, set forth by Reverend Leon H. Sullivan, the Philadelphia minister and General Motors board member. This code calls for fair and equal employment for multinationals operating in the country. Some firms that have not chosen to leave are following these principles very closely. Kellogg, the cereal company, is an example. Kellogg Co. of South Africa Ltd. has banned apartheid in its plant. Additionally, the firm pays 30 percent above the "household subsistence" level which is determined by the South African government. It has also appointed blacks as supervisors, who in some cases directly supervise white workers. The company also pays almost $100,000 annually to subsidize mortgages for new housing in the township where its workers live. At the same time the company has "adopted" a local elementary school. It pays for physical improvements to the facility, contributes money for library materials, and helps provide teacher training. As one of the company's managers put it, "As long as apartheid rules, employers will have to pick up the price tag for the country's political ills."[2] For those who do not feel it is right to leave, South Africa will remain a social responsibility challenge.

[1]"The High Costs of Keeping Blacks on the Bottom," *Business Week*, September 23, 1985, p. 112.
[2]"Kellogg's Private War Against Apartheid," *Business Week*, September 23, 1985, p. 107.
Source: "Leaving South Africa," *Business Week*, September 23, 1985, pp. 104–112.

Managing Operations

Another major social challenge confronting MNCs is the actual management of their foreign operations. These challenges take three basic forms: controlling, deciding the role of women in these operations, and determining the steps to be taken to become truly international. We now examine each of these.

Structuring Operations.   There are a number of types of organization structures that MNCs use in their international operations. The specific structure depends heavily on its degree of involvement and desire for control. There are four types:

1. The simplest form of structure is the *branch organization*, which is merely an outpost or detachment place in a specific location for the purpose of accomplishing certain goals on a local level. Branch organizations are commonly used for selling. The branch manager acts as a sales manager who supervises salespeople, handles orders, and resolves local problems.

2. Another common structure, somewhat more sophisticated than the branch, is the subsidiary. A *subsidiary* is a separate company that is organized under the laws of the foreign country for the purpose of carrying out tasks assigned by the parent company.

3. A third common structure is the world company structure, which is used by very large MNCs. A *world company* is one which has line divisions that are area based and staff departments that support these divisions. Figure 14.2 provides an example.

4. The final type of structure is some form of *matrix*. There are many combinations of this structure. Table 14.5 describes some of their distinguishing characteristics as used by various MNCs.

Controlling Operations.   In deciding the types of control to employ, the MNC has three simple choices: heavy, moderate, and light. Heavy control allows headquarters to make most of the decisions. This would be an example of centralized decision making. Under this arrangement there is seldom a problem of which top management is unaware, and overseas units all operate within the policies and procedures established by headquarters. On the negative side, such centralized control is often expensive in terms of time and money. It also prevents those in the field, in the local situation, who are most likely to understand what really needs to be done and how to do it, from having the freedom to make decisions. Heavy control also tends to damage morale among the overseas personnel and prevents them from developing because they feel they are nothing more than rubber stamps for central management decision making.

Moderate control exists when foreign branches and units continually submit reports to the home office but have freedom in advance. The main advantage of moderate control is that it gives the overseas operation the authority necessary to make day-to-day decisions and deal with operational problems on the spot. On the negative side, this moderate degree of control puts quite a bit of pressure on the manager and the staff, who often find that they have to do everything from selling the company's products to filling out all the reports and other paperwork associated with keeping the central office apprised of what is going on.

Light control exists when the home office gives the foreign units complete operational authority to make whatever decisions it feels are best but holds them accountable for providing periodic information on operations. This is decentralized decision making with centralized control. The major advantage

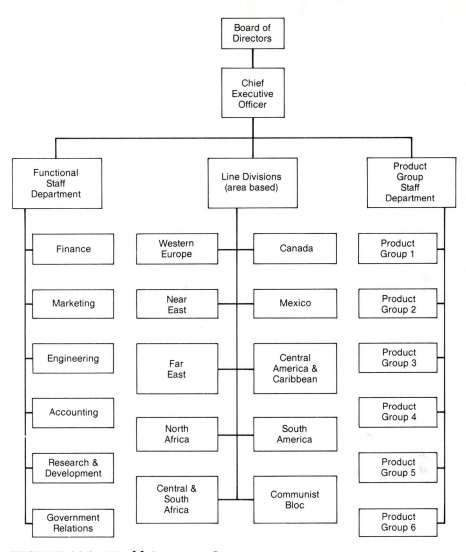

FIGURE 14.2   World Company Structure

of this type of control is that it lets the local personnel turn to their first priority: running the unit on a day-to-day basis and making money for the overall corporation. This type of control has a positive effect on the personnel and also reduces a lot of the expenses associated with paperwork and petty regulatory, bureaucratic controls. On the negative side, under this arrangement the MNC lessens the chance to closely coordinate and integrate world-wide operations. In most cases, however, the trade-offs come down more on the positive side.

TABLE 14.5. Matrix Organizations in Multinational Companies.[a]

Parent Company Characteristic	American Cyanamid Company (U.S.)	CIBA-GEIGY Limited (Switzerland)	The Dow Chemical Company (U.S.)	General Electric Company (U.S.)
Dominant organizational concept	Product divisions with global responsibility	Product divisions with global responsibility, but gradual strengthening of key regional organizations	Decentralized geographically into six regional companies; central coordination through World Headquarters Group	Product-oriented strategic business units on a worldwide basis
Planning and control	Heavy reliance on strategic planning; under guidance of Corporate Planning and Development Department; plans prepared by designated business units; accompanied by annual profit plan; investment priority matrix to facilitate allocation of funds	Moderate reliance on strategic planning by global product divisions; gradual buildup of the role of key regional companies in the planning process; operational plans and capital budgets by country organizations and their product divisions, with the latter playing the more active role	Coordination of geographic regions through World Headquarters Group, particularly the Corporate Product Department; strategic planning at the corporate level on a product basis, and in the operating units on a regional basis; operational plans and capital budgets by geographic region; control function at the corporate level	Heavy reliance on strategic planning; under guidance of Corporate Planning and Development Department; plans prepared by designated strategic business units; investment priority matrix to facilitate allocation of funds

Research and/or product development	Research and product development activities carried out by product divisions at five separate centers, each concentrating on a particular technology and/or market	Research and product development activities carried out by domestic product divisions and certain product divisions in key geographic areas	Research and development activities heavily process-oriented and usually associated with manufacturing facilities reporting to geographic regions; central coordination by World Headquarters Group	Centralized research, with supportive product development activities at the operating level
For U.S.-based companies: handling of international business	Separate international operating divisions organized into two geographic areas; limited authority, serving primarily in staff capacity	(Not applicable)	Highly decentralized organization of six geographic areas, each with almost complete authority over planning and operations	International business sector, together with overseas activities in other sectors; nine country strategic business units, which prepare an international integration plan to coordinate activities with product SBU's
For European-based companies: handling of U.S. business	(Not applicable)	Dual reporting relationship, with U.S. company reporting directly to headquarters and its local divisions also reporting to their counterpart domestic divisions	(Not applicable)	(Not applicable)

TABLE 14.5. Continued

Imperial Chemical Industries Limited (U.K.)	Nestlé S.A. (Switzerland)	N. V. Phillips' Gloeilampen-fabrieken (The Netherlands)	Rhône-Poulenc S.A. (France)	Solvay & Cie S.A. (Belgium)
Product divisions with global responsibility, but gradual strengthening of regional organizations	Decentralized regional and country organizations	Product divisions with global responsibility, but gradual strengthening of geographic organizations; U.S. company financially and legally separate from parent	Product divisions with global responsibility, but major country organizations retain special status	Product divisions with global responsibility, but national and subsidiary organizations allowed to exercise a reasonable degree of autonomy
Coordination of planning through Central Planning Department; strategic planning and operational planning at the divisional and regional levels; tight financial reporting and control by headquarters	Increasing emphasis on strategic planning, with recent formation of Central Planning and Information Services Department; annual plans (budgets) by each major company; tight financial reporting and control by headquarters	Moderate to heavy reliance on strategic planning by planning units in product divisions, selected national organizations, and Central Planning Department; operational plans by division and national organizations, with initiative from the former; monthly review of performance	Moderate reliance on strategic planning by Central Strategy and Planning Department; in addition, strategic planning at the operational level, primarily by product divisions; operational plans and capital budgets by divisions and country organizations; monthly review of performance	Increasing emphasis on strategic planning with the recent formation of Central Planning Department; operational plans and capital budgets by country organizations

Research and product development activities carried out by headquarters and selected regional organizations	Highly centralized research, but local product development by regional and country organizations	Highly centralized research, but with product development by product divisions and large national organizations; other research centers located in four key countries	Research and product development activities carried out by product divisions; several large centers, each focusing on different specializations	Centralized research and product development activities; major national organizations also carry out product development
(Not applicable) U.S. organization oversees ICI activities in the Americas, and reports directly to headquarters; U.S. board has considerable authority regarding local decisions and activities	(Not applicable) U.S. activities divided among three main companies, each with special reporting relationship to headquarters	(Not applicable) No formal chain of command between headquarters and U.S. organization; latter operating under direction of U.S. Philips Trust	(Not applicable) Special reporting relationship directly to headquarters; U.S. company coordinates activities with product divisions at headquarters	(Not applicable) U.S. organization functions as legal entity, overseeing Solvay's activities in the U.S.; however, several of the U.S. businesses report independently to headquarters

a At time of survey.

Source: Rodman L. Drake and Lee M. Caudill, "Management of the Large Multinational: Trends and Future Challenges," *Business Horizons,* May–June 1980, pp. 88–90.

The Role of Women in MNCs

A challenge for MNCs that has definite social implications is that of women executives in foreign subsidiaries. Adler found in a recent survey of over 680 major American and Canadian MNCs that the number of women managers in domestic positions is increasing, but less than 3 percent of international managers are women.[6] Izraeli and his associates uncovered similar results. They found that over 60 percent of the male MNC managers they surveyed felt that women could successfully head and manage a subsidiary in their geographic area. When questioned more closely, however, most of the managers were apprehensive about assigning a woman to a position as a senior executive in an overseas subsidiary. Some of their observations were as follows:

> In most cases, it is desirable that the number one person in the subsidiary be a man. But if there is a woman who is outstandingly capable, she could be the number two. (England, banking.)
>
> A woman could well be a manager in a branch, but not the general manager of the subsidiary. (France, industrial products.)
>
> You could place a woman as manager of sales, but not in a representative function and certainly not as subsidiary chief executive. (Germany, tourism and transportation.)
>
> It is impossible for a woman to be a senior manager, but not the top manager in the branch. (Holland, agricultural products.)[7]

What can be done to deal with this problem? Some of the specific guidelines that have been set forth by researchers and others who are studying the problem include: (1) select women for foreign managerial positions who have both considerable managerial experience and an outstanding record of accomplishment; (2) seek women who are already in midcareer, so that if they do well they can move into top management without question; (3) make women aware of any sex-role stereotypes that exist in the country to which they will be sent and provide them any necessary coaching and counseling regarding the most effective ways of dealing with these problems; (4) before a woman is sent overseas, make the personnel in the subsidiary aware of the decision and the need to establish a positive climate of opinion among themselves; and (5) because it takes a long time to train senior-level managers, businesses should create a large pool of female talent in their overseas subsidiaries by placing women in number two roles and grooming them for promotion.[8]

---

[6]Nancy Adler, "Women in International Management: Where Are They?" *California Management Review*, Summer 1984, pp. 78–89.

[7]Dafna N. Izraeli, Moshe Banai, and Yoram Zeira, "Woman Executives in MNC Subsidiaries," *California Management Review*, Fall 1980, p . 59.

[8]Hodgetts, p. 713.

Becoming Truly International

Another major challenge with social implications for MNCs is that of becoming truly international. In particular, this means hiring more local nationals in place of managers sent over from the host country. Over the last decade, there is evidence that this is beginning to happen more and more. The pattern is often one of sending a manager from the home office and a cadre of support personnel to get things off the ground. Then, as the operation begins to run smoothly, the support people are withdrawn and eventually, the top person is replaced by a local.

In most cases, the biggest problem is replacing the head person with a national. Many MNCs feel uneasy about having someone in charge of the operation who is not an outsider from the host country. To whom will the individual have greatest loyalty: the company of the country? Can the person be trusted with knowledge about how the MNC does business in foreign countries? If a political problem develops, will the manager represent the company or sell it out to the government? These types of questions worry many home office MNC top executives. Until they can resolve in their own mind that foreign operations can often be staffed best with locals and that the latter are trustworthy, the matter of becoming truly international will continue to be a challenge.

SUMMARY

Since the end of World War II, a large number of multinational corporations (MNCs) have sprung up. Although various criteria are often associated with a MNC, three of the most common are: doing business in more than one country, earning a substantial amount of revenue in other countries, and having a nationality mix of managers and a wide distribution of ownership.

There are many reasons that firms go international. Some of the most common include resource extraction, tariff jumping, comparative advantage, and profit. Multinationals offer some very distinct benefits to their host countries. At the same time there are drawbacks that must be considered in putting MNCs in perspective. Both were discussed in this chapter.

In the multinational business arena, MNCs face a number of environments that are quite different from those that they encounter back home. Three of the major ones are cultural, political, and economic. The ramifications of these were described in the chapter together with ways of tempering their negative effects.

Some of the major challenges faced by MNCs are culture shock, value-conflict changes (which have ethical implications), and the problem of managing ongoing international operations. In particular, the problems associated with repatriating personnel back to the home country and the challenge of providing managerial opportunities for women in overseas units were discussed. It was also noted that in becoming truly international, MNCs will have to work ever harder in placing nationals in the top management positions of their foreign operations.

DISCUSSION AND STUDY QUESTIONS

1. In your own words, what is a multinational corporation? Be sure to include some of the criteria that are necessary in order to fit into this category.
2. Why do firms go international? What are some of the major reasons? Identify and describe three.
3. Are there any benefits that MNCs provide to their host country? Explain.
4. Are there any drawbacks that MNCs create for their own home country? Explain.
5. What are some drawbacks that MNCs create for their host country? Identify and describe three of them.
6. In what way does the cultural environment affect MNC operations?
7. How do overseas government attempt to use the political environment to control MNCs? Cite at least two examples.
8. Why is protectionism becoming a major issue in the United States? Is the United States not overreacting? Defend your answer.
9. How can MNCs work to ensure that their operations will not be nationalized by a foreign government? Offer at least four strategies that they can employ.
10. Why do business people taking foreign assignments sometimes suffer culture shock? What causes it? How can it be managed? Be complete in your answer.
11. What kinds of value conflicts do managers in overseas operations sometimes suffer? Cite at least three examples.
12. In managing their overseas operations, many MNCs opt for moderate control. Why?
13. Why are there not more women in top management positions of overseas branches and subsidiaries? What can business do to rectify this situation?
14. For business to become truly international, it must put more nationals into top management positions. Why is this such a major challenge to many MNCs? Explain.

CASES AND INCIDENTS

A Potential Trade War*

Over the last 10 years the trade gap between the United States and Japan has been growing. In the late 1970s it stood at about $7 billion annually; by 1984 it has risen to about $35 billion annually. Nor was the United States

*The material in this case can be found in "Collision Course," *Business Week*, April 8, 1985, pp. 50–55.

alone. Taiwan, Singapore, Hong Kong, and South Korea were also finding their trade gaps with Japan increasing. The result: Many people are beginning to cast around for a villain and they are finding it in the form of Japan. Wrote *Business Week:*

> Top trade officials are suggesting that the Administration for the first time may urge the Federal Communications Commission to use its regulatory authority to squeeze sales of Japanese telecommunications equipment, in effect by nitpicking those exports to death. And that seems to be just the tip of the retaliatory iceberg. An increasingly protectionist Congress now has before it a bill that would limit foreign autos to 15 percent of the U.S. market. Another bill would impose an across-the-board 20 percent surcharge on all imports.[1]

In all fairness to the Japanese, the huge trade gaps are not only a result of their failure to open their doors to foreign goods, although this certainly is one cause of the problem. Other include a strong dollar, which has made American goods less attractive and Japanese goods more attractive; the failure of U.S. corporate officials to learn the Japanese language and to lobby effectively for American interests; and the willingness of American firms to invest in Japan and export the goods back to the States in an effort to improve the bottom line of their financial statements. There is plenty of blame to go around, and everyone has earned some of it.

Regardless of who is to blame, however, a recent *Business Week*/Lou Harris poll reports that there is a deepening U.S. resentment of Japan. Consider the following responses by Americans:

	Yes	*No*	*Unsure*
Why do Japanese products sell well?			
Japanese labor is cheaper	80%	15%	5%
Japanese companies are better managed	56	34	10
Why do American goods sell poorly in Japan?			
U.S. products are too expensive	75%	19%	6%
Japan imposes unfair barriers to U.S. products	54	23	23

Attitudes such as these have many experts convinced that like it or not, the Americans are going to take some action against the Japanese. The only question now is: What will they do?

---

[1]"Collision Course," p. 51.

ANALYSIS

1. What types of government controls can a nation use in regulating or discouraging imports from other countries? Explain.
2. The case reports that some of the problem is being caused by American firms that are importing from Japan. What does this relate about the objectives of MNCs? Can the U.S. government do anything about this? Explain.
3. Do MNCs have any social responsibility to the countries where they sell their products? What are these responsibilities? Explain.

The Proposed Sales Commission

The Andrews Corporation has been a very successful manufacturing firm. Beginning in the early 1950s, it started producing industrial machinery and by 1985 was one of the largest speciality manufacturers in the country. At the same time, it decided to expand by opening an office in a European country. For some time the company had been exporting machinery to Western Europe. By producing the machinery there it could avoid import duties and maintain closer contact with its overseas buyers.

The company opened its new subsidiary last month. The head of the unit, John Williams, had been one of the firm's most successful sales managers in the United States. The company was sure that John could, as the president put it, "work his magic once more."

Two weeks ago John went to visit one of the largest manufacturers in Europe. The latter had expressed an interest in buying some machines from the Andrews Corporation, but they wanted to talk about the specifics of the contract. When John met with the manufacturer's purchasing committee, he was introduced to a Mr. Engel, the purchasing manager. It is he who is responsible for seeing that deliveries are made on time and that the supplier is paid for the goods. The meeting went extremely well. The company seems particularly interested in purchasing seven of Andrews' latest computerized lathes. A decision will be made within 30 days.

Earlier today Mr. Engel called John and met him for a drink. During the meeting, Engel told him the following:

> The company is seriously considering buying your lathe machines. However, I think it would be helpful if you had a sales agent on the inside helping you out. I'd like to be that agent. My fee is 5 percent of the sales price and I use it to handle all of my related expenses, including the members of the committee, many of whom are senior top management officials who you met during our recent meeting. Most top managers, as you know, are badly underpaid and these sales commissions have become standard ways of supplementing their income. Everyone does it. If I were your inside person, I could just about guarantee that you'd get the contract.

Afterward, John returned to the office and began to review what had happened at lunch. He was unsure of what to do. Was Engel telling the truth or lying? More important, was the sales commission legitimate or is this simply a shakedown? Before doing anything, John decided that he should talk to the president back in the States.

ANALYSIS

1. Is there any way for John to check and find out if Engel is telling the truth? Explain.
2. If Engel is telling the truth, is it not unethical to pay this money? After all, is this not a bribe?
3. What does this case relate about doing business in overseas countries? Explain.

Social Issues Funds

Over the past 10 years there have been very active social responsibility strategies implemented by businesses. For example, many firms have chosen to cut back or get out of South Africa because they disapprove of that country's policies. This approach has also been used by brokerage firms. For example, when the Working Assets Money Fund was started in 1983, it had accounts totaling $100,000. Two years later the fund was managing a $63 million portfolio. What makes the fund different from most is that it avoids dealing in debt securities of companies that are involved in South Africa.

There are a number of other funds that also mix investment and ethics. For example, the M.D. Sass Investors Services in New York manages almost $2 billion, including $400 million in public money such as municipal pension funds. Approximately 90 percent of the $400 million has some type of restriction regarding South Africa. In the 1970s there was probably no more than $100 million in social investments. Today that number is in the tens of billions.

There are two types of investors that are most interested in social investments. One consists of middle- and upper-income people who have strong views about political or environmental issues and want their investments to reflect those views. The other is city and state pension funds that are excluded by law from investing in South Africa.

Critics argue that mixing investments and ethics results in problems because it does not always allow the investment fund to take advantage of opportunities. It ties the hands of the money manager. On the other hand, supporters of the policy point to the fact that many of these social-issue funds to do quite well and there seems to be little loss of earnings by excluding certain types of investments from the portfolio.

ANALYSIS

1. If all the investment firms refused to handle stocks of companies in South Africa, would this have much impact on that country? Explain.
2. Are we likely to see a more investment houses adopting a social issues approach to their portfolio management? Why or why not?
3. How important is the financial community in helping control MNCs and ensuring that they act responsibly? Explain.

Individual Social Activism

Chapter Objectives

- To provide a framework of actions for individuals so that they can become more active in promoting social values and attempting to make business more responsive to societal values.

- To develop skills in assessing an organization's responsibilities to its local community through sound research and concerted local action.

- To develop steps in pushing for legislative action directed toward improving an organization's social responsibility.

- To direct attention to the use of class action as an effective means of forcing businesses to assume a more responsive role.

- To discuss the multitude of public-interest groups working for societal goals.

This chapter focuses on the role of the individual and special-interest groups in improving the social responsiveness of business. The perspective of this chapter is that a desired improvement can come about only if people are willing to work for change. Governments will not move and organizations will not be moved unless society demands change. The effectiveness of these demands hinges on their reasonableness and the amount of pressure brought to bear on the business institution. Examples of this type of action abound in popular literature. The unrelenting action that led to California's Proposition 13 to limit taxes was the result of the action of only a few individuals garnering support from the voters. The action of Ralph Nader revolutionized the auto industry and stimulated the whole consumer movement. The actions of minority-led groups such as PUSH, NOW, and FIGHT, in Rochester, New York, have opened corporation doors to individuals formerly discriminated against and the Washington, D.C.–based Ethics Resource Center, which assists companies move from simple truisms on ethics to action programs. In this chapter we offer a framework and strategies for this individual approach to change.

DEVELOPING AN INDIVIDUAL-INITIATED CHANGE STRATEGY

There are four steps in developing an effective individual strategy to improve the social responsiveness of business: (1) defining areas of concern, (2) collecting, analyzing, and interpreting data for the argument for change, (3) determining current political strengths and popular support, and (4) mapping out a tactical strategy.

Defining Areas of Concern

Defining areas of concern means deciding on objectives. For example, before deciding what action should be taken against a steel mill that is polluting, the offending pollution should be identified. Should the individual attack the smokestack emissions, the foul smell from the operations, or the possible corrosive effect of the emissions being released by the company? Attention must be focused on a few issues so that a concerted effort can be made to eliminate one form of pollution. Usually it is a mistake to attack an organization and attempt to correct all of its abuses at once. The efforts would be too diffused over too many fronts, leading to less effective attacks on specific issues. Most actions, if not well channeled, often allow the offender to refute the agruments. A multigrievance action most often leads to the conclusion by the company, the media, and governmental officials that the plaintiff is just antibusiness and not for antipollution, antidiscrimination, or whatever the specific social issue happens to be. The key is to develop credibility with the company, the general public, and potential power sources such as elected and appointed government officials. Once that credibility is achieved, these parties will start listening. It is important to develop a base of support predicated on one's goals and ability to discuss the problems rationally.

Information Gathering and Fact Finding

The second step is information gathering and fact finding. The following questions should be considered:

- What is the problem for the country?
- What is the problem for this locale?
- What is the contribution of this company to the problem?
- What social problems result from this company's action?
- What are these social problems in terms of dollar costs, human suffering, and reduction in the community's quality of life?
- What are other companies doing about the problem?
- What is the company's financial health, and can it make the proposed changes?
- What is the cost of the proposed changes?
- How long will it take to make these changes?
- What sort of commitment would the company have to make in terms of labor time, production disruption, and so on, in order to adopt the proposal?

The person who is advocating action must be fully prepared for the ensuing debate and controversy. Ill-prepared persons lose causes because of their failure to anticipate counterarguments. Government regulatory agencies cannot base their decisions on emotionalism but, instead, must rely on facts and principles that can be justified in an objective, judicial manner. Much of the success of Ralph Nader's approach was based on the use of well-researched arguments and documented cases.

The importance of being well prepared cannot be overemphasized. For example, a midwestern utility filed for a 33 percent rate increase in its domestic electric rates. The company argued that its revenues were inadequate for effective operations. A consumer group that opposed the rate increase did not argue that the utility was less efficient than others; it presented only the petitions of three thousand persons who opposed the rate increase. The public service commission granted a 10 percent increase in this case. The consumer group probably could have successfully argued to maintain existing rates if it had exposed the following facts about this utility:

- The utility was in the upper quartile in consumer electric rates.
- The utility had a greater administrative cost than did 15 other utilities that were surveyed.
- The utility had lost millions of dollars in an Environmental Protection Agency suit against a plant it was building, when it failed to conform to specified plans.
- The suit was filed after repeated warnings by the EPA to meet requirements.

- Administrative salaries ranked in the upper quartile of managerial salaries for the industry.

Time and time again, public-interest groups are frustrated in their attempts because they lack factual knowledge of the issues. That factual knowledge need not necessarily come from a paid consultant; it can be obtained from library sources, public records, and industry survey techniques. The major cost in this research is time, something the individual must be willing to give. Research may show that the questionable business practice presently in effect is really the best that can be done with the present technology or that the firm being challenged cannot really afford to do much without terminating services to the community with a resultant loss of jobs.

Assessing Political Strength

The third step is obtaining information in order to assess the political strength that the cause will muster. The *number* of people who support a proposal is important; yet, the *power* of those who support it is also crucial. Political leaders and other powerful persons can do much to influence a business firm or industry to change its practices. Customers of the company and its investors have a more pronounced effect on a business and its practices than does an unrelated collection of individuals. For example, part of the effort to change the practices of multinational corporations in South Africa was the result of institutional investors pressing reform issues at stockholders' meetings. Boycotts have been organized by church groups against companies that have production facilities in South Africa. These independent interest groups promote actions that can affect the profits of the organization. The women's movement group NOW, in urging passage of the equal rights amendment, attempted to promote economic sanctions against states that did not pass the amendment.

A Strategy for Action

The fourth step is mapping out a strategy. Once the information is gathered, the facts should begin to surface and there should be a clear understanding of the problem and all of its ramifications. In this fourth step it must be determined what, if anything, should be done to change the actions of the offending business that will correct the problem. Once the information is assembled, the person or group can formulate a strategy to effect this change.

One of the preliminary steps of the action strategy might be to decide what, if any, legal action can be taken. If it is found that the company in question is breaking a law, the course of action should be to convince the proper authorities to take the appropriate steps to effect change. If an illegality is not uncovered, some other form of action can be planned.

POLITICAL STRATEGIES TO INCREASE THE SOCIAL RESPONSIVENESS OF BUSINESS

The individual strategy to improve the social responsibility of business includes advocating political actions. An individual or interest group can recommend a social change through legislation and other governmental actions. Political actions should not be overlooked as a way to bring about social change. Even though it may not seem to cause immediate changes, the political approach can lead to more permanent social changes. Often the social responsibility of business is shaped by legal constraints, and so those wishing to change the actions of business firms may well find that a permanent solution to the problem can only be some form of legislative remedy. If the problem cannot be solved through legislative actions or private investment, there may still be recourse through governmental funding of the business to induce the desired social changes. Through either tax write-offs or outright federal subsidies, business can be enticed to make changes for increased social responsibility. An important step for any social action is to find out what the government can do.

Political Action Committees (PACs)

Individuals or interest groups that want to increase the sensitivity of government to the social responsibility of business might build a long-term strategy of drawing up political platforms and approving candidates that support desired social issues. Groups such as the Sierra Club take this approach, speaking out for and against candidates who favor specific social issues. Unions support candidates who support labor. On a smaller scale, individuals and local interest groups can do the same. They can assess the platforms of politicians seeking election or re-election and analyze their voting records. Often a candidate's rhetoric and his or her actions are different. The individual or interest group should publicize the candidate's voting records and promises and then back those who support social responsibility. This active political role is the underpinning of the entire democratic process and should not be ignored.

Lobbying

A second method is lobbying. For those who wish to change the social responsiveness of business, one approach is to change or create laws through a lobbying effort. Local communities' laws can be changed. For example, zoning regulations can do much to improve the quality of life for a local community, and they can also regulate the types of industry that seek to locate in an area. Local pollution and noise-control laws can effectively curb offensive business operations. At the federal level, lobbying activities can shape laws that pertain to corporate responsibility. Passage of the Information Disclosure Act was partly the result of groups seeking to curb the abuses of corporation payoffs to foreign and domestic political leaders. Automobile safety and pollution-control legislation can be tied directly to the lobbying efforts of Nader's and other consumer and environmental groups. Similarly, the Fair Credit Reporting Act and Information Disclosure Act were the result of strong lobbying activities by consumer groups nationwide.

A lobbyist is part of the democratic process. Individuals or groups can hire professional lobbyists full time or part time. An interest group usually submits to the lobbyist a detailed analysis of the proposal and various facts associated with it. The lobbyist can then be hired to argue the proposal before the proper legislative bodies. The individual or group can also, of course, directly contact the particular government representative without going through the lobbying process. But the professional lobbyist will have greater expertise than the amateurs.

Writing Letters to Elected Representatives

Writing letters to elected representatives (at the local, state, or federal level) is an often-maligned method. There is a general feeling that this approach does not produce results. But if legislators receive enough mail on a topic from a variety of constituents, they will be almost forced to act. Often, elected officials use their mail to judge the validity of their constituents' complaints on a particular issue. A volume of mail will definitely influence a politician, always sensitive to reelection. A more organized approach is a write-in campaign. If many individuals are interested enough to compose their own letters on a particular subject and then send them to their elected representatives, the latter will seriously consider the wishes expressed in them.

A letter campaign will be most effective (1) if individuals write to their own representatives, compose their own letters, and not use preprinted or form statements, and (2) if enough individuals write in. Figure 15.1 shows a letter from the Burlington Northern Railroad to its shareholders, recommending that its investors write to their representatives to show their opposition to the coal slurry bills introduced in Congress. Through intense lobbying by the railroads and environmental organizations and the letter-writing campaigns, the slurry pipeline bill was defeated.

Local Political Actions

Most of the discussion so far has been directed toward the federal government, and many of the same processes used to influence federal legislation and policy are equally effective at the local level. Local legislation can also be

BURLINGTON NORTHERN

DEAR BN STOCKHOLDER: June 20, 1978

For the past four years, Burlington Northern has worked with
many other organizations in actively opposing legislation that
would give federal eminent domain to coal slurry pipelines.
We have done this because there is no valid need for a
duplicate system of coal transportation, and because these
pipeline proposals represent a threat to the future coal
traffic of your company.

Thus far, because of the united opposition of many interests--
both public and private--the slurry advocates have been
unsuccessful in obtaining federal authority to condemn private
property for pipeline rights-of-way. They have, however,
managed to move a bill, H.R. 1609, through Congressional
committees to a point where it may be voted on by the House of
Representatives, possibly in early July.

To prepare for the possibility of a vote by the full House--
and perhaps by the Senate--we are asking all interested
employees to get in touch with their congressmen and senators
to urge that they oppose all the coal slurry bills: H.R. 1609
and Senate bills S.707 and S.3046. We also will be enlisting
the assistance of our retirees in a similar manner.

The purpose of this letter is to ask you as a shareholder to
add your voice to those of BN people in opposition to this
legislation. It is particularly important that we get our
viewpoint across to congressmen from outside the territory
directly served by your railroad. In light of our common
interest--and the public interest as well--we urge you to
consider the issues and then make your views known to your
senators and congressman from the district in which you live.
To assist you in doing so there is enclosed a copy of our
GRASS ROOTS REPORT, summarizing major arguments against coal
slurry development.

Sincerely,

Norman M. Lorentzsen   Louis W. Menk
President and Chief Executive Officer   Chairman of the Board

FIGURE 15.1   Letter to Stockholder of Burlington Northern. *Reprinted
with permission.*

directed toward local firms. Even if the government action is only a letter
of censure, its effect on the business firm's practices will be pronounced.
The work of FIGHT against Kodak Corporation effectively elicited support
from the local government for the group's demand for more jobs for blacks
in the Rochester, New York, area.

LEGAL STRATEGIES TO INCREASE THE SOCIAL RESPONSIVENESS OF BUSINESS

Besides political influence, direct legal actions should be considered. In particular, the use of restraint orders, class action suits, individual suits, suits against governmental inaction, and liability suits against corporate officials can be applied to increase the social responsibility of business. Which of these legal approaches to use depends on the situation and the degree of good faith exhibited by the business involved. A legal expert is needed to decide which would be the most effective.

Restraining Orders

One legal action that can be used against an offending business organization is the restraining order. A judge can issue a restraining order when a particular activity appears to be damaging to another party. An individual or interest group can seek a restraining order to curb some business practice that is considered socially irresponsibile *if* that act can be proved to the judge's satisfaction to be harmful to another party. Restraining orders have been used in many stituations. They are invoked only until a full court hearing can be held and the case brought to trial or appeal. For example, if a labor strike will, in the judge's determination, badly harm a third party, or the strike is considered by the judge to be illegal, there are grounds for a restraining order. The dumping of nuclear wastes, the building of a nuclear power plant, dam construction, and strip mining operations all have been delayed by restraining orders. In all cases, the restraining orders were temporary injunctions until the dispute was legally resolved.

Class Action Suits

Class action suits were discussed in the chapter on consumerism but are included here because they can be applied to more than just marketing and product liability. Class action suits can be an effective means of litigation against any company. The combined resources of several groups of people and the power of the suit demanding damages for all concerned have a greater political effect. The costs of such a suit will have a pronounced impact on the firm being sued.

The use of the class action suit mushroomed in the late 1960s after the Supreme Court's decision that an individual could sue in behalf of other injured parties. In 1974, however, the Supreme Court placed a restriction on the use of class action suits, ruling that all parties to the aggrieved suit must be notified as to the litigation, no matter what the cost. This 1974 decision, in effect, made it more difficult to sue in the public interest. If a class action suit was instituted because a company was polluting a given river, what the court decided was that, in effect, all users of the river would have to be notified. Such a notification campaign would be prohibitively costly and difficult, if not impossible, to carry out. Thus, class action suits have diminished in popularity as a legal means of pressing social issues.

Legal Suits Against Government

Still another legal action that may be taken is a suit filed against a governmental body for inaction. Although only a few such suits have been filed, many people are impatient about the lack of action by government, for example, the inaction by consumer protection agencies and other regulatory bodies. The courts have been increasingly receptive to suits against the government. Initially, the general public could not sue the government because individuals suing the government would, in effect, be suing themselves. Since the early 1950s, however, this has not been the case. Through broader interpretations of the law, an individual can now sue governmental agencies.[1]

Another strategy for increasing the social responsibility of business is to act as a watchdog over governmental regulatory bodies to ensure that they are making business organizations obey the law. If the governmental body does little to enforce its regulatory powers or acts in a manner that is contrary to its purpose, then the watchdog or interest group can file suit to force the agency to conform to the law. For example, the United Autoworkers Union filed a lawsuit demanding that the Occupational Safety and Health Administration (OSHA) lower formaldehyde limits, claiming that OSHA had "indefensibly been resisting such changes" to the detriment of the safety and health of members.[2] Agencies such as the Food and Drug Administration, the Corps of Engineers, and the Nuclear Regulatory Commission all have been cited for being unresponsive to society's demands. The Food and Drug Administration has come under increasing attack because of its reluctance to ban carcinogenic substances from foods. The Corps of Engineers has been criticized for its riverbed modifications and dam construction that have little regard for their benefits or damage. The Nuclear Regulatory Agency has been under attack for promoting the use of nuclear energy without ensuring that the construction, maintenance, and operations of the facilities protect society from a nuclear holocaust. In several cases, the courts have issued delays and injunctions in favor of the offended person or interest group. In the future, dissatisfied citizens may more readily question the methods and the data of governmental agencies, and the courts may be more willing to arbitrate between unresponsive government agencies and societal demands.

[1]William L. Prosser, ed., *Handbook of the Law of Torts*, 4th ed. (St. Paul: West Publishing, 1971), pp. 970–987.

[2]"OSHA, UAW Tangle on Formaldehyde," *American Machinist*, November 1982, p. 51.

Liability Suits Against Corporate Officials

A fourth legal approach that individuals or interest groups can use to enforce a business's socially responsible actions is filing liability suits against its managers. As indicated earlier, suits have been filed against businesses for criminal liability. The most noteworthy case was the suit filed in Indiana against the Ford Motor Company. It is reasonable to predict that within the next few years criminal liability suits will be filed against individual corporate officers for actions taken by their organizations. For example, a company that makes an unsafe product may well find that a suit is directed not at the impersonal corporation but at the corporate official who was directly or even indirectly responsible for the product to be manufactured and sold. Liability insurance for teachers, doctors, and other professional groups has recently been expanded to cover corporate officials.[3] If a corporate official allows water pollution to continue in violation of the law, an individual or interest group may try to seek a remedy through the Environmental Protection Agency or may directly sue the corporate manager personally for the infraction. Likewise, corporate managers can be sued for the company's discriminatory actions, product safety violations or false advertising. Well known entertainers are sometimes sued because of the allegedly misleading advertising claims they make. Suits of this type may lead to more corrective actions and more responsive organizations. In the past, a suit against the company hurt only the company, not the managers in control of the company. Because of a suit, a corporate official may suffer economically and personally through adverse public exposure. Even if the organization pays the official's liability insurance premiums, he or she is still not immune. If the official is repeatedly sued, the insurance premium may become so high that the company can no longer afford to retain the sued individual. Such drastic actions by individuals or interest groups can make corporate officials more responsive. The legal system can force companies to be more socially responsible. The statement of one automobile executive that "safety doesn't pay" may not be true in the future. Safety will pay, if not through rewards to the company in increased profits, then through the assessment of penalities for unsafe action on both the corporate and the individual manager levels.

STRATEGIES TO MAKE BUSINESS MORE SOCIALLY RESPONSIBLE

Besides legal and political means, various other tactics can be used against socially irresponsible business firms, such as media campaigns, informational picketing, petition drives, and consumer boycotts. Each of these alone is often not sufficient to produce lasting changes, but they can be used along with political and legal strategies to obtain the desired changes.

[3]Tony McAdams and Robert C. Miljus, "Growing Criminal Liability of Executives," *Harvard Business Review*, April 1977, pp. 36–59.

Using the Media

Media exposure is an effective means of publicizing issues. Such exposure can be through press releases or newsworthy items for newspapers, radio, and/or television. Talk shows on radio or television can also be used. The idea is not just to obtain exposure, but to inform the general public of the issues that need to be reported. The individual or interest group must skillfully present the facts in order to gain support for its cause. Press releases or written position statements can be sent to news outlets (newspapers, radio, and television). Often these news outlets are connected with one of the major news services such as United Press International or Associated Press. These news releases are then sent around the country for use in local and syndicated news outlets. An outlet may use a press release if it seems newsworthy to the audience in its target area. The wording of the press release obviously is important in attracting such widespread attention. Factual data should be presented in a style that will interest the general public. The person or group that can obtain the interest and sympathies of the media can do much to aid a cause, though media exposure alone is not enough; other actions are also needed.

Informational Picketing

Another social action is informational picketing, in which individuals pass out to the general public written information about an issue. Unions use this approach to arouse public sympathies. Although a union cannot formally call a strike against an organization that it does not represent, it can provide information to the public near the site of nonunion organizations. Individuals or interest groups can use the same approach. Giving information to employees and customers can be an effective way to change a business organization's actions. The information packet can list some of the organization's previous actions. The source of the facts should be documented. After the facts are presented, then the arguments for the interest group's proposal should be made. As with all approaches, the informational handout should not be inflammatory, distorted, or undocumented. The purpose of this method is to provide information in order to gain the public's support, not to alienate it. The effectiveness of informational picketing is hard to assess. For example, part of the success of the lettuce and grape boycotts, led by César Chavez, can be attributed to the informational picketing that explained the plight of the migrant workers in California and to Chavez's efforts to change the pay and working conditions of these workers.

Petition Drives

Petition drives can be effective in gathering support from the general population. Petitions in themselves mean little unless there is corresponding pressure for change by either business or government regulators of business. A petition is an instrument of passive support, and what is usually needed in social activism is some form of active support by the larger society. Petitions have somewhat more power than do form letters that are sent to legislators; they show support, but not active support. What is needed is some further demonstration of support. Petition drives alone do not offer enough support to produce changes in most cases, but they are an important tool in the arsenal of planned change that individuals and groups can use in inducing business to become more socially responsible.

Product or Service Boycotts

Another social action is product or service boycotts. A boycott is the consumers' refusal to purchase a particular item or service. Product boycotts have been successfully applied to a multitude of products. Celery, grapes, and grapefruit were targets of boycotts as part of César Chavez's strategy to improve conditions for migrant workers in California. Another widely publicized boycott was that directed against several firms for doing business in South Africa because of its apartheid policies, though it did not change those policies. Other companies such as J. P. Stevens, Farah, and Coors have been targets of boycotts by union groups because of their antiunion stance. Other examples include boycotts of sugar, coffee, and meats that led to reductions in prices. The boycotts supressed demand for the products so that the market forced a lowering of the prices. The key to a boycott is to have enough consumer support to reduce demand.

STRATEGIES FOR EMPLOYEES OF AN UNRESPONSIVE BUSINESS

Extra precautions need to be taken when an individual takes an active stand against a business activity. Such action is called *corporate whistle blowing*.[4] Corporate whistle blowing involves a high degree of personal risk, and an individual could very well lose his or her job. An organization is composed of many power coalitions with many vested interests. Although the upper level of management may support the whistle blower's actions, other levels of management may not, and so the whistle blower must proceed with caution.

The employee also has an obligation to the company. Concern for business practices and procedures should be aired first with established channels within the organization. Legally, this is the most desirable course of action, and it is the fairest. An individual should assume, until proven otherwise, that the officials of an organization really do want to act in a socially responsible way. Therefore, the organization ought to be given a chance to make the necessary corrections on its own, internally, without the adverse publicity associated with a public airing of the issues.

[4] David Clutterbuck, "Blowing the Whistle on Corporate Misconduct," *International Management,* January 1980, pp. 14–18.

One of the best strategies that can be used by the concerned employee is to encourage the upper levels of management to support the employees' exposure of socially irresponsible actions. Internal investigation and resolution will demonstrate management's desire to act in socially responsible ways. Only after exhausting internal sources should the employee seek outside publicity to resolve the problem.

SUMMARY

In this chapter we described actions that individuals can take in order to improve business's social responsiveness. First, steps to develop a strategy for initiating change in a business were outlined, including (1) defining areas of concern, (2) collecting, analyzing, and interpreting data for the argument for change, (3) determining current political strength and popular support, and (4) mapping out a tactical strategy. Strategies can include political and legal actions to build public support for the cause.

Political strategies include political action committees working to support or defeat a candidate for public office, lobbying for a change in public policy, letterwriting campaigns to elected representatives, and local political actions to make businesses more socially responsible.

Legal strategies to increase a business's social responsiveness is a second approach. Obtaining a restraining order can force a business to obey the law. The use of class action suits can bring about corrective actions and deter other businesses from contemplating or committing similar actions. Another legal strategy is suing government agencies that fail to exercise their legal power to protect society. Still another strategy is bringing liability suits against corporate officers, instead of against corporations.

A final way in which change can be instituted is by increasing public pressure on business. Gaining the media's cooperation can help build public support. Informational picketing makes consumers aware of a business's irresponsible actions. Petition drives and boycotts also can affect business actions.

Social activism is an essential to ensure that government curbs business abuses and that business acts responsibly. When the social activist is an employee of the irresponsible business, he or she should proceed carefully. The responsibility that the activist has to himself or herself and to the company is important.

DISCUSSION AND STUDY QUESTIONS

1. The first step toward improving a corporation's social responsibility is defining areas of concern. What is meant by this statement?
2. What are the other strategic steps in improving an organization's social responsibility?

3. How can government use tax write-offs and/or federal subsidies to encourage business to act in a more socially responsible fashion? Cite some examples.
4. What is lobbying, and how can it be of value in enforcing social responsibility?
5. Can local political actions help bring about a more socially responsible business firm? How?
6. What is a restraining order? How does it work? How can it help those seeking to force a company to be more socially responsive?
7. What are class action suits? Are they effective?
8. Can one sue the government for failure to provide, for example, consumer safety? Cite two examples and relate their relevance to social responsibility.
9. Can interest groups bring liability suits against corporate officials? Explain.
10. One form of social action against irresponsive businesses is informational picketing. How does this work?
11. How does a product or service boycott work? Give two examples.

CASES AND INCIDENTS

A Matter of Priority

The Acme Steel Company was located in a medium-sized (population 50,000) midwestern city. It was the largest employer in the area. Acme's president, Richard Yettar, Jr., age 61, had inherited the business from his father. Richard, Sr., founded the company in 1900 and managed it until his death in 1947.

Acme had never been a very profitable firm. A 1 or 2 percent annual return was considered quite good. Because of this low ROI, little money was available to replace or modernize the plant. Most of the equipment was badly out of date and inadequate. Mr. Yettar felt helpless. He could not justify paying 12 percent for a long-term loan to buy new equipment when the most he could derive from the investment would be 2 percent. He reasoned that it was better to continue operating with the poor equipment.

In February Mr. Yettar received a telephone call from the mayor, Mr. Anthony Grouber. The mayor abruptly told Mr. Yettar that a group of irate citizens, calling themselves the Committee for Clean Air (CCA), was in his office demanding that Acme cease polluting the air and install special antipollution devices. The CCA felt that pollution coming from the plant was intolerable. The group was especially angry with Acme because Mr. Yettar's secretary had told them the week before that he was too busy to be bothered by them. The mayor suggested that perhaps it would be best for all parties if a meeting was held the next day. Mr. Yettar reluctantly agreed to attend.

The following afternoon all parties gathered in the mayor's office. After the CCA presented its case, Mr. Yettar took the floor. He quietly outlined Acme's profit picture. He explained that although he appreciated the committee's suggestions, it was nevertheless impossible for the firm to implement them at this time. After answering a few questions regarding the company's profit position, Mr. Yettar kindly thanked them for allowing him to speak. The meeting adjourned shortly thereafter.

The following Monday the mayor called again. "Listen, Richard, you'd better do something about that pollution problem and fast. The CCA attorney, Bob Fairfax, was just here, and he informed me that the committee intends to take your company to court. They're going to ask that you either immediately install antipollution equipment or pay damages to the committee." Mr. Yettar immediately called his attorney, Frank Hopper. The two men were in conference the rest of the day. The company lawyer, Mr. Hopper, offered the following advice:

> This approach is being used by a number of similar groups around the country. In almost all instances the companies have backed down and made the necessary costly changes. However, some firms have chosen to fight the action. My personal feelings are that there is little to be gained by a court fight, and much to lose. Not only would it be expensive, but if you should win the case, you would still create much hostility in the town. For instance, you might have a lot of husbands working here who will support you initially, but their wives may have a different view. Few husbands are going to back you over their wives' objections. Did you count how many women are on the CCA? Why, most of them are females. Furthermore, the leader is none other than Connie Ferguson, the wife of one of our own foremen. I think you should compromise with them now before this emotionally packed issue gets out of hand. Of course, if you choose to fight it, I'll back you all the way. It's all up to you.

The following morning Mr. Yettar called in Les Henderson, the head of his finance department. After relating the events of the last few days, Mr. Yettar asked, "What do you think we should do, Les?" Les answered:

> Well, Mr. Yettar, I've gone over our finances very carefully, and I estimate that it will cost about $100,000 to install antipollution equipment. We just don't have that kind of money available. Conditions are extremely tight, and the way the economy is moving, things will probably get worse before they get better. If we go to court, we might win or, at least, delay an action. This would give us some needed time to put aside some earnings for the new equipment. I realize that sooner or later we will probably have to install the antipollution equipment, but believe me, from a financial standpoint, it isn't possible within the next five years. We're in a very tight financial pinch. It's easy for the CCA to ask for changes; they don't have to meet a payroll and pay suppliers. If we are forced to install this equipment right now, we will have to cut back our work force immediately.

Mr. Yettar thanked him for his analysis of the situation. The president then sat down and began sketching out a list of the company's objectives. When he was finished, he went back over the list and assigned priorities. In this way he hoped to determine whether or not he should agree to the demands of the CCA or pursue a court fight.

ANALYSIS

1. What objectives do you think are on Mr. Yettar's list? Be specific and include at least five objectives.
2. Assign the priorities that you believe Mr. Yettar would give each.
3. What should Mr. Yettar do now? Explain in detail.

A Revised Long-Range Plan

Members of the long-range planning department of a medium-sized utility began filing into the conference room for a meeting. By 8:48 A.M. the eleventh and last member had taken his seat. At 9:00 A.M. sharp Mr. Ralph Russell, the new vice-president of long-range planning, entered. This was Mr. Russell's first meeting since being hired the week before. Although the department members knew very little about their new boss, the grapevine indicated that he was tough, cool, and efficient and that he had been hired away from a major competitor at a substantial increase in salary. The new vice-president walked to the small podium at the end of the table, adjusted his notes, looked up to see if everyone was ready, and addressed the group as follows:

Gentlemen, I am Ralph Russell, your new department vice-president. Over the next few months I am sure I will have ample opportunity to meet you all individually. For the moment, however, I prefer to get right down to business. I have spent the last few days reading over the company's five-year plan that this department has formulated for approval by top management. Overall, it seems very good. I am sure you undoubtedly know your job. However, there seems to be one major void. Social responsibilities are not mentioned anywhere in the plan. I find it difficult to believe that a utility such as ours can overlook such a critical area. In particular, I am concerned with such social issues as hiring disadvantaged persons and protecting the environment.

Let me discuss these in the order that I've presented them. First, let's examine the issue of employment of disadvantaged, hard-core unemployed workers. Many firms around the country are employing individuals who previously were unable to hold down full-time jobs. Some of these workers were poorly educated; others had a very bad attitude toward work. Today, many of these disadvantaged workers are productive employees. Some of you are undoubtedly thinking that the auto makers are in a position to do this but that the utilities are not. This is not a valid conclusion. The fact is that utilities are very interested in and capable of hiring the hard-core unemployed. Consolidated Edison of New York is an example.

They have made an effort to hire blacks and Puerto Ricans over the last two years. This utility has taken the position that social responsibility is much more than good community relations and a maintenance of the status quo. Social responsibility also includes the community's future needs and demands. As more and more attention is given to providing job opportunities for the unemployed, utilities must get involved with hard-core unemployed programs. We cannot wait until public opinion demands action; we must anticipate this trend and take early and effective action. These are some of the reasons that I think this social issue should be included in our long-range plans.

The second issue is the ecological movement that is currently sweeping America. Some people think it is only a passing fad. Whether or not this is true, utilities are much more deeply involved with this issue than most other firms are and, for example, are often accused of polluting the air. According to our chief engineer, Mark Harrison, our firm throws about a half million tons of pollutants into the air every year. So far we have been successful in persuading the local city government that this has had little effect on the quality of air, but how long do you think this will continue? What would happen if the city council suddenly decided to pass and enforce new air-quality regulations? How much would it cost us to adhere to such an ordinance? I hope you get my point. If we do not become cognizant of environmental issues, we may find ourselves in serious trouble when the government steps in to require new standards for environmental control. This concern should not necessarily be confined to air pollution. How much damage are we doing to aquatic life when we draw cold water from the nearby bay and return it five degrees warmer? As the demands for electric power increase, it appears that there will be a corollary increase in thermal pollution. Where does this situation leave us in the future?

In summary, it seems to me that we must recognize these two social issues in our long-range planning. A planner's job is more than extrapolating the present. It also entails anticipating the future. One danger that many utilities face is underestimating the dynamic aspects of society. Destruction of the environment didn't occur overnight. Everyone knew the effects that American industry was having on the environment, but few people were moved to do anything about it. Suddenly everyone seemed to change his or her attitude, and we now have a major problem.

As vice-president of long-range planning, I am determined that this will not happen in this utility. We are going to plan for all contingencies, including social issues. During the next week I want all of you to spend some time carefully thinking about these two issues. Go to the public library and read some of the current literature on the topic. Next Monday we will have another meeting, at which time I want everyone to be prepared to discuss these issues and how they can be incorporated into long-range plans.

ANALYSIS

1. What does Mr. Russell mean by "a planner's job is more than extrapolating the present. It entails anticipating the future"?
2. Do you agree with the theme of Mr. Russell's talk? Explain.

3. How would you account for the fact that some firms do not incorporate social issues into their long-range planning?

Social Responsibility in the Year 2000

Jim Eastwood, a graduate student at a major midwestern university, had been working on a term paper for two months. The title of his paper was "Social Responsibility of Business in the Year 2000." Jim visited with the presidents of five large and 10 medium-sized firms and spent two weeks in the library in preparation for his paper. The abstract for his paper read as follows:

The social responsibility of business can be defined as the obligation that private enterprise owes to society in general and subgroups of that society in particular. Although this is a nebulous definition, two major points can be extracted. First, social responsibility is both a broad and a narrow obligation. Second, to define social responsibility in operational terms, it is necessary to deal with business firms on an individual basis. Because this is not within the scope of this paper, attention will be devoted instead to (1) the general categories of social responsibility and (2) the changes that can be expected over the next quarter century. After interviewing 15 company presidents and doing secondary research in the library, four general categories of business's social responsibility seem to emerge. First, there is an obligation to maintain good community relations. This entails contributing to local projects (for example, serving on the chamber of commerce) and becoming generally integrated into community life. Second, there is a humanistic obligation. During the past decade this second obligation has been to break down the barriers of discrimination in employment and to hire the hard-core unemployables. This is much more action oriented than the first objective because it is directed less at the entire community and more at a specific segment of that community. Third, there is an environmental obligation of business. Air and water pollution are examples. Fourth and last, there is an obligation to the consumer that includes all individuals, groups, and companies that purchase goods or services from the business firm. But principal attention should be given to the retail purchaser.

How will these four social responsibilities of business change between now and the year 2000? The answer is different for each area. For example, community relations will not be radically altered. Business will continue to emphasize good relations with the local community, and the latter will reciprocate. It is a mutually advantageous objective for both business and the community. The other three areas undoubtedly will change a great deal. First, hiring hard-core unemployed will take on new dimensions. At present, business is recruiting and training unemployables in order to turn them into productive workers. By the year 2000 this concept will be expanded to incorporate more than just the traditionally hard-core unemployables. For example, as greater emphasis is placed on creative thinking and computers, modern technology will replace semiskilled and even traditionally skilled employees. Business will have to devote more attention to retraining programs. There should also be strides made by women and minority members in securing more responsible positions. Second, although air and water pollution are ecological targets today, these problems will be largely solved by 2000. In their place will be other ecological problems, specifically, the population explosion. Business will become involved not only in manufacturing birth control devices but also in curbing population growth. More attention also will be given to farming techniques as well as urban problems. Third, the consumerism movement will still be present, with far more legislation to protect the retail purchaser. In addition, political party affiliation will have changed. If only because of the increase in the educational level, people will have begun to vote more for the person than for the party. This will produce a more responsible form of representation, which will lead to an increase of consumer power in Washington.

ANALYSIS

1. Do you agree with Jim's four categories of social responsibility? What changes would you make?
2. Do you think his definition of social responsibility will be valid in 2000? Explain.
3. What do you think of his predictions for social responsibility in 2000?

CASE STUDY FOR PART IV

Weyerhaeuser's Quality-of-Life Strategies Regarding Public Recreation*

The following interview was held with Mr. J. E. Sheppard, a land management executive for Weyerhaeuser Company.

Interviewer: Mr. Sheppard, would you tell me a little history about Weyerhaeuser's high-yield forestry and land use.

Mr. Sheppard: Throughout its history, Weyerhaeuser Company has been characterized by its intention to own, retain, and acquire productive timberlands. Three-quarters of a century of such activity has left us owning nearly 6 million acres of highly productive soils for tree growing. A little more than half is in the mid-South and deep South. The rest is in the Pacific Northwest.

    The pattern of ownership, more than any other single factor, is what throws us right into the middle of outdoor recreation and conservation issues. Running a fast second—

*The research and written case information were presented at the Case Research Association Symposium (New Orleans, 1984) and were evaluated by the CRA's Editorial Board. This case was prepared by Robert D. Hay, University of Arkansas, and Ed Sheppard, Weyerhaeuser Company, distributed by the Case Research Association. All rights reserved to the authors and the Case Research Association. Used with permission.

particularly among those who are critical of how we oper-ate—is the company's highly intensive approach to forest management for commercial tree growth.

Our definition of "conservation" is not the currently ac-cepted, somewhat loose, one of "saving" or "preserving" a resource. The definition we use goes back to that of Gifford Pinchot, at the time of the formation of the National Forest system. He defined conservation as the wise use of re-sources."

Our forestry efforts are aimed at utilizing the timber re-source and the underlying soils wisely, in such a way as to conserve them for future continued use. To that end, most of the company's lands are managed under an inten-sive, even-aged program for growing high-value softwoods; pine, Douglas fir, hemlock, and similar species. This "high-yield forestry" program involves clearcut harvesting, rapid reforestation with nursery-grown seedlings, periodic thin-ning and fertilization, and protection of the timber stands from fire, insects, disease, and heavy brush competition.

The cost of this is extremely high. Weyerhaeuser's total capitalized forestry costs—including road building, prepa-ration of harvest sites for replanting, the planting operation itself, and various silvicultural techniques—average nearly $70 million per year nationwide. Planting alone is a tremen-dous expenditure, because we put between 100 and 150 million seedlings in the ground each year.

Interviewer: The United States does not have a tradition of large private landowners granting use of their "estates" for such pursuits as hiking, hunting, or fishing. We've always had so much open land that we have given over much of our recreation and conservation policy to the government as predominant landowner. Even where the land was privately owned, un-less it was fenced in or otherwise clearly marked, we have tended to recreate on it as though it were *public* land—with little thought to the usually invisible landowner.

Mr. Sheppard: Any private landowner's needs and constraints differ from those of the Park Service, Forest Service, BLM, state agen-cies, or any other public, governmental entity. Very simply, our constituencies are different. Where the public land man-ager responds to one variety of public users groups, from timber bidders to birdwatchers, from hunters to hiking clubs . . . we are focused on a different variety.

In Weyerhaeuser's case, our constituency includes cus-tomers, who may be far distant from our mills and woods, but nonetheless depend on them for reliable supplies of goods at competitive prices . . . employees, whose livelihoods are tied in with the economic and social ramifications of the company's activities . . . shareholders, whose own worth in economic terms is tied to our performance, as gauged by the stock markets of the world.

Nonmanufacturing landowners would have a different set of constituencies. Farm woodlot owners, for example, would probably list family, friends, and future generations as "constituencies" of their decisions about land and forest management. Their economic constraints would be different . . . aesthetics might play a larger role because of their personal closeness to the land they manage.

But neither they nor we are truly constrained to view the hunter, the backpacker, the rock hound as "constituents" of our main job. The governmental agencies *are* so constrained.

I don't think I can stress too much what a differnce that makes. In effect, it is a difference of ownership.

The governmental land, being public, is partly owned by each of us. Each group that can find a voice properly *should* be able to state its preferences and judgments on policy.

In the case of private industrial lands, however, those same judgments are inappropriate—because they are being made, all to often by people who may have an *interest* in what we do, but no *investment* in it, or responsibility to it.

Interviewer: You've mentioned various resource contributors (customers, owners, employees) who have a stake in Weyerhaeuser's operations. Do you think that Weyerhaeuser has a social responsibility to society-at-large?

Mr. Sheppard: Even with purely private land ownership, there is still a strong element of societal stewardship. Whether it be through regulation, or less tangibly through social pressures, the people around the landowner quite frequently let it be known that they, too must be considered in land-use decisions . . . or at least satisfied that your decisions make sense.

Interviewer: So you do recognize your responsibility to society?

Mr. Sheppard: Yes, we do.

Interviewer: Could you expand on this notion?

Mr. Sheppard: The magnitude of its investment in forestry—played off against the fact that the continued ability to operate is a social privelege, not a right—is what leads Weyerhaeuser to a fairly open corporate posture toward recreation. The company began taking that approach four decades ago—when neither our forestry investment nor our expectations for tree growth were as high as today.

In 1941, Weyerhaeuser dedicated the nation's first tree farm, the Clemons, near Montesano, Washington. We declared then our intention to devote those lands to growing trees as a perpetual crop. One major implication of that action was the need to protect our lands from fire, as well as manage them for forestry values.

That meant, in turn, that the old steam rail logging days—which had been coming to an end anyway—would rapidly be replaced by the more flexible use of logging roads and trucks. And roads meant access—not just for the company, but for other people as well.

At the time, Weyerhaeuser was still concentrated in the states of Washington and Oregon. Our logging areas were relatively isolated, in terms of eastern or southern lands, but still near major population centers. Some of our ownership had traditionally been open for recreation use by company employees and families, and by people from nearby communities. But mostly, the company's lands had been inaccessible to the general public.

As our road networks grew, however, bringing the cities and towns of the area closer to our lands, we found ourselves under growing pressure from recreational users of the land. Much like the experience of the Forest Service in early days, we found that public recreation on our lands was an accomplished fact. At that point, we confronted three choices.

First, we could continue as we had been doing for so long: Ignoring most of the technical trespassers . . . paying them just enough attention to minimize their use of our lands . . . and hoping for a mutually beneficial standoff.

Our second choice, as property owners, would be to lock the gates even tighter, and try to prevent all recreational entry, which often posed a threat to good forestry management.

The third alternative was to recognize the public's recreational need, meet it, control it, and encourage it to a mutual advantage if possible.

Interviewer: Did the managerial philosophy of Weyerhaeuser help to dictate what strategy that your firm formulated?

Mr. Sheppard: Yes. Let me expound on that. If we locked the gates and tried to prevent recreational entry, we would have been following a raw self-interest philosophy. We did not believe in that philosophy.

If we continued to ignore the trespassers, we could let them have free access to our land but we (that is, Weyerhaeuser) would not have many benefits. We could act as trustees for the land for anyone who wished to use it, but the reciprocity between them and Weyerhaeuser would be minimal. The users of the land would benefit much more than Weyerhaeuser. We did not believe that would be a fair exchange.

The third alternative was based on a belief of enlightened self-interest. For Weyerhaeuser, the choice of that third alternative was seldom in doubt, once we looked seriously at recreational issues. Thus, Weyerhaeuser steadily expanded access to its lands. The first step was to formalize and define existing practices of access by employees and others; the next was to open gates to the company's lands to the general public during hunting season.

In response to the increased outdoor needs of the postwar affluent, we were well embarked on a program of opening nearly 30 tree farm campgrounds in the Northwest—elaborate, in terms of having camp stoves, picnic tables, well water, and firewood—but still relatively rustic. We hired the timber industry's first full-time public recreation administrator.

The belief that we will do better if we welcome the recreationist, rather than ignore or tolerate him, has been a part of Weyerhaeuser's corporate style. It is reflected in our formal policy, to read as follows:

As a basic aspect of our forest management program, it is Weyerhaeuser Company's policy to extend to the public the privilege of the use and enjoyment of forest lands for recreational purposes.

Weyerhaeuser Company shall manage its timberlands primarily to ensure the continuous and profitable production of raw materials. Except where public recreational use is incompatible with this primary purpose, the lands shall also be made available for the public's enjoyment.

Limitations of public recreational use shall be imposed only as necessary to prevent fire, avoid injury and health hazards to employees or the public, avoid vandalism or damage to timber or other crops, roads or equipment, or protect the contracted rights of others.

Sites of historic interest shall be preserved wherever possible. Sites of outstanding scenic beauty shall be managed with due regard to public enjoyment.

Interviewer: So the philosophy of management did play a role in your strategy and resulting policy statement?

Mr. Sheppard: Yes, it did.

Interviewer: Did you do any research to determine if external environmental factors might influence the recreational strategy?

Mr. Sheppard: As a part of our planning for a more open recreation policy, at Weyerhaeuser, we did try to answer some of the questions—and came up with some surprising results. We decided to see whether approaches by the landowner would make any difference in recreationist behavior. We focused on the hunter, with an experiment called "Operation CHEC"—the initials standing for "Cooperative Hunter Experimental Control"—on some 75 square miles of our Vail Tree Farm in Washington State.

On the test area, the hunter was given a welcome, a map, a printed copy of the local hunting regulations, hunting tips, and a cup of coffee. Once inside the CHEC area, he was free to pursue his game. There were no gates—just polite warning signs.

Meanwhile, on adjacent hunting land, foresters were keeping an eye on the conduct of hunters who were not subject to special conditions, but were subject to all the normal controls we had developed over the years.

At the end of the season, the CHEC hunter had proved to be a model guest. Not one incident of misconduct was noted. Nearby, the uncontrolled hunters had an average incidence of damage and problems.

An analysis of the experiment brought the conclusion that if the visitor was treated as a mature, welcome guest, he would respond in similar fashion. In other words—the attitude of the landowner/host affects the attitude of the visiting recreationist.

Interviewer: As a result of your recreation strategy, what has happened?

Mr. Sheppard: The spirit behind our strategy guides our forest management activities today, in a number of different areas. The hunting program, for example, has moved from a passive opening of the gates to active promotion through the distribution of free recreation maps for each Weyerhaeuser tree farm and operating area, as well as a collaborative effort with other public and private owners to distribute regional maps.

In the South, we have just finished granting an easement to the Arkansas Parks and Tourism Commission, to construct a portion of trail that will bring the Ouachita Trail System all the way east to Pinnacle Mountain State Park, and thus closer to the recreation needs of the populace of Little Rock. In that particular effort, again we worked closely with not only the agency involved, but also with an adjoining private landowner.

Interviewer: Do you think that you are improving the quality of life with all these practices?

Mr. Sheppard: Yes, we do!

Interviewer: A philosophy of enlightened self-interest and an appraisal of external and internal environmental factors has allowed you to determine an objective of improving the quality of life and the resulting recreational strategy. Am I correct?

Mr. Sheppard: Yes, both Weyerhaeuser and society are benefiting from our strategy.

Interviewer: Are there benefits and costs of your strategy?

Mr. Sheppard: The open-land policies followed by Weyerhaeuser and some other private landowners carry both benefits and costs. One thing we know for sure is that increased access for hunters helps counteract the effect our management has in increasing forage for game. For most species of wildlife, high-yield forestry is extremely beneficial since the techniques that increase forest productivity also provide both browse and cover in abundance. Resulting large populations of deer and other large animals can do tremendous damage to young seedlings and plantations. Public hunting, under the supervision of appropriate game departments, is an effective control measure that relates directly to our land-use policy.

Another benefit from having people on our land often turns out to be quicker reporting of wildfires, road washouts, stream damage, and other similar problems. Hunters, backpackers, birdwatchers, and other recreationists often serve as our eyes and ears.

But perhaps the most important benefit to us is the least tangible one. We think that open access to our lands cannot help but increase public understanding of the massive effort under way to grow trees as a perpetual crop, on lands suitable for that purpose.

As society goes through the process of determining land uses in the face of increased population and affluence, such an understanding may well be critical to our continued ability to manage lands for forestry. Whether or not our social privilege is revoked may well depend on whether you—as a camper, hiker, or hunter—understand that *your* recreation and *our* timber are twin crops from the same land base.

Interviewer: What about the costs?

Mr. Sheppard: Counterbalancing such benefits—some would say *overbalancing* them—are some very real and serious costs, problems, and concerns. Three and four decades ago, when the company's managers were putting together the open-lands policy that has characterized the company ever since, we failed to predict two trends. One was the tremendous growth in recreational use of private lands, accompanied by a steady rise in user expectations. The second was a rapid growth in public disregard for private property.

One of the first tasks of the recreation planner was to assess the extent of visitor misconduct. Even today, one of the great voids in the field of public recreation is in-depth knowledge of how and why recreationists act and react. What makes someone pour dirt in the fuel tank of a bulldozer? What factor causes someone to leave a fire untended? Why do some people assume that a sign saying that a road is dangerous is put there merely to challenge their ingenuity?

The growth in public use of our forests has been explosive. With this growth, we have found, comes a growth in expectation of what the landowner should provide for the recreating public. For example, Weyerhaeuser has a program, on most of its holdings, for allowing people from nearby communities to cut their own firewood. The fee, if any, is usually nominal. The rules are relatively clear, and geared as much to the safety to the firewood cutter as to anything else.

Even so, the demands very quickly escalate. People complain that the firewood cutting areas are not close enough to town . . . that we have already taken the best trees (which we have) . . . and that our restrictions are too stringent.

In some areas, hardwood zones that we leave for stream protection, or to provide wildlife habitat diversity, are very difficult to protect from members of the public who cut firewood. I frankly don't know how we will answer the hunters and other wildlife interests the first time a citizen group finds that a hardwood wildlife strip has been cut down for firewood, and then blames the company.

Another cost is governmental standards. I call this aspect of our open land policy one of "rising expectations." Another way to state it is "upping the ante"—every bet you make just means the game gets more expensive. In that sense, the government can be a formidable player.

In the last few years, we have closed many of the campgrounds and free-use parks developed in the Northwest. The reason: Increasingly tighter standards for maintaining such parks, even on a voluntary, no-fee basis.

Well water and pit toilets are out; flush toilets and chlorinated water supplies are a must. The cost has gone out of sight; and the campgrounds, out of existence. Meanwhile, our one experiment in operating a reservation-basis, fee campground floundered—because we couldn't keep our prices as low as those of the tax-supported state and federal campgrounds nearby.

One interesting note—in some cases, the sanitary and other requirements on our campgrounds were a result of state law. Federal campgrounds were thus exempted, and could maintain a more rustic character.

I mentioned the increase in disrespect for private property. Sometimes the public's attitude seems to be "If it isn't gated or fenced, it's ours not just to use, but to use up." Theft, arson, illegal dumping, vandalism, and just general destructiveness are visited on the private landowner to an extent you wouldn't believe unless you could see it.

Although this could ultimately work against public use of private lands, the vast majority of visitors use the land respectfully. With their continued assistance, we believe most problems can be overcome, and our access policy can remain strong.

Interviewer: Do you see any external environmental factors that might alter your open-access strategy?

Mr. Sheppard: From the recreationist's point of view, for example, we see two trends. One is an increased tendency, exemplified by the wilderness setasides of the last couple of decades, to "lock up" lands solely for recreational purposes. Often, the lands included in these proposals are private. They may be in the process of management for some other, equally beneficial use, which is then lost when the land is closed off for single-purpose management.

A second land-user trend seems to be a growing willingness to pay for *quality* recreation. I think, for example, of the number of hunters and fishermen from the Midwest who seem eager to pay for exclusive guided rights to outdoor sports activity on the larger ranches and rangelands of the West.

From the landowner's side, some private owners are beginning to capitalize on the income potential of recreation. Yet there is also a growing recognition in some sectors that free access to private lands, *properly managed by the landowner and appropriate government agencies,* can reduce pressures for taking of those lands through acquistion, condemnation, or such nonpaying mechanisms as scenic easements.

For some of the larger corporate landowners, that reduction in public pressure—superficially only a public relations result, but actually a deeper issue of retaining the right to manage the land—transcends any possible financial return of charging for recreation. This is especially true, of course, where the private lands are near, or intermingled with, public lands on which tax-supported recreation is available at little or no cost, and user fees would not be very competitive.

Interviewer: What about Weyerhaeuser's role?

Mr. Sheppard: The private landowner group already is important in outdoor recreation, and is likely to become more so in the next few decades. When we talk about recreation on the nation's commercial forest lands, for example—that is, those lands productive enough to grow trees on a economically efficient basis—we're talking about a recreation asset that is 72 percent privately owned. As wilderness and roadless areas are carved out of the public forest, and their use restricted by isolation and regulation—the private landowner will probably play an increasing role in forest recreation for the masses of people who are not wilderness users.

Certainly that seems to be the case for the company I work for. Weyerhaeuser has been in the forefront of forestry and land-use issues for decades. Over the years, it has come in for both criticism and grudging admiration from within the ranks of conservationists. Today, both in the West and in the South, our foresters seem to be spending more and more time on recreation-oriented matters. Sometimes, this is in response to public demands or pressures. More often, we are trying to get ahead of public needs, and figure out how to accommodate them as land managers—without compromising our main mission, which is to make money by growing and using trees.

ANALYSIS

1. What is Weyerhaeuser's strategy regarding recreation on its privately owned land?
2. Did the managerial philosophy play a role as a determinant of Weyerhaeuser's strategy? Discuss.
3. Does Weyerhaeuser have either an expressed or implied objective of

improving the quality of life for society? If so, what is one strategy that they follow to accomplish it?

4. What constituents or resources contributors does Weyerhaeuser recognize? Compared to government?

5. What are some of the benefits of enlightened self-interest regarding recreation use of privately owned land? Some costs?

6. Who and what determine whether the benefits outweigh the costs? Discuss.

7. What is the relative importance to Weyerhaeuser of tree growing and profits and quality of life?

PART V

Managing and Controlling the Social Performance of Business

Corporate Social Policy Planning and Strategy

Chapter Objectives

- To define strategy and explain its significance to social responsibility.
- To identify and describe the three most common social responsibility strategy philosophies.
- To discuss the social responsibility strategy options that are available to organizations.
- To examine the major steps in the strategic planning process.

In the final part of this book we examine the ways in which corporations actually manage and control their social performance. This first chapter sets the stage for such social management.

STRATEGY AND SOCIAL RESPONSIBILITY

Strategy is a term that comes from the Greek word *strategos*, which means the "art of the general." Every organization formulates strategy, sometimes implied, other times stated. Small organizations often have implied strategies. Their objectives, plans, and tactics may not be formally spelled out, but the owner-manager has formulated a game plan and knows where the organization is headed. Large enterprises often have stated objectives. The professional manager who heads the organization operates from a predetermined plan with formal objectives and tactics that are clearly spelled out.

In its essence, strategy is "the relationship between an organization and its environment." To some degree at least, an enterprise determines what this relationship will be. When examined from a product-line standpoint, for example, a large business will often use a strategy of low price. Since the firm can produce large quantities of the good, its costs will be lower than those of the competition, and so it will try to capture market share by offering customers the best price available. Small firms will use a different strategy. Since they are low-volume producers, their costs will be higher than those of their giant competitors, and so they will compete on a service basis. They will try to win business by offering timely delivery, better credit terms, and faster and more reliable product maintenance. They will try to convince the buyer that "price is not everything." Intermediate-sized firms will use a strategy that falls between that of the large and small firms. They will often advertise extensively and, from time to time, offer discounts or hold special sales. These companies will compete against their large competitors by differentiating their goods through advertising and trying to convince the buyer that their higher price is a result of superior products. They will compete against their small competitors by offering better prices and, when required, more service.

In each case, the respective organization attempts to compete effectively by creating the "right relationship" between itself and the competition. This is strategy. But when examined in terms of social responsibility, strategy takes on new dimensions. A firm selling TV sets will be competing for sales only within a limited market niche. Of the 1 million people in the city, perhaps 100,000 of them will buy new sets this year. Of these, half may purchase from a national retailer such as Sears or Penney's. Most of the rest may buy from stores located within 10 blocks of their residence so that they can easily bring back the set for repairs. So in the final analysis there may be only 2,500 potential buyers in this business's target market.

The same analogy exists in terms of social responsibility. No organization can address every social issue in every sector of the economy. Mining firms will be most concerned with environmental issues; insurance companies will be most interested in equal employment opportunity issues; and consumer goods manufacturers will be most concerned with consumerism issues. Each firm has its own social responsibility market niche within which it must be responsive to the environment. Yet, regardless of the size and nature of this environment, most firms will use one of three social responsibility strategy philosophies.

Social Responsibility Strategy Philosophies

Small firms have a strategic philosophy of social responsibility different from that of large firms. Small firms typically have, at best, only a passing concern with social responsibility. Large firms usually integrate the issue into their strategic plan. Intermediate-sized firms fall between the two in terms of strategy philosophy. The following will examine the philosophy of each along a reactive, anticipatory, and active preparedness continuum.

Reactive.   Small firms tend to wait until social responsibility issues arise before doing anything about them. This philosophy is representative of their approach to strategy in general. Their objectives typically are informal, often existing only in the mind of the owner-manager. Their strategy is to wait and see what everyone else in the industry is doing, before taking action. If there is a social policy issue with which they should be concerned, they will find out what everyone else is doing and then follow suit. They rely heavily on a "follow the leader" strategy, which is not a bad idea. In the main, most small firms have few social responsibility problems. They are required to obey laws ensuring equal opportunity in the workplace, and they know that their work environments must be safe. However, they are normally less of a target for antitrust suits from the federal government or million-dollar lawsuits from consumers claiming that their products are defective and have resulted in physical injury to the users. As a result, the small firms usually reduce the amount of time and money spent on social responsibility strategy planning by employing a reactive philosophy.

Anticipatory.   Medium-sized firms anticipate what is going to happen in the environment. They know that they are too small to control any major segment of that environment but that they are too large to avoid being hurt should there be a major change in environmental conditions. For example, they would not want to be the first to cut prices because their larger competitors might retaliate and cut prices still more. The result would be a loss of overall revenue to the medium-sized firm. On the other hand, if the large firm cuts prices first, the medium-sized firms will want to be in a position to respond as quickly as possible. As a result, these firms tend to draw up plans that are contingency based; that is, if the competition adopts strategy 1, then we shall counter with strategy 2. The same is true for planning for social responsibility. Medium-sized firms will anticipate changes in both legislation and public opinion. But even these firms' philosophy is somewhat similar to that of the small firms, in that they take a wait-and-see approach. These organizations know that the large firms are those most likely to be affected by any social changes, and so they wait and see what happens to them before implementing their own contingency plans.

Active.   Large firms usually have an active strategy. They want to influence their environments and plan accordingly. For example, rather than waiting to see if a particular product will prove dangerous to the general public, they will conduct research to uncover any problems and work them out before releasing the good for final manufacturing. Additionally, these firms will try to maintain a visible profile so that if anyone questions their social

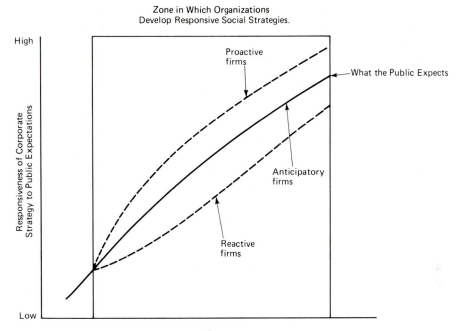

FIGURE 16.1 Corporate Social Responsiveness.

responsibility stance they can point to their well-known programs. Large organizations know that they are the ones most likely to be questioned about their social programs, and so they strive the hardest to develop detailed, meaningful ones. Figure 16.1 contrasts the strategy philosophies of these three types of firms.

Social Responsibility Strategy Options

Regardless of the overall strategy philosophy, not all issues are dealt with similarly. Sometimes a company will find it economically advantageous to drag its feet on a particular issue, even though its overall philosophy is active. Other times a company with a reactive philosophy will adopt an anticipatory approach to a particular issue.

Additionally, a firm will sometimes find that even though trying hard to meet its social responsibility obligations, its strategy turns out to be illegal. This may seem improbable, but it happens all the time. Consider the case of Monsanto Chemical. Before introducing a new plastic container into the market, the company ran tests to ensure that the package was not injurious to health. Other tests related to energy usage, disposal, and recycling were also conducted. Everything looked fine, but that was not how it turned out.

> Monsanto went through this very process in developing Cycle-Safe bottles and spent more than $47 million to market the product. But . . . the FDA banned the bottle because, when stored at 120 degrees for an extended period of time, molecules strayed from the plastic into the contents. Rats, fed with doses that were equivalent to consuming thousands of quarts of soft drink over a human lifetime, developed an above-normal number of tumors.
>
> Monsanto felt that they were providing a product that did something for society—a plastic bottle that could be recycled. But social responsibility is unavoidably a matter of degree and interpretation. Forces outside of the business are liable to interpret a product to be socially unacceptable, even when the company has undertaken an extensive impact analysis.[1]

Sometimes the best of intentions turn out poorly, or deliberate efforts to circumvent or ignore the law are successful. In examining the available options and the strategic response, an analysis of the model in Figure 16.2 is necessary. There are four social responsibility options open to a business.

Illegal/Irresponsible.   The most common examples of illegal/irresponsible strategies occur when (1) an organization stands to lose a great deal of money (or at least has to undertake great expenses) if it complies with the law and (2) the chances of getting caught for a violation are quite small. Given these two conditions, a company may decide to take its chances by adopting an illegal/irresponsible strategy. An example is a firm whose antipollution equipment is substandard, based on new federal guidelines. Should it pay the $1 million to install the equipment or take a chance on getting caught and paying the maximum fine of $20,000? Because there are only a few federal inspectors and over 1 million firms that would need such equipment, the risk is really quite small. So the company may indeed decide to take the chance.

Illegal/Responsible.   The most common examples of the illegal/responsible strategy are those similar to the earlier case of Monsanto. Many organizations that produce a good that is found to be illegal falls into this category. There are other examples, and one of the most interesting is Armour, the meat-packing firm.

> It seems that the Federal Meat Inspection Service ordered an Armour meat-packing plant to create an aperture in a conveyor line so that inspectors could remove samples for testing. Accordingly, the company did so. The Occupational Safety and Health Administration soon arrived and demanded that the aperture on the line constructed a safety hazard. Predictably, each agency threatened to close down the plant if it refused to comply with its orders.[2]

---

[1]Dan R. Dalton and Richard A. Cosier, "The Four Faces of Social Responsibility," *Business Horizons*, May–June 1982, p. 19.
[2]Dalton and Cosier, p. 22.

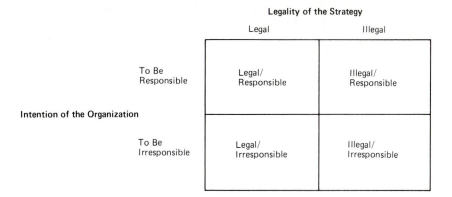

FIGURE 16.2   Social Responsibility Strategy Options.

In this particular no-win case, if each agency maintained its demand, the firm's ideal strategy would be to challenge the law. Of course, the organization is likely to be criticized by those who believe that it violated a federal regulation. But the enterprise should be able to get a ruling regarding what to do, and it can proceed from there.

Another example of illegal/responsible strategy is a business that is judged to be too large and in violation of antitrust. If the company believes that it provides the best product at the best price and ought not to be broken up, it can begin a prolonged court battle, arguing its case each step of the way. IBM is the most recent example. After 20 years in the courts, the computer giant emerged unscathed and intact. Yet even when a firm is found to be engaging in illegal actions, delaying tactics may be called illegal, but can the firm's overall strategy accurately be labeled as irresponsible?

Irresponsible/Legal.   There have been a number of astonishing excesses that provide examples of irresponsible but legal strategies. Before the passage of the Pure Food and Drug Act, there was a diet pill on the market that promised to help people lose weight, regardless of food intake. The product was frighteningly effective. It contained tapeworm larvae that would grow in the intestinal tract and consume everything the person ate. Unfortunately, if not medically treated, these tapeworms would also starve the person to death.

Today there are still may examples of irresponsible but legal strategies, but they usually are subtly presented and implemented. As a result, they often pass unnoticed. In the minds of many, one of the main ones is the production of cigarettes. Do the social short-run benefits of tobacco (employment, taxes, satisfaction of consumer demand) outweigh the long-run costs (medical expenses, pain and suffering, perhaps death)? Many people say they do not. So, despite the legality of cigarette production, many people would put the strategy associated with the manufacture of cigarettes under the heading of legal/irresponsible.

Another example, provided by hundreds of firms each year, is the expansion strategy used for meeting rising consumer demand. When demand is greater than supply, a business has a number of strategy options. One of the most frequently employed is to build new facilities. During this time the business will handle the increased demand by adding a second or third shift at current plants, subcontracting and/or setting up temporary facilities in new locales. The latter often represents a legal but irresponsible strategy because the benefits to the community will be short lived. Typically, the local area has to provide more social services (schooling, housing, recreational facilities) which will no longer be required when the firm's new plant opens and this temporary facility is closed. Does the business always notify the community that the changes are only temporary? If it does, the community will assess it certain costs. Additionally, it is unlikely that the community will make any permanent improvements related to the plant's operation, and local banks will be reluctant to finance building projects, home mortgages, or consumer loans to the company or its personnel. Yet even though such action is irresponsible, there is no legislation that prevents a firm from doing this. When the plant closes, local unemployment will rise, property values will fall, and the tax base will be severely affected. Many firms would call this a risk that every community has to accept and let it go at that. Dalton and Cosier make an argument for the other side, while putting the issue into perspective.

> While organizations may not violate a single law, they may not be socially responsible. What of gambling casinos dealing not only in games of chance but also offering endless free liquor and décolletage? How about the manufacturers of handguns? Automobiles with questionable, if not lethal, fuel systems? Can a society hold organizations to a standard higher than that demanded by law?[3]

Legal/Responsible.   Most firms seek to formulate a strategy that is legal and responsible. Even though this strategy may seem superior to the other three, it is not without criticism:

1. Most businesses are operated by professional managers and not owner-managers. Their relationship is strictly fiduciary; they are there to manage the assets of the firm for the owners. As a result of social responsibility strategy, if profits are reduced or costs increase, stockholder wealth will be diminished, and so these managers will be said to have failed in their duty to the owner.
2. In some cases a company's programs do not benefit the poor or the needy but subsidize the life-style of the more affluent. For example, when a company donates more to support opera or dance companies

[3]Dalton and Cosier, p. 23.

or sends a check to public TV, who really gains? The ballet, symphony, opera, and live theater are more frequently attended by the wealthy than by the poor. Public TV programs are geared to a higher educational level than are the three major networks and are watched disproportionately more by the affluent than by the economically struggling. So these donations are actually directed less toward helping the underprivileged.

3. By getting involved in social programs, businesses begin to shape the form and content of society's environment. Yet it is not their job to lead; it is their responsibility to follow. They are not supposed to be creating demand but to be fulfilling demand. They are usurping authority that does not belong to them.

4. When business becomes involved, it often fails to conduct a cost-benefit analysis. So even though the result may be beneficial to society, the associated outlay is unjustified. The funds might have been more usefully spent on a different project.

Nevertheless, this does not mean that a legal/responsible strategy should be abandoned. What these four points do illustrate, however, is that whatever a company does, it is likely to find someone criticizing its actions. But these comments cannot be allowed to stand in the way of a legal/responsible strategy. What the firm does need to do is to make sure that this strategy complies with three guidelines: (1) to the best of the organization's knowledge, no harm will befall anyone because of the strategy; (2) if there are any problems, the organization will be accountable for them; and (3) the larger the organization is, the greater the responsibility that it will assume in this area.

THE STRATEGIC PLANNING PROCESS

The strategy for social responsibility objectives is put into action through a five-step process, beginning with a scanning of the environment and ending with an evaluation of the results.

Scanning the Environment

The first step, especially for firms developing an active social responsibility strategy, is to scan the environment. What changes are likely to occur over the next three to five years, and how can the organization address them? When examined from a macroviewpoint, there are four types of forecasts typically conducted by businesses: economic, technological, political, and social. These forecasts are designed to help the organization deal with its general and task environment (see Figure 16.3). Commenting on these environments, Kast noted:

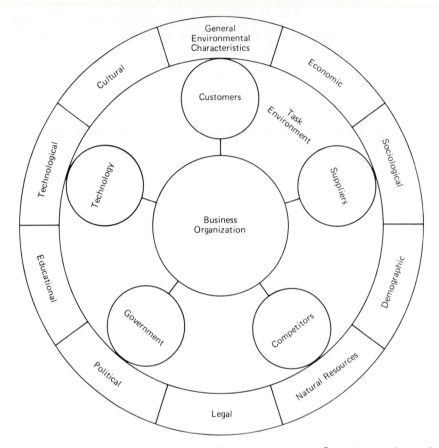

FIGURE 16.3   General and Task Environment of Business Organizations.
From Fremont Kast, "Scanning the Future Environment: Social Indicators," California
Management Review, Fall 1980, p. 24.

Many forces in the general environment influence business, such as the basic
culture, including historical background, ideologies, and values. The level of scientific and technological development, educational attainment, and legal and political processes are important characteristics, as are demographic factors, the nature
of human resources, natural resources, and the general economic and industrial
framework of the society.

The task environment encompasses the forces relevant to an individual business.
Customers, suppliers, competitors, regulators, and specific technologies are part
of the task environment. The distinction between the general and the task environments is not static. Forces in the general environment are continually breaking
through to the task environment.

A close look at the general environment characteristics . . . suggests that there
is an accelerating rate of change. Science and technology are advancing, many
cultural and social changes are apparent, demographic forces are having a profound

TABLE 16.1. United States Peak Electric Demand and Planned Generating Resources (Megawatts).

Summer	1981–1982	1983–1984	1985–1986	1987–1988	1989–1990
Peak demand	444,591	484,563	524,644	565,375	607,974
Planned resources	584,387	633,627	681,336	732,758	772,192
Peak demand as a percentage of resources	76.08%	76.47%	77.00%	77.16%	78.73%
Winter	1981–1982	1983–1984	1985–1986	1987–1988	1989–1990
Peak demand	417,103	545,620	492,480	533,006	573,805
Planned resources	598,131	650,045	698,014	746,609	793,114
Peak demand as a percentage of resources	69.73%	69.78%	70.55%	71.39%	72.35%

Source: National Electric Reliability Council, *1980 Summary* (July 1980).

effect. On all fronts, businesses are facing more heterogeneous, dynamic, and uncertain environments. Growing external turbulence renders traditional, highly structured bureaucracies inadequate; organizations must become more adaptive and responsive.[4]

Of these four forecasts, the social forecast is the one to gain the most recent attention and is the most relevant to the strategic planning process. This forecast helps a firm anticipate and respond to changing values, quality of work life demands, consumerism and ecological issues, and other social challenges. Of course, any scanning of this environment is likely to overlap with other areas, especially economic areas. Electrical utilities are an excellent example. During the next decade, the United States will require more electrical power. Table 16.1 provides a forecast through the end of the 1980s. Without such economically based forecasts, the utility would be unable to meet consumer demand. Commitments for generating capacity during the 2000s have already been completed, and the industry now is forecasting consumer needs during the 2020s. But, this is only one side of the strategic problem; the other side relates to ecology (damage to the environment) and consumerism (costs and safety to consumers). The enterprise must forecast the social changes associated with those economic demands if it is to formulate a complete and viable strategy. This all is typically done through environmental scanning.

[4]Fremont Kast, "Scanning the Future Environment: Social Indicators," *California Management Review*, Fall 1980, p. 23.

Principles of Environmental Scanning. Environmental scanning has two purposes, to monitor current events and to forecast future events that are likely to affect the organization. Researchers like Ian Wilson believe that this process must incorporate a series of principles. The five most important are the following:

1. It must be holistic in its approach to the business environment, i.e. it should view trends—social, economic, political, technological—as a piece, not piece-meal. Ecology and general systems theory both point to the maxim that "everything is related to everything else." . . . The scanning system should, therefore, be comprehensive in its scope and integrative in its approach (cross-impact analyses and scenarios are remarkably useful techniques in this regard).

2. It must also be continuous, iterative in its operation. In a fast-changing world, it makes little sense to rely on one-shot, or even periodic, analyses of the environment. Only constant monitoring, feedback and modification of forecasts can be truly useful.

3. The system must be designed to deal with alternative futures. In an uncertain environment we can never truly know the future, no matter how much we may perfect our forecasting techniques. It is highly misleading, therefore, to claim (or believe) that an early warning system can predict the future. What it can do—and do effectively, if well designed—is to help us clarify our assumptions about the future, speculate systematically about alternative outcomes, assess probabilities, and make more rational choices.

4. It should lay heavy stress on the need for contingency planning. This is a necessary corollary to the preceding point. In fact, there is (or should be) a strong logical connection in our thinking among uncertainty, alternatives and contingencies: the three concepts are strongly bound together. In the final analysis, of course, after considering alternatives, we have to commit to a plan of action based on our assessment of the most probable future. But those lesser probabilities—even the "wild card" scenarios—should not be neglected, for they represent the contingencies for which we should also, in some degree, plan.

5. Most important, the environmental scanning system should be an integral part of the decisionmaking system of the corporation. Speculation about alternative futures makes no real contribution to corporate success if it results merely in interesting studies. To contribute, it must be issue-oriented and help make today's decisions with a better sense of futurity: but it can do this only if the planning and decision-making system is designed to include the requirements of such monitoring and early warning.[5]

---

[5]Ian H. Wilson, "Environmental Scanning and Strategic Planning," *Business Environment/Public Policy: AACSB Conference Papers*, ed. Lee E. Preston (St. Louis: AACSB, 1980), pp. 160–161.

How can an organization gather such environmental information? Usually, this is done by cultivating specialized sources. These can take a number of forms. For example, there are both external personal sources (consultants, conferences, executives and managers in other organizations, government officials, and representatives of public-interest organizations) and impersonal sources (reports from trade associations, government publications, newspapers and magazines, trade and technical journals, special consulting and reporting services, and publications of public-interest organizations). There are also internal personal sources (board of directors, chief executive officer, other executives and managers, and staff specialists) and impersonal sources (management reports and memos, accounting reports, and planning reports and budgets).[6]

Social Forecasting. Most firms have little difficulty addressing the economic, technological, and political environments, as they have been scanning these environments for years. However, how do they deal with the social environment? One of the most direct ways is by identifying social indicators. Exactly what *is* a social indicator? One of the most publicized definitions referred to it as "a statistic of direct normative interest which facilitates concise, comprehensive, and balanced judgments about the condition of a major aspect of society."[7] In essence, social forecasting is identifying and tracking social indicators. These indicators usually have the following seven characteristics:

1. They emphasize noneconomic measures of conditions that are important to the social state of the nation.
2. They are quantifiable, sensitive to change, and are presented as a time series that can be monitored on a quarterly, semi-annual and/or annual basis.
3. They elicit a commitment to the idea that better social information will improve corporate social policy planning.
4. They provide adequate information for evaluation research and social experimentation and offer baseline data for the assessment of future trends.
5. They are anticipatory and suitable for social forecasting, thereby facilitating long-range planning.
6. They offer a limited, yet comprehensive, set of coherent and significant indicators which can be monitored over time and broken down to the level of the relevant social unit.
7. They are systematized and organized around an analytical model or theoretical perspective designed to account for the observed changes.[8]

[6]Francis J. Aguilar, *Scanning the Business Environment* (New York: Macmillan, 1967), p. 68.

[7]U.S. Department of Health, Education and Welfare, *Toward a Social Report* (Washington, D.C.: U.S. Government Printing Office, 1969), p. 97.

[8]Kast, p. 25.

The purpose of these indicators is to provide a more adequate basis for understanding social changes. By being aware of these changes, the organization can then anticipate and devise response strategies that put it in step with society's expectations. To incorporate these forecasts into the enterprise's overall plan, two approaches are available. One is to predict a long-term scenario or development and then work backward by means of deductive reasoning to the present, noting those developments most likely to occur during this time. The other is to begin a logical progression from the current time to a future time when various social events will take place. The two approaches are actually complementary, although for purposes of accuracy many organizations prefer the first. Working one's way back from the future to the present often produces a more detailed and complete scenario than does working from the present to the future. In the latter there is the likelihood of overlooking some important development, if only because the planner begins to rush the analysis in an effort to reach the future social goal.

How common is social forecasting today? The answer is that it is beginning to gain a greater following as organizations realize its value to overall strategy.

> Management needs to develop more sophisticated environmental scanning systems: economic and technological forecasting should be expanded to include other social forces. It is evident that social forecasting is very complex, but this does not minimize its importance. A first step is the acceptance of the inevitability of social change. Historically, business has accepted and even welcomed economic and technological change but has often resisted social change. The prevailing concept has been to emphasize the desirability of social and political stability, for the sake of "business as usual." This view is no longer appropriate.
>
> The development of social indicators is a starting point for obtaining more appropriate environmental information for managerial decision making. Although social indicators are still rudimentary, they do provide the basis for a more adequate and balanced managerial information-decision system.[9]

Identifying and Prioritizing Issues

Based on its environment scanning, an organization will then identify and prioritize those social issues with which it must deal. Not all changes in the environment will require action by the enterprise. Additionally, of those that do, some will be more important than others. At this point, the organization must answer a key question: which social developments can we ignore or assign a low priority to, and which must we address? If the social forecast was carried out properly, the enterprise should be able to identify broadly based trends in public expectations. Sometimes this has not been done and has resulted in both embarrassing and costly outcomes.

[9]Kast, p. 31.

In most cases an organization does not overlook a social issue; rather, it miscalculates its impact. For example, years ago the auto companies knew that they could make safer cars by adding all sorts of padded devices and restraints. However, there was little indication that the public was willing to pay for these "extras." It was not until the 1970s that the firms suddenly realized that these additions would be required by law. Or consider that public utilities for years had urged customers to use as much energy as they needed. Not until the Arab oil embargo and the rising price of electricity in the mid-1970s did these firms realize that they would have to begin using "demarketing" techniques to convince people to conserve energy and reduce their daily consumption. In fact, in many areas around the country, the energy-cost curve has been turned around, and public power commissions are now forcing the utilities to increase their kilowatt cost as customers use more energy. This is a total reversal from a decade ago when the big users were given discounts and urged to increase their usage.

One of the most effective ways of ensuring that a social issue is not overlooked is to develop a prioritizing scheme, by using what often is called *critical questions*. Figure 16.4 presents these questions in the form of a decision-making flow chart. Notice that at each step the organization determines whether it should proceed or simply take no action on the issue. Figures such as Figure 16.4 are useful because they force the organization to answer such key questions as: Should we really address this issue? How much is it going to cost us? What are the benefits or returns to us? Do we have the ability to do the job? These questions help explain why some organizations will not take action on a particular issue: that is, the chances of the issue becoming a problem are minimal, or the risk associated with doing nothing is justified in light of the expenses of taking corrective action. Small companies, for example, will not develop sophisticated equal opportunity employment programs because they know that the chances of their being sued are quite small. On the other hand, large employers will spend thousands of dollars recruiting, hiring, and training minorities and making a concerted effort to retain them. They know that they are much more likely to be targets of discrimination lawsuits, and they are determined to avoid this problem. For small businesses, the expense of such a program does not justify the cost (as least in the minds of the top management), but for large businesses, such expenses cannot be avoided.

Another way of identifying social issues and seeing that they are properly prioritized is to use a two-dimensional priority identification matrix. Such a matrix can be developed by examining such key factors as the likelihood that a particular social issue or trend will develop and the impact of such an issue or trend on the organization. Of the two, the latter tends to receive the greater weight. After all, not every issue will affect the firm, but the ones that do can cause severe problems.

These two factors can be brought together in a priority identification

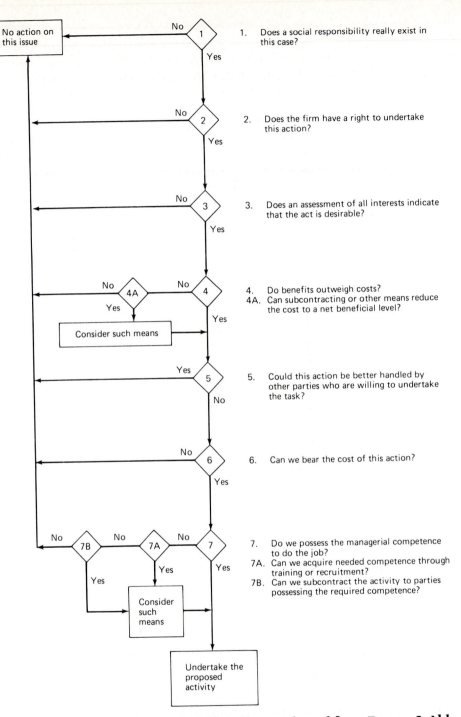

FIGURE 16.4 Decision-Making Flow Chart. Adapted from Ramon J. Aldag and Donald W. Jackson, Jr., "A Managerial Framework for Social Decision Making," MSU Business Topics, Spring 1975; p. 34. *Reprinted by permission of the publisher, Division of Research, Graduate School of Business Administration, Michigan State University.*

matrix (see Figure 16.5). Notice that in the figure the probability of a social issue or trend is contrasted with its impact on the enterprise. The result is the determination of the issue's priority. By working from priority 1 issues down to priority 4 issues, the organization can allocate the requisite time and money for appropriate responses. The important thing is not to overlook priority 1 issues or to develop detailed plans for dealing with priority 4 issues.

In prioritizing social issues, it is common to find business firms first dividing the issues into two categories, those with a direct impact on the firm and those with an indirect impact on the firm. Those with a direct impact, using Figure 16.5 as an example, are then further divided into first, second, or third priority. Those with an indirect impact are simply assigned to a fourth priority.

Each organization will make its own assignment of issues according to

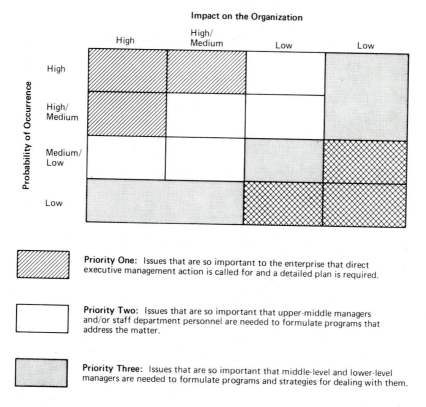

Priority One: Issues that are so important to the enterprise that direct executive management action is called for and a detailed plan is required.

Priority Two: Issues that are so important that upper-middle managers and/or staff department personnel are needed to formulate programs that address the matter.

Priority Three: Issues that are so important that middle-level and lower-level managers are needed to formulate programs and strategies for dealing with them.

Priority Four: Issues that are no so important to the enterprise but require limited planning attention.

FIGURE 16.5. Priority Identification Matrix.

the values of the top managers, the philosophy of the organization, the market niche the firm is pursuing, and the enterprise's current and future strategies. In the case of a well-known firm such as Sears, the agenda of public issues is staggering. In contrast with a small firm that may have a total of five issues with which it must be concerned, the giant Sears has no less than 50. Sample illustrations of first priority issues for the retailer include equal employment opportunity, product liability, credit income/financing/interest costs, and Federal Trade Commission requirements. Second-priority issues include equal pay, product safety, energy costs, advertising regulations, and labeling and packaging specifications. Third-priority issues include copyright laws, product usage, environmental protection, product restrictions, and coporate governance. Finally, fourth-priority issues include inflation, monetary policy, public confidence in institutions, national energy programs, and full employment.[10]

Formulation of Objectives

Having decided which issues will receive the highest priority, the organization will then formulate specific objectives for each. These objectives also provide a basis for action, in that they help point out the type of program the enterprise will have to develop. Table 16.2 identifies typical objectives and objective descriptions. Notice that in each case, the description relates how the objective will be pursued and the cost that will be involved. In writing objective descriptions, the organization has given itself a basis for later control and follow-up. The data in the table also show that social responsibility objectives can be drawn up for virtually any issue, from the support of minority enterprises to female employment to product safety to international sales.

Determining a Strategic Implementation Posture

For each objective, the organization will devise a specific program or plan. The organization will also decide how active or passive it wants to be in implementing the program. If the goal is one of hiring 25 percent more female managers at the middle ranks of the hierarchy in order to meet a directive from its board of directors, a very aggressive posture may be assumed. The organization will try to accomplish this objective in record time. On the other hand, if the objective is complying with new federal health standards in the manufacture of its products, the organization may seek government clarification and deliberately proceed slowly. The difference between the two strategic postures is that the firm is setting its own rules in

[10]Robert E. Barmeier, "The Role of Environmental Forecasting and Public Issues Analysis in Corporate Planning," *Business Environment/Public Policy: AACSB Conference Papers*, ed. Lee E. Preston (St. Louis: AACSB, 1980), p. 158.

TABLE 16.2. Examples of Social Responsibility Objectives.

Area of Objectives	Description of Objectives
Community development, support of minority enterprises	Local outlets will be chosen for products; minority ownership will be a factor. If product quality meets minimum criteria or beyond and price is not greater than 10 percent over nonminority organization, the minority organization will be chosen. Estimated additional cost to our organization: $200,000 per year.
Job training program	Each plant will hire at least 10 percent of each year's entry hirees from job service pool of hard-core unemployed. A training program will be instituted to teach the required skills and other work habits. Program cost: $80,000 per year.
Female employment	A special program will be initiated to recruit qualified female applicants for managerial positions. A goal of 20 percent of first-level managerial jobs that become vacant will be filled with female applicants. Cost: $30,000.
Consumer affairs	An institutional advertising campaign will be developed by 12/31 that will run monthly ads in 10 major nationwide publications. The institutional ads will stress a hot-line phone number for consumer complaints; 12 monthly ads will be written. Cost: $500,000.
Product safety	All existing products will be submitted to the National Laboratory Testing Agency for safety testing by 1/31. Cost: $500,000.
Worker safety	The safety inspector will conduct a comprehensive study of one department per month to ensure that each department meets OSHA requirements. Cost: Office staff and supervisor—$50,000 per year.
Pollution control, water	A review committee will be formed by 7/31 to study the water pollution-control system to determine if it meets standards. The committee will determine the most cost-effective technology that industry can provide to meet the company's needs. Final report due 9/15. Cost: Committee time $80,000. Travel 20,000. Office staff 20,000.
Air	Preliminary plans will be adopted to purchase the smokestack scrubber to meet future air-quality standards. Cost: $3.5 million.
Legislative lobbying	Promote the fair trade act through industry association lobbying. Annual fee: $30,000.

TABLE 16.2. Continued

Area of Objectives	Description of Objectives
Product labeling	Each product will contain information about repairs. To be done by 12/31. Cost: $70,000; $50,000 per year after first year.
Warranty product recalls information	Each product will have a serial code, and each sale will include a warranty card. Do by 12/31. Cost: $400,000 per year.
International sales	No product that is considered unsafe and banned in the United States will be sold in any foreign country. All such products will be phased out by 12/31. Cost: $1 million per year in current dollars in lost revenues.

the first but is complying with someone else's in the second. Whenever government regulation of any sort enters the picture, strategic posturing becomes an implementation issue.

This posture generally takes one of three forms: sensing, progressive, and aggressive. Though similar to the philosophies discussed earlier—reactive, anticipatory, and active—these postures are used in dealing with individual programs or issues. A firm can have an overall active philosophy but use a reactive posture with some of its programs, an anticipatory posture with others, and an active posture with the remainder. The following examines each of them.

Sensing. A sensing posture is used when a firm wants to monitor changes in the environment via an early warning system. This is often done by actively participating in the Better Business Bureau, the national chamber of commerce, and/or other industry-wide associations. Through these sources, business firms learn of proposed government regulation and can move to lobby for or against it. As seen in Figure 16.6, the retail clothing industry uses this type of posturing for general regulatory intervention.

The retail clothing industry is relatively unshackled by specific government regulations, but it is subject to short-term issues. One that it faced was how to dispose of children's pajamas that did not meet new inflammability regulations. No sooner did it conform to these regulations then the industry was confronted with the problems of disposing of pajamas treated with a fire retardant that was believed to be carcinogenic. Thanks to the channels of political communication, such as the trade associations that it cultivated, the industry was able to deal with the problem.

Progressive. A progressive posture is typically undertaken whenever an organization's product or production process and/or its competitive abilities

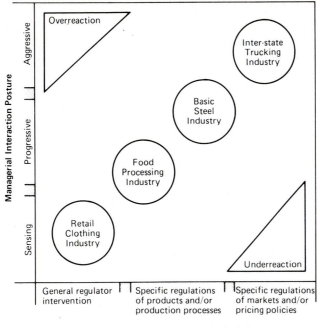

FIGURE 16.6. A Profile of Management–Political Intervention. *Copyright 1981, by the Foundation for the School of Business at Indiana University. Reprinted by permission.*

are affected. This posture includes all the elements of sensing plus more active steps such as lobbying, informing people about current industry processes and practices, and trying to influence regulation by getting the right person in the right place.

> For example, the history of the Federal Communications Commission (FCC) illustrates that lobbying for the right man in the right position can save business funds later on. Appointments in administrative agencies can affect industry profits, for appointed heads influence the direction of the regulatory agency and its attitude toward industry and profits. Throughout FCC history, those commissioners appointed from the broadcast industry have been less stringent in their policies and enforcement, while those heads appointed from outside the industry have been more harsh.[11]

Aggressive. An aggressive posture is used when market availability and pricing policies are affected. At this point the organization will begin mount-

---

[11]Marianne M. Jennings and Frank Shipper, "Strategic Planning for Managerial-Political Interaction," *Business Horizons*, July–August 1981, p. 48.

ing a counteroffensive of its own. Lobby action is one of the most common tactics. Another is the use of lawsuits. For example, an association of California truckers brought federal state, administrative, and judicial proceedings to stop applicants from obtaining operating rights in the state. The association was successful in the courts. On the national level, the trucking industry lobby, in conjunction with the Teamsters Union, was also successful in both securing and maintaining a protected market environment until recently.

> The Teamsters Union has established itself, in part, by obtaining and maintaining one of the highest average hourly wages for its members. Since the rate to be charged shippers by all interstate truckers is established in a collective manner, the need for hard-bargaining for labor rates at the negotiating table is minimized. The additional costs of higher wages are simply passed on to consumers through the collective bargaining rate-making process. Thus, a profitable and protected environment is maintained by the regulators for the truckers and their employees.[12]

Depending on environmental conditions, the firm's strategic response will vary. For example, as seen in Figure 16.6, if the organization faces general regulatory intervention, it should use a sensing posture. A progressive posture would be too strong, and an aggressive one would be an overreaction. Conversely, if the organization faces specific market regulations and/or pricing policies, an aggressive posture should be used. A progressive posture would be too unresponsive, and a sensing one would even be less appropriate.

Implementation and Assessment

The last stages of strategy are implementation and assessment. At this point, the strategy formulation ends and the strategy implementation begins; the process gives way to action.

Implementation Techniques.   The methods of implementation will depend on the program itself and will also be influenced by the environment. In some instances the organization will choose a very aggressive posture; in others the firm will simply do the minimum. An organization with a dedicated commitment to a particular program, such as hiring five hundred youths for summer jobs, will actively recruit and employ young people. A company forced to provide copious and repetitive reports to a federal agency will provide the least amount of information necessary and will repeat portions of the report in answering redundant inquiries.

Another phase in implementation is the formation of the necessary organization structure. How will the program be coordinated? Who will be responsible for each of its parts? More will be said about this in Chapter 17, in which strategy implementation will be discussed in more detail.

[12]Jennings and Shipper, p. 49.

A third consideration is the development of any requisite alliances with outside organizations. If the business is working with the Urban League, the Chamber of Commerce, or United Way, channels of communication will have to be established. If the company is coordinating its efforts with those of another firm, an integrative implementation strategy must be agreed upon. To help promote the program, if the firm needs the support of local organizations, such as newspaper or TV coverage or cooperation from the mayor's office, these alliances must be cemented during this phase.

Evaluation of Results.   The last phase of strategy, which will be explained in more detail in Chapter 18, is evaluating the results. How well did the strategy work out? Were there any problems? Can they be addressed now, or will the firm simply have to live with them? How will the results affect future strategy formulation? These are the types of questions asked in the strategy assessment phase.

But when social programs or public issues are the focus of the evaluation, the process is more subjective. One reason is that the objective may be difficult to measure. A goal of being a "good corporate citizen" is very vague. A second reason is that the goal is often arbitrary. An objective of hiring 25 minority salespeople is measurable, but can the organization prove that this is the right number to hire? Why not 30 or 35? A third reason is that the evaluation criteria might not have been determined when the program was initially established, and the firm may not know which now to use in making a final evaluation.

Issues such as these can be at least partially resolved by following the five steps in formulating and implementing strategy that were described in this chapter, which represent the basic framework used by most firms. However, in every case certain phases of the strategy will end up being given more attention than others. Companies developing a social strategy for the first time are more likely to emphasize planning things. Businesses that have carried out these programs before will give more attention to implementation and control. They already know what has to be accomplished; their goal is to get it done more efficiently and effectively.

Subjectivity is often an inherent part of social program evaluation. It cannot be eliminated, but it can be kept to an acceptable level. Sometimes the only accurate answer that business can give to a critic who asks how a firm knows that it is socially responsible is, "we know."

SUMMARY

Strategy is the relationship between an organization and its environment. Every corporation attempts to establish a relationship that offers it the most benefits. For some, such as small firms, this means adopting a reactive strategy. For others, especially medium-sized firms, this calls for an anticipatory strategy. For large firms, an active strategy is typically used.

Regardless of overall strategy philosophy, however, not all social issues are dealt with similarly. Sometimes a company will find it economically advantageous to drag its feet on a particular issue, even though its overall philosophy is active. Other times, a corporation will be basically anticipatory in its approach, but reactive on a particular issue. In all there are four patterns of social responsibility strategy options: illegal/irresponsible, illegal/responsible, legal/irresponsible, and legal/responsible. Each was described.

The strategic planning process consists of five steps. The first is scanning the environment, typically done by means of four forecasts: economic, technological, political, and social. The social forecast has received the most recent attention and helps organizations anticipate and respond to changing values, quality of work life demands, consumerism and ecological issues, and other social challenges. In forecasting the social environment, corporations try to identify and track social indicators in order to understand social changes. On the basis of their analysis, they determine the effects of these changes.

The second step in the strategy planning process is identifying and prioritizing social issues. Based on its environmental scanning, an organization will identify and rank those social issues with which it must deal. This identification and prioritization will often be done through a decision-making flowchart or a priority identification matrix. In either, the organization will decide which issues it should deal with first and which can wait.

The third step is the formulation of objectives. Besides identifying these objectives the organization will also describe them, thereby providing a basis for developing both programs to accompany the objectives and bases on which they can be evaluated.

The fourth step in the strategic planning process is determining a strategic implementation posture. This posture can be sensing, progressive, or aggressive. Each was described.

The last two stages of strategic planning are implementation and assessment. Implementation involves not only decisions regarding how to put the program into action but also how to form the necessary organization structure and develop the necessary alliances for implementing the program. The assessment phase is determining how well everything went and the types of changes that need to be made in the future.

DISCUSSION AND STUDY QUESTIONS

1. "Strategy is the relationship between an organization and its environment." What is meant by this statement?
2. What kind of responsive social strategy will be used by an active firm? Anticipatory firm? Reactive firm? Identify and describe each strategy.
3. When will a corporation use a reactive strategy? An anticipatory strategy? An active strategy? Give an example of each.

4. How do each of the following social responsibility strategy options work: illegal/irresponsible, legal/irresponsible, illegal/responsible, legal/responsible? Describe each.

5. When would a corporation be likely to implement each of the following social responsibility strategy options: illegal/irresponsible, legal/irresponsible, illegal/responsible, legal/responsible? Give an example of each.

6. In scanning their environments, organizations must consider both their general and their task environments. What forces exist in each of these two environments? Explain your answer in detail.

7. How does a corporation go about scanning its environment? Briefly describe the process.

8. What are some of the principles of environmental scanning? Identify and describe four of them.

9. What is a social indicator and what are its characteristics?

10. One way of prioritizing social issues is to use a decision-making flowchart. A second is to use a form of priority identification matrix. How would each of these be used? Describe how to use each.

11. What are some of the social responsibility objectives that organizations formulate? Identify three and describe each.

12. In determining a strategic implementation posture, a corporation may use sensing, progressive, and aggressive postures. When would each be used? When would each be considered inappropriate? Be complete in your answer.

13. The last phases of strategy are implementation and assessment. Describe each. Which presents the greater problem to management? Why?

CASES AND INCIDENTS

Dealing With Social Change

Christopher Brothers, Inc., a retail chain, currently has 47 stores in five states. But it was not always like this. When Paul Christopher started out in 1914, he had just one small retail store located on the corner of a main thoroughfare in a large midwestern city. Over the years he enlarged the store, and in 1927 he opened a second one. During the Great Depression when his competitors were closing their stores or cutting back their operations, Christopher very conservatively began to increase his retail line and started offering revolving credit-charge lines.

By 1950, when he retired and turned the operation over to his sons, Paul, Ir. and Simon, they had eleven retail outlets in two states. Since then the two brothers have increased sales by almost 2,000 percent and in the last five years have opened a new store each year.

Earlier this month the two brothers went into semiretirement, turning the operation over to their own sons, Michael and Mark. The fathers continue to be active consultants, whereas the sons are responsible for the daily operations. One of the principal issues in which the young brothers have found themselves involved is predicting social change. The retail business is very much affected by changes in life-style and personal values. Those changes, of course, are much more important than they were during the early years of the company's operations. Paul, Jr. explained it this way:

When dad started this company, the only real social concern he had was giving the customer the best value for his money. If there were any social responsibilities besides this, they certainly were not issues of primary concern. However, as the company began to grow and we increased the number of stores, we found ourselves having to pay closer attention to more social issues, especially in the personnel area. Equality in pay and opportunity and, in the late 1960s, hiring quotas all became important. I think about this time we began to realize that we could no longer take a reactive approach to forecasting and dealing with social change. We had to become more responsive and adopt an anticipatory philosophy. Today, as large as we are, we attempt to be as active as possible. We want to know what is going to happen, help shape it if possible, and be prepared to deal with it. We are content to sense the environment in terms of a strategic posture, but we are prepared to act when we see something that requires our attention. For example, last year we actively recruited 250 kids for summer employment. We found this to be not only good social strategy but also good business. Lots of people do business with us because they know we are interested in community affairs and are willing to take a social stand and support it. Our strategy has changed a lot over the last fifty years, and if we are going to remain successful, it will have to change a lot more. You know, sometimes I look at how difficult it can be to formulate a well-thought out strategy for dealing with social change and begin to wonder how we ever did it. I have to admit, though, I don't envy our sons. They have a heavy responsibility to carry, and they are going to have to be even better strategists than we were.

ANALYSIS

1. How can a firm like Christopher Brothers, Inc. go about scanning its environment? What principles should it follow in doing so?
2. What philosophy (reactive, anticipatory, active) and strategy posture (sensing, progressive, aggressive) does the firm use? Explain.
3. What changes is the company likely to see in its social environment over the next decade? How can strategic planning help the firm deal with these changes? Be complete in your answer.

Greg's Dilemma

Greg Morris is really sore. Earlier this week he was informed by his general counsel that the Environmental Protection Agency had passed a rule that companies such as his must install a new type of smokestack scrubber. The cost will be in the neighborhood of $100,000.

Last year Morris's company installed a new scrubber at a cost of $65,000. However, because of new technology, there is now a much better one available, which allows companies to cut their air pollution by almost 98 percent, whereas the one installed last year is equipped to deal with only 95 percent of the pollution. Morris is seriously thinking of bringing legal action to delay and, if possible, to prevent the government from requiring the installation of the new scrubber. He feels that his company's desire to maintain clean air and meet its social responsibility is clear to all. His firm did not have to put in the new scrubber last year. It did so because it learned that the apparatus would reduce air pollution, and this was one of the company's social responsibility objectives. But the firm planned on keeping the scrubber for three years, at which time it would be fully depreciated and then be replaced with the most modern scrubber available. Another thing that made Morris angry is that three of his competitors installed only the minimum air pollution equipment. If they are inspected, they will be fined heavily and required to install new equipment immediately. But they have been playing the odds. There are only a few inspectors in the three-state area, and they feel that it will, on the average, take almost fifteen years before they are inspected. They believe that the risk is worth the penalty.

The other thing that made Morris angry is a decision yesterday by a state product-safety agency, requiring all equipment produced by firms like his to have special warning labels regarding how to operate the machinery. Morris's company spent over $25,000 creating a brochure illustrating how to run the machine and the proper steps to take in ensuring that no one is hurt during operations. However, the state agency has argued that the person running the machine may not have the booklet at hand or may not be given a copy of it before being assigned to operate the machine. In either event, an accident could occur. In order to prevent this, the agency wants a small plate, eight inches square, mounted on the side of all machines produced after the end of next month. The plate will provide important safety instructions to the operator. Morris estimates that the cost to prepare this plate will be approximately $3,000 and that another $4,000 will be lost in time and effort expended in putting these plates on machinery that is currently being used.

ANALYSIS

1. Using Figure 16.2 where would you place Morris's current social responsibility options for both the scrubber and the safety warning? Explain your logic.
2. What strategies are available to Morris's company in dealing with the scrubber issue? The warning label issue? Identify and describe each, being sure to use Figure 16.2 in your answer.
3. How can Morris's firm prevent problems like this? In your answer use social responsibility strategy philosophies.

Implementation of Social Policy and Strategy

Chapter Objectives

- To describe the impact of corporate philosophy and investment criteria on strategy implementation.
- To explain how enterprises are organizing for social responsiveness.
- To discuss the changing nature of managerial processes and action.
- To relate the ways in which modern organizations go about making strategy implementation pay off.

In this chapter we examine the implementation of social policy and strategy. The implementation process consists of two phases: changing the organization's structure so as to accommodate the predetermined strategy and changing the managerial processes and actions so as to carry out the strategy more efficiently.

IMPLEMENTATION

As noted in our discussion of strategy at the end of Chapter 16, implementation is part of the strategic planning process, beginning with strategy formulation and ending with strategy implementation. Commenting on this process, Thomas Jones observed that

Once this concept of corporate social responsibility is accepted, the problem . . . becomes one of implementation. The new concept leads to an altered set of criteria for evaluating corporate social performance. Emphasis is shifted to the inputs of the decision-making process. Corporate managers would be expected, by whatever means, to fully examine the potential social impact of their decisions before the fact.

The means by which this might be done are varied. Some firms might choose to institute social policy study groups within the existing corporate structure. Some might wish to hire outside consultants. Others might feel that the decision-making process should be formally altered through the addition of special purpose directors—environmentalists, racial minorities, women, consumer advocates—or general purpose "public" directors. Regardless of the method or methods chosen, the important concern is that the social impact of corporate decisions be given full consideration in the process itself.[1]

There are a number of key implementation areas. The two that we shall consider are organization structure and managerial processes and actions. Organization structure is important because the enterprise must be organized in such a way as to carry out its social responsibility strategy efficiently and effectively. Managerial processes and actions are important because individual managers must assume new duties and tasks as well as, sometimes, a different philosophy regarding the organization's social obligations.

Corporate Philosophy

Strategy implementation may reflect corporate philosophy. The Polaroid Corporation is an example. This successful company was pressured by numerous groups to abandon its South African operations. These groups argued that Polaroid was helping perpetuate an illegitimate, corrupt, and racially prejudiced regime. Polaroid responded by setting up a committee, consisting of both black and white employees, to study the problem and make recommendations. Based on the committee's recommendations, Polaroid (1) stated its opposition to apartheid, (2) halted direct sales to the South African government, (3) gave equal pensions to South African blacks, and (4) donated money for educational programs for blacks.[2]

In this case, implementation was a result of corporate philosophy. The firm's management decided that the company's objectives could be pursued more effectively if the firm changed its way of doing business in South Africa.

Investment Criteria

Strategy implementation also can be tied to investment criteria. For example, the managers of some pension funds refuse to invest in certain types of operations and/or insist on investing in other types. The implementation of

---

[1]Thomas M. Jones, "Corporate Social Responsibility Revisited, Redefined," *California Management Review*, Spring 1980, p. 65.

[2]"Polaroid to Continue South African Program to Aid Black Workers," *Wall Street Journal*, December 31, 1971, p. 13.

this financial-social strategy can take such forms as the disinvestment of certain companies (investment exclusion) and/or the concentration of investments in certain firms or regions (investment targeting). Investment exclusion by money managers of pension funds includes (1) divestment of companies doing business with or in South Africa, Chile, or other countries whose governments attract significant public disapproval; (2) exclusion of "sin" stocks such as liquor, tobacco, or war-related industries; and (3) exclusion of nonunion companies or competitors of the sponsor corporation. Examples of investment targeting are (1) concentration of investments in a local region, (2) concentration of investments in the sponsor corporation or prounion companies, and (3) concentration of investment in the beneficiaries' liabilities (such as mortgages for plan participants).[3]

Critics may ask whether the decision to invest in a particular firm is based on certain social criteria or whether the decision to disinvest in a particular firm is based on the failure to meet these criteria or to influence the total worth of the pension fund? In fact, social responsibility criteria bias the portfolio by excluding some assets and/or forcing a concentration of investment into other assets. The effect of the bias is permanent, and in some cases, the money manager actually makes less for the fund contributors than he or she would if these social criteria were not used to decide where to invest. For example, although armament firms may be viewed as targets for investment exclusion, these companies often return very high dividends to their investors. Or consider the cigarette and liquor industries. Regardless of how one feels about the social value of these products, many of them have been financially successful for years. Yet because of the corporate management's social goals, financial performance is secondary in deciding where to invest the pension funds. So although there may be some risk in using this type of strategy, it is often regarded as acceptable.

> The imposition of social responsibility criteria may bias the portfolio and cause, except in rare circumstances, an increase in the investment risk. Financially, these criteria are no different from many other exclusionary and targeting criteria such as dividend or quality requirements which are imposed on portfolio management. There can be few managers who are able to purchase the assets they want irrespective of external or internal regulations. Each time that a manager is constrained, the portfolio performance suffers. Social responsibility criteria are merely incremental to the traditional investment approach.[4]

Corporate philosophy and investment criteria are but two factors that affect strategy implementation, but they do illustrate the implementation process. This process is put into action through the careful formulation of an organization design that addresses the company's strategic social responsibility goals.

---

[3]Andrew Rudd, "Social Responsibility and Portfolio Performance," *California Management Review*, Summer 1981, pp. 55–56.

[4]Rudd, p. 60.

ORGANIZING FOR SOCIAL RESPONSIVENESS

Organization structure is vital to strategy implementation. For social policies and strategy, the structure must be designed to facilitate social responsiveness. Before the 1960s, a corporation's social conscience was often that of the chief executive officer (CEO). Over the last 20 years, many corporations have added directors who have an interest in public affairs. Some have also hired public affairs directors and affirmative action officers. At the same time, business firms have begun experimenting with a variety of structural arrangements designed to accommodate their objectives of social responsibility.

Typical Organizational Arrangements

How have organizations altered their structures to accommodate social responsibility? Smaller firms tend to use individual executives, temporary task forces, or permanent committees of senior officers to make social decisions. Large firms usually have permanent departments or a combination of departments, committees, and task forces to make such decisions.

The selection of organizational arrangement is also related to the industry's characteristics. For example, the transportation, communication, and utilities industries seem to prefer individual executives or a permanent committee of senior executives to make decisions with social implications. Oil, gas, finance, insurance, real estate, and wholesale and retail firms favor permanent departments. Manufacturing firms fall between these two groups, having an almost equal preference for individual executive and permanent departments. Commenting on her overall findings and the reasons for organizations' different structural arrangements in various industries, Holmes reported:

> The results of this investigation indicate that the selection of structural means for making social decisions is related to a number of interdependent factors including industry characteristics (such as the nature of technology and interface with the public), size of the firm, and areas of social involvement. Firms that are especially large in terms of either assets or number of employees tend to prefer permanent arrangements and smaller firms are more likely to prefer more temporary arrangements. The relationship between size and organizational arrangements is complicated by pronounced industry preferences for organizational arrangements, which are at least partially attributable to mainstream social efforts into areas closely related to the economic functions of the firm. A tendency to "follow the leader" may also contribute to pronounced industry patterns. Similar preferences for areas of social involvement seem to result in similar structural adaptations even across industrial classifications.[5]

[5]Sandra L. Holmes, "Adapting Corporate Structures for Social Responsiveness," *California Management Review*, Fall 1978, p. 52–53.

Structural Design and Personnel Function

Most organizations handle social issues programs using either a decentralized or a centralized arrangement. Under a decentralized arrangement, each functional department is responsible for these issues that fall within the purview of its expertise. For example, the finance department handles investor relations; the public relations department takes care of stockholder relations; the public affairs department assumes responsibility for government relations; and the marketing department deals with customer relations. An example of this arrangement is given in Figure 17.1.

Under a centralized arrangement, all of these functions are handled through one department. The head of this department reports directly to the CEO and coordinates all activities related to external relations. An example of this arrangement is shown in Figure 17.2.

Most corporate organizations designed to handle external affairs operate between the two extremes illustrated in Figures 17.1 and 17.2. It is becoming more common to find these departments carrying the title of public affairs, as opposed to the old title of public relations. The reason for the change is that public relations has some negative connotations: that is, (1) public relations is typically identified as a media relations; (2) the title is often interpreted to be nothing more than image building; (3) public relations has lost credibility in the business world and elsewhere; and (4) the title of public affairs more accurately describes the functions carried out by this department.

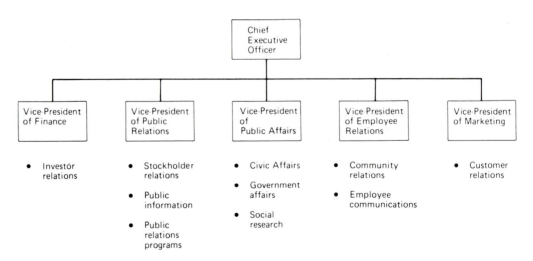

FIGURE 17.1   Decentralized Arrangements for Handling External Affairs.

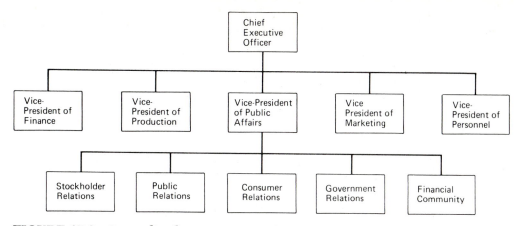

FIGURE 17.2   Centralized Arrangements for Handling External Affairs.

The Rise of Specialists

Another organizational structure change is the rise of social responsibility experts. An example is the person with a knowledge of equal opportunity legislation and company personnel policy. This individual is often found heading the firm's EEO (equal employment opportunity) or affirmative action section and is responsible for seeing that the corporation complies with federal government guidelines and laws. Another example is the vice-president of environmental affairs:

> Interlake, Inc., for example, a producer of steel and powdered metals in Oak Brook, Illinois, reports that its environmental staff has grown to 40 people. A vice-president of the company spends about 95 percent of his time on environmental matters and states that his advice is sought on all company activities that affect the environment. *Business Week* states that this case is not unusual. "Increasingly, corporations are upgrading the status and responsibilities of their environmental managers. Their staffs and budgets are being enlarged, and many are gaining more clout with top management."[6]

The same pattern occurs in other social responsibility areas, from quality of work life to consumer relations. But this does not mean that staff specialists, rather than line managers, will assume responsibility for the company's policies and programs.

---

[6]Rogene A. Buchholz, *Business Environment and Public Policy: Implications for Management* (Englewood Cliffs, N.J.: Prentice-Hall, 1982), p. 441.

Dealing with the Government

Government relations continues to be a major concern for business. In fact, as corporations increase in size, it is common to find them establishing offices in Washington. When the company has a Washington office only, this representative typically reports directly to the CEO. If there is an internal public affairs office, then the Washington representative commonly reports to the head of this department. However, if the Washington connection is extremely important, as in the case of companies that rely heavily on government contracts, both the head of this office and the head of public affairs will report to the CEO. The reason for this trend was explained in a Conference Board study:

> Government relations is gaining greater status within the organization, as government relations executives report direct involvement in the decision-making process of their companies. More and more chief executives are emphasizing the importance of this function and are taking a more direct, personal role in it. So, too, are other senior executives, and those in charge of technical areas, R and D, personnel, finance, and so on throughout the management team.[7]

Are corporations likely to continue to organize for government relations? Executives report that they believe that the trend will continue. When asked how much their involvement in federal government relations had increased over the past three years and what they expected over the next three years, they reported that

Relations were the same over the last three years and should remain that way over the next three.	3%
Relations were the same over the last three years but should increase moderately over the next three.	4
Relations were the same over the last three years but should increase strongly over the next three.	1
Relations have increased moderately over the last three years but should remain this way over the next three.	3
Relations have increased moderately over the last three years and should continue to increase moderately over the next three.	28
Relations have increased moderately over the last three years but should increase strongly over the next three.	5
Relations have increased strongly over the last three years but should remain this way over the next three.	2

[7]Phyllis McGrath, *Redefining Corporate-Federal Regulations* (New York: The Conference Board, 1979), pp. 2–3.

Relations have increased strongly over the last three years and should
   increase moderately over the next three.   25
Relations have increased strongly over the last three years and should
   continue to do so for the next three years.[8]   29

The Role of Committees

Few firms use committees as their primary tool to implement social responsibility strategies, but many use variations of the permanent committee to supplement their efforts. After analyzing organizational arrangements in different industries, Holmes offered the following partial listing of committee variations:

> Senior management makes the initial decision, then delegates to the Community Affairs Officers.
>
> A permanent division is assigned all recurring decisions, but new issues are brought before a Public Affairs Committee which includes the Division Manager. Extremely significant new issues which affect company policy may be brought to the Executive Committee before a decision is made.
>
> Decisions are made by top management after recommendations by department heads. On minor items, decisions are made by department heads.
>
> Social problems are the responsibility of the Vice President for Corporate Relations. Decisions are made by the Chief Executive (or Board of Directors) on recommendation from the Vice President of Corporation Relations and the Senior Vice President.
>
> A Corporate Responsibilities Committee, consisting of members from all layers of management and including a member of the Board of Directors.
>
> A Corporate Responsibilities Committee of the Board of Directors.
>
> Consensus among senior management.
>
> A combination of committee supported by a staff function in which staff recommends through committee to top management.
>
> The Corporation Executive Committee.
>
> Public Affairs Officer in consultation with senior management.
>
> A Board of Directors Committee which studies, audits, and formulates policy on major items.
>
> Various committees review specific social issues on their own initiative or because a department which is responsible has requested or recommended their review.[9]

[8]McGrath, *Redefining*, p. 3.
[9]Holmes, pp. 49–50.

Buchholz reported the growing popularity of public responsibility commit-tees at the board level.[10] These committees are responsible for (1) identifying the major constituencies (both internal and external) that judge the corpora-tion's behavior and performance, (2) examining the company's performance from both social and environmental standpoints, (3) recommending specific issues for board and management consideration, (4) determining the relative priority of these issues, (5) recommending corporate policy for responding to these issues, (6) considering and recommending new areas of public policy and their possible impact on the corporations, (7) examining and reporting to the board on corporate attitudes toward the needs and concerns of the company's major constituencies, and (8) recommending where duties and responsibilities should lie in the firm regarding important public policy issues.[11]

One of the reasons for the evolution of these committees is that they supplement board activity by investigating social issue areas that are too time-consuming for direct board involvement. The committee can also help by implementing board directives stemming from its research and recom-mendations.

Some firms have carried the committee idea farther by using two or more of them, often in conjunction with a social policy department or its equivalent, to address its corporate social responsibility. The Bank of America is one such firm. No one person or group is responsible for identifying social issues and implementing strategy; instead, three are used: a public policy commit-tee, a social policy committee, and a social policy department:

> *Public Policy Committee.* Composed of six outside directors and two inside direc-tors, this committee meets monthly and is charged with advising management on public policy issues and monitoring performance. The purpose of the commit-tee is to underscore the bank's commitment to corporate responsibility and to provide an objective assessment of performance by independent directors.
>
> *Social Policy Committee.* Ten senior bank officers from a cross section of line and staff units, sit on this Committee. Meeting at least once a month, the group provides the link which transforms issues into policy decisions and, ultimately, into line management responsibilities. The committee seeks to initi-ate those changes in bank policies and practices necessary to ensure that the company's operations reflect the values of its core constituencies and the expec-tations of the public at large.
>
> *Social Policy Department.* This department provides staff support to the Public Policy and Social Policy Committees. It is also broken into three sections, each of which focuses on a different aspect of bank operations. The Retail Section addresses issues affecting California communities, small businesses and consum-ers. The Wholesale Section is concerned with international issues and works

[10]Buchholz, p. 445.

[11]Michael L. Lovdal, Raymond A. Bauer, and Nancy H. Treverton, "Public Responsibility Committees of the Board," *Harvard Business Review*, May–June 1977, pp. 40–41.

closely with the bank's World Banking Division. The Administration/Corporate Section handles issues related to the bank's administrative units, and works with subsidiaries of the overall bank in establishing their own corporate responsibility systems. All three sections are responsible for providing management and the board with early identification and analysis of social issues and social trends. They also determine the relevance of these issues and trends for the bank and formulate recommendations for changes in the way the company conducts the business. Additionally, the department is responsible for monitoring performance in areas where line management already exists such as customer relations, corporate giving, minority purchasing, and equal employment opportunity. Finally, this unit serves as a clearing house for the social impact of the bank's operations.[12]

Committee organizations and other structural arrangements are also changing managerial behavior.

CHANGING MANAGERIAL BEHAVIOR

The effective implementation of social policy and strategy brings about a dramatic change in managerial behavior as reflected in management's philosophy and role, the increasing paperwork, and the personal liability issue confronting top management.

Management's Philosophy and Role

Management's behavior toward social policy implementation is described in Table 17.1. Whether the organization operates from social obligation, social responsibility, or social responsiveness, a particular dimension of behavior (proscriptive, prescriptive, or anticipatory and preventive) can be used to describe corporate behavior. Anticipatory and preventive behavior best describes managerial activities in large organizations.

In implementing their respective strategies, business programs, policies, and procedures can be described according to their behavioral dimensions, as in Table 17.1. Notice that these range from a search for legitimacy, ethical norms, and social accountability for corporate action (the philosophical side of management behavior) to operating strategy, response to social pressures, activities pertaining to government actions, legislative and political activities, and philanthropy (the action-oriented side of management behavior). This table is intended for descriptive purposes only; it is not meant to be a moral statement. If one accepts the social responsibility tenet that "with power comes obligation," then the social policy strategy of large firms will be best described by the behavioral dimensions of state 3. Additionally, as

[12]Bank of America Corporate Responsibility Report, *Community and the Bank*, 1979, pp. 46–47.

TABLE 17.1. Three-State Schema for Classifying Corporate Behavior.

Dimension of Behavior	State One: Social Obligation Proscriptive	State Two: Social Responsibility Prescriptive	State Three: Social Responsiveness Anticipatory and Preventive
Search for legitimacy	Confines legitimacy to legal and economic criteria only; does not violate laws; equates profitable operations with fulfilling social expectations.	Accepts the reality of limited relevance of legal and market criteria of legitimacy in actual practice. Willing to consider and accept broader—extralegal and extramarket—criteria for measuring corporate performance and social role.	Accepts its role as defined by the social system and therefore subject to change; recognizes importance of profitable operations but includes other criteria.
Ethical norms	Considers business value-neutral; managers expected to behave according to their own ethical standards	Defines norms in community—related terms (i.e., good corporate citizen). Avoids taking moral stand on issues which may harm its economic interests or go against prevailing social norms (majority views).	Takes definite stand on issues of public concern; advocates institutional ethical norms even though they may be detrimental to its immediate economic interest or prevailing social norms.
Social accountability for corporate actions	Construes narrowly as limited to stockholders; jealously guards its prerogative against outsiders.	Construes narrowly for legal purposes, but broadened to include groups affected by its actions; management more outward looking.	Willing to account for its actions to other groups, even those not directly affected by its actions.
Operating strategy	Exploitative and defensive adaptation. Maximum externalization of costs.	Reactive adaptation. Where identifiable internalize previously external costs. Maintain current standards of physical and social environment. Compensate victims of pollution and other corporate-related activities even in the absence of clearly established legal grounds. Develop industry-wide standards.	Proactive adaptation. Takes lead in developing and adapting new technology for environmental protectors. Evaluates side effects of corporate actions and eliminates them prior to the action's being taken. Anticipates future social changes and develops internal structures to cope with them.

Response to social pressures	Maintains low public profile, but if attacked, uses PR methods to upgrade its public image; denies any deficiencies; blames public dissatisfaction on ignorance or failure to understand corporate functions; discloses information only where legally required.	Accepts responsibility for solving current problems; will admit deficiencies in former practices and attempt to persuade public that its current practices meet social norms; attitude toward critics conciliatory; freer information disclosures than state one.	Willingly discusses activities with outside groups; makes information freely available to public; accepts formal and informal inputs from outside groups in decision making. Is willing to be publicly evaluated for its various activities.
Activities pertaining to governmental actions	Strongly resists any regulation of its activities except when it needs help to protect its market position; avoids contact; resists any demands for information beyond that legally required.	Preserves management discretion in corporate decisions, but cooperates with government in research to improve industry-wide standards; participates in political processes and encourages employees to do likewise.	Openly communicates with government; assists in enforcing existing laws and developing evaluations of business practices; objects publicly to governmental activities that it feels are detrimental to the public good.
Legislative and political activities	Seeks to maintain status quo; actively opposes laws that would internalize any previously externalized costs; seeks to keep lobbying activities secret.	Willing to work with outside groups for good environment laws; concedes need for change in some status quo laws; less secrecy in lobbying than state one.	Avoids meddling in politics and does not pursue special-interest laws; assists legislative bodies in developing better laws where relevant; promotes honesty and openness in government and its own lobbying activities.
Philanthropy	Contributes only when direct benefit to it clearly shown; otherwise, views contributions as responsibility of individual employees.	Contributes to noncontroversial and established causes; matches employee contributions.	Activities of state two, *plus* support and contributions to new, controversial groups whose needs it sees as unfulfilled and increasingly important.

Source: S. Prakash Sethi, "Dimensions of Corporate Social Performance: An Analytical Framework," *California Management Review*, Spring 1975, p. 63.

business firms increase in size, one should expect their behavior to change from that in state 1 to that in state 3.

Top management's involvement in implementing strategy is more active than ever before, ranging from in-house activities, such as making decisions about worker safety protection systems, to speaking out on public issues, talking to public-interest group leaders, and testifying before Congress. One of the CEO's most important roles is as the firm's principal external representative. In this role, there are many different public groups to whom the chief executive officer must be responsible. Gone are the days when this executive was responsible only to the stockholders and the customers. On the other hand, when supported by a well-managed public affairs staff that researches public issues and is active in both formulating and implementing social policy, the CEO's overall effectiveness in conducting social responsibility strategy can be greatly enhanced.

Paperwork

One big change associated with strategy implementation is the paperwork. The Federal Paperwork Commission, created to study the cost to society of paperwork, estimated that the costs to private industry alone are in the billions of dollars annually. The largest companies spend well over $1 million a year.

Types of Reports.   Where is all this money spent? Some of the most common paperwork expenses are (1) statistical information requested by federal agencies such as the Bureau of the Census, International Trade Commission, Bureau of Labor Statistics, and Bureau of Economic Analysis; (2) financial information filed with the Federal Trade Commission and/or the Securities and Exchange Commission; (3) affirmative action plans filed with the Department of Labor and annual statistics on women and minorities as requested by the Equal Employment Opportunity Commission; (4) information about salaried and hourly pension plans supplied to the government in compliance with the Employee Retirement Income Security Act; (5) energy usage information supplied to the Department of Energy; (6) data related to occupational injuries and illnesses on the work site filed and maintained at each workplace or company plant; and (7) environmental information related to air, water, and disposal pollution as required by industry and processed and filed with the appropriate governmental agency.

The Cost Factor.   As noted, the cost of these reports can run into the millions of dollars. Some of these expenses are easily identified, but others are hidden.

One expense that businesses will have to continue to bear are start-up costs. These expenses begin when the enterprise decides what types of reports it will have to provide to meet governmental regulations. Some of these early expenses relate to finding out just what the governmental agency wants, in what form, and how many copies. Commenting on this, Buchholz noted:

Compliance with the new Toxic Substances Control Act provides a current example of a start-up cost. The act requires the EPA to compile and make public an inventory of chemical substances manufactured, imported, or processed in the United States for commercial purposes. Any substance not on this list will then be considered a new chemical subject to premanufacture notification requirements. This inventory will be compiled from inventories that manufacturers, importers, processors, or users of chemical substances are required to prepare and submit to the agency.[13]

A second cost is direct reporting costs. These are the expenses associated with gathering the data and having them analyzed by the computer and entered in the proper place on the reports. It also includes the cost associated with employee time expended on these efforts, as well as any expenses for hiring consultants, lawyers, accountants, and other professionals. The latter expenses are sometimes referred to as *variable* because they depend to a large degree on the number of times the report has to be submitted and the detail that is required in each case.

A third cost is typically referred to as avoidance cost. These are expenses incurred by corporations in avoiding disclosing information to the government. Examples are the costs of lobbying efforts, legal assistance, and research on advertising and public relations and ways and means of avoiding reporting certain types of information.

A fourth cost is that of legal exposure. As more and more information is requested by the federal government, corporate executives have to assume more and more risks when they sign these reporting forms. What if the data are incomplete or inaccurate? Who is responsible? What if the information is misleading or false? To what degree is the person signing the form legally liable? These may seem like rhetorical questions, but they are not. Management's personal liability is becoming a very important issue. In fact, before agreeing to serve on a board of directors, many executives, are now asking, What kinds of protection or liability insurance are you willing to give me?

Personal Liability and Top Management

In implementing social responsibility strategy, executives are finding that they can become personally liable for a particular action. An executive signs many different memos, forms, letters, reports, and other pieces of correspondence. If one of these contains incomplete or inaccurate information, is the executive personally responsible? If so, to what degree?

Traditionally, top managers have been shielded from the unlawful acts of their subordinates. For example, if a top executive's subordinate deliberately issues memos to subsidiary managers urging them not to hire a minority member or to engage in certain types of questionable safety practices, it is

---

[13]Buchholz, p. 459.

not uncommon for the executive to initial the memo without reading it. He or she assumes that the subordinate is following both corporate and government policy and that there is nothing illegal in the correspondence. But what if there is? Is the executive liable? In the past, executives were responsible only when they were personally involved in a wrongdoing. But since the late 1970s, the courts, regulatory agencies, state legislators, and Congress seem to have changed their minds. Now there is a movement toward making the executive responsible for the actions of his or her subordinates and, in some cases, for almost every person in the enterprise. Sethi offered the following evidence:

> The President of a Philadelphia-based supermarket chain . . . was convicted . . . of violating the Federal Food and Drug Act and fined $250 after inspectors found evidence of rat infestations at a warehouse in Baltimore. The U.S. Supreme Court upheld his conviction. . . .
>
> Four managers of American Chicle and an executive of its parent company, Warner-Lambert, were charged with manslaughter and criminally negligent homicide after six workers were killed and 55 others injured in an explosion and fire at a Long Island City chewing gum plant. . . . A New York state judge dismissed the case earlier this year, but the state intends to appeal.
>
> The manager of an H. J. Heinz Company plant in Tracy, California, received a six-month suspended sentence and probation after being cited by California food and drug authorities for unsanitary working conditions in his plant.
>
> A Minneapolis municipal judge ordered Illinois-based Lloyd A. Fry Roffling Co. to select one of its executives to serve a 30-day jail term for the plant's violations of city air pollution standards. The sentence was rescinded because of a legal technicality.[14]

Such illustrations indicate that executive liability is no joking matter. When implementing a social responsibility strategy, or failing to implement one, top managers can find themselves in serious legal straits. Increasingly, the courts are rejecting the old interpretation of the law, in which responsibility is placed with the individual who made the mistake, and placing more and more of the blame at the top. Anyone who holds a responsible position in an enterpise can find himself or herself in trouble. What kinds of risks do executives face under federal law? Table 17.2 offers some answers to this question. It is increasingly likely that managers will end up having to pay these penalties:

> A top enforcement official for the Food and Drug Administration (FDA) tells the story of a business executive who recently assembled his senior personnel and had a lawyer explain the concept of executive liability. When the presentation was done, the executive turned to his subordinates and said: "Gentlemen, as I

---

[14]S. Prakash Sethi, "Who Me? Jail as an Occupational Hazard," *The Wharton Magazine*, Summer 1978, pp. 19–20.

TABLE 17.2. Risks Executives Face Under Federal Law.

Agency	Year Enforcement Began	Complaint May Name Individual	Maximum Individual Penalty	Maximum Corporate Penalty	Private Suit Allowed Under Applicable Statute
Internal Revenue Service	1862	Yes	$5,000, three years, or both	$10,000, 50% assessment, prosecution costs	No
Antitrust Division (Justice Department)	1890	Yes	$100,000, three years, or both	$1 million, injunction, divestiture	Yes
Food and Drug Administration	1907	Yes	$1,000, one year, or both for first offense; $10,000, three years, or both thereafter	$1,000 for first offense; $10,000 thereafter; seizure of condemned products	No
Federal Trade Commission	1914	Yes	Restitution, injunction	Restitution; injunction, divestiture, $10,000 per day for violation or rules, orders	No
Securities and Exchange Commission	1934	Yes	$10,000, two years, or both	$10,000, injunction	Yes
Equal Employment Opportunity Commission	1965	No		Injunction, back-pay award, reinstatement	Yes
Office of Federal Contract Compliance	1965	No		Suspension, cancellation of contract	Yes
Environmental Protection Agency	1970	Yes	$25,000 per day, one year, or both for first offense; $50,000 per day, two years, or both thereafter	$25,000 per day, first offense; $50,000 per day thereafter; injunction	Yes
Occupational Safety and Health Administration	1970	No[a]	$10,000, six months, or both	$10,000	No
Consumer Product Safety Commission	1972	Yes	$50,000, one year, or both	$500,000	Yes
Office of Employee Benefits Security (Labor Dept.)	1975	Yes	$10,000, one year, or both; barring from future employment with plan; reimbursement	$100,000, reimbursement	Yes

[a] Except sole proprietorship

Source: Business Week, May 10, 1976, p. 113.

understand it, if you screw up, I can be prosecuted. If that happens, you can bet that you will be out of a job here, and I'll see to it that no one else hires you either."[15]

On the positive side, executives are finding that the public will not accept extremely harsh measures and that the company will often pay all fines and penalties. For example, the sentence of a business executive to five years in jail for an error committed by a subordinate is not only distasteful to the public in general but also is unlikely to be meted out by the courts. On the other hand, if a fine or penalty is assessed, it is likely that the corporation will pick it up. In either event, the executive escapes unscathed. So where is the danger or the risk to top management? The answer is somewhere in between: shorter jail sentences (more likely to be used by the courts) and larger financial fines (more likely to be felt by the corporations). Commenting on these developments, Sethi found:

> The trend toward stiffer penalties also is showing up in the traditional areas of corporate crime, such as antitrust and securities fraud, in which executives often are found to have direct knowledge or involvement. In 1976, 175 persons were convicted of antitrust violations and one went to jail. In 1977, the number of antitrust convictions declined to 161 but five violators went to jail. This year, in an antitrust case in which several makers of electrical wiring devices were convicted of price-fixing, 11 present and former officers received fines totalling $200,000 and 10 of them received prison terms of one-to-three months. The total time actually to be served—19 months with no parole—exceeds the total prison time previously served in the history of antitrust actions in the United States.[16]

Additionally, amendments to the Sherman Act increased the maximum penalty for corporate crime to three years in jail and a fine of $100,000 per individual. The Justice Department's latest guidelines regarding sentencing recommend that the severity of the punishment be tied directly to the defendant's relative position in the management hierarchy. In 1977, the Foreign Corrupt Practices Act provided for maximum penalties of up to $1 million for corporations and five years in jail and $10,000 in fines for officers and directors. No wonder some researchers and writers in the field of business and its environment are recommending that corporations educate their managers in how to handle their external relations more effectively. Some of the recommendations include the following:

1. Internal management development programs that have environmental concerns as part of the curriculum.
2. Company-developed and-operated continuing education programs in Washington, D.C., to teach management employees how government functions.

[15]Sethi, p. 22.
[16]Sethi, p. 25.

3. Company publications or internal management monographs devoted in part or in whole to public issues of concern to the company.
4. Educational programs dealing with legislative issues of concern to the company, designed to stimulate grass-roots political activity.
5. Attendance at outside institutes or university seminars and conferences dealing with environmental or public policy matters.
6. Participation in advanced management programs at colleges and universities where public policy material constitutes at least part of the content.
7. Attendance at programs and seminars in Washington, D.C., to learn about government.
8. Management retreats and seminars, some of which are devoted to environmental issues where many outside speakers are invited.
9. Participation in professional societies or industry and trade associations.
10. Participation in the President's Interchange Program—an exchange of executives between business and government.
11. Involving employees and managers in creating social programs or in developing social policy for the company.
12. Service by employees on a foundation advisory committee helping to make decisions about charitable contributions.
13. Regular management meetings at which public issues are discussed—these meetings become something of an educational process, particularly for new managers.
14. Faculty forums where university faculty are invited to discuss public issues with younger managers for a two- or three-day period.[17]

MAKING STRATEGY IMPLEMENTATION PAY

Strategy implementation requires changing the organizational structure and managerial behavior. If an enterprise analyzes its position, such implementation can prove to be cost beneficial. For example, if properly addressed, it is possible to turn consumer issues to an organization's competitive advantage. Becker illustrated this by using what he called an "opportunity matrix," such as the one presented in Figure 17.3. This matrix addresses marketing decision variables (product, place, price, and promotion) and consumer issues (information, health and safety, repair and servicing, pricing, pollution, market concentration, product quality, and consumer representation before government.

Each cell in the consumerism opportunity matrix represents how an issue can be approached. Pollution is an example. If a corporation wants to implement a pollution strategy related to each of the four marketing decision variables, it can do so while turning the issue to its own competitive advantage.

[17]Buchholz, p. 456.

Marketing Decision Variables

Consumer Issues	Product	Price	Place	Promotion
Information				
Health and safety				
Repair and servicing				
Pricing				
Pollution				
Market concentration				
Product quality				
Consumer representation before government				

FIGURE 17.3   Consumerism Opportunity Matrix.

Product Strategy

In product strategy, the firm must decide how it can meet its responsibility of not polluting the environment while at the same time producing its product for a profit. One of the best examples of this strategy is that used by firms creating recyclable products. For example, some paper companies have turned out quality writing paper made entirely of recycled beer cartons and magazines, and aerosol can manufacturers have eliminated fluorocarbons, allegedly harmful to the ozone layer around the earth, from all of their products.

Pricing Strategy

Perhaps the most popular approach to pricing strategy is recycling. Reusable materials are purchased from the consumer and put back into the production process. With this implementation process, manufacturers have created a positive image among the general public, and by cooperating with the company, consumers have been able to reduce the cost of the recycled product.

Distribution Strategy

Some firms are also using their marketing channels to deal with pollution. A number of grocery chains, for example, are using their retail outlets as centers for the return of recyclable products.

> Red Owl stores in Milwaukee began to accept the return of shopping bags, egg cartons, and milk and beverage containers made of glass. Furthermore, the chain offered shoppers cash refunds ranging from two to three cents for the above materials; these amounts represent the original cost to the store. Because of the subsequent paper shortages, the idea seemed even more attractive and . . . was extended to all the chain's outlets. National Tea subsequently substituted a similar program, as did a number of smaller grocery chains.[18]

Promotion Strategy

One of the main ways that promotion strategies deal with pollution is to emphasize the organization's response to the consumer complaint about its product. ARCO, for example, voluntarily abandoned its 1,000 billboards along highways and at service stations in an effort to help clean up the environment. Another and more imaginative use of promotion to improve a company's social responsibility image was that of Hunt-Wesson, which started a "save the eagle" campaign. The firm offered to buy 15 square feet of land near an eagle-nesting area for each label sent in from three of its products.

Extensions of the Matrix

Not all consumer issues are equally relevant to all consumers. Some people are more interested in the price of a product than in the recyclability of its carton. Others are more concerned with the availability of a good than in the fact that the company will contribute ten cents to a wildlife preserve for every label from the product that is cut off and sent in. So in implementing a social responsibility strategy that allows the corporation to use its competitive advantages, consumer segmentation is necessary. The firm must carefully choose its marketing strategy (product, price, place, promotion). The same approach can be used in dealing with other publics, including employees, the government, and suppliers. Becker put it this way:

> The Opportunity Matrix can assist management in identifying potential consumer problems and converting apparently threatening situations into challenges for gaining market advantage. It can be further developed to analyze specific products, market segments, and operations objectives.

[18]Boris W. Becker, "Using Consumer Issues for Competitive Advantage," *Business Horizons*, May–June 1981, p. 45.

Consumerism can be viewed as a threat or a challenge. It will surely be a threat to the recalcitrant, who may fall under the ever-vigilant eye of government regulation, or worse yet, may fall victim to their more aggressive competitors. But consumerism has already been turned into a source of competitive advantage by the numerous firms alert enough to take advantage of opportunity.[19]

SUMMARY

Strategy implementation is a natural follow-up to strategy formulation. Implementation is influenced by many factors, particularly corporate philosophy and investment criteria.

In organizing for social responsiveness, the selection of the organizational arrangement is usually determined by the size of the enterprise and its industry characteristics. Some firms use a decentralized arrangement, and others prefer a more centralized structure. In either case, it is becoming more and more common to find social responsibility coordinated by a director for external relations. This person generally provides advice or counsel, service, and control. Another emerging organizational structure change is the rise of experts in a particular social responsibility area. A third development is the modification of structures to help enterprises deal more effectively with government relations. A fourth development is the use of committees, often to supplement board activity by investigating social issues areas that would be too time consuming to warrant direct board involvement.

The effective implementation of social policy and strategy has also changed managerial behavior, management philosophy and role, and the paperwork required by government regulatory agencies. Such changes are also being brought about because of the personal liability of top management if their subordinates (if not themselves) are involved in unlawful acts.

In the last part of the chapter we discussed how to make strategy implementation pay. Through the effective use of the marketing mix (product, price, place, and promotion), it is often possible for a corporation to use social issues to its competitive advantage. One way is through the effective use of the consumerism opportunity matrix presented in Figure 17.3.

DISCUSSION AND STUDY QUESTIONS

1. How does corporate philosophy influence strategy implementation? Give an example. How do investment criteria influence strategy implementation? Cite an example.
2. How do the organizational arrangements of small companies differ from those of large companies?
3. What areas of social involvement most affect organizational arrangements

---

[19]Becker, p. 47.

in the following industries: oil and gas; finance, insurance, and real estate; wholesale and retail; manufacturing; and transportation, communication, and utilities?

4. How do decentralized organizational arrangements differ from centralized organizational arrangements? Draw an organization chart showing each arrangement, and discuss these charts in your answer.

5. Why are more and more firms dropping the title of public relations and substituting external relations or some similar departmental title?

6. External relations executives usually have three roles. Describe each.

7. "Another organizational structure change is the rise of experts in a social responsibility area." What does this statement mean?

8. How are many modern enterprises organizing so as to handle most effectively their government relations? Describe the changes.

9. How likely is it that corporations will have to continue to organize for government relations? Be as complete as possible in your answer, citing statistics when possible.

10. How are corporations using committees to help organize for and implement their social responsibility strategies?

11. Using Table 17.2 as a reference, how does corporate behavior change as a corporation moves from proscriptive to prescriptive and then to an anticipatory and preventive behavior? Be as complete as possible in your answer.

12. Do corporations spend much money keeping up with the paperwork demands of government regulation and compliance? In your answer be sure to discuss the various costs associated with such compliance.

13. Can executives be liable for the unlawful acts of their subordinates? Do managers have any responsibility? Explain.

14. How can business firms train their managers to handle external relations more effectively? Cite at least five suggestions.

15. How can the consumerism opportunity matrix in Figure 17.3 help business make strategy implementation pay?

CASE AND INCIDENTS

The New Department

A medium-sized consumer goods firm swept the soap market a few years ago with a newly developed dishwashing liquid. After this initial success, the company began expanding its offerings and moved to nationwide coverage. At the rate it is growing, the firm will be grossing over $100 million within five years.

As the corporation began its rapid growth, the CEO started paying closer attention to the enterprise's environment and how the company should be organized. One area that had not received a great deal of organizational attention was social policy and strategy. Realizing that no large consumer goods firm could afford not to have a socially responsive posture, the CEO decided to bring in a public relations expert to head up a newly created public affairs department. The CEO hopes that this person will be able to pull together all of the social programs and play an active role in their implementation.

At the present time, investor relations are handled by the vice-president of finance; stockholder relations and public relations are handled by the vice-president of public relations; community relations and employee communications are taken care of by the vice-president of employee relations; and customer relations are managed by the vice-president of marketing. The company has also been trying to land some government orders and has a small office in Washington which is managed by a senior staff official.

The person who will head up this new public affairs department will be responsible for coordinating all of the social responsibility activities and will also be responsible for seeing that all consumer regulations are adhered to by manufacturing and marketing and that any reports or other information required by federal agencies are provided in a complete and timely manner.

ANALYSIS

1. Will a centralized or a decentralized organizational arrangement be more effective for this firm? Make a rough draft of what its organization chart will look like after it adds this new department.
2. What kinds of activities will the head of the public affairs department handle? What will the person's role entail?
3. In what way can the creation of a new department of public affairs be of value to this company? What advantages does it offer to the enterprise? Cite and describe at least three benefits.

Paula's Shock

Paula Higgins does not know whether to call her personal attorney or just wait and see how bad the situation is before she seeks any legal assistance. Paula is the president of a small design and manufacturing company located in the Midwest. A year ago a friend of Paula's called her up to tell her about a retail chain's expansion plans. The chain was interested in developing and selling a wide array of new merchandise, including electrical toys. Since Paula's firm had designed and manufactured two very successful toys in the past, he wondered whether Paula would be interested in a contract to develop and produce a half dozen more. Paula said she was, and the retail chain agreed on the six toys to be produced.

Five of these toys were quite simple and presented no problem at all.

However, the last, a plastic talking doll, was difficult. The toy was to be run by battery and able to be taken into the bath. The three biggest challenges were to prevent corrosion of the mechanical system, stop the battery from getting wet, and ensure that there was no danger from electric shock.

Realizing that the developmental expertise was beyond her firm's capability, Paula signed a subcontract with a research and development (R&D) firm to design and test a doll that would meet these three specifications. After seven weeks of intensive effort, coupled with countless tests, Paula was provided with the manufacturing blueprints for producing the doll.

The actual manufacture and delivery only took 90 days, thanks to the detailed specifications from the R&D firm. The dolls were delivered three months ago, and after a nationwide advertising campaign, sales began last week.

Early this morning Paula heard the bad news. Two children who were playing with their dolls in the bath were shocked by its electrical system. The parents immediately contacted their attorneys. The retail chain is in the process of pulling all of these dolls off the shelf, and it also wants to see all of the test data from the R&D firm.

Paula has had her assistant gather this information and make a copy for the retailer. While looking through the file, Paula noticed that on four occasions she signed reports that were sent to her by the R&D firm. These reports all said basically the same thing: (1) here are our latest test results; (2) please look them over carefully, and if you see a problem, let us know; and (3) if you agree that we are on the right track in complying with our contract, sign below. Paula also noticed that in the original contract that the R&D firm sent to her, both it and she were listed as copartners in this R&D project. Paula never read the reports or the contract; her assistant simply put the reports in front of her for a signature, and then the contract was drawn up by the R&D firm, read by Paula's attorney and then signed by her.

Paula is now wondering what the extent of her liability might be. She realizes that she signed certain forms that might make her a party to the problem. On the other hand, she had no idea that there was anything wrong with the doll. If anything, she feels like an innocent dupe. Nevertheless, just to be on the safe side, she thinks she should call her lawyer.

ANALYSIS

1. What mistake did Paula make?
2. Does Paula have any personal liability? Explain, being sure to support your argument.
3. How can Paula avoid problems like this in the future? Be complete in your answer.

Measuring and Reporting Corporate Social Performance

Chapter Objectives

- To explain the nature of social performance quality.
- To relate the ways in which business firms go about measuring social performance.
- To discuss the area of social accounting and the ways in which financial statements can be extended and new reporting formats developed.
- To relate the way specific firms go about setting and measuring their social performance.

In this chapter we focus on measuring and reporting corporate social performance. How do business firms determine how well they meet their social responsibility objectives? How is this information conveyed to internal personnel and to external sources? These questions will be answered in this chapter.

SOCIAL PERFORMANCE REPORTING

Social programs are now a part of virtually every large corporation's strategic plan. How does an enterprise measure its performance after these programs are put into action? This can be a difficult question to answer, because sometimes it is hard to determine performance, and other times the evaluation is highly subjective.

The Measurement Issue

Most firms gauge their social performance by means of statistics on hiring, environmental programs, consumer action projects, or whatever areas they have addressed, though this approach does have shortcomings. For example, consider the case of a corporation whose minority employment grew from 3 percent ten years ago to 13 percent today. Should the firm be given (or give itself) a good rating? This is difficult to say because several related employment questions must be answered: What is the minority representation in the local community? How much of this hiring was legally required? What percentage of this hiring would have occurred in the normal course of operations? What is the financial cost or benefit of such discrimination to those concerned?

Or, consider the business that has set up first-rate quality control procedures and, as a result, has greatly increased its product's performance. What rating should the company get? Before this question can be answered, a number of supporting questions must be addressed: What consumer benefit has been generated by the new procedure? What is this benefit worth? What net social asset has been created?

Answering these questions is not always easy, and for this reason, many companies confine their social responsibility evaluation to merely reporting the results. Some, however, have detailed programs for evaluating their progress. Those interested in quantifying the results have recommended varying approaches to reporting this so-called social accounting on the company's financial statement, and this will be the focus of attention later in the chapter. The important thing to remember now is that many groups are interested in corporate social performance information. Some of these groups are internal (e.g., board members, union officials, law, personnel, and public relations departments, and top management) and some are external (e.g., government agencies, public-interest groups, and the news media).

SOCIAL ACCOUNTING

Much of social responsibility reporting is commonly referred to as *social accounting*, the measurement and reporting, internal or external, of information concerning the impact on society of an entity and its activities.[1] Social accounting is not restricted to merely gathering information on social performance and reporting the results. There has also been a move toward reporting the effects of such performance in terms of financial outcomes. The following examines some proposed approaches to corporate social accounting.

[1]Ralph Estes, *Corporate Social Accounting* (New York: Wiley, 1976), p. 3.

Extension of Financial Statements

One of the most popular approaches is including on the financial statement descriptions of both social programs and social costs. The American Accounting Association's Committee on Environmental Effects of Organization Behavior recommended that these descriptions be placed in footnotes and accompany the financial statements. The descriptions would cover such things as

1. Identification of environmental problems—specific organizational problems with regard to control, imposed control standards, compliance deadlines, penalties for noncompliance, environmental considerations contained in executory contracts, and other contingent aspects.
2. Abatement goals of the organization—detailed description of plans for abatement, projection of time schedules, estimates of costs and/or budgeted expenditures.
3. Progress of the organization—description of tangible progress, cost to date, expected future costs and pertinent nonmonetary information relative to the organization's attainment of environment goals.
4. Disclosure of material environmental effects on financial position, earnings and business activities of the organization.[2]

These types of disclosures would be useful not only to members of the general public concerned about environmental matters but also to investors interested in the future liabilities and assessments that might result from the problems and progress reported in the footnotes.

Others have recommended that additional environmental information be provided. Beams, for example, suggested that the accounts list industrial site deterioration caused by pollution.[3] This information would be provided by firms engaged in strip-mining, agribusiness, resort development, and other industries to which soil, land surface conditions, and still bodies of water are important.

New Reporting Formats

More of the interest in corporate social reporting, however, is in developing new and/or distinctive reporting formats. Current financial statements, argue social accounting proponents, have been traditionally too restricted to include the types of social accounting information that should be reported. In the area of pollution control, for example, there is a need to report how well the company's pollution controls compare with the state-of-the-art standards. The firm's actual pollution emission figures should also be compared with relevant federal standards. The results could be reported in the auditor's

[2]"Report of the Committee on Environmental Effects on Organization Behavior," *The Accounting Review*, suppl. to vol. 1008, 1974, p. 110.

[3]Floyd A. Beams, "Accounting for Environmental Pollution," *The New York Certified Public Accountant*, August 1970, pp. 657–661.

comments that accompany that financial statement. Others have suggested that annual reports be extended to cover health and safety matters as well as minority recruitment and promotion.[4] Corcoran and Leininger proposed an environmental exchange in which all the exchanges between a firm and its environment would be reported.[5] The report would contain sections on the inputs out outputs of both human resources and physical resources and would include selected financial data relevant to social concerns.

> The report is similar to a statement of cash flows that reflects all money exchanges between an entity and the rest of society, but the analogy is not complete. For example, the input of human resources would seem to be the hours of human services diverted by the firm from other activities in society, and this is reported. But the firm can produce no output of human resources (only humans can do that), and thus, the output information provided in this category can only be supplemental and explanatory. Further, a complete report on financial exchanges would simply require reproduction of some version of a funds flow statement; Corcoran and Leininger recognize this and seem to assume that the Environment Exchange Report would be provided along with a flow of funds statement. On the other hand, the analogy with respect to input and output of physical resources appears to be complete—and quite informative.[6]

Another suggestion is that by Linowes, who feels that first social audits will be required of most business firms and then "socioeconomic operating statements" (SEOS).[7] Thus he proposed a periodic SEOS to accompany a firm's regular financial statements. An example is given in Table 18.1.

This SEOS would be put together by an internal interdisciplinary team consisting of an accountant, a seasoned business executive, an economist, and others (such as a sociologist and a public health administrator). This statement would report the costs of improving relations with people, relations with the environment, and relations with the product. Such costs (see Table 18.1) would be those incurred voluntarily to improve the welfare of employees and the public, to enhance the safety of the product, and/or to protect or improve the environment. The detriments would be those costs avoided or not incurred for needed actions that are brought to management's attention by a responsible authority, as long as the needed action is such that a reasonably productive and socially aware business manager would have responded favorably.

Linowes's approach has some important advantages. For example, it uses money values so as to produce a single net result. This is important in communicating the company's total social performance. On the other hand,

---

[4] Steven C. Dilley and Jerry J. Weygandt, "Measuring Social Responsibility: An Empirical Test," *Journal of Accountancy*, September 1973, pp. 62–70.

[5] A. Wayne Corcoran and Wayne E. Leininger, Jr., "Financial Statements—Who Needs Them?" *Financial Executive*, August 1970, pp. 34–38, 45–47.

[6] Estes, p. 76.

[7] David F. Linowes, "An Approach to Socio-Economic Accounting," *Conference Board Record*, November 1972, pp. 58–61.

TABLE 18.1. XXXX Corporation.

Socioeconomic Operating Statement for the Year Ending December 31, 19--

I. Relations with People

A. *Improvements*
1. Training program for handicapped workers — $ 10,000
2. Contribution to educational institution — 4,000
3. Extra turnover costs because of minority hiring program — 5,000
4. Cost of nursery school for children of employees, voluntarily set up — 11,000

Total improvements — $ 30,000

B. *Less: Detriments*
1. Postponed installing new safety devices on cutting machines (cost of the devices) — 14,000

C. Net improvements in people actions for the year — $ 16,000

II. Relations with Environment

A. *Improvements*
1. Cost of reclaiming and landscaping old dump on company property — $ 70,000
2. Cost of installing pollution control devices on plant A smokestacks — 4,000
3. Cost of detoxifying waste from finishing process this year — 9,000

Total improvements — $ 83,000

B. *Less: Detriments*
1. Cost that would have been incurred to relandscape strip mining site used this year — $ 80,000
2. Estimated costs to have installed purification process to neutralize poisonous liquid being dumped into stream — $100,000

C. Net deficit in environment actions for the year — ($ 97,000)

III. Relations with Product:

A. *Improvements:*
1. Salary of V.P. while serving on government product safety commission — $ 25,000
2. Cost of substituting lead-free paint for previously used poisonous lead paint — 9,000

Total improvements — $ 34,000

B. *Less: Detriments*
1. Safety device recommended by safety council but not added to product — $ 22,000

C. Net Improvements in product actions for the year — $ 12,000

Total socioeconomic deficit for the year — ($ 69,000)

Add: Net cumulative socioeconomic improvements as at January 1, 19-- — $249,000

GRAND TOTAL NET SOCIOECONOMIC ACTIONS TO DECEMBER 31, 19-- — $180,000

Source: David F. Linowes, "An Approach to Socio-Economic Accounting," *Conference Board RECORD*, November 1972, p. 60. © The Conference Board. Reprinted with permission.

the approach is subjective, and the possibility of reporting the wrong cost limits its usefulness for external social reporting.

A final example of new reporting formats is that suggested by Seidler, who recommended two types of social income statements (see Tables 18.2 and 18.3), one for profit-seeking firms and the other for nonprofit organizations.[8] The reason that these statements are so well regarded by social accountants is that they are capable of reflecting all of an entity's social effects.

> In addition to reflecting the contribution of a profit-seeking entity from its basic economic activity (approximated by the revenues and costs reported in the traditional income statement), the social income statement adds socially desirable outputs for which no money is received (external economies) and deducts costs that the entity imposes on society but does not pay (external diseconomies). The result is a net social profit or loss reflecting the net contribution of the entity to society.
>
> Because of the difficulty of estimating value added for an institution, such as a university in which payments for services rendered do not come exclusively from the beneficiaries of those services (but also from grants, legislative appropriations, and the like), the social income statement for many not-for-profit organizations would simply have two sections: one for benefits to society . . . and another for costs to society. As in the statement for profit-seeking organizations, this format allows for recognition of benefits and costs that are not formalized through market transactions, such as contributions to knowledge or air pollution.[9]

OTHER MEASUREMENT APPROACHES

Social accounting is one way of measuring and reporting corporate social strategy. But because of its heavily theoretical nature and its accounting orientation, many firms prefer to use other approaches to supplement, at least, such efforts. Some of these seem to be designed most for internal use; others are more oriented toward external use. Some are formulated to measure a product's orientation; others are developed to measure a social orientation. General Electric provides an example of the former and the First Bank Minneapolis provides an example of the latter.

General Electric's Approach

General Electric's (GE) social measurement approach was developed in a joint effort with the national accounting firm of Peat, Marwick, Mitchell & Company. The purpose of the reporting system was to (1) help the firm

---

[8]Lee J. Seidler, "Dollar Values in the Social Income Statement," *World* (Peat, Marwick, Mitchell & Co.), Spring 1973, pp. 14, 16–23.

[9]Estes, p. 87.

TABLE 18.2. Social Income Statement for a Profit-Seeking Organization

Value added by enterprise's production		$XXX
Add: socially desirable outputs not sold		
Job training	$XXX	
Health improvement of workers	XXX	
Employment of disadvantaged minorities	XXX	
Other	XXX	XXX
		$XXX
Less: socially undesirable effects not paid for		
Air pollution	$XXX	
Water pollution	XXX	
Health problems caused by products	XXX	
Other	XXX	XXX
Net social profit (or loss)		$XXX

Source: Adapted with minor modifications from Lee J. Seidler, "Dollar Values in the Social Income Statement," *World* (Peat, Marwick, Mitchell & Co.), Spring 1973, p. 21.

establish both corporate and component goals and objectives, by using a more complete accounting of both business needs and public expectations, (2) provide more in-depth reporting on the company's use of resources, (3) point out the consequences of managerial actions, and (4) clarify the differences among various courses of action, thereby simplifying the selection.

GE began by designing a social accounting matrix that identified those constituencies to which the firm felt a social obligation and the types of product and technical performance for each constituency. The initial matrix was modified a number of times, and the final one is presented in Table 18.4. The factor analysis to which each constituency interest was subjected

TABLE 18.3. Social Income Statement for a University.

Revenues		
Value of instruction to society		$XXX
Value of research to society		XXX
Total revenues		$XXX
Less Costs		
Tuition paid to university	$XXX	
Cost of research	XXX	
State aid	XXX	
Others—lost production, etc.	XXX	
Total costs		XXX
Profit to Society		$XXX

Source: Adapted with minor modification from Lee J. Seidler, "Dollar Values in the Social Income Statement," *World* (Peat, Marwick, Mitchell & Co.), Spring 1973, p. 18.

TABLE 18.4. GE Measurement Project Eyeball Assessment of Constituency Interests.

	Customers	Investors	Employees	Suppliers Dealers- Distributors	Competitors	Communities	Public	Government
Product and technical performance	×		×	×	×			×
Employment performance			×			×		×
Environment and natural resources						×	×	×
Community welfare						×	×	×
Government-business relations								×
International trade and development	×		×		×			×

is described in Table 18.5. A close look at each of the cells in Table 18.5 shows that every constituency was affected, at least to some extent, by every aspect of corporate performance.

The last step in GE's approach was to devise a set of measures that could provide feedback on performance related to each cell in Table 18.5. This was done by means of a factor analysis form (Table 18.6). The purpose of this form was to develop operational measures for each cell factor which would (1) define each factor; (2) explore the possibilities for comparisons, norms, quantification, and "dollarization" in making operational statements about the constituency's interest; and (3) suggest measures of performance. In filling out the factor analysis form, the manager is given a detailed list of instructions, seven steps in all. Summarized, they are:

1. Review all factors in the cell. Should any of these factors be deleted or combined? Are there any that should be added? Can these factors be measured?
2. Determine what each factor means to the respective constituency. For example, how is "novelty" viewed by buyers? What does a worker think of when evaluating "pride in job"? How is "social utility/acceptance of product" expressed? What does "market acceptance of products" mean? The reason for examining these definitions is to ensure that follow-up measures of corporate performance are keyed closely to significant constituency interests.
3. In making comparisons, establishing norms, or quantifying factors, (a) be imaginative, (b) be credible, (c) compare performance between one component of a company and another and between one time period and another, and (d) be specific in describing how implementation can be carried out.
4. In developing measurements of performance, focus on outputs and the

TABLE 18.5.   Product and Technical Performance: Cell-by-Cell Factor Analysis.

Customers	*Employees*	*Investors, creditors*
Utility of products	Market acceptance of products	Markets acceptance of products
Efficiency/ease of operation	"Pride in product" and craftsmanship	Risk/payoff of (large) ventures
Technological innovation	Job structuring ("pride in job")	Technological leadership
Novelty	"Productivity improvements"	Patent licensing policies
Aesthetic values	Impact of process equipment on labor content (labor intensity)	Product safety and quality
Standardization (versus options): compatibility	Scheduling of operations and production	Advertising image
Safety	Occupational health and safety (re products and processes)	
"Practical" life/ "technological obsolescence"		
"Psychological" life/ "planned obsolescence"		
Product information/ advertising accuracy; availability		
Delivery		
Maintenance/service		

Dealers, distributors	*Suppliers*	*Competitors*
Market acceptance of products	Market acceptance of products	Technological leadership/ product innovation
Product reliability/safety	Value analysis (quality of suppliers)	Patent licensing policies
Impact on service requirements	Production scheduling	Consortium arrangements on R&D
Advertising (including "cop-op" programs)	Inventory requirements	Compatibility of products
Product information	Purchasing practices (ethical versus unethical)	Policy on "tie-in" sales
Warranty specifications		
Inventory requirements		
Availability of parts		
Dealer training programs		
Policing integrity		

Public	*Government*	*Communities*
Social utility/acceptability of product	Company contributions to: material standard of living	Community pride in corporate "leadership," e.g.,
Technology assessment	defense	R&D leader
National "image" of a technological superiority	social problem solving (e.g., housing transportation, medical care)	first in industry
Company contributions to: material defense		

TABLE 18.5.   Continued

Public	Government	Communities
social problem solving (e.g., housing transportation, medical care) protection of persons and property	protection of persons and property Developing/protecting technological leadership Safety in: product process workplace Truth in: advertising packaging lending Technology assessment	

impact of constituency interests. Determine how the information will help management in decision making. Make sure that the measurement figures accurately describe corporate performance and facilitate comparisons. In suggesting measures of performance, consider actual or potential availability of required data.

5. Since there are sixty-three cells in the overall matrix, try to reduce the number of measurements to a manageable number. Look for places where one measurement will evaluate the effectiveness of corporate performance of two or more factors.

6. Formulate a cost-benefit statement with respect to the interaction of corporate operations and constituency interests. The cost-benefit statement should be made at either the factor level or a higher level (such as a whole cell) if possible. In formulating these statements, recognize that the firm can either incur costs or avoid them. When possible, translate the costs and benefits into dollars and cents.

7. When the factor analysis forms have been completed for all factors in a cell, review the factors so as to assign priorities in rank or importance. In this ranking, consider any evidence regarding which factors the constituency considers most important, the relative credibility of factors and measurements, and the relative availability of needed data.

Tables 18.7 and 18.8 show two completed factor analysis forms. Notice that in each case the seven guidelines were followed in filling them out.

The GE approach has been useful to other organizations that want to develop a social accounting reporting system. Of greatest value is how the company constructed its matrix before it decided on operational measures. This matrix approach has been copied by other firms with only slight modification.

The second segment of the GE approach, the development of factor lists for each cell of the matrix and the formulation of operational measures for

TABLE 18.6.   GE Measurement Project Factor Analysis Form.

1. Factor:

2. Definition of elements:

3. Possibility of:	Yes/No	How?	What?
Comparisons?			
Normative goals?			
Quantification?			
Dollarization?			

4. Measures of performance:

5. Data needed:

6. Feasibility of cost-benefit analysis:

TABLE 18.7. GE Measurement Project Factor Analysis Form.

Factor: Product information

Definition of elements
1. Accuracy of information.
2. Completeness of information.
3. Clarity of information.
4. Availability of information.
5. Promptness in responding to requests for information.

Possibility of:	*Yes/No*	*How?*	*What?*
Comparisons?	Yes	Over time; with competing products.	
Normative goals?	Yes	Zero charges/complaints about inaccuracy, incompleteness, obscurity, unavailability.	
Quantification?	Yes	Number of complaints/charges about inadequate information. Number of participants in information seminars, workshops, trade fairs, etc. Number of bulletins to newspapers, trade journals, etc. Number of relevant facts in ads, tags, labels, etc. Average time period between receipt of, and response to, requests for information.	
Dollarization?	Yes	Dollars spent on supplying information.	

Measures of performance
1. Descriptive analysis of advertisements, tags, labels, instructions, warranties, and special information services (e.g., General Electric Consumer's Institute).
2. Use of newsletters, bulletins, publicity releases by media.
3. Extent of review procedures for information to be disseminated.
4. $ spent on supplying information.

Data needed
Samples of advertisements, tags, labels, instructions, warranties
Description of activities of General Electric Consumer's Institute
Measures of use by media of publicity releases, etc.
Description of review procedures for information to be disseminated
Dollars spent on information services

Feasibility of cost-benefit analysis
Yes, in a limited way.
(e.g., dollar cost of supplying information vs. description of benefits customers derive from information.)

Source: Reported in Marc J. Epstein, Eric G. Flamholtz, and John J. McDonough, *Corporate Social Performance: The Measurement of Product and Service Contributions* (New York: National Association of Accountants, 1977), p. 44. Copyright © 1977 by National Association of Accountants. All rights reserved.

TABLE 18.8 GE Measurement Project Factor Analysis Form.

Factor: Safety

Definition of elements
1. Compliance with National Electrical Code (where applicable).
2. Compliance with Underwriters' Laboratories safety standards (where applicable).
3. Compliance with all other legal or trade association safety requirements.
4. Systematic procedures for identifying and minimizing potential hazards.
5. Warnings to customers of potential hazards; clear directions on how to avoid them and what to do in case of accidents.
6. Clear assignment of responsibility for assuring that products are safe.
7. Prompt recalls of products found to be hazardous. Full publicity about hazards and how to avoid them.

Possibility of:	*Yes/No*	*How?*	*What?*
Comparisons?	Yes	Over time; with competing products.	
Normative goals?	Yes	Zero accidents.	
Quantitive?	Yes.	Numbers of accidents.	
Dollarization?	Yes	Dollar cost of making products safe	
		Dollar cost of settling legal actions resulting from unsafe products	

Measures of performance
1. Accidents (perhaps weighted by severity) due to faulty products as a percent of all products sold or in use; comparisons with accident records of competing products.
2. Completeness and effectiveness of procedures for identifying and minimizing hazards.
3. Completeness and clarity of safety instructions to customers.
4. Promptness of recalls of hazardous products.

Data needed
Records of accidents due to faulty products
Procedures for identifying and minimizing hazards
Safety instructions to consumers
Records on recalls

Feasibility of cost-benefit analysis:
Yes, probably.
(e.g., dollar cost of accident-free products vs. benefits of numerically low accident record)

each factor, unfortunately, has proved to be of less value to other firms. Companies found it necessary to use the matrix to make up their own list of cell factors.

> The very essence of the GE exercise was to broaden the overall concept of corporate impact by systematically examining each of the areas of corporate performance across the interests of nine constituencies. Specifically, the notion of product and technical performance was broadened beyond the traditional customer or market view to incorporate the interests of employees, dealer/distributors, suppliers, competitors, communities, the public, government and investors/creditors.
>
> The power of the GE approach lies in its ability to help managers break out of the "tangible product" concept of industrial organizations and to begin to see more fully the interdependent set of constituents whose interests are intertwined with those of the organization.[10]

First Bank Minneapolis Approach

First Bank Minneapolis offers another example of how firms measure their social performance. The bank's management decided that the health of the community and the banking industry were intertwined, and so the bank established an Urban Development Department. The mission of the department was to expand the bank's economic and human investment in the community and to make it more effective. The overall objective was to make the bank an active presence in the civic community and to improve its investment of time and money in community affairs.

One of the first areas to receive attention from the department was charitable contributions. Annual requests for funding far exceeded what the bank could justify. In order to approach the issue systematically, the Urban Development Department decided to set up a process for making allocation decisions. It also realized that it had no way of assessing community problems or deciding on the bank's general priorities. So the bank publicly announced that it was going to develop a social-environmental audit.

The bank identified 10 constituents to which it felt responsible: job opportunities, housing, education, public safety, income, health, transportation, citizen participation, physical environment, and cultural life. The bank then set objectives for itself in each of these areas and began measuring its performance. By 1974 the bank had increased the number of areas to thirteen, adding human relations, community investment, and consumer protection and services.

By the 1980s First Bank Minneapolis had refined its social report and provided a detailed plan and a record of its performance for the previous year and a plan for the upcoming year. Table 18.9 shows one of its most recent audits. Notice that the bank did not succeed in every area. Residential mortgage performance was quite low, and so the bank drastically revised

[10]Estes, p. 63.

TABLE 18.9. Social Audit.

Credit Investments	1981 Plan	1981 Performance	1982 Plan
Residential			
Mortgages originating to Minneapolis residents ($)	8,200,000	2,997,600	5,900,000
Mortgages originating to Hennepin County residents ($)	12,200,000	3,182,300	6,100,000
Mortgages originating to non-Hennepin County Metro residents ($)	11,640,000	2,993,810	5,900,000
Mortgages originating to Minneapolis residents (no.)	162	53	103
Mortgages originating to Hennepin County residents (no.)	207	51	101
Mortgages originating to non-Hennepin County residents (no.)	229	48	98
Home improvement loans outstanding to Minneapolis residents (no.)	200	47	55
Home improvement loans outstanding to non-Minneapolis residents (no.)	300	83	95
Construction			
Commercial construction and development loan commitments originated in Minneapolis ($)	10,000,000	10,364,100	13,060,000
Commercial construction and development loan commitments originating outside Minneapolis ($)	63,622,000	169,045,000	154,677,750
Business			
Loan commitments to Minneapolis businesses ($)	649,193,000	623,197,350	728,940,125
Loan commitments to non-Minneapolis businesses ($)	2,037,233,000	1,891,949,000	2,248,575,740
Special Loans and Purchases			
Civic loan commitments less than market terms ($)	630,000	10,780,100	10,400,000
Commercial line commitments to cultural institutions ($)	550,000	346,000	390,400
Small Business minority loans • No. approved	26	32	38
• $ value	4,450,000	3,964,300	4,700,000
Level of minority business purchases	180,000	155,049	131,400

Mortgages
☐ Minneapolis Residents
☐ Hennepin County and Other Non-Minneapolis Residents

$50 Million
40
30
20
10
78 79 80 81 82

Home Improvement Loans
☐ Minneapolis
☐ Non-Minneapolis

$500 Million
400
300
200
100
78 79 80 81 82

Commercial Construction and Land Development Commitments in Minneapolis

$30 Million
20
10
78 79 80 81 82

Loan Commitment to Minneapolis Business
$800 Million

600 — 400 — 200 — 78 79 80 81 82

Small Business Minority Loans
$5 Million

4 — 3 — 2 — 1 — 78 79 80 81 82

Total Contributions
$1.5 Million

1.2 — .9 — .6 — .3 — 78 79 80 81 82

Individual Time and Demand Deposits			
Originating in Minneapolis ($)	158,000,000	177,000,000	186,000,000
Originating outside Minneapolis ($)	186,000,000	208,000,000	219,000,000
Environmental Investments			
Energy			
Bank steam consumption (lb)	26,500,000	20,874,900	20,870,000
Bank electricity consumption (kWh)	12,000,000	11,623,360	11,623,000
Average mpg bank pool cars	12.0	14.3	16.0
Ecology			
Loans to antipollution enterprises ($)	17,000,000	17,150,000	17,150,000
Transportation			
Percent employees traveling to work by:			
Bus	69	73	74
Carpool/van pool	19	18	19
Driving alone	9	7	5
Walking/biking/other	3	2	2
Philanthropic Investments			
Corporate Contributions			
Total ($)	1,133,280	1,138,153	1,304,360
Housing	104,000	92,500	119,000
Education	200,000	253,331	240,000
Environment	35,000	19,102	20,000
Culture	150,000	147,997	195,000
Human and social relations	285,430	267,055	361,360
Health	25,000	22,802	25,000
United Way corporate gift	320,850	313,649	319,000
employee gift	111,000	131,400	150,000
employee donors (percent)ª	—	89%	91%
College Grant Matching Program			
Dollar amount gifts matched	13,000	21,717	25,000
Number of employee donors	80	92	100
Employee Community Involvement			
Monthly hours volunteered	9,000	9,254	9,500
Personal time	8,000	8,140	8,300
Bank time	1,000	1,114	1,200

TABEL 18.9.   Continued

	1981 Plan	1981 Performance	1982 Plan
Credit Investments			
Breakdown by interest area			
Artistic/cultural	2,350	1,955	2,000
Civic/human relations/environmental	900	908	930
Credit Investments			
Educational	1,600	2,011	2,060
Fraternal/service	960	1,002	1,000
Health/social welfare	2,000	2,556	2,500
Housing/community development	665	528	500
Political/governmental	525	294	510
Average total monthly hours per employee[b]		3.6	3.9
Exempt	—	3.3	3.7
Nonexempt	—	4.0	4.2
Employee Investments			
Job Opportunities			
Female officers/managers/professionals as percent of total	37.5%	37.3%	38.5%
Minority officers/managers/professionals as percent of total	5.5%	4.4%	5.5%
Percent jobs posted internally	69.0%	70.4%	71.0%
Special employment			
Handicapped and other target groups	24	14	26
Summer youth	15	37	15
Career Development			
Number of internal classes taken by employees	—	1,746	—
Number of external classes taken by employees	—	879	—
Health			
Number HMO plans offered	7	7	7
Percent employee participants enrolled in HMO plans	—	48.7%	—

[a] New category.
[b] New criteria includes all employee average, not merely those volunteering.

Source: Reprinted with permission of the First National Bank Minneapolis/Urban Development Department. Minneapolis, MN 55480.

United Way
☐ Employee Gift
☐ Corporate Gift

$400 Thousand
300
200
100
78 79 80 81 82

Percent Female Officers, Managers and Professionals
50 Percent
40
30
20
10
78 79 80 81 82

610

its planned performance. It did much better with construction loans, and job opportunities was also successful.

The bank has also begun turning out a Community Quality of Life Report, indicating performance and trends for quality of life indicators (education, public safety, housing, jobs) in the Minneapolis area. The results are a summary of a bank poll of area residents and public- and private-sector community leaders to determine local priorities among basic public services that contribute to the area's quality of life. Figure 18.1 presents the overall findings of the poll.

The bank's approach to reporting corporate social performance is important for a number of reasons. The major one is that it offers a substantive picture of its operations in regard to the general public. It not only set forth a list of community priorities and areas of bank impact but also has established a tracking system for monitoring performance. (In fact, the audit received an award from the Bank Marketing Association).

Some critics have charged that the First Bank Minneapolis approach is designed specifically for public relations purposes. This charge is hard to substantiate. If anything, the audit has been of more value to the bank in defining its priorities than it has been to any other outside organization. The annual audits have helped pinpoint those areas in which the bank has had the most direct impact on the community and showed the closest fit between its assessment of community priorities and the areas of the bank's most significant social impact: job opportunities for women and minorities, volume and distribution of residential- and home-improvement loan commitments, minority-business loan commitments, purchases from minority businesses, loan commitments to businesses operating within the inner city, community involvement by bank employees in human relations activities, and direct contributions to civic and welfare organizations whose objectives are defined by their contribution to the inner city. One comment on the overall impact of the bank's efforts was:

> From an internal standpoint, the audit appears to have made considerable impact in terms of establishing a heightened consciousness among key personnel as to both the areas of most significant social impact and the areas in which socioeconomic interests compete most actively for attention. The audit process has focused attention among senior officers of the bank on a number of basic allocation issues:
>
> 1. The proportion of residential mortgage, home improvement and interim construction loan commitments in the city as opposed to the suburbs.
> 2. The level of loan commitments to manufacturers of antipollution equipment and/or companies working to make pollution control-related capital improvements.
> 3. The level of loan commitments to cultural and civic organizations and the determination of appropriate rates of interest.
> 4. The dollar allocations for minority business loans.

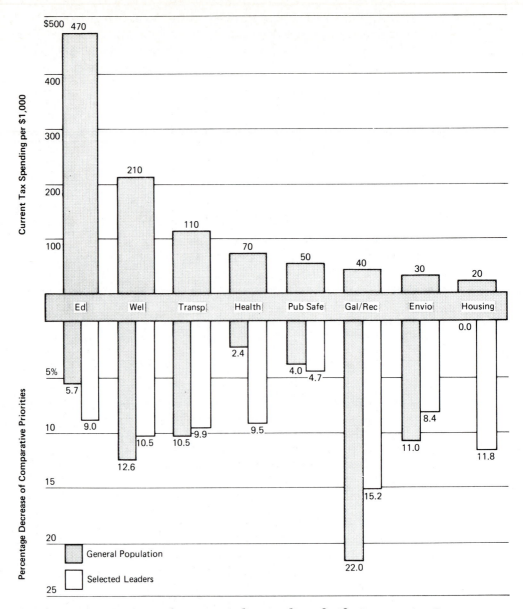

FIGURE 18.1   First Bank Minneapolis: Quality of Life Community Survey: Results Summary. *Reprinted with permission of the First National Bank of Minneapolis/Urban Development Department, Minneapolis, Minnesota 55480.*

5. The proportion of commercial loans made to businesses located within the inner city.
6. The proportion of commercial mortgage loans associated specifically with downtown development projects.[11]

Perhaps the greatest benefit of the First Bank Minneapolis approach is its effort to measure social performance. The bank identified those areas in which its actions had had social impact and strove to develop a program that would provide feedback on its progress.

FUTURE TRENDS

What does the future hold for social measurement and reporting trends? In order to answer this question, two areas need to be addressed: social accounting direction and social measurement and reporting trends.

Social Accounting Direction

Regardless of how social accounting is done, there are rules that must be followed. The principal one is specifying the social report's objective. Companies must concentrate on what they are trying to do with these reports and the relationship between them and corporate objectives.

> Social reporting might contribute to at least three corporate objectives: public wage, learning, and social responsibility. Improved public image might be sought for greater product acceptance, name identification, and avoidance of confrontations (including legal actions, disruption of stockholder meetings, strikes, and boycotts). Management of a corporation might undertake preparation of a social report to see what it could learn about the organization, both internally and in terms of its impact on society. And of course social reports may be issued because of a feeling of social responsibility within the organization—an attitude that society should be informed fully of the corporation's behavior and impact.[12]

Second, in reporting social performance, the most highly recommended rules include (1) relevance—the information should pertain to some need or interest of society, be timely, and be significant; (2) no bias—the information should be fair, verifiable, and complete; and (3) understandability—the information should be clear, concise, comparable, consistent, and, if possible, quantifiable.

How are companies interested in social reporting actually doing so? Most follow six steps. First, they secure the support of top management, critical in overcoming resistance by personnel who do not want to participate in the program. Second, one person is made responsible for reviewing the social

[11]Estes, p. 56.
[12]Estes, p. 151.

accounting literature and keeping abreast of what other firms are doing. Third, an initial inventory or enumeration of all social benefits and social costs attributable to the firm is drawn up. In this inventory, the corporation identifies its major constituencies and examines its overall effect (social contribution and social cost) on the community. Fourth, the firm begins to assign numbers to its social benefits and costs. Some corporations begin by choosing a social responsibility program that is expected to cost more than it returns: this gets them thinking about cost assignment. Fifth, this social accounting effort, in the main, is carried out by inhouse people, and the reports (at least for now) are used only for internal purposes. Finally, having completed the first round of social accounting, corporations find that they have an abundance of ideas and proposals useful for extensions and follow-up. The ball is now rolling, and in the future the firm will provide social accounting reports for both internal and external use. Having learned what social accounting actually is, the enterprise can now begin to derive the maximum benefit from its use.

Reporting Trends

There has been a marked increase in the amount of social responsibility disclosure in corporate annual reports. One of the Big Eight accounting firms, which often collect data on such disclosures, reported that in the early 1970s, 59.6 percent of the Fortune 500 firms were making social responsibility disclosures in their annual statements. Ten years later this had increased to almost 90 percent.[13]

The types of information reported varies by firm. Mining and smelting firms are more likely to report on their environmental efforts; insurance companies and banks are more likely to discuss community involvement and human resource programs. Overall, some of the most popular categories of social responsibility disclosures are the environment, energy, fair business practices, human resources, community involvement, and product information. Excerpts from some of these reports are the following:

Commercial Banks

Ninety-four percent of the Fortune 50 Commercial Banks made SR disclosures. Fair Business Practices, Human Resources, and Community Involvement were the topics receiving the most attention.

The average number of pages devoted to SR disclosure was .43. However, at least eight banks reported SR information outside the annual report by publishing an additional booklet specifically devoted to social responsibility.

Forty percent of the disclosing banks provided quantified disclosure. Community Involvement was the category in which the largest number of monetary disclosures were made while nonmonetary disclosures were most often made in the category of Fair Business Practices.

[13]*Social Responsibility Disclosure: 1978 Survey* (Cleveland, Ohio: Ernst R. Ernst), p. 3.

Life Insurance Companies

Eighty-eight percent of the life insurance companies provided SR information in their annual reports. Disclosing companies devoted an average of 0.50 page to SR information with the highest number being 3.25 pages.

Extensive disclosure was provided on Fair Business Practices. Human Resources and Community Involvement. In particular, the topic of employee training was frequently mentioned.

Forty-eight percent of the disclosing life insurance companies provided quantified information. The greatest number of monetary disclosures were in the category of Community Involvement while most of the nonmonetary disclosures were in the area of Human Resources.[14]

Many companies use a section of their annual report for social responsibility reporting. This often is a discussion of what the corporation has done, how it turned out, and, in many cases, what its plans are for the future. Sometimes, although not as commonly, this information is contained in the president's letter to the stockholders. In rare cases the company will prepare a separate booklet and send it to the stockholders along with the annual report.

Regardless of the specific content of corporate reporting, one thing is clear. More and more firms are beginning to measure and report their social responsibility performance. This development should mean both more constructive feedback regarding past performance and improved strategy formulation for future performance.

SUMMARY

Social responsibility programs are now a part of virtually all large corporate strategic plans. One of the biggest problems faced by these companies is how to measure their social responsibility performance. A second problem is how to report this performance. This chapter addressed both of these problems.

There are a variety of monitoring/measurement activities currently used by businesses to account for their social performance. The four areas of performance are product and service contributions, human resources, community involvement, and physical resources and environment. Much of social responsibility reporting is called social accounting, which is the measurement and reporting, internal or external, of information concerning the impact on society of an entity and its activities. Social accounting may use such approaches as extension of financial statements and new reporting formats.

Some firms have their own methods of reporting social responsibility performance. Examples are those of General Electric and First Bank Minneapolis. General Electric identifies its major constituencies and then uses cell-

---

[14]*Social Responsibility*, pp. 3–6.

by-cell analysis of product and technical performance. The results are reported by means of a project factor analysis form for each factor. First Bank Minneapolis uses a social audit and supplements it with a community quality of life report.

DISCUSSION AND STUDY QUESTIONS

1. Who would be interested in corporate social performance information? Identify three internal and three external groups.
2. What kinds of information about social performance would be most useful?
3. What is meant by the term *social accounting?*
4. How are some corporations extending their financial statement so as to improve their social responsibility reporting?
5. What new types of reporting formats are some accountants recommending for reporting social responsibility performance? Describe three.
6. Why have many firms found General Electric's identification and assessment of constituency interests useful in developing their own social responsibility measurement formats?
7. In what way does its cell-by-cell factor analysis (see Table 18.5) help General Electric evaluate its social responsibility performance?
8. How useful is the project factor analysis form (see Table 18.6) to General Electric?
9. How useful is First Bank Minneapolis's social audit in evaluating and reporting its social performance?
10. What is the likely future direction of social accounting? Be complete in your answer.
11. In reporting social performance, three of the rules that should be followed are relevance, no bias, and understandability. What does this statement mean?
12. What are some of the social responsibility reporting trends for the future? Be complete in you answer.

CASES AND INCIDENTS

A Social Evaluation Tool

A fully integrated eastern corporation recently decided to evaluate its social responsibility progress. The major problem was the specific steps to take. After several meetings, a committee was formed to look into the matter. A month later the committee recommended the development of a social audit worksheet. This worksheet was to be designed to cover all areas in which the company had programs. In each of these a continuum was to be drawn, showing the degrees of success or progress in meeting the particular social issue. Some of these were the following:

0	20	40	60	80	100
Little effort to hire the hard-core unemployed.	Some effort to hire the hard-core; occasionally employment ads directed at this objective.	Fairly active campaign to hire the hard-core; advertising and personal recruiting used.	Very active efforts designed toward hiring the hard-core, including close cooperation with local community employment.	Vigorous program designed to both hire and maintain the hard-core unemployed. Some members of the staff work on this program on a full-time basis.	

0	20	40	60	80	100
Most ecological efforts are directed toward fighting implementation of current ecological legislation.	Some attempts to fight present legislation; minimum attempts to clean up operations.	General adherence to ecological legislation; operations meet all legislative requirements.	In addition to meeting all ecological requirements, some attention is focused on working with legislative groups in providing information useful in drafting future laws or modifying current ones.	All ecological legislative requirements are met; company is working closely with legislative groups to provide substantive input for any future legislation.	

0	20	40	60	80	100
Advertising to designed only to sell the product.	Advertising copy is reviewed by advertising staff to eliminate any misleading comments or implications.	Advertising is reviewed by nonadvertising personnel in an effort to eliminate any misleading information.	Advertising is tested in a local market to work out any "bugs" before being transmitted to the general public.	Advertising is as complete and factual as possible; all charges of "misleading advertising" by the public are reviewed and acted upon within the earliest possible time period.	

Some of the members on the committee felt that this type of audit worksheet would help the company evaluate its social responsibility progress. Others, however, were not sure and thought that a more definitive instrument could be developed, although they were unsure of what this might be.

ANALYSIS

1. How useful can a social audit worksheet be in evaluating social responsibility progress?
2. What are the advantages of such a worksheet? What are the disadvantages?
3. What other techniques could a firm use to evaluate its social responsibility?

Getting Started

The president of a large hotel chain, based in New York City, is very active in community affairs. Last month, while meeting with other top managers regarding a summer jobs program, the president was shown a social audit. It had been turned out by the urban department of a large manufacturing firm. The audit provided a wealth of information on what the company had done over the past year and how well its social performance had compared with its social goals. Some of the areas covered in the audit were philanthropy, environmental programs, jobs in the inner city, and career development of minorities.

The president was impressed with the brief yet informative report. In four pages the audit had managed to convey a feeling of genuine social concern. At first glance the report seemed to be a slick public relations effort. But each section of the audit revealed that a great deal of time had been spent identifying social performance factors and gathering and measuring data on each.

The president of the hotel chain would like to see his enterprise develop a social audit. If nothing else, he feels that such information would be useful in providing the company with feedback on how well it was meeting its social obligations. On the other hand, he is somewhat concerned about the time and effort that would have to be expended to produce such an audit. He is also unsure of exactly what belongs in such an audit. What can be measured? How should it be measured? What constitutes excellent, good, fair, or poor performance? All of these questions are making the president think that maybe a social audit effort will be more trouble than it is worth. Nevertheless, the president intends to talk to his senior vice-president about it and at least make some progress toward a preliminary audit by this time next year.

ANALYSIS

1. What activities should the hotel chain measure in a social audit? Describe three.
2. How can General Electric's social audit efforts help the hotel chain devise its own audit?
3. How can the social audit report of First Bank Minneapolis help the hotel chain present its social performance?

Now What?

Two years ago Betty Whiskin became head of external affairs at a national insurance company. One of her duties was to formulate an overall corporate social responsibility strategy. During her first six months she coordinated her efforts with those of the functional department managers so that this strategy had a uniform direction. This was the first time the corporation had ever formulated an integrated approach to its social efforts.

At the end of the first year, Whiskin had her assistant pull together all of the results and put them in graphic and tabular form. The company had been very socially responsive, and the data showed it. For this reason, Whiskin decided to go a step farther and ask the functional managers to set for the next year measurable social goals in their respective areas. These objectives were submitted to her 13 months ago. At the same time Whiskin worked with other top executives and members of the board to develop additional objectives. The overall list was quite impressive, extending from recruiting and hiring practices to philanthropic and community programs. Each objective was examined in light of past performance, and a one-year target was set. Whiskin felt that all these goals would be attained and planned to secure as much press coverage and external notice of them as possible.

Last week Whiskin received the results from the year's performance. They are quite disappointing. Of the 19 areas for which data were collected, in only five were the results better than the expectations. Two were exactly as expected, and the last 12 were below projections. The main reason was undoubtedly the downturn in the economy. From the time the annual social plan was drawn up until the results were measured, national unemployment increased by 29 percent, and the firm had to curtail its social efforts.

As a result, Whiskin is now in a quandary. She would like to report the positive results but is concerned about what to do with the negative data. She had thought that everything would turn out well and that each goal would be reached. Since this is not the case, Whiskin is wondering how to handle the situation.

ANALYSIS

1. How should Whiskin report the results? What should the social audit summary look like?
2. How should Whiskin deal with the results? Offer her a plan of action.
3. Is there any way that Whiskin can avoid a similar problem in the future?

CASE STUDY FOR PART V

American Engineering

American Engineering, located in the southwestern part of Michigan, specializes in the design and production of machines that make an assortment of materials for diverse purposes. For example, one major machine that the company designed and produced was a stamping machine that makes automobile parts. The company has been owned by Albert Coy since 1976. The success of American Engineering since the 1976 purchase has necessitated a threefold increase in the size of the plant, as there has been a tenfold increase in business.

Sales have grown rapidly especially as American Engineering moved into international markets. The 1986 breakdown of sales revealed the following:

60 percent sales to U.S. customers.
10 percent sales to Canadian customers.
20 percent sales to European customers.
10 percent sales to Japan, India, and southeast Asia.

Albert Coy, the 46-year-old president, attributes the sales growth to aggressive marketing, being on the cutting edge of computer-assisted machine design and engineering, designing machines noted for high quality, and in the development of a product that is considered to be far advanced. In addition, American Engineering has sale licensing agreements for sales of special European and Asian products in the United States. All the products that American Engineering designs and sells are covered through patents, thereby ensuring that American Engineering (AE) is the only producer of the product.

AE has grown from a staff of 25 highly skilled production workers and five engineers to 100 production staff and 25 engineers. Even with this increase in staff, there has been a consistent three-year backlog of orders.

Albert Coy Wanted to maintain a backlog to ensure a stable supply of work for both the design and engineering staff.

AE's plant was located between two small towns in an area noted for a good supply of highly skilled workers, primarily a carryover of the Studebaker plant located in South Bend, Indiana. This plant closed in the 1960s, but there were still many smaller companies that had a strong need for high-quality staff.

On New Year's Day of 1986, Albert Coy was looking out the window of his office onto a 4-foot drift of snow that came nearly up to the window. In spite of the snow, Albert was pleased with the success of the organization and the progress it had made over the past 10 years. It was a lot of hard work, but it had really paid off both in the growth of the firm and in the personal wealth of Albert and his partner Loomis. Albert was in his 40s and a millionaire, and he was grateful. In the back of his mind he wanted to do something to reflect appreciation for those who made the success story all possible. He guessed he wanted to become more socially responsible but he was not quite sure how he wanted to do it. His main concern was simply to understand social responsibility. Albert decided to talk to a friend, a professor at a nearby university who was known for his work in social responsibility.

They discussed Albert's concerns at the plant later that month. It was after hours and they walked around the plant reviewing operations, profits, and future goals. Albert finally got to the topic of being socially responsible. His friend, Willard, was delighted.

Albert: I think I want to be more socially responsible.

Willard: Aren't you now?

Albert: Well, I think so, but I want to have a better feeling about my work. I want to do something that reflects my feelings about the success we have had.

Willard: To who do you want to be responsible?

Albert: Those that have contributed to my success . . . but even beyond that. I want to do more to help others. I have made a lot of money and now I am in a position to do something to help others.

Willard: OK, I guess we need to look at your current levels of social responsiveness and build from there.

Albert: Why?

Willard: Well, tell me how you want to be responsible? Are you responsible now?

Albert: I think we are now. But I haven't really thought about it much. There are a lot of problems in my community . . . a lot of suffering in the world . . . maybe can do something about that. . . . But I guess I do want to begin with trying to do those things that would more directly reward those people that have helped to make this business successful. . . . But, well, you know you bring up a good point. I am not even sure if we are being socially responsible right now. We have just spent the last decade plus in building a successful business. We made it last year when we reached sales of $50 million and a profit of over $5 million. We can easily grow larger, but I don't know if we want to do that. I feel I am about at the limit of what I can manage.

Willard: I think I understand what you want to do. Let's first decide what areas you want to consider in measuring the social responsiveness of your company right now in the direct contacts it has with the community, its sales clients, and its employees. Then we will move on to try to establish some degree of a framework to evaluate the different alternatives that you may want to consider after you feel that we have committed a sufficient amount of resources to ensure that we are being as responsive as we can be within the day-to-day operation of our organization.

Albert: Good, but how are you going to develop a criterion to judge the effectiveness of other programs? How can I judge the merits of contributing to the local fine-arts group with that of contributing for world disaster relief?

Willard: We can and we should. It will be based on what your preferences are and a determination of the effectiveness and efficiency of a particular organization to which you may consider making a donation.

Albert: Won't that take a lot of time and resources?

Willard: Well, did you want to give away money . . . or did you want to do some good for it?

Albert: What organization is going to open the books for me to see how effective they are?

Willard: How much are you going to contribute?

Albert: Up to $500,000.

Willard: I think they would want to talk to you some. . . . I sure would if I was a potential recipient.

Albert: I see what you mean. You aren't on the clock now, are you?

Willard: Wait until you see my bill.

Albert: Seeing a bill and getting paid for it is another matter.

They both laugh and head off to the restaurant for a social evening. Later that month, they get together again to set up criteria by which to judge the effectiveness of the company's social responsiveness. Willard first determined major areas and groups of people for whom the company had a responsibility. The next stage was to develop criteria by which to measure the degree of social responsibility that the organization is exhibiting. These measures would constitute an index that could then be used to develop a baseline index of the company's social responsiveness. For example, employee compensation might be one measure of responsiveness. Another criterion might be the salary paid at American Engineering (AE) compared with that of other organizations in the surrounding community for comparable jobs. The logic underpinning this criterion is that a responsible employer is one that pays employees in an equitable fashion. A comparison of like salaries with those at AE would be one measure.

Willard continued until a set of 10 areas were covered with roughly five criterion for each area. Although these were, admittedly, not a perfect measure of social responsiveness, it did move the orientation of the organization from thinking they were responsive toward developing measures to demonstrate their action.

Albert and Willard then worked to develop a system to evaluate the appropriateness of responsiveness efforts for projects outside the organization. They finally decided that Albert wanted to fund programs based on (1) the visibility they gave the company; and (2) that the programs directly help to improve the company's image in the community or in the eyes of customers of American Engineering. To measure the internal effectiveness of a proposal, a criterion was developed such that the effectiveness of an alternative was measured by (1) comparing the proposal's budget and determining how much cost went to administration and how much directly to the goals of the project or program, and (2) whether the organization had developed some degree of quantified results from their previous activities. For example, contributions to the Red Cross would be rated high, as administrative costs are relatively low and they have a history of effectiveness. However, the ratings might be low on the visibility dimension and in improving the company image.

ANALYSIS

1. Define six groups or areas that AE could define as areas in which social responsiveness can be measured.
2. For three of the six groups or areas, develop three objective measures or criteria by which to measure the degree of social responsiveness of AE.
3. How might AE establish a criterion to measure the visibility of an external social program? Give four examples of a criterion that might be applied.
4. Do the four criteria used to evaluate social responsiveness seem reasonable?
5. Make a case that AE is *not* acting responsibly in using the criterion that Willard developed.
6. Establish an alternative criterion that may be more responsible than the one that Willard established.
7. Make a case that AE should not consider *any* program beyond those that affect the organization directly. Why might it be appropriate that AE be concerned with responsibilities beyond those affecting its immediate clientel?

Name Index

Subject Index